McDougal Littell

CLASSZONE

Visit classzone.com and get connected.

ClassZone resources provide instruction, practice and learning support for students and parents.

Help with the Math

- @Home Tutor enables students to focus on the math and be more prepared for class, using animated examples and instruction.
- Extra examples similar to those in the book provide additional support.

Games and Activities

- Crossword puzzles, memory games, and other activities help students connect to essential math concepts.
- Math Vocabulary Flipcards are a fun way to learn math terminology.

Assessment

- Section Quizzes show students what concepts they still need further practice on.
- Students can take Unit Tests online and then view test reports to see whether they need more practice.

Access the online version of your textbook at **classzone.com**

Your complete text is available for immediate use!

McDougal Littell

Where Great Lessons Begin

McDougal Littell

GEORGIA HIGH SCHOOL MATHEMATICS 3

McDougal Littell
A DIVISION OF HOUGHTON MIFFLIN COMPANY
Evanston, Illinois • Boston • Dallas

Cover Photo Credits: Clockwise from top: *Okefenokee Swamp* © Farrell Grehan/Corbis; *Peach* © Comstock Images/Age Fotostock; *St. Simons Island Lighthouse* © James Schwabel/Alamy; *Horse-drawn carriage, Savannah* © Bob Krist/Corbis; *The Rock Eagle Effigy Mound* © Tami Chappell/America 24-7/Getty Images; *Tybee Island boat marina* © Walter Bibikow/Age Fotostock; *Georgia State Capitol Building* © W. Cody/Corbis

ISBN-10: 0-618-92008-0
ISBN-13: 978-0-618-92008-2 56789—0918—11 10

Internet Web Site: http://www.mcdougallittell.com

About This Book

McDougal Littell Georgia High School Mathematics 3

The Georgia High School Mathematics 3 book covers all of the Georgia Performance Standards for Mathematics 3. Its content has been organized into a convenient sequence that corresponds to the strands of the Georgia Performance Standards. Georgia standards that correlate to the content of each lesson are given at point of use in the Student Edition and Teacher's Edition of *Georgia High School Mathematics 3*.

At the front of this book, you will find a complete listing of all the Georgia Performance Standards for Mathematics 3, along with a correlation of these standards to appropriate lessons in *Georgia High School Mathematics 3*.

Advisers and Reviewers

Curriculum Advisers and Reviewers

Michele Borror Long
Mathematics Teacher
LaGrange High School
LaGrange, GA

Sandye Ashley
Mathematics Teacher
Rome Middle School
Rome, GA

Georgia Panel

Ernest Adams
Mathematics Teacher, Department Chair
Northview High School
Duluth, GA

Salvatore Angelica
Mathematics Teacher
Luella High School
Locust Grove, GA

Sandra Campagnone
Mathematics Teacher
Pebblebrook High School
Mableton, GA

Mack Graham
Mathematics Teacher
Benjamin E. Mays High School
Atlanta, GA

Debra Hodge
Mathematics Teacher
Dunwoody High School
Dunwoody, GA

Carletta Malcom
Mathematics Teacher, Department Chair
Cedar Grove High School
Ellenwood, GA

Yvonne Pringle
Mathematics Teacher, Department Chair
North Atlanta High School
Atlanta, GA

Maria Travitz
Mathematics Teacher
Kennesaw Mountain High School
Kennesaw, GA

Melissa Walker
Mathematics Teacher, Department Chair
Martin Luther King, Jr. High School
Lithonia, GA

Contents

UNIT 1

Algebra: Linear Systems, Matrices, and Vertex-Edge Graphs

1.1 **Use Problem Solving Strategies and Models** (MM3P1d, MM3P3a) 2

1.2 **Solve Linear Systems by Graphing** (MM3A5c) 6

1.3 **Solve Linear Systems Algebraically** (MM3A5c) 13
• Investigating Math Activity: Systems with Many or No Solutions (MM3A5c) 12

1.4 **Graph Linear Inequalities in Two Variables** (MM3A6a) 17

1.5 **Graph Systems of Linear Inequalities** (MM3A6a) 23
• Problem Solving Workshop (MM3A6a) 29

1.6 **Linear Programming** (MM3A6b) 30

1.7 **Solve Systems of Linear Equations in Three Variables** (MM3A5c) 34

1.8 **Perform Basic Matrix Operations** (MM3A4a, MM3A4c) 38

1.9 **Multiply Matrices** (MM3A4a, MM3A4c) 43
• Technology Activity: Matrix Operations (MM3A4a) 48

1.10 **Evaluate Determinants and Apply Cramer's Rule** (MM3A5c) 49

1.11 **Use Inverse Matrices to Solve Linear Systems** (MM3A4b, MM3A5a, MM3A5b) 54
• Investigating Math Activity: Inverse Matrices (MM3A4a, MM3A4b) 53

1.12 **Use Vertex-Edge Graphs** (MM3A7a, MM3A7b) 59

Unit 1 Test 63

UNIT 2

Algebra: Polynomial Functions

2.1 **Evaluate and Graph Polynomial Functions** (MM3A1b, MM3A1c, MM3A1d) 66

2.2 **Translate Graphs of Polynomial Functions** (MM3A1a, MM3A1c, MM3A1d) 71

2.3 **Factor and Solve Polynomial Equations** (MM3A3b, MM3A3d) 76
• Problem Solving Workshop (MM3A3b, MM3A3d) 80

2.4 **Solve Polynomial Inequalities** (MM3A3c) 81

2.5 **Apply the Remainder and Factor Theorems** (MM3A3a, MM3A3d) 85

2.6 **Find Rational Zeros** (MM3A3a, MM3A3d) 89

2.7 **Apply the Fundamental Theorem of Algebra** (MM3A3a, MM3A3d) 94
• Investigating Math Activity: Zeros of a Polynomial Function (MM3A1b, MM3A1d, MM3A3a) 93

2.8 **Analyze Graphs of Polynomial Functions** (MM3A1b, MM3A1d) 98
• Technology Activity: Local Maximums and Minimums (MM3A1d) 104

Unit 2 Test 105

UNIT 3

Algebra: Rational Exponents and Square Root Functions

3.1 **Evaluate *n*th Roots and Use Rational Exponents** (MM3A2a, MM3A2b, MM3A3d) 109
• Investigating Math Activity: Radicals and Rational Exponents (MM3A2a) 108

3.2 **Apply Properties of Rational Exponents** (MM3A2b) 113
• Problem Solving Workshop (MM3A2b) 117

3.3 **Graph Square Root and Cube Root Functions** (MM3A3d) 118

3.4 **Solve Radical Equations** (MM3A3d) 122
• Technology Activity: Radical Equations (MM3A3d) 126

Unit 3 Test 127

UNIT 4

Algebra: Exponential and Logarithmic Functions

4.1 **Graph Exponential Growth Functions** (MM3A2e, MM3A2f, MM3A2g) 130
• Problem Solving Workshop (MM3A2g, MM3A3d) 134

4.2 **Graph Exponential Decay Functions** (MM3A2e, MM3A2f, MM3A2g) 135
• Technology Activity: Evaluate Exponential Decay Models (MM3A2g) 139

4.3 **Use Functions Involving *e*** (MM3A2e, MM3A2f, MM3A2g, MM3A3d) 140

4.4 **Evaluate Logarithms and Graph Logarithmic Functions** (MM3A2c, MM3A2e, MM3A2f) 145
• Investigating Math Activity: Explore Exponential and Logarithmic Equations (MM3A2c) 144

4.5 **Interpret Graphs of Exponential and Logarithmic Functions** (MM3A2e, MM3A2f) 149

4.6 **Apply Properties of Logarithms** (MM3A2d, MM3A2g) 155

4.7 **Solve Exponential and Logarithmic Equations** (MM3A3b, MM3A3d) 159

4.8 **Solve Exponential and Logarithmic Inequalities** (MM3A3c) 163

4.9 **Write and Apply Exponential and Power Functions** (MM3A2g) 169

Unit 4 Test 173

UNIT 5

Geometry

5.1 Graph and Write Equations of Parabolas (MM3G2b, MM3G2c) 176

5.2 Graph and Write Equations of Circles (MM3G1a, MM3G1b, MM3G1c) 180
- Problem Solving Workshop (MM3G1a) 184

5.3 Graph and Write Equations of Ellipses (MM3G2b, MM3G2c) 186
- Investigating Math Activity: Draw an Ellipse (MM3G2b) 185

5.4 Graph and Write Equations of Hyperbolas (MM3G2b, MM3G2c) 190

5.5 Translate and Classify Conic Sections (MM3G2a, MM3G2b, MM3G2c) 194

5.6 Solve Quadratic Systems (MM3G1d, MM3G1e) 200
- Technology Activity: Solve Quadratic Systems (MM3G1d) 204

5.7 Use Figures in Three-Dimensional Space (MM3G3a, MM3G3b, MM3G3c) 205

Unit 5 Test 209

UNIT 6

Data Analysis and Probability

6.1 Construct and Interpret Binomial Distributions (MM3D1) 212
- Technology Activity: Create a Binomial Distribution (MM3D1) 217

6.2 Use Normal Distributions (MM3D2a, MM3D2b, MM3D2c) 219
- Investigating Math Activity: Explore a Normal Curve (MM3D2a) 218

6.3 Approximate Binomial Distributions and Test Hypotheses (MM3D2b, MM3D2c, MM3D3) 224
- Investigating Math Activity: Collecting Data (MM3D3) 223

6.4 Select and Draw Conclusions from Samples (MM3D3) 228
- Problem Solving Workshop (MM3D3) 232

6.5 Experimental and Observational Studies (MM3D3) 233

Unit 6 Test 237

Student Resources

Tables .... pages 240–248

Refer to the tables for information about mathematical symbols, measures, formulas, postulates, theorems, properties, squares, square roots, and the Standard Normal Table.

- Table of Symbols 240
- Time and Measures 241
- Area and Volume Formulas 242
- Other Formulas 243–244
- Theorems 244
- Properties 245–246
- Squares and Square Roots 247
- Standard Normal Table 248

English–Spanish Glossary .... page 250

Use the English–Spanish Glossary to see definitions in English and Spanish, as well as examples illustrating vocabulary.

Index .... page 276

Look up items in the alphabetical Index to find where a particular math topic is covered in the book.

Selected Answers .... page SA1

Use the Selected Answers to check your work.

Correlation to Standards

Correlation of *McDougal Littell Georgia High School Mathematics 3* to the Georgia Performance Standards for Mathematics 3

ALGEBRA

Students will investigate exponential, logarithmic and polynomial functions of degree higher than 2. Students will understand matrices and use them to solve problems.

Georgia Performance Standard		Lesson / Activity
MM3A1	**Students will analyze graphs of polynomial functions of higher degree.**	
MM3A1a	Graph simple polynomial functions as translations of the function $f(x) = ax^n$.	Lesson 2.2
MM3A1b	Understand the effects of the following on the graph of a polynomial function: degree, lead coefficient, and multiplicity of real zeros.	Lesson 2.1, Lesson 2.8
MM3A1c	Determine whether a polynomial function has symmetry and whether it is even, odd, or neither.	Lesson 2.1, Lesson 2.2
MM3A1d	Investigate and explain characteristics of polynomial functions, including domain and range, intercepts, zeros, relative and absolute extrema, intervals of increase and decrease, and end behavior.	Lesson 2.1, Lesson 2.2, Investigating Math Activity 2.7, Lesson 2.8, Technology Activity 2.8
MM3A2	**Students will explore logarithmic functions as inverses of exponential functions.**	
MM3A2a	Define and understand properties of nth roots.	Lesson 3.1, Investigating Math Activity 3.1
MM3A2b	Extend properties of exponents to include rational exponents.	Lesson 3.1, Lesson 3.2, Problem Solving Workshop 3.2
MM3A2c	Define logarithmic functions as inverses of exponential functions.	Lesson 4.4, Investigating Math Activity 4.4
MM3A2d	Understand and use properties of logarithms by extending laws of exponents.	Lesson 4.6
MM3A2e	Investigate and explain characteristics of exponential and logarithmic functions including domain and range, asymptotes, zeros, intercepts, intervals of increase and decrease, and rate of change.	Lesson 4.1, Lesson 4.2, Lesson 4.3, Lesson 4.4, Lesson 4.5
MM3A2f	Graph functions as transformations of $f(x) = a^x$, $f(x) = \log_a x$, $f(x) = e^x$, $f(x) = \ln x$.	Lesson 4.1, Lesson 4.2, Lesson 4.3, Lesson 4.4, Lesson 4.5

Georgia Performance Standard		Lesson / Activity
MM3A2g	Explore real phenomena related to exponential and logarithmic functions including half-life and doubling time.	Lesson 4.1, Problem Solving Workshop 4.1, Lesson 4.2, Technology Activity 4.2, Lesson 4.3, Lesson 4.6, Lesson 4.9
MM3A3	**Students will solve a variety of equations and inequalities.**	
MM3A3a	Find real and complex roots of higher degree polynomial equations using the factor theorem, remainder theorem, rational root theorem, and fundamental theorem of algebra, incorporating complex and radical conjugates.	Lesson 2.5, Lesson 2.6, Lesson 2.7, Investigating Math Activity 2.7
MM3A3b	Solve polynomial, exponential, and logarithmic equations analytically, graphically, and using appropriate technology.	Lesson 2.3, Problem Solving Workshop 2.3, Lesson 4.7
MM3A3c	Solve polynomial, exponential, and logarithmic inequalities analytically, graphically, and using appropriate technology. Represent solution sets of inequalities using interval notation.	Lesson 2.4, Lesson 4.8
MM3A3d	Solve a variety of types of equations by appropriate means choosing among mental calculation, pencil and paper, or appropriate technology.	Lesson 2.3, Problem Solving Workshop 2.3, Lesson 2.5, Lesson 2.6, Lesson 2.7, Lesson 3.1, Lesson 3.3, Lesson 3.4, Technology Activity 3.4, Problem Solving Workshop 4.1, Lesson 4.3, Lesson 4.7
MM3A4	**Students will perform basic operations with matrices.**	
MM3A4a	Add, subtract, multiply, and invert matrices, when possible, choosing appropriate methods including technology.	Lesson 1.8, Lesson 1.9, Technology Activity 1.9, Investigating Math Activity 1.11
MM3A4b	Find the inverses of two-by-two matrices using pencil and paper, and find inverses of larger matrices using technology.	Lesson 1.11, Investigating Math Activity 1.11
MM3A4c	Examine the properties of matrices, contrasting them with properties of real numbers.	Lesson 1.8, Lesson 1.9
MM3A5	**Students will use matrices to formulate and solve problems.**	
MM3A5a	Represent a system of linear equations as a matrix equation.	Lesson 1.11
MM3A5b	Solve matrix equations using inverse matrices.	Lesson 1.11
MM3A5c	Represent and solve realistic problems using systems of linear equations.	Lesson 1.2, Lesson 1.3, Investigating Math Activity 1.3, Lesson 1.7, Lesson 1.10

Georgia Performance Standard		Lesson/Activity
MM3A6	**Students will solve linear programming problems in two variables.**	
MM3A6a	Solve systems of inequalities in two variables, showing the solutions graphically.	Lesson 1.4, Lesson 1.5, Problem Solving Workshop 1.5
MM3A6b	Represent and solve realistic problems using linear programming.	Lesson 1.6
MM3A7	**Students will understand and apply matrix representations of vertex-edge graphs.**	
MM3A7a	Use graphs to represent realistic situations.	Lesson 1.12
MM3A7b	Use matrices to represent graphs, and solve problems that can be represented by graphs.	Lesson 1.12

GEOMETRY

Students will understand and use the analytic geometry of conic sections and of planes and spheres in space.

MM3G1	**Students will investigate the relationships between lines and circles.**	
MM3G1a	Find equations of circles.	Lesson 5.2, Problem Solving Workshop 5.2
MM3G1b	Graph a circle given an equation in general form.	Lesson 5.2
MM3G1c	Find the equation of a tangent line to a circle at a given point.	Lesson 5.2
MM3G1d	Solve a system of equations involving a circle and a line.	Lesson 5.6, Technology Activity 5.6
MM3G1e	Solve a system of equations involving two circles.	Lesson 5.6
MM3G2	**Students will recognize, analyze, and graph the equations of the conic sections (parabolas, circles, ellipses, and hyperbolas).**	
MM3G2a	Convert equations of conics by completing the square.	Lesson 5.5
MM3G2b	Graph conic sections, identifying fundamental characteristics.	Lesson 5.1, Lesson 5.3, Investigating Math Activity 5.3, Lesson 5.4, Lesson 5.5
MM3G2c	Write equations of conic sections given appropriate information.	Lesson 5.1, Lesson 5.3, Lesson 5.4, Lesson 5.5
MM3G3	**Students will investigate planes and spheres.**	
MM3G3a	Plot the point (x, y, z) and understand it as a vertex of a rectangular prism.	Lesson 5.7
MM3G3b	Apply the distance formula in 3-space.	Lesson 5.7

Georgia Performance Standard		Lesson / Activity
MM3G3c	Recognize and understand equations of planes and spheres.	Lesson 5.7

DATA ANALYSIS AND PROBABILITY

Students will use a normal distribution to calculate probabilities. They will organize, represent, investigate, interpret, and make inferences using data from both observational studies and experiments.

MM3D1	Students will create probability histograms of discrete random variables, using both experimental and theoretical probabilities.	Lesson 6.1, Technology Activity 6.1
MM3D2	**Students will solve problems involving probabilities by interpreting a normal distribution as a probability histogram for a continuous random variable (z-scores are used for a general normal distribution).**	
MM3D2a	Determine intervals about the mean that include a given percent of data.	Lesson 6.2, Investigating Math Activity 6.2
MM3D2b	Determine the probability that a given value falls within a specified interval.	Lesson 6.2, Lesson 6.3
MM3D2c	Estimate how many items in a population fall within a specified interval.	Lesson 6.2, Lesson 6.3
MM3D3	Students will understand the differences between experimental and observational studies by posing questions and collecting, analyzing, and interpreting data.	Lesson 6.3, Investigating Math Activity 6.3, Lesson 6.4, Problem Solving Workshop 6.4, Lesson 6.5

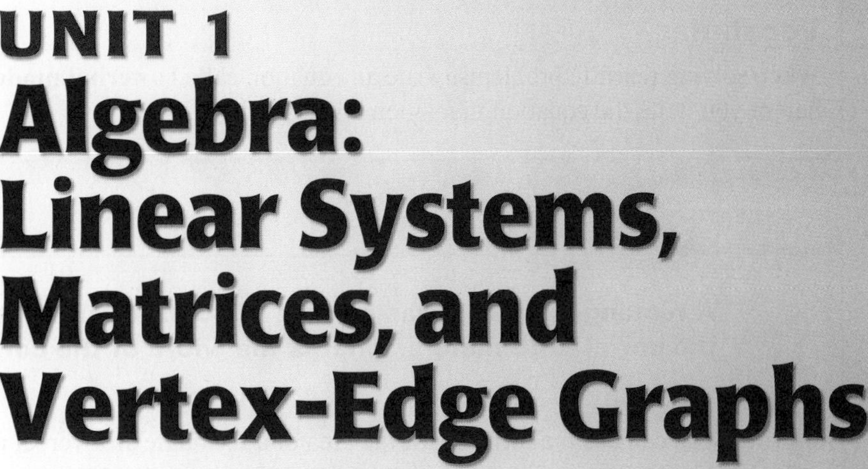

UNIT 1 Algebra: Linear Systems, Matrices, and Vertex-Edge Graphs

1.1 Use Problem Solving Strategies and Models (MM3P1d, MM3P3a)

1.2 Solve Linear Systems by Graphing (MM3A5c)

1.3 Solve Linear Systems Algebraically (MM3A5c)

1.4 Graph Linear Inequalities in Two Variables (MM3A6a)

1.5 Graph Systems of Linear Inequalities (MM3A6a)

1.6 Linear Programming (MM3A6b)

1.7 Solve Systems of Linear Equations in Three Variables (MM3A5c)

1.8 Perform Basic Matrix Operations (MM3A4a, MM3A4c)

1.9 Multiply Matrices (MM3A4a, MM3A4c)

1.10 Evaluate Determinants and Apply Cramer's Rule (MM3A5c)

1.11 Use Inverse Matrices to Solve Linear Systems (MM3A4b, MM3A5a, MM3A5b)

1.12 Use Vertex-Edge Graphs (MM3A7a, MM3A7b)

LESSON 1.1

Use Problem Solving Strategies and Models

Georgia Performance Standards: MM3P1d, MM3P3a

Goal Solve problems using verbal models.

Vocabulary

When solving real-life problems, write an equation called a **verbal model** in words before you write the equation in mathematical symbols.

Example 1 Use a formula

A rectangular corral has an area of 3500 square meters. If the length of the corral is 75 meters, what is the width of the corral?

Solution

You can use the formula for the area of a rectangle as a verbal model.

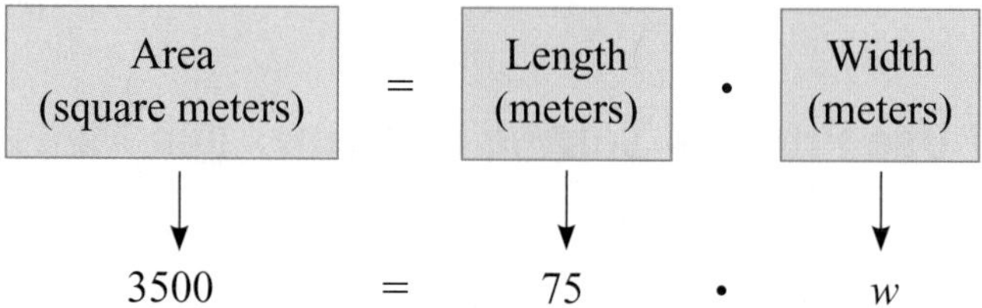

An equation for this situation is $3500 = 75w$. Solve for w.

$3500 = 75w$ Write equation.

$46.7 \approx w$ Divide each side by 75.

The width of the corral is about 46.7 meters.

Guided Practice for Example 1

1. The perimeter of a rectangular city park is 1260 yards. The width of the park is 290 yards. What is the length of the park?

2. A boat travels at a speed of 32 miles per hour. How long will it take the boat to travel 144 miles?

Example 2 Look for a pattern

Look for a pattern in the table. Then write an equation that represents the table.

x	0	1	2	3
y	0	6	12	18

Solution

The x-values increase by 1 and the y-values increase by 6. You can use this pattern to write the equation $y = 6x$.

UNIT 1

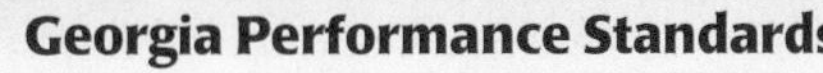

Georgia Performance Standards

MM3P1d Monitor and reflect on the process of mathematical problem solving. ☑

MM3P3a Organize and consolidate their mathematical thinking through communication. ☑

Guided Practice for Example 2

Look for a pattern in the table. Then write an equation that represents the table.

3.

x	0	1	2	3
y	0	−3	−6	−9

4.

x	0	1	2	3
y	1	8	15	22

Example 3 Draw a diagram

Rock Pond You are designing a square rock pond surrounded by a brick sidewalk of uniform width. The pond has a side length of 32 feet. The side length of the outside square is 40 feet. Draw a diagram to find the width of the sidewalk.

Solution

Begin by drawing and labeling a diagram, as shown below.

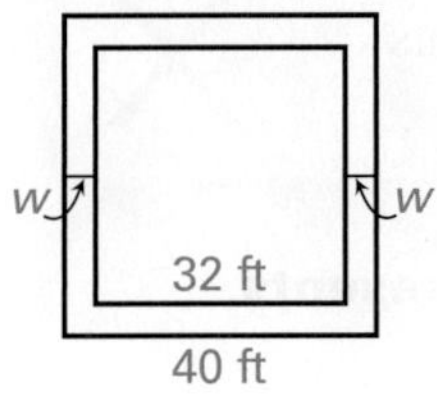

From the diagram, you can write and solve an equation to find w.

$w + 32 + w = 40$ Write equation.

$2w + 32 = 40$ Combine like terms.

$2w = 8$ Subtract 32 from each side.

$w = 4$ Divide each side by 2.

The width of the sidewalk is 4 feet.

Guided Practice for Example 3

5. **Fabric** A piece of fabric is 50 inches long. You cut the fabric into two pieces. The first piece is x inches long. The second piece is 16 inches longer than the first piece. Draw and label a diagram of the fabric. Then write and solve an equation to find x.

6. **Construction** You want to create an open rectangular box from a square piece of cardboard. The cardboard is 24 inches by 24 inches and you will cut 3 inch squares from each corner. Draw a diagram to find the length of the box.

UNIT 1

LESSON 1.1

Exercise Set A

MM3P1d Monitor and reflect on the process of mathematical problem solving.

MM3P3a Organize and consolidate their mathematical thinking through communication.

UNIT 1

Use the formula $d = rt$ for distance traveled to solve for the missing variable.

1. $d = \underline{?}$, $r = 45$ mi/h, $t = 7$ h
2. $d = 420$ mi, $r = 70$ mi/h, $t = \underline{?}$
3. $d = 504$ mi, $r = \underline{?}$, $t = 8$ h
4. $d = 577.5$ mi, $r = 55$ mi/h, $t = \underline{?}$

Use the formula $A = bh$ for the area of a parallelogram to solve for the missing variable.

5. $A = \underline{?}$, $b = 9$ ft, $h = 6$ ft
6. $A = 62$ in.^{2}, $b = \underline{?}$, $h = 4$ in.
7. $A = 195$ m^2, $b = 15$ m, $h = \underline{?}$
8. $A = \underline{?}$, $b = 26$ cm, $h = 17$ cm
9. Error Analysis *Describe* and correct the error in writing an equation.

x	0	5	10	15
y	9	19	29	39

An equation that represents the table is $y = 9 + 10x$.

Look for a pattern in the table. Then write an equation that represents the table.

10.

x	0	1	2	3
y	9	17	25	33

11.

x	0	1	2	3
y	34	37	40	43

12.

x	0	1	2	3
y	79	74	69	64

13.

x	0	1	2	3
y	58	47	36	25

14. **Windsurfing** The highest speed reached by a windsurfer is about 56.04 miles per hour. How far could a windsurfer travel in 1.5 hours at this speed?
15. **Shopping** You buy a pair of jeans for \$29.99. T-shirts are on sale for \$8.95 each. You have \$80 to spend for clothes. How many T-shirts can you purchase?
16. **Travel** You and a friend take turns driving on a 530 mile trip. Your friend drives for 4.5 hours at an average speed of 60 miles per hour. What must your average speed be for the remainder of the trip if you want to reach your hotel in 4 more hours?
17. **Remodeling** A five gallon bucket of polyurethane can seal 3200 square feet of floor space. If you need to cover 9000 square feet, how many buckets of polyurethane must be purchased in order to cover it?

LESSON 1.1

Exercise Set B

MM3P1d Monitor and reflect on the process of mathematical problem solving.

MM3P3a Organize and consolidate their mathematical thinking through communication.

Look for a pattern in the table. Then write an equation that represents the table.

1.

x	0	1	2	3
y	22	28	34	40

2.

x	0	4	8	12
y	60	52	44	36

3. **Multiple Representations** Your cell phone plan costs $52 per month plus $.10 per text message. You receive a bill for $69.20.

a. **Making a Table** Copy and complete the table below. Use the table to estimate how many text messages you sent.

Text messages	0	50	100	150	200
Monthly bill	$52	?	?	?	?

b. **Writing a Model** Write an equation for the situation. Solve it to find exactly how many text messages you sent.

c. **Comparing Answers** Is your estimate from part (a) compatible with the exact answer from part (b)? *Explain.*

4. **Commission** A salesman earns a base salary of $12,000 per year. The salesman also receives a 7% commission on his sales. If his total sales exceed $500,000 for the year, a bonus of $5000 is paid in December. Last year the salesman reported an income of $56,921 to the IRS. What were his total sales?

5. **Wood Shop** You have a piece of wood that is 84 inches long. You cut the wood into three pieces. The second piece is 8 inches longer than the first piece. The third piece is 16 inches longer than the first piece. Draw a diagram and then write and solve an equation to find the lengths of the three pieces.

6. **Painting** You and a group of friends volunteer to help paint a house. You need to paint 4 rooms in 8 hours. If each person can paint one room in 10 hours, how many people will it take to paint all of the rooms on time?

7. **Art Gallery** The owner of an art gallery wants to hang five paintings on a wall so that the spaces between the paintings are the same. The owner also wants the spaces at the left and right of the group of paintings to be twice the space between any two adjacent paintings. The wall is 24 feet wide and the paintings are 2 feet wide. Draw a diagram and then write and solve an equation to find how to position the paintings.

LESSON 1.2

Solve Linear Systems by Graphing

Georgia Performance Standards: MM3A5c

Goal Solve systems of linear equations.

Vocabulary

A **system of two linear equations** in two variables x and y, also called a linear system, consists of two equations that can be written in the following form:
$Ax + By = C$ and $Dx + Ey = F$.

A **solution of a system** of linear equations in two variables is an ordered pair (x, y) that satisfies each equation.

A system that has at least one solution is **consistent.**

If a system has no solution, the system is **inconsistent.** The graph of this system is a pair of parallel lines.

A consistent system that has exactly one solution is **independent.**

A consistent system that has infinitely many solutions is **dependent.** The graph of this system is a pair of lines that coincide.

UNIT 1

Example 1 Solve a system graphically

Graph the linear system and estimate the solution. Then check the solution algebraically.

$y + 3x = 5$ Equation 1

$y - 2x = -5$ Equation 2

Solution

Begin by graphing both equations, as shown at the right. From the graph, the lines appear to intersect at $(2, -1)$. The solution can be checked algebraically:

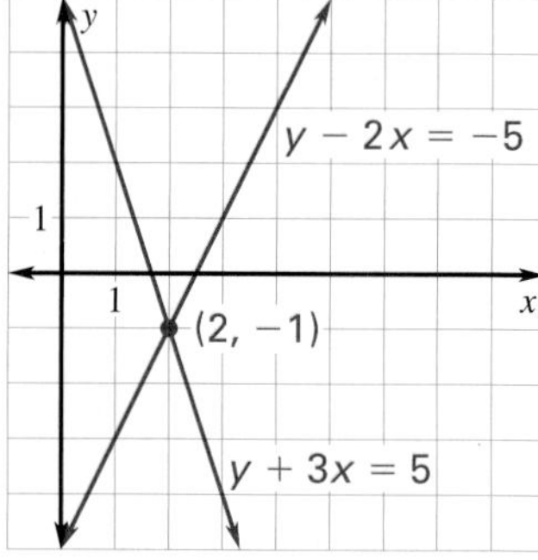

Equation 1	Equation 2
$y + 3x = 5$	$y - 2x = -5$
$(-1) + 3(2) \stackrel{?}{=} 5$	$-1 - 2(2) \stackrel{?}{=} -5$
$-1 + 6 \stackrel{?}{=} 5$	$-1 - 4 \stackrel{?}{=} -5$
$5 = 5$ ✓	$-5 = -5$ ✓

The solution is $(2, -1)$.

Guided Practice for Example 1

Graph the linear system and estimate the solution. Then check the solution algebraically.

1. $y = 4x - 1$
$y = 3x$

2. $3x + y = 7$
$y = 2x - 3$

3. $2x + 3y = 5$
$3x - 4y = -1$

Georgia Performance Standards

MM3A5c Represent and solve realistic problems using systems of linear equations.

Example 2 Classify a system of two linear equations

Classify each system as *consistent and independent, consistent and dependent,* or *inconsistent.*

a. $10x - 2y = 14$ Equation 1

$5x - y = 7$ Equation 2

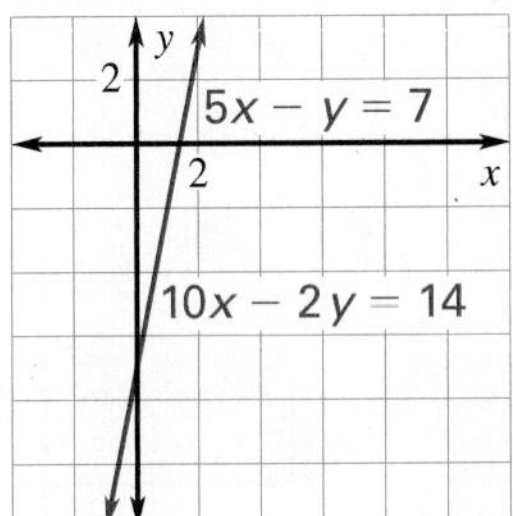

The graphs of the equations are the same line. The system is consistent and dependent.

b. $3x + 2y = 2$ Equation 1

$3x + 2y = 4$ Equation 2

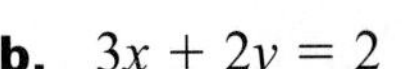

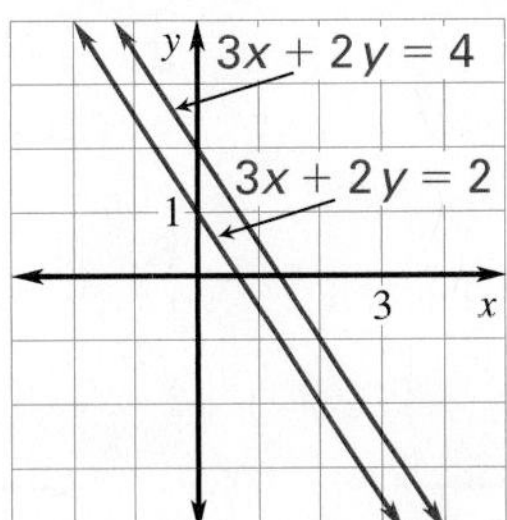

The graphs of the equations are parallel lines. The system is inconsistent.

Example 3 Write and use a linear system

Resort Costs Resort A charges \$70 per night, plus a one-time surcharge of \$5. Resort B charges \$65 per night, plus a one-time surcharge of \$20. After how many nights will the total cost of the two options be the same?

Let x represent the number of nights at the resort.
Let y represent the total cost of the stay at the resort.

$y = 70x + 5$ Equation 1 (Resort A)

$y = 65x + 20$ Equation 2 (Resort B)

To solve the system, graph the equations. The lines appear to intersect at (3, 215). So, after 3 nights the total cost of the two options is the same.

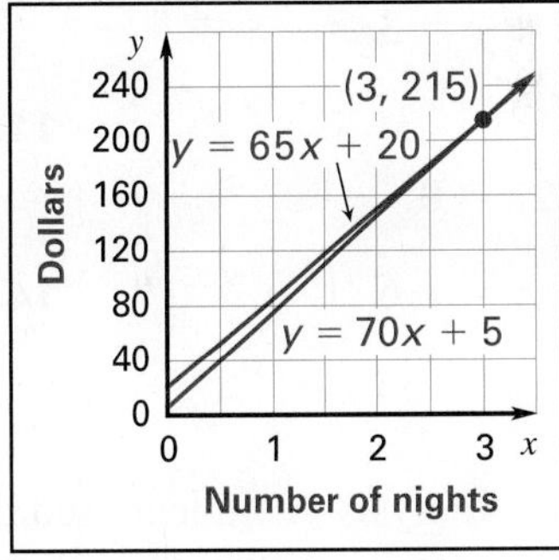

Guided Practice for Examples 2 and 3

Solve the system. Then classify the system as *consistent and independent, consistent and dependent,* or *inconsistent.*

4. $y = -2x$
$y = x + 3$

5. $y - 3x = 2$
$y - 3x = 3$

6. $x + y = 6$
$-2x - 2y = -12$

7. **What If?** In Example 3, suppose Resort A charges \$70 per night, plus a one-time surcharge of \$10 and Resort B charges \$60 per night, plus a one-time surcharge of \$30. After how many nights will the total cost of the two options be the same?

LESSON 1.2 **Exercise Set A**

MM3A5c Represent and solve realistic problems using systems of linear equations.

Match the linear system with its graph. Then classify the system as *consistent and independent, consistent and dependent,* or *inconsistent.*

1. $3x - 2y = 2$
$-2x + y = -2$

2. $4x - y = 3$
$-8x + 2y = -6$

3. $x + 3y = 2$
$-3x - 9y = 18$

A.

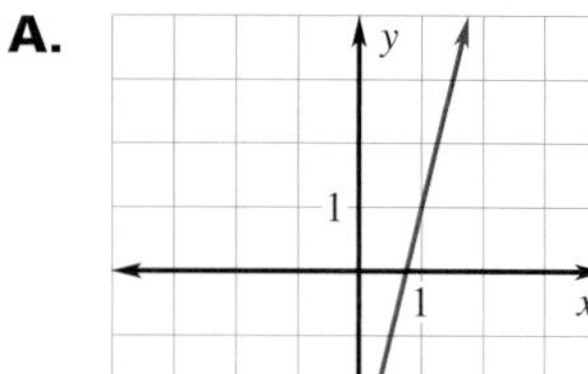

B.

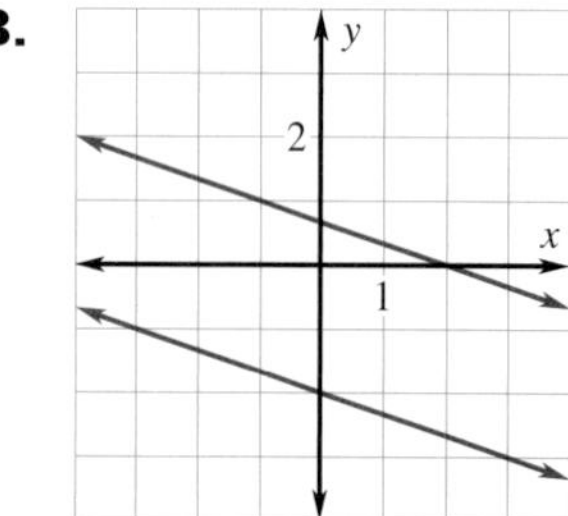

C.

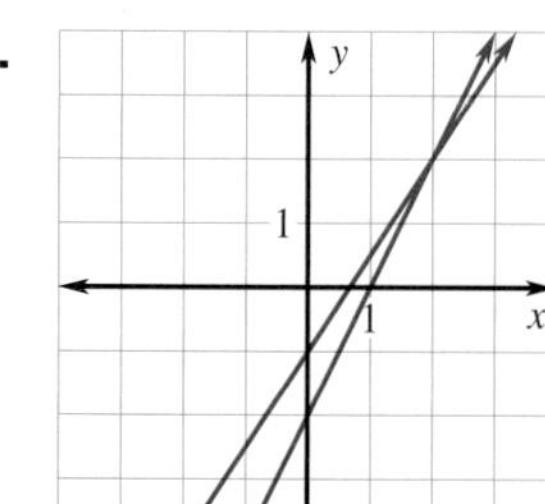

Graph the linear system and estimate the solution. Then check the solution algebraically.

4. $2x + 3y = 8$
$-x + y = -4$

5. $3x + 5y = -4$
$2x - y = -7$

6. $x - 2y = 4$
$4x + 2y = 6$

7. $3x + y = 3$
$-2x + y = 3$

8. $5x - 2y = -1$
$x - 3y = 5$

9. $x - 2y = -5$
$-2x + 6y = 18$

10. $3x + 3y = 3$
$x + 2y = 0$

11. $2x - 4y = 2$
$-2x + 3y = 0$

12. $5x - 3y = -17$
$4x + 5y = 16$

13. $4x - y = -6$
$3x + 7y = 11$

14. $5x - 3y = 3$
$-x - y = -7$

15. $6x + y = -26$
$-4x - 7y = -8$

16. Error Analysis A student used the check shown to conclude that $(1, -2)$ is a solution of this system:

$5x - y = 7$

$x + 4y = -5$

Describe and correct the student's error.

$5x - y = 7$

$5(1) - (-2) \stackrel{?}{=} 7$

$7 = 7$

So, $(1, -2)$ is a solution of the system.

Solve the system. Then classify the system as *consistent and independent, consistent and dependent,* or *inconsistent.*

17. $y = -1$
$5x + y = 9$

18. $4x - y = 10$
$x - 4y = -5$

19. $y = 5x + 3$
$y = 5x - 3$

Exercise Set A *(continued)*

20. $y = 2x - 1$

$-8x + 4y = -4$

21. $-20x + 16y = -24$

$5x - 4y = 6$

22. $4x - 5y = -9$

$3x - 5y = -13$

23. $3x + 7y = 9$

$2x + 9y = 6$

24. $4x + 5y = 4$

$6x + 9y = 12$

25. $8x + 9y = 7$

$5x - 2y = 12$

26. $x - 2y = 5$

$2x - 4y = 10$

27. $5x + y = 16$

$-3x + y = 0$

28. $2x + \frac{1}{2}y = 4$

$12x - 6y = -12$

29. **Work Schedule** You worked 18 hours last week and earned a total of \$124 before taxes. Your job as a lifeguard pays \$8 per hour, and your job as a cashier pays \$6 per hour. How many hours did you work at each job?

30. **Law Enforcement** During one calendar year, a state trooper issued a total of 385 citations for warnings and speeding tickets. Of these, there were 31 more warnings than speeding tickets. How many warnings and how many speeding tickets were issued?

31. **Concert** A vendor sold 200 tickets for an upcoming rock concert. Floor seats were \$36 and stadium seats were \$28. The vendor sold \$6080 in tickets. How many \$36 and \$28 tickets did the vendor sell?

32. **Multiple Representations** The price of refrigerator A is \$800, and the price of refrigerator B is \$1300. The cost of electricity needed to operate the refrigerators is \$50 per year for refrigerator A and \$40 per year for refrigerator B.

a. **Writing Equations** Write an equation for the cost of owning refrigerator A and an equation for the cost of owning refrigerator B.

b. **Graphing Equations** Graph the equations from part (a). After how many years are the total costs of owning the refrigerators equal?

c. **Checking Reasonableness** Is your solution from part (b) reasonable in this situation? *Explain.*

In Exercises 33–36, use the following information.

Break-Even Analysis You purchase a music store for \$115,000. The estimated monthly revenue is \$5500 and expected monthly costs are \$3200.

33. Let R represent the revenue during the first t months. Write a linear model for R.

34. Let C represent the costs during the first t months including the purchase price. Write a linear model for C.

35. Graph the linear models for revenue and cost on the same coordinate plane.

36. How many months will it take until revenue and costs are equal (at the "break-even point")?

UNIT 1

LESSON 1.2 **Exercise Set B**

MM3A5c Represent and solve realistic problems using systems of linear equations.

Graph the linear system and estimate the solution. Then check the solution algebraically.

1. $x + 2y = 7$
$3x + y = 6$

2. $2x + 3y = 1$
$2x - y = 5$

3. $4x - 3y = 8$
$4x + 2y = -12$

4. $-3x - y = 1$
$x + y = 3$

5. $6x - 3y = 3$
$2x + 3y = 1$

6. $2x + 3y = 3$
$-x + 6y = -4$

7. $4x + 4y = 3$
$-2x + 5y = 2$

8. $3x - 4y = -5$
$-6x - 4y = 1$

9. $9x - 2y = 0$
$3x + 4y = 7$

10. $y = 3x + 2$
$15x - 5y = -10$

11. $x - 7y = 4$
$-3x + 21y = -12$

12. $2x + 9y = 4$
$-6x - 3y = -4$

Solve the system. Then classify the system as *consistent and independent, consistent and dependent,* or *inconsistent.*

13. $3x - 4y = 5$
$2x + y = 7$

14. $-2x + 6y = -2$
$-3x + 2y = 4$

15. $5x + 2y = -3$
$3x + y = -1$

16. $4x + 3y = -1$
$-2x - 3y = -4$

17. $8x + 4y = -4$
$x - 2y = 6$

18. $x - 5y = -5$
$3x - 15y = 9$

19. $3x + 4y = 8$
$-6x - 8y = -16$

20. $\frac{3}{2}x - y = 1$
$\frac{2}{3}x - y = \frac{3}{4}$

21. $2x + y = -5$
$\frac{1}{2}x - y = -3$

22. Write a system of equations that has no solutions.

23. Write a system of equations that has infinitely many solutions.

24. Write a system of equations that has exactly one solution.

Graph the system and estimate the solution(s). Then check the solution(s) algebraically.

25. $y = |x + 1|$
$y = x$

26. $y = |x - 4|$
$y = x$

27. $y = |x - 1|$
$y = -x + 2$

28. $y = |x + 1|$
$y = x - 2$

29. $y = |x| - 5$
$y = 5$

30. $y = |x| + 3$
$y = 3$

UNIT 1

In Exercises 31 and 32, use the following information.

Test Questions A math test is to have 20 questions. The test format uses multiple choice worth 4 points each and problem solving questions worth 6 points each. The test has a total of 100 points.

31. Write a system of equations to determine how many of each type of question are used.

32. Solve the system.

33. Multiple Representations The price of washer A is \$756, and the price of washer B is \$1424. The cost needed to operate the washers is \$90.25 per year for washer A and \$48.50 per year for washer B.

   a. Writing Equations Write an equation for the cost of owning washer A and an equation for the cost of owning washer B.

   b. Graphing Equations Graph the equations from part (a). Estimate the number of years before the total costs of owning the washers are equal. Use a graphing calculator to check your estimate.

   c. Checking Reasonableness Is your solution from part (b) reasonable in this situation? *Explain.*

In Exercises 34–36, use the following information.

Buying a Computer Store 1 is advertising that all desktop computers are 20% off for a limited time. Store 2 is advertising a \$250 rebate on all desktop computers. Assume that the lowest priced desktop computer is \$700.

34. Let x represent the original price and y represent the sale price. Write a system of equations that describes the prices of the computers in both stores.

35. Graph the system.

36. Under what circumstances does Store 1 have a better deal than Store 2?

In Exercises 37–40, use the following information.

Business Investing A business invests \$10,000 in equipment to produce a product. Each unit of the product costs \$.75 to produce and is sold for \$1.25.

37. Let R represent the revenue obtained by selling x units. Write a linear model for R.

38. Let C represent the total cost of producing x units. Write a linear model for C.

39. Graph the linear models for revenue and total cost on the same coordinate plane.

40. How many units must be sold before the revenue and costs are equal (at the "break-even point")?

Georgia Performance Standards

MM3A5c Represent and solve realistic problems using systems of linear equations.

Investigating Math Activity

Systems with Many or No Solutions

Use before Lesson 1.3

Materials graphing calculator

Question

How can you determine whether a system of linear equations has no solution or an infinite number of solutions without solving or graphing the system?

Explore

Determine whether the system has many or no solutions.

Graph the system of linear equations. Use the graph to determine whether the system has no solutions or an infinite number of solutions.

$$x + 2y = 6$$
$$3x + 6y = 3$$

STEP 1 Enter the equations in slope-intercept form.

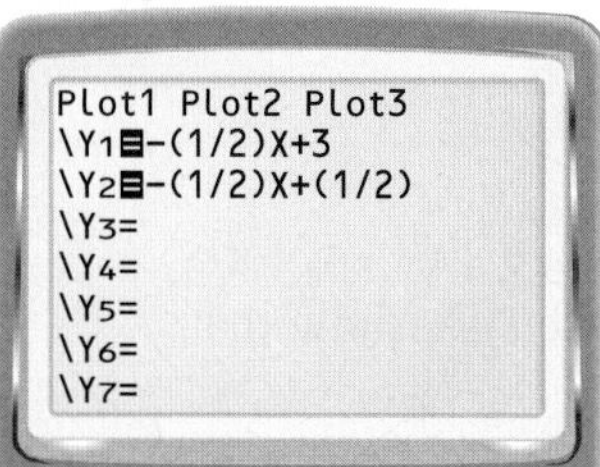

STEP 2 Graph the equations in a standard viewing window.

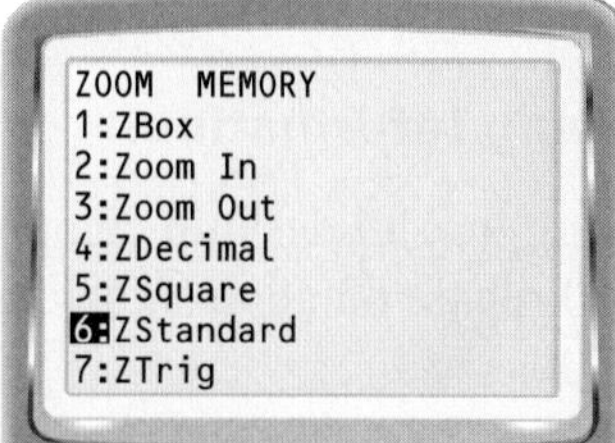

STEP 3 The graph shows that the number of solutions is zero.

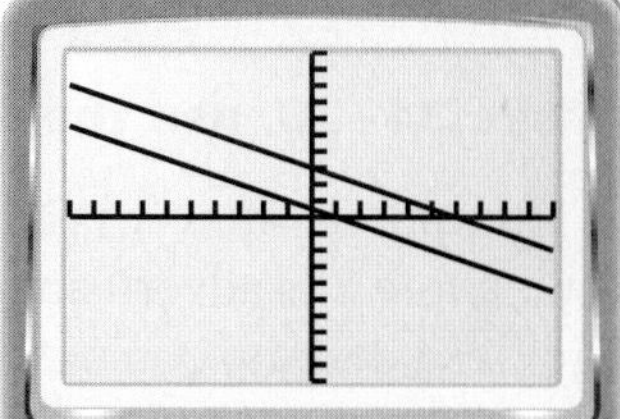

Draw Conclusions

In Exercises 1–3, graph the system of linear equations. Use the graph to determine whether the system has no solutions or an infinite number of solutions.

1. $5x - 2y = 9$
$20x - 8y = -28$

2. $x - 4y = 10$
$2x - 8y = 20$

3. $8x - 6y = 10$
$-12x + 9y = -15$

4. What types of lines were graphed in the Explore and Exercise 1? In each system, how do the coefficients of x compare? the coefficients of y? the constants?

5. What types of lines were graphed in Exercise 2 and Exercise 3? In each system, how do the coefficients of x compare? the coefficients of y? the constants?

6. Reasoning Based on your results, make a conjecture about the relationship between the equations in a system and whether it has no solutions or an infinite number of solutions.

LESSON 1.3

Solve Linear Systems Algebraically

Georgia Performance Standards: MM3A5c

Goal Solve linear systems algebraically.

Vocabulary

To use the **substitution method,** Step 1 is to *solve* one of the equations for one of its variables. Step 2 is to *substitute* the expression from Step 1 into the other equation and solve for the other variable. Step 3 is to *substitute* the value from Step 2 into the revised equation from Step 1 and solve.

To use the **elimination method,** Step 1 is to *multiply* one or both of the equations by a constant to obtain coefficients that differ only in sign for one of the variables. Step 2 is to *add* the revised equations from Step 1 and solve for the remaining variable. Step 3 is to *substitute* the value obtained in Step 2 into either of the original equations and solve for the other variable.

Example 1 Use the substitution method

Solve the system using the substitution method.

$6x + 3y = 12$ **Equation 1**

$3x + y = 5$ **Equation 2**

Solution

STEP 1 **Solve** Equation 2 for y.

$y = 5 - 3x$

STEP 2 **Substitute** the expression for y into Equation 1 and solve for x.

$6x + 3(5 - 3x) = 12$ Substitute $5 - 3x$ for y.

$x = 1$ Solve for x.

STEP 3 **Substitute** the value of x into the revised equation from Step 1 and solve for y.

$y = 5 - 3(1)$ Substitute 1 for x.

$y = 2$ Solve for y.

The solution is (1, 2).

Guided Practice for Example 1

Solve the system using the substitution method.

1. $2x + y = 4$
$3x - 5y = 6$

2. $3x + 6y = 3$
$x - 2y = 5$

3. $2x - y = 6$
$-3x + 2y = -8$

UNIT 1

Georgia Performance Standards

MM3A5c Represent and solve realistic problems using systems of linear equations.

Example 2 Use the elimination method

School T-Shirts Your school sells short sleeve T-shirts that cost the school \$5 each and are sold for \$8 each. Long sleeve T-shirts cost the school \$7 each and are sold for \$13 each. The school spends a total of \$2450 on T-shirts and sells all of them for \$4325. How many of each type of T-shirt are sold?

STEP 1 **Write** a system of equations. Let x represent the number of short sleeve T-shirts and let y represent the number of long sleeve T-shirts.

$5x + 7y = 2450$ Equation 1: Total cost for all T-shirts

$8x + 13y = 4325$ Equation 2: Total revenue from all T-shirts sold

STEP 2 **Multiply** Equation 1 by -8 and Equation 2 by 5 so that the coefficients of x differ only in sign. Then add the revised equations and solve for y.

$5x + 7y = 2450$ → $\times -8$ → $-40x - 56y = -19{,}600$

$8x + 13y = 4325$ → $\times 5$ → $40x + 65y = 21{,}625$

$9y = 2025$ → $y = 225$

STEP 3 **Substitute** the value of y into one of the original equations and solve for x.

$5x + 7(225) = 2450$ Substitute 225 for y in Equation 1.

$x = 175$ Simplify and solve for x.

The school sold 175 short sleeve T-shirts and 225 long sleeve T-shirts.

Example 3 Solve linear systems with many or no solutions

a. **Solve:** $9x - 3y = 6$
$3x - y = 2$

b. **Solve:** $x - 2y = 5$
$4x - 8y = 3$

a. $y = 3x - 2$ Solve second equation for y.

$9x - 3(3x - 2) = 6$ Substitute $3x - 2$ for y in first equation.

$6 = 6$ Simplify.

Because the equation $6 = 6$ is always true, there are infinitely many solutions.

b. $-4x + 8y = -20$ Multiply first equation by -4.

$4x - 8y = 3$ Add the second equation.

$0 = -17$

Because the equation $0 = -17$ is never true, there is no solution.

Guided Practice for Examples 2 and 3

Solve the linear system by any algebraic method.

4. $7x + 2y = -5$
$3x - 4y = -7$

5. $2x - 3y = 3$
$4x - 5y = 9$

6. $3x - y = 5$
$6x - 2y = 10$

7. $x - 2y = 5$
$4x - 8y = -3$

UNIT 1

LESSON 1.3

Exercise Set A

MM3A5c Represent and solve realistic problems using systems of linear equations.

Solve the system using the substitution method.

1. $x + 2y = 6$
$3x - 2y = 2$

2. $x + 3y = 3$
$2x - 4y = 6$

3. $4x + y = 7$
$2x + 5y = -1$

4. $2x - 3y = 3$
$-2x + y = -4$

5. $3x + 2y = -2$
$6x - y = 6$

6. $8x + 2y = 2$
$x + 3y = 14$

Solve the system using the elimination method.

7. $-3x + 3y = 3$
$3x + y = 9$

8. $5x - y = -9$
$2x + y = 2$

9. $-5x + 12y = 20$
$x - 2y = -6$

10. $4x - 2y = -2$
$6x + y = 5$

11. $3x + 2y = 1$
$4x + 6y = 7$

12. $7x - 3y = 6$
$-2x + 5y = -10$

Solve the system using any algebraic method.

13. $5x + 7y = -2$
$2x - 7y = 9$

14. $x + 3y = 1$
$3x + 7y = 1$

15. $4x + 6y = 8$
$2x + 3y = 3$

16. $8x - 5y = -17$
$-2x + y = 6$

17. $3x - 8y = 0$
$-2x + 5y = -2$

18. $4x - 6y = 2$
$5x + 3y = 1$

19. $2x - 5y = 3$
$-4x + 10y = -6$

20. $8x + 3y = 10$
$-6x + y = -12$

21. $\frac{5}{4}x + y = -\frac{9}{2}$
$x + \frac{3}{2}y = -12$

22. Business A nut wholesaler sells a mix of peanuts and cashews. The wholesaler charges \$2.65 per pound for peanuts and \$4.90 per pound for cashews. The mix is to sell for \$3.28 per pound. How many pounds of peanuts and how many pounds of cashews should be used to make 125 pounds of the mix?

23. Hair Salon A hair salon receives a shipment of 84 bottles of hair conditioner to use and sell to customers. The two types of conditioners received are type A, which is used for regular hair, and type B, which is used for dry hair. Type A costs \$6.50 per bottle and type B costs \$8.25 per bottle. The hair salon's invoice for the conditioner is \$588. How many of each type of conditioner are in the shipment?

24. Birthday Gift You and your sister decide to combine your weekly overtime earnings to buy a birthday gift for your mother. Your overtime rate is \$18 per hour and your sister's overtime rate is \$24 per hour. The total amount earned for the gift was \$288. If you worked two more hours of overtime than your sister, how many overtime hours did each of you work?

LESSON 1.3 **Exercise Set B**

MM3A5c Represent and solve realistic problems using systems of linear equations.

UNIT 1

Solve the system using the substitution method.

1. $2x + 4y = -4$
$x - 2y = 10$

2. $2x + y = -3$
$-6x - 4y = 0$

3. $4x + y = -1$
$8x + 2y = -2$

4. $6x - 3y = 12$
$-2x + y = -4$

5. $x + 2y = 11$
$4x + 3y = 9$

6. $\frac{1}{5}x + 2y = \frac{4}{3}$
$x + \frac{2}{3}y = 2$

Solve the system using the elimination method.

7. $2x + 4y = -10$
$-3x - 2y = -1$

8. $6x + 12y = -7$
$x + 2y = 2$

9. $5x + 4y = -3$
$3x - 7y = 17$

10. $-2x + \frac{5}{3}y = -5$
$3x - \frac{7}{2}y = \frac{9}{2}$

11. $\frac{1}{2}x + 3y = 9$
$\frac{1}{3}x + y = 4$

12. $\frac{4}{3}x + 6y = -1$
$4x - 4y = \frac{13}{3}$

Solve the system using any algebraic method.

13. $0.25x + 0.5y = 7.5$
$0.4x + 0.5y = 9$

14. $0.5x - 0.3y = 1.3$
$-1.4x + 1.2y = -2.2$

15. $2x - 3y = 1$
$x + 2y = 5$

16. $3x - \frac{5}{3}y = 5$
$-\frac{3}{5}x + \frac{1}{3}y = -5$

17. $0.3x - 0.2y = 1.4$
$0.12x - 0.8y = 0.56$

18. $3.3x - 1.5y = 5.22$
$1.1x + 2.6y = 7.32$

19. Aviation Flying with the wind, a plane flew 600 miles in 3 hours. Flying against the wind, the plane could fly only 300 miles in the same amount of time. Find the speed of the plane in calm air and the speed of the wind.

20. Business For a recent job, an electrician earned \$50 per hour, and the electrician's apprentice earned \$20 per hour. The electrician worked 6 hours more than the apprentice, and together they earned a total of \$650. How much money did each person earn?

21. DVD Cable In order to connect your DVD player to your TV set, you need a cable with a special adapter at both ends. An 8 foot cable costs \$24.50 and a 4 foot cable costs \$15.50. The total cost is the sum of the cost of the adapters and the cost of the cable itself. What would you expect to pay for a 6 foot cable?

22. Challenge Find a and b so that $(-2, -1)$ is the unique solution to the system below.

$ax + by = -7$
$-ax + 2by = -2$

LESSON 1.4

Graph Linear Inequalities in Two Variables

Georgia Performance Standards: MM3A6a

Goal Graph linear inequalities in two variables.

Vocabulary

A **linear inequality in two variables** can be written in one of four forms: $Ax + By < C$, $Ax + By \leq C$, $Ax + By > C$, $Ax + By \geq C$.

An ordered pair (x, y) is a **solution of a linear inequality** in two variables if the inequality is true when the values of x and y are substituted into the inequality.

The **graph of a linear inequality** in two variables is the set of all points in a coordinate plane that represent solutions of the inequality.

A line divides the plane into two **half-planes.**

Example 1 Solution of a linear inequality in two variables

Tell whether the ordered pairs (5, −1) and (−2, 6) are solutions of the inequality $2x + 3y > 9$.

Ordered Pair	Substitute	Conclusion
$(5, -1)$	$2(5) + 3(-1) = 7 \not> 9$	$(5, -1)$ is not a solution.
$(-2, 6)$	$2(-2) + 3(6) = 14 > 9$	$(-2, 6)$ is a solution.

Guided Practice for Example 1

Tell whether the given ordered pairs are solutions of the inequality.

1. $4x - y \leq 2$; $(2, 4)$, $(1, -3)$

2. $\frac{3}{2}x + 5y \geq 15$; $(-2, 4)$, $(0, -3)$

Example 2 Graph linear inequalities in one or two variables

a. Graph $y \geq 1$ in a coordinate plane.

Graph the boundary line $y = 1$. Use a solid line because the inequality symbol is $\geq$. Because $(0, 2)$ is a solution, shade the half-plane that contains $(0, 2)$.

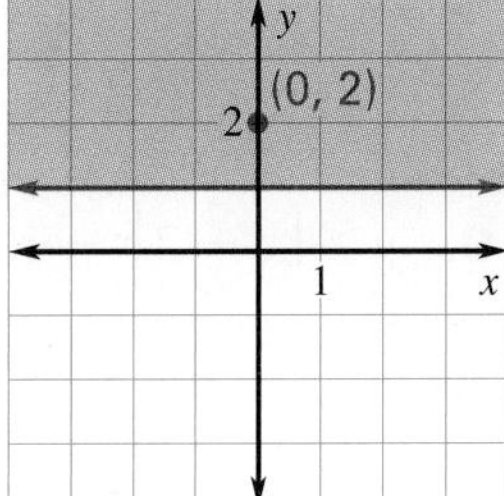

b. Graph $2x + y < -3$.

Graph the boundary line $2x + y = -3$. Use a dashed line because the inequality symbol is $<$. Because $(0, 0)$ is *not* a solution, shade the half-plane that does *not* contain $(0, 0)$.

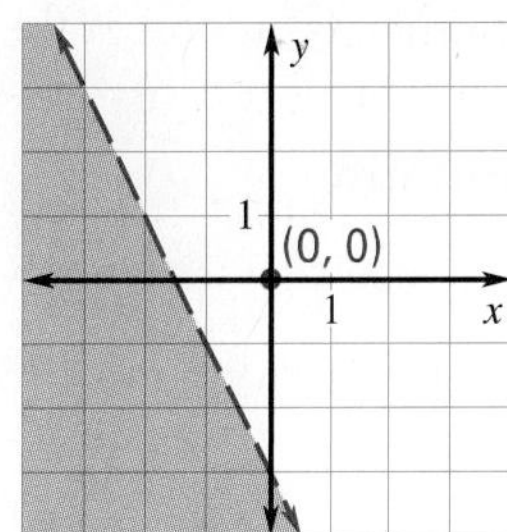

Georgia Performance Standards

MM3A6a Solve systems of inequalities in two variables, showing the solutions graphically.

Guided Practice for Example 2

Graph the inequality in a coordinate plane.

3. $x < -1$ **4.** $y \leq 3x$ **5.** $x + 4y < 8$

Example 3 Solve a multi-step problem

The perimeter of a rectangle is to be more than 16 inches. Write an inequality describing the possible dimensions of the rectangle. Then graph the inequality and identify three solutions.

STEP 1 **Write** an inequality. An inequality is $2x + 2y > 16$.

STEP 2 **Graph** the inequality. First graph the boundary line $2x + 2y = 16$. Use a dashed line because the inequality symbol is >. Because (0, 0) is *not* a solution, shade the half-plane that does *not* contain (0, 0). Because x and y cannot be negative, shade only points in Quadrant I.

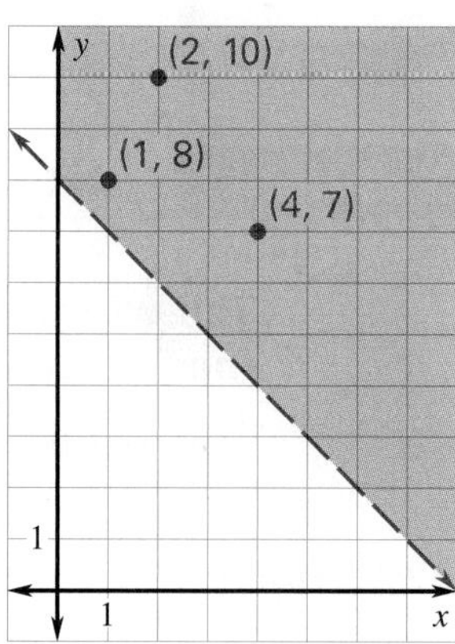

STEP 3 **Identify** solutions on the graph. Three solutions of the inequality are (1, 8), (2, 10), and (4, 7).

Example 4 Graph an absolute value inequality

Graph $y \leq |x| + 1$.

STEP 1 **Graph** the equation of the boundary, $y = |x| + 1$. Use a solid line because the inequality is ≤.

STEP 2 **Test** the point (0, 0). Because (0, 0) is a solution of the inequality, shade the portion of the coordinate plane outside the absolute value graph.

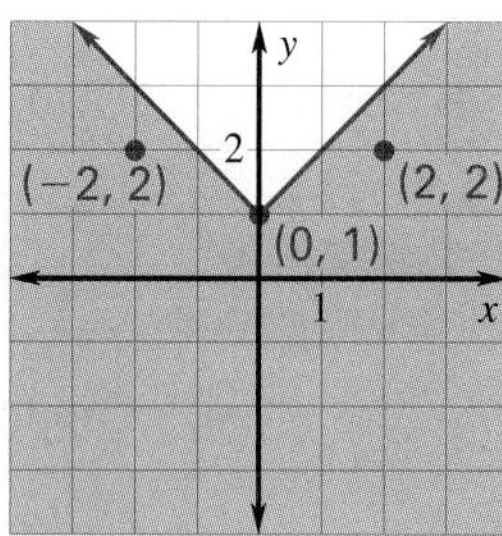

Guided Practice for Examples 3 and 4

6. Rework Example 3 if the perimeter of the rectangle is to be no less than 20 centimeters.

Graph the inequality.

7. $y \leq 3|x|$ **8.** $y > -|x| + 3$ **9.** $y \geq |x + 2| - 1$

LESSON 1.4 **Exercise Set A**

MM3A6a Solve systems of inequalities in two variables, showing the solutions graphically.

Tell whether the given ordered pairs are solutions of the inequality.

1. $x - y < 4$; (5, 4), (−1, −4)

2. $2x + 3y \leq -3$; (0, −1), (−3, 2)

3. $4x - 2y > 5$; (5, 8), (−1, −4)

4. $8y - 2x \geq 15$; (1, 2), (3, 3)

5. $2y < 5x + 10$; (−2, −1), (−1, 2)

6. $10x \geq 14 - 8y$; (2, 4), (4, −3)

Match the inequality with its graph.

7. $3x - 2y \geq -4$

8. $3x - 2y \leq -4$

9. $3x - 2y > -4$

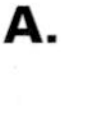

A.

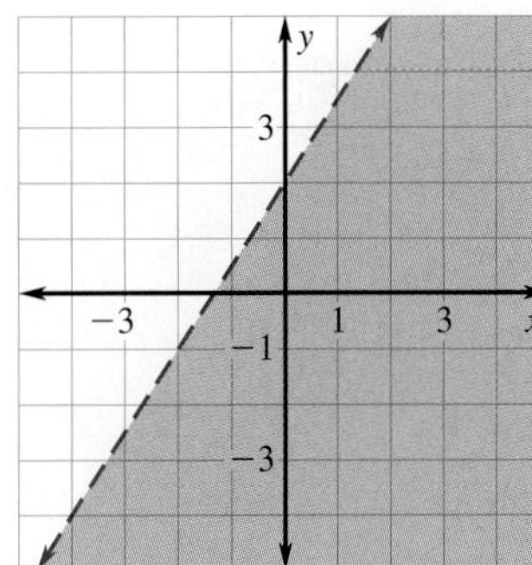

B.

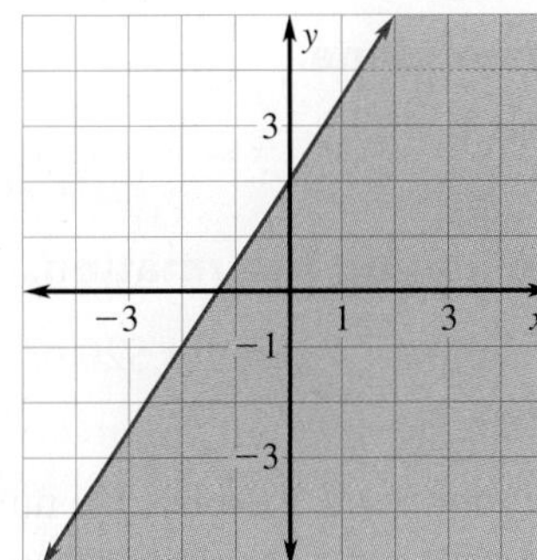

C.

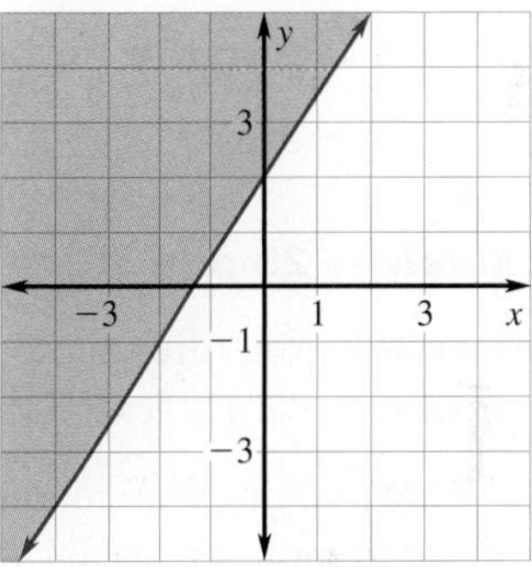

Graph the inequality in a coordinate plane.

10. $x > 2$

11. $x \leq -1$

12. $2x \leq 8$

13. $y \geq -2$

14. $y < 3$

15. $\frac{1}{4}y \leq 1$

16. $y < 2x - 1$

17. $y \geq \frac{1}{2}x + 2$

18. $3x + y > -3$

19. $x + 3y \leq 6$

20. $x - 3y > -3$

21. $-6x - 2y \leq 4$

Error Analysis ***Describe*** **and correct the error in graphing the inequality.**

22. $y < x + 3$

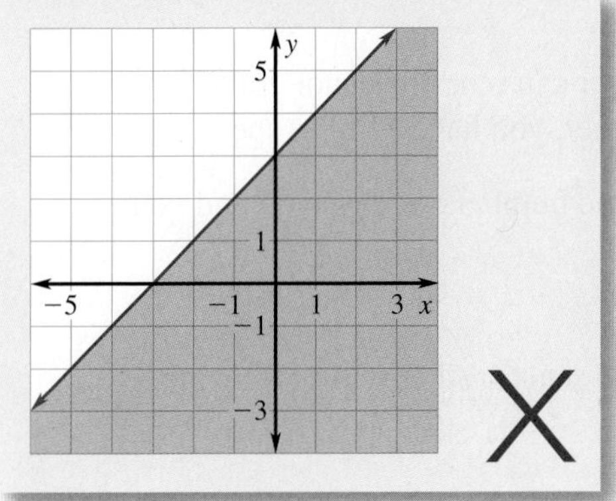

23. $y \geq -3x - 4$

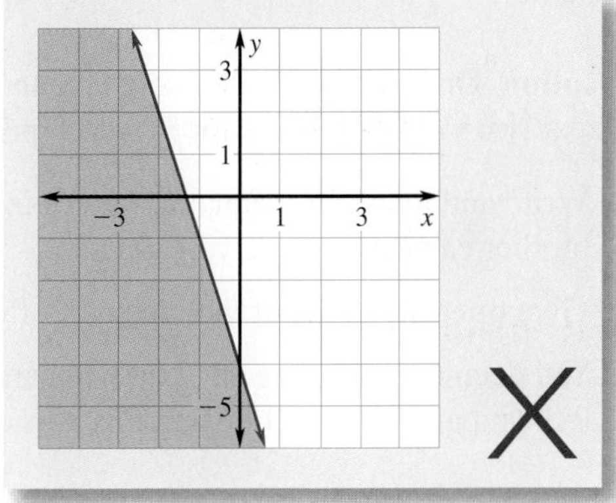

Exercise Set A *(continued)*

Write an inequality represented by the graph.

24. 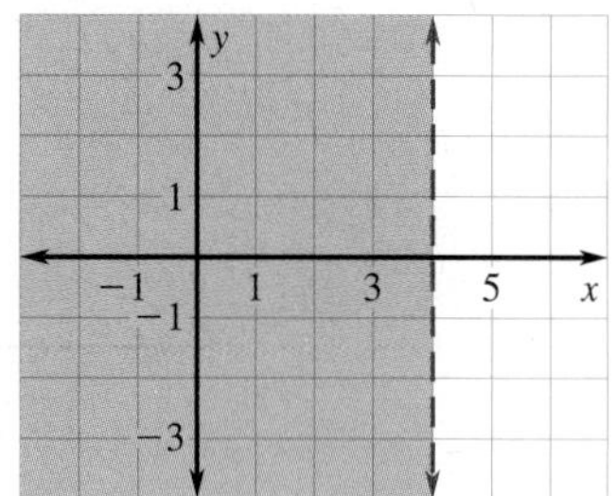

25. 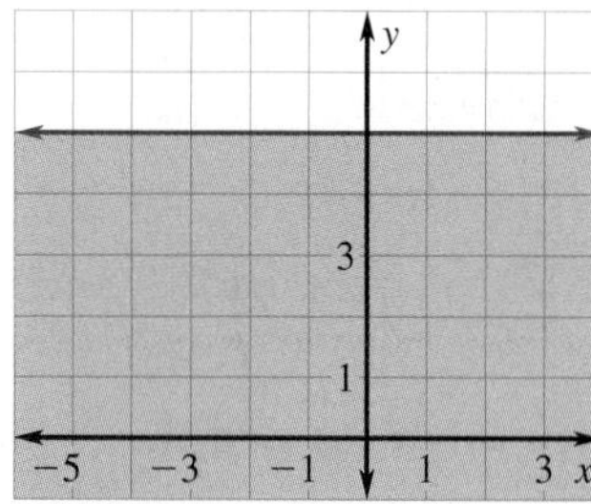

Graph the inequality in a coordinate plane.

26. $y > |x - 3|$

27. $y \leq |x| + 4$

28. $y \geq |x + 2| - 1$

In Exercises 29 and 30, use the following information.

Summer Job You offer to mow your neighbors' lawns for \$20 or to wash their cars for \$10. Your goal is to earn at least \$1500 this summer.

29. Write and graph an inequality that represents the possible number of lawns you would have to mow x and cars you would have to wash y in order to reach your goal.

30. What ordered pair represents mowing 50 lawns and washing 65 cars? Is this ordered pair a solution of the inequality?

In Exercises 31–33, use the following information.

Music Lessons Your parents have budgeted \$550 for you to take music lessons on the piano for \$25 and on the saxophone for \$20.

31. Write and graph an inequality that represents the possible number of piano lessons x and saxophone lessons y you can take this summer.

32. Is it possible to take 12 piano lessons and 15 saxophone lessons this summer?

33. If you take 14 piano lessons, what is the maximum number of saxophone lessons you can take?

34. **Vacation** On a two week vacation, you and your brother can rent one canoe for \$12 per day or rent two mountain bikes for \$15 each per day. Together, you have \$140 to spend.

a. Write and graph an inequality describing the possible numbers of days you and your brother can canoe or bicycle together.

b. Give three solutions of the inequality from part (a).

c. You decide that on one day you will canoe alone and your brother will bicycle alone. Repeat parts (a) and (b) using this new condition.

LESSON 1.4

Exercise Set B

MM3A6a Solve systems of inequalities in two variables, showing the solutions graphically.

Tell whether the given ordered pairs are solutions of the inequality $-1.5y - 3x > 4$.

1. $(-1.5, -1)$ **2.** $(-2.5, 2)$ **3.** $(-3, -4)$ **4.** $(3.5, -2.5)$

Match the inequality with its graph.

5. $y > |x + 4| - 3$ **6.** $y < |x + 4| - 3$ **7.** $y \geq |x + 4| - 3$

A.

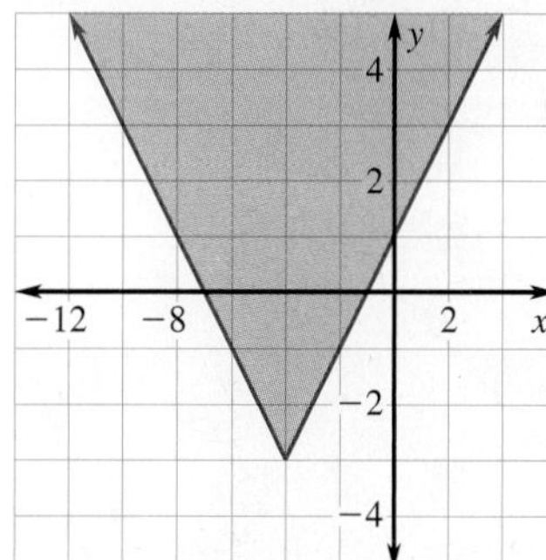

B.

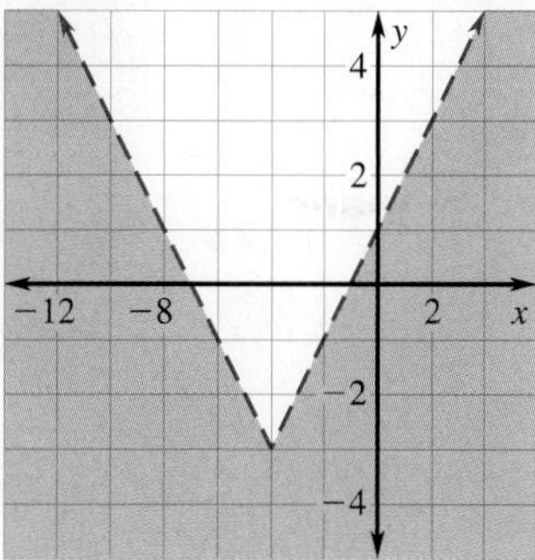

C.

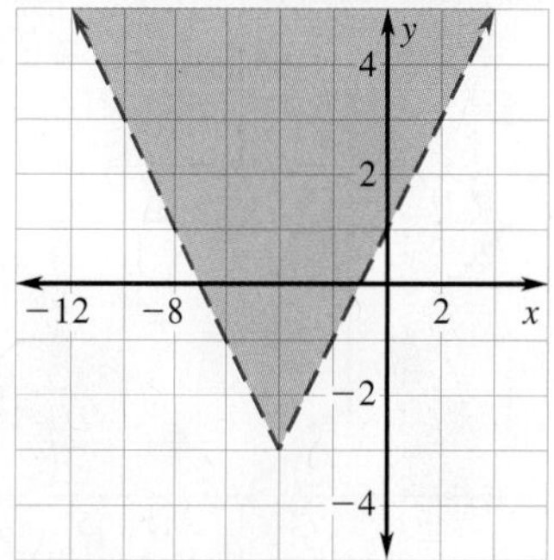

Graph the inequality in a coordinate plane.

8. $x + 2 < 6$

9. $y - 2 \geq -1$

10. $2x + y \leq 0$

11. $5x - 2y \leq 3$

12. $-7x + 4y < 2$

13. $3x - 6y > -12$

14. $-x - 3y \geq -8$

15. $4x - 5y \leq -7$

16. $-6x + 8y < 4$

17. $y \geq 3|x - 2| + 1$

18. $y > -\frac{1}{2}|x + 1| + \frac{3}{2}$

19. $3 - 2y \geq 6|x - 3| - 3$

Error Analysis ***Describe*** **and correct the error in graphing the inequality.**

20. $y > 2|x - 3| - 2$

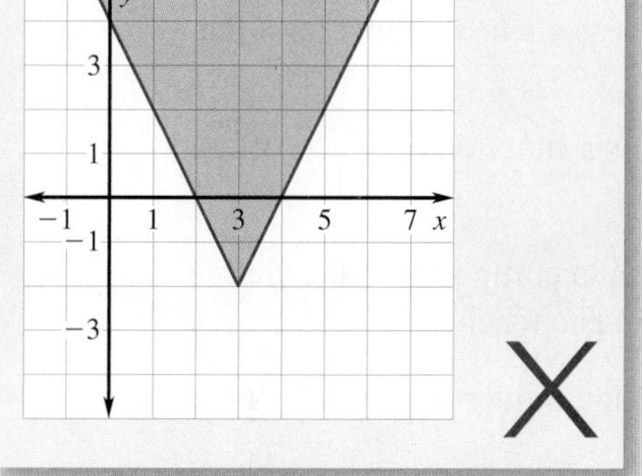

21. $y \leq \frac{1}{2}|x + 1| + 4$

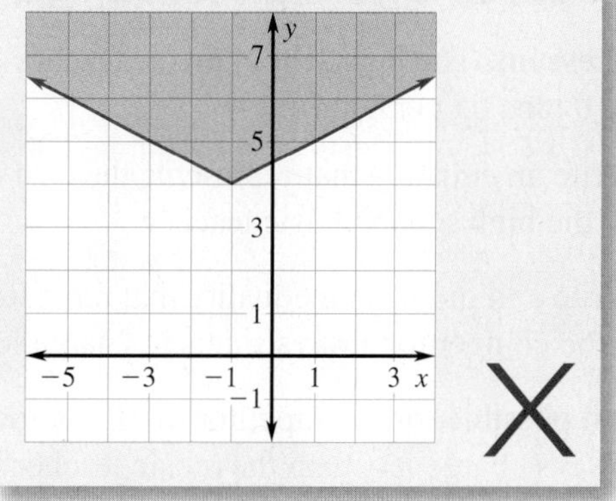

UNIT 1

Exercise Set B *(continued)*

Write an inequality represented by the graph.

22.

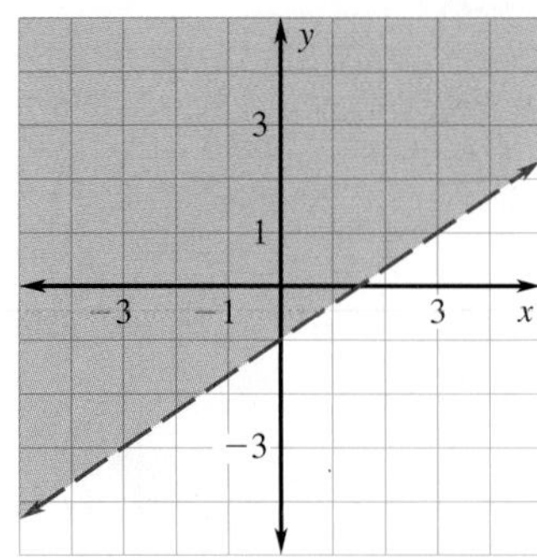

23.

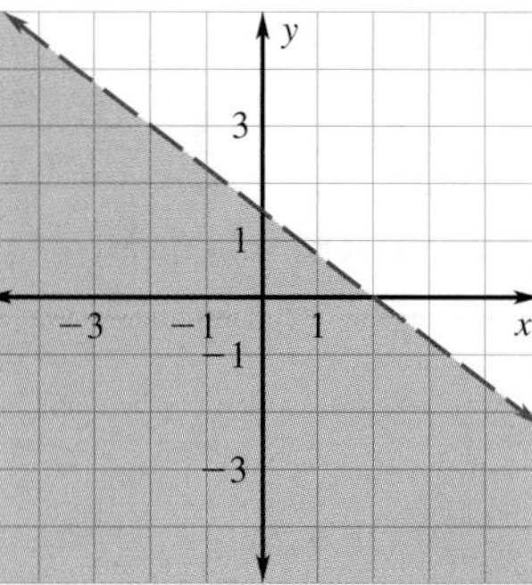

24.

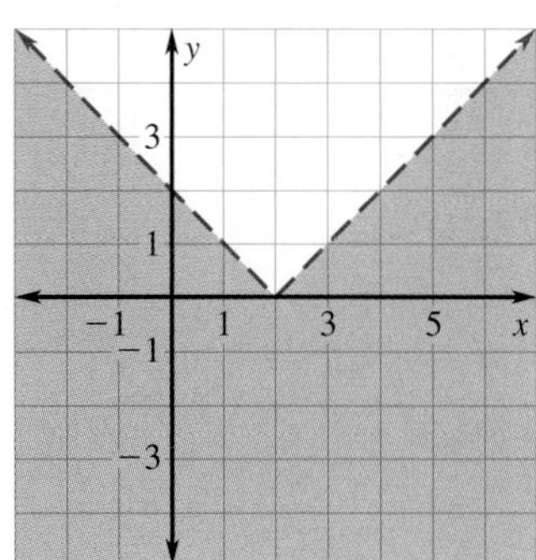

25.

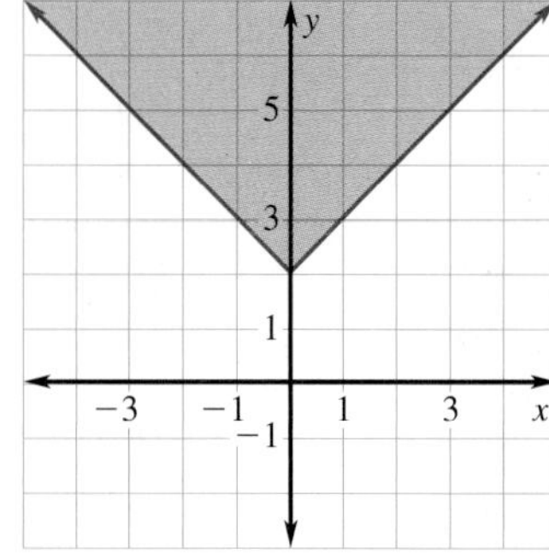

In Exercises 26–28, use the following information.

Test Scores A chemistry exam included multiple choice questions that were worth 3 points each and fill-in-the-blank questions that were worth 2 points each. The highest score in the class was 88 out of a possible 100 points.

26. Write an inequality that represents the number of x multiple choice and y fill-in-the-blank questions that could have been answered correctly by any student in the class.

27. Graph the inequality.

28. Is it possible that someone in the class answered 13 multiple choice questions and 25 fill-in-the-blank questions correctly?

In Exercises 29–31, use the following information.

Music Lessons The high school music teacher offers piano lessons to students for a flat fee of $10 plus $5 per hour.

29. Write an equation that represents the cost c of lessons as a function of time t offered by the high school music teacher.

30. Write and graph an inequality that represents the amount a competitor must charge if the competitor always wants to charge less than the music teacher.

31. Is it possible for a competitor to offer a lower flat fee but a higher hourly rate and always charge less than the music teacher? *Explain.*

LESSON 1.5

Graph Systems of Linear Inequalities

Georgia Performance Standards: MM3A6a

Goal Graph systems of linear inequalities.

Vocabulary

The following is an example of a **system of linear inequalities** in two variables: $x + y \leq 6$ and $2x - y > 6$.

A **solution of a system of inequalities** is an ordered pair that is a solution of each inequality in the system.

The **graph of a system of inequalities** is the graph of all solutions of the system.

Example 1 Graph a system of two inequalities

Graph the system of inequalities.

$y < x + 2$ **Inequality 1**

$y \geq -2x$ **Inequality 2**

Solution

STEP 1 **Graph** each inequality in the system. Use red for $y < x + 2$ and blue for $y \geq -2x$.

STEP 2 **Identify** the region that is common to both graphs. It is the region that is shaded purple.

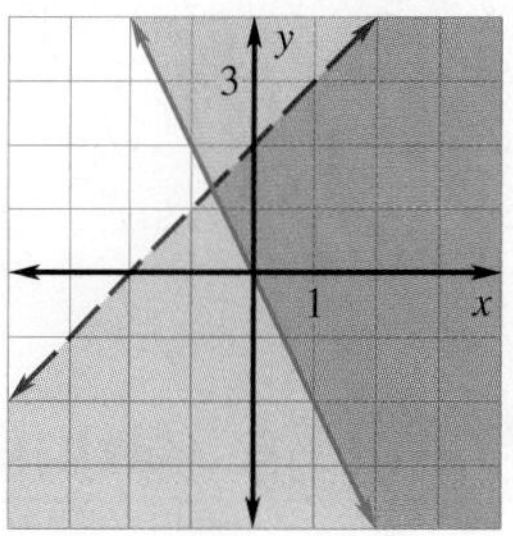

Example 2 Graph a system with no solution

Graph the system of inequalities.

$y > x + 2$ **Inequality 1**

$y \leq x + 1$ **Inequality 2**

Solution

STEP 1 **Graph** each inequality in the system. Use red for $y > x + 2$ and blue for $y \leq x + 1$.

STEP 2 **Identify** the region that is common to both graphs. There is no common region shaded by both inequalities. So, the system has no solution.

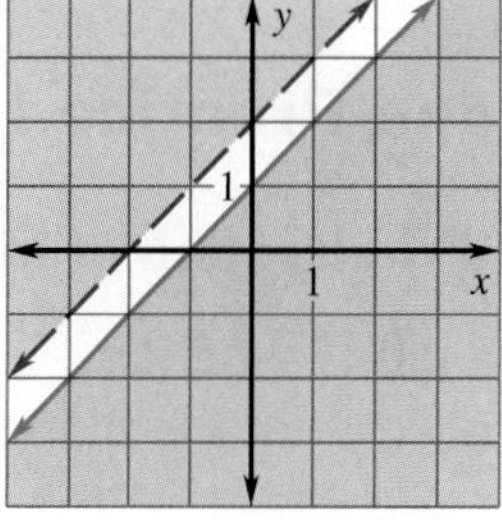

UNIT 1

Georgia Performance Standards

MM3A6a Solve systems of inequalities in two variables, showing the solutions graphically.

Example 3 Graph a system with an absolute value inequality

Graph the system of inequalities.

$y \geq 0$ **Inequality 1**

$y < |x - 1|$ **Inequality 2**

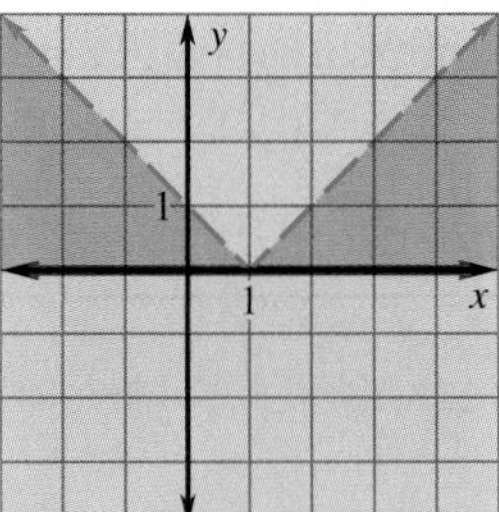

STEP 1 **Graph** each inequality in the system. Use red for $y \geq 0$ and blue for $y < |x - 1|$.

STEP 2 **Identify** the region that is common to both graphs. It is the region that is shaded purple.

Guided Practice for Examples 1, 2, and 3

Graph the system of inequalities.

1. $y > 1$, $y \leq 3$

2. $x < 3$, $y < 4$

3. $y \leq -x - 1$, $y \leq \frac{1}{2}x - 1$

4. $y \geq 2$, $y < -2$

5. $y > -x$, $y < -x - 2$

6. $y \geq x + 1$, $y \leq x - 1$

7. $y < |x|$, $y \geq 0$

8. $y \leq -|x| + 2$, $y \geq 0$

9. $y \geq |x - 1|$, $y < 2$

Example 4 Graph a system of three or more inequalities

Graph the system of inequalities.

$y \leq -x + 2$ **Inequality 1**

$x \geq 1$ **Inequality 2**

$y > -2$ **Inequality 3**

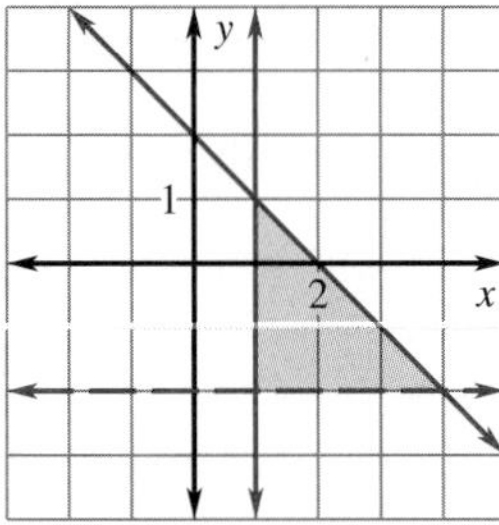

Graph each inequality in the system. Then identify the region that is common to all the graphs. The solution of the system is the region that is shaded.

Guided Practice for Example 4

Graph the system of inequalities.

10. $x \geq 0$, $y \geq 0$, $y < x$

11. $x \geq -2$, $y \leq 0$, $y \geq x$

12. $x \geq 0$, $y > x$, $y < 2$

UNIT 1

LESSON 1.5 **Exercise Set A**

MM3A6a Solve systems of inequalities in two variables, showing the solutions graphically.

Match the system of inequalities with its graph.

1. $x + y > 1$
$-2x + 3y \geq -6$

2. $x + y < 1$
$-2x + 3y < -6$

3. $x + y \leq 1$
$-2x + 3y > -6$

A. 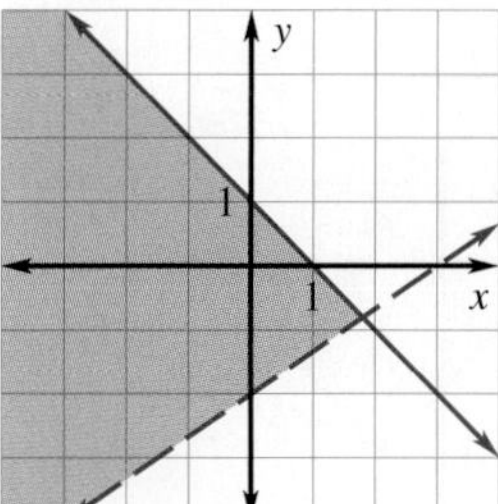

B. 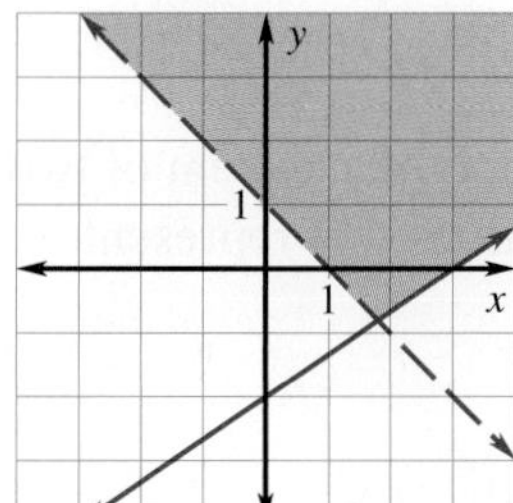

C. 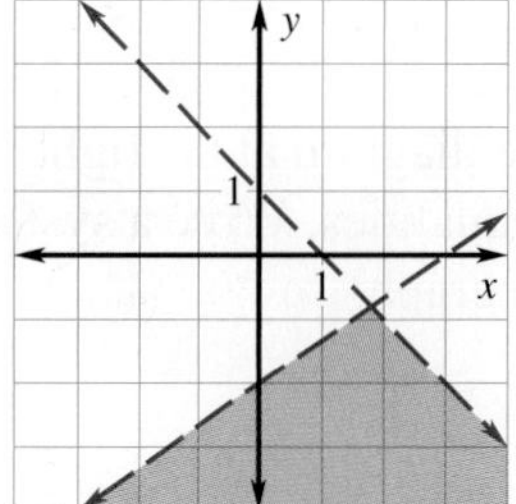

4. Error Analysis *Describe* and correct the error in graphing the system of inequalities.

$y \geq -4$

$y \leq 2x - 2$

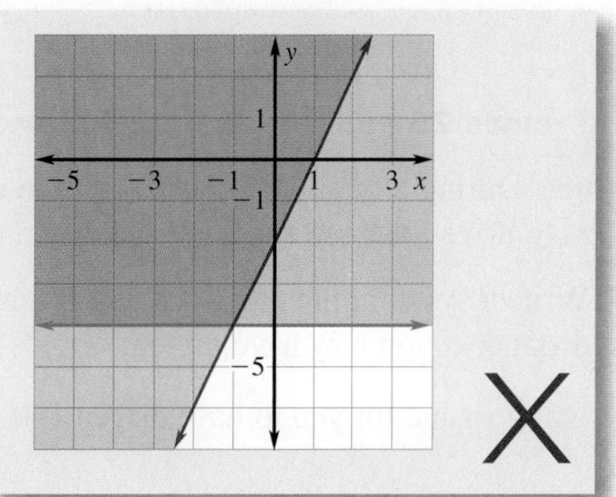

Graph the system of inequalities.

5. $x > -1$
$y > -1$

6. $x \geq -2$
$y < 1$

7. $y \leq 3$
$y > 1$

8. $x + y \geq 0$
$-x + y \geq 0$

9. $y > -2x$
$2x - y > 1$

10. $2x + y < 5$
$y > 2|x - 1|$

11. $x + 2y < 2$
$3x + y \leq 3$

12. $y > 2x - 3$
$x > -1$
$y < 3$

13. $y \leq |x| + 4$
$x < 2$
$y \geq 2$

14. $y < \frac{1}{2}x + 3$
$y \geq -2x - 3$
$x \leq 3$

15. $x + y > -2$
$-x + y > -2$
$y \geq 0$

16. $y \leq -\frac{1}{3}x + 2$
$y > 3x - 3$
$x > -1$

17. $x + 2y \leq 8$
$x + 4y \geq 8$
$x \geq 0$

18. $x + 2y \leq 10$
$2x + y \leq 8$
$2x - 5y < 20$

19. $x + 2y \leq 5$
$2x - 4y \leq -10$
$3x + 6y > -12$

UNIT 1

Exercise Set A *(continued)*

Write a system of two linear inequalities that has the ordered pair as a solution.

20. $(2, -3)$

21. $(-1, -6)$

22. $(-4, 0)$

23. $(0, -5)$

24. The diagram at the right shows the graph of a system of two inequalities. Write a system of inequalities that represents the graph.

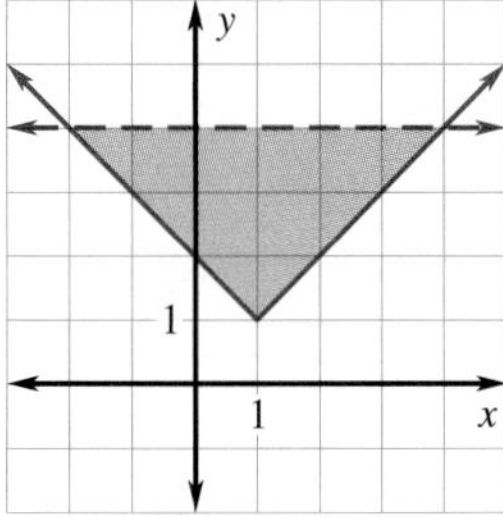

In Exercises 25 and 26, use the following information.

Distance During a family trip, you share the driving with your dad. At most, you are allowed to drive for three hours. While driving, your maximum speed is 55 miles per hour.

25. Write a system of inequalities describing the possible number of hours t and distance d you may have driven.

26. Is it possible for you to have driven 160 miles?

27. **Summer Jobs** You can work at most 24 hours next week. You need to earn at least \$100 to cover your weekly expenses. Your babysitting job pays \$7 per hour and your job at the grocery store pays \$6.50 per hour.

- **a.** Write a system of inequalities to describe the situation.
- **b.** Graph the system you wrote in part (a).
- **c.** Give three possible solutions for the number of hours you can work at each job.

28. **Multiple Representations** The homecoming committee must consist of 9 to 12 representatives from the junior and senior classes. The committee must include at least 4 juniors and at least 4 seniors. Let x be the number of juniors and y be the number of seniors.

- **a.** **Writing a System** Write a system of inequalities to describe the situation.
- **b.** **Graphing a System** Graph the system you wrote in part (a).
- **c.** **Finding Solutions** Give two possible solutions for the numbers of juniors and seniors on the homecoming committee.

LESSON 1.5

Exercise Set B

MM3A6a Solve systems of inequalities in two variables, showing the solutions graphically.

Match the system of inequalities with its graph.

1. $x \le 3$
   $y \ge -2$
   $y < x$
   $3x + 2y \le 8$

2. $x \le 3$
   $y \ge -2$
   $y > x$
   $3x + 2y \ge 8$

3. $x \le 3$
   $y \le -2$
   $y < x$
   $3x + 2y \le 8$

A. 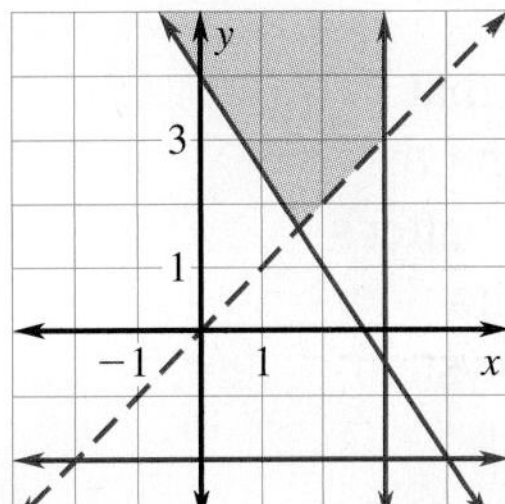

B. 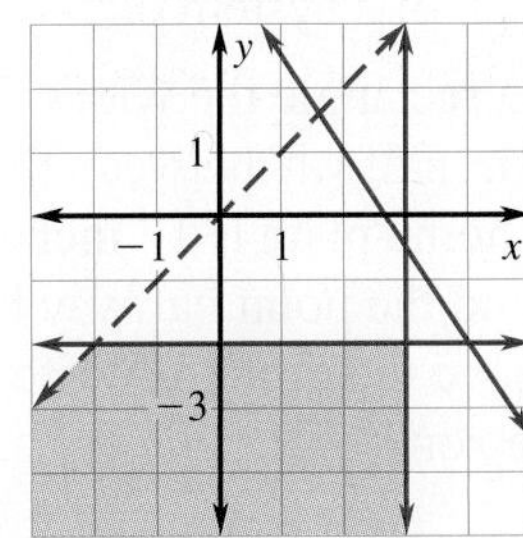

C. 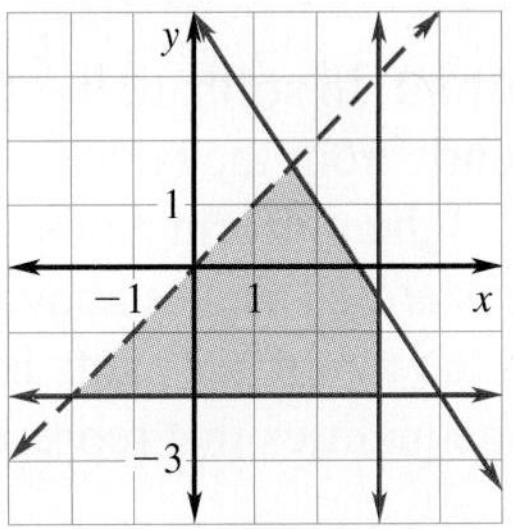

Graph the system of inequalities.

4. $x - y > -1$
   $2x + y < -1$

5. $y \le -3x$
   $x + 4y < 8$

6. $3x + 4y \ge -10$
   $2x - 3y > -6$

7. $2x + y \le 3$
   $y \ge |x| + 1$

8. $y > -2|x + 1| - 2$
   $2x - y < 4$

9. $x + y < 1$
   $y > \frac{1}{2}|x - 2| - 3$

10. $-x + y < 4$
    $x + 3y > -9$
    $x > -3$

11. $2x + y < 3$
    $x - y > -1$
    $x + 2y \ge 0$

12. $3x + 6y > 4$
    $3x - 4y > 4$
    $x - y < 5$

13. $-2x + y < 3$
    $x + y > 1$
    $y \le 0$
    $y > -2$

14. $-2x + 4y < 8$
    $2x + 4y > -8$
    $-4x + y \ge 0$
    $x \ge -2$

15. $3x + 2y \le 6$
    $-3x + 2y \le 6$
    $3x + 2y \ge -6$
    $-3x + 2y \ge -6$

Write a system of four linear inequalities that has the ordered pair as a solution.

16. $(2, -1)$

17. $(-2, -4)$

18. $(-3, 0)$

19. $(6, 7)$

Write a system of linear inequalities for the shaded region.

20. 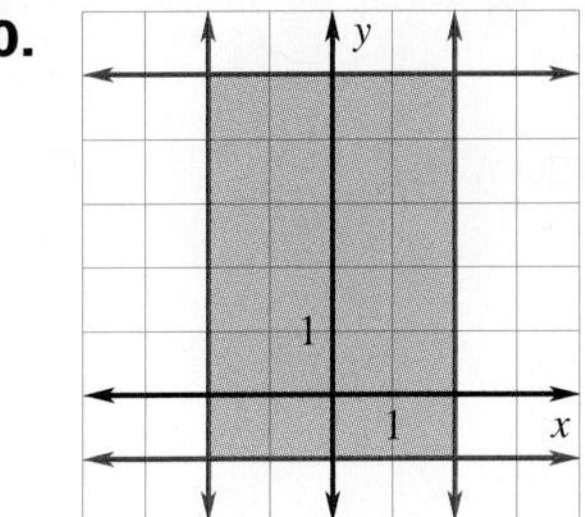

21. 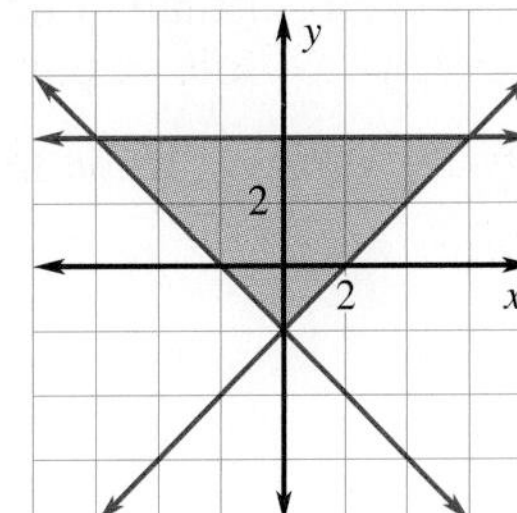

22. 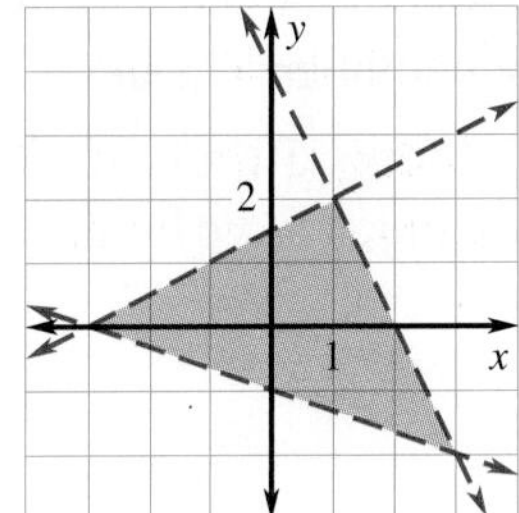

UNIT 1

Exercise Set B *(continued)*

23. Visual Thinking Write a system of linear inequalities whose graph is a pentagon and its interior.

24. **Arena Seating** For an upcoming event, a 2500 seat arena is selling tickets for \$25 and \$15. At least 1000 tickets must be priced at \$15 and total sales need to exceed \$10,000 to make a profit. Let x represent the number of tickets priced at \$25 and y represent the number of tickets priced at \$15. Write a system of inequalities that shows the possible combinations of ticket sales in order to make a profit.

25. **Softball** In softball, the strike zone is a rectangle the width of home plate that extends from the batter's knees to a point halfway between the shoulders and the top of the uniform pants. The width of home plate is 17 inches. Suppose a batter's knees are 18 inches above the ground and the point halfway between her shoulder and the top of her pants is 40 inches above the ground. Write and graph a system of inequalities that represents the strike zone.

26. Multiple Representations Near the end of summer, a department store has a summer clothes sale to make room for winter attire. The sale allows customers to save 20% to 50% on all clothing items regularly priced at \$15 or more.

a. **Writing a System** Write a system of inequalities with x as the regular price and y as the sale price.

b. **Graphing a System** Graph the system of inequalities.

c. **Describing Solutions** Give the range of possible sale prices for an item regularly priced at \$45.

27. **Heart Rate** A person's theoretical maximum heart rate (in heartbeats per minute) is $220 - x$ where x is the person's age in years ($20 \le x \le 65$). When a person exercises, it is recommended that the person strive for a heart rate that is at least 50% of the maximum and at most 75% of the maximum.

a. Write a system of linear inequalities that describes the given information.

b. Graph the system you wrote in part (a).

c. A 36-year-old person has a heart rate of 145 heartbeats per minute when exercising. Is the person's heart rate in the recommended range? *Explain.*

28. Challenge You and a friend are trying to guess the number of peanuts in a jar. You both agree that the jar contains at least 500 peanuts. You guess that there are x peanuts, and your friend guesses that there are y peanuts. The actual number of peanuts in the jar is 1000. Write and graph a system of inequalities describing the values of x and y for which your guess is closer than your friend's guess to the actual number of peanuts.

UNIT 1

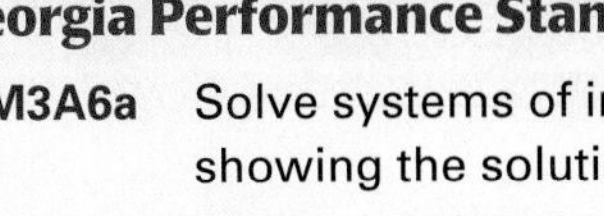

Georgia Performance Standards

MM3A6a Solve systems of inequalities in two variables, showing the solutions graphically.

LESSON 1.5

Problem Solving Workshop

Problem A furniture store is having a sale. All chairs that have a regular price of \$50 to \$250 are on sale for 15% to 75% off. Write a system of linear inequalities for the regular chair prices and possible sale prices. Graph the system of inequalities. Find the range of possible sale prices for a chair that is regularly priced at \$160.

STEP 1 **Read and Understand**

What do you know? The regular prices of chairs and the sale percentages

What do you want to find out? The possible sale prices for a chair that is regularly priced at \$160

STEP 2 **Make a Plan** Use what you know to write and graph a system of linear inequalities.

STEP 3 **Solve the Problem** Let x be the regular chair price and y be the sale price. From the information, you can write the following four inequalities.

$x \geq 50$	Regular price must be at least \$50.
$x \leq 250$	Regular price can be at most \$250.
$y \geq 0.25x$	Sale price is at least (100 − 75)% = 25% of regular price.
$y \leq 0.85x$	Sale price is at most (100 − 15)% = 85% of regular price.

Graph each inequality in the system. The region that is common to all is shaded.

Identify the sale prices for \$160 chairs. From the graph, when $x = 160$, the value of y is between 40 and 136, inclusive.

Therefore, chairs regularly priced at \$160 sell for between \$40 and \$136, inclusive, during the sale.

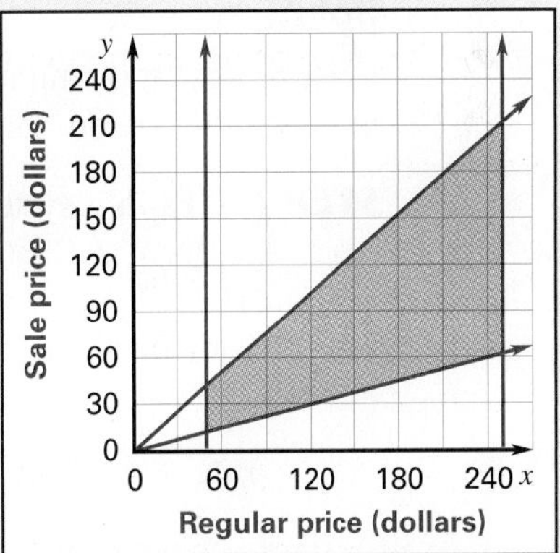

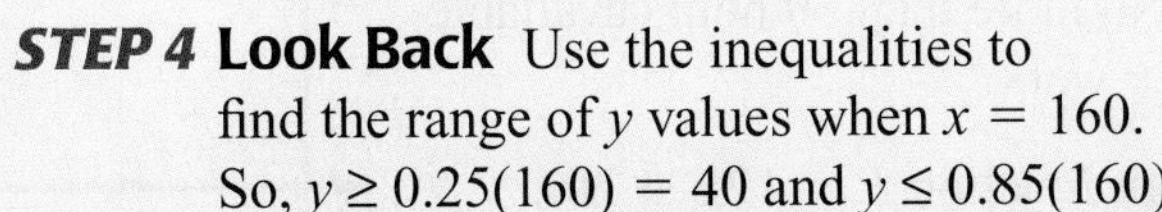

STEP 4 **Look Back** Use the inequalities to find the range of y values when $x = 160$. So, $y \geq 0.25(160) = 40$ and $y \leq 0.85(160) = 136$. The value of y is between 40 and 136, inclusive. The answer is correct.

Practice

1. **Shopping** All MP3 players at an electronics store that have a regular price of \$100 to \$330 are on sale for 10% to 35% off. Write a system of linear inequalities for the regular MP3 player prices and possible sale prices. Graph the system of inequalities. Use the graph to estimate the range of possible sale prices for an MP3 player that is regularly priced at \$200.

2. **Garden** You are designing a rectangular garden that is to be enclosed by a fence no longer than 500 feet. The length of the garden must be greater than 50 feet and the width of the garden must be greater than 25 feet. Write a system of linear inequalities for the dimensions of the garden. Graph the system of inequalities. Find the range of possible widths for a length of 120 feet.

UNIT 1

LESSON 1.6

Linear Programming

Georgia Performance Standards: MM3A6b

Goal Solve linear programming problems.

Vocabulary

Linear programming is a process of maximizing or minimizing a linear *objective function*. The **objective function** gives a quantity that is to be maximized (or minimized), and is subject to **constraints** that are linear inequalities.

If all the constraints in a linear programming problem are graphed, the intersection of the graph is called the **feasible region.** If this region is bounded, then the objective function has a maximum value and a minimum value on the region. Moreover, the maximum and minimum values each occur at a vertex of the feasible region.

Example 1 Use linear programming to maximize profit

Crafts Toy wagons are made to sell at a craft fair. It takes 4 hours to make a small wagon and 6 hours to make a large wagon. The owner of the craft booth will make a profit of \$12 for a small wagon and \$20 for a large wagon. The craft booth owner has no more than 60 hours available to make wagons and wants to have at least 6 small wagons to sell. How many of each size should be made to maximize profit?

Solution

Let x represent the number of small wagons made and let y represent the number of large wagons made. The total profit P is given by the equation $P = 12x + 20y$.

STEP 1 **Graph** a system of constraints.

$x \geq 6$	Make at least 6 small wagons.
$y \geq 0$	Number of large wagons cannot be negative.
$4x + 6y \leq 60$	No more than 60 hours available to work.

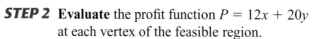

STEP 2 **Evaluate** the profit function $P = 12x + 20y$ at each vertex of the feasible region.

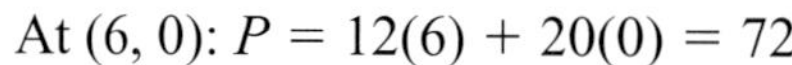

At (6, 0): $P = 12(6) + 20(0) = 72$

At (6, 6): $P = 12(6) + 20(6) = 192$ ← **Maximum**

At (15, 0): $P = 12(15) + 20(0) = 180$

The owner can maximize profit by making 6 small wagons and 6 large wagons.

Guided Practice for Example 1

1. Rework Example 1 if the owner of the craft booth has no more than 40 hours available to make wagons and wants to have at least 4 small wagons to sell.

Georgia Performance Standards

MM3A6b Represent and solve realistic problems using linear programming.

Example 2 Solve a linear programming problem

Find the minimum value and the maximum value of the objective function $C = 3x + 2y$ subject to the following constraints.

$x \geq 0$

$y \geq 0$

$x + 3y \leq 15$

$4x + y \leq 16$

Solution

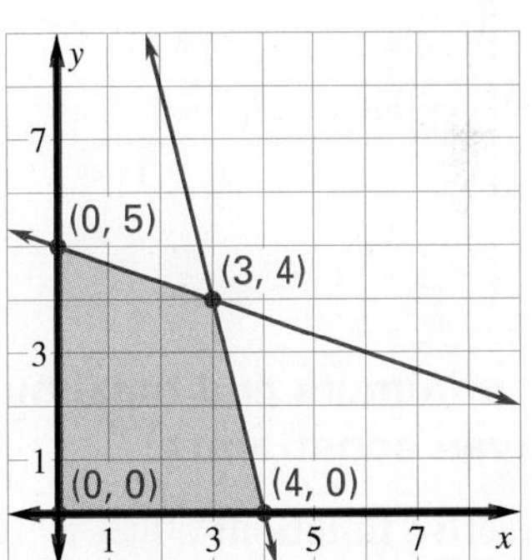

STEP 1 **Graph** the system of constraints. Find the coordinates of the vertices of the feasible region by solving systems of two linear equations. The solution of the system

$x + 3y = 15$

$4x + y = 16$

gives the vertex (3, 4). The other three vertices are (0, 0), (4, 0), and (0, 5).

STEP 2 **Evaluate** the function $C = 3x + 2y$ at each vertex.

At (0, 0): $C = 3(0) + 2(0) = 0$ ← **Minimum**

At (4, 0): $C = 3(4) + 2(0) = 12$

At (3, 4): $C = 3(3) + 2(4) = 17$ ← **Maximum**

At (0, 5): $C = 3(0) + 2(5) = 10$

The minimum value of C is 0. It occurs when $x = 0$ and $y = 0$.

The maximum value of C is 17. It occurs when $x = 3$ and $y = 4$.

Guided Practice for Example 2

Find the minimum and maximum values of the objective function subject to the given constraints.

2. Objective function:
$C = 4x + 3y$
Constraints:
$x \geq 0$
$y \geq 0$
$x + y \leq 8$

3. Objective function:
$C = 7x + 5y$
Constraints:
$x \geq 2$
$y \geq 0$
$2x + y \leq 10$

4. Objective function:
$C = 2x + 8y$
Constraints:
$x \geq 0$
$y \geq 0$
$x + 2y \leq 14$
$6x + y \leq 18$

UNIT 1

LESSON 1.6 **Exercise Set A**

MM3A6b Represent and solve realistic problems using linear programming.

Find the minimum and maximum values of the objective function for the given feasible region.

1. $C = x + 2y$

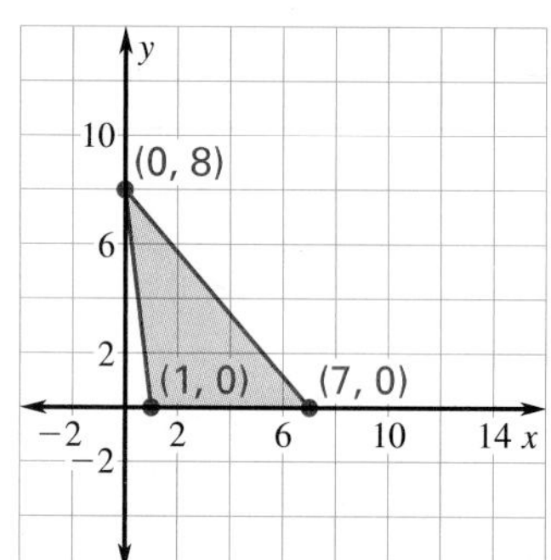

2. $C = 6x - 4y$

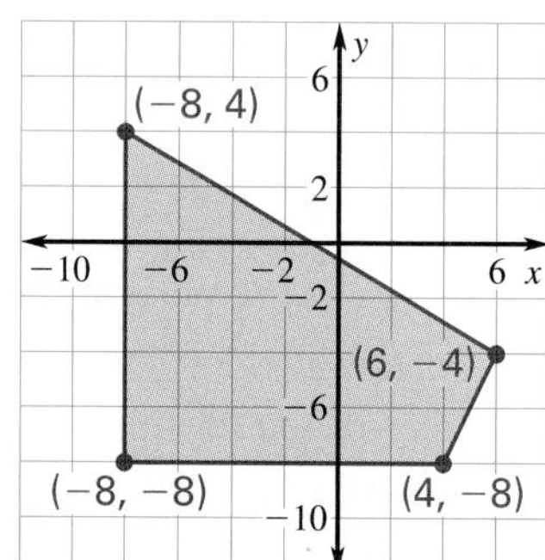

3. $C = 5x + 7y$

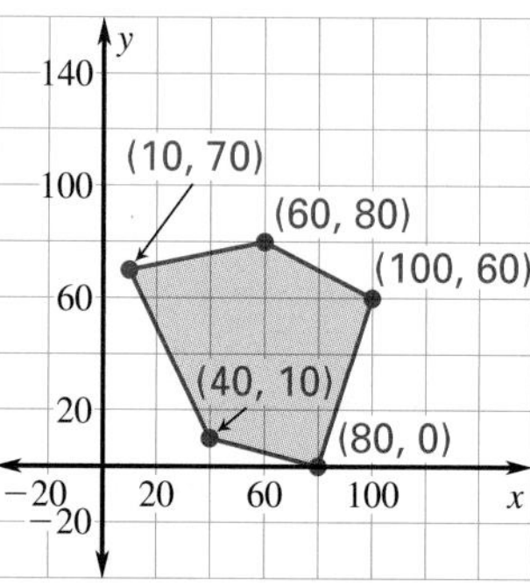

Find the minimum and maximum values of the objective function subject to the given constraints.

4. **Objective function:**
$C = 3x + 4y$
Constraints:
$x \geq 0$
$y \geq 0$
$x + y \leq 6$

5. **Objective function:**
$C = 2x + 5y$
Constraints:
$x \leq 5$
$y \geq 4$
$-2x + 5y \leq 30$

6. **Objective function:**
$C = 7x + 3y$
Constraints:
$x \geq 1$
$y \geq 2$
$6x + 4y \leq 38$

7. **Objective function:**
$C = 4x + 6y$
Constraints:
$x \geq 0$
$y \leq 8$
$-2x + 3y \geq 12$

8. **Objective function:**
$C = 8x + 7y$
Constraints:
$x \geq 0$
$y \geq 0$
$4x + 4y \leq 20$
$x + 2y \leq 8$

9. **Objective function:**
$C = 3x + 5y$
Constraints:
$x \geq 0$
$2x + 3y \geq 6$
$3x - y \leq 9$
$x + 4y \leq 16$

10. **Craft Fair** Piñatas are made to sell at a craft fair. It takes 2 hours to make a mini piñata and 3 hours to make a regular-sized piñata. The owner of the craft booth will make a profit of $14 for each mini piñata sold and $22 for each regular-sized piñata sold. If the craft booth owner has no more than 40 hours available to make piñatas and wants to have at least 16 piñatas to sell, how many of each size piñata should be made to maximize profit?

11. **Manufacturing** A company manufactures inkjet printers and laser printers. The company can make a total of 60 printers per day, and it has 120 labor-hours per day available. It takes 1 labor-hour to make an inkjet printer and 3 labor-hours to make a laser printer. The profit is $45 per inkjet printer and $65 per laser printer. How many of each type of printer should the company make to maximize its daily profit?

LESSON 1.6

Exercise Set B

MM3A6b Represent and solve realistic problems using linear programming.

Find the minimum and maximum values of the objective function subject to the given constraints.

1. Objective function:
$C = 6x + 7y$
Constraints:
$x \geq 3$
$y \geq 4$
$2x + 6y \leq 48$

2. Objective function:
$C = 8x + 3y$
Constraints:
$x \geq 0$
$y \geq 0$
$x + \frac{1}{2}y \leq 4$

3. Objective function:
$C = 5x + 2y$
Constraints:
$x \geq 0$
$y \geq 0$
$4x - y \leq 20$
$x + 2y \leq 14$

4. Objective function:
$C = 20x + 30y$
Constraints:
$x \geq 0$
$y \geq 0$
$7x + 8y \leq 5600$
$7x + 8y \geq 2800$

5. Objective function:
$C = 3x + y$
Constraints:
$x \geq 0$
$y \geq -3$
$y \geq -x$
$x - 4y \geq -20$

6. Objective function:
$C = x + 2y$
Constraints:
$x \geq 0$
$y \geq 0$
$2x + 3y \leq 60$
$2x + y \leq 28$
$4x + y \leq 48$

7. Error Analysis *Describe* and correct the error in finding the minimum and maximum values of the objective function $C = 2x + 5y$ subject to the following constraints.

$x \geq 2$
$y \geq 2$
$x + y \leq 16$
$3x + y \leq 32$
$-\frac{1}{2}x + y \geq \frac{1}{2}$

The minimum value of C is 14. It occurs when $x = 2$ and $y = 2$. The maximum value of C is 56. It occurs when $x = 8$ and $y = 8$.

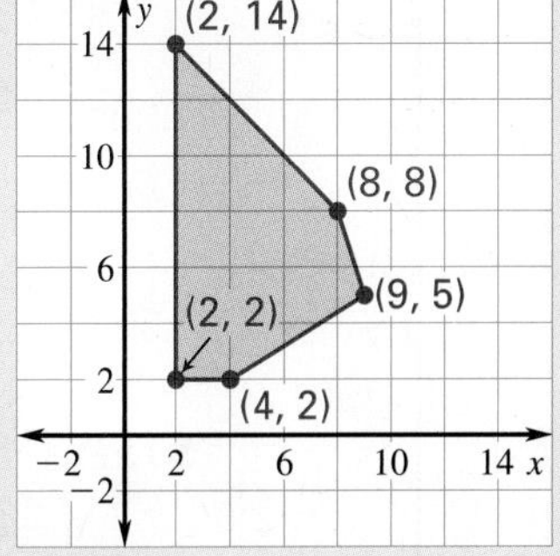

8. Manufacturing A bicycle company produces two models of bicycles. The table below shows the number of hours it takes for assembling, painting, and packaging each model. The total times available are 4000 hours for assembling, 4800 hours for painting, and 1500 hours for packaging. The profits are \$55 for model A and \$60 for model B. How many of each model of bicycle should the company make to maximize profit? What is the maximum profit?

	Assembling	Painting	Packaging
Hours, Model A	2	4	1
Hours, Model B	2.5	1	0.75

UNIT 1

LESSON 1.7

Solve Systems of Linear Equations in Three Variables

Georgia Performance Standards: MM3A5c

Goal Solve systems of equations in three variables.

Vocabulary

A **linear equation in three variables** x, y, and z is an equation of the form $ax + by + cz = d$ where a, b, and c are not all zero.

An example of a **system of three linear equations** in three variables is:

$x + 2y + z = 3$ Equation 1

$2x + y + z = 4$ Equation 2

$x - y - z = 2$ Equation 3

A **solution of a system with three variables** is an **ordered triple** (x, y, z) whose coordinates make each equation true.

UNIT 1

Example 1 Use the elimination method

Solve the system. $\mathbf{2x + 3y - z = 13}$ **Equation 1**

$\mathbf{3x + y - 3z = 11}$ **Equation 2**

$\mathbf{x - y + z = 3}$ **Equation 3**

STEP 1 **Rewrite** the system as a linear system in *two* variables.

$$\begin{array}{r} 2x + 3y - z = 13 \\ 3x - 3y + 3z = 9 \\ \hline 5x \qquad + 2z = 22 \end{array}$$

Add 3 times Equation 3 to Equation 1.

New Equation 1

$$\begin{array}{r} 3x + y - 3z = 11 \\ x - y + z = 3 \\ \hline 4x \qquad - 2z = 14 \end{array}$$

Add Equations 2 and 3.

New Equation 2

STEP 2 **Solve** the new linear system for both of its variables.

$$\begin{array}{r} 5x + 2z = 22 \\ 4x - 2z = 14 \\ \hline 9x \qquad = 36 \\ x = 4 \\ z = 1 \end{array}$$

Add new Equation 1 and new Equation 2.

Solve for x.

Substitute into new Equation 1 or 2 to find z.

STEP 3 **Substitute** $x = 4$ and $z = 1$ into an original equation and solve for y.

$x - y + z = 3$ Write original Equation 3.

$4 - y + 1 = 3$ Substitute 4 for x and 1 for z.

$y = 2$ Solve for y.

Because $x = 4$, $y = 2$, and $z = 1$, the solution is the ordered triple $(4, 2, 1)$.

Georgia Performance Standards

MM3A5c Represent and solve realistic problems using systems of linear equations.

Example 2 Solve a three-variable system with no solution

Solve the system.

$$\begin{aligned} 2x - 2y + 2z &= 9 \quad \textbf{Equation 1} \\ x - y + z &= 5 \quad \textbf{Equation 2} \\ 3x + y + 2z &= 4 \quad \textbf{Equation 3} \end{aligned}$$

When you multiply Equation 2 by -2 and add the result to Equation 1, you obtain a false equation.

$$\begin{aligned} 2x - 2y + 2z &= 9 \\ -2x + 2y - 2z &= -10 \\ \hline 0 &= -1 \end{aligned}$$

Add -2 times Equation 2 to Equation 1.

New Equation 1

Because you obtain a false equation, the original system has no solution.

Example 3 Solve a three-variable system with many solutions

Solve the system.

$$\begin{aligned} x + y + z &= 3 \quad \textbf{Equation 1} \\ x + y - z &= 3 \quad \textbf{Equation 2} \\ 3x + 3y + z &= 9 \quad \textbf{Equation 3} \end{aligned}$$

STEP 1 **Rewrite** the system as a linear system in *two* variables.

$$\begin{aligned} x + y + z &= 3 \\ x + y - z &= 3 \\ \hline 2x + 2y \quad &= 6 \end{aligned}$$

Add Equation 1 to Equation 2.

New Equation 1

$$\begin{aligned} x + y - z &= 3 \\ 3x + 3y + z &= 9 \\ \hline 4x + 4y \quad &= 12 \end{aligned}$$

Add Equation 2 to Equation 3.

New Equation 2

STEP 2 **Solve** the new linear system for both of its variables.

$$\begin{aligned} -4x - 4y &= -12 \\ 4x + 4y &= 12 \\ \hline 0 &= 0 \end{aligned}$$

Add -2 times new Equation 1 and new Equation 2.

Because you obtain the identity $0 = 0$, the system has infinitely many solutions.

STEP 3 **Describe** the solution. Divide new Equation 1 by 2 to get $x + y = 3$, or $y = -x + 3$. Substituting this into the original Equation 1 produces $z = 0$. Any ordered triple of the form $(x, -x + 3, 0)$ is a solution of the system.

Guided Practice for Examples 1, 2, and 3

Solve the system.

1. $2x + y + z = 5$
$x - y + 2z = 4$
$x + y + z = 4$

2. $x + 2y + z = 7$
$x - y + z = 4$
$3x + 6y + 3z = 9$

3. $x + y + z = 2$
$x + y - z = 2$
$2x + 2y + z = 4$

UNIT 1

LESSON 1.7 **Exercise Set A**

MM3A5c Represent and solve realistic problems using systems of linear equations.

Tell whether the given ordered triple is a solution of the system.

1. $(2, 1, 3)$

$2x - y + 5z = 16$
$x - 3y + 2z = 5$
$x + 2y + z = 7$

2. $(5, -2, 2)$

$2x - y + z = 5$
$x + 2y - z = -1$
$-2x + y - 3z = -15$

3. $(3, 3, 4)$

$x + 2y - 2z = 1$
$7x - 4y + z = 11$
$2x - 3y + 2z = 5$

Solve the system using any algebraic method.

4. $x + y - 5z = -5$
$y - 2z = 14$
$4y - 2z = 8$

5. $x - y + z = 5$
$2y + 3z = 14$
$-3y + 2z = 5$

6. $-3x + y - z = -2$
$2x - y - 2z = -12$
$4x + 2y + z = 1$

7. $x - 2y + z = -1$
$x + 2y - z = 7$
$x + y + z = 2$

8. $x - 2y + 4z = -19$
$2x + y - 3z = 14$
$3x + y + 2z = 5$

9. $x - 2y - 3z = -7$
$4x + 5y - 2z = -7$
$-2x + y + z = -7$

10. $8x - 2y + z = -6$
$-x + 3y - 2z = -15$
$3x - y + 4z = 13$

11. $2x + 2y + z = -5$
$2x + y + 3z = 7$
$-4x - 2y - 6z = -14$

12. $3x - 4y - 4z = 8$
$4x + 2y - 2z = 11$
$-5x + 8y + 3z = -9$

13. Harvest Yields A farmer makes three deliveries to the feed mill during one harvest. The harvest produced 2885 bushels of corn, 1335 bushels of wheat, and 1230 bushels of soybeans. Use the table to write and solve a system of equations to find the total number of bushels in each delivery.

Crop	First Delivery	Second Delivery	Third Delivery
Corn	50%	75%	40%
Wheat	30%	10%	30%
Soybeans	20%	15%	30%

14. Harvest Earnings The feed mill pays a farmer \$6930.00 for the first delivery, \$5475.00 for the second delivery, and \$8879.50 for the third delivery. The table shows the number of bushels included in each delivery. Use the table to write and solve a system of equations to find the price per bushel that the farmer received for each crop.

Delivery	Corn	Wheat	Soybeans
First Delivery	900	540	360
Second Delivery	1125	150	225
Third Delivery	860	645	645

LESSON 1.7

Exercise Set B

MM3A5c Represent and solve realistic problems using systems of linear equations.

Solve the system using the elimination method.

1. $x + 2y + 2z = -2$
$2x - y + 3z = -6$
$x - 3y + 2z = -7$

2. $-3x + y - 3z = -13$
$2x - y + z = 8$
$4x + 2y + 3z = 2$

3. $2x + 4y - 4z = 6$
$x + 2y - 2z = 1$
$5x - 3y + z = 5$

Solve the system using the substitution method.

4. $2x + 2y - z = 9$
$3x - y + 3z = -1$
$x - 2y + z = 3$

5. $x - 3y - z = -1$
$2x + 2y + 2z = 0$
$3x + y + 3z = -2$

6. $4x - 2y + 3z = 19$
$x + 4y - 2z = -3$
$2x + 6y + z = 5$

Solve the system using any algebraic method.

7. $2x + 5y - 4z = -3$
$4x + 2y - 2z = 4$
$2x - 8y - 2z = 21$

8. $2x + 2y - z = -1$
$-2x + 2y + 3z = -1$
$3x - y + 4z = 3$

9. $3x - y - 2z = 6$
$2x + 3y + 3z = 5$
$4x + 2y + z = 4$

10. $x + 2y - z = 4$
$3x - y + 4z = -2$
$6x + 5y + z = 10$

11. $x - 2y + z = \frac{7}{6}$
$2x + y - 3z = \frac{53}{12}$
$3x + 3y + 2z = \frac{23}{12}$

12. $x - 2y + 3z = 8$
$4x - 2y - 2z = -6$
$-2x + y + z = 3$

13. $w + x - 2y + z = 1$
$2w - x + 3y - 2z = 2$
$w + 3x - y + 4z = 7$
$3w + x - y + 2z = 5$

14. $w + x + 2y + z = 2$
$2w + 2x + y + 3z = 0$
$2w - 4x - 2y - z = 7$
$-w + 2x + y - z = -2$

15. $-w + 3x - y - 4z = 6$
$2w + 4x + 2y - z = 6$
$w - x + y + 3z = -4$
$3w - x + 3y + z = 4$

In Exercises 16–18, use the following information.

Polynomial Curve Fitting You can use a system of equations to find a polynomial of degree n whose graph passes through $(n + 1)$ points. Consider a polynomial of degree 2, $y = ax^2 + bx + c$. Suppose $(1, -2)$, $(-2, 7)$, and $(-5, -2)$ lie on the graph. Using the point $(1, -2)$, the following equation can be derived:

$$y = ax^2 + bx + c$$
$$-2 = a(1)^2 + b(1) + c$$
$$-2 = a + b + c$$

The equation $a + b + c = -2$ becomes the first equation in the system.

16. Write the equations in the system that correspond to the points $(-2, 7)$ and $(-5, -2)$.

17. Write a system of equations for the coefficients of a polynomial of degree 2 whose graph passes through $(1, -2)$, $(-2, 7)$, and $(-5, -2)$. Solve the system.

18. Write the polynomial.

UNIT 1

LESSON 1.8

Perform Basic Matrix Operations

Georgia Performance Standards: MM3A4a, MM3A4c

Goal Perform operations with matrices.

Vocabulary

A **matrix** is a rectangular arrangement of numbers in rows and columns. The **dimensions** of a matrix with m rows and n columns are $m \times n$. The numbers in a matrix are its **elements. Equal matrices** have the same dimensions and the elements in corresponding positions are equal.

To add or subtract two matrices, simply add or subtract elements in corresponding positions. You can add or subtract matrices only if they have the same dimensions.

In matrix algebra, a real number is often called a **scalar.** To perform **scalar multiplication,** you multiply each element in the matrix by the scalar.

Properties of Matrix Operations

Many of the properties you have used with real numbers can be applied to matrices. In the properties below, let A, B, and C be matrices with the same dimensions, and let k be a scalar.

Associative Property of Addition	$(A + B) + C = A + (B + C)$
Commutative Property of Addition	$A + B = B + A$
Distributive Property of Addition	$k(A + B) = kA + kB$
Distributive Property of Subtraction	$k(A - B) = kA - kB$

Example 1 Add and subtract matrices

Perform the indicated operation, if possible.

a. $\begin{bmatrix} -9 & 0 \\ -1 & 5 \end{bmatrix} + \begin{bmatrix} 1 & 7 \\ 10 & -2 \end{bmatrix} = \begin{bmatrix} -9 + 1 & 0 + 7 \\ -1 + 10 & 5 + (-2) \end{bmatrix} = \begin{bmatrix} -8 & 7 \\ 9 & 3 \end{bmatrix}$

b. $\begin{bmatrix} -8 & -5 \\ 7 & 9 \end{bmatrix} - \begin{bmatrix} 1 & 2 \\ 8 & -2 \end{bmatrix} = \begin{bmatrix} -8 - 1 & -5 - 2 \\ 7 - 8 & 9 - (-2) \end{bmatrix} = \begin{bmatrix} -9 & -7 \\ -1 & 11 \end{bmatrix}$

Guided Practice for Example 1

1. $\begin{bmatrix} 3 & -4 \\ 0 & 6 \end{bmatrix} + \begin{bmatrix} -7 & 5 \\ 10 & -2 \end{bmatrix}$

2. $\begin{bmatrix} -6 & -4 \\ 3 & 7 \end{bmatrix} - \begin{bmatrix} -1 & 3 \\ -5 & -4 \end{bmatrix}$

3. $\begin{bmatrix} 2 & -1 & 3 \\ 8 & -9 & 6 \end{bmatrix} + \begin{bmatrix} -3 & 1 & -2 \\ 4 & 6 & 7 \end{bmatrix}$

4. $\begin{bmatrix} 0 & -5 & 8 \\ 3 & -3 & 6 \\ 4 & 7 & -2 \end{bmatrix} - \begin{bmatrix} -4 & 1 & -1 \\ 9 & -5 & 3 \\ 5 & 8 & 1 \end{bmatrix}$

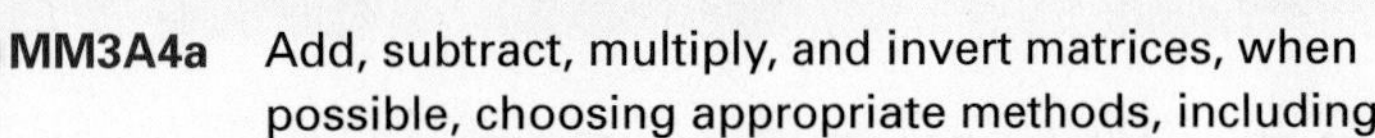

Georgia Performance Standards

MM3A4a Add, subtract, multiply, and invert matrices, when possible, choosing appropriate methods, including technology. 

MM3A4c Examine the properties of matrices, contrasting them with properties of real numbers. 

Example 2 Multiply a matrix by a scalar

Perform the indicated operation, if possible.

$$-3\begin{bmatrix} 0 & 3 \\ -2 & 5 \\ 1 & 4 \end{bmatrix} = \begin{bmatrix} -3(0) & -3(3) \\ -3(-2) & -3(5) \\ -3(1) & -3(4) \end{bmatrix} = \begin{bmatrix} 0 & -9 \\ 6 & -15 \\ -3 & -12 \end{bmatrix}$$

Guided Practice for Example 2

Perform the indicated operation, if possible.

5. $2\begin{bmatrix} -3 & 0 \\ -2 & 1 \end{bmatrix}$

6. $4\begin{bmatrix} 1 & -7 \\ -3 & 0 \\ -1 & 2 \end{bmatrix}$

7. $-3\begin{bmatrix} 5 & 4 & -2 \\ 0 & 3 & 1 \end{bmatrix}$

Example 3 Solve a multi-step problem

Gardening Last year you planted 12 geraniums, 36 begonias, and 20 petunias. This year you planted 10 geraniums, 40 begonias, and 32 petunias. Organize the data using two matrices. Write and interpret a matrix that gives the average number of flowers for the two year period.

Solution

STEP 1 **Organize** the data using two 3×1 matrices, as shown.

	Last year (A)	This year (B)
Geraniums	12	10
Begonias	36	40
Petunias	20	32

STEP 2 **Write** a matrix for the average number of flowers by multiplying the sum of A and B by $\frac{1}{2}$. You can use the distributive property to rewrite the expression as shown.

$$\frac{1}{2}(A + B) = \frac{1}{2}A + \frac{1}{2}B = \frac{1}{2}\begin{bmatrix} 12 \\ 36 \\ 20 \end{bmatrix} + \frac{1}{2}\begin{bmatrix} 10 \\ 40 \\ 32 \end{bmatrix}$$

$$= \begin{bmatrix} 6 \\ 18 \\ 10 \end{bmatrix} + \begin{bmatrix} 5 \\ 20 \\ 16 \end{bmatrix} = \begin{bmatrix} 11 \\ 38 \\ 26 \end{bmatrix}$$

STEP 3 **Interpret** the matrix from Step 2. You planted an average of 11 geraniums, 38 begonias, and 26 petunias over the last two years.

UNIT 1

Guided Practice for Example 3

8. In Example 3, find $A - B$ and explain what information this matrix gives.

9. **Bakery** A local bakery keeps track of their sales as shown below.

Last Month Store 1: 620 rolls, 240 cakes, and 38 pies

Store 2: 510 rolls, 190 cakes, and 30 pies

This Month Store 1: 860 rolls, 270 cakes, and 54 pies

Store 2: 780 rolls, 230 cakes, and 46 pies

Organize the data using two matrices. Write and interpret a matrix that gives the average number of bakery items sold per store over the two month period.

Example 4 Solve a matrix equation

Solve the matrix equation for *x* and *y*.

$$3\left(\begin{bmatrix} 5x & -2 \\ 6 & -4 \end{bmatrix} + \begin{bmatrix} 3 & 7 \\ -5 & -y \end{bmatrix}\right) = \begin{bmatrix} -36 & 15 \\ 3 & -27 \end{bmatrix}$$

Solution

Simplify the left side of the equation.

$$3\left(\begin{bmatrix} 5x & -2 \\ 6 & -4 \end{bmatrix} + \begin{bmatrix} 3 & 7 \\ -5 & -y \end{bmatrix}\right) = \begin{bmatrix} -36 & 15 \\ 3 & -27 \end{bmatrix}$$ Write original equation.

$$3\begin{bmatrix} 5x + 3 & 5 \\ 1 & -4 - y \end{bmatrix} = \begin{bmatrix} -36 & 15 \\ 3 & -27 \end{bmatrix}$$ Add matrices inside parentheses.

$$\begin{bmatrix} 15x + 9 & 15 \\ 3 & -12 - 3y \end{bmatrix} = \begin{bmatrix} -36 & 15 \\ 3 & -27 \end{bmatrix}$$ Perform scalar multiplication.

Equate corresponding elements and solve the two resulting equations.

$15x + 9 = -36$ $\qquad$ $-12 - 3y = -27$

$x = -3$ $\qquad$ $y = 5$

The solution is $x = -3$ and $y = 5$.

Guided Practice for Example 4

Solve the matrix equation for *x* and *y*.

10. $\begin{bmatrix} 10 & -3y \\ 6 & 13 \end{bmatrix} = \begin{bmatrix} 10 & -15 \\ 6x & 13 \end{bmatrix}$

11. $\begin{bmatrix} 12 & 3 \\ 6y & 5 \end{bmatrix} = \begin{bmatrix} -4x & 3 \\ 24 & 5 \end{bmatrix}$

12. Solve $-2\left(\begin{bmatrix} -3x & -1 \\ 4 & y \end{bmatrix} + \begin{bmatrix} 9 & -4 \\ -6 & 3 \end{bmatrix}\right) = \begin{bmatrix} 6 & 10 \\ 4 & -20 \end{bmatrix}$ for x and y.

LESSON 1.8 **Exercise Set A**

MM3A4a Add, subtract, multiply, and invert matrices, when possible, choosing appropriate methods, including technology.

MM3A4c Examine the properties of matrices, contrasting them with properties of real numbers.

Perform the indicated operation, if possible. If not possible, state the reason.

1. $\begin{bmatrix} 2 & 1 \\ 6 & 4 \end{bmatrix} - \begin{bmatrix} -2 & 1 \\ -4 & 0 \end{bmatrix}$

2. $\begin{bmatrix} 5 & 2 \\ -1 & 4 \\ -3 & 6 \end{bmatrix} + \begin{bmatrix} -2 & 4 \\ 6 & -2 \\ 7 & -5 \end{bmatrix}$

3. $\begin{bmatrix} 6 & 4 & 3 \\ 1 & -3 & 2 \\ 8 & 7 & 1 \end{bmatrix} - \begin{bmatrix} 4 & 5 & -4 \\ 5 & 1 & 0 \\ 6 & 4 & 7 \end{bmatrix}$

4. $\begin{bmatrix} -4 & 2 & 3 \end{bmatrix} + \begin{bmatrix} -2 \\ 0 \\ -1 \end{bmatrix}$

5. $\begin{bmatrix} 10 & -5 & 7 \\ 2 & -12 & 0 \\ 8 & -4 & 6 \end{bmatrix} + \begin{bmatrix} -7 & 14 & 6 \\ 0 & 12 & -4 \\ 2 & 7 & 3 \end{bmatrix}$

6. $\begin{bmatrix} 10 & -7 & 14 \\ -5 & -10 & 0 \\ 9 & -3 & -7 \end{bmatrix} - \begin{bmatrix} -1 & -3 & 8 \\ -12 & 0 & 6 \\ 10 & -5 & 5 \end{bmatrix}$

Perform the indicated operation.

7. $-3\begin{bmatrix} 4 & 2 \\ 3 & 2 \end{bmatrix}$

8. $-2\begin{bmatrix} 3 & 0 & -1 \\ 0.5 & -6 & 4 \\ 7 & -1.25 & 9 \end{bmatrix}$

9. $-4\begin{bmatrix} 4 & 1 \\ -5 & 0 \\ 1 & -3 \end{bmatrix}$

Solve the matrix equation for *x* and *y*.

10. $\begin{bmatrix} -2x & 6 \\ 3y & 9 \end{bmatrix} = \begin{bmatrix} -8 & 6 \\ -12 & 9 \end{bmatrix}$

11. $\begin{bmatrix} 4 & 5x \\ -2 & 5 \end{bmatrix} + \begin{bmatrix} -11 & 2 \\ 6 & 5 \end{bmatrix} = \begin{bmatrix} y & 12 \\ 4 & 10 \end{bmatrix}$

In Exercises 12–15, use the following information.

Book Prices The matrices below show the number of books sold and the average price (in dollars) for the years 2002, 2003, and 2004.

	2002 (D)		2003 (E)		2004 (F)	
	Sold	Price	Sold	Price	Sold	Price
Book A	125,000	52.00	110,000	55.50	90,000	47.50
Book B	85,000	83.50	95,000	85.50	100,000	89.00
Book C	190,000	45.60	210,000	56.25	225,000	75.25

12. You purchased book A in 2002, book C in 2003, and book B in 2004. How much did you spend on these three books?

13. How many more (or less) volumes of book B were sold in 2004 than in 2002?

14. How much more (or less) is the price of book A in 2004 than in 2002?

15. In 2005, would you expect book C sales to be *more* or *less* than 100,000?

UNIT 1

LESSON 1.8 **Exercise Set B**

MM3A4a Add, subtract, multiply, and invert matrices, when possible, choosing appropriate methods, including technology.

MM3A4c Examine the properties of matrices, contrasting them with properties of real numbers.

Perform the indicated operation, if possible. If not possible, state the reason.

1. $\begin{bmatrix} 3 & 4 \\ -1 & 8 \end{bmatrix} - \begin{bmatrix} -2 & 6 \\ -5 & 0 \end{bmatrix}$

2. $\begin{bmatrix} 3 & 8 \\ 2 & 0 \\ -4 & 4 \end{bmatrix} + 3\begin{bmatrix} 4 & 3 \\ 1 & -2 \\ 2 & 6 \end{bmatrix}$

3. $-2\begin{bmatrix} 2 & 1 \\ 0 & -3 \end{bmatrix} - 6\begin{bmatrix} 0 & 3 \\ -1 & 4 \end{bmatrix}$

4. $\begin{bmatrix} 4 & 0 & 9 \\ 1 & -2 & 0 \\ 8 & 7 & 11 \end{bmatrix} - \begin{bmatrix} 0 & -2 \\ 2 & 0 \\ 5 & 7 \end{bmatrix}$

5. $3\left(\begin{bmatrix} 2 \\ -1 \end{bmatrix} + 2\begin{bmatrix} 0 \\ 2 \end{bmatrix}\right) - \begin{bmatrix} 5 \\ 8 \end{bmatrix}$

6. $\frac{1}{2}\begin{bmatrix} 1 & 2 \\ -2 & 3 \end{bmatrix} + \begin{bmatrix} 9 \\ 5 \end{bmatrix}$

7. $\frac{1}{3}\begin{bmatrix} -1 & 3 & 0 \\ 4 & -6 & 12 \\ 7 & 5 & -3 \end{bmatrix} + \begin{bmatrix} 2 & -1 & 2 \\ 0 & 5 & -2 \\ 4 & 7 & 3 \end{bmatrix}$

8. $\frac{1}{2}\left(\begin{bmatrix} 3 & -1 \\ 4 & 5 \end{bmatrix} + \begin{bmatrix} 5 & -3 \\ 0 & 7 \end{bmatrix}\right) - \begin{bmatrix} 4 & 2 \\ 1 & 0 \end{bmatrix}$

9. $6\left(\frac{2}{3}\begin{bmatrix} 2 & 3 \\ 6 & -5 \\ -1 & 0 \end{bmatrix} + \frac{1}{2}\begin{bmatrix} -4 & 2 \\ 3 & 0 \\ 1 & -8 \end{bmatrix}\right)$

10. $\begin{bmatrix} 1 & 3 \\ 4 & 0 \end{bmatrix} - \frac{3}{2}\left(\begin{bmatrix} 4 & -1 \\ 5 & 8 \end{bmatrix} + \frac{1}{2}\begin{bmatrix} 6 & 3 \\ 0 & -1 \end{bmatrix}\right)$

Solve the matrix equation for *x* and *y*.

11. $2\begin{bmatrix} 2x & 0 \\ 3 & -3y \end{bmatrix} = \begin{bmatrix} -12 & 0 \\ 6y & -6y \end{bmatrix}$

12. $3\begin{bmatrix} 3 & -2x \\ 2 & 4 \\ -y & 2 \end{bmatrix} - \begin{bmatrix} 2 & -2x \\ 0 & 5 \\ -2y & -2 \end{bmatrix} = \begin{bmatrix} 7 & 8 \\ 6 & 7 \\ 0 & 8 \end{bmatrix}$

13. **Sun Block** With the growing health concerns about sun exposure and skin protection, it is very important to wear sun block when outdoors. Two department stores had the following sales of the most popular sun block.

Store A: x in May, $2x$ in June, $3x - 150$ in July

Store B: y in May, $1.5y + 220$ in June, $3y - 60$ in July

Write a matrix that represents the sun block sales for the given months.

14. **Medical Insurance** A company offers medical, vision, and dental insurance to its employees. The annual employee costs for this year and next year are shown in the following matrices. Use the matrices to write a matrix that shows the *monthly* changes from this year to next year. Round to the nearest penny.

	This Year		Next Year	
	Single	Family	Single	Family
Medical	725.52	2243.64	780.36	2352.28
Vision	29.76	220.08	35.24	236.12
Dental	57.36	198.36	46.78	172.88

UNIT 1

LESSON 1.9 Multiply Matrices

Georgia Performance Standards: MM3A4a, MM3A4c

Goal Multiply matrices.

Vocabulary

The product of two matrices A and B is defined provided the number of columns in A is equal to the number of rows in B. If A is an $m \times n$ matrix and B is an $n \times p$ matrix, then the product AB is an $m \times p$ matrix.

When multiplying matrices, to find the element in the ith row and jth column of the product matrix AB, multiply each element in the ith row of A by the corresponding element in the jth column of B, then add the products, as shown below.

$$\underset{A}{\begin{bmatrix} a & b \\ c & d \end{bmatrix}}\underset{B}{\begin{bmatrix} e & f \\ g & h \end{bmatrix}} = \underset{AB}{\begin{bmatrix} ae + bg & af + bh \\ ce + dg & cf + dh \end{bmatrix}}$$

Properties of Matrix Operations

To evaluate expressions involving matrices, use the properties below. Let A, B, and C be matrices and let k be a scalar.

Associative Property of Matrix Multiplication	$A(BC) = (AB)C$
Left Distributive Property	$A(B + C) = AB + AC$
Right Distributive Property	$(A + B)C = AC + BC$
Associative Property of Scalar Multiplication	$k(AB) = (kA)B = A(kB)$

It is important to note that, in general, matrix multiplication is *not* commutative. So, the product BA is usually not the same as the product AB.

Example 1 Describe matrix products

State whether the product *AB* is defined. If so, give the dimensions of *AB*.

a. A: 5×3, B: 3×2

b. A: 2×3, B: 2×4

Solution

a. Because A is a **5** $\times$ **3** matrix and B is a **3** $\times$ **2** matrix, the product AB is defined and is a **5** $\times$ **2** matrix.

b. Because the number of columns in A (three) does not equal the number of rows in B (two), the product AB is not defined.

Guided Practice for Example 1

State whether the product *AB* is defined. If so, give the dimensions of *AB*.

1. A: 4×2, B: 2×2

2. A: 5×2, B: 5×2

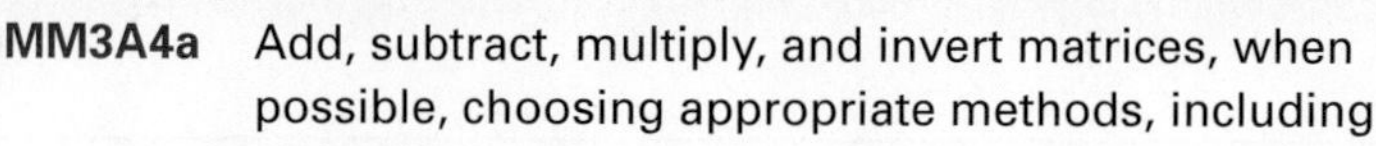

Georgia Performance Standards

MM3A4a Add, subtract, multiply, and invert matrices, when possible, choosing appropriate methods, including technology. 

MM3A4c Examine the properties of matrices, contrasting them with properties of real numbers. 

Example 2 Find the product of two matrices

Find AB if $A = \begin{bmatrix} 3 & 6 \\ 7 & -1 \end{bmatrix}$ and $B = \begin{bmatrix} 4 & 2 \\ -3 & 8 \end{bmatrix}$.

Because the number of columns in A (two) equals the number of rows in B (two), the product AB is defined and is a 2×2 matrix.

STEP 1 **Multiply** the numbers in the first row of A by the numbers in the first column of B, add the products, and put the result in the first row, first column of AB.

$$\begin{bmatrix} 3 & 6 \\ 7 & -1 \end{bmatrix}\begin{bmatrix} 4 & 2 \\ -3 & 8 \end{bmatrix} = \begin{bmatrix} 3(4) + 6(-3) & \\ & \end{bmatrix}$$

STEP 2 **Multiply** the numbers in the first row of A by the numbers in the second column of B, add the products, and put the result in the first row, second column of AB.

$$\begin{bmatrix} 3 & 6 \\ 7 & -1 \end{bmatrix}\begin{bmatrix} 4 & 2 \\ -3 & 8 \end{bmatrix} = \begin{bmatrix} 3(4) + 6(-3) & 3(2) + 6(8) \\ & \end{bmatrix}$$

STEP 3 **Multiply** the numbers in the second row of A by the numbers in the first column of B, add the products, and put the result in the second row, first column of AB.

$$\begin{bmatrix} 3 & 6 \\ 7 & -1 \end{bmatrix}\begin{bmatrix} 4 & 2 \\ -3 & 8 \end{bmatrix} = \begin{bmatrix} 3(4) + 6(-3) & 3(2) + 6(8) \\ 7(4) + (-1)(-3) & \end{bmatrix}$$

STEP 4 **Multiply** the numbers in the second row of A by the numbers in the second column of B, add the products, and put the result in the second row, second column of AB.

$$\begin{bmatrix} 3 & 6 \\ 7 & -1 \end{bmatrix}\begin{bmatrix} 4 & 2 \\ -3 & 8 \end{bmatrix} = \begin{bmatrix} 3(4) + 6(-3) & 3(2) + 6(8) \\ 7(4) + (-1)(-3) & 7(2) + (-1)(8) \end{bmatrix}$$

STEP 5 **Simplify** the product matrix.

$$\begin{bmatrix} 3(4) + 6(-3) & 3(2) + 6(8) \\ 7(4) + (-1)(-3) & 7(2) + (-1)(8) \end{bmatrix} = \begin{bmatrix} -6 & 54 \\ 31 & 6 \end{bmatrix}$$

Guided Practice for Example 2

Find the product. If it is not defined, state the reason.

3. $\begin{bmatrix} 4 \\ -2 \end{bmatrix}\begin{bmatrix} 1 & 3 \end{bmatrix}$

4. $\begin{bmatrix} 2 & 3 \\ 4 & 7 \end{bmatrix}\begin{bmatrix} -5 & -2 \\ 1 & 6 \end{bmatrix}$

5. $\begin{bmatrix} 1 & -3 \\ 5 & 8 \end{bmatrix}\begin{bmatrix} -9 & 7 \\ -2 & -4 \end{bmatrix}$

Example 3 Use matrix operations

Using the given matrices, evaluate the expression *B*(*A* + *C*).

$$A = \begin{bmatrix} 2 & -1 \\ -6 & 4 \end{bmatrix},\ B = \begin{bmatrix} 4 & 2 \\ 1 & -5 \end{bmatrix},\ C = \begin{bmatrix} 0 & -3 \\ 4 & 5 \end{bmatrix}$$

$$B(A + C) = \begin{bmatrix} 4 & 2 \\ 1 & -5 \end{bmatrix}\left(\begin{bmatrix} 2 & -1 \\ -6 & 4 \end{bmatrix} + \begin{bmatrix} 0 & -3 \\ 4 & 5 \end{bmatrix}\right)$$

$$= \begin{bmatrix} 4 & 2 \\ 1 & -5 \end{bmatrix} \cdot \begin{bmatrix} 2 & -4 \\ -2 & 9 \end{bmatrix} = \begin{bmatrix} 4 & 2 \\ 12 & -49 \end{bmatrix}$$

Guided Practice for Example 3

Using the given matrices, evaluate the expression.

$$A = \begin{bmatrix} -2 & 6 \\ 1 & 3 \end{bmatrix},\ B = \begin{bmatrix} 0 & 2 \\ 4 & -5 \end{bmatrix},\ C = \begin{bmatrix} 5 & -1 \\ -2 & 0 \end{bmatrix}$$

6. $AB + C$ **7.** $2AB$ **8.** $A(B + C)$

Example 4 Use matrices to calculate total cost

School Supplies You and a friend are purchasing school supplies. You buy 4 binders and 1 notepad. Your friend buys 2 binders and 3 notepads. Each binder costs \$3.50 and each notepad costs \$2. Write a supplies matrix and a cost per item matrix. Then use matrix multiplication to write a total cost matrix.

Solution

	Supplies	
	Binders	**Notepads**
You	4	1
Friend	2	3

	Cost
	Dollars
Binders	3.5
Notepads	2

The total cost can be found by multiplying the 2×2 supplies matrix by the 2×1 cost per item matrix. The product is a 2×1 total cost matrix.

$$\begin{bmatrix} 4 & 1 \\ 2 & 3 \end{bmatrix} \cdot \begin{bmatrix} 3.5 \\ 2 \end{bmatrix} = \begin{bmatrix} 16 \\ 13 \end{bmatrix}$$

The total cost of the school supplies is the sum of the rows of the total cost matrix, or \$29.

Guided Practice for Example 4

9. Rework Example 3 if a binder costs \$3 and a notepad costs \$2.50.

UNIT 1

LESSON 1.9 **Exercise Set A**

MM3A4a Add, subtract, multiply, and invert matrices, when possible, choosing appropriate methods, including technology.

MM3A4c Examine the properties of matrices, contrasting them with properties of real numbers.

State the dimensions of each matrix and determine whether the product *AB* is defined. If so, give the dimensions of *AB*.

1. $A = \begin{bmatrix} 2 & 1 \\ 5 & 0 \\ 1 & 2 \end{bmatrix}, B = \begin{bmatrix} 2 & 1 & 5 \end{bmatrix}$

2. $A = \begin{bmatrix} 2 & -3 & 4 \\ -2 & 1 & 0 \end{bmatrix}, B = \begin{bmatrix} 1 & 2 & 0 \\ 5 & 4 & 3 \\ -4 & 2 & -5 \end{bmatrix}$

Find the product. If it is not defined, state the reason.

3. $\begin{bmatrix} 3 & 2 \end{bmatrix}\begin{bmatrix} 1 \\ 4 \end{bmatrix}$

4. $\begin{bmatrix} 1 & -1 \\ 2 & 1 \end{bmatrix}\begin{bmatrix} 2 & -2 \\ 1 & 2 \end{bmatrix}$

5. $\begin{bmatrix} 2 \\ -1 \\ 3 \end{bmatrix}\begin{bmatrix} -1 & 3 \end{bmatrix}$

6. $\begin{bmatrix} 3 & 5 \\ -2 & 4 \end{bmatrix}\begin{bmatrix} 2 & -1 \\ 4 & 0 \end{bmatrix}$

7. $\begin{bmatrix} 5 & 1 & 0 \\ -2 & 3 & 1 \\ 0 & 2 & 4 \end{bmatrix}\begin{bmatrix} -1 & 2 & -3 \\ 0 & 5 & 4 \\ 2 & -1 & 2 \end{bmatrix}$

8. $\begin{bmatrix} 2 \\ 1 \end{bmatrix}\begin{bmatrix} 1 & 2 & 4 \\ -2 & 3 & 1 \end{bmatrix}$

9. $\begin{bmatrix} -1 & 6 & 2 & 4 \end{bmatrix}\begin{bmatrix} 1 \\ -1 \\ 4 \\ 0 \end{bmatrix}$

10. $\begin{bmatrix} 2 & -3 \\ 4 & -2 \\ 0 & -1 \end{bmatrix}\begin{bmatrix} 2 & 1 & -1 \\ 5 & 3 & 2 \end{bmatrix}$

11. $\begin{bmatrix} 0 & 1 & 0 \\ 2 & 3 & -1 \\ -2 & 4 & 0 \\ 5 & 0 & -2 \end{bmatrix}\begin{bmatrix} 2 \\ -3 \\ 1 \end{bmatrix}$

Using the given matrices, evaluate the expression.

$A = \begin{bmatrix} 2 & -1 \\ 3 & 2 \end{bmatrix}, B = \begin{bmatrix} 1 & 0 \\ 3 & -2 \end{bmatrix}, C = \begin{bmatrix} 3 & -2 \\ -1 & 4 \end{bmatrix}$

12. $-2BC$

13. $AC - AB$

14. $BA + BC$

15. Football Tickets to the football game cost \$2.50 for students, \$5.00 for adults, and \$4.00 for senior citizens. Attendance for the first game of the postseason was 120 students, 185 adults, and 34 senior citizens. Attendance for the second game of the postseason was 150 students, 210 adults, and 50 senior citizens. Use matrix multiplication to find the revenue from ticket sales for each game.

UNIT 1

LESSON 1.9

Exercise Set B

MM3A4a Add, subtract, multiply, and invert matrices, when possible, choosing appropriate methods, including technology.

MM3A4c Examine the properties of matrices, contrasting them with properties of real numbers.

Find the product. If it is not defined, state the reason.

1. $\begin{bmatrix} -4 & 2 \\ -1 & 0 \\ 3 & 1 \end{bmatrix}\begin{bmatrix} 2 & 1 \\ 3 & 5 \end{bmatrix}$

2. $\begin{bmatrix} 3 & -1 & 0 \\ 2 & 5 & -4 \end{bmatrix}\begin{bmatrix} 1 & 0 \\ 0 & 1 \end{bmatrix}$

3. $\begin{bmatrix} 5 & 0 & -2 \\ 1 & 6 & 0 \\ -2 & 3 & 1 \end{bmatrix}\begin{bmatrix} 1 & 0 \\ -3 & 2 \\ 2 & -1 \end{bmatrix}$

4. $\begin{bmatrix} -2 \\ -1 \\ 3 \\ 4 \end{bmatrix}\begin{bmatrix} 2 & 3 & -1 \end{bmatrix}$

Using the given matrices, evaluate the expression.

$A = \begin{bmatrix} 2 & -1 \\ 1 & 3 \end{bmatrix}, B = \begin{bmatrix} 2 & 3 \\ 0 & -2 \end{bmatrix}, C = \begin{bmatrix} 4 & -1 \\ 1 & 2 \\ 3 & -2 \end{bmatrix}, D = \begin{bmatrix} 1 & 0 & -2 \\ 4 & 1 & 6 \\ 2 & -1 & 2 \end{bmatrix}, E = \begin{bmatrix} -3 & 0 & 1 \\ 2 & 5 & -3 \\ -1 & 0 & 2 \end{bmatrix}$

5. $-AB$

6. $\frac{1}{2}CB$

7. $CA - CB$

8. DC

9. CAB

10. $EC(A + B)$

Solve for *x* and *y*.

11. $\begin{bmatrix} 1 & 2 & -1 \\ 3 & -2 & 1 \\ 0 & 2 & 4 \end{bmatrix}\begin{bmatrix} x \\ 2 \\ -1 \end{bmatrix} = \begin{bmatrix} 8 \\ y \\ 0 \end{bmatrix}$

12. $\begin{bmatrix} 3 & 2 & -1 \\ -2 & 0 & 2 \end{bmatrix}\begin{bmatrix} 2 & x \\ -1 & 4 \\ 3 & y \end{bmatrix} = \begin{bmatrix} 1 & 0 \\ 2 & 4 \end{bmatrix}$

13. **Geometry** Matrix B contains the coordinates of the vertices of the triangle shown in the graph. Calculate AB and determine what effect the multiplication of matrix A has on the graph.

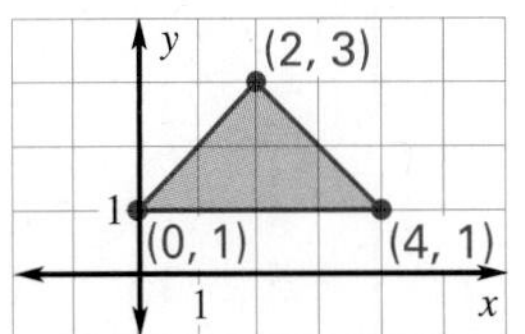

$A = \begin{bmatrix} -1 & 0 \\ 0 & -1 \end{bmatrix} \quad B = \begin{bmatrix} 0 & 2 & 4 \\ 1 & 3 & 1 \end{bmatrix}$

14. **Mayor Election** Candidate A and candidate B are running for mayor of a small town. After attending a debate, some citizens change their minds about the candidate for whom they will vote. Let $m = 25\%$ be the percent of citizens that switch from candidate A to candidate B. Let $n = 16\%$ be the percent of citizens that switch from candidate B to candidate A. Before the debate, candidate A was expected to win the election 1200 votes to 950 votes. After the debate, how many votes will candidate A and candidate B receive? Use the transition matrix T to help answer the question.

$T = \begin{bmatrix} 1 - m & n \\ m & 1 - n \end{bmatrix}$

UNIT 1

Georgia Performance Standards

MM3A4a Add, subtract, multiply, and invert matrices, when possible, choosing appropriate methods, including technology.

Technology Activity
Matrix Operations

Use after Lesson 1.9

Question

How can you use a graphing calculator to perform matrix operations?

Example

Use a graphing calculator to perform operations with matrices.

Using matrices A and B below, find $A + B$ and $2A + 3B$.

$$A = \begin{bmatrix} 7 & -2 & 1 \\ 4 & -8 & 9 \end{bmatrix} \quad B = \begin{bmatrix} -1 & 3 & -4 \\ 0 & 6 & 12 \end{bmatrix}$$

STEP 1

Enter Matrix *A*

Enter the dimensions and elements of matrix A.

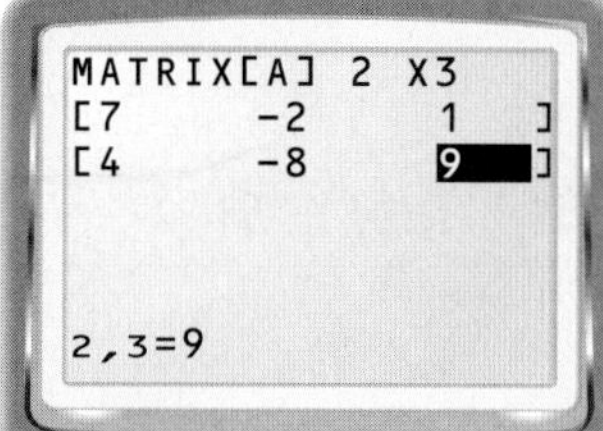

STEP 2

Enter Matrix *B*

Enter the dimensions and elements of matrix B.

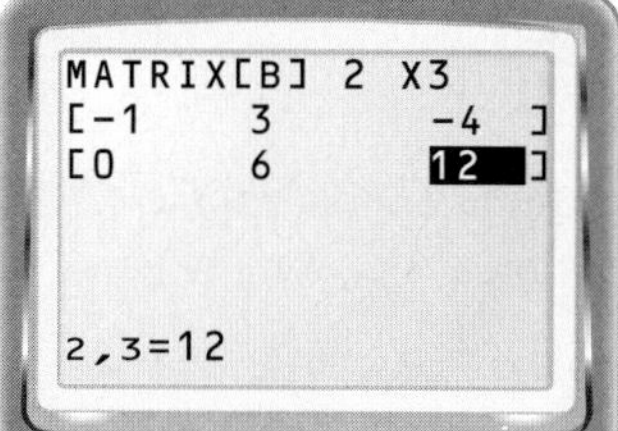

STEP 3

Perform calculations

From the home screen, calculate $A + B$ and $2A - 3B$.

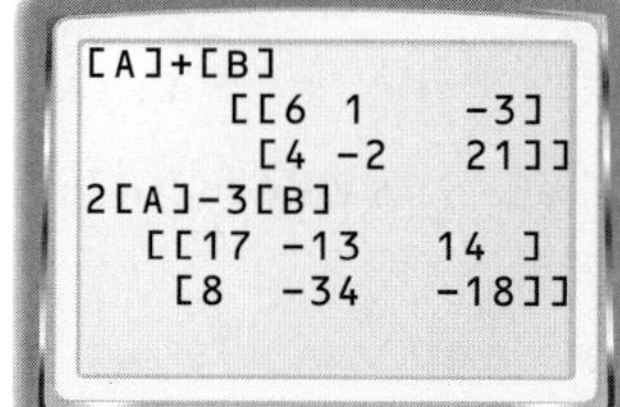

Practice

Use a graphing calculator to perform the indicated operation(s).

1. $\begin{bmatrix} -7 & 2 \\ 4 & 8 \end{bmatrix} + \begin{bmatrix} 10 & -6 \\ 5 & -8 \end{bmatrix}$

2. $3.5\begin{bmatrix} 11.6 & 7.8 & -4.2 \\ -0.6 & 5.4 & -2.1 \end{bmatrix}$

3. $\begin{bmatrix} 4 & 9 & 14 \\ -5 & -13 & -10 \\ 8 & 11 & 7 \end{bmatrix} + \begin{bmatrix} -8 & 10 & 0 \\ -7 & 12 & 3 \\ -1 & -9 & -5 \end{bmatrix}$

4. $2\begin{bmatrix} 5 & -2 \\ 7 & -5 \\ -3 & -1 \end{bmatrix} - 4\begin{bmatrix} 4 & 1 \\ -9 & 0 \\ -2 & 15 \end{bmatrix}$

5. **Book Sales** The matrices below show book sales (in thousands of dollars) at a chain of bookstores for August and September. The book formats are hardcover and paperback. The categories of books are romance (R), mystery (M), science fiction (S), and children's (C). Use a graphing calculator to find the total sales of each format and category for August and September.

	August				September			
	R	M	S	C	R	M	S	C
Hardcover	20	18	23	12	24	20	19	9
Paperback	34	21	15	30	38	25	10	27

LESSON 1.10

Evaluate Determinants and Apply Cramer's Rule

Georgia Performance Standards: MM3A5c

Goal Evaluate determinants of matrices.

Vocabulary

Associated with each square matrix ($n \times n$) is a real number called its **determinant.** The determinant of a matrix A is denoted by det A or by $|A|$.

Determinant of a 2 × 2 Matrix

$$\det\begin{bmatrix} a & b \\ c & d \end{bmatrix} = \begin{vmatrix} a & b \\ c & d \end{vmatrix} = ad - cb$$

The determinant of a 2 × 2 matrix is the difference of the products of the elements on the diagonals.

Determinant of a 3 × 3 Matrix

Repeat the first two columns to the right of the determinant. Then **subtract** the sum of the **red products** from the sum of the **blue products.**

$$\det\begin{bmatrix} a & b & c \\ d & e & f \\ g & h & i \end{bmatrix} = \left|\begin{matrix} a & b & c \\ d & e & f \\ g & h & i \end{matrix}\right|\begin{matrix} a & b \\ d & e \\ g & h \end{matrix} = (aei + bfg + cdh) - (gec + hfa + idb)$$

The **coefficient matrix** of the linear system $ax + by = e$ and $cx + dy = f$ is $\begin{bmatrix} a & b \\ c & d \end{bmatrix}$.

Cramer's rule is another method for solving linear systems.

Cramer's rule for a 2 × 2 System: Let A be the coefficient matrix of the linear system $ax + by = e$ and $cx + dy = f$. If det $A \neq 0$, then the system has exactly one solution.

The solution is $x = \dfrac{\begin{vmatrix} e & b \\ f & d \end{vmatrix}}{\det A}$ and $y = \dfrac{\begin{vmatrix} a & e \\ c & f \end{vmatrix}}{\det A}$.

Cramer's rule for a 3 × 3 System: Let A be the coefficient matrix of the linear system $ax + by + cz = j$, $dx + ey + fz = k$ and $gx + hy + iz = \ell$. If det $A \neq 0$, then the system has exactly one solution.

The solution is $x = \dfrac{\begin{vmatrix} j & b & c \\ k & e & f \\ \ell & h & i \end{vmatrix}}{\det A}$, $y = \dfrac{\begin{vmatrix} a & j & c \\ d & k & f \\ g & \ell & i \end{vmatrix}}{\det A}$, and $z = \dfrac{\begin{vmatrix} a & b & j \\ d & e & k \\ g & h & \ell \end{vmatrix}}{\det A}$.

Example 1 Evaluate determinants

a. $\det\begin{bmatrix} 8 & -2 \\ 4 & 7 \end{bmatrix} = \begin{vmatrix} 8 & -2 \\ 4 & 7 \end{vmatrix} = 8(7) - 4(-2) = 56 + 8 = 64$

b. $\det\begin{bmatrix} 3 & 0 & 1 \\ -3 & 4 & 2 \\ -2 & 1 & -1 \end{bmatrix} = \left|\begin{matrix} 3 & 0 & 1 \\ -3 & 4 & 2 \\ -2 & 1 & -1 \end{matrix}\right|\begin{matrix} 3 & 0 \\ -3 & 4 \\ -2 & 1 \end{matrix}$

$= [(-12) + 0 + (-3)] - (-8 + 6 + 0) = -15 - (-2) = -13$

UNIT 1

Georgia Performance Standards

MM3A5c Represent and solve realistic problems using systems of linear equations.

Example 2 Use Cramer's rule for a 2 × 2 system

Use Cramer's rule to solve the linear system: $7x + 5y = 16$
$4x - 2y = 14$

STEP 1 **Evaluate** the determinant of the coefficient matrix. $\begin{vmatrix} 7 & 5 \\ 4 & -2 \end{vmatrix} = -14 - 20 = -34$

STEP 2 **Apply** Cramer's rule because the determinant is not zero.

$$x = \frac{\begin{vmatrix} 16 & 5 \\ 14 & -2 \end{vmatrix}}{-34} = \frac{-32 - 70}{-34} = 3 \qquad y = \frac{\begin{vmatrix} 7 & 16 \\ 4 & 14 \end{vmatrix}}{-34} = \frac{98 - 64}{-34} = -1$$

The solution is (3, −1).

Example 3 Solve a multi-step problem

Pricing Two bottles of water and 1 bottle of juice sell for \$2.55. Two bottles of juice and 1 bottle of milk sell for \$2.45. One bottle of water, 1 bottle of juice, and 1 bottle of milk sell for \$2.30. Use a linear system and Cramer's rule to find the prices of the water, juice, and milk.

STEP 1 **Write** a linear system using w, j, and m to represent the various number of bottles.

$$2w + j = 2.55$$
$$2j + m = 2.45$$
$$w + j + m = 2.30$$

STEP 2 **Evaluate** the determinant of the coefficient matrix.

$$\begin{vmatrix} 2 & 1 & 0 \\ 0 & 2 & 1 \\ 1 & 1 & 1 \end{vmatrix}\begin{matrix} 2 & 1 \\ 0 & 2 \\ 1 & 1 \end{matrix} = 4 + 1 + 0 - (0 + 2 + 0) = 3$$

STEP 3 **Apply** Cramer's rule because the determinant is not zero.

$$w = \frac{\begin{vmatrix} 2.55 & 1 & 0 \\ 2.45 & 2 & 1 \\ 2.30 & 1 & 1 \end{vmatrix}}{3} = 0.80 \quad j = \frac{\begin{vmatrix} 2 & 2.55 & 0 \\ 0 & 2.45 & 1 \\ 1 & 2.30 & 1 \end{vmatrix}}{3} = 0.95 \quad m = \frac{\begin{vmatrix} 2 & 1 & 2.55 \\ 0 & 2 & 2.45 \\ 1 & 1 & 2.30 \end{vmatrix}}{3} = 0.55$$

The price of water is \$.80, the price of juice is \$.95, and the price of milk is \$.55.

Guided Practice for Examples 1, 2, and 3

1. Evaluate $\begin{vmatrix} -6 & 2 \\ 4 & -3 \end{vmatrix}$.

2. Evaluate $\begin{vmatrix} 4 & 1 & 5 \\ -2 & 0 & 1 \\ 3 & 2 & -1 \end{vmatrix}$.

Use Cramer's rule to solve the linear system.

3. $2x + y = 11$
$-3x + 2y = 1$

4. $4x - 5y = 6$
$7x - 12y = 4$

5. $-6x + 4y + z = 32$
$5x + 2y + 3z = 13$
$x - y + z = -5$

LESSON 1.10 **Exercise Set A**

MM3A5c Represent and solve realistic problems using systems of linear equations.

Evaluate the determinant of the matrix.

1. $\begin{bmatrix} 5 & -2 \\ 4 & -4 \end{bmatrix}$

2. $\begin{bmatrix} 3 & -5 \\ -2 & -3 \end{bmatrix}$

3. $\begin{bmatrix} \frac{1}{2} & \frac{2}{3} \\ 6 & 5 \end{bmatrix}$

4. $\begin{bmatrix} 5 & -1 & 3 \\ 4 & 0 & 2 \\ 1 & -2 & -5 \end{bmatrix}$

5. $\begin{bmatrix} 3 & 2 & 9 \\ 0 & 1 & -4 \\ 5 & -1 & 2 \end{bmatrix}$

6. $\begin{bmatrix} 1 & 15 & 2 \\ 0 & 1 & 3 \\ 2 & 12 & 2 \end{bmatrix}$

In Exercises 7–9, use the formula below to find the area of a triangle with vertices (x_1, y_1), (x_2, y_2), and (x_3, y_3). The symbol $\pm$ indicates that the appropriate sign should be chosen to yield a positive value.

$$\text{Area} = \pm\frac{1}{2}\begin{vmatrix} x_1 & y_1 & 1 \\ x_2 & y_2 & 1 \\ x_3 & y_3 & 1 \end{vmatrix}$$

7.

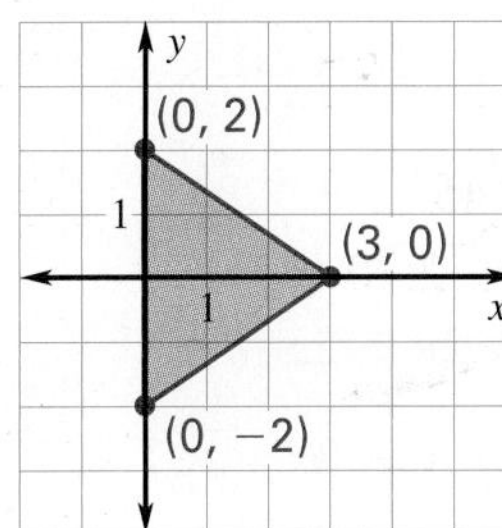

8.

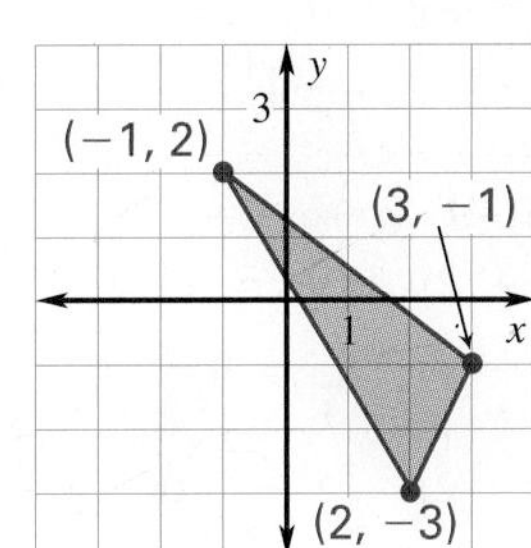

9.

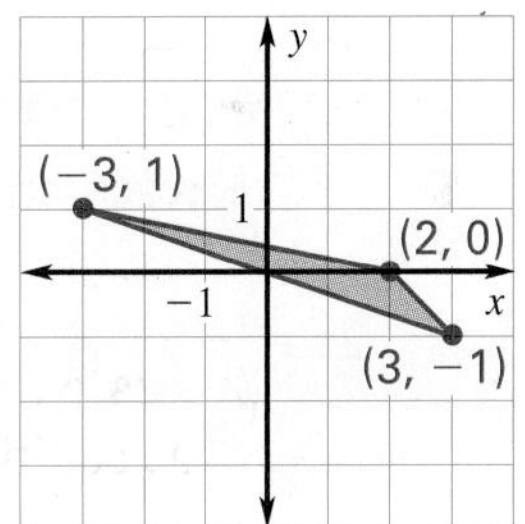

Use Cramer's rule to solve the linear system.

10. $x - 5y = -1$
$-2x + 5y = -3$

11. $x + 2y = 1$
$-3x - 7y = -6$

12. $2x + 6y = 12$
$-x + 7y = -6$

13. $2x + 2y + z = 2$
$-x + 3y + z = -2$
$3x + 2z = 7$

14. $2x - 5y + 2z = 2$
$-3x + y - 6z = 3$
$x + y + z = 1$

15. $3x + 2y + 3z = -1$
$2x - 8y + 2z = -3$
$x + 6y + 4z = -2$

In Exercises 16 and 17, use the following information.

Gasoline You fill up your car with 15 gallons of premium gasoline and fill up a 5 gallon gas can with regular gasoline for various appliances around the house. You pay the cashier \$42. The price of regular gasoline y is 20 cents less per gallon than the price of premium gasoline x.

16. Write a system of linear equations that models the price per gallon for regular and premium gasoline.

17. Use Cramer's rule to find the price per gallon of regular and premium gasoline.

UNIT 1

LESSON 1.10 **Exercise Set B**

MM3A5c Represent and solve realistic problems using systems of linear equations.

Evaluate the determinant of the matrix.

1. $\begin{bmatrix} 3 & 5 \\ -2 & 4 \end{bmatrix}$

2. $\begin{bmatrix} 4 & -2 \\ 3 & 2 \end{bmatrix}$

3. $\begin{bmatrix} 2 & 0 & -1 \\ 3 & 2 & 1 \\ 1 & 4 & 2 \end{bmatrix}$

4. $\begin{bmatrix} 2 & 0 & 0 \\ 0 & -5 & 0 \\ 0 & 0 & -2 \end{bmatrix}$

5. $\begin{bmatrix} 6 & 1 & -2 \\ 4 & -2 & 0 \\ -2 & 4 & 3 \end{bmatrix}$

6. $\begin{bmatrix} 7 & -2 & 6 \\ 3 & -1 & 5 \\ -6 & 2 & 4 \end{bmatrix}$

Use the formula on the previous page to find the area of the triangle with the given vertices.

7. $A(0, -4), B\left(-3, \frac{1}{2}\right), C(2, -1)$

8. $A\left(\frac{1}{2}, 3\right), B(-3, -1), C\left(3, \frac{1}{2}\right)$

Use Cramer's rule to solve the linear system.

9. $3x - 3y = -6$
$4x + y = 22$

10. $2x + 3y = 0$
$5x + 7y = -1$

11. $4x + 3y = 4$
$-2x - 3y = 10$

12. $3x + 6y + z = 3$
$x + 3y + z = 3$
$3x + y - 2z = -5$

13. $x - 3y + 2z = 2$
$5x + 2y + 9z = 11$
$3x - y + 6z = 9$

14. $4x + 3y + z = 3$
$3x + 5y + 2z = 2$
$2x + 2y + 2z = 4$

15. $x + 2y + z = 8$
$-2x + 2y - 2z = 2$
$3x + 4y + z = 0$

16. $x - 3y + 2z = -6$
$-3x + y - 6z = 2$
$9x + y + 3z = 7$

17. $2x - 2y + 3z = -1$
$6x - 7y + 5z = 5$
$5x + 2y - 7z = -16$

In Exercises 18 and 19, use the following information.

Electoral College In the 1976 presidential election, 538 electoral votes were cast. Of these, x went to Jimmy Carter, y went to Gerald Ford, and z went to Ronald Reagan. The value of x is 57 more than y. The value of y is 239 more than z.

18. Write a system of linear equations that models the electoral votes cast in the 1976 presidential election.

19. Use Cramer's rule to find the values of x, y, and z.

20. **Determinant Relationships** Let $A = \begin{bmatrix} 2 & 3 \\ 4 & 1 \end{bmatrix}$ and $B = \begin{bmatrix} 5 & 6 \\ 7 & 8 \end{bmatrix}$. How is det AB related to det A and det B? How is det AB related to det BA?

21. **Challenge** Let $A = \begin{bmatrix} a & b \\ c & d \end{bmatrix}$ and $B = \begin{bmatrix} w & x \\ y & z \end{bmatrix}$. Show that the det AB = (det A)(det B).

UNIT 1

Georgia Performance Standards

MM3A4a Add, subtract, multiply, and invert matrices, when possible, choosing appropriate methods, including technology. 

MM3A4b Find the inverses of two-by-two matrices using pencil and paper, and find inverses of larger matrices using technology. ☑

Investigating Math Activity

Inverse Matrices

Use before Lesson 1.11

Question

How can you determine whether or not two matrices are inverses of each other?

Explore

Multiply matrices.

Use the matrices below to calculate AB, BA, CD, and DC.

$$A = \begin{bmatrix} 2 & 3 \\ 1 & 2 \end{bmatrix} \qquad B = \begin{bmatrix} 2 & -3 \\ -1 & 2 \end{bmatrix}$$

$$C = \begin{bmatrix} 0 & -1 & 2 \\ 1 & 1 & -1 \\ 2 & 0 & 3 \end{bmatrix} \qquad D = \begin{bmatrix} 3 & 3 & -1 \\ -5 & -4 & 2 \\ -2 & -2 & 1 \end{bmatrix}$$

Draw Conclusions

1. *Compare* the products AB and BA.

2. *Compare* the products CD and DC.

3. **Reasoning** Based on your observations, make a conjecture about the products of inverse matrices.

4. Test your conjecture using matrices E and F, which are inverses of each other. Revise your answer to Exercise 3 if necessary.

$$E = \begin{bmatrix} -3 & -2 \\ 8 & 5 \end{bmatrix} \qquad F = \begin{bmatrix} 5 & 2 \\ -8 & -3 \end{bmatrix}$$

5. **Reasoning** Based on your observations, what is the inverse of the matrix $\begin{bmatrix} -5 & -3 \\ 3 & 2 \end{bmatrix}$?

A. $\begin{bmatrix} -2 & 3 \\ 3 & 5 \end{bmatrix}$ **B.** $\begin{bmatrix} -2 & 3 \\ -3 & 5 \end{bmatrix}$ **C.** $\begin{bmatrix} 2 & -3 \\ 3 & 5 \end{bmatrix}$ **D.** $\begin{bmatrix} -2 & -3 \\ 3 & 5 \end{bmatrix}$

UNIT 1

LESSON 1.11

Use Inverse Matrices to Solve Linear Systems

Georgia Performance Standards: MM3A4b, MM3A5a, MM3A5b

Goal Solve linear systems using inverse matrices.

Vocabulary

The $n \times n$ **identity matrix** is a matrix with 1's on the main diagonal and 0's elsewhere. If A is any $n \times n$ matrix and I is the $n \times n$ identity matrix, then $AI = A$ and $IA = A$.

2 × 2 Identity Matrix

$$I = \begin{bmatrix} 1 & 0 \\ 0 & 1 \end{bmatrix}$$

3 × 3 Identity Matrix

$$I = \begin{bmatrix} 1 & 0 & 0 \\ 0 & 1 & 0 \\ 0 & 0 & 1 \end{bmatrix}$$

Two $n \times n$ matrices A and B are **inverses** of each other if their product (in both orders) is the $n \times n$ identity matrix. That is, $AB = I$ and $BA = I$. An $n \times n$ matrix A has an inverse if and only if $\det A \neq 0$. The symbol for the inverse of A is A^{-1}.

Inverse of 2 × 2 Matrix: The inverse of the matrix

$$A = \begin{bmatrix} a & b \\ c & d \end{bmatrix} \text{ is } A^{-1} = \frac{1}{|A|}\begin{bmatrix} d & -b \\ -c & a \end{bmatrix} = \frac{1}{ad - cb}\begin{bmatrix} d & -b \\ -c & a \end{bmatrix} \text{ provided } ad - cb \neq 0.$$

The inverse of a 3×3 matrix is difficult to compute by hand. In this case, a graphing calculator can be used to find the inverse matrix.

In the matrix equation $AX = B$, matrix A is the coefficient matrix, X is **the matrix of variables,** and B is the **matrix of constants.**

Example 1 Find the inverse of a 2 × 2 matrix

Find the inverse of $A = \begin{bmatrix} 4 & 7 \\ 3 & 5 \end{bmatrix}$.

Solution

$$A^{-1} = \frac{1}{20 - 21}\begin{bmatrix} 5 & -7 \\ -3 & 4 \end{bmatrix}$$

$$= -1\begin{bmatrix} 5 & -7 \\ -3 & 4 \end{bmatrix}$$

$$= \begin{bmatrix} -5 & 7 \\ 3 & -4 \end{bmatrix}$$

Guided Practice for Example 1

Find the inverse of the matrix.

1. $\begin{bmatrix} 2 & 1 \\ 7 & 3 \end{bmatrix}$

2. $\begin{bmatrix} -4 & 4 \\ -5 & 6 \end{bmatrix}$

3. $\begin{bmatrix} -3 & -8 \\ -2 & -1 \end{bmatrix}$

Georgia Performance Standards

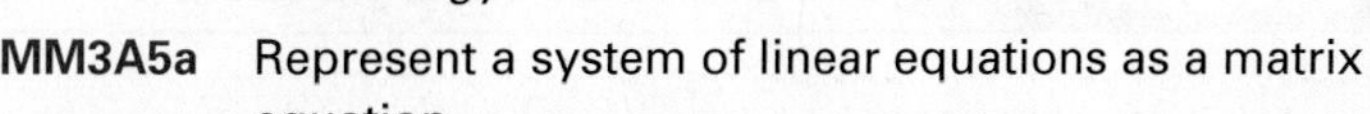
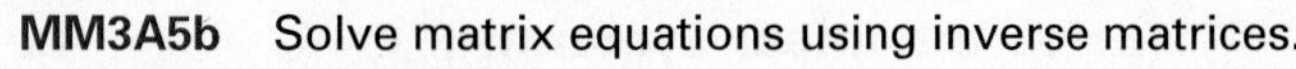

MM3A4b	Find the inverses of two-by-two matrices using pencil and paper, and find inverses of larger matrices using technology.	☑
MM3A5a	Represent a system of linear equations as a matrix equation.	☑
MM3A5b	Solve matrix equations using inverse matrices.	☑

Example 2 Solve a matrix equation

Solve the matrix equation $AX = B$ for the 2×2 matrix X.

$$\overbrace{\begin{bmatrix} 1 & 1 \\ 6 & 7 \end{bmatrix}}^{A} X = \overbrace{\begin{bmatrix} 2 & 3 \\ 1 & 4 \end{bmatrix}}^{B}$$

Begin by finding the inverse of A.

$$A^{-1} = \frac{1}{7-6}\begin{bmatrix} 7 & -1 \\ -6 & 1 \end{bmatrix} = \begin{bmatrix} 7 & -1 \\ -6 & 1 \end{bmatrix}$$

To solve the equation for X, multiply both sides of the equation by A^{-1} on the left.

$$\begin{bmatrix} 7 & -1 \\ -6 & 1 \end{bmatrix}\begin{bmatrix} 1 & 1 \\ 6 & 7 \end{bmatrix} X = \begin{bmatrix} 7 & -1 \\ -6 & 1 \end{bmatrix}\begin{bmatrix} 2 & 3 \\ 1 & 4 \end{bmatrix} \qquad A^{-1}AX = A^{-1}B$$

$$\begin{bmatrix} 1 & 0 \\ 0 & 1 \end{bmatrix} X = \begin{bmatrix} 13 & 17 \\ -11 & -14 \end{bmatrix} \qquad IX = A^{-1}B$$

$$X = \begin{bmatrix} 13 & 17 \\ -11 & -14 \end{bmatrix} \qquad X = A^{-1}B$$

Guided Practice for Example 2

Solve the matrix equation.

4. $\begin{bmatrix} 1 & 1 \\ 2 & 3 \end{bmatrix} X = \begin{bmatrix} 6 & 4 \\ 2 & 8 \end{bmatrix}$ **5.** $\begin{bmatrix} 1 & 1 \\ 3 & 4 \end{bmatrix} X = \begin{bmatrix} 1 & 2 \\ 1 & 3 \end{bmatrix}$ **6.** $\begin{bmatrix} 9 & 4 \\ 2 & 1 \end{bmatrix} X = \begin{bmatrix} 0 & -1 \\ 3 & 2 \end{bmatrix}$

Example 3 Find the inverse of a 3 × 3 matrix

Use a graphing calculator to find the inverse of A. Then use the calculator to verify the result.

$$A = \begin{bmatrix} 4 & 0 & -1 \\ 6 & -2 & 0 \\ 3 & 1 & -4 \end{bmatrix}$$

Enter matrix A into a graphing calculator and calculate A^{-1}. Then compute AA^{-1} and $A^{-1}A$ to verify that you obtain the 3×3 identity matrix.

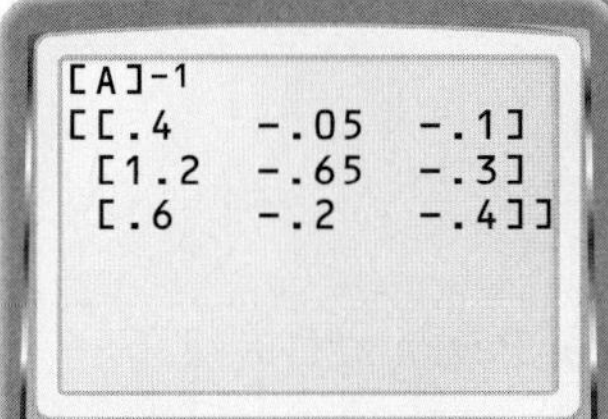

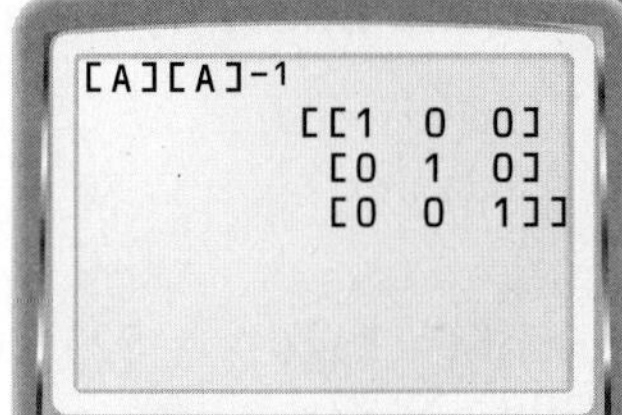

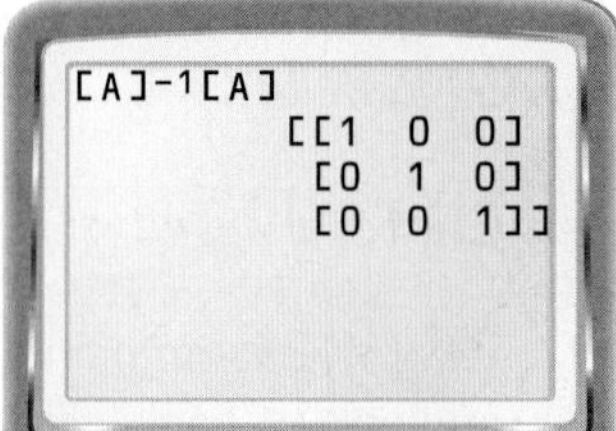

Example 4 Solve a linear system

Use an inverse matrix to solve the linear system.

$3x + 2y = 1$ **Equation 1**

$4x + y = -2$ **Equation 2**

STEP 1 **Write** the linear system as a matrix equation $AX = B$.

$$\begin{bmatrix} 3 & 2 \\ 4 & 1 \end{bmatrix}\begin{bmatrix} x \\ y \end{bmatrix} = \begin{bmatrix} 1 \\ -2 \end{bmatrix}$$

STEP 2 **Find** the inverse of matrix A.

$$A^{-1} = \frac{1}{3-8}\begin{bmatrix} 1 & -2 \\ -4 & 3 \end{bmatrix} = \begin{bmatrix} -0.2 & 0.4 \\ 0.8 & -0.6 \end{bmatrix}$$

STEP 3 **Multiply** the matrix of constants by A^{-1} on the left.

$$X = A^{-1}B = \begin{bmatrix} -0.2 & 0.4 \\ 0.8 & -0.6 \end{bmatrix}\begin{bmatrix} 1 \\ -2 \end{bmatrix} = \begin{bmatrix} -1 \\ 2 \end{bmatrix} = \begin{bmatrix} x \\ y \end{bmatrix}$$

The solution of the system is $(-1, 2)$.

Example 5 Solve a multi-step problem

Gift Shop A gift shop sells three beach packages. Package A that includes 2 towels, 1 tube of sunscreen, and 1 beach chair costs \$21. Package B that includes 3 towels and 2 beach chairs costs \$31. Package C that includes 1 tube of sunscreen and 2 beach chairs costs \$19. Find the cost of each package item.

STEP 1 **Write** a system of equations. Let t be the cost of a towel, s be the cost of the tube of sunscreen, and c be the cost of a beach chair.

$2t + s + c = 21$ Package A

$3t + 2c = 31$ Package B

$s + 2c = 19$ Package C

STEP 2 **Rewrite** the system as a matrix equation and solve $X = A^{-1}B$ with a graphing calculator.

$$\begin{bmatrix} 2 & 1 & 1 \\ 3 & 0 & 2 \\ 0 & 1 & 2 \end{bmatrix} \cdot \begin{bmatrix} t \\ s \\ c \end{bmatrix} = \begin{bmatrix} 21 \\ 31 \\ 19 \end{bmatrix}$$

A towel costs \$5, sunscreen costs \$3, and a chair costs \$8.

Guided Practice for Examples 3, 4, and 5

7. Use a graphing calculator to find the inverse of $A = \begin{bmatrix} 1 & 1 & 2 \\ 2 & 4 & -3 \\ 3 & 6 & -5 \end{bmatrix}$.

Use an inverse matrix to solve the linear system.

8. $2x - y = -4$
$x + y = 13$

9. $3x - y = 1$
$-x + 2y = 3$

10. $2x + y = -1$
$3x - y = -4$

11. Rework Example 5 with cost of Package A = \$23, cost of Package B = \$36, and cost of Package C = \$20.

LESSON 1.11 **Exercise Set A**

MM3A4b Find the inverses of two-by-two matrices using pencil and paper, and find inverses of larger matrices using technology.

MM3A5a Represent a system of linear equations as a matrix equation.

MM3A5b Solve matrix equations using inverse matrices.

Find the inverse of the matrix, if it exists.

1. $\begin{bmatrix} 4 & 7 \\ 1 & 2 \end{bmatrix}$ **2.** $\begin{bmatrix} 3 & 2 \\ 4 & 2 \end{bmatrix}$ **3.** $\begin{bmatrix} 4 & -2 \\ 3 & 1 \end{bmatrix}$

4. $\begin{bmatrix} 7 & 14 \\ 3 & 6 \end{bmatrix}$ **5.** $\begin{bmatrix} -4 & -2 \\ 5 & 2 \end{bmatrix}$ **6.** $\begin{bmatrix} 3 & -3 \\ -3 & -2 \end{bmatrix}$

Use a graphing calculator to find the inverse of the matrix.

7. $\begin{bmatrix} 1 & 3 & 5 \\ 0 & 3 & 5 \\ 0 & 0 & 5 \end{bmatrix}$ **8.** $\begin{bmatrix} 0 & 1 & 0 \\ 2 & 1 & -2 \\ 0 & 2 & 2 \end{bmatrix}$

Solve the matrix equation.

9. $\begin{bmatrix} 2 & 1 \\ 3 & 2 \end{bmatrix} X = \begin{bmatrix} 5 & 1 \\ 2 & 1 \end{bmatrix}$ **10.** $\begin{bmatrix} 4 & 3 \\ 2 & 2 \end{bmatrix} X = \begin{bmatrix} -2 & 3 \\ -1 & 2 \end{bmatrix}$

11. $\begin{bmatrix} 3 & 1 \\ 6 & 3 \end{bmatrix} X = \begin{bmatrix} 1 & 4 & -2 \\ 6 & 0 & -3 \end{bmatrix}$ **12.** $\begin{bmatrix} 6 & 2 \\ 5 & 1 \end{bmatrix} X = \begin{bmatrix} 9 & 12 & 6 \\ -4 & 3 & 8 \end{bmatrix}$

Use an inverse matrix to solve the linear system.

13. $3x - 2y = 2$
$2x - y = 2$

14. $5x + 3y = 4$
$2x + 2y = 8$

15. $3x + y + 2z = 9$
$-2x + 2y + 3z = 6$
$2x - y + z = 8$

16. $3x + 3y + 3z = -12$
$5x + 2y + 2z = -17$
$2x - 4y - z = -20$

17. **Multiple Representations** During the 2004–2005 NBA season, Shaquille O'Neal scored 1669 points while making 1011 shots. Shaq's points were a combination of 3-point field goals, 2-point field goals, and 1-point free throws. He made 305 more 2-point field goals than free throws.

a. **Writing a System** Write a system of equations for the number of shots made during the season.

b. **Writing a Matrix Equation** Write the system of equations from part (a) as a matrix equation $AX = B$.

c. **Solving a System** Use an inverse matrix to solve the system of equations. How many of each type of shot did Shaq make during the season?

LESSON 1.11 **Exercise Set B**

MM3A4b Find the inverses of two-by-two matrices using pencil and paper, and find inverses of larger matrices using technology.

MM3A5a Represent a system of linear equations as a matrix equation.

MM3A5b Solve matrix equations using inverse matrices.

Find the inverse of the matrix, if it exists.

1. $\begin{bmatrix} 3 & 6 \\ 2 & 4 \end{bmatrix}$

2. $\begin{bmatrix} -2 & 6 \\ 4 & -10 \end{bmatrix}$

3. $\begin{bmatrix} 3 & 7 \\ -1 & 2 \end{bmatrix}$

Use a graphing calculator to find the inverse of the matrix, if it exists.

4. $\begin{bmatrix} 3 & 2 & 2 \\ 1 & 2 & 0 \\ 4 & -4 & 1 \end{bmatrix}$

5. $\begin{bmatrix} -2 & -1 & 4 \\ 2 & -4 & 0 \\ 0 & 1 & 1 \end{bmatrix}$

6. $\begin{bmatrix} 2 & 4 & 2 \\ 3 & 1 & 0 \\ 0 & 5 & 1 \end{bmatrix}$

Solve the matrix equation.

7. $\begin{bmatrix} -2 & 6 \\ -3 & 8 \end{bmatrix} X - \begin{bmatrix} -3 & 4 & 2 \\ 5 & -6 & 0 \end{bmatrix} = \begin{bmatrix} 9 & 2 & -7 \\ -3 & 4 & 8 \end{bmatrix}$

8. $\begin{bmatrix} 3 & 0 & -2 \\ 0 & 2 & 0 \\ 4 & -1 & 4 \end{bmatrix} X + \begin{bmatrix} 5 \\ -2 \\ 4 \end{bmatrix} = \begin{bmatrix} 7 \\ 12 \\ -9 \end{bmatrix}$

Use an inverse matrix to solve the linear system.

9. $4x + 5y = 7$
$-2x - y = 7$

10. $2x + 2y = 12$
$3x - 3y = 6$

11. $-4x + 7y = -9$
$2x - y = 2$

12. $2x + 3y + 4z = 7$
$-x + 5y + 2z = 6$
$-3x + 6y = 3$

13. $3x + y - 2z = 3$
$-2x + 2y + 3z = -14$
$5x - y - 3z = 25$

14. $4x - 3y + 4z = -5$
$-2x + 3y + 2z = 5$
$8x - 6y + 14z = -7$

15. **Inverse Properties** Let $A = \begin{bmatrix} 3 & 2 \\ 4 & 3 \end{bmatrix}$. How is A related to $(A^{-1})^{-1}$?

16. **Multiple Representations** An accountant for a company is creating part of the fiscal budget for next year. She has \$500,000 to allocate between salaries, insurance, and general expenses. Based on previous financial statements, she expects to spend eight times as much on salaries x as on insurance y. Also, general expenses z historically cost 20% of the amount spent on salaries and insurance combined.

a. Writing a System Write a system of equations for the amount allocated to each category.

b. Writing a Matrix Equation Write the system of equations from part (a) as a matrix equation $AX = B$.

c. Solving a System Use an inverse matrix to solve the system of equations. How much is allocated to each category?

LESSON 1.12

Use Vertex-Edge Graphs

Georgia Performance Standards: MM3A7a, MM3A7b

Goal Use vertex-edge graphs to represent real-life situations.

Vocabulary

A **vertex-edge graph** is a collection of points and line segments connecting some (possibly empty) subset of the points.

An **edge of a vertex-edge graph** is a line segment connecting the vertices of a graph. A **vertex of a vertex-edge graph** is a point that is either the endpoint of an edge or not part of an edge.

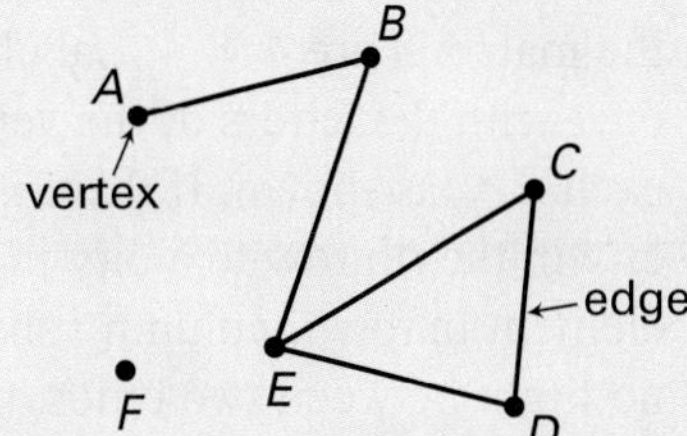

Example 1 Use a vertex-edge graph to represent a situation

Transportation An airline serves four cities: Bedford, Columbia, Dunwich, and Exton. There are flights between Bedford and Columbia, Bedford and Dunwich, and Columbia and Exton. Draw a vertex-edge graph to represent this situation.

Solution

STEP 1 **Represent** the cities using points. Let the points B represent Bedford, C represent Columbia, D represent Dunwich, and E represent Exton.

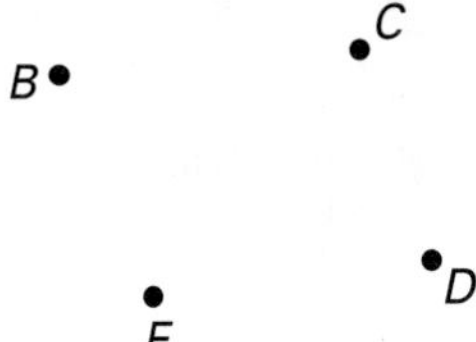

STEP 2 **Draw** the edges for the graph. Two vertices are connected by an edge if there are flights between the corresponding cities. Draw edges connecting B and C, B and D, and C and E.

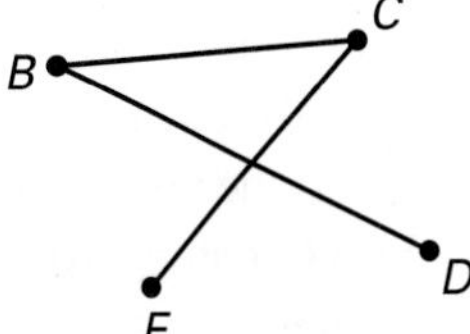

UNIT 1

Guided Practice for Example 1

1. **Transportation** An airline serves five cities: Lowell, Montour, Newman, Peoria, and Orlando. There are flights between Lowell and Montour, Lowell and Orlando, Montour and Orlando, Newman and Orlando, and Newman and Peoria. Draw a vertex-edge graph to represent this situation.

Georgia Performance Standards

MM3A7a Use graphs to represent realistic situations.

MM3A7b Use matrices to represent graphs, and solve problems that can be represented by graphs.

Example 2 Use a matrix to represent a vertex-edge graph

Use a matrix *A* to represent the vertex-edge graph from Example 1.

Because there are four cities, the dimensions of the matrix A are 4×4. Label the rows and columns of A with the letters of the vertices that represent each city, as shown. If there is a flight from a city in the ith row to a city in the jth column, the element in row i, column j should be 1. If there is no flight between two cities, then enter a 0 in the appropriate position of the matrix.

$$A = \begin{array}{c} \\ B \\ C \\ D \\ E \end{array} \begin{array}{c} \begin{array}{cccc} B & C & D & E \end{array} \\ \begin{bmatrix} 0 & 1 & 1 & 0 \\ 1 & 0 & 0 & 1 \\ 1 & 0 & 0 & 0 \\ 0 & 1 & 0 & 0 \end{bmatrix} \end{array}$$

Example 3 Use a matrix representing a vertex-edge graph

Use the matrix you found in Example 2 to calculate A^2. What does A^2 represent?

Solution

Enter matrix A into a graphing calculator and calculate A^2.

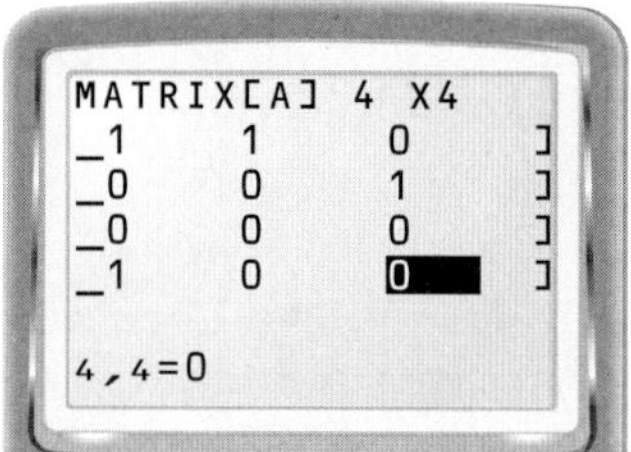

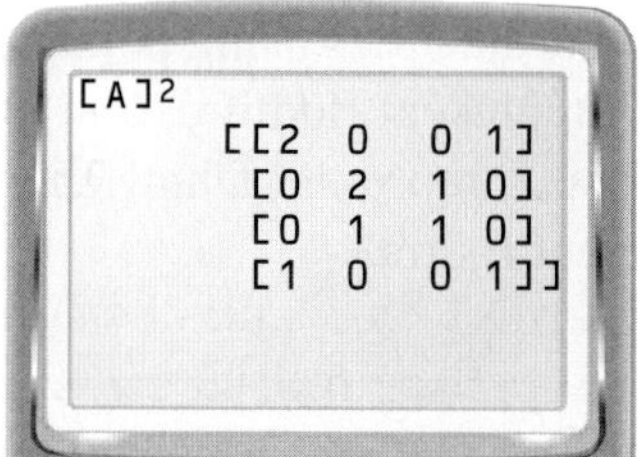

The matrix A^2 gives the number of ways you can fly from one city to another using exactly two flights. For instance, to find the number of two-flight trips from Columbia to Dunwich, locate the element in row C, column D. Because the element is 1, you can conclude that there is exactly 1 way you can fly from Columbia to Dunwich using exactly two flights.

$$A^2 = \begin{array}{c} \\ B \\ C \\ D \\ E \end{array} \begin{array}{c} \begin{array}{cccc} B & C & D & E \end{array} \\ \begin{bmatrix} 2 & 0 & 0 & 1 \\ 0 & 2 & 1 & 0 \\ 0 & 1 & 1 & 0 \\ 1 & 0 & 0 & 1 \end{bmatrix} \end{array}$$

row C, column D

Guided Practice for Examples 2 and 3

2. Use the information from Examples 2 and 3 and a graphing calculator to calculate A^3. What does this matrix represent?

3. Why is there a 0 in the first row, first column of A but a 2 in the first row, first column of A^2?

UNIT 1

LESSON 1.12 **Exercise Set A**

MM3A7a Use graphs to represent realistic situations.

MM3A7b Use matrices to represent graphs, and solve problems that can be represented by graphs.

In Exercises 1–3, determine the number of vertices and edges in the vertex-edge graph.

1. 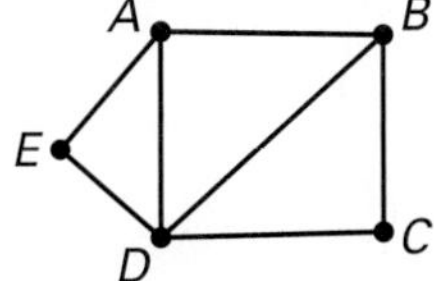

2. 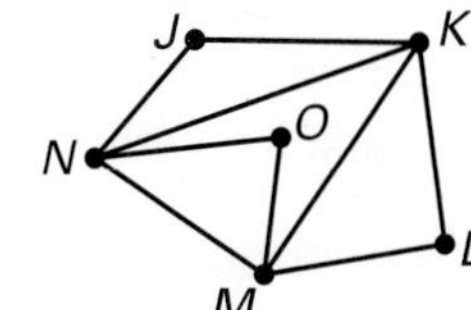

3. 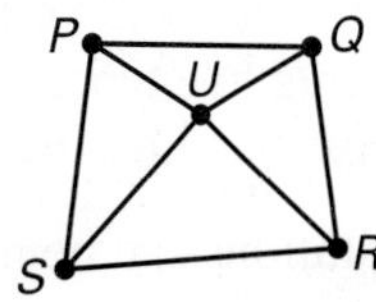

In Exercises 4–6, determine whether the statement is *true* or *false*.

You want to buy four types of fish for your new aquarium. Some fish can live together in the same tank while others cannot. The vertex-edge graph at the right represents four types of fish: gouramis (G), tetras (T), black mollies (B), and angelfish (A). An edge connecting two vertices indicates that those two types of fish can live together.

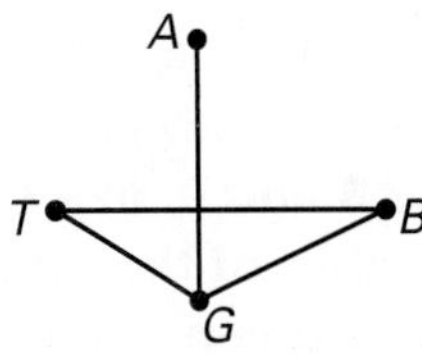

4. All four types of fish can live in the same tank.

5. Angelfish can live in the same tank with black mollies.

6. Gouramis can share a tank with any of the other fish.

7. Use the information above to give two examples of the number of tanks you could use to house all the fish. State the type(s) of fish living in each tank.

In Exercises 8 and 9, each vertex of the vertex-edge graph represents a city. An edge connecting two vertices indicates the cities are connected by a highway. Write a matrix that represents the vertex-edge graph.

8. 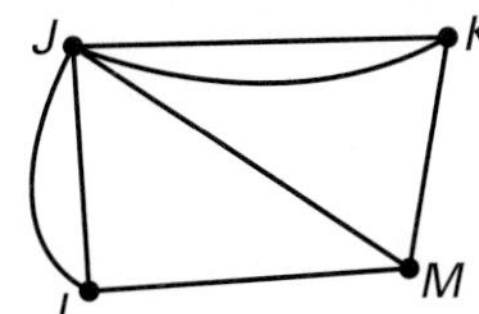

9. 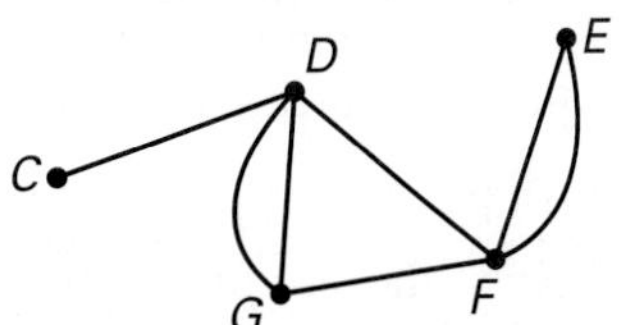

In Exercises 10–12, draw a vertex-edge graph to represent the portion of the United States. Let each state be represented by a vertex, then draw an edge between two vertices if the states share a border.

10. 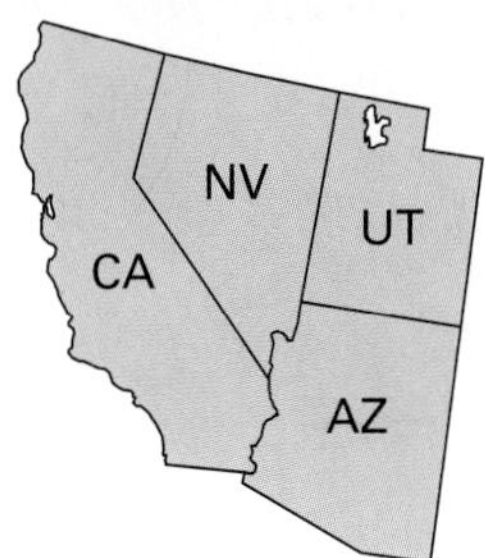

11. 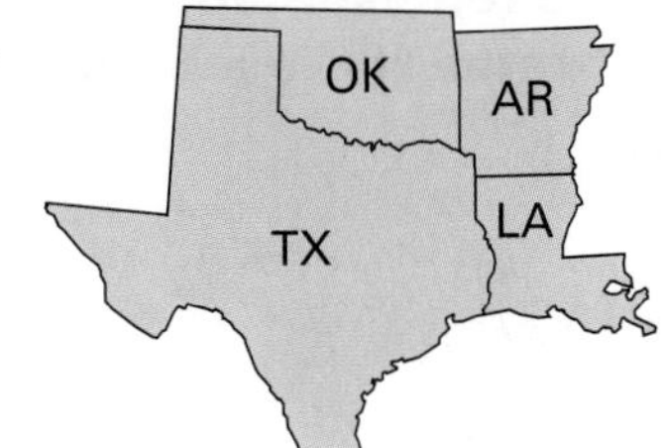

12. 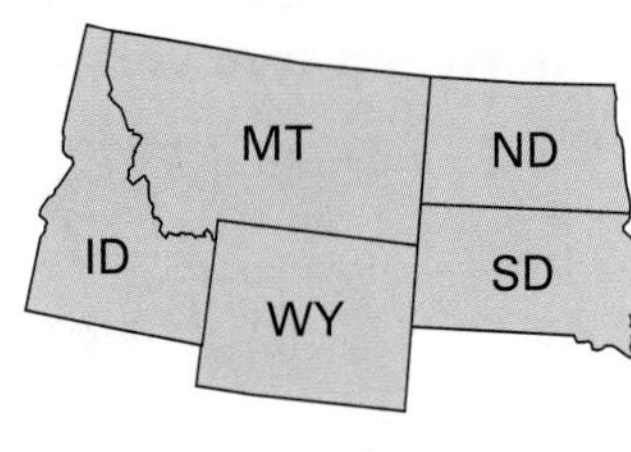

UNIT 1

LESSON 1.12 **Exercise Set B**

MM3A7a Use graphs to represent realistic situations.

MM3A7b Use matrices to represent graphs, and solve problems that can be represented by graphs.

In Exercises 1–4, determine whether the statement is *true* or *false*.

You are mixing different solutions in a chemistry lab. Some solutions can be mixed together while others cannot. The vertex-edge graph at the right represents five types of solutions. An edge connecting two vertices indicates that those two solutions can be mixed together.

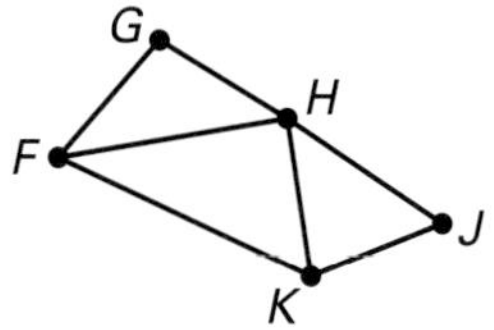

1. All the solutions can be mixed together.
2. Solution F can be mixed with any other solution.
3. Solution H can be mixed with any other solution.
4. Solution K can be mixed with exactly three other solutions.

In Exercises 5 and 6, use the vertex-edge graph that shows a portion of the city or town where you live. The distances given are in miles.

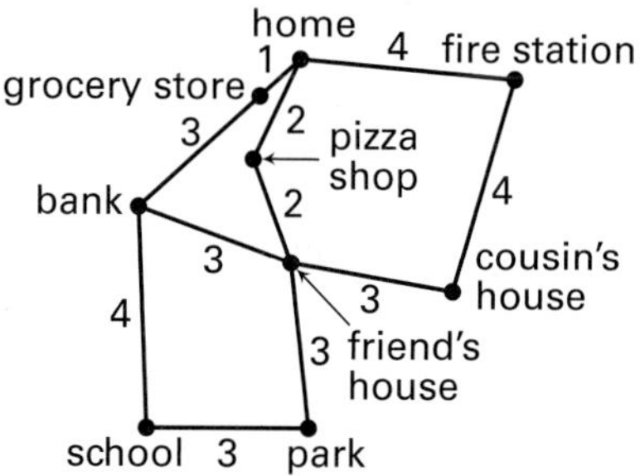

5. You are going from home to your cousin's house. What is the shortest route and its distance?
6. You are at home. You need to go to your friend's house and stop at school. What is the shortest distance including your return home?

In Exercises 7–9, each vertex of the vertex-edge graph represents a town. An edge connecting two vertices indicates the towns are connected by a road.

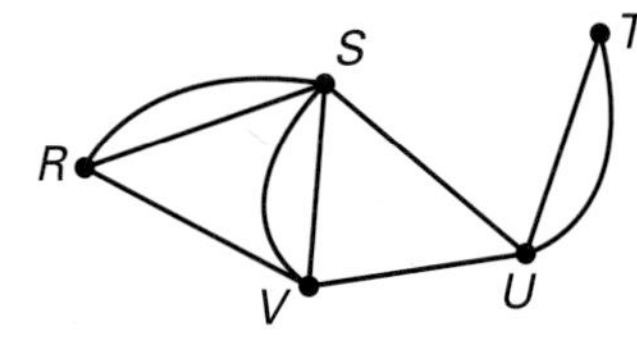

7. Write a matrix M that represents the vertex-edge graph.
8. Use a graphing calculator to calculate M^2.
9. Use the matrix from Exercise 8 to find the number of ways you can travel between the two given towns using 2 roads.

   a. Town R to Town V b. Town T to Town S

   c. Town V to Town S d. Town S back to Town S

In Exercises 10–12, draw a vertex-edge graph to represent the portion of the United States. Let each state be represented by a vertex, then draw an edge between two vertices if the states share a border.

10. 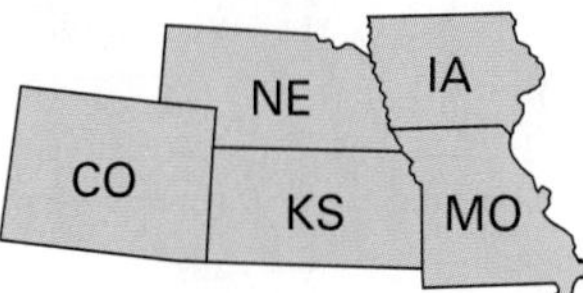

11. 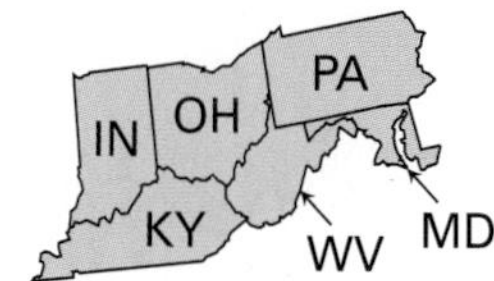

12. 

UNIT 1

TEST | for Unit 1

1. Look for a pattern in the table shown. Then write an equation that represents the table.

x	0	1	2	3
y	25	36	47	58

Solve the system using any method.

2. $3x + 5y = -1$
$2x - y = -5$

3. $x - 2y = 6$
$5x - 10y = 3$

4. $-4x + 3y = 19$
$6x + y = -1$

Graph the inequality.

5. $\frac{1}{3}y \leq 2$

6. $6x - 3y > -12$

7. $y \geq |x + 3| - 4$

Graph the system of inequalities.

8. $y \geq |x - 3|$
$y < 4$

9. $y > 2x - 5$
$x \geq -1$
$y \leq 3$

10. $x - y < 4$
$3x - y > -1$
$6x + 2y \leq 3$

11. Find the minimum and maximum values of the objective function $C = 3x + 5y$ subject to the constraints $x \geq 0$, $y \geq 0$, $-3x + 6y \leq 18$, and $x + y \leq 6$.

Solve the system using any algebraic method.

12. $x + y - 2z = -6$
$y - 3z = -10$
$5y - 2z = -11$

13. $-2x + y - z = 6$
$3x - y + z = -7$
$6x + y - z = -2$

14. $x - y + z = 8$
$3x - 3y + 3z = 1$
$4x + y + 5z = 3$

Using the given matrices, evaluate the expression.

$$A = \begin{bmatrix} -1 & 3 \\ -4 & 5 \end{bmatrix}, B = \begin{bmatrix} 0 & 2 \\ 3 & -4 \end{bmatrix}, C = \begin{bmatrix} -7 & -2 \\ 0 & -3 \end{bmatrix}, D = \begin{bmatrix} 3 & -1 & 2 \\ 4 & -2 & 0 \\ 0 & -3 & -4 \end{bmatrix}, E = \begin{bmatrix} 2 & 5 & -3 \\ 7 & 2 & -6 \\ 1 & -5 & -1 \end{bmatrix}$$

15. $A + 2B$

16. $4D - E$

17. $A(B + C)$

18. $2AC + 3AB$

Evaluate the determinant of the matrix.

19. $\begin{bmatrix} -5 & -7 \\ -4 & 6 \end{bmatrix}$

20. $\begin{bmatrix} 10 & 9 \\ -8 & 3 \end{bmatrix}$

21. $\begin{bmatrix} 3 & 0 & 2 \\ -4 & 6 & 4 \\ 5 & -1 & 1 \end{bmatrix}$

Use Cramer's rule to solve the linear system.

22. $x - 4y = 10$
$-2x + 5y = -11$

23. $3x + 7y = 5$
$x - 2y = 6$

24. $2x + 3y + 2z = 3$
$x - 7y + 3z = -26$
$x + 5y + 4z = 9$

25. Find the inverse, if it exists, of the matrices (a) $\begin{bmatrix} -3 & 7 \\ 2 & -5 \end{bmatrix}$ and (b) $\begin{bmatrix} -4 & -3 \\ -8 & -6 \end{bmatrix}$.

UNIT 1

26. Shipping A shipment of machine parts was trucked from Georgia to Kentucky in 11 hours. The trip covered about 649 miles. What was the average speed of the truck?

27. School A student advisory board at your school must consist of 7 to 10 representatives from junior and senior classes. The board must include at least 3 juniors and 3 seniors. Write and graph a system of inequalities to describe the situation. Then give two solutions for the numbers of juniors and seniors on the board.

28. Craft Fair You are decorating jewelry boxes to sell at a fair. It takes you 3 hours to decorate a small jewelry box and 4 hours to decorate a large jewelry box. You make a profit of \$12 for a small jewelry box and \$18 for a large jewelry box. If you have no more than 36 hours available and want at least 10 jewelry boxes to sell, how many of each size should you decorate to maximize your profit?

29. Shopping Before taxes, two pairs of jeans and a T-shirt cost \$59.48. Two T-shirts and a pair of sandals cost \$33.00. One pair of jeans, one T-shirt, and one pair of sandals cost \$48.49. Use a linear system and Cramer's rule to find the prices of a pair of jeans, a T-shirt, and a pair of sandals.

30. Geography Draw a vertex-edge graph to represent the counties shown in the map: Mitchell (M), Colquitt (C), Decatur (D), Grady (G), Thomas (T), and Brooks (B). Let each county be represented by a vertex, then draw an edge between two vertices if the counties share a border.

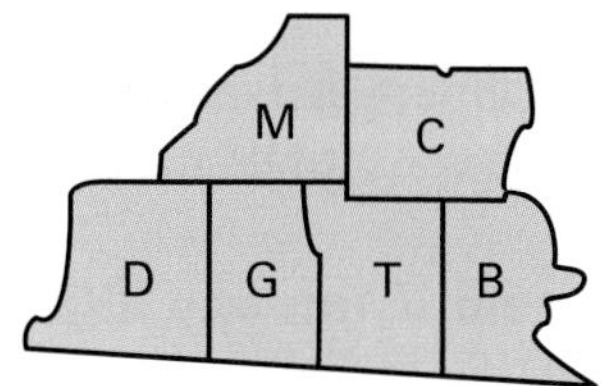

Performance Task

Inventory

A company manufactures three models of MP3 players: music only (M), music/photo (MP), and music/photo/video (MPV). The MP3 players are shipped to two warehouses. The number of units shipped to each warehouse this month and last month are given in matrices A and B.

This month (A):

	M	MP	MPV
Warehouse 1	12,000	14,000	8000
Warehouse 2	10,000	12,000	6000

Last month (B):

	M	MP	MPV
Warehouse 1	15,000	18,000	10,000
Warehouse 2	14,000	16,000	9000

Price (C):

M	\$99.99
MP	\$179.99
MPV	\$249.99

a. Write a matrix M that gives the total number of each type of MP3 player shipped to the two warehouses for the two months.

b. Calculate $\frac{1}{2}M$. What does this matrix represent?

c. The prices of the models are given in matrix C. Use your result from part (a) and a graphing calculator to write a matrix that gives the total value of the MP3 players shipped to each warehouse in the last two months.

d. In one week, an electronics store sells 64 MP3 players for a total of \$9339.36. There were twice as many music-only MP3 players sold than music/photo MP3 players. Write a system of equations to represent this situation. How many of each type of MP3 player were sold at the store?

UNIT 2
Algebra: Polynomial Functions

2.1 Evaluate and Graph Polynomial Functions (MM3A1b, MM3A1c, MM3A1d)

2.2 Translate Graphs of Polynomial Functions (MM3A1a, MM3A1c, MM3A1d)

2.3 Factor and Solve Polynomial Equations (MM3A3b, MM3A3d)

2.4 Solve Polynomial Inequalities (MM3A3c)

2.5 Apply the Remainder and Factor Theorems (MM3A3a, MM3A3d)

2.6 Find Rational Zeros (MM3A3a, MM3A3d)

2.7 Apply the Fundamental Theorem of Algebra (MM3A3a, MM3A3d)

2.8 Analyze Graphs of Polynomial Functions (MM3A1b, MM3A1d)

LESSON 2.1

Evaluate and Graph Polynomial Functions

Georgia Performance Standards: MM3A1b, MM3A1c, MM3A1d

Goal Evaluate and graph other polynomial functions.

Vocabulary

A **polynomial** is a monomial or a sum of monomials. A **polynomial function** is a function of the form $f(x) = a_n x^n + a_{n-1}x^{n-1} + \cdots + a_1 x + a_0$ where $a_n \neq 0$, the exponents are all whole numbers, and the coefficients are all real numbers.

The **degree of a polynomial function** is the exponent in the term where the variable is raised to the greatest power.

The **leading coefficient** is the coefficient in the term of a polynomial function that has the greatest exponent.

A polynomial function is in **standard form** if its terms are written in descending order of exponents from left to right.

Synthetic substitution is another way to evaluate a polynomial function, involving fewer operations than direct substitution.

The **end behavior** of a polynomial function's graph is the behavior of the graph as x approaches positive infinity ($+\infty$) or negative infinity ($-\infty$).

If the degree of a polynomial function is odd and the leading coefficient is positive, then $f(x) \to +\infty$ as $x \to +\infty$ and $f(x) \to -\infty$ as $x \to -\infty$.

If the degree of a polynomial function is odd and the leading coefficient is negative, then $f(x) \to -\infty$ as $x \to +\infty$ and $f(x) \to +\infty$ as $x \to -\infty$.

If the degree of a polynomial function is even and the leading coefficient is positive, then $f(x) \to +\infty$ as $x \to +\infty$ and $f(x) \to +\infty$ as $x \to -\infty$.

If the degree of a polynomial function is even and the leading coefficient is negative, then $f(x) \to -\infty$ as $x \to +\infty$ and $f(x) \to -\infty$ as $x \to -\infty$.

A function f is **even** if $f(-x) = f(x)$. The graph of an even function is symmetric with respect to the y-axis. A function f is **odd** if $f(-x) = -f(x)$. The graph of an odd function is symmetric with respect to the origin.

Example 1 Identify polynomial functions

Decide whether the function is a polynomial function. If so, write it in standard form and state its degree and leading coefficient.

a. $g(x) = -5x + 6x^{-2}$ **b.** $t(x) = -\sqrt{5}x + 2$

Solution

a. The function $g(x)$ is not a polynomial function because the term $6x^{-2}$ has an exponent that is not a whole number.

b. The function $t(x)$ is a polynomial function written in standard form. It has degree 1 and a leading coefficient of $-\sqrt{5}$.

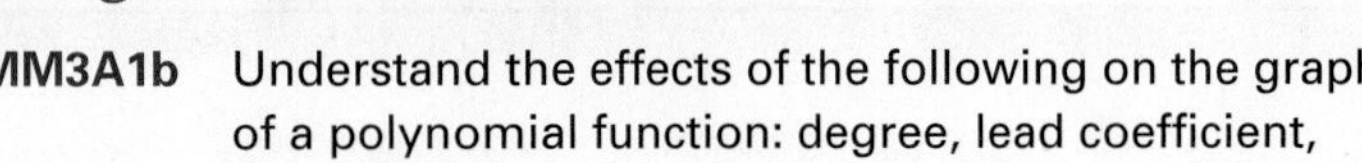

Georgia Performance Standards

MM3A1b	Understand the effects of the following on the graph of a polynomial function: degree, lead coefficient, and multiplicity of real zeros.	☑
MM3A1c	Determine whether a polynomial function has symmetry and whether it is even, odd, or neither.	☑
MM3A1d	Investigate and explain characteristics of polynomial functions, including domain and range, intercepts, zeros, relative and absolute extrema, intervals of increase and decrease, and end behavior.	☑

Example 2 Evaluate a polynomial function

Use (a) direct substitution and (b) synthetic substitution to evaluate $g(x) = -4x^3 + 3x^2 - 7$ when $x = -2$.

Solution

a. $g(x) = -4x^3 + 3x^2 - 7$ Write original function.

$g(-2) = -4(-2)^3 + 3(-2)^2 - 7$ Substitute -2 for x.

$= 37$ Simplify.

b.

STEP 1 **Write** the coefficients of $g(x)$ in order of descending exponents. Write the x-value at which $g(x)$ is being evaluated to the left.

$$\begin{array}{r|rrrr} -2 & -4 & 3 & 0 & -7 \\ & & & & \\ \hline \end{array}$$

STEP 2 **Bring** down the leading coefficient. Multiply the leading coefficient by the x-value. Write the product under the second coefficient. Add.

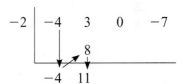

$$\begin{array}{r|rrrr} -2 & -4 & 3 & 0 & -7 \\ & & 8 & & \\ \hline & -4 & 11 & & \end{array}$$

STEP 3 **Multiply** the previous sum by the x-value. Write the product under the third coefficient. Add. Repeat for all the remaining coefficients. The final sum is the value of $g(x)$ at the given x-value.

$$\begin{array}{r|rrrr} -2 & -4 & 3 & 0 & -7 \\ & & 8 & -22 & 44 \\ \hline & -4 & 11 & -22 & 37 \end{array}$$

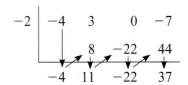

Synthetic substitution gives $g(x) = 37$, which matches the result in part (a).

Guided Practice for Examples 1 and 2

Decide whether the function is a polynomial function. If so, write it in standard form and state its degree and leading coefficient.

1. $g(x) = ix + 7$ **2.** $s(x) = 2x^2 + x^{-1}$ **3.** $d(x) = 3\pi x^2$

4. Evaluate $g(x) = -4x^2 + 6$ when $x = 3$ using direct substitution. Check with synthetic substitution.

UNIT 2

Example 3 Describe end behavior

Describe the end behavior of the graph. Then describe the degree and leading coefficient of the polynomial function.

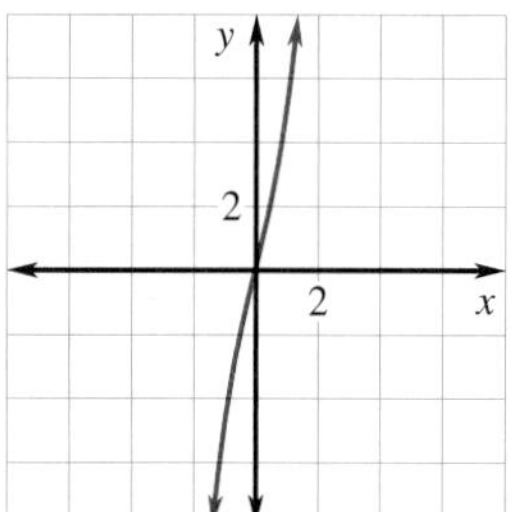

Solution

From the graph, $f(x) \to -\infty$ as $x \to -\infty$ and $f(x) \to +\infty$ as $x \to +\infty$. The degree is odd and the leading coefficient is positive.

Example 4 Graph and analyze a polynomial function

Graph and analyze the function $f(x) = -2x^4 + 4x^2 - 2$.

a. Graph the function.

b. Find the domain and range of the function.

c. Describe the degree and leading coefficient of the function.

d. Decide whether the function is *even, odd,* or *neither*. Describe any symmetries in the graph.

e. Identify where the function increases and decreases.

Solution

a. Make a table of values and plot the corresponding points. Connect the points with a smooth curve.

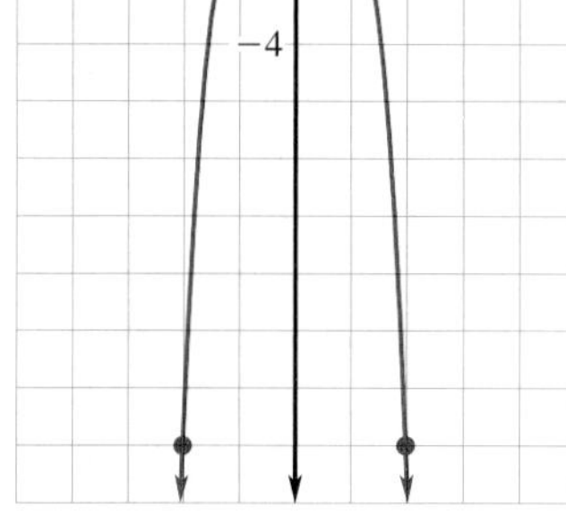

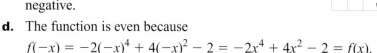

x	−2	−1	0	1	2
y	−18	0	−2	0	−18

b. The domain is all real numbers and the range is $y \leq 0$.

c. The degree is even and the leading coefficient is negative.

d. The function is even because

$f(-x) = -2(-x)^4 + 4(-x)^2 - 2 = -2x^4 + 4x^2 - 2 = f(x)$.

The graph of the function is symmetric with respect to the y-axis.

e. The function increases for $x < -1$ and $0 < x < 1$. The function decreases for $-1 < x < 0$ and $x > 1$.

Guided Practice for Examples 3 and 4

Describe **the end behavior of the graph of the polynomial function by completing these statements: $f(x) \to$ _?_ as $x \to -\infty$ and $f(x) \to$ _?_ as $x \to +\infty$.**

5. $f(x) = x^4 - 2x^2 + 1$

6. $f(x) = x^3 - 7x - 6$

7. Graph and analyze the function $f(x) = x^3 - 2x$.

LESSON 2.1

Exercise Set A

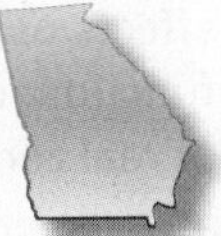

MM3A1b Understand the effects of the following on the graph of a polynomial function: degree, lead coefficient, and multiplicity of real zeros.

MM3A1c Determine whether a polynomial function has symmetry and whether it is even, odd, or neither.

MM3A1d Investigate and explain characteristics of polynomial functions, including domain and range, intercepts, zeros, relative and absolute extrema, intervals of increase and decrease, and end behavior.

Decide whether the function is a polynomial function. If it is, write the function in standard form and state the degree and leading coefficient.

1. $f(x) = 7 - 2x$ **2.** $g(x) = 2x - x^3 + 8$ **3.** $h(x) = x^4 - x^{-3}$

Use direct substitution to evaluate the polynomial function for the given value of *x*.

4. $f(x) = 6x^4 - x^3 + 3x^2 - 5x + 9; x = -1$ **5.** $g(x) = 7x - x^4 + 1; x = -4$

Use synthetic substitution to evaluate the polynomial function for the given value of *x*.

6. $f(x) = 7x^4 - 3x^3 + x^2 + 5x - 9; x = 2$ **7.** $g(x) = x^3 - 8x + 6; x = -3$

***Describe* the end behavior of the graph of the polynomial function by completing these statements: *f(x)* → _?_ as *x* → −∞ and *f(x)* → _?_ as *x* → +∞.**

8. $f(x) = -5x^3$ **9.** $f(x) = 2x^5 - 7x^2 - 4x$ **10.** $f(x) = -12x^6 - 2x + 5$

Decide whether the function is *even, odd,* or *neither*. *Describe* any symmetries in the graph.

11. $f(x) = x^2 - 3$ **12.** $g(x) = x^3 - 5x$ **13.** $f(x) = -2x^5 + 8x$

Graph the polynomial function.

14. $f(x) = -x^3 - 2$ **15.** $g(x) = x^4 + 2x$ **16.** $h(x) = -x^4 + 2x^3 - 5x + 1$

For the polynomial function, (a) graph the function, (b) find the domain and range, (c) describe the degree and leading coefficient, and (d) identify where the function increases and decreases.

17. $f(x) = -x^3$ **18.** $f(x) = x^4 + 1$ **19.** $f(x) = 3(x^3 - 13x + 12)$

20. **Multiple Representations** The retail space in shopping centers in the United States from 1986 to 2003 can be modeled by $S = -0.0388t^4 + 1.723t^3 - 28t^2 + 309t + 3481$ where S is the amount of retail space (in millions of square feet) and t is the number of years since 1986.

a. **Graphing a Function** Graph the function on the domain $0 \le t \le 17$.

b. **Using a Graph** Use the graph to estimate the first year that the amount of retail space was greater than 5 billion square feet.

c. **Predicting a Value** Use the model to predict the amount of retail space in the year 2010. Is it appropriate to use the model to make this prediction? *Explain.*

LESSON 2.1 **Exercise Set B**

MM3A1b Understand the effects of the following on the graph of a polynomial function: degree, lead coefficient, and multiplicity of real zeros.

MM3A1c Determine whether a polynomial function has symmetry and whether it is even, odd, or neither.

MM3A1d Investigate and explain characteristics of polynomial functions, including domain and range, intercepts, zeros, relative and absolute extrema, intervals of increase and decrease, and end behavior.

Decide whether the function is a polynomial function. If it is, write the function in standard form and state the degree and leading coefficient.

1. $f(x) = x^3\sqrt{5} + 7 - 2x^2$

2. $g(x) = \pi - 4x^2 + 2x^{-1}$

Use direct substitution to evaluate the polynomial function for the given value of *x*. Then check your answer using synthetic substitution.

3. $f(x) = 2x^5 - 3x^4 + x^3 - 6x + 20; x = 2$

4. $g(x) = -8x^3 + 5x^2 + 14; x = -3$

Describe **the end behavior of the graph of the polynomial function by completing these statements: $f(x) \to$ __?__ as $x \to -\infty$ and $f(x) \to$ __?__ as $x \to +\infty$.**

5. $f(x) = -x^7 + 10x$

6. $f(x) = 0.6x^3 - 2x^2 + 27$

7. $f(x) = x^{102} + 4x^{99}$

Decide whether the function is *even, odd, or neither. Describe* any symmetries in the graph.

8. $f(x) = -x^4 + 3$

9. $g(x) = 2x^3 + 6x$

10. $f(x) = x^6 - x^4 - 2$

Graph the polynomial function.

11. $f(x) = 0.5 - 2x^4$

12. $g(x) = -2x^7 - 4$

13. $h(x) = \sqrt{2}x^3 - 2x + 3$

For the polynomial function, (a) graph the function, (b) find the domain and range, (c) describe the degree and leading coefficient, and (d) identify where the function increases and decreases.

14. $f(x) = -x^4 + 6x^2$

15. $f(x) = 2x^4 - 4x^2 + 8$

16. $f(x) = -x^3 + 3x^2 - 2x + 5$

17. Critical Thinking Give an example of a polynomial function f such that $f(x) \to -\infty$ as $x \to -\infty$ and $f(x) \to -\infty$ as $x \to +\infty$.

18. **Child Development** The average heights B and G (in inches) for boys and girls ages 2 to 20, respectively, can be modeled by the functions $B = -0.001t^4 + 0.04t^3 - 0.57t^2 + 5.7t + 25$ and $G = 0.000007t^4 - 0.00276t^3 - 0.012t^2 + 3.1t + 27$ where t is the age (in years).

a. According to the models, what is the difference in average height between 16-year-old boys and girls?

b. Sketch the graphs of the two models in the same coordinate plane.

c. During an annual physical, a doctor measures a 14-year-old to be 60 inches tall. Is the 14-year-old more likely to be male or female? *Explain.*

LESSON 2.2

Translate Graphs of Polynomial Functions

Georgia Performance Standards: MM3A1a, MM3A1c, MM3A1d

Goal Graph translations of polynomial functions.

Example 1 Translate a polynomial function vertically

Graph $g(x) = x^4 + 5$. Compare the graph with the graph of $f(x) = x^4$.

STEP 1 **Make** a table of values and plot the corresponding points.

x	−2	−1	0	1	2
y	21	6	0	6	21

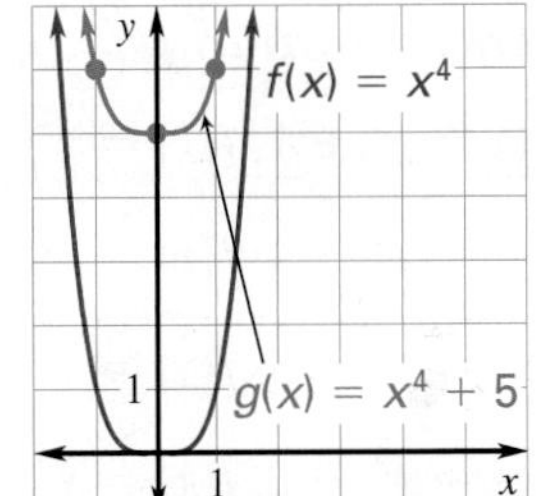

STEP 2 **Connect** the points with a smooth curve and check the end behavior. The degree is even and the leading coefficient is positive. So, $g(x) \to +\infty$ as $x \to -\infty$ and $g(x) \to +\infty$ as $x \to +\infty$.

STEP 3 **Compare** with $f(x) = x^4$. The graph of $g(x) = x^4 + 5$ is the graph of $f(x) = x^4$ translated up 5 units. The domains of f and g are all real numbers. The range of f is $y \geq 0$ and the range of g is $y \geq 5$. The function f has x- and y-intercepts of 0 and g has a y-intercept of 5. Notice that both f and g are symmetric with respect to the y-axis and are even functions because $f(-x) = (-x)^4 = f(x)$ and $g(-x) = (-x)^4 + 5 = g(x)$.

Example 2 Translate a polynomial function vertically

Graph $g(x) = x^3 - 2$. Compare the graph with the graph of $f(x) = x^3$.

STEP 1 **Make** a table of values and plot the corresponding points.

x	−2	−1	0	1	2
y	−10	−3	−2	−1	6

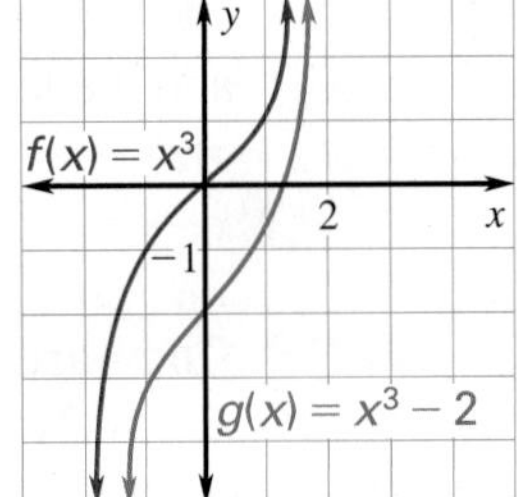

STEP 2 **Connect** the points with a smooth curve and check the end behavior. The degree is odd and the leading coefficient is positive. So, $g(x) \to -\infty$ as $x \to -\infty$ and $g(x) \to +\infty$ as $x \to +\infty$.

STEP 3 **Compare** with $f(x) = x^3$. The graph of $g(x) = x^3 - 2$ is the graph of $f(x) = x^3$ translated down 2 units. The domains and ranges of both functions are all real numbers. The function f has x- and y-intercepts of 0, and g has an x-intercept of about 1.3 and a y-intercept of –2. Notice that f is symmetric with respect to the origin and is odd because $f(-x) = -x^3 = -f(x)$. Notice that g is neither even nor odd because $g(-x) = -x^3 - 2$, which is not equal to $g(x)$ or $-g(x)$. Also, g is symmetric with respect to (0, –2), the image of the origin for this translation.

UNIT 2

Georgia Performance Standards

MM3A1a Graph simple polynomial functions as translations of the function $f(x) = ax^n$. 

MM3A1c Determine whether a polynomial function has symmetry and whether it is even, odd, or neither. 

MM3A1d Investigate and explain characteristics of polynomial functions, including domain and range, intercepts, zeros, relative and absolute extrema, intervals of increase and decrease, and end behavior.

Guided Practice for Examples 1 and 2

Graph the function $g(x)$. *Compare* the graph with the graph of $f(x)$.

1. $g(x) = x^3 + 1, f(x) = x^3$
2. $g(x) = x^3 - 4, f(x) = x^3$
3. $g(x) = x^4 - 3, f(x) = x^4$
4. $g(x) = x^4 + 2, f(x) = x^4$

UNIT 2

Example 3 Translate a polynomial function horizontally

Graph $g(x) = 2(x - 2)^3$. Compare the graph with the graph of $f(x) = 2x^3$.

Solution

STEP 1 **Make** a table of values and plot the corresponding points.

x	−1	0	1	2	3
y	−54	−16	−2	0	2

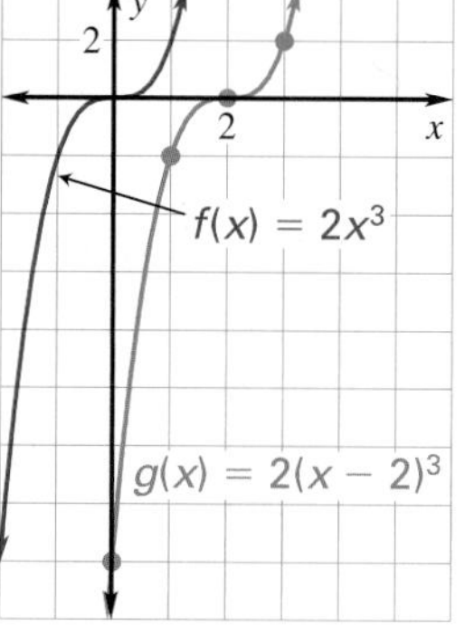

STEP 2 **Connect** the points with a smooth curve and check the end behavior. The degree is odd and the leading coefficient is positive. So, $g(x) \to -\infty$ as $x \to -\infty$ and $g(x) \to +\infty$ as $x \to +\infty$.

STEP 3 **Compare** with $f(x) = 2x^3$. The graph of $g(x) = 2(x - 2)^3$ is the graph of $f(x) = 2x^3$ translated to the right 2 units. The domains and ranges of both functions are all real numbers. The function f has x- and y-intercepts of 0 and g has an x-intercept of 2 and a y-intercept of -16. Notice that f is symmetric with respect to the origin and is an odd function because $f(-x) = 2(-x)^3 = -f(x)$. Notice that g is neither even nor odd because $g(-x) = 2(-x - 2)^3$, which is not equal to $-g(x)$ or $g(x)$. Also, g is symmetric with respect to $(2, 0)$, the image of the origin for this translation.

Guided Practice for Example 3

Graph the function *g*(*x*). *Compare* the graph with the graph of *f*(*x*).

5. $g(x) = (x - 1)^3, f(x) = x^3$

6. $g(x) = (x + 4)^4, f(x) = x^4$

7. $g(x) = 3(x - 3)^4, f(x) = 3x^4$

8. $g(x) = \frac{1}{2}(x + 2)^3, f(x) = \frac{1}{2}x^3$

Example 4 Translate a polynomial function

Graph $g(x) = -\frac{1}{2}(x + 1)^4 - 3$. Compare the graph with the graph of $f(x) = -\frac{1}{2}x^4$.

Solution

STEP 1 **Make** a table of values and plot the corresponding points.

x	-3	-2	-1	0	1
y	-11	-3.5	-3	-3.5	-11

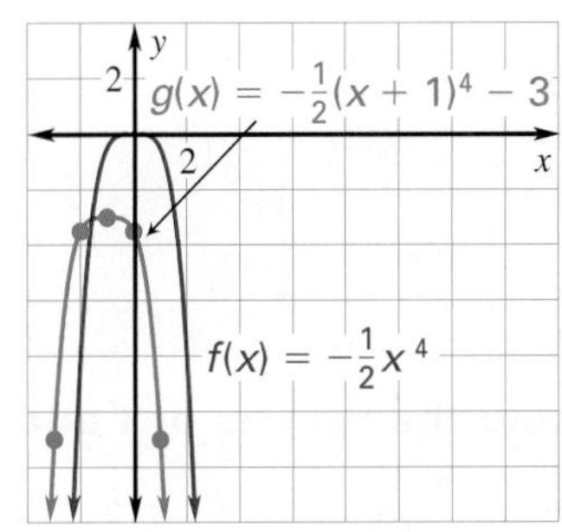

STEP 2 **Connect** the points with a smooth curve and check the end behavior. The degree is even and the leading coefficient is negative. So, $g(x) \to -\infty$ as $x \to -\infty$ and $g(x) \to -\infty$ as $x \to +\infty$.

STEP 3 **Compare** with $f(x) = -\frac{1}{2}x^4$. The graph of $g(x) = -\frac{1}{2}(x + 1)^4 - 3$ is the graph of $f(x) = -\frac{1}{2}x^4$ translated to the left 1 unit and down 3 units. The domains of f and g are all real numbers. The range of f is $y \le 0$ and the range of g is $y \le -3$. The function f has x- and y-intercepts of 0 and g has a y-intercept of -3.5. Notice that f is symmetric with respect to the y-axis and is an even function because $f(-x) = -\frac{1}{2}(-x)^4 = f(x)$. Notice that g is neither even nor odd because $g(-x) = -\frac{1}{2}(-x + 1)^4 - 3$, which is not equal to $-g(x)$ or $g(x)$. Also, g is symmetric with respect to the line $x = -1$, the image of the y-axis for this translation.

Guided Practice for Example 4

Graph the function *g*(*x*). *Compare* the graph with the graph of *f*(*x*).

9. $g(x) = (x + 4)^3 - 2, f(x) = x^3$

10. $g(x) = -\frac{3}{2}(x - 1)^3 + 3,\ f(x) = -\frac{3}{2}x^3$

11. $g(x) = -(x - 2)^4 + 1, f(x) = -x^4$

12. $g(x) = \frac{2}{3}(x + 2)^4 - 2,\ f(x) = \frac{2}{3}x^4$

Exercise Set A

MM3A1a Graph simple polynomial functions as translations of the function $f(x) = ax^n$.

MM3A1c Determine whether a polynomial function has symmetry and whether it is even, odd, or neither.

MM3A1d Investigate and explain characteristics of polynomial functions, including domain and range, intercepts, zeros, relative and absolute extrema, intervals of increase and decrease, and end behavior.

Match the function with its graph.

1. $y = x^3 + 4$

2. $y = (x + 4)^3$

3. $y = -x^3 + 4$

A.

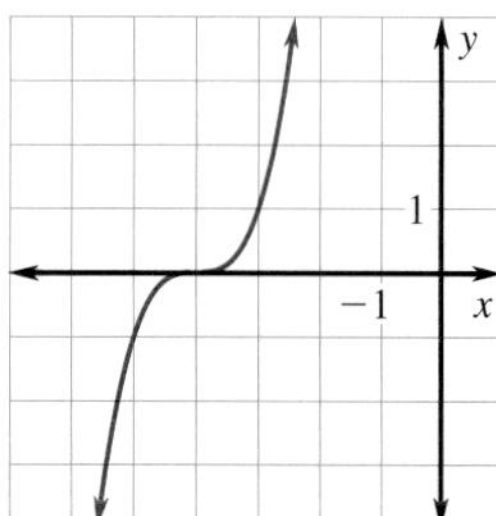

B.

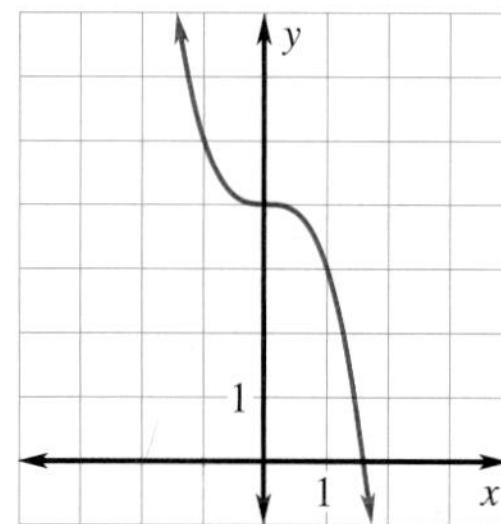

C.

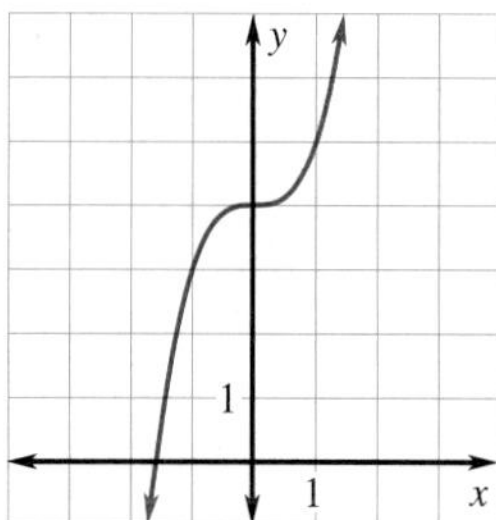

Explain **how the graphs of *f* and *g* are related.**

4. $f(x) = -x^3, g(x) = -(x - 8)^3$

5. $f(x) = 2x^4, g(x) = 2x^4 - 6$

Graph the function. ***Compare*** **the graph with the graph of $f(x) = x^3$.**

6. $g(x) = x^3 - 1$

7. $g(x) = x^3 + 2$

8. $g(x) = (x - 4)^3$

Graph the function. ***Compare*** **the graph with the graph of $f(x) = -2x^3$.**

9. $g(x) = -2x^3 + 3$

10. $g(x) = -2(x - 1)^3$

11. $g(x) = -2(x + 2)^3 + 4$

Graph the function. ***Compare*** **the graph with the graph of $f(x) = x^4$.**

12. $g(x) = (x + 1)^4$

13. $g(x) = x^4 - 5$

14. $g(x) = (x - 3)^4$

Graph the function. ***Compare*** **the graph with the graph of $f(x) = \frac{1}{3}x^4$.**

15. $g(x) = \frac{1}{3}x^4 - 2$

16. $g(x) = \frac{1}{3}(x + 3)^4$

17. $g(x) = \frac{1}{3}(x - 1)^4 + 1$

Write an equation for the function that is described by the given characteristics.

18. The shape of $f(x) = x^3$, but moved 7 units down.

19. The shape of $f(x) = x^4$, but moved 5 units to the left.

20. Geometry The volume of a cube with side length x feet is given by $V_1 = x^3$. The volume of a cube with side length $(x + 2)$ feet is given by $V_2 = (x + 2)^3$.

a. Graph V_1 and V_2. *Explain* how the graphs are related.

b. Find the volume of each cube when $x = 6$.

LESSON 2.2 **Exercise Set B**

MM3A1a Graph simple polynomial functions as translations of the function $f(x) = ax^n$.

MM3A1c Determine whether a polynomial function has symmetry and whether it is even, odd, or neither.

MM3A1d Investigate and explain characteristics of polynomial functions, including domain and range, intercepts, zeros, relative and absolute extrema, intervals of increase and decrease, and end behavior.

***Explain* how the graphs of *f* and *g* are related.**

1. $f(x) = x^3, g(x) = x^3 - 7$
2. $f(x) = x^4, g(x) = (x + 6)^4$
3. $f(x) = \frac{1}{4}x^3, g(x) = \frac{1}{4}(x + 3)^3 - 1$
4. $f(x) = -4x^4, g(x) = -4(x - 1)^4 + 0.5$

Graph the function. *Compare* the graph with the graph of $f(x) = -x^3$.

5. $g(x) = -x^3 + 4$
6. $g(x) = -(x + 2)^3$
7. $g(x) = -(x - 5)^3 + 1$

Graph the function. *Compare* the graph with the graph of $f(x) = \frac{3}{2}x^3$.

8. $g(x) = \frac{3}{2}x^3 - 2$
9. $g(x) = \frac{3}{2}(x - 4)^3$
10. $g(x) = \frac{3}{2}(x + 1)^3 - 3$

Graph the function. *Compare* the graph with the graph of $f(x) = x^4$.

11. $g(x) = (x - 3)^4$
12. $g(x) = x^4 + 4$
13. $g(x) = (x + 3)^4 - 5$

Graph the function. *Compare* the graph with the graph of $f(x) = 0.5x^4$.

14. $g(x) = 0.5x^4 + 1$
15. $g(x) = 0.5(x - 6)^4$
16. $g(x) = 0.5(x - 2)^4 + 3$

17. **Error Analysis** A student tried to explain how the graphs of $f(x) = -2x^3$ and $g(x) = -2(x - 5)^3 + 4$ are related. *Describe* and correct the error.

> The graph of $g(x) = -2(x - 5)^3 + 4$ is the graph of $f(x) = -2x^3$ translated left 5 units and down 4 units.

Write an equation for the function that is described by the given characteristics.

18. The shape of $f(x) = -x^3$, but moved 4 units to the right and 6 units down.

19. The shape of $f(x) = 3x^4$, but moved 7 units to the left and 1 unit up.

20. **Multiple Representations** The volume of a ball with radius r inches is given by $V_1 = \frac{4}{3}\pi r^3$. The radius of a second ball is 1 inch greater than the radius of the first ball.
    a. **Writing a Function** Write a function that represents the volume V_2 of the second ball.
    b. **Graphing Functions** Graph V_1 and V_2.
    c. **Analyzing Graphs** *Explain* how the graphs are related.
    d. **Calculating a Value** Find the volume of each ball when $r = 4.5$ inches.

UNIT 2

LESSON 2.3

Factor and Solve Polynomial Equations

Georgia Performance Standards: MM3A3b, MM3A3d

Goal Factor and solve polynomial equations.

Vocabulary

A factorable polynomial with integer coefficients is **factored completely** if it is written as a product of unfactorable polynomials with integer coefficients. To factor the sum of two cubes, use the pattern $a^3 + b^3 = (a + b)(a^2 - ab + b^2)$. To factor the difference of two cubes, use the pattern $a^3 - b^3 = (a - b)(a^2 + ab + b^2)$.

For some polynomials you can **factor by grouping** pairs of terms that have a common monomial factor.

An expression of the form $au^2 + bu + c$, where u is any expression in x, is said to be in **quadratic form.**

UNIT 2

Example 1 Factor the sum or difference of two cubes

Factor the polynomial completely.

a. $4x^4 - 108x = 4x(x^3 - 27)$ Factor common monomial.

$= 4x(x - 3)(x^2 + 3x + 9)$ Difference of two cubes

b. $2b^3 + 16a^3 = 2(b^3 + 8a^3)$ Factor common monomial.

$= 2(b + 2a)(b^2 - 2ab + 4a^2)$ Sum of two cubes

Example 2 Factor by grouping

Factor the polynomial $x^3 + 2x^2 - x - 2$ completely.

$x^3 + 2x^2 - x - 2 = x^2(x + 2) - 1(x + 2)$ Factor by grouping.

$= (x^2 - 1)(x + 2)$ Distributive property

$= (x + 1)(x - 1)(x + 2)$ Difference of two squares

Example 3 Factor polynomials in quadratic form

Factor completely: (a) $3x^8 + 18x^5 + 24x^2$ and (b) $81g^4 - 256$.

a. $3x^8 + 18x^5 + 24x^2 = 3x^2(x^6 + 6x^3 + 8)$ Factor common monomial.

$= 3x^2(x^3 + 2)(x^3 + 4)$ Factor trinomial in quadratic form.

b. $81g^4 - 256 = (9g^2)^2 - (16)^2$ Write as difference of two squares.

$= (9g^2 + 16)(9g^2 - 16)$ Difference of two squares

$= (9g^2 + 16)(3g + 4)(3g - 4)$ Difference of two squares

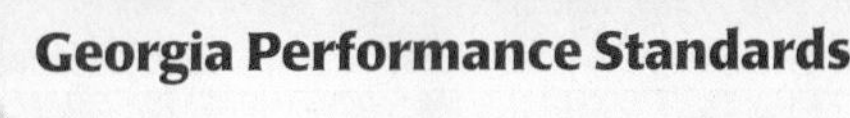

Georgia Performance Standards

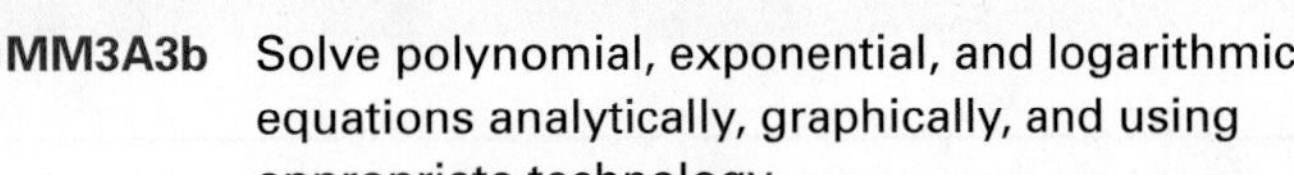

MM3A3b Solve polynomial, exponential, and logarithmic equations analytically, graphically, and using appropriate technology. 

MM3A3d Solve a variety of types of equations by appropriate means choosing among mental calculation, pencil and paper, or appropriate technology. 

Example 4 Find real-number solutions

Find the real-number solutions of the equation $x^4 - 7x^2 = -12$.

$x^4 - 7x^2 + 12 = 0$	Write in standard form.
$(x^2 - 4)(x^2 - 3) = 0$	Factor trinomial.
$(x + 2)(x - 2)(x^2 - 3) = 0$	Difference of two squares
$x = -2, x = 2, x = \sqrt{3}$, or $x = -\sqrt{3}$	Zero product property

Example 5 Solve a polynomial equation

Box Dimensions The dimensions (in inches) of a jewelry box are: length $4x$, width $(x - 1)$, and height $(x - 2)$. If the volume of the box is 24 cubic inches, find the dimensions of the box.

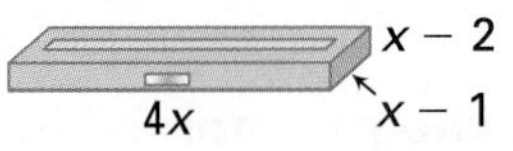

Solution

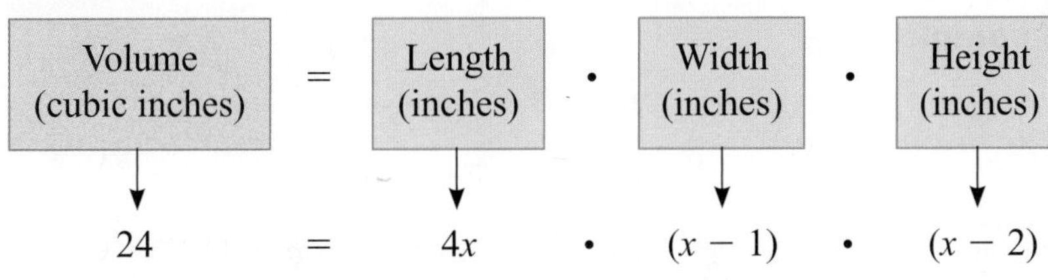

$24 = (4x)(x - 1)(x - 2)$	Write equation.
$0 = 4x^3 - 12x^2 + 8x - 24$	Write in standard form.
$0 = 4x^2(x - 3) + 8(x - 3)$	Factor by grouping.
$0 = (4x^2 + 8)(x - 3)$	Distributive property

The only real solution is $x = 3$. The jewelry box is 12 in. long, 2 in. wide, and 1 in. high.

Guided Practice for Examples 1, 2, 3, 4, and 5

Factor the polynomial completely.

1. $7x^5 - 56x^2$ **2.** $128y^6 + 2$ **3.** $x^3 - 3x^2 - 4x + 12$

4. $y^3 + 7y^2 - 9y - 63$ **5.** $3b^6 + 6b^4 + 3b^2$ **6.** $z^8 - 16$

Find the real-number solutions of the equation.

7. $x^4 - 3x^2 + 2 = 0$ **8.** $x^5 - 8x^3 = -12x$ **9.** $x^5 - 12x^3 = -27x$

10. The dimensions (in inches) of a jewelry box are: length $2x$, width $(x - 1)$, and height $(x - 3)$. If the volume of the box is 24 cubic inches, find the dimensions of the box.

LESSON 2.3 **Exercise Set A**

MM3A3b Solve polynomial, exponential, and logarithmic equations analytically, graphically, and using appropriate technology.

MM3A3d Solve a variety of types of equations by appropriate means choosing among mental calculation, pencil and paper, or appropriate technology.

Factor the sum or difference of cubes.

1. $x^3 + 125$

2. $y^3 - 8$

3. $64n^3 - 27$

4. $27g^3 + 343$

5. $w^3 + 27$

6. $8v^3 - 125$

Factor the polynomial by grouping.

7. $r^3 - 3r^2 + 6r - 18$

8. $x^3 + 6x^2 + 7x + 42$

9. $c^3 + 4c^2 - 9c - 36$

10. $9m^3 + 18m^2 - 4m - 8$

Factor the polynomial in quadratic form.

11. $x^4 - 36$

12. $x^4 + x^2 - 20$

13. $6y^6 - 5y^3 - 4$

Factor the polynomial completely.

14. $x^6 - 4$

15. $d^4 - 7d^2 + 10$

16. $24q^3 - 81$

17. $a^6 + 7a^3 + 6$

18. $-4x^4 + 26x^2 - 30$

19. $2b^4 + 14b^3 - 16b - 112$

Find the real-number solutions of the equation.

20. $n^4 = -6n^3$

21. $4k^3 = 9k^2$

22. $x^3 + 2x^2 - 25x - 50 = 0$

23. $6w^3 + 30w^2 - 18w - 90 = 0$

24. $y^4 + 45 = 14y^2$

25. $3r^5 + 15r^3 - 18r = 0$

26. Error Analysis *Describe* and correct the error in finding all real-number solutions.

$$2x^3 - 50x = 0$$
$$2x(x^2 - 25) = 0$$
$$x^2 - 25 = 0$$
$$x = -5 \text{ or } x = 5$$

X

27. **City Park** You are designing a marble planter for a city park. You want the length of the planter to be six times the height and the width to be three times the height. The sides should be one foot thick. Because the planter will be on the sidewalk, it does not need a bottom. What should the outer dimensions of the planter be if it is to hold 4 cubic feet of dirt?

UNIT 2

LESSON 2.3 **Exercise Set B**

MM3A3b Solve polynomial, exponential, and logarithmic equations analytically, graphically, and using appropriate technology.

MM3A3d Solve a variety of types of equations by appropriate means choosing among mental calculation, pencil and paper, or appropriate technology.

Factor the polynomial completely using any method.

1. $x^3 - 512$
2. $2a^3 + 432$
3. $7h^3 + 448$
4. $-3c^3 + 24$
5. $12x^3 - 6x^2 + 2x - 1$
6. $3k^4 + 27k^3 - 7k - 63$
7. $3n^3 - 10n^2 - 48n + 160$
8. $x^6 + x^5 - x^4 - x^3$
9. $y^4 - 81$
10. $2z^4 - 1250$
11. $6a^4 + 13a^2 - 5$
12. $6b^4 - 17b^2 - 28$
13. $r^5 + r^3 - r^2 - 1$
14. $-4w^8 - 8w^6 + 4w^4 + 8w^2$
15. $a^6b^3 + 125$
16. $2ac^2 - 5bc^2 - 2ad^2 + 5bd^2$

Find the real-number solutions of the equation.

17. $x^3 + 1000 = 0$
18. $27g^3 - 8 = 0$
19. $6v^3 = 384$
20. $p^3 + 4p^2 - 9p = 36$
21. $125q^4 - 27 = 125q^3 - 27q$
22. $s^4 - 11s^2 + 28 = 0$
23. $162y^4 = 2$
24. $m^6 - 64 = 0$
25. $3z^{11} - 3z^5 = 0$
26. $16h^5 - 25h^3 + 9h = 0$
27. $12n^7 + 2n^5 = 30n^3$
28. $6r^7 + 6r^5 = 9r^6 + 9r^4$

29. **Critical Thinking** Write a polynomial that can be factored using grouping and the sum of cubes. Show the complete factorization of your polynomial.

30. **Theater** A stage crew is assembling a three-level semi-circular platform on a stage for a performance. The platform has the dimensions shown in the diagram and a total volume of 756π cubic feet.

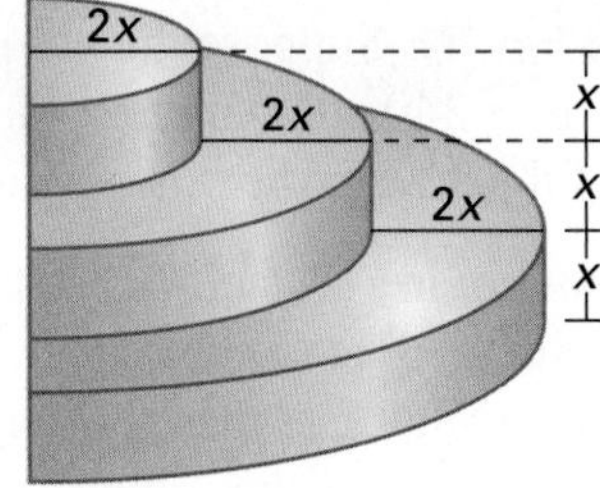

   a. What is the volume, in terms of x, of each of the three levels of the platform?

   b. Use what you know about the total volume to write an equation involving x.

   c. Solve the equation from part (b).

   d. Use your solution from part (c) to calculate the dimensions (radius and height) of each of the levels of the platform.

Georgia Performance Standards

MM3A3b Solve polynomial, exponential, and logarithmic equations analytically, graphically, and using appropriate technology. 

MM3A3d Solve a variety of types of equations by appropriate means choosing among mental calculation, pencil and paper, or appropriate technology. 

LESSON 2.3

Problem Solving Workshop

Problem In Example 5 on page 77, you solved a polynomial equation by factoring. You can also solve a polynomial equation *using a graph*. The dimensions (in inches) of a jewelry box are: length $4x$, width $(x - 1)$, and height $(x - 2)$. If the volume of the box is 24 cubic inches, find the dimensions of the box.

STEP 1 **Write** a function for the volume of the jewelry box. The volume of a rectangular prism is length • width • height. So, the volume y of the jewelry box is given by this function: $y = 4x(x - 1)(x - 2)$.

STEP 2 **Graph** the equations $y = 24$ and $y = 4x(x - 1)(x - 2)$. Choose a viewing window that shows the intersection of the graphs.

STEP 3 **Identify** the coordinates of the intersection point. On a graphing calculator, you use the *intersect* feature. The intersection point is (3, 24).

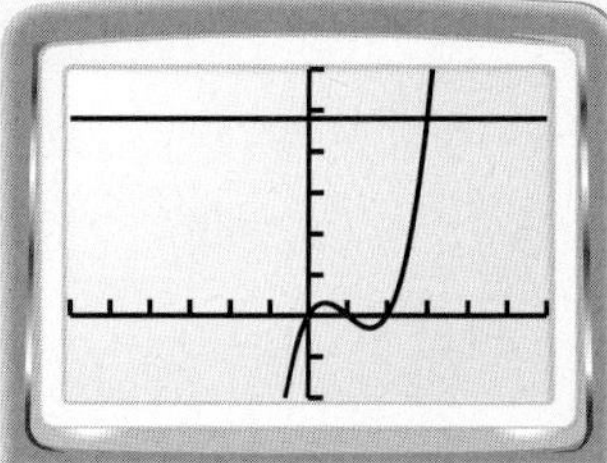

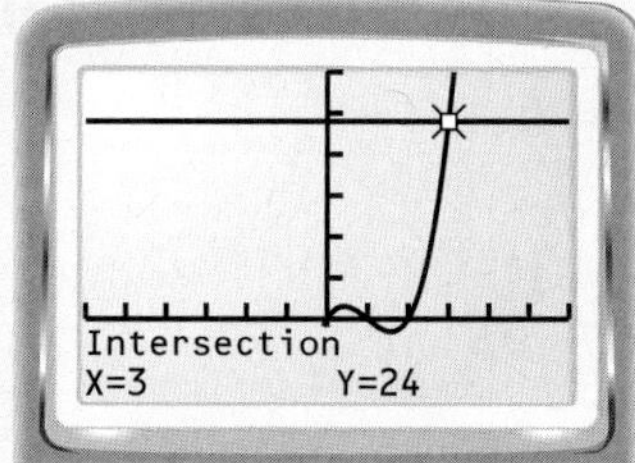

The volume of the jewelry box is 24 cubic inches when x is 3. So, the dimensions of the jewelry box should be as follows:

Length = 4(3) = 12 inches, width = 3 − 1 = 2 inches, height = 3 − 2 = 1 inch

Practice

1. **What If?** Suppose the volume of the jewelry box is 240 cubic inches. Find the dimensions of the jewelry box using a graph.

2. **Packaging** A factory needs a box that has a volume of 1485 cubic inches. The width should be 2 inches less than the height, and the length should be 4 inches greater than the height. Find the dimensions of the box using a graph.

3. **Population** From 1980 to 2005, the population P (in thousands) of Columbus, Georgia can be modeled by the function

$$P(x) = -0.0018x^3 + 0.039x^2 + 0.79x + 169$$

where x is the number of years since 1980. In what year was the population of Columbus, Georgia about 179 thousand? Solve the problem using a graph.

UNIT 2

LESSON 2.4

Solve Polynomial Inequalities

Georgia Performance Standards: MM3A3c

Goal Solve polynomial inequalities.

Vocabulary

A **polynomial inequality** in one variable can be written as one of the following:

$a_nx^n + a_{n-1}x^{n-1} + \cdots + a_1x + a_0 < 0$, $a_nx^n + a_{n-1}x^{n-1} + \cdots + a_1x + a_0 > 0$,

$a_nx^n + a_{n-1}x^{n-1} + \cdots + a_1x + a_0 \le 0$, $a_nx^n + a_{n-1}x^{n-1} + \cdots + a_1x + a_0 \ge 0$

where $a_n \ne 0$.

Inequalities can be used to describe subsets of real numbers called **intervals.** In the bounded intervals below, the real numbers a and b are the endpoints of each interval.

Inequality	$a \le x \le b$	$a < x < b$	$a \le x < b$	$a < x \le b$
Notation	$[a, b]$	(a, b)	$[a, b)$	$(a, b]$

Unbounded intervals are also written in this notation.

Inequality	$x \ge a$	$x > a$	$x \le b$	$x < b$
Notation	$[a, +\infty)$	$(a, +\infty)$	$(-\infty, b]$	$(-\infty, b)$

UNIT 2

Example 1 Solve a polynomial inequality algebraically

Solve $x^3 - 3x^2 > 10x$ algebraically.

First, write and solve the equation obtained by replacing > with =.

$x^3 - 3x^2 = 10x$	Write equation that corresponds to original inequality.
$x^3 - 3x^2 - 10x = 0$	Write in standard form.
$x(x - 5)(x + 2) = 0$	Factor.
$x = 0, x = 5,$ or $x = -2$	Zero product property

The numbers 0, 5, and -2 are the critical x-values of the inequality $x^3 - 3x^2 > 10x$. Plot 0, 5, and -2 on a number line, using open dots because the values do not satisfy the inequality. The critical x-values partition the number line into four intervals. Test an x-value in each interval to see if it satisfies the inequality.

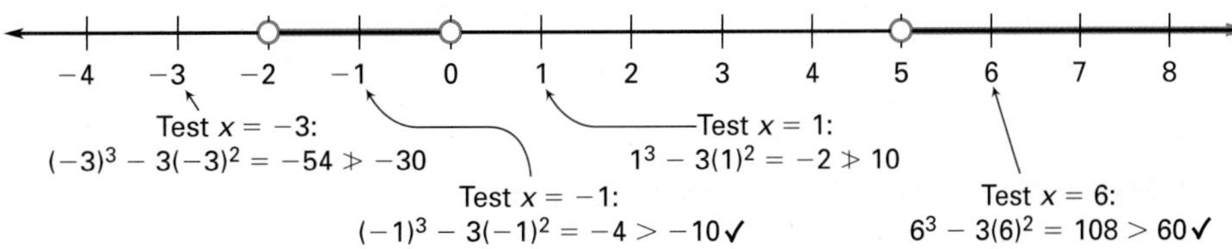

The solution set consists of all real numbers in the intervals $(-2, 0)$ and $(5, \infty)$.

Guided Practice for Example 1

Solve the inequality algebraically.

1. $x^3 - 4x \ge 0$ **2.** $-3x^3 + 10x^2 \le -8x$ **3.** $x^3 - 3x^2 - x + 3 < 0$

Georgia Performance Standards

MM3A3c Solve polynomial, exponential, and logarithmic inequalities analytically, graphically, and using appropriate technology. Represent solution sets of inequalities using interval notation.

Example 2 Solve a polynomial inequality by graphing

Solve $2x^3 + x^2 - 6x \leq 0$ by graphing.

The solution consists of the x-values for which the graph of $y = 2x^3 + x^2 - 6x$ lies on or below the x-axis. Find the graph's x-intercepts by letting $y = 0$ and solve for x.

$2x^3 + x^2 - 6x = 0$ Set y equal to 0.

$x(2x - 3)(x + 2) = 0$ Factor.

$x = 0, x = \frac{3}{2}, \text{ or } x = -2$ Zero product property

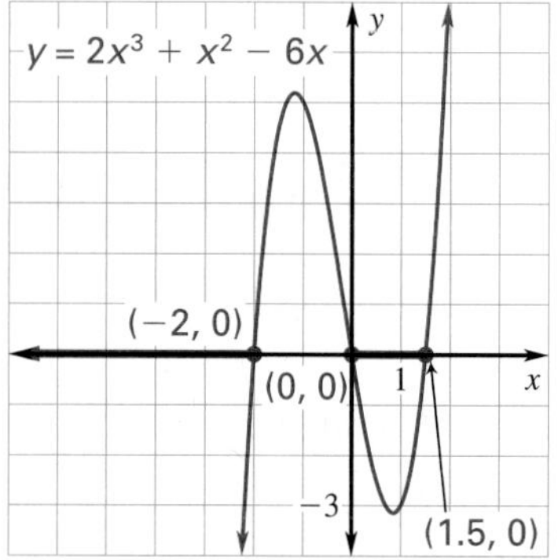

Graph the polynomial and plot the x-intercepts $0, \frac{3}{2}$, and -2. The graph lies on or below the x-axis to the left of (and including) $x = -2$ and between (and including) $x = 0$ and $x = \frac{3}{2}$.

The solution set consists of all real numbers in the intervals $(-\infty, -2]$ and $\left[0, \frac{3}{2}\right]$.

Example 3 Use a polynomial inequality as a model

Cruise Ships The number C of North American cruise ships can be modeled by $C(x) = -0.067x^3 + 0.37x^2 + 9.0x + 131, 0 \leq x \leq 8$ where x is the number of years since 1997. For what years was the number of cruise ships greater than 175?

Solution

You want to find the values of x for which:

$$C(x) > 175$$

$$-0.067x^3 + 0.37x^2 + 9.0x + 131 > 175$$

$$-0.067x^3 + 0.37x^2 + 9.0x - 44 > 0$$

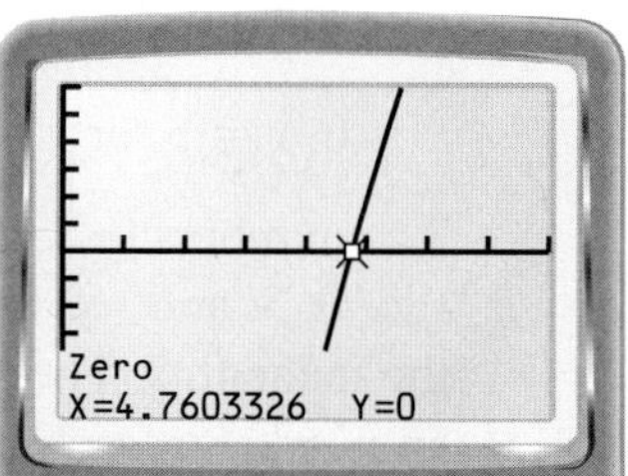

Graph $y = -0.067x^3 + 0.37x^2 + 9.0x - 44$ on the domain $0 \leq x \leq 8$. The graph's x-intercept is about 4.8. The graph lies above the x-axis when $4.8 < x \leq 8$.

There were more than 175 cruise ships in the years 2002–2005.

Guided Practice for Examples 2 and 3

Solve the inequality using a graph.

4. $x^3 - 5x^2 + 4x \geq 0$ **5.** $2x^3 + 8x^2 < -6x$ **6.** $x^4 - 8x^2 - 9 \leq 0$

7. Use the information in Example 3 to determine in what years there were at least 155 cruise ships.

UNIT 2

LESSON 2.4 **Exercise Set A**

MM3A3c Solve polynomial, exponential, and logarithmic inequalities analytically, graphically, and using appropriate technology. Represent solution sets of inequalities using interval notation.

Solve the inequality algebraically.

1. $x^3 + x^2 - 20x < 0$

2. $x^3 - 9x \geq 0$

3. $x^4 - 16 > 0$

4. $x^3 - 5x^2 \leq 24x$

5. $2x^4 - 7x^2 > 4$

6. $x^4 + x^2 < 2$

7. $x^3 - x^2 - 16x + 16 \geq 0$

8. $x^4(x - 3) \leq 0$

9. $2x^3 - 3x^2 - 32x > -48$

Solve the inequality using a graph.

10. $x^3 + x^2 - 4x - 4 > 0$

11. $x^4 - 11x^2 + 18 \leq 0$

12. $3x^4 - 1 \leq 11$

13. $x^5 - 36x > 0$

14. $3x^3 - 6x^2 - 2x \leq 7x$

15. $-6x^3 + 19x^2 \geq 10x$

16. $x^4 - 14 < 0$

17. $-\frac{1}{2}x^3 + 4x^2 \geq 1$

18. $x^3 - 0.2x^2 - 3.16x + 1.4 < 0$

19. **Error Analysis** *Describe* and correct the error in solving the inequality $x^3 - 4x^2 + 3x > 0$ by graphing.

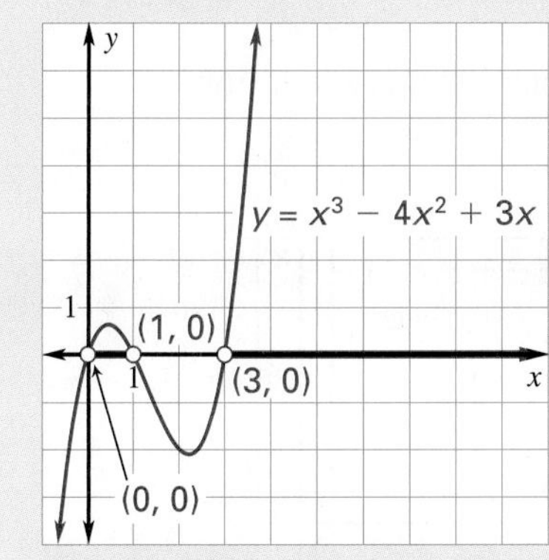

The solution set is all real numbers in the intervals $[0, 1]$ and $[3, \infty)$.

20. **Picnic Cooler** A rectangular picnic cooler has length 3 inches more than its width and height 6 inches more than its width. If the volume of the cooler is more than 648 cubic inches, what are the possible widths of the cooler?

21. **Investment** P dollars, invested at interest rate r compounded annually, increases to an amount A where

$$A = P(1 + r)^3$$

in 3 years. An investment of \$1000 is to increase to an amount greater than \$1200 in 3 years.

a. Write an inequality that represents the situation.

b. Use a graph to solve the inequality and interpret your answer.

LESSON 2.4 **Exercise Set B**

MM3A3c Solve polynomial, exponential, and logarithmic inequalities analytically, graphically, and using appropriate technology. Represent solution sets of inequalities using interval notation.

Solve the inequality algebraically.

1. $x^3 - 4x^2 - 20x + 48 > 0$
2. $x^4 + 4x^3 - 12x^2 \leq 0$
3. $4x^4 + 4 \leq 17x^2$
4. $x^3 - 2x < 0$
5. $2x^3 + 3x^2 - 18x > 27$
6. $x^4 + x^3 - 2x^2 \geq 2x$

Solve the inequality using a graph.

7. $x^3 - 5x^2 - 22x + 56 > 0$
8. $x^4 - 8x^2 + 15 \leq 0$
9. $2x^3 + x^2 - 5x - 2 \leq 0$
10. $\frac{1}{4}x^4 - 4x < -3$
11. $1.2x^3 + 3.07x^2 - x > 3.71$
12. $-0.3x^3 + 15.2x^2 \geq -2.3x$

Solve the inequality using any method.

13. $x^3 + 4x^2 - 8x > 96$
14. $(x^2 - 4)(x - 1)^2 \leq 0$
15. $2x^3 - 11x^2 + 3x \geq 54$
16. $(x + 4)^2(x - 4)(x - 3) < 0$
17. $11x^3 - 11x^2 - x + 1 \leq 0$
18. $1.8x^4 - x^3 + 3.2x > 0.5$

19. **Critical Thinking** *Describe* how the solution of the inequality $x^3 + 7x^2 - x - 7 < 0$ changes if $<$ is replaced with $\leq$.

20. **Critical Thinking** Write a polynomial inequality in one variable that has a solution set consisting of the intervals $(0, 3)$ and $(6, \infty)$.

21. **Packaging** An open box is to be made from a square piece of material, 36 centimeters on a side, by cutting equal squares with sides of length x from the corners and folding up the sides as shown in the figure. If the volume of the box is to be greater than 2700 cubic centimeters, what are the possible heights of the box?

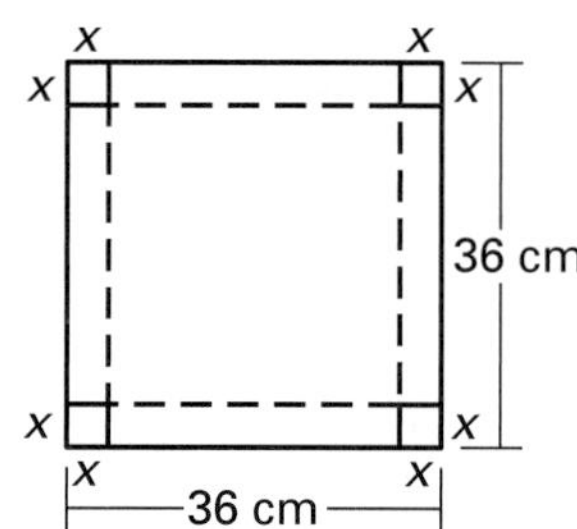

22. **Multiple Representations** The numbers $M(x)$ of morning newspapers and $E(x)$ of evening newspapers in the United States can be modeled by

$M(x) = -0.035x^3 + 0.31x^2 + 20.5x + 555, 0 \leq x \leq 15$

$E(x) = 0.035x^3 + 0.35x^2 - 42.1x + 1083, 0 \leq x \leq 15$

where x is the number of years since 1990.

a. **Writing an Inequality** Write an inequality that you can use to find the years for which $M(x)$ is less than $E(x)$.

b. **Finding a Solution** Use a table to find the solution of the inequality from part (a). Your table should contain x-values from 0 to 15. Interpret your answer.

c. **Checking a Solution** Check the solution you found in part (b) by using a graphing calculator to solve the inequality $M(x) < E(x)$ graphically.

UNIT 2

LESSON 2.5

Apply the Remainder and Factor Theorems

Georgia Performance Standards: MM3A3a, MM3A3d

Goal Use theorems to factor polynomials.

Vocabulary

Polynomial long division can be used to divide a polynomial $f(x)$ by a divisor polynomial $d(x)$, producing a quotient polynomial $q(x)$ and a remainder polynomial $r(x)$.

Synthetic division can be used to divide any polynomial by a divisor of the form $x - k$.

Remainder Theorem: If a polynomial $f(x)$ is divided by $x - k$, then the remainder is $r = f(k)$.

Factor Theorem: A polynomial $f(x)$ has a factor $x - k$, if and only if $f(k) = 0$.

Example 1 Use polynomial long division

Divide $f(x) = x^3 + 2$ by $x + 1$ using long division.

Solution

$$\begin{array}{r} x^2 - x + 1 \\ x + 1 \overline{)\, x^3 + 0x^2 + 0x + 2} \end{array}$$

$x^3 + x^2$	Multiply divisor by $x^3/x = x^2$.
$-x^2 + 0x$	Subtract.
$-x^2 - x$	Multiply divisor by $-x^2/x = -x$.
$x + 2$	Subtract.
$x + 1$	Multiply divisor by $x/x = 1$.
1	Subtract.

$$\frac{x^3 + 2}{x + 1} = x^2 - x + 1 + \frac{1}{x + 1}$$

Example 2 Use synthetic division

Divide $f(x) = x^3 + 2$ by $x + 1$ using synthetic division.

Write $x + 1$ in the form $x - k$: $x + 1 = x - (-1)$. So, write -1 to the left of the coefficients of $f(x)$, as shown.

$$\begin{array}{r|rrrr} -1 & 1 & 0 & 0 & 2 \\ & & -1 & 1 & -1 \\ \hline & 1 & -1 & 1 & 1 \end{array}$$

coefficients of quotient → 1 −1 1 | 1 ← remainder

So, $\frac{x^3 + 2}{x + 1} = x^2 - x + 1 + \frac{1}{x + 1}$, which is the same result as in Example 1.

UNIT 2

Georgia Performance Standards

MM3A3a Find real and complex roots of higher degree polynomial equations using the factor theorem, remainder theorem, rational root theorem, and fundamental theorem of algebra, incorporating complex and radical conjugates. 

MM3A3d Solve a variety of types of equations by appropriate means choosing among mental calculation, pencil and paper, or appropriate technology. 

Guided Practice for Examples 1 and 2

Divide using polynomial long division.

1. $(2x^4 + 2x^3 + x^2 - x - 1) \div (x + 1)$ **2.** $(x^3 + 3x^2 - x - 3) \div (x^2 - 1)$

Divide using synthetic division.

3. $(x^4 + 2x^3 - 5x^2 + 3x - 1) \div (x - 1)$ **4.** $(-x^4 + 4x^2 + 5x + 5) \div (x + 2)$

Example 3 Factor a polynomial

Factor $f(x) = x^3 - 4x^2 + x + 6$ completely given that $x - 3$ is a factor.

Because $x - 3$ is a factor of $f(x)$, you know that $f(3) = 0$. Use synthetic division to find the other factors.

Use the result to write $f(x)$ as a product of two factors and then factor completely.

3	1	−4	1	6
		3	−3	−6
	1	−1	−2	0

$f(x) = x^3 - 4x^2 + x + 6 = (x - 3)(x^2 - x - 2) = (x - 3)(x - 2)(x + 1)$

Guided Practice for Example 3

Factor the polynomial completely given that $x - 3$ is a factor.

5. $x^3 - 3x^2 - x + 3$ **6.** $x^3 - 2x^2 - 5x + 6$ **7.** $x^3 - 6x^2 + 11x - 6$

Example 4 Finding zeros of functions

Find the other zeros of $f(x) = x^3 + 2x^2 - x - 2$ given that $f(-1) = 0$.

Because $f(-1) = 0$, $x + 1$ is a factor of f. Use synthetic division to find the other factors.

Use the result to write $f(x)$ as a product of two factors and then factor completely.

−1	1	2	−1	−2
		−1	−1	2
	1	1	−2	0

$f(x) = x^3 + 2x^2 - x - 2 = (x + 1)(x^2 + x - 2) = (x + 1)(x + 2)(x - 1)$

The zeros are -1, -2, and 1.

Guided Practice for Example 4

A polynomial f and one zero of f are given. Find the other zeros of f.

8. $f(x) = x^3 - 3x^2 + 4;\ 2$ **9.** $f(x) = x^3 - x^2 - 4x + 4;\ -2$

LESSON 2.5

Exercise Set A

MM3A3a Find real and complex roots of higher degree polynomial equations using the factor theorem, remainder theorem, rational root theorem, and fundamental theorem of algebra, incorporating complex and radical conjugates.

MM3A3d Solve a variety of types of equations by appropriate means choosing among mental calculation, pencil and paper, or appropriate technology.

Divide using polynomial long division.

1. $(x^2 + 5x - 14) \div (x - 2)$
2. $(x^2 - 2x - 48) \div (x + 5)$
3. $(x^3 + x + 30) \div (x + 3)$
4. $(6x^2 - 5x + 9) \div (2x - 1)$
5. $(8x^3 + 5x^2 - 12x + 10) \div (x^2 - 3)$
6. $(5x^4 + 2x^3 - 9x + 12) \div (x^2 - 3x + 4)$

Divide using synthetic division.

7. $(x^2 + 7x + 12) \div (x + 4)$
8. $(x^3 - 3x^2 + 8x - 5) \div (x - 1)$
9. $(x^4 - 7x^2 + 9x - 10) \div (x - 2)$
10. $(2x^4 - x^3 + 4) \div (x + 1)$
11. $(2x^4 - 11x^3 + 15x^2 + 6x - 18) \div (x - 3)$
12. $(x^4 - 6x^3 - 40x + 33) \div (x - 7)$

A polynomial *f* and a factor of *f* are given. Factor *f* completely.

13. $f(x) = x^3 - 3x^2 - 16x - 12;\ x - 6$
14. $f(x) = x^3 - 12x^2 + 12x + 80;\ x - 10$
15. $f(x) = x^3 - 18x^2 + 95x - 126;\ x - 9$
16. $f(x) = x^3 - x^2 - 21x + 45;\ x + 5$
17. $f(x) = 4x^3 - 4x^2 - 9x + 9;\ x - 1$
18. $f(x) = 3x^3 - 16x^2 - 103x + 36;\ x + 4$

A polynomial *f* and one zero of *f* are given. Find the other zeros of *f*.

19. $f(x) = x^3 + 2x^2 - 20x + 24;\ -6$
20. $f(x) = x^3 + 11x^2 - 150x - 1512;\ -14$
21. $f(x) = 2x^3 + 3x^2 - 39x - 20;\ 4$
22. $f(x) = 15x^3 - 119x^2 - 10x + 16;\ 8$
23. $f(x) = x^3 - 3x^2 - 45x + 175;\ -7$
24. $f(x) = x^3 - 9x^2 - 5x + 45;\ 9$

25. **Geometry** The volume of the box shown at the right is given by $V = 2x^3 - 11x^2 + 10x + 8$. Find an expression for the missing dimension.

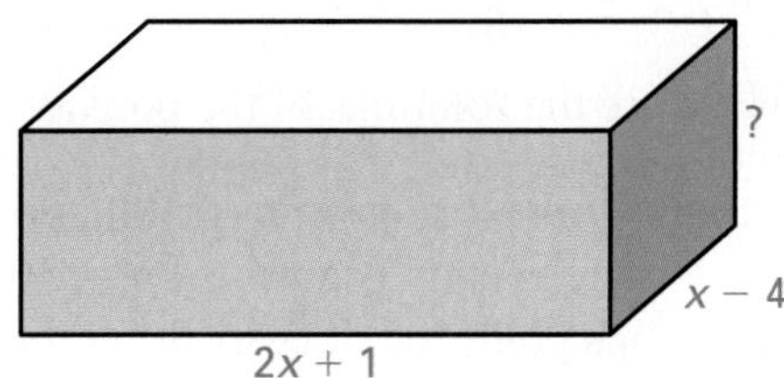

26. **Fuel Consumption** From 1995 to 2002, the total fuel consumption T (in billions of gallons) by cars in the United States and the U.S. population P (in millions) can be modeled by

$$T = -0.003x^3 - 0.02x^2 + 1.3x + 68 \text{ and } P = 3x + 267$$

where x is the number of years since 1995. Write a function for the average amount of fuel consumed by each person from 1995 to 2002.

UNIT 2

LESSON 2.5 **Exercise Set B**

MM3A3a Find real and complex roots of higher degree polynomial equations using the factor theorem, remainder theorem, rational root theorem, and fundamental theorem of algebra, incorporating complex and radical conjugates.

MM3A3d Solve a variety of types of equations by appropriate means choosing among mental calculation, pencil and paper, or appropriate technology.

Divide using polynomial long division.

1. $(4x^3 - 2x^2 + 6x - 1) \div (2x + 3)$

2. $(5x^4 + 8x - 9) \div (x^2 - 4)$

3. $(2x^4 + 2x^3 - 10x - 9) \div (x^3 + x^2 - 5)$

4. $(8x^4 + 2x^2 - 12x + 9) \div (x^2 + x - 3)$

Divide using synthetic division.

5. $(x^4 + 5x^3 - 2x^2 - 4x + 4) \div (x + 3)$

6. $(3x^4 - x^2 + 6x) \div (x - 3)$

7. $(4x + 2x^3 + 7x^2 - 1) \div (x + 1)$

8. $(2x^3 + 3x^5 + 1 - 5x) \div (x - 1)$

A polynomial *f* and a factor of *f* are given. Factor *f* completely.

9. $f(x) = x^3 + 9x^2 - 37x - 165; x - 5$

10. $f(x) = 4x^3 + 8x^2 - 25x - 50; x + 2$

11. $f(x) = 4x^4 + 26x^3 - 8x^2 + 39x - 21; x + 7$

12. $f(x) = 6x^5 - 38x^4 + 12x^3 - 15x^2 + 95x - 30; x - 6$

A polynomial *f* and one zero of *f* are given. Find the other zeros of *f*.

13. $f(x) = 2x^3 + 11x^2 + 9x + 2; -\frac{1}{2}$

14. $f(x) = x^3 + x^2 + 2x + 24; -3$

15. Consider the polynomial function $f(x) = x^3 + 3x^2 - 36x + 32$.

a. Given that $f(4) = 0$, find the other zeros of f.

b. Based on your results from part (a), what are the factors of the polynomial $x^3 + 3x^2 - 36x + 32$?

c. What are the solutions of the polynomial equation $x^3 + 3x^2 - 36x + 32 = 0$?

16. Company Profit The price p (in dollars) that a television manufacturer is able to charge for a television is given by $p = 300 - 8x^2$ where x is the number (in millions) of televisions produced. It costs the company \$175 to make a television.

a. Write an expression for the company's total revenue in terms of x.

b. Write a function for the company's profit P as a function of x.

c. Currently, the company produces 2.5 million televisions and makes a profit of \$187,500,000. Write and solve an equation to find a lesser number of televisions that the company could produce and still yield the same profit.

d. Do all of the solutions in part (c) make sense in this situation? *Explain.*

UNIT 2

LESSON 2.6

Find Rational Zeros

Georgia Performance Standards: MM3A3a, MM3A3d

Goal Find all real zeros of a polynomial function.

Example 1 Find zeros when the leading coefficient is 1

Find all real zeros of $f(x) = x^3 - 7x^2 + 14x - 8$.

The rational root theorem states if $a_n x^n + \cdots + a_1 x + a_0$ has integer coefficients, then every rational zero of f has the form $\frac{p}{q} = \frac{\text{factor of constant term } a_0}{\text{factor of leading coefficient } a_n}$.

STEP 1 **List** the possible rational zeros. The leading coefficient is 1 and the constant term is -8. The possible rational zeros are: $x = \pm 1, \pm 2, \pm 4, \pm 8$

STEP 2 **Test** these zeros using synthetic division. Test $x = 4$:

$$\begin{array}{r|rrrr} 4 & 1 & -7 & 14 & -8 \\ & & 4 & -12 & 8 \\ \hline & 1 & -3 & 2 & 0 \end{array}$$

← 4 is a zero.

Because 4 is a zero of f, write $f(x) = (x - 4)(x^2 - 3x + 2)$.

STEP 3 **Factor** the trinomial and use the factor theorem.

$f(x) = (x - 4)(x^2 - 3x + 2) = (x - 4)(x - 2)(x - 1)$

The zeros are 1, 2, and 4.

Example 2 Find zeros when the leading coefficient is not 1

Find all real zeros of $f(x) = 3x^3 - 17x^2 + 18x + 8$.

STEP 1 **List** the possible rational zeros of f: $x = \pm 1, \pm 2, \pm 4, \pm 8, \pm\frac{1}{3}, \pm\frac{2}{3}, \pm\frac{4}{3}, \pm\frac{8}{3}$

STEP 2 **Choose** a reasonable value to check using the graph of the function.

STEP 3 **Check** $x = -\frac{1}{3}$:

$$\begin{array}{r|rrrr} -\frac{1}{3} & 3 & -17 & 18 & 8 \\ & & -1 & 6 & -8 \\ \hline & 3 & -18 & 24 & 0 \end{array}$$

← $-\frac{1}{3}$ is a zero.

STEP 4 **Factor** out a binomial using the result of synthetic division.

$$\begin{aligned} f(x) &= \left(x + \frac{1}{3}\right)(3x^2 - 18x + 24) \\ &= \left(x + \frac{1}{3}\right)(3)(x^2 - 6x + 8) \\ &= (3x + 1)(x - 2)(x - 4) \end{aligned}$$

The real zeros of f are $-\frac{1}{3}$, 2, and 4.

UNIT 2

Georgia Performance Standards

MM3A3a Find real and complex roots of higher degree polynomial equations using the factor theorem, remainder theorem, rational root theorem, and fundamental theorem of algebra, incorporating complex and radical conjugates.

MM3A3d Solve a variety of types of equations by appropriate means choosing among mental calculation, pencil and paper, or appropriate technology. 

Guided Practice for Examples 1 and 2

Find all real zeros of the function.

1. $f(x) = x^3 + x^2 - 4x - 4$

2. $f(x) = x^3 + 2x^2 - 11x - 12$

3. $f(x) = 2x^3 - 5x^2 + x + 2$

4. $g(x) = x^3 - 3x^2 - x + 3$

5. $g(x) = x^3 - 2x^2 - 5x + 6$

6. $g(x) = x^3 - 6x^2 + 11x - 6$

Example 3 Solve a multi-step problem

Desk Organizer The length of a rectangular desk organizer is 4 inches greater than the width. The height is $\frac{1}{3}$ of the width and the volume is 21 cubic inches. What are the dimensions of the organizer?

STEP 1 **Write** an equation for the volume of the organizer.

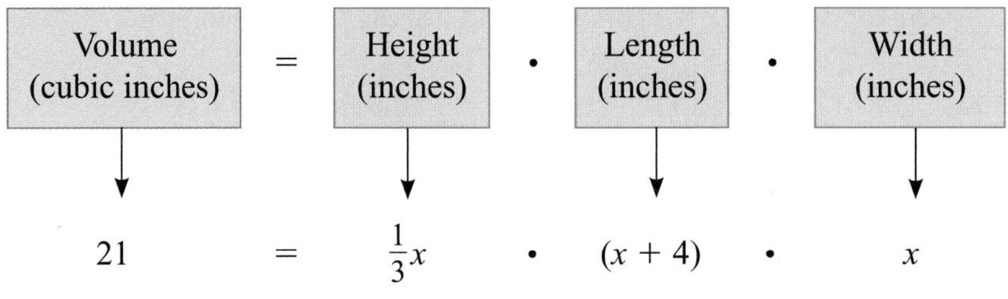

$$21 = \frac{1}{3}x \cdot (x + 4) \cdot x$$

$63 = x^3 + 4x^2$ Multiply each side by 3 and simplify.

$0 = x^3 + 4x^2 - 63$ Subtract 63 from each side.

STEP 2 **List** the possible rational solutions: $\pm1, \pm3, \pm7, \pm9, \pm21, \pm63$

STEP 3 **Test** the possible rational solutions. Only positive x-values make sense.

$$\begin{array}{r|rrrr} 3 & 1 & 4 & 0 & -63 \\ & & 3 & 21 & 63 \\ \hline & 1 & 7 & 21 & 0 \end{array}$$

$\leftarrow$ 3 is a solution.

STEP 4 **Check** for other solutions. The other solutions are imaginary numbers and can be discarded.

The width is 3 inches, the length is $3 + 4 = 7$ inches, and the height is $\frac{1}{3}(3) = 1$ inch.

Guided Practice for Example 3

7. A pyramid has a square base with sides of length x, a height of $x - 2$, and a volume of 3. Write a polynomial equation to model the situation. List the possible rational solutions of the equation, and then find the dimensions of the pyramid.

LESSON 2.6

Exercise Set A

MM3A3a Find real and complex roots of higher degree polynomial equations using the factor theorem, remainder theorem, rational root theorem, and fundamental theorem of algebra, incorporating complex and radical conjugates.

MM3A3d Solve a variety of types of equations by appropriate means choosing among mental calculation, pencil and paper, or appropriate technology.

List the possible rational zeros of the function using the rational root theorem.

1. $f(x) = x^4 - 6x^3 + 8x^2 - 21$

2. $h(x) = 2x^3 + 7x^2 - 7x + 30$

3. $h(x) = 5x^4 + 12x^3 - 16x^2 + 10$

4. $g(x) = 9x^5 + 3x^3 + 7x - 4$

Find all real zeros of the function.

5. $f(x) = x^3 - 3x^2 - 6x + 8$

6. $g(x) = x^3 + 4x^2 - x - 4$

7. $f(x) = x^3 + 72 - 5x^2 - 18x$

8. $f(x) = x^3 + x^2 - 2x - 2$

Use the graph to shorten the list of possible rational zeros of the function. Then find all real zeros of the function.

9. $f(x) = 4x^3 - 8x^2 - 15x + 9$

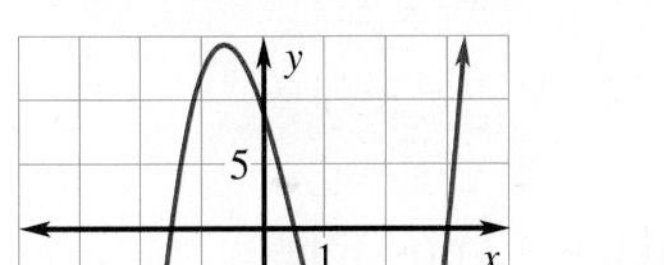

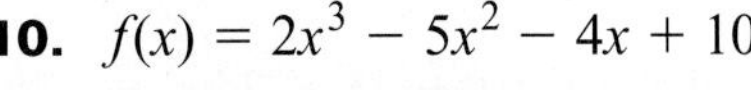

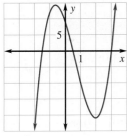

10. $f(x) = 2x^3 - 5x^2 - 4x + 10$

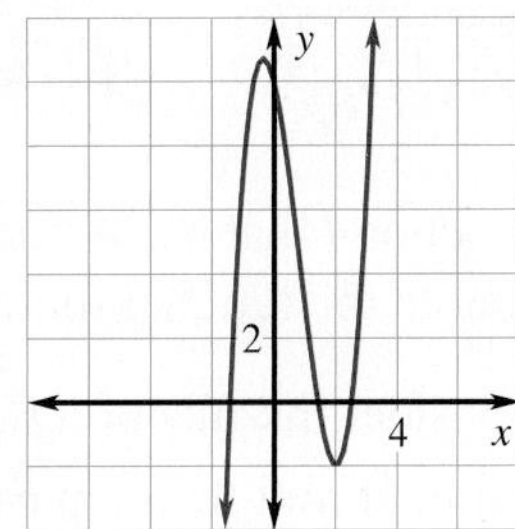

Find all real zeros of the function.

11. $g(x) = 2x^3 + 4x^2 - 2x - 4$

12. $f(x) = 2x^3 - 5x^2 - 14x + 8$

13. $h(x) = 2x^4 + 5x^3 - 5x^2 - 5x + 3$

14. $f(x) = 2x^4 + 3x^3 - 6x^2 - 6x + 4$

15. Mail From 1995 to 2003, the amount of mail M (in billions of pieces) handled by the U.S. Postal Service can be modeled by $M = 0.05(t^4 - 18t^3 + 89t^2 - 32t + 3680)$ where t is the number of years since 1995. In which year were there about 204,000,000,000 pieces of mail handled?

a. Write a polynomial equation that can be used to answer the question.

b. List the possible whole-number solutions of the equation in part (a) that are less than or equal to 8.

c. Use synthetic division to determine which of the possible solutions in part (b) is an actual solution. Then answer the question in the problem statement.

d. Use a graphing calculator to graph and identify any additional real solutions of the equation that are reasonable.

LESSON 2.6 **Exercise Set B**

MM3A3a Find real and complex roots of higher degree polynomial equations using the factor theorem, remainder theorem, rational root theorem, and fundamental theorem of algebra, incorporating complex and radical conjugates.

MM3A3d Solve a variety of types of equations by appropriate means choosing among mental calculation, pencil and paper, or appropriate technology.

Find all real zeros of the function.

1. $f(x) = x^3 - 4x^2 - 7x + 10$
2. $g(x) = x^5 - x^4 - 7x^3 + 11x^2 - 8x + 12$
3. $h(x) = x^4 + 4x^3 + x^2 - 8x - 6$
4. $g(x) = x^3 + 2x^2 - 34x + 7$
5. $f(x) = x^4 + 4x^3 - 14x^2 - 20x - 3$
6. $h(x) = x^5 + 15x^4 + 72x^3 + 80x^2 - 225x - 375$
7. $h(x) = 24x^4 - 26x^3 - 45x^2 - x + 6$
8. $f(x) = 8x^3 + 28x^2 + 14x - 15$
9. $f(x) = 18x^5 + 51x^4 - 60x + 75 - 34x^3 - 178x^2$
10. $g(x) = 6x^5 - 116x^3 - x^4 - 53x^2 + 24 + 50x$
11. Write a polynomial function f that has a leading coefficient of 6 and has 12 possible rational zeros according to the rational root theorem.
12. **Critical Thinking** Consider the function $f(x) = 2x^4 + 5x^3 - 21x^2 - 36x$.
    a. *Explain* why the rational root theorem cannot be directly applied to this function.
    b. Factor out the common monomial factor of f.
    c. Apply the rational root theorem to find all the real zeros of f.
    d. Find all the real zeros of $f(x) = 3x^5 - x^4 - 6x^3 + 2x^2$.
13. **Critical Thinking** Consider the functions
    $f(x) = x^3 + 2x^2 - 19x - 20$, $g(x) = -x^3 - 2x^2 + 19x + 20$,
    $h(x) = 2x^3 + 4x^2 - 38x - 40$, and $j(x) = 4x^3 + 8x^2 - 76x - 80$.
    a. Use the rational root theorem to find all of the real zeros of each function.
    b. Note that $g(x) = -f(x)$, $h(x) = 2f(x)$, and $j(x) = 4f(x)$. What can you conclude about the zeros of $f(x)$ and $af(x)$?
    c. *Explain* why the rational root theorem cannot be directly applied to
    $f(x) = \frac{4}{3}x^3 + 3x^2 - \frac{10}{3}x - 1$.
    d. Use the conclusion from part (b) to find the real zeros of the function in part (c).

UNIT 2

Georgia Performance Standards

MM3A1b Understand the effects of the following on the graph of a polynomial function: degree, lead coefficient, and multiplicity of real zeros. 

MM3A1d Investigate and explain characteristics of polynomial functions, including domain and range, intercepts, zeros, relative and absolute extrema, intervals of increase and decrease, and end behavior. 

MM3A3a Find real and complex roots of higher degree polynomial equations using the factor theorem, remainder theorem, rational root theorem, and fundamental theorem of algebra, incorporating complex and radical conjugates.

Investigating Math Activity

Zeros of a Polynomial Function

Use before Lesson 2.7

Materials graphing calculator

Question

How many zeros can a polynomial function have?

Explore

Find the zeros of a function.

Graph the function $y = x^2 + 2x - 8$ on a graphing calculator and determine the number of zeros of the function.

STEP 1 Enter the function in the equation editor window.

STEP 2 Set the screen to a standard viewing window.

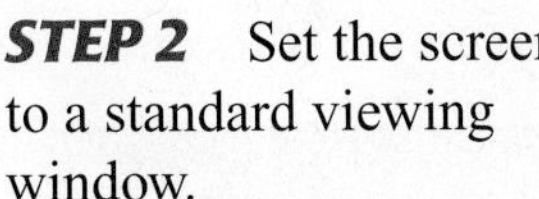

STEP 3 Use the graph to determine the number of zeros.

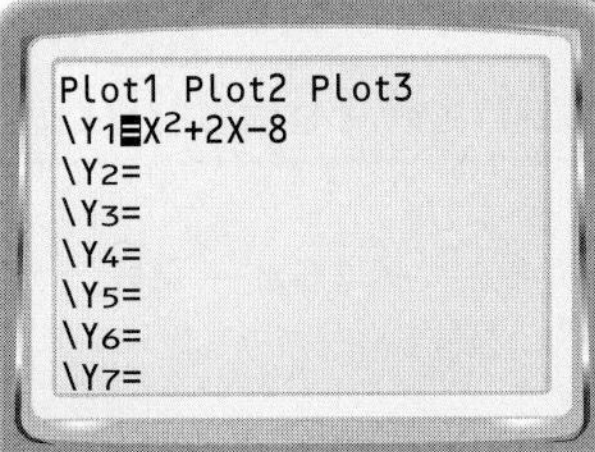

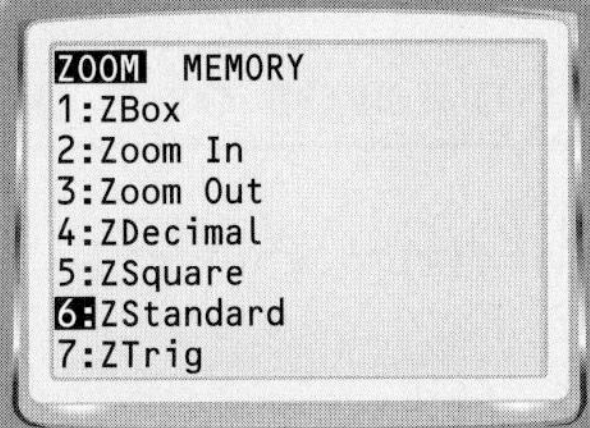

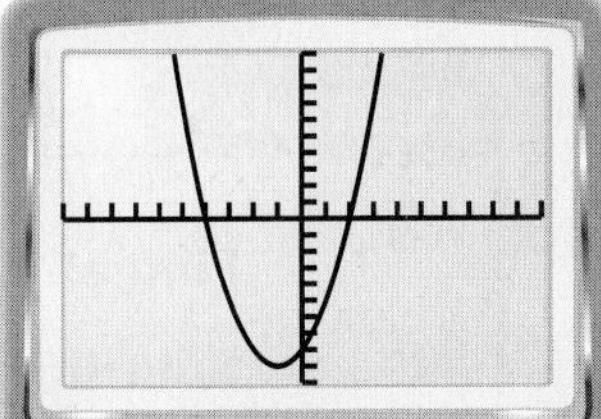

STEP 4 Look at the function and determine its degree.

Draw Conclusions

1. Determine the number of zeros and the degree of each function.

 a. $y = x^2 + 2x - 8$

 b. $y = x^3 + 5x^2 + 4x - 3$

 c. $y = x^4 + 6x^3 - 3x^2 - 8x + 1$

2. Reasoning What relationship do you notice between the degree of a function and the number of zeros of the function?

LESSON 2.7

Apply the Fundamental Theorem of Algebra

Georgia Performance Standards: MM3A3a, MM3A3d

Goal Classify the zeros of polynomial functions.

Vocabulary

When a factor of a polynomial appears more than once, you can count its solution more than once. The repeated factor produces a **repeated solution.**

The Fundamental Theorem of Algebra: If $f(x)$ is a polynomial of degree n where $n > 0$, then the equation $f(x) = 0$ has at least one solution in the set of complex numbers.

Corollary to the Fundamental Theorem of Algebra: If $f(x)$ is a polynomial of degree n where $n > 0$, then the equation $f(x) = 0$ has exactly n solutions provided each solution repeated twice is counted as 2 solutions, each solution repeated three times is counted as 3 solutions, and so on.

Complex Conjugates Theorem: If f is a polynomial function with real coefficients, and $a + bi$ is an imaginary zero of f, then $a - bi$ is also a zero of f.

Irrational Conjugates Theorem: Suppose f is a polynomial function with rational coefficients, and a and b are rational numbers such that $\sqrt{b}$ is irrational. If $a + \sqrt{b}$ is a zero of f, then $a - \sqrt{b}$ is also a zero of f.

Descartes' Rule of Signs: Let $f(x) = a_nx^n + a_{n-1}x^{n-1} + \cdots + a_2x^2 + a_1x + a_0$ be a polynomial function with real coefficients. The number of *positive real zeros* of f is equal to the number of changes in sign of the coefficients of $f(x)$ or is less than this by an even number. The number of *negative real zeros* of f is equal to the number of changes in sign of the coefficients of $f(-x)$ or is less than this by an even number.

Example 1 Find the zeros of a polynomial function

Find all zeros of $f(x) = x^5 - x^4 - 7x^3 + 11x^2 + 16x - 20$.

Solution

STEP 1 **Find** the rational zeros of f. The possible rational zeros are: $x = \pm 1, \pm 2, \pm 4, \pm 5, \pm 10$, and ± 20. Using synthetic division you find that -2 is a zero repeated twice and 1 is also a zero.

STEP 2 **Write** $f(x)$ in factored form. Dividing f by its known factors $x + 2$, $x + 2$, and $x - 1$ gives a quotient of $x^2 - 4x + 5$.
So, $f(x) = (x - 1)(x + 2)^2(x^2 - 4x + 5)$.

STEP 3 **Find** the complex zeros of f. Use the quadratic formula to factor the trinomial into linear factors.

$$f(x) = (x - 1)(x + 2)^2[x - (2 + i)][x - (2 - i)]$$

The zeros are $-2, -2, 1, 2 + i$, and $2 - i$.

Georgia Performance Standards

MM3A3a Find real and complex roots of higher degree polynomial equations using the factor theorem, remainder theorem, rational root theorem, and fundamental theorem of algebra, incorporating complex and radical conjugates. 

MM3A3d Solve a variety of types of equations by appropriate means choosing among mental calculation, pencil and paper, or appropriate technology. 

Example 2 Use zeros to write a polynomial function

Write a polynomial function of least degree that has rational coefficients, a leading coefficient of 1, and 4 and $1 + \sqrt{2}$ as zeros.

By the irrational conjugates theorem, $1 - \sqrt{2}$ is a zero. Use the zeros and the factor theorem to write $f(x)$ as a product of three factors.

$f(x) = (x - 4)[x - (1 + \sqrt{2})][x - (1 - \sqrt{2})]$	Write $f(x)$ in factored form.
$= (x - 4)[(x - 1) - \sqrt{2}][(x - 1) + \sqrt{2}]$	Regroup terms.
$= (x - 4)[(x - 1)^2 - (\sqrt{2})^2]$	Multiply.
$= (x - 4)(x^2 - 2x - 1)$	Simplify.
$= x^3 - 6x^2 + 7x + 4$	Write in standard form.

Example 3 Solve a polynomial equation

Determine the possible numbers of positive real zeros, negative real zeros, and imaginary zeros for $f(x) = x^4 + 2x^3 - x^2 + 3x + 5$.

The coefficients of $f(x) = x^4 + 2x^3 - x^2 + 3x + 5$ have 2 sign changes, so f has 2 or 0 positive real zero(s).

$f(-x) = (-x)^4 + 2(-x)^3 - (-x)^2 + 3(-x) + 5 = x^4 - 2x^3 - x^2 - 3x + 5$

The coefficients in $f(-x)$ have 2 sign changes, so f has 2 or 0 negative real zero(s).

The function has a total of 4 zeros, so the possible combinations are 2 positive real zeros and 2 negative real zeros, 2 positive real zeros and 2 imaginary zeros, 2 negative real zeros and 2 imaginary zeros, or 4 imaginary zeros.

Guided Practice for Examples 1, 2, and 3

Find all zeros of the function.

1. $f(x) = x^3 - 2x^2 + 3x - 2$

2. $f(x) = x^4 - 4x^3 + 5x^2 - 2x - 12$

Write a polynomial function *f* of least degree that has rational coefficients, a leading coefficient of 1, and the given zeros.

3. $-2, -1, 1$

4. $i, 4$

5. $i, 2 - \sqrt{3}$

Determine the possible numbers of positive real zeros, negative real zeros, and imaginary zeros for the function.

6. $g(x) = x^3 + x^2 - 3x - 7$

7. $h(x) = x^4 - 3x^3 + 4x - 2$

LESSON 2.7

Exercise Set A

MM3A3a Find real and complex roots of higher degree polynomial equations using the factor theorem, remainder theorem, rational root theorem, and fundamental theorem of algebra, incorporating complex and radical conjugates.

MM3A3d Solve a variety of types of equations by appropriate means choosing among mental calculation, pencil and paper, or appropriate technology.

Identify the number of solutions or zeros.

1. $f(x) = 5x^3 - 6x^2 + 2x - 3$

2. $g(s) = 8s^6 - 3s^4 - 11s^3 - 2s^2 + 4$

3. $-3y^7 + 5y^5 - 12y + 2 = 6$

4. $4 - 7x = x^2 - 3x^5$

Find all the zeros of the polynomial function.

5. $h(x) = x^3 - 3x^2 - x + 3$

6. $f(x) = x^4 - 4x^3 - 20x^2 + 48x$

7. $g(x) = x^3 + 5x^2 + x + 5$

8. $g(x) = x^4 - 9x^3 + 23x^2 - 81x + 126$

9. $f(x) = x^3 - x^2 - 11x + 3$

10. $h(x) = 2x^4 + x^3 + x^2 + x - 1$

Write a polynomial function *f* of least degree that has rational coefficients, a leading coefficient of 1, and the given zeros.

11. $-7, -4$

12. $1, 2, 5$

13. $-3, 0, 1$

14. $4, i, -i$

15. $-5, 0, -2i, 2i$

16. $8, 2 + i$

17. **Error Analysis** *Describe* and correct the error in writing a polynomial function with rational coefficients and zeros 3 and $2 + i$.

$$\begin{aligned} f(x) &= (x - 3)[x - (2 + i)] \\ &= x(x - 2 - i) - 3(x - 2 - i) \\ &= x^2 - 2x - ix - 3x + 6 + 3i \\ &= x^2 - (5 + i)x + (6 + 3i) \end{aligned}$$

X

Use a graphing calculator to graph the function. Then use the *zero* (or *root*) feature to approximate the real zeros of the function.

18. $g(x) = x^3 - x^2 - 5x + 3$

19. $h(x) = 2x^3 - x^2 - 3x - 1$

20. $f(x) = x^4 - 2x - 1$

21. $g(x) = x^4 - x^3 - 20x^2 + 10x + 27$

22. **Sporting Goods** For 1998 through 2005, the sales S (in billions of dollars) of sporting goods can be modeled by $S = 0.007t^3 + 0.1t^2 + 1.4t + 70$ where t is the number of years since 1998. In which year were sales about \$78 billion?

23. **Grocery Store Revenue** For the 25 years that a grocery store has been open, its annual revenue R (in millions of dollars) can be modeled by

$$R = \frac{1}{10{,}000}(-t^4 + 12t^3 - 77t^2 + 600t + 13{,}650)$$

where t is the number of years since the opening of the store. In what year(s) was the revenue about \$1.5 million?

UNIT 2

LESSON 2.7 **Exercise Set B**

MM3A3a Find real and complex roots of higher degree polynomial equations using the factor theorem, remainder theorem, rational root theorem, and fundamental theorem of algebra, incorporating complex and radical conjugates.

MM3A3d Solve a variety of types of equations by appropriate means choosing among mental calculation, pencil and paper, or appropriate technology.

Find all the zeros of the polynomial function.

1. $f(x) = x^4 + 4x^3 - 6x^2 - 36x - 27$

2. $h(x) = x^4 - 4x^3 + 4x - 1$

3. $g(x) = 2x^5 - 4x^4 - 2x^3 + 28x^2$

4. $g(x) = 2x^4 - x^3 - 42x^2 + 16x + 160$

5. $h(x) = 2x^4 - 7x^3 - 27x^2 + 63x + 81$

6. $f(x) = x^3 + 2x^2 + 4x - 7$

7. $g(x) = x^4 + 2x^3 + 2x - 1$
(*Hint:* $-i$ is a zero.)

8. $h(x) = x^4 - 2x^3 + 14x^2 + 6x - 51$
(*Hint:* $1 + 4i$ is a zero.)

Write a polynomial function *f* of least degree that has rational coefficients, a leading coefficient of 2, and the given zeros.

9. $-4, 0, 2, 4$

10. $2i, -2i, 5i, -5i$

11. $-5, \sqrt{3}$

12. $0, 3 + 4i$

13. $1, 2, 4 + \sqrt{2}$

14. $0, 3, i, 5 - 2i$

Determine the possible numbers of positive real zeros, negative real zeros, and imaginary zeros for the function.

15. $h(x) = x^3 - 4x^2 + 5x + 9$

16. $g(x) = x^4 + 3x^2 - 10x + 16$

17. $f(x) = x^5 - 6x^4 - 3x^3 + 7x^2 - 8x + 1$

18. $g(x) = x^{10} - x^8 + x^6 - x^4 + x^2 - 1$

Use a graphing calculator to graph the function. Then use the *zero* (or *root*) feature to approximate the real zeros of the function.

19. $g(x) = x^4 + 3x^2 - 2$

20. $h(x) = x^5 + 12x^3 - 4x^2 + 16x + 25$

21. $f(x) = -x^6 + 4x^5 - 2x^2 + 9$

22. $g(x) = 3x^6 + 5x^5 - 30x^4 - 37x^3 - 25x^2$

23. Critical Thinking The graph of a polynomial of degree 5 has four distinct x-intercepts. What can be said about one of its zeros? Sketch a graph of this situation.

24. Critical Thinking Find a counterexample to disprove the following statement.
The polynomial function of least degree with integer coefficients and zeros at $x = -4$, $x = 2$, and $x = 5$ is unique.

25. **College Tuition** For 1998 through 2005, the enrollment E and cost of tuition T (in dollars) can be modeled by

$E = -29.881t^2 + 190t + 4935$ and $T = 10.543t^3 - 118.83t^2 + 921t + 9979$

where t is the number of years since 1998.

a. Write a model that represents the total tuition R brought in by the college in a given year.

b. In which year did the college take in \$62,638,000 in tuition?

UNIT 2

LESSON 2.8

Analyze Graphs of Polynomial Functions

Georgia Performance Standards: MM3A1b, MM3A1d

Goal Use intercepts to graph polynomial functions.

Vocabulary

The graph of a polynomial function of degree n has *at most* $n - 1$ turning points.

The y-coordinate of a turning point is a **local maximum** of the function if the point is higher than all nearby points. The y-coordinate of a turning point is a **local minimum** of the function if the point is lower than all nearby points.

The **multiplicity of a root** is the number of times a given polynomial equation has a value as a root. For the polynomial equation $f(x) = 0$, k is a repeated solution, or a root with a multiplicity greater than 1, if and only if the factor $x - k$ has an exponent greater than 1 when $f(x)$ is factored completely. If the exponent is odd, the graph of f crosses the x-axis at the zero. If the exponent is even, the graph of f touches the x-axis at the zero.

UNIT 2

Example 1 Use x-intercepts to graph a polynomial function

Graph the function $f(x) = 0.2(x - 3)^2(x + 1)^2$.

STEP 1 **Plot** the x-intercepts, $(-1, 0)$ and $(3, 0)$.

STEP 2 **Plot** points between and beyond the x-intercepts.

x	−2	0	1	2	4
y	5	1.8	3.2	1.8	5

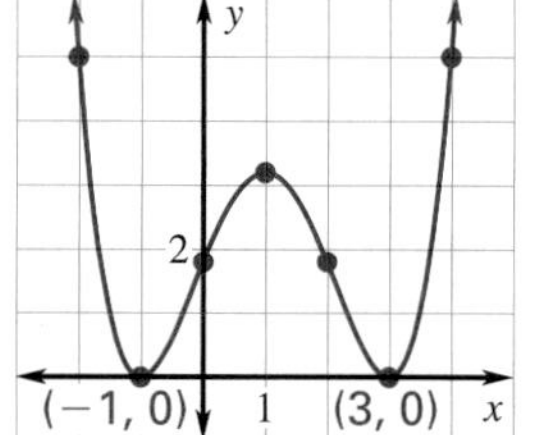

STEP 3 **Determine** end behavior and multiplicity. Because f has four factors of the form $x - k$ and a constant factor of 0.2, it is a quartic function with a positive leading coefficient. So, $f(x) \to +\infty$ as $x \to -\infty$ and $f(x) \to +\infty$ as $x \to +\infty$. The zeros -1 and 3 are both repeated twice. So, the graph of f touches the x-axis at $(-1, 0)$ and $(3, 0)$.

STEP 4 **Draw** the graph so that it passes through the plotted points and has the appropriate end behavior.

Example 2 Find turning points

Graph the function $h(x) = -x^4 - 2x^3 + 3x^2 + 4x - 4$. Identify the x-intercepts and the points where the local maximums and local minimums occur.

Use a graphing calculator to graph the function. The graph of h has two x-intercepts and three turning points. Use the calculator's *zero*, *minimum*, and *maximum* features to approximate the coordinates of the points. The x-intercepts are $x = -2$ and $x = 1$. The function has a local minimum at $(-0.5, -5.0625)$. The function has local maximums at $(-2, 0)$ and $(1, 0)$.

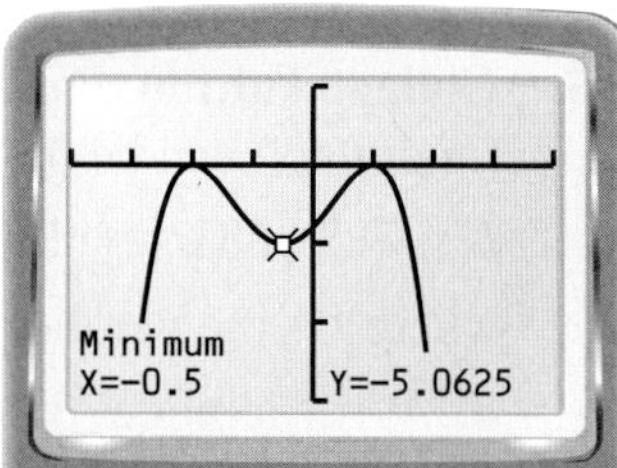

Georgia Performance Standards

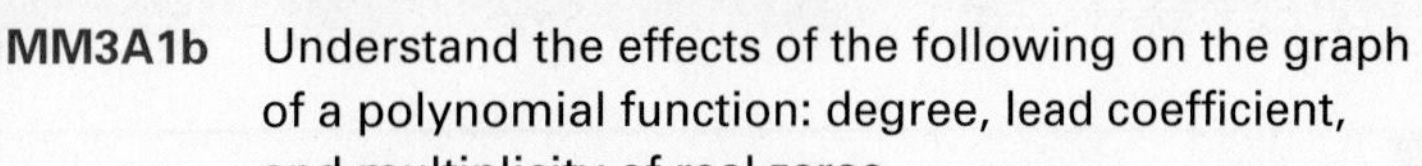

MM3A1b Understand the effects of the following on the graph of a polynomial function: degree, lead coefficient, and multiplicity of real zeros. 

MM3A1d Investigate and explain characteristics of polynomial functions, including domain and range, intercepts, zeros, relative and absolute extrema, intervals of increase and decrease, and end behavior. 

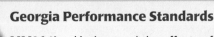

Example 3 Maximize a polynomial model

Metal Box You are making an open rectangular box out of a 4-inch by 12-inch piece of metal. The box will be formed by making the cuts shown in the diagram and folding up the sides so that the flaps are square. You want the box to have the greatest volume possible.

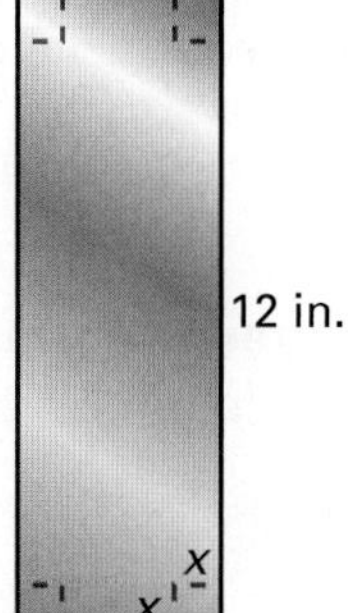

- How long should you make the cuts?
- What is the maximum volume?
- What will be the dimensions of the finished box?

Solution

Write a verbal model for the volume. Then write a function.

Volume (cubic inches)	=	Length (inches)	•	Width (inches)	•	Height (inches)
V	=	$(12 - 2x)$	•	$(4 - 2x)$	•	x

$= (48 - 32x + 4x^2)\,x$ Use FOIL method.

$= 4x^3 - 32x^2 + 48x$ Write in standard form.

To find the maximum volume, graph the volume function on a graphing calculator using $0 < x < 2$ from the physical restrictions on the size of the flaps. From the graph, you can see that the maximum is about 20.2 and occurs when $x \approx 0.9$.

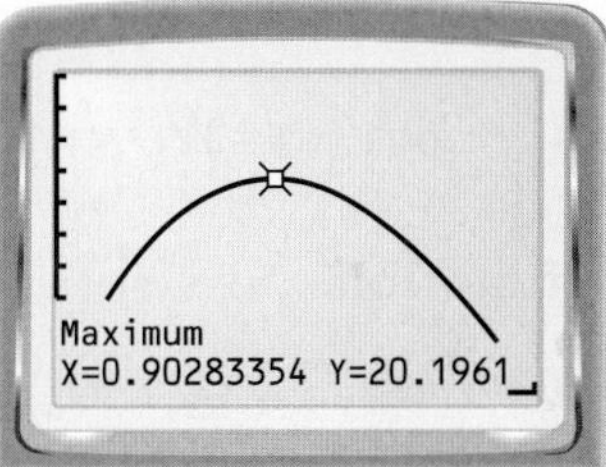

The maximum volume is about 20.2 cubic inches. The dimensions of the box are about 10.2 inches, by 2.2 inches by 0.9 inch.

Guided Practice for Examples 1, 2 and 3

Graph the function. Identify the *x*-intercepts and the points where the local maximums and local minimums occur.

1. $f(x) = \frac{1}{2}x^3 - 6x - 8$

2. $f(x) = x^3 + 5x^2 + 7x + 3$

3. In Example 3, how do the answers change if the piece of metal is 6 inches by 12 inches?

LESSON 2.8 **Exercise Set A**

MM3A1b Understand the effects of the following on the graph of a polynomial function: degree, lead coefficient, and multiplicity of real zeros.

MM3A1d Investigate and explain characteristics of polynomial functions, including domain and range, intercepts, zeros, relative and absolute extrema, intervals of increase and decrease, and end behavior.

1. Error Analysis *Describe* and correct the error in the following statement.

If -6 is a solution of the polynomial equation $f(x) = 0$, then -6 is a factor of $f(x)$.

For the given degree *n* of a polynomial function, determine the maximum number of turns in the graph of the function.

2. $n = 3$ **3.** $n = 5$ **4.** $n = 2$ **5.** $n = 4$

Determine the *x*-intercepts of the function.

6. $g(x) = (x + 3)(x - 2)(x - 5)$

7. $h(x) = (x + 4)(x - 6)(x - 8)$

8. $f(x) = (x + 3)^2(x - 2)$

9. $f(x) = (x + 5)(x + 1)(x - 7)$

10. $g(x) = (x + 6)^3(x + 2)$

11. $h(x) = (x - 8)^5$

Find all the real zeros of the function. Then determine the multiplicity of each zero and the exact number of turning points of the graph.

12. $f(x) = x^2(x + 1)$

13. $g(x) = (x + 2)^2(x - 5)$

14. $h(x) = (x - 4)^3(x - 1)$

15. $f(x) = (x + 6)^2(3x - 2)^2$

16. $g(x) = x(4x + 3)(x - 8)^2$

17. $h(x) = x^2(x + 4)(2x - 3)^3$

Graph the function.

18. $f(x) = (x - 3)(x + 2)(x + 1)$

19. $g(x) = (x - 3)^2(x + 2)$

20. $h(x) = 0.3(x + 6)(x - 1)(x - 4)$

21. $g(x) = \frac{5}{6}(x + 1)^2(x - 1)(x - 4)$

22. $h(x) = (x - 1)(x^2 + x + 1)$

23. $f(x) = (x + 2)(x^2 + 2x + 2)$

Estimate the coordinates of each turning point and state whether each corresponds to a local maximum or a local minimum. Then estimate all real zeros and determine the least degree the function can have.

24.

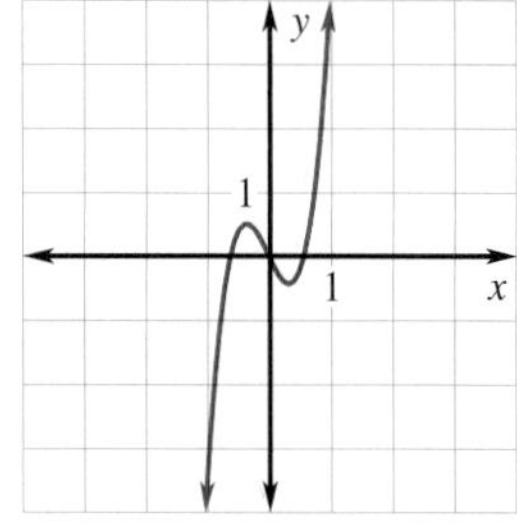

25.

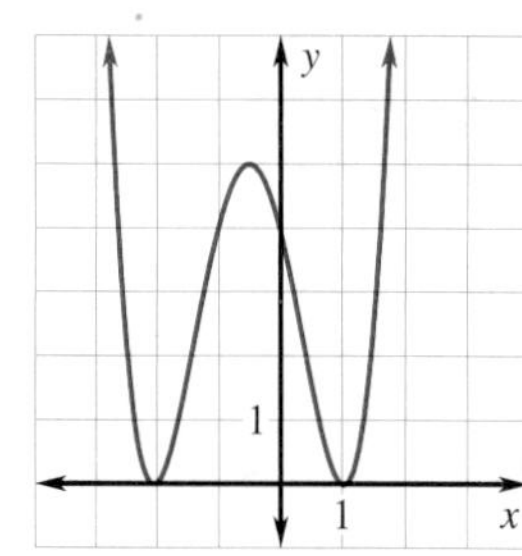

26.

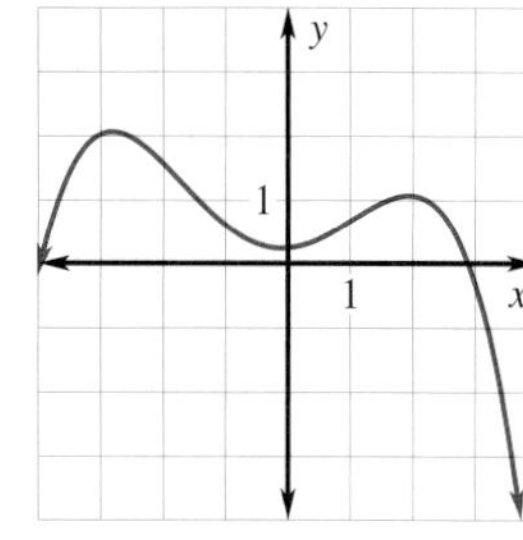

Exercise Set A *(continued)*

Use a graphing calculator to graph the function. Identify the *x*-intercepts and points where local maximums or local minimums occur.

27. $f(x) = 3x^3 - 9x + 1$

28. $h(x) = -\frac{1}{3}x^3 + x - \frac{2}{3}$

29. $g(x) = -\frac{1}{4}x^4 + 2x^2$

30. $f(x) = x^5 - 6x^3 + 9x$

31. $h(x) = x^5 - 5x^3 + 4x$

32. $g(x) = x^4 - 2x^3 - 3x^2 + 5x + 2$

In Exercises 33 and 34, assume that the box is constructed using the method illustrated in Example 3 on page 99.

33. **Jewelry** Lila wants to make a box to hold her jewelry from a piece of metal that is 8 inches by 10 inches. What is the maximum volume of the box? What are the dimensions of the box with the maximum volume?

34. **DVDs** Chris is making a box for his DVD collection from a piece of cardboard that is 24 inches by 30 inches. What is the maximum volume of the box? What are the dimensions of the box with the maximum volume?

35. **Food** The average number E of eggs eaten per person each year in the United States from 1970 to 2000 can be modeled by

$$E = 0.000944t^4 - 0.052t^3 + 0.95t^2 - 9.4t + 308$$

where t is the number of years since 1970.

a. Graph the function.

b. Identify any turning points on the domain $0 \leq t \leq 30$. What real-life meaning do these points have?

36. **Quonset Huts** A Quonset hut is a dwelling shaped like half a cylinder. You have 600 square feet of material with which to build a Quonset hut.

a. The formula for the surface area of the hut is $S = \pi r^2 + \pi r\ell$ where r is the radius of the semicircle and ℓ is the length of the hut. Substitute 600 for S and then write an equation that gives ℓ in terms of r.

b. The formula for the volume of the hut is $V = \frac{1}{2}\pi r^2 \ell$. Write an equation for the volume V of the Quonset hut as a polynomial function of r by substituting the expression for ℓ from part (a) into the volume formula.

c. Graph the volume function from part (b). Use the function from part (b) to find the maximum volume of a Quonset hut with a surface area of 600 square feet. What are the hut's dimensions?

LESSON 2.8

Exercise Set B

MM3A1b Understand the effects of the following on the graph of a polynomial function: degree, lead coefficient, and multiplicity of real zeros.

MM3A1d Investigate and explain characteristics of polynomial functions, including domain and range, intercepts, zeros, relative and absolute extrema, intervals of increase and decrease, and end behavior.

For the given degree *n* of a polynomial function, determine the maximum number of turns in the graph of the function.

1. $n = 9$

2. $n = 6$

FInd all the real zeros of the function. Then determine the multiplicity of each zero and the exact number of turning points of the graph.

3. $f(x) = (x + 2)^2(3 - x)(2x - 9)$

4. $g(x) = (x + 4)^2(3x - 5)^2$

5. $h(x) = x^3(x^2 - 1)(x + 1)$

6. $f(x) = -x(x + 6)(x + 3)(2x - 1)^2$

7. $g(x) = x^4 + x^3 - 10x^2 - 4x + 24$

8. $h(x) = 2x^5 + 9x^4 + 9x^3 - 8x^2 - 12x$

Graph the function and state the domain and range.

9. $f(x) = (x + 1)(x^2 + 1)$

10. $g(x) = x(x + 2)^2(x - 1)^2$

11. $h(x) = (x - 1)(x + 1)^3(x - 2)^2$

12. $h(x) = -x^2(x - 3)(x - 2)^3$

13. $g(x) = x(x + 1)(x - 1)^2(x - 3)^3$

14. $f(x) = x^3(x + 3)^2(x^2 + x + 2)$

15. $f(x) = x^2(x + 1)(x - 1)^2(x - 3)^3$

16. $g(x) = (x + 7)^2(x + 4)^2(x + 2)^3$

Estimate the coordinates of each turning point and state whether each corresponds to a local maximum or a local minimum. Then estimate all real zeros and determine the least degree of the function.

17.

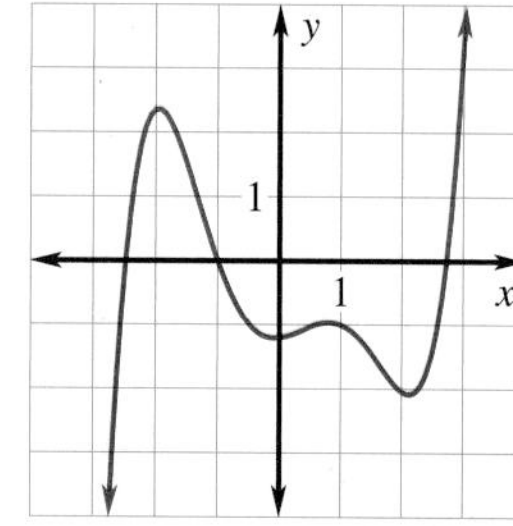

18.

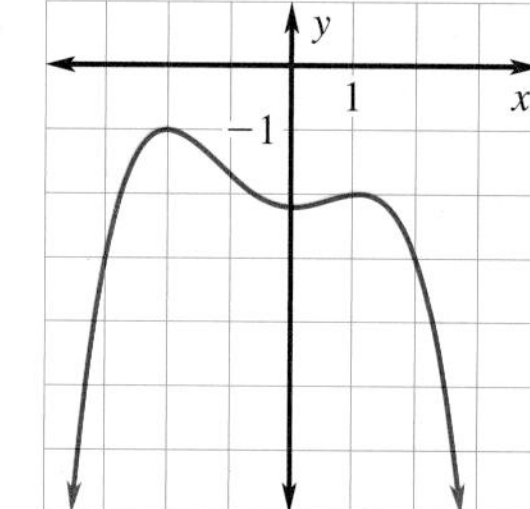

19.

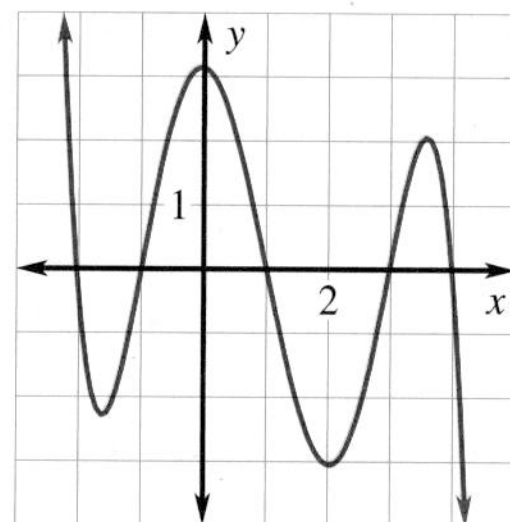

Use a graphing calculator to graph the function. Identify the *x*-intercepts and points where local maximums or local minimums occur.

20. $f(x) = x^5 - 2x^4 - x^3 + 3x + 1$

21. $g(x) = 3x^3 - 6x + x^4$

22. $g(x) = 3x^4 + 4x^3 - 3$

23. $f(x) = x^5 - 5x^3 + 4x$

24. $h(x) = -\frac{1}{5}x^5 - \frac{7}{8} + x^2$

25. $f(x) = x^4 + 2.6x^3 - 10.56x^2 + 7.2x$

UNIT 2

Exercise Set B *(continued)*

26. **Critical Thinking** Does a quartic function *always, sometimes,* or *never* have a turning point? *Justify* your answer.

27. **Critical Thinking** Write a cubic function, a quartic function, and a fifth-degree polynomial function whose graphs have x-intercepts only at $x = -1$, 3, and 4.

Consider the graphs $f(x) = (x + 1)^n$ where $n = 1, 2, 3, 4,$ and 5.

28. What is the x-intercept for all of the functions?

29. For what values of n does the graph have a turning point at the x-intercept?

30. For what values of n does the graph not have a turning point at the x-intercept?

31. Generalize your findings in Exercises 29 and 30. Test your theory by graphing $f(x) = (x + 1)^6$ and $g(x) = (x + 1)^7$.

32. **Storage** A silo is a storage building shaped like a cylinder with half a sphere on top. A farmer has 1000 square feet of material with which to build a silo.
    - **a.** The formula for the surface area of the silo is $S = 4\pi r^2 + 2\pi rh$ where r is the radius of the cylinder and h is the height of the cylinder. Substitute 1000 for S and then write an equation for h in terms of r.
    - **b.** The formula for the volume of the silo is $V = \frac{2}{3}\pi r^3 + \pi r^2 h$. Write an equation for the volume V of the silo as a polynomial function of r by substituting the expression for h from part (a) into the volume formula.
    - **c.** Graph the volume function for part (b). Use the function from part (b) to find the maximum volume of a silo with a surface area of 1000 square feet. What are the silo's dimensions?

33. **Temperature** During a 24-hour period, the temperature T (in degrees Fahrenheit) in a city can be approximated by the model

    $T = 0.026x^3 - 1.03x^2 + 10.2x + 34, 0 \le x \le 24$

    where x is the number of hours since 6 A.M.
    - **a.** Graph the function.
    - **b.** Identify any turning points on the domain $0 \le x \le 24$. What real-life meaning do these points have?
    - **c.** What is the range of the function?

34. **Volume** A cylinder is inscribed in a sphere of radius 6. Write an equation for the volume of the cylinder as a function of h. Find the value of h that maximizes the volume of the inscribed cylinder. What is the maximum volume of the cylinder?

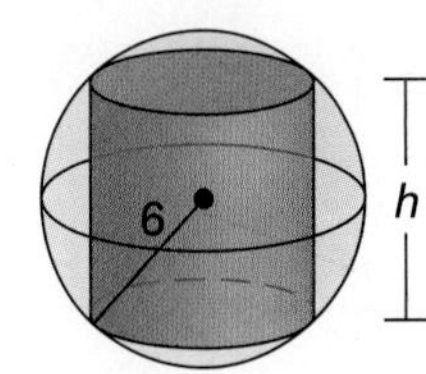

UNIT 2

Georgia Performance Standards

MM3A1d Investigate and explain characteristics of polynomial functions, including domain and range, intercepts, zeros, relative and absolute extrema, intervals of increase and decrease, and end behavior.

Technology Activity
Local Maximums and Minimums

Use after Lesson 2.8

Question

How can you use a graphing calculator to find local maximums and minimums of a polynomial function?

An important characteristic of graphs of polynomial functions is that they have turning points corresponding to the local maximum and minimum values.

You can use a graphing calculator to find these local maximums and minimums.

Example

Find local maximums and minimums on a graphing calculator.

Use a graphing calculator to find the local maximums and minimums of the given function.

$y = x^3 - 7x + 6$

Solution

STEP 1 **Enter** the function in the equation editor.

STEP 2 **Graph** the function.

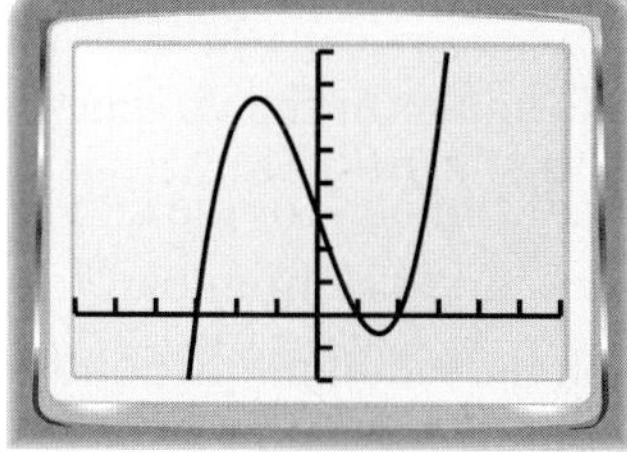

STEP 3 **Adjust** your viewing window so that you can see the local maximum and minimum.

STEP 4 **Use** the *maximum* feature to find the local maximum. The local maximum is about $(-1.53, 13.13)$.

STEP 5 **Use** the *minimum* feature to find the local minimum. The local minimum is about $(1.53, -1.13)$.

Practice

Use a graphing calculator to find the local maximums and minimums of the given function.

1. $y = x^4 - 2x^3 - 10x^2 + 8x + 12$

2. $y = x^3 + 4x^2 + x - 6$

3. $y = x^4 - 13x^2 + 36$

4. $y = 2(x - 4)(x + 4)(x + 1)$

5. $y = -\frac{2}{3}(x - 1)(x + 2)(x + 1)(x - 3)$

6. $y = 0.4(x + 6)(x - 6)(x + 2)$

TEST | for Unit 2

Use direct substitution to evaluate the polynomial function for the given value of *x*. Then check your answer using synthetic substitution.

1. $f(x) = -2x^3 + 8x^2 + 3x - 1; x = 4$

2. $f(x) = x^4 + 2x^2 - 16; x = -3$

For the polynomial function, (a) graph the function, (b) find the domain and range, (c) describe the degree and leading coefficient, and (d) identify where the function increases and decreases.

3. $f(x) = x^3 - x^2 - 2x$

4. $f(x) = \frac{1}{4}x^4 - 2x^2 + 16$

5. $f(x) = -2x^3 + 6x^2 - \frac{9}{2}x$

Graph the function. *Compare* the graph with the graph of $f(x) = \frac{1}{2}x^4$.

6. $g(x) = \frac{1}{2}x^4 + 2$

7. $g(x) = \frac{1}{2}(x - 1)^4$

8. $g(x) = \frac{1}{2}(x + 4)^4 - 3$

Find the real-number solutions of the equation.

9. $20x^3 = 125x$

10. $x^4 - 3x^2 + 2 = 0$

11. $2x^3 - 6x^2 - 6x + 18 = 0$

12. $x^4 + 2x^3 - 8x - 16 = 0$

Solve the inequality using any method.

13. $2x^3 - 5x^2 - 3x \leq 0$

14. $x^4 - 4x^2 + 3 < 0$

15. $x^4 - 12 > 0$

A polynomial *f* and a factor of *f* are given. Factor *f* completely.

16. $f(x) = 2x^3 + x^2 - 5x + 2; x + 2$

17. $f(x) = x^4 - 4x^3 + 8x - 32; x - 4$

Find all real zeros of the function.

18. $g(x) = x^3 + 6x^2 - 31x - 36$

19. $g(x) = 2x^3 + 9x^2 - 11x - 30$

20. $f(x) = 2x^4 + 5x^3 - 6x^2 - 7x + 6$

21. $f(x) = 6x^4 + 35x^3 + 35x^2 - 55x - 21$

Write a polynomial function *f* of least degree that has rational coefficients, a leading coefficient of 1, and the given zeros.

22. $-2, 4, 6$

23. $3, 1 + \sqrt{2}$

24. $-1, 0, -i, i$

25. $-4, 1, 1 - 2i$

Find all the real zeros of the function. Then determine the multiplicity of each zero and the exact number of turning points of the graph.

26. $f(x) = x^3(x + 4)$

27. $g(x) = (x - 9)^2(x - 1)$

28. $h(x) = x^2(x + 2)^3(x - 7)$

29. $f(x) = (x + 1)^2(4x - 3)^2$

Use a graphing calculator to graph the function. Identify the *x*-intercepts and the points where the local maximums and local minimums occur.

30. $f(x) = -3x^3 - 4x^2 + x - 3$

31. $h(x) = 2x^4 - 6x^2 + 1$

32. Telephone Bills From 1995 to 2003, the average monthly local telephone bill T (in dollars) for subscribers in the United States can be modeled by

$$T = -0.0097x^4 + 0.148x^3 - 0.56x^2 + 0.5x + 20$$

where x is the number of years since 1995.

a. Classify the function by degree and type.

b. Make a table of values for the function for $x = 0, 3, 5, 7, 8$.

c. Sketch a graph of the function. Do you think the model will accurately predict local telephone bills for years beyond 2003? *Explain.*

33. Company Profit The profit P (in millions of dollars) for a video game manufacturer can be modeled by $P = -3x^3 + 7x^2 + 11x$ where x is the number of video games produced (in millions). Currently, the company produces 3 million video games and makes a profit of \$15,000,000. What lesser number of video games could the company produce and still make the same profit?

34. Candles Wes is making a candle by filling a mold with wax. It is to be shaped like a pyramid with a height that is 4 inches greater than the length of each side of its square base, as shown in the diagram. The volume of the candle is 21 cubic inches. What are the dimensions of the mold?

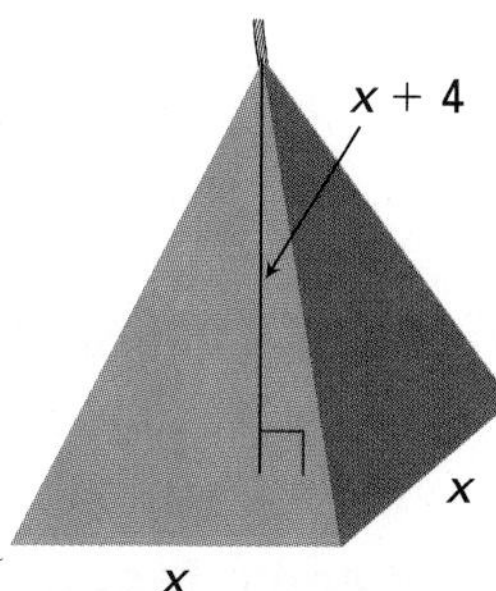

Performance Task

Art

You are making a clay sculpture that is a rectangular prism. You want the height of the sculpture to be 10 inches greater than the width of the base. The length is to be twice the width.

a. Let x represent the width (in inches) of the sculpture's base. Draw a diagram of the sculpture, and label the dimensions in terms of x.

b. Write a function that gives the volume V of the sculpture in terms of x.

c. Graph the function in part (b). Use the graph to estimate the value of x when the volume is 234 cubic inches.

d. Write a polynomial equation that you can use to find the value of x when the volume is 234 cubic inches.

e. Identify the possible rational solutions of the equation in part (d). Then solve the equation.

f. *Compare* your answer in part (e) with your estimate from part (c). What are the dimensions of the sculpture?

g. Does the sculpture have a maximum volume? Use the end behavior of the graph in part (b) to explain your reasoning.

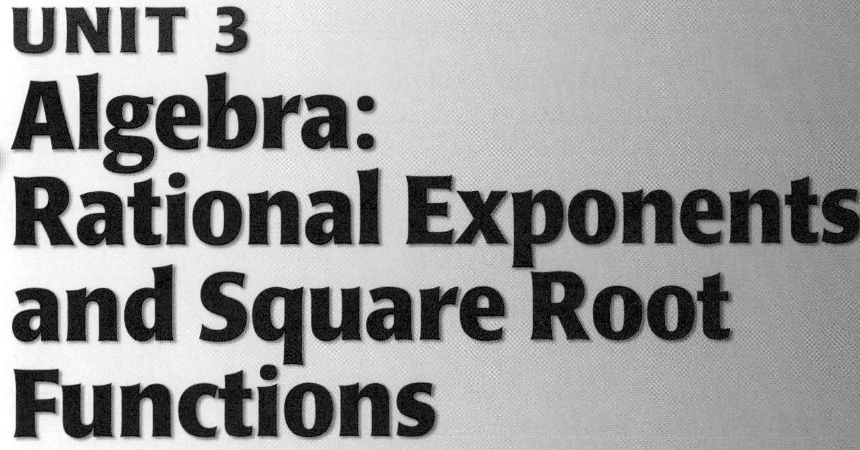

UNIT 3
Algebra: Rational Exponents and Square Root Functions

3.1 Evaluate *n*th Roots and Use Rational Exponents (MM3A2a, MM3A2b, MM3A3d)

3.2 Apply Properties of Rational Exponents (MM3A2b)

3.3 Graph Square Root and Cube Root Functions (MM3A3d)

3.4 Solve Radical Equations (MM3A3d)

Georgia Performance Standards

MM3A2a Define and understand the properties of nth roots. 

Investigating Math Activity

Radicals and Rational Exponents

Use before Lesson 3.1

Materials graphing calculator

Question

How can you write the root of an integer using an exponent?

An nth root of x is written as $\sqrt[n]{x}$ where n is the index of the radical.

index — $\sqrt[n]{x}$ — radicand

Explore

Evaluate radical and exponential expressions.

Use a graphing calculator to evaluate each expression.

	Radical Expression	Exponential Expression
a.	$\sqrt{4}$	$4^{1/2}$
b.	$\sqrt[3]{27}$	$27^{1/3}$
c.	$\sqrt[4]{625}$	$625^{1/4}$
d.	$\sqrt[5]{32}$	$32^{1/5}$
e.	$\sqrt[6]{729}$	$729^{1/6}$

Draw Conclusions

1. What is the relationship of the values of each pair of radical and exponential expressions?

2. Reasoning *Compare* the indexes in the radical expressions with the denominators of the exponents in the exponential expressions. What is the relationship of these numbers?

3. Writing Write a rule that explains how to rewrite a radical expression as an exponential expression.

4. Use your rule from Exercise 3 to rewrite the following radical expressions as exponential expressions. Then, use your calculator to verify your rule.

a. $\sqrt[3]{64}$ **b.** $\sqrt[4]{81}$ **c.** $\sqrt[5]{3125}$

5. Writing Modify your rule to explain how you would rewrite the following radical expressions as exponential expressions. Then, rewrite the radical expressions as exponential expressions. Use your calculator to help you verify your new rule.

a. $(\sqrt[3]{8})^2$ **b.** $(\sqrt[5]{32})^4$

UNIT 3

LESSON 3.1

Evaluate *n*th Roots and Use Rational Exponents

Georgia Performance Standards: MM3A2a, MM3A2b, MM3A3d

Goal Evaluate *n*th roots and study rational exponents.

Vocabulary

For an integer n greater than 1, if $b^n = a$, then b is an ***n*th root of *a*.**

An *n*th root of a is written as $\sqrt[n]{a}$ where n is the **index of the radical.** If n is odd, then a has one real *n*th root. If n is even, then a has two real *n*th roots if $a > 0$, one real *n*th root if $a = 0$, and no real *n*th roots if $a < 0$.

Example 1 Find *n*th roots

Find the indicated real *n*th root(s) of *a*.

a. $n = 6, a = 64$

b. $n = 5, a = -32$

Solution

a. Because $n = 6$ is even and $a = 64 > 0$, 64 has two real sixth roots. Because $2^6 = 64$ and $(-2)^6 = 64$, you can write $\pm\sqrt[6]{64} = \pm 2$ or $\pm 64^{1/6} = \pm 2$.

b. Because $n = 5$ is odd, -32 has one real fifth root. Because $(-2)^5 = -32$, you can write $\sqrt[5]{-32} = -2$ or $(-32)^{1/5} = -2$.

Example 2 Evaluate expressions with rational exponents

Evaluate (a) $9^{5/2}$ and (b) $27^{-2/3}$.

	Rational Exponent Form	Radical Form
a.	$9^{5/2} = (9^{1/2})^5 = 3^5 = 243$	$9^{5/2} = (\sqrt{9})^5 = 3^5 = 243$
b.	$27^{-2/3} = \frac{1}{27^{2/3}} = \frac{1}{(27^{1/3})^2} = \frac{1}{3^2} = \frac{1}{9}$	$27^{-2/3} = \frac{1}{(\sqrt[3]{27})^2} = \frac{1}{3^2} = \frac{1}{9}$

Guided Practice for Examples 1 and 2

1. Find the real cube root of -343.
2. Evaluate the expression $36^{3/2}$ without using a calculator.

Example 3 Approximate roots with a calculator

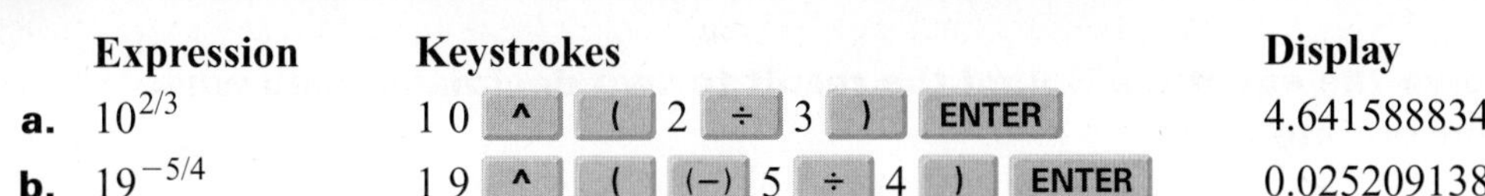

	Expression	Keystrokes	Display
a.	$10^{2/3}$	1 0 ^ (2 ÷ 3) ENTER	4.641588834
b.	$19^{-5/4}$	1 9 ^ ((–) 5 ÷ 4) ENTER	0.0252091382

UNIT 3

Georgia Performance Standards

MM3A2a Define and understand the properties of *n*th roots. ☑

MM3A2b Extend properties of exponents to include rational exponents. ☑

MM3A3d Solve a variety of types of equations by appropriate means choosing among mental calculation, pencil and paper, or appropriate technology. ☑

Example 4 Solve equations using *n*th roots

Solve the equation.

a. $-2x^6 = -1458$

$x^6 = 729$ Divide each side by -2.

$x = \pm\sqrt[6]{729}$ Take sixth root of each side.

$x = \pm 3$ Simplify.

b. $(x + 2)^5 = 35$

$x + 2 = \sqrt[5]{35}$ Take fifth root of each side.

$x = -2 + \sqrt[5]{35}$ Solve for x.

$x \approx 0.04$ Use a calculator.

Example 5 Use *n*th roots in problem solving

Beach Ball The volume of a beach ball can be approximated using the model $V = \frac{4}{3}\pi r^3$ where r is the radius of the ball in inches. Estimate the radius of the ball if the volume is 382 cubic inches.

Solution

$V = \frac{4}{3}\pi r^3$ Write model for volume.

$382 = \frac{4}{3}\pi r^3$ Substitute 382 for volume.

$\frac{3(382)}{4\pi} = r^3$ Multiply each side by $\frac{3}{4\pi}$.

$91.20 \approx r^3$ Simplify.

$4.50 \approx r$ Take cube root of each side.

Guided Practice for Examples 3, 4, and 5

Evaluate the expression using a calculator. Round the result to two decimal places when appropriate.

3. $10^{1/3}$ **4.** $\sqrt[6]{13}$ **5.** $21^{-1/4}$ **6.** $(\sqrt[4]{81})^{-2}$

Solve the equation. Round the result to two decimal places when appropriate.

7. $-6x^2 = -180$ **8.** $x^3 - 9 = 31$ **9.** $(x + 8)^4 = 2$

10. Rework Example 5 if the volume of a ball is 268 cubic inches.

LESSON 3.1 **Exercise Set A**

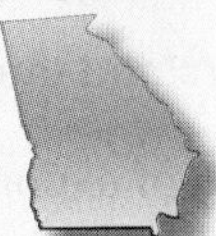

MM3A2a	Define and understand the properties of *n*th roots.
MM3A2b	Extend properties of exponents to include rational exponents.
MM3A3d	Solve a variety of types of equations by appropriate means choosing among mental calculation, pencil and paper, or appropriate technology.

Rewrite the expression using rational exponent notation.

1. $\sqrt[3]{7}$
2. $(\sqrt[3]{6})^2$
3. $(\sqrt[5]{14})^4$
4. $(\sqrt[7]{-21})^3$
5. $(\sqrt[8]{11})^7$
6. $(\sqrt[9]{-2})^4$

Rewrite the expression using radical notation.

7. $17^{1/3}$
8. $44^{1/6}$
9. $33^{2/3}$
10. $9^{5/3}$
11. $(-28)^{7/5}$
12. $39^{4/7}$

Evaluate the expression without using a calculator.

13. $(\sqrt[3]{8})^2$
14. $(\sqrt[4]{16})^3$
15. $(\sqrt[4]{81})^4$
16. $36^{3/2}$
17. $4^{5/2}$
18. $27^{2/3}$
19. $125^{4/3}$
20. $(-8)^{1/3}$
21. $(-32)^{3/5}$

Evaluate the expression using a calculator. Round the result to two decimal places when appropriate.

22. $\sqrt[3]{38}$
23. $\sqrt[6]{112}$
24. $\sqrt[7]{-215}$
25. $(241)^{1/5}$
26. $(-133)^{1/3}$
27. $(69)^{1/4}$
28. $(96)^{2/3}$
29. $(356)^{5/9}$
30. $(-2427)^{4/7}$

31. Geometry Find the radius of a sphere with a volume of 589 cubic centimeters.

Solve the equation. Round the result to two decimal places when appropriate.

32. $x^3 + 17 = 132$
33. $2x^5 + 73 = 53$
34. $(x + 3)^4 = 362$

In Exercises 35and 36, use the following information.

Water and Ice Water, in its liquid state, has a density of 0.9971 gram per cubic centimeter. Ice has a density of 0.9168 gram per cubic centimeter. A cubic container is filled with 600 grams of liquid water. A different cubic container is filled with 600 grams of ice. Round the answers to two decimal places when appropriate.

35. Find the volume of the container filled with liquid water. Then find the length of the edges of the cubic container that is filled with liquid water.

36. Find the volume of the container filled with ice. Then find the length of the edges of the cubic container that is filled with ice.

Exercise Set B

MM3A2a Define and understand the properties of nth roots.

MM3A2b Extend properties of exponents to include rational exponents.

MM3A3d Solve a variety of types of equations by appropriate means choosing among mental calculation, pencil and paper, or appropriate technology.

Rewrite the expression using rational exponent notation.

1. $(\sqrt[5]{63})^3$
2. $(\sqrt[3]{-25})^4$
3. $(\sqrt[6]{124})^7$

Rewrite the expression using radical notation.

4. $(-57)^{4/3}$
5. $13^{3/2}$
6. $204^{5/8}$

Evaluate the expression without using a calculator.

7. $(\sqrt[3]{27})^2$
8. $(\sqrt[4]{256})^3$
9. $(\sqrt[3]{-64})^2$
10. $36^{3/2}$
11. $(25)^{-3/2}$
12. $16^{1/4}$
13. $(-32)^{-3/5}$
14. $(81)^{-5/2}$
15. $(-125)^{-5/3}$

Evaluate the expression using a calculator. Round the result to two decimal places when appropriate.

16. $(\sqrt[3]{23})^5$
17. $(\sqrt[4]{65})^3$
18. $(\sqrt[5]{-124})^4$
19. $(39)^{4/3}$
20. $(-128)^{-2/5}$
21. $(256)^{5/8}$
22. $(-325)^{3/5}$
23. $(215)^{-4/9}$
24. $(-1012)^{8/5}$

Solve the equation. Round the result to two decimal places when appropriate.

25. $x^5 = 1321$
26. $3x^5 + 3 = 213$
27. $(x - 3)^6 = 502$
28. $-4x^3 = 132$
29. $2x^4 = 36$
30. $(3x + 2)^4 = 232$
31. $7 - x^5 = 3$
32. $4x^5 + 96 = 24$
33. $12 - (2x + 3)^3 = 84$

34. **Geometry** Find the radius of a sphere with a volume of 994 cubic centimeters.

35. **Volume** A cylindrical container holds 20 ounces of liquid. One fluid ounce is approximately 1.8 cubic inches. The height of the container is 3.5 inches. Use the formula for the volume of a cylinder to find the radius of the container.

36. **Critical Thinking** Use the following examples to determine when $\sqrt[n]{a^n} \neq a$.
    a. $\sqrt[3]{(-2)^3}$
    b. $\sqrt{(-2)^2}$
    c. $\sqrt[3]{2^3}$
    d. $\sqrt{2^2}$

UNIT 3

LESSON 3.2

Apply Properties of Rational Exponents

Georgia Performance Standards: MM3A2b

Goal Simplify expressions involving rational exponents.

Vocabulary

A radical with index n is in **simplest form** if the radicand has no perfect nth powers as factors and any denominator has been rationalized.

Two radical expressions with the same index and radicand are **like radicals.**

The expressions $a + \sqrt{b}$ and $a - \sqrt{b}$ are called **radical conjugates** of each other.

For a list of properties of rational exponents and radicals, see pages 245 and 246.

Example 1 Use properties of exponents

Use the properties of rational exponents to simplify the expression.

a. $(8^2 \cdot 3^2)^{-1/2} = [(8 \cdot 3)^2]^{-1/2} = (24^2)^{-1/2} = 24^{-1} = \frac{1}{24}$

b. $(4^{1/5} \cdot 2^{1/5})^{10} = (4^{1/5})^{10} \cdot (2^{1/5})^{10} = 4^2 \cdot 2^2 = 16 \cdot 4 = 64$

c. $\frac{5^{3/4}}{5^{1/2}} \cdot 5^2 = 5^{3/4 - 1/2} \cdot 5^2 = 5^{1/4} \cdot 5^2 = 5^{1/4 + 2} = 5^{9/4}$

Example 2 Use properties of radicals

Use the properties of radicals to simplify the expression.

a. $\sqrt{8} \cdot \sqrt{50} = \sqrt{8 \cdot 50} = \sqrt{400} = 20$ Product property

b. $\sqrt[3]{\frac{192}{24}} = \frac{\sqrt[3]{192}}{\sqrt[3]{24}} = \frac{\sqrt[3]{64 \cdot 3}}{\sqrt[3]{8 \cdot 3}} = \frac{4\sqrt[3]{3}}{2\sqrt[3]{3}} = 2$ Quotient property

Example 3 Write radicals in simplest form

a. $\sqrt[5]{64} = \sqrt[5]{32 \cdot 2}$ Factor out perfect fifth powers.

$= \sqrt[5]{32} \cdot \sqrt[5]{2}$ Product property

$= 2\sqrt[5]{2}$ Simplify.

b. $\frac{\sqrt[3]{3}}{\sqrt[3]{4}} = \frac{\sqrt[3]{3}}{\sqrt[3]{4}} \cdot \frac{\sqrt[3]{2}}{\sqrt[3]{2}}$ Make denominator a perfect cube.

$= \frac{\sqrt[3]{6}}{\sqrt[3]{8}}$ Product property

$= \frac{\sqrt[3]{6}}{2}$ Simplify.

UNIT 3

Georgia Performance Standards

MM3A2b Extend properties of exponents to include rational exponents. ☑

Example 4 Add and subtract like radicals and roots

Simplify the expression.

a. $\sqrt[4]{162} - \sqrt[4]{32} = \sqrt[4]{81} \cdot \sqrt[4]{2} - \sqrt[4]{16} \cdot \sqrt[4]{2} = 3\sqrt[4]{2} - 2\sqrt[4]{2} = (3 - 2)\sqrt[4]{2} = \sqrt[4]{2}$

b. $7^{3/2} + 4(7^{3/2}) = (1 + 4)7^{3/2} = 5(7^{3/2})$

Guided Practice for Examples 1, 2, 3, and 4

Simplify the expression.

1. $(8^{1/2} \cdot 9^{1/4})^2$ **2.** $\left(\frac{10}{10^{2/3}}\right)^2$ **3.** $125^{-1/3}$ **4.** $11^{-1/2} \cdot 11^{5/2}$

5. $\sqrt{18} \cdot \sqrt{27}$ **6.** $\sqrt[3]{16} \cdot \sqrt[3]{24}$ **7.** $\frac{\sqrt{200}}{\sqrt{8}}$ **8.** $\frac{\sqrt[5]{160}}{\sqrt[5]{5}}$

9. $\sqrt[3]{432}$ **10.** $\frac{\sqrt[4]{2}}{\sqrt[4]{3}}$ **11.** $3(6)^{1/4} + 5(6)^{1/4}$ **12.** $9(54)^{1/2} - 54^{1/2}$

Example 5 Simplify expressions involving variables

Simplify the expression. Assume all variables are positive.

a. $\sqrt[3]{\frac{8y^6}{z^{12}}} = \frac{\sqrt[3]{8y^6}}{\sqrt[3]{z^{12}}} = \frac{\sqrt[3]{(2y^2)^3}}{\sqrt[3]{(z^4)^3}} = \frac{2y^2}{z^4}$

b. $\sqrt[3]{\frac{a^2}{b}} = \sqrt[3]{\frac{a^2 \cdot b^2}{b \cdot b^2}} = \sqrt[3]{\frac{a^2b^2}{b^3}} = \frac{\sqrt[3]{a^2b^2}}{\sqrt[3]{b^3}} = \frac{\sqrt[3]{a^2b^2}}{b}$

c. $\frac{2}{c + \sqrt{d}} = \frac{2}{c + \sqrt{d}} \cdot \frac{c - \sqrt{d}}{c - \sqrt{d}} = \frac{2(c - \sqrt{d})}{c^2 - c\sqrt{d} + c\sqrt{d} - d} = \frac{2(c - \sqrt{d})}{c^2 - d}$

Example 6 Add and subtract expressions involving variables

Perform the indicated operation. Assume all variables are positive.

a. $-4\sqrt{k} - 5\sqrt{k} = (-4 - 5)\sqrt{k} = -9\sqrt{k}$

b. $9a^{1/3}b - 2a^{1/3}b = (9 - 2)a^{1/3}b = 7a^{1/3}b$

Guided Practice for Examples 5 and 6

Simplify the expression. Assume all variables are positive.

13. $\sqrt[4]{\frac{81m^4}{16n^8}}$ **14.** $(8p^6q^3)^{2/3}$ **15.** $\frac{3}{x - \sqrt{2y}}$

16. $6\sqrt{h} - 8\sqrt{h}$ **17.** $11a^{1/2}b - 4a^{1/2}b$ **18.** $3\sqrt{5y^4} - y\sqrt{20y^2}$

UNIT 3

LESSON 3.2

Exercise Set A

MM3A2b Extend properties of exponents to include rational exponents.

Simplify the expression using the properties of radicals and rational exponents.

1. $7^{1/3} \cdot 7^{4/3}$

2. $\frac{4^{2/3}}{4^{1/3}}$

3. $(6^{2/3})^{3/4}$

4. $5^{1/4} \cdot 3^{1/4}$

5. $\sqrt[4]{2} \cdot \sqrt[4]{8}$

6. $\frac{\sqrt[4]{192}}{\sqrt[4]{6}}$

7. $\frac{11}{\sqrt[4]{11}}$

8. $\sqrt[3]{7} \cdot \sqrt[3]{49}$

9. $(3^{3/2})^2$

10. $\left(\frac{54}{64}\right)^{1/3}$

11. $\frac{\sqrt[4]{32}}{\sqrt[4]{2}}$

12. $\frac{\sqrt[5]{5}}{\sqrt[5]{27}}$

Simplify the expression. Assume all variables are positive.

13. $x^{5/3} \cdot x^{4/3}$

14. $\sqrt{x^{2/5}}$

15. $(x^{1/2})^{2/7}$

16. $\left(\frac{x^2}{27}\right)^{1/3}$

17. $\sqrt[3]{16x^4}$

18. $(x^{-3})^{2/5}$

19. $\frac{x^{7/5}}{x^{4/5}}$

20. $\frac{\sqrt[3]{64x^3y}}{4x^{-3}y}$

21. $x^5 \cdot x^{\sqrt{3}}$

22. $(x^{\sqrt{2}})^{3\sqrt{2}}$

23. $\frac{x^{4\sqrt{3}}}{2x^{2\sqrt{3}}}$

24. $\frac{4x}{x + \sqrt{5y}}$

Perform the indicated operation. Assume all variables are positive.

25. $6\sqrt[3]{5} + 2\sqrt[3]{5}$

26. $5\sqrt{5} - \sqrt{45}$

27. $2\sqrt{27} - 3\sqrt{48}$

28. $2\sqrt{x} + 7\sqrt{x}$

29. $3(x^{1/2}y^3)^2 - (x^3y^{18})^{1/3}$

30. $4x^{\sqrt{3}} + x^{\sqrt{3}}$

Write the expression in simplest form. Assume all variables are positive.

31. $\sqrt[4]{3x^7y^9z^3}$

32. $\sqrt{x^3y^4z} \cdot \sqrt{xyz^4}$

33. $\sqrt[3]{\frac{81x^2y^3}{8xy^4z}}$

34. **Earth Science** The equatorial circumference of Earth is 4.01×10^4 kilometers. One kilometer is equivalent to 3.94×10^4 inches. What is the equatorial circumference of Earth in inches?

35. **Swimming Pool** A wooden deck and a circular swimming pool cover an area of 514.16 square feet of the lawn. The rectangular deck is 20 feet wide and 10 feet long. What is the radius of the pool?

UNIT 3

LESSON 3.2

Exercise Set B

MM3A2b Extend properties of exponents to include rational exponents.

Simplify the expression using the properties of radicals and rational exponents.

1. $(4^{2/3} \cdot 5^{3/4})^3$
2. $(3^{3/2} \cdot 3^3)^{1/3}$
3. $[(7^{2/3})^{3/5}]^3$
4. $\left(\frac{5^2}{5^{7/2}}\right)^{-1/3}$
5. $\left(\frac{16^{1/3}}{2^{1/3}}\right)^2$
6. $\sqrt[4]{\sqrt[3]{\sqrt{6}}}$
7. $\sqrt{\frac{\sqrt{32}}{\sqrt{72}}}$
8. $\sqrt[5]{(3^3)^2 \cdot (3^4)^2}$
9. $\frac{\sqrt{\frac{5}{7}} \cdot \sqrt{\frac{4}{5}}}{\sqrt{10}}$

Simplify the expression. Assume all variables are positive.

10. $x^{\sqrt{3}} \cdot x^{\sqrt{12}}$
11. $\sqrt[4]{\frac{x^{17}}{y^8}}$
12. $\left(\frac{x^{1/4}}{x^{1/2}}\right)^{-1}$
13. $\frac{x^{4/3}y^{7/6}}{xy}$
14. $\left(\frac{2x^3y^{2/3}}{x^{5/3}y^{3/5}z}\right)^3$
15. $\left(\frac{xy^2}{3y^{4/3}z^{1/2}}\right)^{-1/2}$
16. $\left[\frac{(12xz^2)^{1/2}}{(3y^3z)^{1/2}}\right]^{-3}$
17. $\sqrt[4]{(3x^3)^3(3x^2)^5}$
18. $\frac{8x}{x - \sqrt{3y}}$

19. Error Analysis *Describe* and correct the error in simplifying the expression.

$$\frac{y^{1/2}}{y^{-3/4}} = y^{-1/4} = \frac{1}{y^{1/4}} \quad \text{X}$$

Perform the indicated operation. Assume all variables are positive.

20. $\sqrt{10\sqrt{3} - 6\sqrt{3}}$
21. $2x\sqrt[3]{x^4yz^5} + \sqrt[3]{x^7yz^5}$
22. $\sqrt{\sqrt[4]{16x} - \sqrt[4]{x}}$
23. $\sqrt[3]{\frac{2x}{5}} + \sqrt{\frac{x}{25}}$
24. $\sqrt[3]{8x} + \sqrt[6]{x^2} - \sqrt[9]{x^3}$
25. $\sqrt{xyz^2}\,\sqrt{9x^3z}\,\sqrt{x} + x\sqrt{yz}\,\sqrt{x^3z^2}$

26. **Astronomy** The equatorial circumference of the Moon is 1.09×10^4 kilometers. One kilometer is equivalent to 3.94×10^4 inches. What is the equatorial circumference of the Moon in inches?

27. **Bowling Ball** A bowling ball is submerged in a tub of water. As a result, a total of 333 cubic inches of water is displaced. Use the formula for the volume of a sphere to find the radius of the bowling ball.

UNIT 3

Georgia Performance Standards

MM3A2b Extend properties of exponents to include rational exponents.

Problem Solving Workshop

Problem The surface area S (in square centimeters) of a large dog's body can be approximated by the model $S = 11.2m^{2/3}$ where m is the mass (in grams) of the dog. Approximate the surface area of a dog that has a mass of 9 kilograms (9×10^3 grams).

STEP 1 **Read and Understand**

What do you know? The function that models surface area of a large dog

What do you want to find out? The surface area of a dog that has a mass of 9 kilograms

STEP 2 **Make a Plan** Use what you know to substitute and solve the equation.

STEP 3 **Solve the Problem** Substitute for m in the equation and simplify.

$S = 11.2m^{2/3}$	Write model.
$= 11.2(9 \times 10^3)^{2/3}$	Substitute 9000 for m.
$= 11.2(9)^{2/3}(10^3)^{2/3}$	Power of a product property
$\approx 11.2(4.33)(10^2)$	Power of a power property
≈ 4850	Simplify.

The dog's surface area is about 4850 square centimeters.

STEP 4 **Look Back** Use a graphing calculator to make a table of values for the function. The table shows that the dog has a surface area of about 4846 square centimeters. The answer is correct.

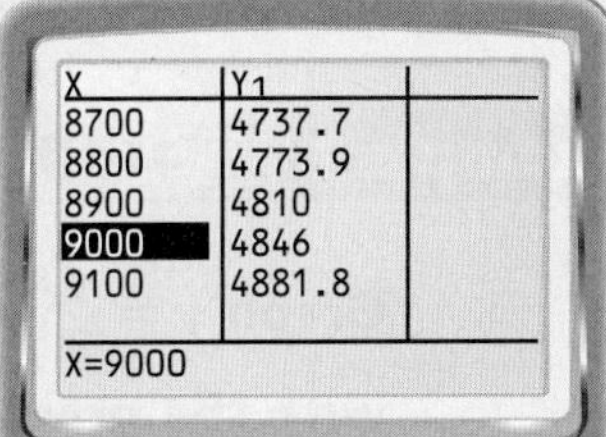

Practice

1. **Biology** An ant is basically cylindrical in shape, so its surface area S can be approximated by the formula for the surface area of a cylinder, $S = 2\pi rh + 2\pi r^2$, where h is the length of the ant and r is the radius. Approximate the surface area of an ant that is 5 millimeters long and has a radius of 1.1 millimeters.

2. **What If?** Because the ant is cylindrical in shape, the volume of the ant can be approximated by the formula $V = \pi r^2 h$ where h is the length of the ant and r is the radius. Approximate the volume of the ant in Exercise 1.

3. **Volume** The formula for the volume of a square pyramid is $V = \frac{1}{3}\ell^2 h$ where ℓ is the length of a side of the base and h is the height. Find the length of a pyramid that has a volume of 162 cubic feet and a height of 6 feet.

4. **Biology** Let m be the mass of an average house cat. Then the mass of the Canadian lynx is $2m$. The surface areas of the house cat and the Canadian lynx can be modeled by $S_{cat} = 10m^{2/3}$ and $S_{lynx} = 10(2m)^{2/3}$. Find the ratio of the surface area of the Canadian lynx to the surface area of the cat. *Explain* what the ratio means.

UNIT 3

LESSON 3.3

Graph Square Root and Cube Root Functions

Georgia Performance Standards: MM3A3d

Goal Graph square root and cube root functions.

Vocabulary

Radical functions include functions of the form $y = a\sqrt{x - h} + k$ and $y = a\sqrt[3]{x - h} + k$.

Example 1 Graph a square root function

Graph $y = 2\sqrt{x}$, and state the domain and range. Compare the graph with the graph of $y = \sqrt{x}$.

Solution

Make a table of values and sketch the graph.

x	0	1	2	3	4
y	0	2	2.83	3.46	4

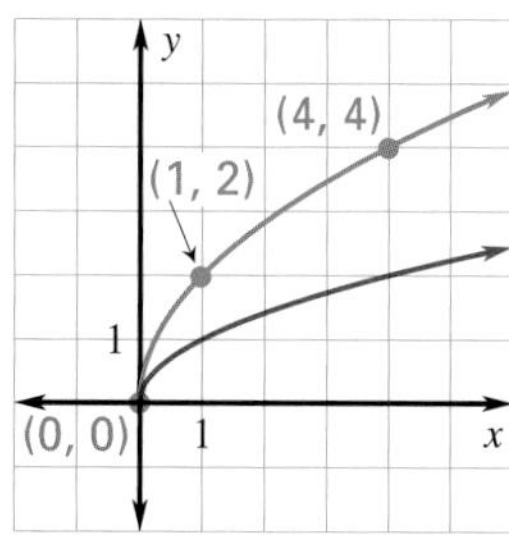

The domain is $x \geq 0$. The range is $y \geq 0$. The graph of $y = 2\sqrt{x}$ is a vertical stretch of the parent graph of $y = \sqrt{x}$.

Example 2 Graph a cube root function

Graph $y = \frac{1}{3}\sqrt[3]{x}$, and state the domain and range. Compare the graph with the graph of $y = \sqrt[3]{x}$.

Solution

Make a table of values and sketch the graph.

x	−2	−1	0	1	2	8
y	−0.42	−0.33	0	0.33	0.42	0.67

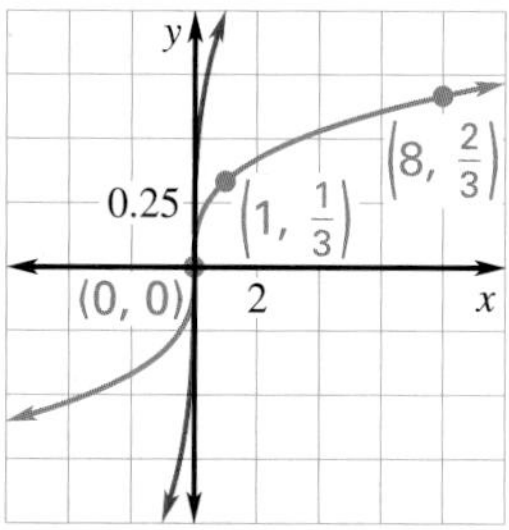

The domain and range are all real numbers. The graph of $y = \frac{1}{3}\sqrt[3]{x}$ is a vertical shrink of the parent graph of $y = \sqrt[3]{x}$ by a factor of $\frac{1}{3}$.

Guided Practice for Examples 1 and 2

Graph the function. Then state the domain and range.

1. $y = \frac{1}{4}\sqrt{x}$ **2.** $y = -2\sqrt{x}$ **3.** $y = 3\sqrt[3]{x}$ **4.** $y = -\frac{1}{2}\sqrt[3]{x}$

UNIT 3

Georgia Performance Standards

MM3A3d Solve a variety of types of equations by appropriate means choosing among mental calculation, pencil and paper, or appropriate technology. ☑

Example 3 Solve a multi-step problem

The period of a pendulum can be modeled by $T = 1.34\sqrt{\ell}$ where ℓ is the length of the pendulum in feet.

a. Use a graphing calculator to graph the model.

b. Find the length of a pendulum that has a period of 2 seconds.

Solution

a. Graph the model. Enter $y = 1.34\sqrt{x}$. Use a viewing window of $0 \le x \le 3$ and $0 \le y \le 3$.

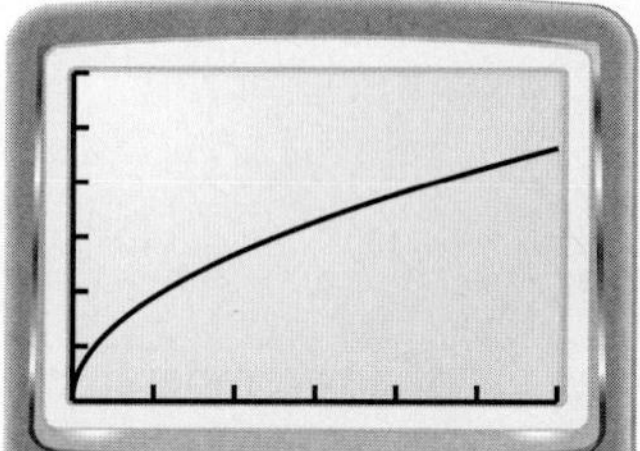

b. Use the *trace* feature to find the x-coordinate when $y = 2$. The graph shows $x \approx 2.234$.

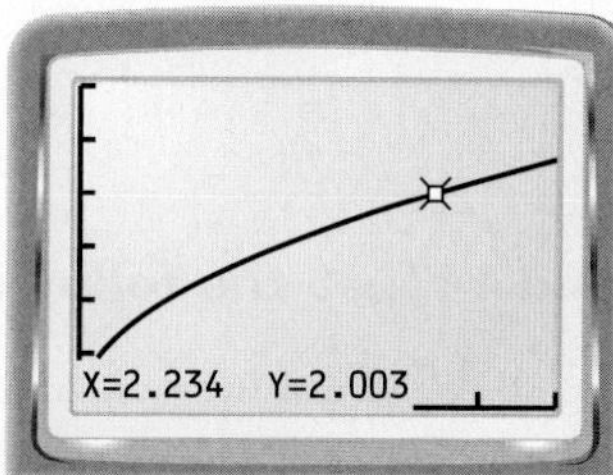

A pendulum with a period of 2 seconds is about 2.23 feet long.

Guided Practice for Example 3

5. Rework Example 3 to find the length of a pendulum with a period of 3 seconds.

Example 4 Graph a translated radical function

Graph $y = -\sqrt[3]{x + 2} + 1$. Then state the domain and range.

STEP 1 **Sketch** the graph of $y = -\sqrt[3]{x}$. It passes through $(-1, 1)$, $(0, 0)$ and $(1, -1)$.

STEP 2 **Note** that for $y = -\sqrt[3]{x + 2} + 1$, $h = -2$ and $k = 1$. Shift the graph left 2 units and up 1 unit. The resulting graph passes through $(-3, 2)$, $(-2, 1)$, and $(-1, 0)$. The domain and the range of the function are both all real numbers.

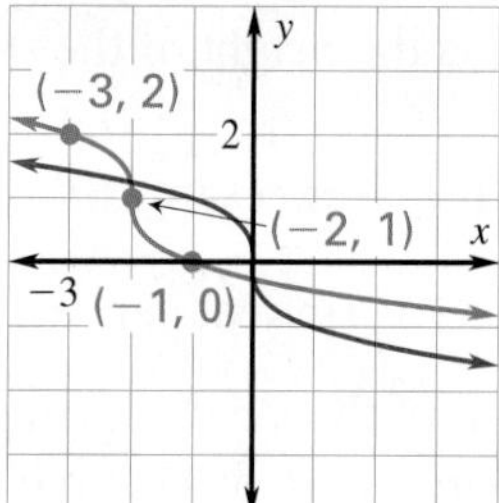

Guided Practice for Example 4

6. Graph $y = -\sqrt{x + 1} + 3$. Then state the domain and range.

7. Graph $y = 2\sqrt[3]{x - 1} + 1$. Then state the domain and range.

UNIT 3

LESSON 3.3 **Exercise Set A**

MM3A3d Solve a variety of types of equations by appropriate means choosing among mental calculation, pencil and paper, or appropriate technology.

Graph the square root function. Then state the domain and range.

1. $f(x) = \sqrt{x} - 2$

2. $f(x) = \sqrt{x - 2}$

3. $f(x) = 3\sqrt{x + 1}$

4. $f(x) = \sqrt{x + 2} - 2$

5. $f(x) = \sqrt{x - 1} + 1$

6. $f(x) = -\sqrt{x - 3}$

Graph the cube root function. Then state the domain and range.

7. $f(x) = \sqrt[3]{x} + 1$

8. $f(x) = \sqrt[3]{x - 4}$

9. $f(x) = 3\sqrt[3]{x}$

10. $f(x) = \sqrt[3]{x + 2}$

11. $f(x) = -\sqrt[3]{x} - 1$

12. $f(x) = \sqrt[3]{x + 2} - 2$

In Exercises 13 and 14, use the following information.

Speed of Sound The speed of sound V in feet per second through air of any temperature is given by $V = \frac{1087\sqrt{t + 273}}{16.52}$ where t is the temperature (in degrees Celsius).

13. Identify the domain and range of the function.

14. What is the temperature of the air if the speed of sound is 1250 feet per second?

In Exercises 15 and 16, use the following information.

Falling Object A stone is dropped from a height of 200 feet. The time it takes for the stone to reach a height of h feet is given by the function $t = \frac{1}{4}\sqrt{200 - h}$ where t is the time in seconds.

15. Identify the domain and range of the function.

16. What is the height of the stone after 3 seconds?

17. **Multiple Representations** Under certain conditions, a skydiver's terminal velocity v_t (in feet per second) is given by $v_t = 33.7\sqrt{\frac{W}{A}}$ where W is the weight of the skydiver (in pounds) and A is the skydiver's cross-sectional surface area (in square feet). Note that skydivers can vary their cross-sectional surface area by changing positions as they fall.

a. **Writing an Equation** Write an equation that gives v_t as a function of A for a skydiver who weighs 175 pounds.

b. **Making a Table** Make a table of values for the equation from part (a).

c. **Drawing a Graph** Use your table to graph the equation.

LESSON 3.3 **Exercise Set B**

MM3A3d Solve a variety of types of equations by appropriate means choosing among mental calculation, pencil and paper, or appropriate technology.

Graph the function. Then state the domain and range.

1. $f(x) = \sqrt{x + 4} - 2$

2. $f(x) = 2\sqrt{x - 2} + 3$

3. $f(x) = -3\sqrt{x} + 3$

4. $f(x) = -\sqrt{x + 2} + 2$

5. $f(x) = \sqrt[3]{x} + 3$

6. $f(x) = 3\sqrt[3]{x + 2}$

7. $f(x) = \sqrt[3]{x - 3} + 4$

8. $f(x) = \sqrt[3]{x - 4} + 1$

9. $f(x) = -2\sqrt[3]{x} - 3$

10. Error Analysis A student tried to explain how the graphs of $y = -2\sqrt[3]{x}$ and $y = -2\sqrt[3]{x - 1} - 3$ are related. *Describe* and correct the error.

> The graph of $y = -2\sqrt[3]{x - 1} - 3$ is the graph of $y = -2\sqrt[3]{x}$ translated left 1 unit and down 3 units.

Visual Thinking Using a graphing calculator, graph the functions $f(x) = \sqrt{x}$, $g(x) = \sqrt[4]{x}$, $h(x) = \sqrt[6]{x}$, and $j(x) = \sqrt[8]{x}$ on the same coordinate plane. Use the window Xmin $= -1$, Xmax $= 2$, Xscl $= 1$, Ymin $= -1$, Ymax $= 2$, and Yscl $= 1$.

11. What two points do all the graphs have in common?

12. *Describe* how the graphs are related.

13. Using what you have learned in Exercises 11 and 12, graph $f(x) = \sqrt[4]{x + 2} - 1$.

Visual Thinking Using a graphing calculator, graph the functions $f(x) = \sqrt[3]{x}$, $g(x) = \sqrt[5]{x}$, $h(x) = \sqrt[7]{x}$, and $j(x) = \sqrt[9]{x}$ on the same coordinate plane. Use the window Xmin $= -2$, Xmax $= 2$, Xscl $= 1$, Ymin $= -2$, Ymax $= 2$, and Yscl $= 1$.

14. What three points do all the graphs have in common?

15. *Describe* how the graphs are related.

16. Using what you have learned in Exercises 14 and 15, graph $f(x) = \sqrt[5]{x - 1} + 1$.

In Exercises 17–20, use the following information.

Falling Object A stone is dropped from a height of 175 feet. The time it takes for the stone to reach a height of h feet is given by the function $t = \frac{1}{4}\sqrt{175 - h}$ where t is the time in seconds.

17. Identify the domain and range of the function.

18. What is the height of the stone after 1 second?

19. What is the height of the stone after 3 seconds?

20. When does the stone hit the ground?

LESSON 3.4

Solve Radical Equations

Georgia Performance Standards: MM3A3d

Goal Solve radical equations.

Vocabulary

Equations with radicals that have variables in their radicands are called **radical equations.**

Example 1 Solve a radical equation

$\sqrt[3]{5 - 11x} = 3$ Original equation

$(\sqrt[3]{5 - 11x})^3 = 3^3$ Cube each side to eliminate the radical.

$5 - 11x = 27$ Simplify.

$x = -2$ Subtract 5 from each side. Then divide each side by -11.

CHECK Check $x = -2$ in the original equation.

$\sqrt[3]{5 - 11(-2)} \stackrel{?}{=} 3$ Substitute -2 for x.

$3 = 3$ ✓ Solution checks.

Example 2 Solve a radical equation given a function

Power Consumption The amount of power used by an appliance is given by $I = \sqrt{\frac{P}{R}}$ where I is the current (in amps), R is the resistance (in ohms), and P is the power (in watts). If the appliance uses $I = 12$ amps, and $R = 25$ ohms, find the power P.

$I = \sqrt{\frac{P}{R}}$ Write given function.

$12 = \sqrt{\frac{P}{25}}$ Substitute 12 for I and 25 for R.

$144 = \frac{P}{25}$ Square each side.

$3600 = P$ Multiply each side by 25.

The power consumed is 3600 watts.

Guided Practice for Examples 1 and 2

Solve the equation and check the solution.

1. $\sqrt{x + 2} = 3$

2. $\sqrt[3]{6x - 10} = 2$

3. $\sqrt[4]{x} - 5 = -3$

4. $2\sqrt[3]{x - 3} = 6$

5. Rework Example 2 to find R when $I = 10$ amps and $P = 2000$ watts.

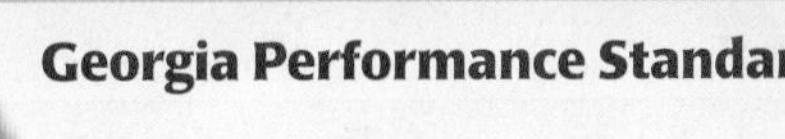

Georgia Performance Standards

MM3A3d Solve a variety of types of equations by appropriate means choosing among mental calculation, pencil and paper, or appropriate technology.

Example 3 Solve an equation with a rational exponent

$(x-1)^{3/2} - 2 = 6$	Original equation
$(x-1)^{3/2} = 8$	Add 2 to each side.
$[(x-1)^{3/2}]^{2/3} = 8^{2/3}$	Raise each side to the power $\frac{2}{3}$.
$x - 1 = (8^{1/3})^2$	Apply properties of exponents.
$x - 1 = 2^2$	Simplify.
$x = 5$	Add 1 to each side and simplify.

The solution is 5. Check this in the original equation.

Example 4 Solve an equation with two radicals

$\sqrt{x+1} = \sqrt{3x} - 1$	Original equation
$(\sqrt{x+1})^2 = (\sqrt{3x} - 1)^2$	Square each side.
$x + 1 = 3x - 2\sqrt{3x} + 1$	Expand right side and simplify left side.
$-2x = -2\sqrt{3x}$	Isolate radical expression.
$x = \sqrt{3x}$	Divide each side by -2.
$x^2 = 3x$	Square each side again.
$x^2 - 3x = 0$	Write in standard form.
$x(x-3) = 0$	Factor.
$x = 0$ or $x = 3$	Zero product property

CHECK $x = 0$ in the original equation.

$\sqrt{0+1} \stackrel{?}{=} \sqrt{3(0)} - 1$

$1 \neq -1$

CHECK $x = 3$ in the original equation.

$\sqrt{3+1} \stackrel{?}{=} \sqrt{3(3)} - 1$

$2 = 2$ ✓

The only solution is 3. (The apparent solution 0 is extraneous.)

Guided Practice for Examples 3 and 4

Solve the equation. Check for extraneous solutions.

6. $2x^{3/4} = 16$

7. $\frac{1}{2}x^{5/2} = 16$

8. $\sqrt{4 - x} = x - 4$

9. $\sqrt{5x} = 4 + \sqrt{x - 4}$

UNIT 3

LESSON 3.4 **Exercise Set A**

MM3A3d Solve a variety of types of equations by appropriate means choosing among mental calculation, pencil and paper, or appropriate technology.

Solve the equation. Check your solution.

1. $\sqrt{x} + 3 = 12$

2. $x^{1/2} - 4 = 1$

3. $3\sqrt{x+2} = 6$

4. $(2x - 3)^{1/2} + 2 = 2$

5. $5\sqrt{3x} = 15$

6. $3\sqrt{4 - 3x} = 21$

7. $7 - \sqrt{x - 4} = -6$

8. $\sqrt{3x + 4} + \frac{3}{2} = 3$

9. $2(x - 1)^{1/2} - 3 = 7$

Solve the equation. Check your solution.

10. $\sqrt[3]{x} + 1 = -2$

11. $4\sqrt[3]{x} + 2 = 0$

12. $\sqrt[3]{2x + 7} = 5$

13. $(x + 4)^{1/3} - 2 = -6$

14. $8\sqrt[3]{x} + 3 = 11$

15. $3x^{1/3} - 2 = -4$

16. $-2\sqrt[3]{2x + 5} + 7 = 15$

17. $\frac{1}{2}(5x + 1)^{1/3} + \frac{5}{2} = 4$

18. $6\sqrt[3]{x - 3} + 2 = \frac{1}{2}$

Solve the equation. Check for extraneous solutions.

19. $x^{5/3} = 243$

20. $x^{3/2} + 3 = 11$

21. $2x^{5/3} = -64$

22. $(x - 2)^{3/4} = 8$

23. $(3x + 12)^{3/2} - 3 = 24$

24. $(3x + 21)^{3/4} + 9 = 36$

Solve the equation. Check for extraneous solutions.

25. $\sqrt{x - 3} = \sqrt{2x - 7}$

26. $\sqrt{x + 3} = \sqrt{4x - 8}$

27. $\sqrt[3]{4x - 9} = \sqrt[3]{2x - 4}$

28. $\sqrt[4]{3x + 3} = \sqrt[4]{2x - 7}$

29. $\sqrt{x} + 1 = \sqrt{3x - 3}$

30. $\sqrt[3]{3x + 9} = \sqrt[3]{x + 6}$

31. $x + 2 = \sqrt{2x + 7}$

32. $\sqrt{2x + 3} = 1 + \sqrt{x + 1}$

In Exercises 33–35, use the following information.

Velocity The velocity of a free falling object is given by $V = \sqrt{2gh}$ where V is velocity (in meters per second), g is acceleration due to gravity (in meters per second squared), and h is the distance (in meters) the object has fallen. The value of g depends on which body/planet is attracting the object. If an object hits the surface with a velocity of 30 meters per second, from what height was it dropped in each of the following situations?

33. You are on Earth where $g = 9.81 \text{ m/s}^2$.

34. You are on the moon where $g = 1.57 \text{ m/s}^2$.

35. You are on Mars where $g = 3.72 \text{ m/s}^2$.

LESSON 3.4

Exercise Set B

MM3A3d Solve a variety of types of equations by appropriate means choosing among mental calculation, pencil and paper, or appropriate technology.

Solve the equation. Check your solution.

1. $(2x + 1)^{1/2} - 2 = 2$

2. $9 - \sqrt{x + 4} = 4$

3. $3\sqrt{4 - 3x} + 5 = 17$

4. $\sqrt{x^2 - 9} + 3 = 7$

5. $2\sqrt{x^2 - 3} + 3 = 15$

6. $(3x^2 - 2)^{1/2} + 4 = 9$

Solve the equation. Check your solution.

7. $(x - 2)^{1/3} - 3 = -5$

8. $8\sqrt[3]{x} + 7 = 31$

9. $\sqrt[3]{x + 5} + 2 = 7$

10. $10 - 3\sqrt[3]{2x + 5} = -11$

11. $(3x - 2)^{1/3} + \frac{2}{3} = 3$

12. $\sqrt[3]{x^3 + 3} + 1 = 4$

Solve the equation. Check for extraneous solutions.

13. $x^{3/2} = 125$

14. $(x + 3)^3 + 6 = -21$

15. $3(x - 5)^{3/2} - 6 = 18$

16. $\frac{1}{2}(x - 3)^{3/4} + 6 = 9$

17. $(5x + 14)^{2/3} + 10 = 6$

18. $2(4x^3 - 13)^{3/5} - 5 = 49$

Solve the equation. Check for extraneous solutions.

19. $\sqrt{2x - 6} = \sqrt{5x - 15}$

20. $\sqrt[3]{6x - 5} - \sqrt[3]{3x + 2} = 0$

21. $\sqrt[5]{8x + 11} = \sqrt[5]{5x - 4}$

22. $\sqrt{3x + 7} = x + 1$

23. $\sqrt{x} + 3 = \sqrt{x + 4}$

24. $\sqrt{x - 5} = \sqrt{x} - 2$

25. $\sqrt{x + 9} = 3 - \sqrt{x}$

26. $\sqrt{x + 3} = 1 + \sqrt{x + 1}$

27. $\sqrt{x - 7} = \sqrt{x + 1} + 2$

28. $\sqrt{x + 8} = \sqrt{x} + \sqrt{3}$

29. Geometry The lateral surface area S of a cone is given by $S = \pi r\sqrt{r^2 + h^2}$ where r is the radius and h is the height of the cone. The surface area of the base B of the cone is given by $B = \pi r^2$ where r is the radius of the cone. The total surface area of a cone with a radius of 9 inches is 216π square inches. What is the height of the cone?

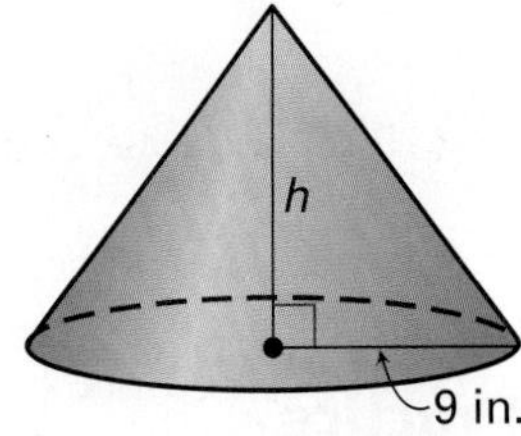

30. Geometry A container is to be made in the shape of a cylinder with a conical top. The lateral surface areas of the cylinder S_1 and cone S_2 are $S_1 = 2\pi rh$ and $S_2 = \pi r\sqrt{r^2 + h^2}$ where r is the radius and h is the height of the object. The surface area of the base B of the container is $B = \pi r^2$ where r is the radius of the container. The height of the cone is half the height of the cylinder. The radius of the container is 6 inches and its total surface area is 288π square inches. Find the total height of the container.

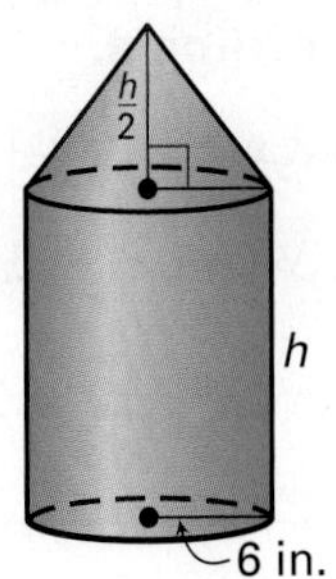

Georgia Performance Standards

MM3A3d Solve a variety of types of equations by appropriate means choosing among mental calculation, pencil and paper, or appropriate technology. 

Technology Activity

Radical Equations

Use after Lesson 3.4

Question

How can you use a graphing calculator to solve an equation with two radicals?

You can use a graphing calculator to solve an equation with two radicals by treating each side of the equation as a function. The solution of the equation will be the point of intersection of the graphs of the two functions.

Example

Solve equations with two radicals.

Use a graphing calculator to solve the equation with two radicals.

$\sqrt{4x + 28} = 3\sqrt{2x}$

Solution

Let the left side of the equation represent one function, so $Y_1 = \sqrt{4x + 28}$.

Let the right side of the equation represent another function, so $Y_2 = 3\sqrt{2x}$.

STEP 1 **Enter** the equations in the equation editor window.

STEP 2 **Graph** the functions in a standard viewing window.

STEP 3 **Use** the *intersect* feature of the calculator to find the point of intersection.

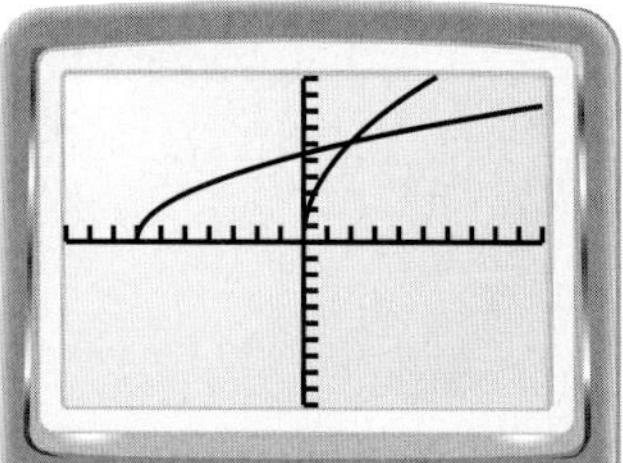

You can see that the point of intersection is (2, 6). So, the solution is $x = 2$.

Practice

Use a graphing calculator to find the solution of the equation with two radicals.

1. $\sqrt{x + 2} = \sqrt{10 - 3x}$

2. $\sqrt{x + 5} = 5 - \sqrt{x}$

3. $\sqrt{2x + 3} = 3 - \sqrt{2x}$

4. $\sqrt{2x - 1} = \sqrt{x + 4}$

5. $\sqrt{2x + 10} = 2\sqrt{x}$

6. $\sqrt{x - 6} = \sqrt{\frac{1}{3}x}$

UNIT 3

TEST | for Unit 3

Evaluate the expression without using a calculator.

1. $(\sqrt[3]{8})^5$

2. $(\sqrt[4]{256})^3$

3. $(\sqrt[4]{81})^2$

4. $16^{3/4}$

5. $125^{4/3}$

6. $49^{3/2}$

Solve the equation. Round the result to two decimal places when appropriate.

7. $x^5 = 327$

8. $2x^4 + 17 = 209$

9. $5x^3 - 12 = 83$

10. $(x + 6)^4 = 334$

11. $(2x - 5)^5 = 728$

12. $(x + 7)^3 - 27 = 531$

Simplify the expression. Assume all variables are positive.

13. $\sqrt{x^{2/3}}$

14. $x^{3/4} \cdot x^{7/4}$

15. $(x^{2/3})^{6/5}$

16. $\left(\dfrac{x^4}{64}\right)^{1/3}$

17. $\sqrt[3]{81x^5}$

18. $\dfrac{6}{x + \sqrt{7y}}$

Perform the indicated operation. Assume all variables are positive.

19. $7\sqrt{5} + 5\sqrt{5}$

20. $\sqrt{54} - 5\sqrt{6}$

21. $2\sqrt{18} + \sqrt{8}$

22. $6\sqrt{x} - \sqrt{4x}$

23. $\sqrt{(11\sqrt{2} - 2\sqrt{2})}$

24. $5x\sqrt[3]{xy^7} - 3y\sqrt[3]{x^4y^4}$

Graph the function. Then state the domain and range.

25. $f(x) = \sqrt{x} + 5$

26. $f(x) = \sqrt{x - 4} + 6$

27. $f(x) = -3\sqrt[3]{x}$

28. $f(x) = 2\sqrt{x + 2} - 2$

29. $f(x) = \frac{3}{5}\sqrt[3]{x + 4} - 1$

30. $f(x) = -\frac{1}{2}\sqrt[3]{x - 2} + 2$

31. $f(x) = -2\sqrt{x + 3} + 1$

32. $f(x) = -\frac{1}{3}\sqrt[3]{x - 1} + 3$

33. $f(x) = \frac{1}{2}\sqrt[3]{x + 3} + 2$

Solve the equation. Check your solution.

34. $\sqrt{x} - 4 = 5$

35. $7\sqrt[3]{x} - 4 = 3$

36. $(x + 1)^{1/2} + 5 = 8$

37. $4 = \sqrt[3]{2x - 8}$

38. $\sqrt{3x + 12} = 6$

39. $(4x + 7)^{1/3} - 5 = -2$

Solve the equation. Check for extraneous solutions.

40. $(x + 12)^{3/2} - 15 = 12$

41. $x + 2 = \sqrt{28 - x}$

42. $x - 1 = \sqrt{x + 41}$

43. $x + 1 = \sqrt{19 - x}$

44. $\sqrt{3x + 5} = \sqrt{4x - 2}$

45. $\sqrt[3]{5x + 4} = \sqrt[3]{2x - 8}$

46. Geometry Find the radius of a circle with an area of 907 square centimeters.

47. Geometry Find the radius of a sphere with a volume of 2.14 cubic feet.

48. **Physics** In physics, transitional kinetic energy E (in Joules) is given by the equation $E = \frac{1}{2}mv^2$ where m represents the mass in kilograms, and v represents the velocity (in meters per second). Find the velocity of a thrown baseball at time of release whose mass is 0.148 kilogram, and whose transitional kinetic energy is 90.65 Joules.

49. **Placemat** A rectangular placemat on a table is 15 inches long and 9 inches wide. A circular plate is sitting on the placemat. The area of the placemat that is not covered by the plate is 84.76 square inches. What is the radius of the plate?

50. **Pendulum** The period T (in seconds) of a pendulum can be modeled by $T = 1.11\sqrt{\ell}$ where ℓ is the pendulum's length (in feet). How long is a pendulum with a period of 5 seconds?

51. **Pendulum** Use the equation from Exercise 50 to determine the length of a pendulum with a period of 1.4 seconds.

52. **Velocity** The velocity of a free falling object is given by $V = \sqrt{19.62h}$, where V is velocity (in meters per second) and h is the distance (in meters) the object has fallen. If an object hit the ground with a velocity of 55 meters per second, from what height was it dropped?

53. Surface Area The lateral surface area of a cone is given by $S = \pi r\sqrt{r^2 + h^2}$ where r is the radius and h is the height of the cone. A cone has a radius of 12 inches and a lateral surface area of 912 square inches. What is the height of the cone?

Performance Task

Park Design

A park has a circular pond and a square picnic area. The length of a side of the picnic area is the same as the diameter of the pond.

a. The area of the picnic area is 2809 square feet. What is the radius of the pond?

b. Solve the equation $A = \pi r^2$ for r.

c. Write the equation you found in part (b) using rational exponents.

d. Graph the equation you found in part (b). How does the graph of the equation differ from the graph of $f(x) = \sqrt{x}$?

e. Suppose the park is going to build a cone-shaped cover for the pond, without a bottom. The amount of material needed for the cover is 2387 square feet. Use the formula for the lateral surface area of a cone, $S = \pi r\sqrt{r^2 + h^2}$, to determine the height of the cone-shaped cover.

f. Find the height of the cone-shaped cover if only 2230 square feet of material is available.

UNIT 4
Algebra: Exponential and Logarithmic Functions

4.1 Graph Exponential Growth Functions (MM3A2e, MM3A2f, MM3A2g)

4.2 Graph Exponential Decay Functions (MM3A2e, MM3A2f, MM3A2g)

4.3 Use Functions Involving *e* (MM3A2e, MM3A2f, MM3A2g, MM3A3d)

4.4 Evaluate Logarithms and Graph Logarithmic Functions (MM3A2c, MM3A2e, MM3A2f)

4.5 Interpret Graphs of Exponential and Logarithmic Functions (MM3A2e, MM3A2f)

4.6 Apply Properties of Logarithms (MM3A2d, MM3A2g)

4.7 Solve Exponential and Logarithmic Equations (MM3A3b, MM3A3d)

4.8 Solve Exponential and Logarithmic Inequalities (MM3A3c)

4.9 Write and Apply Exponential and Power Functions (MM3A2g)

LESSON 4.1

Graph Exponential Growth Functions

Georgia Performance Standards: MM3A2e, MM3A2f, MM3A2g

Goal Graph and use exponential growth functions.

Vocabulary

An **exponential function** has the form $y = ab^x$, where $a \neq 0$ and the base b is a positive number other than 1.

If $a > 0$ and $b > 1$, then the function $y = ab^x$ is an **exponential growth function,** and b is called the **growth factor.**

An **asymptote** is a line that a graph approaches more and more closely.

Exponential Growth Model When a real-life quantity increases by a fixed percent each year (or other time period), the amount y of the quantity after t years can be modeled by the equation $y = a(1 + r)^t$, where a is the initial amount and r is the percent increase expressed as a decimal. Note that the quantity $1 + r$ is the growth factor.

UNIT 4

Example 1 Graph $y = b^x$ for $b > 1$

Graph $y = 5^x$.

STEP 1 **Make** a table of values.

x	-2	-1	0	1	2
y	$\frac{1}{25}$	$\frac{1}{5}$	1	5	25

STEP 2 **Plot** the points from the table.

STEP 3 **Draw,** from *left* to *right*, a smooth curve that begins just above the x-axis, passes through the plotted points, and moves up to the right.

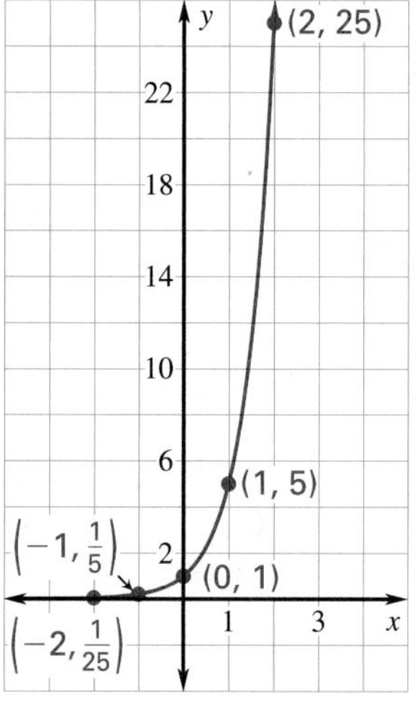

Example 2 Graph $y = ab^x$ for $b > 1$

Graph $y = \left(-\frac{1}{4}\right) \cdot 2^x$.

Plot $\left(0, -\frac{1}{4}\right)$ and $\left(1, -\frac{1}{2}\right)$. From *left* to *right*, draw a curve that begins just below below the x-axis, passes through the two points, and moves down to the right.

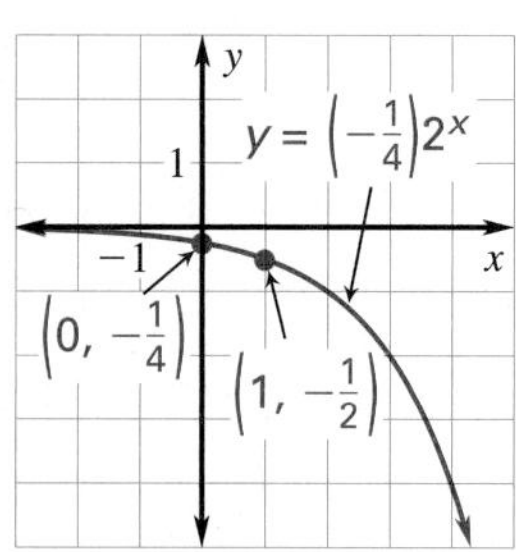

Georgia Performance Standards

MM3A2e Investigate and explain characteristics of exponential and logarithmic functions including domain and range, asymptotes, zeros, intercepts, intervals of increase and decrease, and rate of change. 

MM3A2f Graph functions as transformations of $f(x) = a^x$, $f(x) = \log_a x$, $f(x) = e^x$, $f(x) = \ln x$. 

MM3A2g Explore real phenomena related to exponential and logarithmic functions including half-life and doubling time. 

Example 3 Graph $y = ab^{x-h} + k$ for $b > 1$

Graph $y = 3 \cdot 2^{x+1} + 2$. State the domain and range.

Begin by sketching the graph of $y = 3 \cdot 2^x$, which passes through (0, 3) and (1, 6). Because the function is of the form $y = ab^{x-h} + k$ where $h = -1$ and $k = 2$, translate the graph of $y = 3 \cdot 2^x$ left 1 unit and up 2 units.

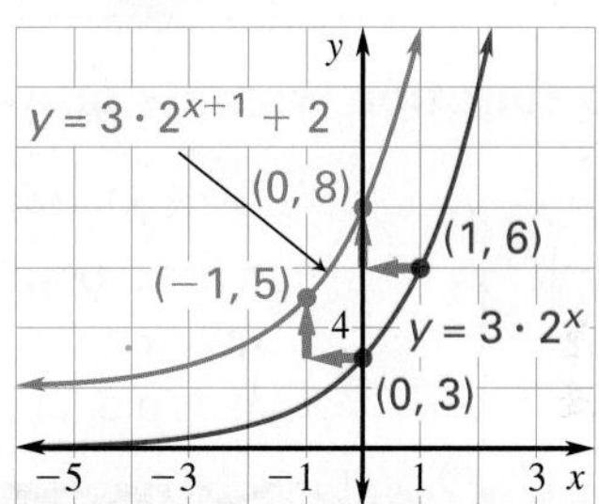

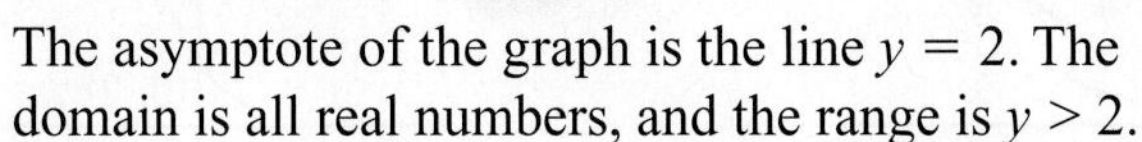

The asymptote of the graph is the line $y = 2$. The domain is all real numbers, and the range is $y > 2$.

Example 4 Find the doubling time for an account

Finance You deposit \$3000 in an account that pays 6% interest compounded annually. In about how many years will the balance double?

STEP 1 **Write** an exponential growth function using the compound interest formula.

$$A = P\left(1 + \frac{r}{n}\right)^{nt}$$

$$A = 3000\left(1 + \frac{0.06}{1}\right)^{(1)t}$$

$$A = 3000(1.06)^t$$

STEP 2 **Graph** the model.

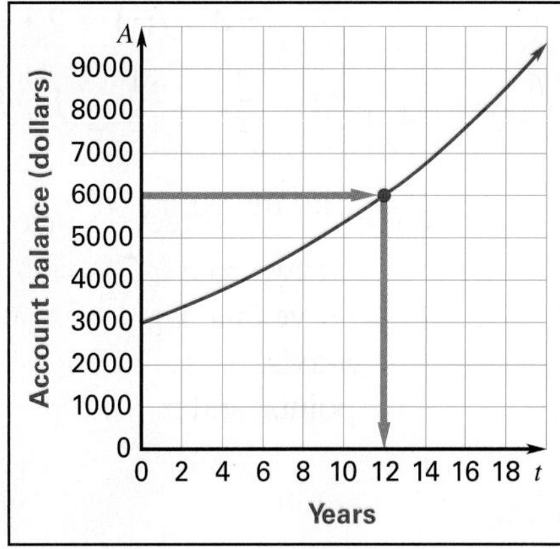

STEP 3 **Use** the graph to estimate the year when the balance of the account is \$6000, double the initial balance.

The balance of the account doubles in about 12 years.

Guided Practice for Examples 1, 2, 3, and 4

Graph the function. State the domain and range.

1. $y = 6^x$

2. $f(x) = -\left(\frac{1}{4}\right) \cdot 8^x$

3. $y = \frac{1}{2} \cdot 3^{x-5} + 4$

4. You deposit \$2000 in an account that pays 4.75% interest compounded annually. In about how many years will the balance double?

UNIT 4

LESSON 4.1

Exercise Set A

MM3A2e Investigate and explain characteristics of exponential and logarithmic functions including domain and range, asymptotes, zeros, intercepts, intervals of increase and decrease, and rate of change.

MM3A2f Graph functions as transformations of $f(x) = a^x$, $f(x) = \log_a x$, $f(x) = e^x$, $f(x) = \ln x$.

MM3A2g Explore real phenomena related to exponential and logarithmic functions including half-life and doubling time.

Match the function with its graph.

1. $y = 4 \cdot 2^x$

2. $y = 2 \cdot 4^x$

3. $y = -4 \cdot 2^x$

A.

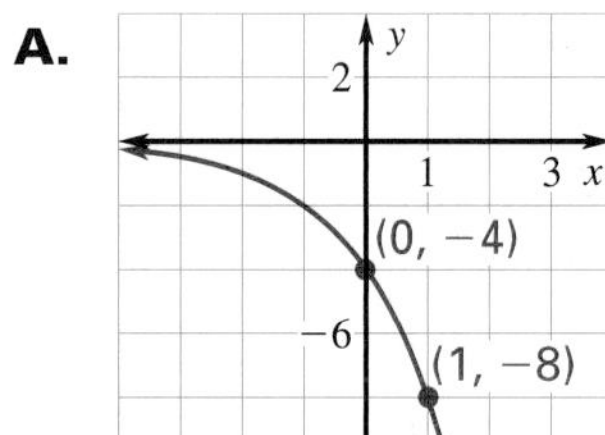

B.

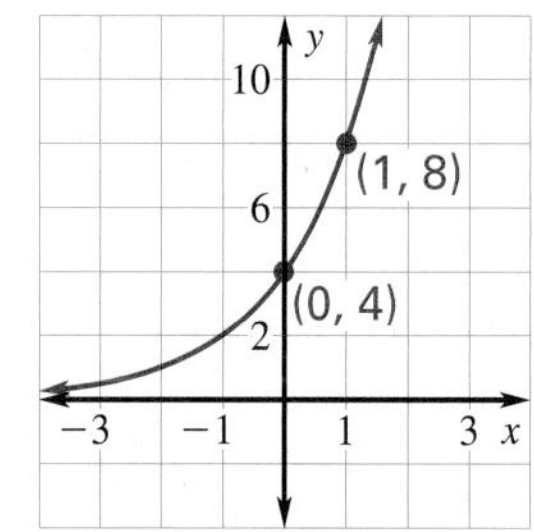

C.

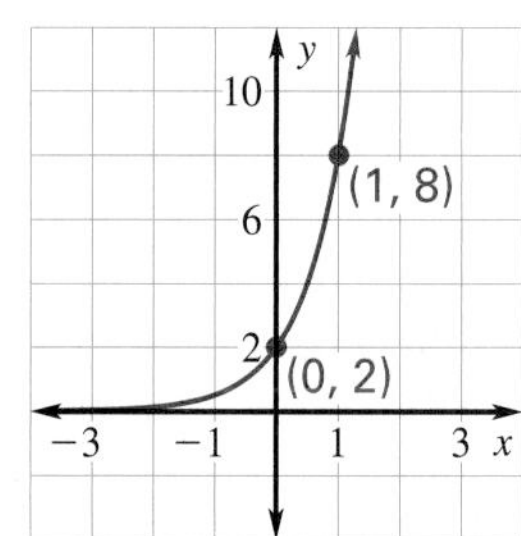

Graph the function. State the domain and range.

4. $y = 5^x$

5. $f(x) = 9^x$

6. $y = \frac{1}{3} \cdot 6^x$

7. $f(x) = -\left(\frac{3}{2}\right)^x$

8. $f(x) = 2 \cdot \left(\frac{5}{4}\right)^x$

9. $y = 5^x + 1$

10. $f(x) = -3 \cdot 2^{x+3} + 1$

11. $y = 2 \cdot 5^{x-3} - 5$

12. $y = 5 \cdot 3^{x-4} - 6$

13. **Error Analysis** *Describe* and correct the error in graphing the function $y = \frac{1}{2} \cdot 6^x$.

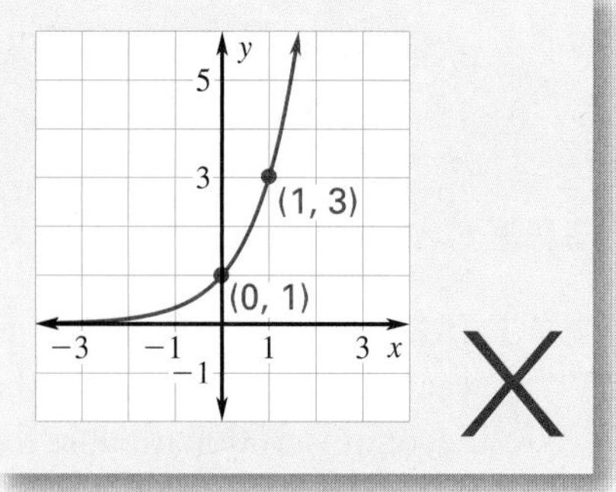

14. **Account Balance** You deposit \$2000 in an account that pays 4.5% interest compounded annually. Write a model giving the account balance A after t years. In about how many years will the balance double?

15. **Enrollment** The student enrollment of a high school was 1350 in 2008 and increases by 9% each year.

a. Write a model giving the enrollment E of the high school t years after 2008. What is the student enrollment in 2011?

b. Estimate when the enrollment will double.

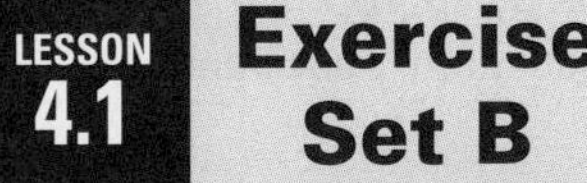

LESSON 4.1 **Exercise Set B**

MM3A2e Investigate and explain characteristics of exponential and logarithmic functions including domain and range, asymptotes, zeros, intercepts, intervals of increase and decrease, and rate of change.

MM3A2f Graph functions as transformations of $f(x) = a^x$, $f(x) = \log_a x$, $f(x) = e^x$, $f(x) = \ln x$.

MM3A2g Explore real phenomena related to exponential and logarithmic functions including half-life and doubling time.

Graph the function. State the domain and range.

1. $y = 7^x$

2. $f(x) = 5 \cdot 2^x$

3. $y = -2(2.5)^x$

4. $f(x) = -3 \cdot 2^{x+4}$

5. $f(x) = 5 \cdot 4^x - 7$

6. $y = 3^{x+1} + 3$

7. $f(x) = 8 \cdot 2^{x-3} - 1$

8. $y = -3.5^{x-1} + 2$

9. $y = 5 \cdot 2^{x-1} - 2$

In Exercises 10–12, use the following information.

Account Balance You deposit $4500 in an account that earns 3.5% annual interest. Find the balance after one year if the interest is compounded with the given frequency.

10. annually

11. monthly

12. quarterly

13. Population In 1990, the population of Austin, Texas, was 494,290. During the next 10 years, the population increased by about 3% per year.

a. Write a model giving the population P (in thousands) of Austin t years after 1990. What was the population in 2000?

b. Graph the model and state the domain and range.

c. Estimate the year when the population was about 540,000.

14. Antiques You purchase an antique end table in 2008 for $325. The value of the table is expected to increase by 5% per year.

a. Write a model giving the value v of the end table t years after 2008. What was the value of the table in 2010?

b. Graph the model and state the domain and range. Use the graph to estimate the year when the value of the end table will double its initial value.

15. Multiple Representations In 1977, there were 41 breeding pairs of bald eagles in Maryland. Over the next 24 years, the number of breeding pairs increased by about 8.9% per year.

a. Writing a Model Write a model giving the number n of breeding pairs of bald eagles in Maryland t years after 1977.

b. Making a Table Make a table of values for the model.

c. Graphing a Model Graph the model.

d. Estimating a Value Estimate the year in which the number of breeding pairs was double the number in 1977.

Georgia Performance Standards

MM3A2g Explore real phenomena related to exponential and logarithmic functions including half-life and doubling time. 

MM3A3d Solve a variety of types of equations by appropriate means choosing among mental calculation, pencil and paper, or appropriate technology.

LESSON 4.1

Problem Solving Workshop

Problem In 1998, there were about 29,670,000 Internet hosts. During the next 7 years, the number of hosts increased by about 39% each year. Write an exponential growth model giving the number h (in millions) of hosts t years after 1998. Use a graph to estimate the year when there were about 80 million hosts.

STEP 1 **Read and Understand**

What do you know? The number of Internet hosts in 1998 and the percent increase for the next 7 years

What do you want to find out? The exponential growth model and points on the model

STEP 2 **Make a Plan** Use what you know to substitute and solve the equation.

STEP 3 **Solve the Problem** The initial amount is $a = 29.67$ million and the percent increase is $r = 0.39$. So the exponential growth model is:

$h = a(1 + r)^t$	Write exponential growth model.
$= 29.67(1 + 0.39)^t$	Substitute 29.67 for a and 0.39 for r.
$= 29.67(1.39)^t$	Simplify.

The graph passes through the points (0, 29.67) and (1, 41.24). Plot a few other points. Then draw a smooth curve through the points.

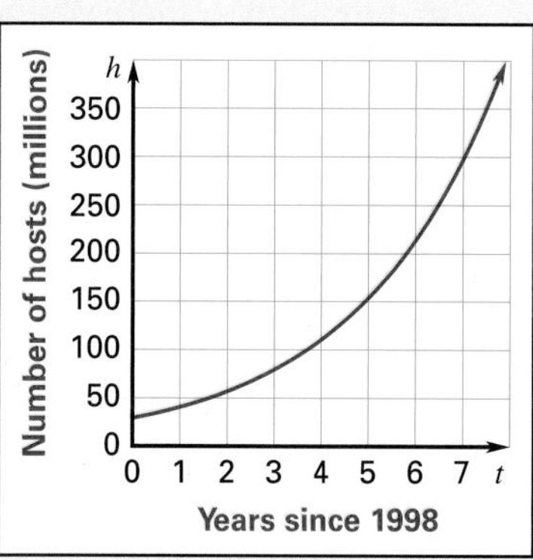

Using the graph, you can estimate that the number of hosts was about 80 million during 2001 ($t \approx 3$).

STEP 4 **Look Back** Substitute $t = 3$ into the equation to see that there were about $29.67(1.39)^3 \approx 79.68$ million hosts in 2001 which is reasonably close to 80 million. The answer is correct.

Practice

1. **Medicare** In 2000, the amount of federal budget outlays for Medicare was \$197.1 billion. During the next 5 years, the amount increased by about 8% each year. Write an exponential growth model giving the amount M (in billions of dollars) of outlays for Medicare t years after 2000. Use a graph to estimate the year when about \$250 billion was given to Medicare.

2. **Population** In 2000, the population of a town was 2200. During the next 15 years, the population of the town increased by about 3% each year. Write an exponential growth model giving the number p of people in the town t years after 2000. Use a graph to estimate the year when there were about 2800 people in the town.

LESSON 4.2

Graph Exponential Decay Functions

Georgia Performance Standards: MM3A2e, MM3A2f, MM3A2g

Goal Graph and use exponential decay functions.

Vocabulary

An **exponential decay function** has the form $y = ab^x$, where $a > 0$ and $0 < b < 1$.

The base b of an exponential decay function is called the **decay factor.**

The time required for a substance to fall to half its initial value is called **half-life.**

Exponential Decay Model When a real-life quantity decreases by a fixed percent each year (or other time period), the amount y of the quantity after t years can be modeled by the equation $y = a(1 - r)^t$, where a is the initial amount and r is the percent decrease expressed as a decimal. Note that the quantity $1 - r$ is the decay factor.

Example 1 Graph $y = b^x$ for $0 < b < 1$

Graph $y = \left(\frac{1}{2}\right)^x$.

Solution

STEP 1 **Make** a table of values.

x	-2	-1	0	1	2
y	4	2	1	$\frac{1}{2}$	$\frac{1}{4}$

STEP 2 **Plot** the points from the table.

STEP 3 **Draw,** from *right* to *left*, a smooth curve that begins just above the x-axis, passes through the plotted points, and moves up to the left.

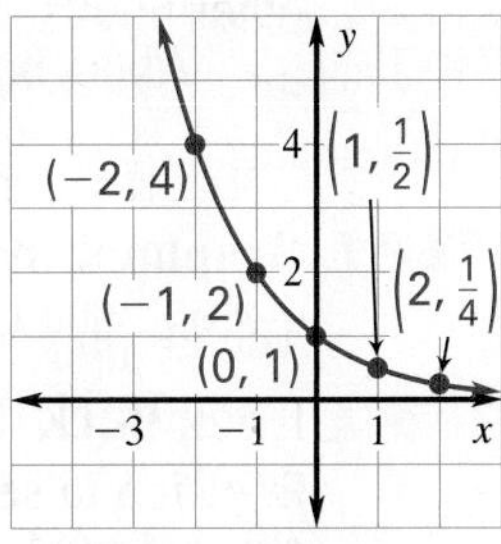

Example 2 Graph $y = ab^x$ for $0 < b < 1$

Graph $y = -3\left(\frac{2}{5}\right)^x$.

Solution

Plot $(0, -3)$ and $\left(1, -\frac{6}{5}\right)$. From *right* to *left*, draw a curve that begins just below the x-axis, passes through the two points, and moves down to the left.

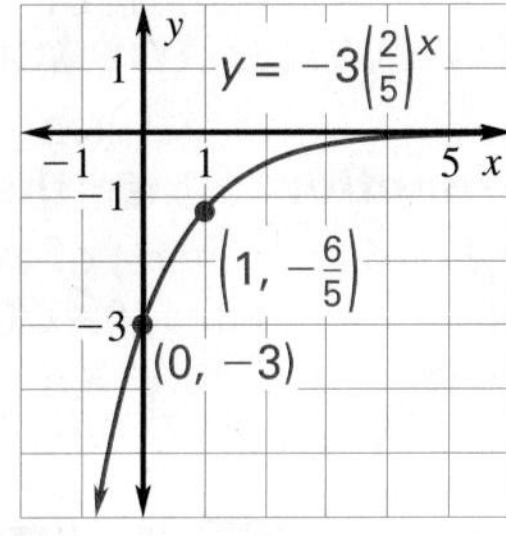

UNIT 4

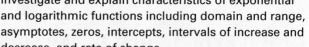

Georgia Performance Standards

MM3A2e Investigate and explain characteristics of exponential and logarithmic functions including domain and range, asymptotes, zeros, intercepts, intervals of increase and decrease, and rate of change. 

MM3A2f Graph functions as transformations of $f(x) = a^x$, $f(x) = \log_a x$, $f(x) = e^x$, $f(x) = \ln x$. 

MM3A2g Explore real phenomena related to exponential and logarithmic functions including half-life and doubling time.

Example 3 Graph $y = ab^{x-h} + k$ for $0 < b < 1$

Graph $y = 3\left(\frac{1}{2}\right)^{x+1} - 2$. State the domain and range.

Begin by sketching the graph of $y = 3\left(\frac{1}{2}\right)^x$ which passes through (0, 3) and $\left(1, \frac{3}{2}\right)$. Then translate the graph left 1 unit and down 2 units. The graph passes through (−1, 1) and $\left(0, -\frac{1}{2}\right)$.

The asymptote of the graph is the line $y = -2$. The domain is all real numbers, and the range is $y > -2$.

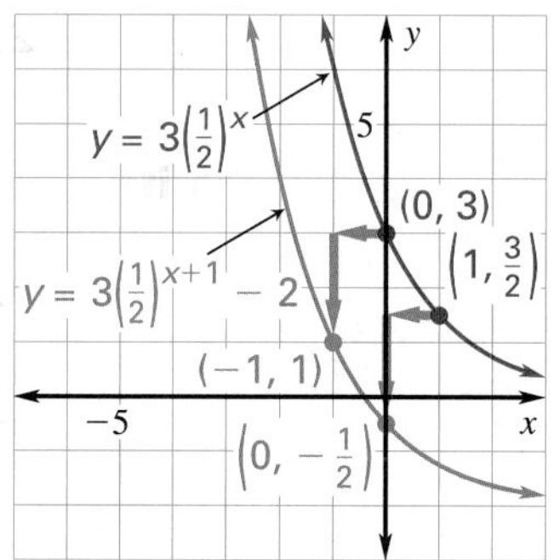

Example 4 Using a half-life model

Biology When a plant dies, it stops acquiring carbon-14 from the atmosphere. Carbon-14 decays over time with a half-life of about 5730 years. The percent P (in decimal form) of the original amount of carbon-14 that remains in a sample after t years is given by $P = 1\left(\frac{1}{2}\right)^{t/5730}$. About how many years after a plant dies will 60% of the carbon-14 in the plant remain?

STEP 1 **Graph** the model.

The graph passes through the point (0, 1). Plot a few other points. Then draw a smooth curve through the points.

STEP 2 **Use** the graph to estimate.

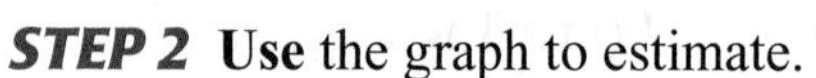

About 4200 years after the plant dies, 60% of the carbon-14 remains in the plant.

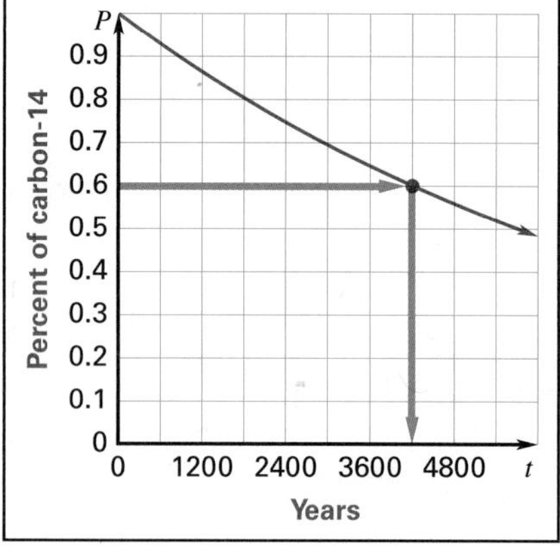

Guided Practice for Examples 1, 2, 3, and 4

Graph the function. State the domain and range.

1. $y = \left(\frac{1}{5}\right)^x$

2. $f(x) = -2\left(\frac{2}{3}\right)^x$

3. $y = 5\left(\frac{1}{3}\right)^{x+2} - 1$

4. About how many years after a plant dies will 50% of the carbon-14 in the plant remain?

LESSON **4.2**

Exercise Set A

MM3A2e Investigate and explain characteristics of exponential and logarithmic functions including domain and range, asymptotes, zeros, intercepts, intervals of increase and decrease, and rate of change.

MM3A2f Graph functions as transformations of $f(x) = a^x$, $f(x) = \log_a x$, $f(x) = e^x$, $f(x) = \ln x$.

MM3A2g Explore real phenomena related to exponential and logarithmic functions including half-life and doubling time.

Tell whether the function represents *exponential growth* or *exponential decay*.

1. $y = 9 \cdot \left(\frac{3}{4}\right)^x$ **2.** $y = 3 \cdot \left(\frac{5}{2}\right)^x$ **3.** $y = 5 \cdot (0.5)^x$

Match the function with its graph.

4. $y = 4 \cdot \left(\frac{1}{4}\right)^x$ **5.** $y = 4 \cdot 4^x$ **6.** $y = \left(\frac{1}{4}\right)^x + 4$

A.

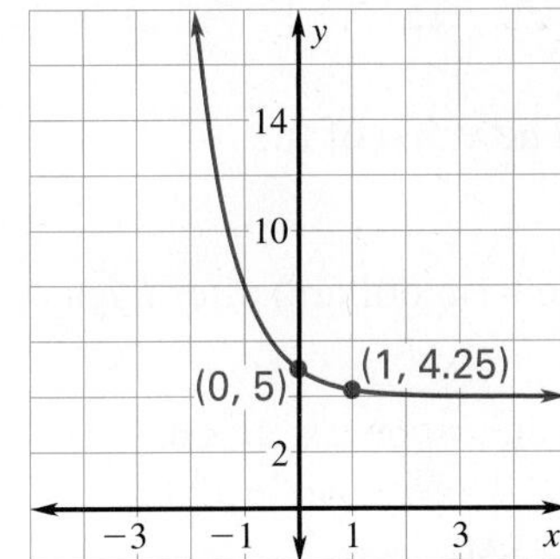

B.

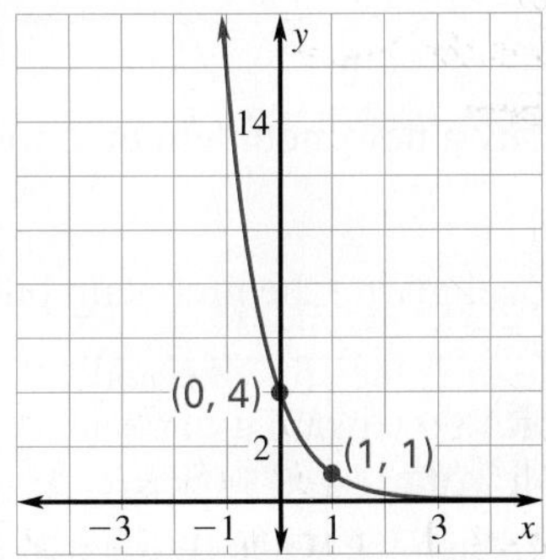

C.

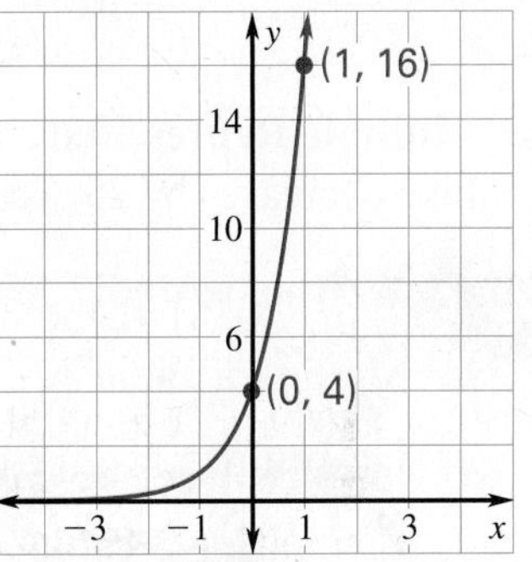

Graph the function. State the domain and range.

7. $y = \left(\frac{1}{6}\right)^x$ **8.** $f(x) = \left(\frac{1}{3}\right)^x + 1$ **9.** $y = -\left(\frac{1}{2}\right)^{x+3}$

10. $f(x) = -8\left(\frac{1}{2}\right)^{x-4}$ **11.** $y = 6\left(\frac{1}{3}\right)^{x-4} + 2$ **12.** $y = \left(\frac{2}{5}\right)^{x+1} - 2$

13. **Medicine** The half-life of a drug is the amount of time it takes for half of the active elements to be eliminated from the body. The amount A (in milligrams) of 200 milligrams of a certain drug that remains in the bloodstream after t hours is given by $A = 200\left(\frac{1}{2}\right)^{t/3}$. In about how many hours will 100 milligrams of the drug remain in the bloodstream?

14. **Radioactive Decay** The half-life of radium-226 is about 1600 years. The amount A (in grams) of radioactive radium-226 that remains in a sample after t years is given by $A = 10(0.5)^{t/1600}$.

a. What is the initial amount of radium-226? ($t = 0$)

b. In about how many years will 2.5 grams of radium-226 remain?

LESSON 4.2 **Exercise Set B**

MM3A2e Investigate and explain characteristics of exponential and logarithmic functions including domain and range, asymptotes, zeros, intercepts, intervals of increase and decrease, and rate of change.

MM3A2f Graph functions as transformations of $f(x) = a^x$, $f(x) = \log_a x$, $f(x) = e^x$, $f(x) = \ln x$.

MM3A2g Explore real phenomena related to exponential and logarithmic functions including half-life and doubling time.

Graph the function. State the domain and range.

1. $f(x) = 3\left(\frac{1}{5}\right)^x$ **2.** $y = -(0.2)^x$ **3.** $f(x) = -3\left(\frac{1}{4}\right)^x$

4. $f(x) = \left(\frac{1}{5}\right)^x - 4$ **5.** $y = -\left(\frac{2}{3}\right)^{x+3}$ **6.** $f(x) = -2\left(\frac{1}{2}\right)^{x+2} - 5$

7. $y = -\left(\frac{1}{2}\right)^{x+8} - 2$ **8.** $y = 10\left(\frac{1}{4}\right)^{x-5} + 1$ **9.** $y = \left(\frac{3}{5}\right)^{x+1} - 2$

10. **Multiple Representations** You buy a new mountain bike for \$200. The value of the bike decreases by 25% each year.

a. Writing a Model Write a model giving the mountain bike's value y (in dollars) after t years.

b. Making a Table Make a table of values for the model.

c. Graphing a Model Graph the model.

d. Estimating a Value Estimate when the value of the model will be \$50.

11. **Error Analysis** You invest \$700 in the stock of a company. The value of the stock decreases 3% each year. *Describe* and correct the error in writing a model for the value of the stock after t years.

$y = \left(\begin{array}{c}\text{Initial} \\ \text{amount}\end{array}\right)\left(\begin{array}{c}\text{Decay} \\ \text{factor}\end{array}\right)^t$

$y = 700(0.03)^t$

12. **Medicine** The amount A (in milligrams) of a certain drug that remains in the bloodstream after t hours is given by $A = 500\left(\frac{1}{2}\right)^{t/4}$. The initial amount of the drug is 500 milligrams. What is the half-life of the medication?

13. **Half-life Models** The half-life of phosphorus-32 is about 14 days. The amount A (in grams) of radioactive phosphorus-32 that remains in a sample after t days is given by $A = 400\left(\frac{1}{2}\right)^{t/14}$.

a. What is the initial amount of phosphorus-32? ($t = 0$)

b. How much phosphorus-32 is present after 10 days?

c. In about how many days will 100 grams of phosphorus-32 remain?

Georgia Performance Standards

MM3A2g Explore real phenomena related to exponential and logarithmic functions including half-life and doubling time. 

Technology Activity

Evaluate Exponential Decay Models

Use after Lesson 4.2

Question

How can you use the *table* feature of a graphing calculator to evaluate an exponential decay model?

When a real-life quantity decreases by a fixed percent each year (or other time period), the amount y of the quantity after t years can be modeled by the equation $y = a(1 - r)^t$ where a is the initial amount and r is the percent decrease expressed as a decimal. Note that the quantity $1 - r$ is the decay factor. You can use the *table* feature of a graphing calculator to evaluate a model at different times.

Example

Use the *table* feature of a graphing calculator.

A new car costs \$23,000. The value of the car will depreciate 14% each year for the first three years. Find the value of the car after two years.

Solution

The exponential decay model is $y = 23{,}000(1 - 0.14)^x$ or $y = 23{,}000(0.86)^x$, where x represents the number of years.

X	Y1
1	19780
2	17011
3	14629
4	12581
5	10820

Y1=17010.8

Use the *table* feature of a graphing calculator to find the value of the car after two years.

STEP 1 **Enter** the equation in the equation editor window.

STEP 2 **Set** up a table to display the x-values starting at 1 and increasing in increments of 1.

STEP 3 **View** the table. In the table, x represents the number of years and Y_1 represents the value of the car. So, you can easily see that the value of the car after two years is about \$17,011.

Practice

Use the *table* feature of a graphing calculator to complete the following.

1. A new motorcycle costs \$18,000. The value of the motorcycle will depreciate 12% each year. Write an exponential decay model for the situation. What is the value of the motorcycle after three years?

2. You buy a used motorcycle for \$10,000. The value of the motorcycle will depreciate 15% each year. Write an exponential decay model for the situation. When will the value of the motorcycle be about \$2700?

UNIT 4

LESSON 4.3

Use Functions Involving *e*

Georgia Performance Standards: MM3A2e, MM3A2f, MM3A2g, MM3A3d

Goal Study functions involving the natural base *e*.

Vocabulary

The number denoted by the letter e is called the **natural base e** or the *Euler number*. It is an irrational number defined as follows: As n approaches $+\infty$, $\left(1 + \frac{1}{n}\right)^n$ approaches $e \approx 2.718281828$.

A function of the form $f(x) = ae^{rx}$ is called a *natural base exponential function*.

Continuously Compounded Interest When interest is compounded *continuously*, the amount A in an account after t years is given by the formula $A = Pe^{rt}$, where P is the principal and r is the annual interest rate expressed as a decimal.

UNIT 4

Example 1 Simplify natural base expressions

Simplify the expression.

a. $e^6 \cdot e^4 = e^{6+4} = e^{10}$

b. $\frac{21e^8}{7e^2} = 3e^{8-2} = 3e^6$

c. $(-2e^x)^3 = (-2)^3(e^x)^3 = -8e^{3x}$

Example 2 Graph natural base functions

Graph the function. State the domain and range.

a. $y = 4e^{-x} + 5$

Because $a = 4$ is positive and $r = -1$ is negative, the function is an exponential decay function. Translate the graph of $y = 4e^{-x}$ up 5 units.

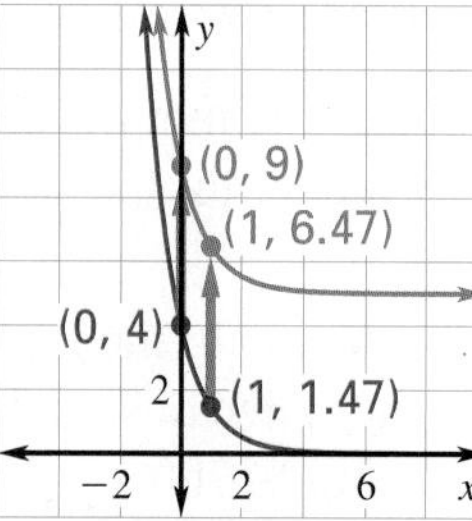

The domain is all real numbers, and the range is $y > 5$.

b. $y = e^{2(x+1)} - 2$

Because $a = 1$ is positive and $r = 2$ is positive, the function is an exponential growth function. Translate the graph of $y = e^{2x}$ left 1 unit and down 2 units.

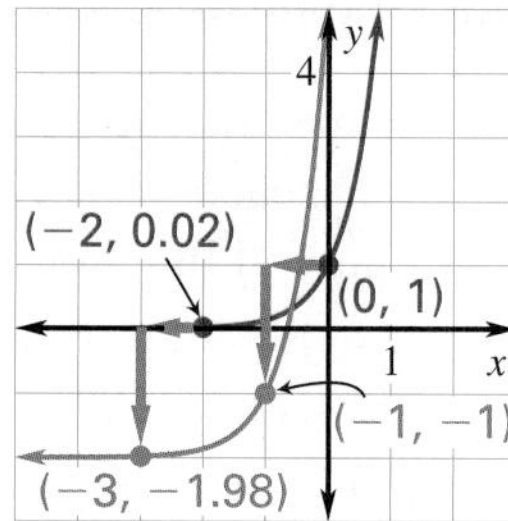

The domain is all real numbers, and the range is $y > -2$.

Georgia Performance Standards

MM3A2e Investigate and explain characteristics of exponential and logarithmic functions including domain and range, asymptotes, zeros, intercepts, intervals of increase and decrease, and rate of change. 

MM3A2f Graph functions as transformations of $f(x) = a^x$, $f(x) = \log_a x$, $f(x) = e^x$, $f(x) = \ln x$. 

MM3A2g Explore real phenomena related to exponential and logarithmic functions including half-life and doubling time.

MM3A3d Solve a variety of types of equations by appropriate means, choosing among mental calculation, pencil and paper, or appropriate technology.

Example 3 Solve a multi-step problem

Bacteria Growth A population of bacteria can be modeled by the function $P = 70e^{0.22t}$ where t is the time (in hours). Graph the model and use the graph to estimate the population after 4 hours.

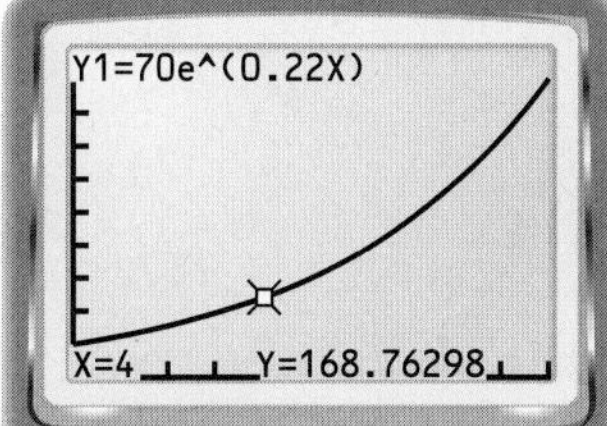

STEP 1 **Graph** the model, as shown.

STEP 2 **Use** the *trace* feature to find that $P \approx 168.76298$ when $t = 4$.

The population of bacteria is about 169 after 4 hours.

Example 4 Model continuously compounded interest

Compound Interest You deposit \$500 in an account that pays 3% annual interest compounded continuously. What is the balance after 2 years?

Solution

Use the formula for continuously compounded interest.

$A = Pe^{rt}$	Write formula.
$= 500e^{0.03(2)}$	Substitute 500 for P, 0.03 for r, and 2 for t.
≈ 530.92	Use a calculator.

The balance at the end of 2 years is \$530.92.

Guided Practice for Examples 1, 2, 3, and 4

Simplify the expression.

1. $e^8 \cdot e$ **2.** $4e^{-5} \cdot 7e^8$ **3.** $\frac{18e^{10}}{3e^5}$ **4.** $(11e^{-3x})^2$

Graph the function. State the domain and range.

5. $y = 2e^{0.6x} - 1$ **6.** $y = 5e^{-2x}$ **7.** $y = \frac{2}{3}e^{x+3} + 2$

8. You deposit \$2000 in an account that pays 4% annual interest compounded continuously. Find the balance after each amount of time.

a. 1 year **b.** 3 years **c.** 5.5 years

UNIT 4

LESSON 4.3 **Exercise Set A**

MM3A2e Investigate and explain characteristics of exponential and logarithmic functions including domain and range, asymptotes, zeros, intercepts, intervals of increase and decrease, and rate of change.

MM3A2f Graph functions as transformations of $f(x) = a^x$, $f(x) = \log_a x$, $f(x) = e^x$, $f(x) = \ln x$.

MM3A2g Explore real phenomena related to exponential and logarithmic functions including half-life and doubling time.

MM3A3d Solve a variety of types of equations by appropriate means, choosing among mental calculation, pencil and paper, or appropriate technology.

Simplify the expression.

1. $e^{-5} \cdot e^2$ **2.** $e^3 \cdot e^{-3}$ **3.** $(e^4)^{-3}$

4. $(2e^3)^2$ **5.** $\left(\frac{3e^3}{6e^2}\right)^2$ **6.** $\left(\frac{8e^2}{2e^5}\right)^{-1}$

7. $3e^x \cdot 2e^{4x}$ **8.** $\sqrt{9e^4} \cdot 2e^{-3}$ **9.** $\frac{e^3}{e^{x+3}}$

10. Error Analysis *Describe* and correct the error in simplifying the expression.

$$(3e^{5x})^2 = 3e^{(5x)(2)} = 3e^{10x}$$ X

Use a calculator to evaluate the expression. Round the result to three decimal places.

11. e^7 **12.** $e^{-3/2}$ **13.** $e^{0.6}$ **14.** $e^{\sqrt{3}}$

Tell whether the function is an example of *exponential growth* or *exponential decay*.

15. $f(x) = 4e^{2x}$ **16.** $f(x) = e^{-5x}$ **17.** $f(x) = 6e^{-x}$

18. $f(x) = \frac{1}{4}e^{4x}$ **19.** $f(x) = \frac{1}{8}e^{-x}$ **20.** $f(x) = -e^{-x/2}$

Graph the function. State the domain and range.

21. $f(x) = 3e^x$ **22.** $f(x) = 3e^{-x}$ **23.** $f(x) = -e^x + 3$

24. $f(x) = 2e^{x-1} + 1$ **25.** $f(x) = \frac{1}{2}e^{x-2} - 3$ **26.** $f(x) = e^{2x+1} + 2$

In Exercises 27 and 28, use the following information.

Finance You deposit \$2200 in an account that pays 3% annual interest. After 15 years, you withdraw the money.

27. What is the balance if the interest is compounded quarterly?

28. What is the balance if the interest is compounded continuously?

UNIT 4

LESSON 4.3

Exercise Set B

MM3A2e Investigate and explain characteristics of exponential and logarithmic functions including domain and range, asymptotes, zeros, intercepts, intervals of increase and decrease, and rate of change.

MM3A2f Graph functions as transformations of $f(x) = a^x$, $f(x) = \log_a x$, $f(x) = e^x$, $f(x) = \ln x$.

MM3A2g Explore real phenomena related to exponential and logarithmic functions including half-life and doubling time.

MM3A3d Solve a variety of types of equations by appropriate means, choosing among mental calculation, pencil and paper, or appropriate technology.

Simplify the expression.

1. $\frac{1}{2}e^{-2}(2e^4)^3$
2. $\left(\frac{e^3}{3e}\right)^{-2}$
3. $\left(\frac{2e^{-4}}{6}\right)^{-3}$
4. $(2e^{1.2x})^5$
5. $\left(\frac{e^{4x-1}}{\sqrt{4e^{2x}}}\right)^3$
6. $\sqrt[3]{16e^{10x}}$

Use a calculator to evaluate the expression. Round the result to three decimal places.

7. e^5
8. $e^{-\sqrt{3}/2}$
9. $e^{-1.6}$
10. e^e

Graph the function. State the domain and range.

11. $f(x) = 2e^x - 3$
12. $f(x) = \frac{1}{2}e^{-x} + 1$
13. $f(x) = -e^{x+2} + 2$
14. $f(x) = \frac{1}{4}e^{2x-1} + 1$
15. $f(x) = \frac{3}{5}e^{2-x} - 4$
16. $f(x) = \frac{3}{2}e^{3(x-2)} - 3$

In Exercises 17–21, use the following information.

Learning Curve The management at a factory has determined that a worker can produce a maximum of 45 units per day. The model $y = 45 - 42e^{-0.05t}$ indicates the number of units y that a new employee can produce per day after t days on the job.

17. Is the model an example of exponential growth or exponential decay?
18. Graph the function.
19. How many units can be produced by an employee on the first day?
20. How many units can be produced per day by an employee who has been on the job 13 days?
21. Use the graph to estimate how many days of employment are required for a worker to produce 30 units per day.

UNIT 4

Georgia Performance Standards

MM3A2c Define logarithmic functions as inverses of exponential functions.

Investigating Math Activity

Explore Exponential and Logarithmic Equations

Use before Lesson 4.4

Question

How can you rewrite an exponential equation as a logarithmic equation?

It is simple to evaluate a numerical exponential expression. For example, the exponential expression 4^2 has a value of 16. It is more difficult, however, to determine the value of x that would satisfy $3^x = 15$. Mathematicians define this x-value as a logarithm and write $x = \log_3 15$.

Explore

Evaluate exponential expressions.

Evaluate the exponential expression. Notice how the resulting equation compares with the corresponding logarithmic equation.

	Exponential Equation	Logarithmic Equation
a.	$3^2 = \underline{\ ?\ }$	$\log_3 9 = 2$
b.	$2^{-3} = \underline{\ ?\ }$	$\log_2 \frac{1}{8} = -3$
c.	$5^0 = \underline{\ ?\ }$	$\log_5 1 = 0$
d.	$\left(\frac{1}{6}\right)^{-2} = \underline{\ ?\ }$	$\log_{1/6} 36 = -2$

Draw Conclusions

1. *Compare* your answers in the *Exponential Equation* column with a classmate.
2. In an exponential expression, the number being raised to a power is called the *base*. In a logarithmic expression, the number that is written as the subscript of *log* is known as the *base*. How does the base in the exponential equation compare with the base in the logarithmic equation for each pair of equations?
3. How does the exponent in the exponential equation compare with the value of the logarithmic equation for each pair of equations? How does the value of the exponential equation compare with the number following the subscript in the logarithmic equation for each pair of equations?
4. Writing *Explain* how to rewrite exponential equations as logarithmic equations. Then rewrite the following exponential equations as logarithmic equations.

   a. $2^5 = 32$ **b.** $4^{-2} = \frac{1}{16}$ **c.** $3^4 = 81$

LESSON 4.4

Evaluate Logarithms and Graph Logarithmic Functions

Georgia Performance Standards: MM3A2c, MM3A2e, MM3A2f

Goal Evaluate logarithms and graph logarithmic functions.

Vocabulary

Let b and y be positive numbers with $b \neq 1$. The **logarithm of y with base b** is denoted by $\log_b y$ and is defined as follows: $\log_b y = x$ if and only if $b^x = y$.

A **common logarithm** is a logarithm with base 10, denoted by log.

A **natural logarithm** is a logarithm with base e, denoted by ln.

A **logarithmic function** is a function of the form $f(x) = \log_b x$.

By definition of a logarithm, it follows that the logarithmic function $g(x) = \log_b x$ is the inverse of the exponential function $f(x) = b^x$. This means that $g(f(x)) = \log_b b^x = x$ and $f(g(x)) = b^{\log_b x} = x$.

Example 1 Rewrite logarithmic equations

	Logarithmic Form	Exponential Form
a.	$\log_2 16 = 4$	$2^4 = 16$
b.	$\log_4 1 = 0$	$4^0 = 1$
c.	$\log_9 9 = 1$	$9^1 = 9$
d.	$\log_{1/5} 25 = -2$	$\left(\frac{1}{5}\right)^{-2} = 25$

Example 2 Evaluate logarithms

Evaluate the logarithm.

a. $\log_3 81$ **b.** $\log_4 0.25$ **c.** $\log_{1/6} 36$ **d.** $\log_{27} 3$

Solution

a. $3^4 = 81$, so $\log_3 81 = 4$.

b. $4^{-1} = 0.25$, so $\log_4 0.25 = -1$.

c. $\left(\frac{1}{6}\right)^{-2} = 36$, so $\log_{1/6} 36 = -2$.

d. $27^{1/3} = 3$, so $\log_{27} 3 = \frac{1}{3}$.

Guided Practice for Examples 1 and 2

Rewrite the equation in exponential form.

1. $\log_5 125 = 3$ **2.** $\log_{11} 11 = 1$ **3.** $\log_8 1 = 0$ **4.** $\log_{1/3} 27 = -3$

Evaluate the logarithm.

5. $\log_6 216$ **6.** $\log_5 \frac{1}{25}$ **7.** $\log_{1/2} 64$ **8.** $\log_{32} 2$

Georgia Performance Standards

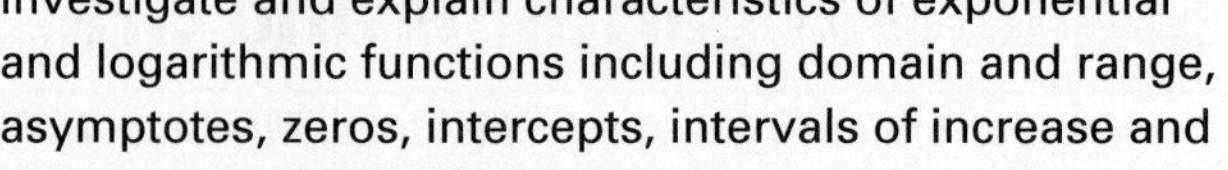

MM3A2c Define logarithmic functions as inverses of exponential functions. ☑

MM3A2e Investigate and explain characteristics of exponential and logarithmic functions including domain and range, asymptotes, zeros, intercepts, intervals of increase and decrease, and rate of change. ☑

MM3A2f Graph functions as transformations of $f(x) = a^x$, $f(x) = \log_a x$, $f(x) = e^x$, $f(x) = \ln x$. ☑

Example 3 Simplify using inverse properties

a. $10^{\log 9.6} = 9.6$ $\quad$ $b^{\log_b x} = x$

b. $\log_7 49^{2x} = \log_7(7^2)^{2x}$ $\quad$ Express 49 as a power with base 7.

$= \log_7(7)^{4x}$ $\quad$ Power of a power property

$= 4x$ $\quad$ $\log_b b^x = x$

Example 4 Find inverse functions

Find the inverse of the function.

a. $y = 8^x$; From the definition of logarithm, the inverse of $y = 8^x$ is $y = \log_8 x$.

b.

$y = \ln(x - 2)$	Original function
$x = \ln(y - 2)$	Switch x and y.
$e^x = y - 2$	Write in exponential form.
$e^x + 2 = y$	Solve for y.

The inverse of $y = \ln(x - 2)$ is $y = e^x + 2$.

Example 5 Translate a logarithmic graph

Graph $y = \log_3(x + 1) - 2$. State the domain and range.

STEP 1 **Sketch** the graph of the parent function $y = \log_3 x$, which passes through (1, 0), (3, 1), and (9, 2).

STEP 2 **Translate** the parent graph left 1 unit and down 2 units. The translated graph passes through (0, −2), (2, −1), and (8, 0). The graph's asymptote is $x = -1$.

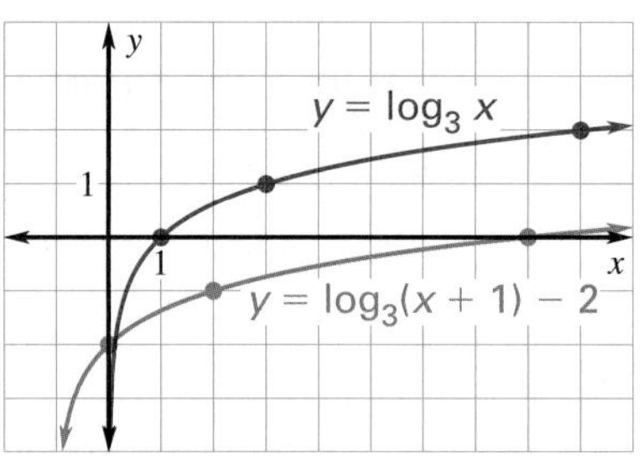

The domain is $x > -1$, and the range is all real numbers.

Guided Practice for Examples 3, 4, and 5

Simplify the expression.

9. $e^{\ln 4.5}$ **10.** $\ln e^{-2x}$ **11.** $\log_4 4^{7x}$ **12.** $10^{\log 3x}$

13. Find the inverse of $y = \ln(x + 1)$. **14.** Find the inverse of $y = 5^x$.

15. Graph $y = \log_2(x - 4) - 3$. State the domain and range.

LESSON 4.4 **Exercise Set A**

MM3A2c Define logarithmic functions as inverses of exponential functions.

MM3A2e Investigate and explain characteristics of exponential and logarithmic functions including domain and range, asymptotes, zeros, intercepts, intervals of increase and decrease, and rate of change.

MM3A2f Graph functions as transformations of $f(x) = a^x$, $f(x) = \log_a x$, $f(x) = e^x$, $f(x) = \ln x$.

Rewrite the equation in exponential form.

1. $\log_7 49 = 2$ **2.** $\log_2 16 = 4$ **3.** $\log_5 125 = 3$

4. $\log_{16} 4 = \frac{1}{2}$ **5.** $\log_4 \frac{1}{4} = -1$ **6.** $\log_3 \frac{1}{9} = -2$

Evaluate the logarithm without using a calculator.

7. $\log_9 81$ **8.** $\log_8 1$ **9.** $\log_3 \frac{1}{3}$

10. $\log_4 2$ **11.** $\log_{27} 3$ **12.** $\log_4 4^{2/3}$

Use a calculator to evaluate the logarithm. Round the result to three decimal places.

13. $\ln \sqrt{5}$ **14.** $\log 110$ **15.** $\ln \frac{1}{2}$

Find the inverse of the function.

16. $y = \log_5 x$ **17.** $y = \ln x$ **18.** $y = \log_{1/5} x$

19. $y = \log \frac{x}{2}$ **20.** $y = \log_6(x + 2)$ **21.** $y = \log_3 9x$

Graph the function. State the domain and range.

22. $f(x) = \log_3 x$ **23.** $f(x) = \log_3(x + 2)$ **24.** $f(x) = -\log_3 x - 1$

25. Galloping Speed Four-legged animals run with two different types of motion: trotting and galloping. An animal that is trotting has at least one foot on the ground at all times. An animal that is galloping has all four feet off the ground at times. The number S of strides per minute at which an animal breaks from a trot to a gallop is related to the animal's weight w (in pounds) by the model $S = 256.2 - 47.9 \log w$. Approximate the number of strides per minute for a 450 pound horse when it breaks from a trot to a gallop.

26. Tornadoes The wind speed S (in miles per hour) near the center of a tornado is related to the distance d (in miles) the tornado travels by the model $S = 93 \log d + 65$. Approximate the wind speed of a tornado that traveled 75 miles.

UNIT 4

LESSON 4.4

Exercise Set B

MM3A2c Define logarithmic functions as inverses of exponential functions.

MM3A2e Investigate and explain characteristics of exponential and logarithmic functions including domain and range, asymptotes, zeros, intercepts, intervals of increase and decrease, and rate of change.

MM3A2f Graph functions as transformations of $f(x) = a^x$, $f(x) = \log_a x$, $f(x) = e^x$, $f(x) = \ln x$.

Rewrite the equation in exponential form.

1. $\log_4 2 = \frac{1}{2}$ **2.** $\log_3 81 = 4$ **3.** $\log_{1/4} 64 = -3$

Evaluate the logarithm without using a calculator.

4. $\log_4 \frac{1}{64}$ **5.** $\log 10\sqrt{10}$ **6.** $\log_4 32$

7. $\log_8 4$ **8.** $\log_{16} \frac{1}{2}$ **9.** $\log_{25} 125$

Use a calculator to evaluate the logarithm. Round the result to three decimal places.

10. $1 + \ln 7$ **11.** $\frac{\log 82}{0.24}$ **12.** $\frac{\ln 15}{2 - \ln 10}$

Find the inverse of the function.

13. $y = \log_7 x$ **14.** $y = \log_3 4x$

15. $y = \log_{1/2}(2x) + 3$ **16.** $y = \ln x + 2$

17. $y = \ln(x - 1) - 3$ **18.** $y = \log_2 8^{x-1}$

Graph the function. State the domain and range.

19. $f(x) = \log_2(x + 2)$ **20.** $f(x) = -\log_2(x + 2) - 1$ **21.** $f(x) = 5(\log(x - 1))$

In Exercises 22–24, use the following information.

400-Meter Relay The winning time (in seconds) in the women's 400-meter relay at the Olympic Games from 1928 to 1996 can be modeled by the function $f(t) = 67.99 - 5.82 \ln t$ where t is the number of years since 1900.

22. What was the winning time in 1976?

23. Graph the model.

24. Use the graph to approximate the winning time in the 2004 Olympic Games.

UNIT 4

LESSON 4.5

Interpret Graphs of Exponential and Logarithmic Functions

Georgia Performance Standards: MM3A2e, MM3A2f

Goal Interpret graphs of exponential and logarithmic functions.

Vocabulary

The **zeros** of a function $f(x)$ are the values of x for which $f(x) = 0$. The zero of a function is the x-coordinate of the x-intercept.

A function $f(x)$ is increasing on an interval if the graph moves upward as you move from left to right.

A function $f(x)$ is decreasing on an interval if the graph moves downward as you move from left to right.

For nonlinear functions, the **average rate of change** r between two points (x_1, y_1) and (x_2, y_2) is given by the formula $r = \frac{y_2 - y_1}{x_2 - x_1}$.

Example 1 Analyzing the graph of an exponential function

Analyze the graph of the function $y = 2^x - 4$.

a. Identify the intercepts of the graph and the zeros of the function, if any.

b. Determine the intervals over which the function is increasing and decreasing.

c. Determine whether the average rate of change is greater between (2, 0) and (3, 4) or (3, 4) and (4, 12).

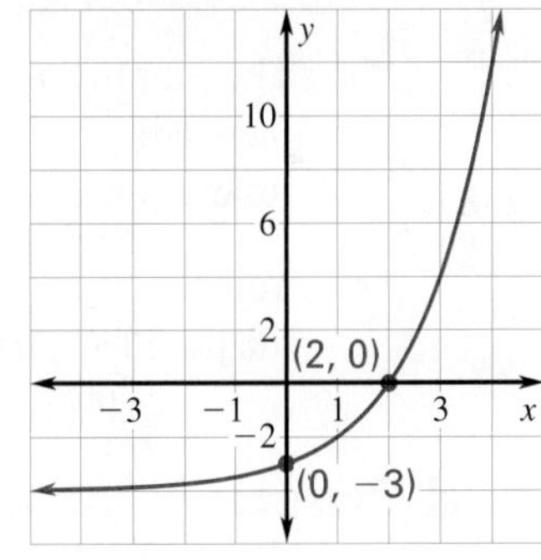

Solution

a. The graph intersects the x-axis at point (2, 0). So the x-intercept is 2 and the zero of the function is $x = 2$. The graph intersects the y-axis at point $(0, -3)$. So the y-intercept is -3.

You can check your answer using a graphing calculator. Graph the function $y = 2^x - 4$. Then use the *zero* and *table* features.

b. The graph is moving upward as you move from left to right. So, the function is increasing over the entire real number line. There are no intervals of decrease because the function is always increasing.

c. The average rate of change between (2, 0) and (3, 4) is $\frac{y_2 - y_1}{x_2 - x_1} = \frac{4 - 0}{3 - 2} = 4$.

The average rate of change between (3, 4) and (4, 12) is $\frac{y_2 - y_1}{x_2 - x_1} = \frac{12 - 4}{4 - 3} = 8$.

So, the average rate of change is greater between (3, 4) and (4, 12).

UNIT 4

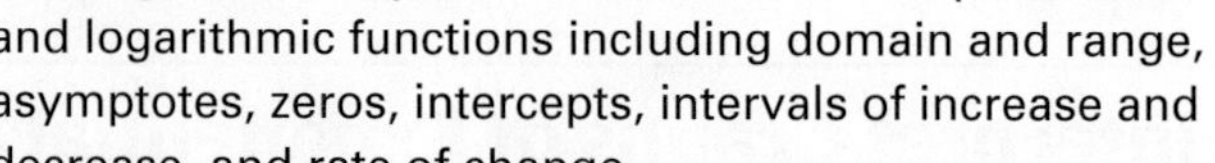

Georgia Performance Standards

MM3A2e Investigate and explain characteristics of exponential and logarithmic functions including domain and range, asymptotes, zeros, intercepts, intervals of increase and decrease, and rate of change. 

MM3A2f Graph functions as transformations of $f(x) = a^x$, $f(x) = \log_a x$, $f(x) = e^x$, $f(x) = \ln x$.

Example 2 Analyzing the graph of a logarithmic function

Analyze the graph of the function $y = \log_2 x$.

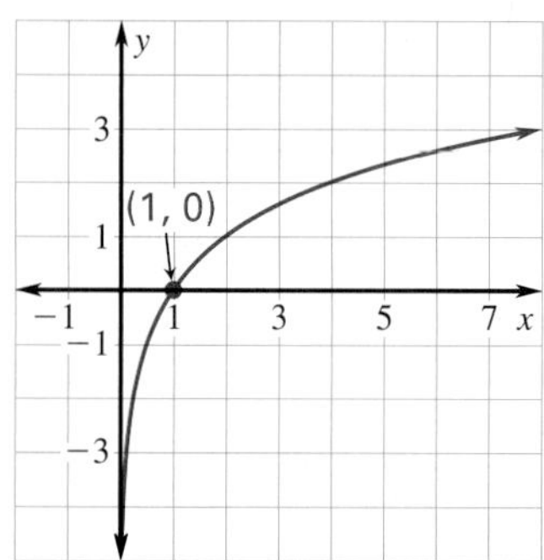

a. Identify the zeros of the function, if any.

b. Determine the intervals over which the function is increasing and decreasing.

c. Determine whether the average rate of change is greater between (1, 0) and (2, 1) or (3, 1.585) and (4, 2).

Solution

a. The graph intersects the x-axis at point (1, 0). So the zero of the function is $x = 1$.

b. The graph is moving upward as you move from left to right. So, the function is increasing over the interval $x > 0$. There are no intervals of decrease because the function is always increasing.

c. You can see from the graph that the average rate of change is greater between the points (1, 0) and (2, 1).

Guided Practice for Examples 1 and 2

For Exercises 1 and 2, analyze the graph.

a. Identify the intercepts of the graph and the zeros of the function, if any.

b. Determine the intervals for which the function is increasing and decreasing.

c. Determine whether the average rate of change is greater between points A and B or between C and D.

1.

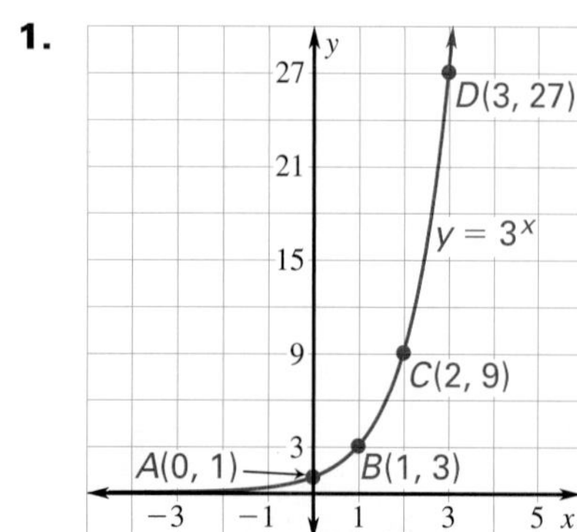

2.

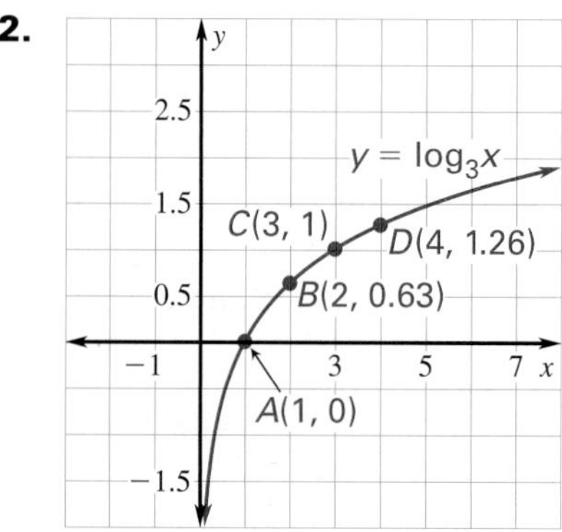

UNIT 4

Example 3 Graph a natural logarithmic function

Graph the function $y = \ln x$.

Solution

STEP 1 **Make** a table of values.

x	1	2	3	4	5
y	0	0.693	1.099	1.386	1.609

STEP 2 **Plot** the points from the table. The y-axis is a vertical asymptote.

STEP 3 **Draw,** from left to right, a smooth curve that starts just to the right of the y-axis and moves up through the plotted points.

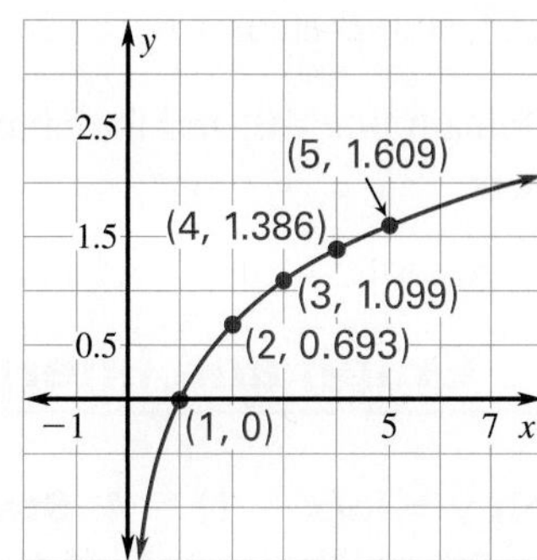

You can translate the graph of a function of the form $y = \ln(x - h) + k$ by translating the graph of the parent function $y = \ln x$.

Example 4 Translate a natural logarithmic graph horizontally

Graph $y = \ln(x + 2)$. State the domain and the range.

Solution

STEP 1 **Sketch** the graph of the parent function $y = \ln x$.

STEP 2 **Translate** the parent graph left 2 units. The translated graph passes through $(-1, 0)$, $(0, 0.693)$, $(1, 1.099)$. The graph's asymptote is $x = -2$.

The domain is $x > -2$, and the range is all real numbers.

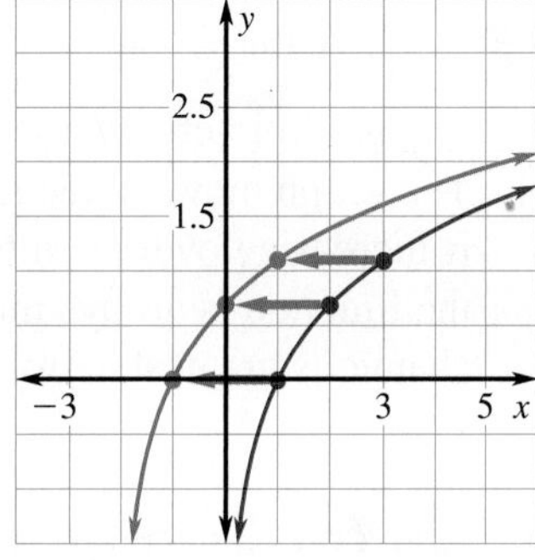

Guided Practice for Examples 3 and 4

Graph the function. State the domain and range.

3. $y = \ln(x - 8)$

4. $y = \ln(x + 4)$

Example 5 Translate a natural logarithmic graph vertically

Graph $y = \ln x + 5$. State the domain and the range.

Solution

STEP 1 **Sketch** the graph of the parent function $y = \ln x$.

STEP 2 **Translate** the parent graph up 5 units. The translated graph passes through (1, 5), (2, 5.693), (3, 6.099). The graph's asymptote is $x = 0$.

The domain is $x > 0$, and the range is all real numbers.

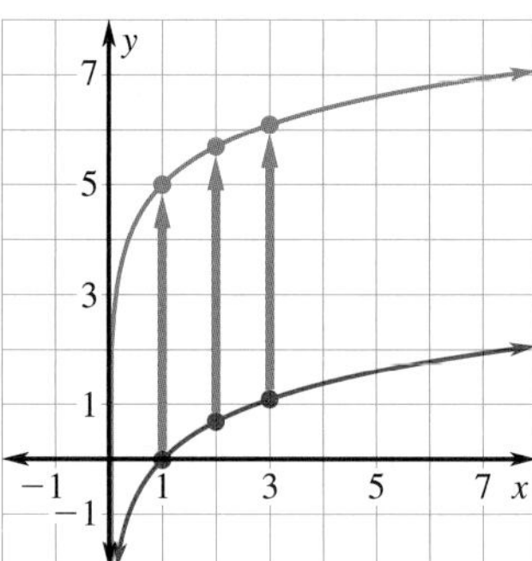

Example 6 Graph and interpret a natural logarithmic function

Graph $y = \ln(x - 1) - 4$. State the domain and the range and analyze the graph of the function.

Solution

STEP 1 **Sketch** the graph of the parent function $y = \ln x$.

STEP 2 **Translate** the parent graph right 1 unit and down 4 units. The translated graph passes through (2, −4), (3, −3.307), (4, −2.901). The graph's asymptote is $x = 1$. The domain is $x > 1$, and the range is all real numbers.

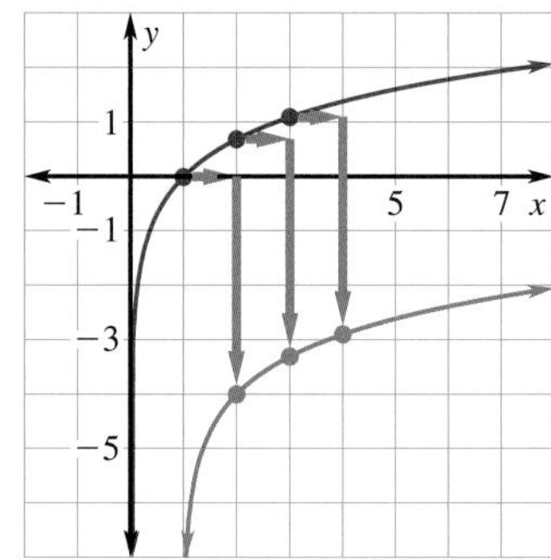

STEP 3 **Analyze** the graph.

The graph intersects the x-axis at about (55.6, 0), so $x \approx 55.6$ is a zero. The graph moves upward as you move from left to right. So, the function is increasing over the interval $x > 1$. There are no intervals of decrease because the function is always increasing. Of the points shown, the average rate of change is greatest between points (2, −4) and (3, −3.307).

Guided Practice for Examples 5 and 6

Graph the function. State the domain and range.

5. $y = \ln x + 0.5$

6. $y = \ln(x + 2) + 3$

7. $y = \ln x - 3$

8. $y = \ln(x - 4) - 5$

LESSON 4.5

Exercise Set A

MM3A2e Investigate and explain characteristics of exponential and logarithmic functions including domain and range, asymptotes, zeros, intercepts, intervals of increase and decrease, and rate of change.

MM3A2f Graph functions as transformations of $f(x) = a^x$, $f(x) = \log_a x$, $f(x) = e^x$, $f(x) = \ln x$.

Analyze the graph. (a) Identify the intercepts of the graph and the zeros of the function, if any. (b) Determine the intervals for which the function is increasing and decreasing. (c) Determine whether the average rate of change is greater between points *A* and *B* or between *C* and *D*.

1.

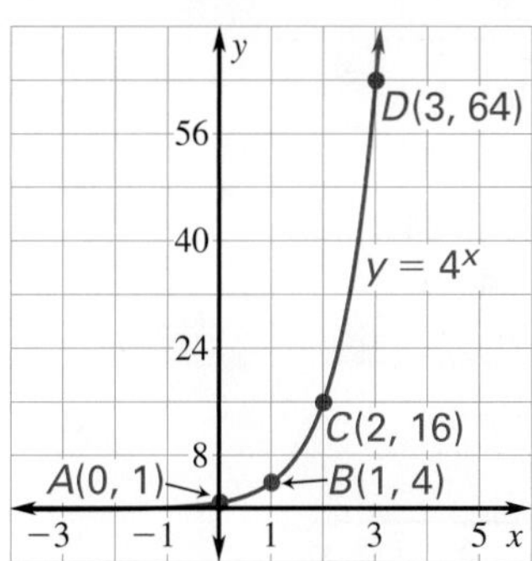

2.

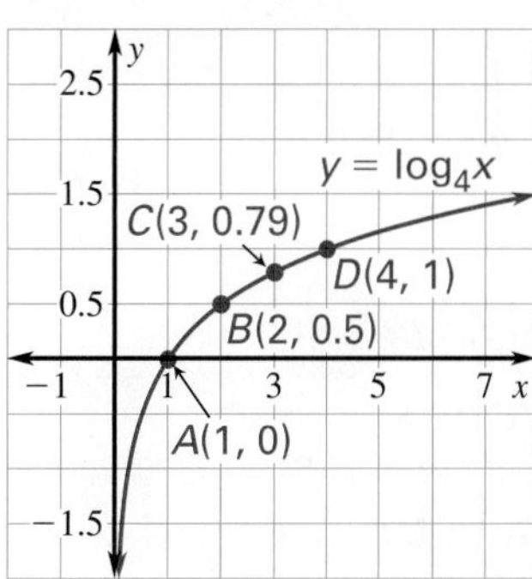

3. **Error Analysis** *Describe* and correct the error in identifying the zeros of the function $y = -3^x + 9$.

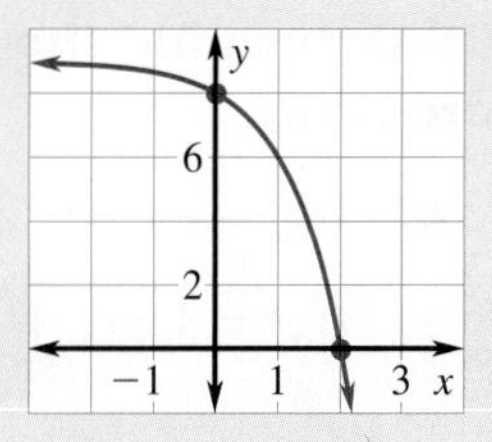

The zero of the function is $x = 8$.

Graph the function. State the domain and range.

4. $y = \ln(x + 12)$

5. $y = \ln x - 0.25$

6. $f(x) = \ln(x - 1) + 5$

Use a graphing calculator to graph the function. (a) Approximate the zeros of the function, if any. (b) Determine the intervals for which the function is increasing and decreasing.

7. $f(x) = -5^x$

8. $f(x) = \log_5 x$

9. $f(x) = -\ln x$

10. **Car Value** The value V (in dollars) of a car t years after it is purchased is shown.

a. Identify the zeros of the function and the interval(s) for which the function is increasing and decreasing. What does this mean?

b. Determine whether the average rate of change is greater between years 1 and 2 or between 4 and 5. What does this mean in the context of the problem?

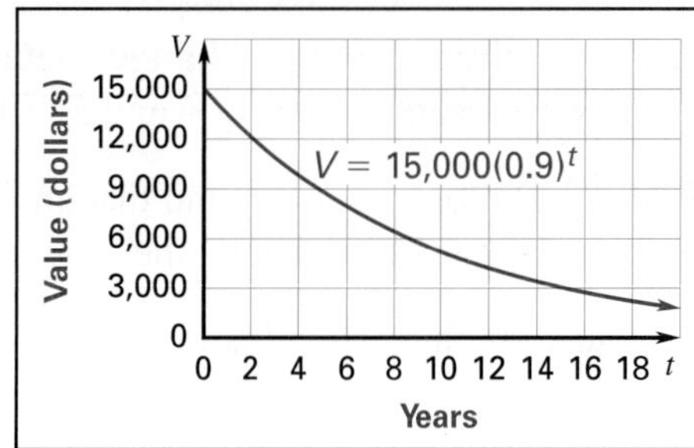

UNIT 4

LESSON 4.5

Exercise Set B

MM3A2e Investigate and explain characteristics of exponential and logarithmic functions including domain and range, asymptotes, zeros, intercepts, intervals of increase and decrease, and rate of change.

MM3A2f Graph functions as transformations of $f(x) = a^x$, $f(x) = \log_a x$, $f(x) = e^x$, $f(x) = \ln x$.

Analyze the graph. (a) Identify the zeros of the function, if any. (b) Determine the intervals for which the function is increasing and decreasing. (c) Determine whether the average rate of change is greater between points *A* and *B* or between *C* and *D*.

1.

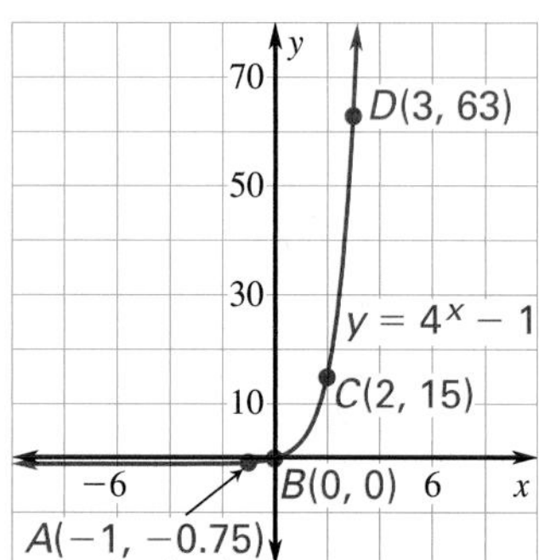

2.

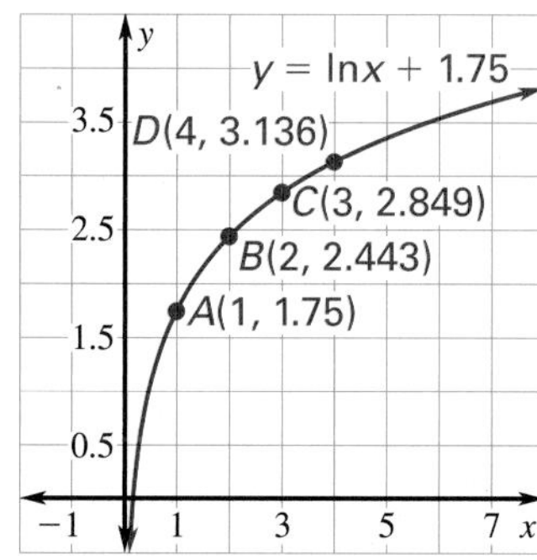

Use a graphing calculator to graph the function. (a) Approximate the zeros of the function, if any. (b) Determine the intervals for which the function is increasing and decreasing.

3. $y = 3^{x+1}$

4. $f(x) = -8^x - 2$

5. $y = 2^{x+1} + 3$

6. $f(x) = \log_9 x + 3$

7. $f(x) = \log(x + 1) - 1$

8. $y = \log_4 x + \log_2 x$

Graph the function. State the domain and range.

9. $y = \ln(x + 1.2)$

10. $y = \ln(x - 0.5) + 1.5$

11. $f(x) = \ln(x + 7.8) - 3.2$

12. **Multiple Representations** You buy an antique chair. The value V (in dollars) of a chair can be modeled by the function $V = 250(1.1)^t$, where t is the number of years since the date of purchase.

- **a.** **Making a Table** Make a table with t-values of 0, 1, 2, 3, 4, and 5.
- **b.** **Graphing a Model** Graph the model. Identify the zeros of the function, if any. What does this mean?
- **c.** **Identifying Intervals** Identify the interval(s) for which the value of the chair is increasing and decreasing. What does this mean in the context of the problem?
- **d.** **Determining Rate of Change** Determine whether the average rate of change is greater between years 1 and 2 or 4 and 5. What does this mean in the context of the problem?

13. **Biology** Biologists have found that an alligator's length ℓ (in inches) and weight w (in pounds) can be related by the function $\ell = 27.1 \ln w - 32.8$ when $w > 4$.

- **a.** Use a graphing calculator to graph the model. Identify the zeros of the function, if any.
- **b.** Find the intervals for which the function is increasing and decreasing. What does this mean in the context of the problem?

LESSON 4.6

Apply Properties of Logarithms

Georgia Performance Standards: MM3A2d, MM3A2g

Goal Rewrite logarithmic expressions.

Vocabulary

Properties of logarithms

Because of the relationship between logarithms and exponents, the properties of exponents have corresponding properties involving logarithms.

Let *b, m,* and *n* be positive numbers such that $b \neq 1$.

Product Property: $\log_b mn = \log_b m + \log_b n$

Quotient Property: $\log_b \frac{m}{n} = \log_b m - \log_b n$

Power Property: $\log_b m^n = n \log_b m$

Example 1 Use properties of logarithms

Use $\log_3 5 \approx 1.465$ and $\log_3 6 \approx 1.631$ to evaluate the logarithm.

a. $\log_3 \frac{6}{5} = \log_3 6 - \log_3 5$ Quotient property

$\approx 1.631 - 1.465$ Use the given values of $\log_3 5$ and $\log_3 6$.

$= 0.166$ Simplify.

b. $\log_3 30 = \log_3(5 \cdot 6)$ Write 30 as $5 \cdot 6$.

$= \log_3 5 + \log_3 6$ Product property

$\approx 1.465 + 1.631$ Use the given values of $\log_3 5$ and $\log_3 6$.

$= 3.096$ Simplify.

c. $\log_3 36 = \log_3 6^2$ Write 36 as 6^2.

$= 2 \log_3 6$ Power property

$\approx 2(1.631)$ Use the given value of $\log_3 6$.

$= 3.262$ Simplify.

Example 2 Expand a logarithmic expression

$\log_8 \frac{3x}{y} = \log_8 3x - \log_8 y$ Quotient property

$= \log_8 3 + \log_8 x - \log_8 y$ Product property

Example 3 Condense a logarithmic expression

$\ln x + 3 \ln y - 2 \ln 4 = \ln x + \ln y^3 - \ln 4^2$ Power property

$= \ln(x \cdot y^3) - \ln 4^2$ Product property

$= \ln \frac{xy^3}{16}$ Quotient property

UNIT 4

Georgia Performance Standards

MM3A2d Understand and use properties of logarithms by extending laws of exponents.

MM3A2g Explore real phenomena related to exponential and logarithmic functions including half-life and doubling time.

Guided Practice for Examples 1, 2, and 3

Use $\log_2 7 \approx 2.807$ and $\log_2 3 \approx 1.585$ to evaluate the logarithm.

1. $\log_2 \frac{7}{3}$ **2.** $\log_2 21$ **3.** $\log_2 49$ **4.** $\log_2 27$

5. Expand $\ln x^5y^2z$. **6.** Condense $8 \log x + \frac{1}{2} \log y$.

Change-of-Base Formula Logarithms with any base other than 10 or e can be written in terms of common or natural logarithms using the change-of-base formula. Let x and c be positive numbers with $c \neq 1$. Then $\log_c x = \frac{\log x}{\log c}$ and $\log_c x = \frac{\ln x}{\ln c}$.

Example 4 Use the change-of-base formula

Evaluate $\log_2 12$ using common logarithms and natural logarithms.

Using common logarithms:

$$\log_2 12 = \frac{\log 12}{\log 2} \approx \frac{1.0792}{0.3010} \approx 3.585$$

Using natural logarithms:

$$\log_2 12 = \frac{\ln 12}{\ln 2} \approx \frac{2.4849}{0.6931} \approx 3.585$$

Example 5 Use properties of logarithms in real life

Average student scores on a memory exam are modeled by the function $f(t) = 100 - 12 \log(t + 1)$ where t is the time in months.

a. Use properties of logarithms to write the model in condensed form.

b. Find the average score after 3 months.

Solution

a. $f(t) = 100 - 12 \log(t + 1)$ Write original model.

$f(t) = 100 - \log(t + 1)^{12}$ Power property

b. $f(3) = 100 - \log(3 + 1)^{12}$ Substitute 3 for t.

≈ 92.775 Use a calculator.

Guided Practice for Examples 4 and 5

Use the change-of-base formula to evaluate the logarithm.

7. $\log_2 6$ **8.** $\log_4 18$ **9.** $\log_9 4$ **10.** $\log_{12} 26$

11. Rework Example 5 to find the average score after 6 months.

LESSON 4.6 **Exercise Set A**

MM3A2d Understand and use properties of logarithms by extending laws of exponents.

MM3A2g Explore real phenomena related to exponential and logarithmic functions including half-life and doubling time.

Match the expression with the logarithm that has the same value.

1. $\log \sqrt{2} + \log \sqrt{8}$ **2.** $\log 4 - \log 10$ **3.** $2 \log 4 - \log 2$ **4.** $-3 \log \frac{1}{3}$

A. $\log \frac{2}{5}$ **B.** $\log 27$ **C.** $\log 4$ **D.** $\log 8$

Use $\log 4 \approx 0.602$ and $\log 7 \approx 0.845$ to evaluate the logarithm.

5. $\log 28$ **6.** $\log \frac{7}{4}$ **7.** $\log 16$

8. $\log 49$ **9.** $\log \frac{1}{4}$ **10.** $\log \frac{49}{64}$

Expand the expression.

11. $\log_7 x^2y$ **12.** $\log_2 \frac{x^2}{4}$ **13.** $\log 5\sqrt[3]{x}$

14. $\ln \frac{1}{2x^2}$ **15.** $\log_9 \frac{2x^3}{3}$ **16.** $\log_6 \frac{xy^2}{\sqrt{z}}$

Condense the expression.

17. $\log_3 4 + \log_3 2 + \log_3 2$ **18.** $2 \ln x - \ln 3 + \ln 6$

19. $3 \log x + \log 4 - \log x - \log 6$ **20.** $3 \ln(x + 1) - 2 \ln y + \ln y + \ln 2$

Use the change-of-base formula to evaluate the logarithm. Round your result to three decimal places.

21. $\log_7 12$ **22.** $\log_4 112$ **23.** $\log_5 1.25$

24. $\log_{2.2} 22$ **25.** $\log_{4.2} 18.1$ **26.** $\log_{1/3} 0.0005$

27. Henderson-Hasselbach Formula The pH of a patient's blood can be calculated using the Henderson-Hasselbach Formula, $\text{pH} = 6.1 + \log \frac{B}{C}$, where B is the concentration of bicarbonate and C is the concentration of carbonic acid. The normal pH of blood is approximately 7.4.

a. Expand the right side of the formula.

b. Find the pH of blood that has bicarbonate concentration of 38 and carbonic acid concentration of 2.0.

c. Is the pH in part (b) above normal or below normal?

UNIT 4

LESSON 4.6 **Exercise Set B**

MM3A2d Understand and use properties of logarithms by extending laws of exponents.

MM3A2g Explore real phenomena related to exponential and logarithmic functions including half-life and doubling time.

Use ln 2 ≈ 0.693, ln 3 ≈ 1.099, and ln 7 ≈ 1.946 to evaluate the logarithm.

1. $\ln 28$ **2.** $\ln \frac{7}{4}$ **3.** $\ln 16$

4. $\ln 42$ **5.** $\ln \frac{21}{4}$ **6.** $\ln \frac{24}{9}$

Expand the expression.

7. $\log_2 \frac{x^3}{yz^2}$ **8.** $\ln \sqrt{x^3 y}$ **9.** $\log \frac{\sqrt{4x}}{y^2}$

10. $\ln \frac{7y}{x^2}$ **11.** $\log_9 (2x^2yz)^5$ **12.** $\log_6 \frac{(x+3)^2}{3y^3}$

Condense the expression.

13. $\log_3 4 + \log_3 5 - \log_3 2 - \log_3 6$ **14.** $2 \log 5 - 2 \log x + \log y$

15. $2\left(\log_2 3 + \frac{1}{2} \log_2 x\right) - \log_2 y - 4 \log_2 x$ **16.** $2 \ln(x - 3) - \ln 6 - 3 \ln(x + 2)$

17. $\frac{3}{2} \log (x + 4) - 3 \log x - \log 6$ **18.** $\frac{1}{2}[\ln 3 + 4 \ln x - 2 \ln(x - 1)]$

Use the change-of-base formula to evaluate the logarithm. Round your result to three decimal places.

19. $\log_{15} 158$ **20.** $\log_{0.05} 22$ **21.** $\log_{32} 10{,}254$

22. Annuities An ordinary annuity is an account in which you make a fixed deposit at the end of each compounding period. You want to use an annuity to help you save money for college. The formula

$$t = \frac{\ln\left[\frac{Sr + Pn}{Pn}\right]}{n \ln\left[\frac{n + r}{n}\right]}$$

gives the time t (in years) required to have S dollars in the annuity if your periodic payments P (in dollars) are made n times a year and the annual interest rate is r (in decimal form).

a. Expand the right side of the formula.

b. How long will it take you to save \$35,000 in an annuity that earns an annual interest rate of 5% if you make monthly payments of \$150?

c. How long will it take you to save \$35,000 in an annuity that earns an annual interest rate of 4% if you make monthly payments of \$250?

UNIT 4

LESSON 4.7

Solve Exponential and Logarithmic Equations

Georgia Performance Standards: MM3A3b, MM3A3d

Goal Solve exponential and logarithmic equations.

Vocabulary

Exponential equations are equations in which variable expressions occur as exponents.

Logarithmic equations are equations that involve logarithms of variable expressions.

Property of Equality for Exponential Equations If b is a positive number other than 1, then $b^x = b^y$ if and only if $x = y$.

Property of Equality for Logarithmic Equations If b, x, and y are positive numbers with $b \neq 1$, then $\log_b x = \log_b y$ if and only if $x = y$.

Example 1 Solve by equating exponents

Solve $8^x = 4^{x+1}$.

Solution

$8^x = 4^{x+1}$	Write original equation.
$(2^3)^x = (2^2)^{x+1}$	Rewrite 8 and 4 as powers with base 2.
$2^{3x} = 2^{2x+2}$	Power of a power property
$3x = 2x + 2$	Property of equality for exponential equations
$x = 2$	Solve for x.

CHECK Check the apparent solution using a graph. Graph $y = 8^x$ and $y = 4^{x+1}$ in the same coordinate plane. The graphs intersect when $x = 2$. So, the solution is 2.

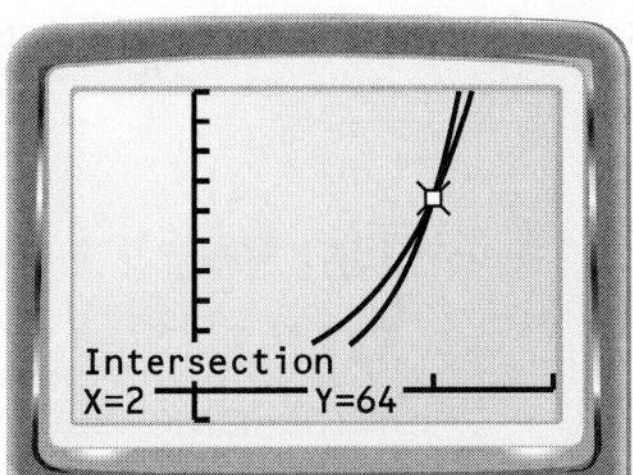

Example 2 Solve by taking a logarithm of each side

Solve $8^x = 23$.

Solution

$8^x = 23$	Write original equation.
$\log_8 8^x = \log_8 23$	Take $\log_8$ of each side.
$x = \log_8 23$	$\log_b b^x = x$
$x = \dfrac{\log 23}{\log 8}$	Use change-of-base formula.
$x \approx 1.51$	Use a calculator.

Georgia Performance Standards

MM3A3b Solve polynomial, exponential, and logarithmic equations analytically, graphically, and using appropriate technology. 

MM3A3d Solve a variety of types of equations by appropriate means choosing among mental calculation, pencil and paper, or appropriate technology.

Example 3 Solve a logarithmic equation

$\log_8(x + 6) = \log_8(4 - x)$	Original equation
$x + 6 = 4 - x$	Property of equality for logarithmic equations
$2x + 6 = 4$	Add x to each side.
$2x = -2$	Subtract 6 from each side.
$x = -1$	Divide each side by 2.

Example 4 Exponentiate each side of an equation

Find the solution(s) of $\log x + \log(x + 3) = 1$.

METHOD 1 Solve analytically.

$\log x + \log(x + 3) = 1$	Write original equation.
$\log[x(x + 3)] = 1$	Product property of logarithms
$10^{\log[x(x + 3)]} = 10^1$	Exponentiate each side using base 10.
$x(x + 3) = 10$	$b^{\log_b x} = x$
$x^2 + 3x = 10$	Distributive property
$x^2 + 3x - 10 = 0$	Write in standard form.
$(x + 5)(x - 2) = 0$	Factor.
$x = -5$ or $x = 2$	Zero product property

METHOD 2 Use a graph.

STEP 1 Graph $y = \log x + \log(x + 3)$ and $y = 1$ in the same viewing window. Set the viewing window to show $-6 \le x \le 6$ and $-4 \le y \le 4$.

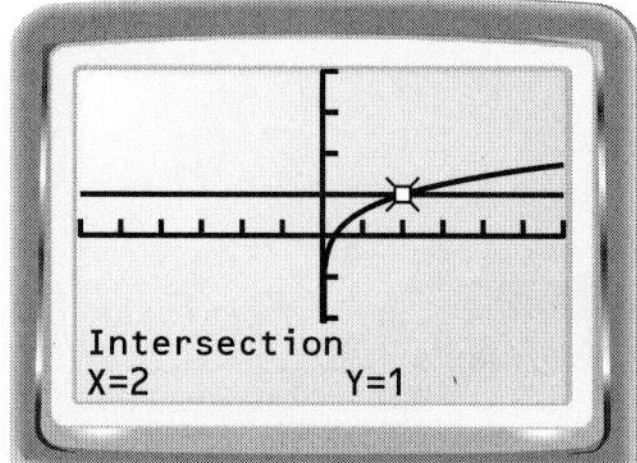

STEP 2 Use the *intersect* feature to determine where the graphs intersect. The graphs intersect only when $x = 2$.

So, 2 is the only solution.

Guided Practice for Examples 1, 2, 3, and 4

Solve the equation. Check for extraneous solutions.

1. $5^{3x + 1} = 25^{x + 1}$
2. $4^{3x} = 9$
3. $\log_7(x + 2) = \log_7(2 - 3x)$
4. $\ln(4 - 5x) = \ln(x + 10)$
5. $\log_6 x + \log_6(x - 5) = 2$
6. $2 \ln x = \ln(2x - 3) + \ln(x - 2)$

LESSON 4.7 **Exercise Set A**

MM3A3b Solve polynomial, exponential, and logarithmic equations analytically, graphically, and using appropriate technology.

MM3A3d Solve a variety of types of equations by appropriate means choosing among mental calculation, pencil and paper, or appropriate technology.

Solve the exponential equation. Check for extraneous solutions. Round the result to three decimal places if necessary.

1. $e^x = 1$ **2.** $e^x + 1 = 7$ **3.** $5^x = 12$

4. $4^x - 6 = 4$ **5.** $3e^{3x} = 12$ **6.** $10^{2x-3} + 3 = 19$

7. $3^{-3x+1} = 3^{x-9}$ **8.** $8^{2x} = 8^{x+7}$ **9.** $7^{2x-3} - 4 = 14$

10. $4e^{3x} = 1$ **11.** $e^{5x+2} = e^{3x+12}$ **12.** $3e^{3-x} = 15$

13. $9^{2x} = 3^{2x+4}$ **14.** $25^{x-4} = 5^{3x+1}$ **15.** $8^{x-1} = \left(\frac{1}{2}\right)^{2x-1}$

16. $3(2^{x+6}) = 17$ **17.** $5^{0.5x} + 12 = 21$ **18.** $-5e^x - 3 = 24$

19. $\frac{3}{4}e^{3x} - 8 = -6$ **20.** $\frac{2}{3}(4^{3x}) - 5 = -2$ **21.** $10^{2x+1} + 2 = 2$

Solve the logarithmic equation. Check for extraneous solutions. Round the result to three decimal places if necessary.

22. $\log x = 3$ **23.** $\ln x = 4$ **24.** $\log_3 x = 5$

25. $\log_7(2 - x) = \log_7 5x$ **26.** $\ln(3x - 3) = \ln(x - 6)$ **27.** $7 - \log_3 8x = 2$

28. $2 \log_7(1 - 2x) = 12$ **29.** $3 \ln x - 7 = 4$ **30.** $\ln(1 - 3x) + 3 = 9$

31. $\log 7x + 4 = 5$ **32.** $4 + \log_9(3x - 7) = 6$ **33.** $\log_2 2x + \log_2 x = 5$

34. $\log_6(2x - 6) + \log_6 x = 2$ **35.** $\ln 3x - \ln 2 = 4$ **36.** $\ln(-5x + 3) = \ln 2x + 2$

37. **Multiple Choice** You deposit \$500 in an account that pays 3.25% annual interest compounded monthly. About how long does it take for the balance to quadruple?

A. 36.3 years **B.** 42.7 years **C.** 45.1 years

In Exercises 38–40, use the following information.

Compounding Interest You deposit \$700 in an account that pays 2.75% annual interest. How long does it take the balance to reach the following amounts?

38. \$1000 when interest is compounded quarterly

39. \$1500 when interest is compounded yearly

40. \$2000 when interest is compounded continuously

41. **Rocket Velocity** Disregarding the force of gravity, the maximum velocity v of a rocket is given by $v = t \ln M$ where t is the velocity of the exhaust and M is the ratio of the mass of the rocket with fuel to its mass without fuel. A solid propellant rocket has an exhaust velocity of 2.3 kilometers per second. Its maximum velocity is 7.2 kilometers per second. Find its mass ratio M.

UNIT 4

LESSON 4.7

Exercise Set B

MM3A3b Solve polynomial, exponential, and logarithmic equations analytically, graphically, and using appropriate technology.

MM3A3d Solve a variety of types of equations by appropriate means choosing among mental calculation, pencil and paper, or appropriate technology.

Solve the exponential equation. Check for extraneous solutions. Round the result to three decimal places if necessary.

1. $e^x = 5$

2. $e^{x-2} = 14$

3. $e^{2x} + 5 = 12$

4. $2^x = 22$

5. $3^x - 4 = 6$

6. $4^{4x+2} = 54$

7. $e^{2x-3} + 6 = 13$

8. $2e^{2-3x} - 3 = 11$

9. $9^{x-5} + 4 = 15$

10. $3^{x+1} + 4 = 8$

11. $\frac{1}{2}(10^{x+6}) - 5 = 14$

12. $4^{3-x} + 2 = \frac{5}{2}$

13. $3e^{3x} - 1 = 1$

14. $e^{x^2-2} = e^x$

15. $3^{x^2} + 5 = 6$

16. $27^x = 3^{2x+3}$

17. $216^{2x-1} = 36^{4x+3}$

18. $16^{x-5} = \left(\frac{1}{2}\right)^{2x-1}$

Solve the logarithmic equation. Check for extraneous solutions. Round the result to three decimal places if necessary.

19. $\log(x + 2) = 4$

20. $2 \ln x - 7 = -5$

21. $\log_3(x - 3) + 3 = 5$

22. $\log_7(2 - x) = 3$

23. $\ln(2x - 1) + \ln x = 0$

24. $\log_2 x + \log_2(x + 1) = 1$

25. $\log_3 x + \log_3(x + 8) = 2$

26. $\log_4(x - 3) + \log_4(x - 4) = \frac{1}{2}$

27. $\log(x - 5) = \log(x - 2) + 1$

28. $2 \log_7(1 - x) = \log_7(7 - x)$

29. $\ln(2x^2 - 3) = \ln(9x - 13)$

30. $\log_2(x - 3) + \log_2(x + 1) = \log_2(6x - 18)$

31. $\log_2 x + \log_2(x + 4) - \log_2(x - 2) = 4$

32. $\log_2(7x - 8) - \log_2(x + 1) - \log_2(x - 1) = 1$

Solve the exponential equation. Round the result to three decimal places.

33. $3^{x+1} = 2^{4x}$

34. $e^{x-2} = 10^{2-x}$

35. $4^{2x+3} = 5^{x-4}$

In Exercises 36–38, use the following information.

Loan Repayment The formula $L = P\left[\dfrac{1 - \left(1 + \frac{r}{n}\right)^{-nt}}{\frac{r}{n}}\right]$ gives the amount of a loan L in terms of the amount of each payment P, the interest rate r as a decimal, the number of payments per year n, and the number of years t.

36. How long will it take to pay off a \$120,000 loan at 6% interest when making monthly payments of \$860?

37. When the loan is paid off, how much money will you have paid the bank?

38. How much did you pay in interest?

UNIT 4

LESSON 4.8

Solve Exponential and Logarithmic Inequalities

Georgia Performance Standards: MM3A3c

Goal Solve exponential and logarithmic inequalities.

Vocabulary

An **exponential inequality in one variable** is an inequality that can be written in the form $ab^x + k < 0$, $ab^x + k > 0$, $ab^x + k \le 0$, or $ab^x + k \ge 0$, where $a \ne 0$, $b > 0$, and $b \ne 1$.

A **logarithmic inequality in one variable** is an inequality that can be written in the form $\log_b x + k < 0$, $\log_b x + k > 0$, $\log_b x + k \le 0$, or $\log_b x + k \ge 0$, where $b > 0$, and $b \ne 1$.

The same methods used to solve polynomial inequalities in Lesson 2.4 can be used to solve exponential and logarithmic inequalities.

Example 1 Solve an exponential inequality analytically

Solve $4^{x+1} \ge 32$.

Solution

STEP 1 **Write** and solve the equation obtained by replacing $\ge$ with $=$.

$4^{x+1} = 32$	Write equation that corresponds to inequality.
$\log_4 4^{x+1} = \log_4 32$	Take $\log_4$ of each side.
$x + 1 = \log_4 32$	$\log_b b^x = x$
$x = \log_4 32 - 1$	Subtract 1 from each side.
$x = \dfrac{\log 32}{\log 4} - 1$	Change-of-base formula
$x = 1.5$	Use a calculator.

STEP 2 **Plot** the solution from Step 1 on a number line. Use a solid dot to indicate 1.5 is a solution of the inequality. The solution $x = 1.5$ represents the *critical x-value* of the inequality $4^{x+1} \ge 32$. The critical x-value partitions the number line into two intervals. Test an x-value in each interval to see if it is a solution of the inequality.

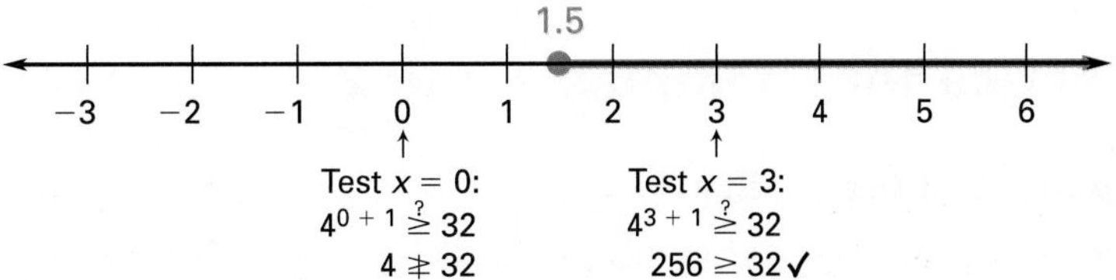

The solution consists of all real numbers in the interval $[1.5, +\infty)$.

UNIT 4

Georgia Performance Standards

MM3A3c Solve polynomial, exponential, and logarithmic inequalities analytically, graphically, and using appropriate technology. Represent solution sets of inequalities using interval notation.

Example 2 Solve an exponential inequality using technology

Car Value Your family purchases a new car for \$25,000. Its value depreciates by 12% each year. During what interval of time does the car's value exceed \$16,000?

Solution

Let y represent the value of the car (in dollars) x years after it is purchased. A function relating x and y is:

$y = 25{,}000(1 - 0.12)^x$ Original function

$y = 25{,}000(0.88)^x$ Simplify.

To find the values of x for which y exceeds 16,000, solve the inequality $25{,}000(0.88)^x > 16{,}000$.

METHOD 1 Use a table.

STEP 1 **Enter** the function $y = 25{,}000(0.88)^x$ into a graphing calculator. Set up a table to display the x-values starting at 0 and increasing in increments of 0.1.

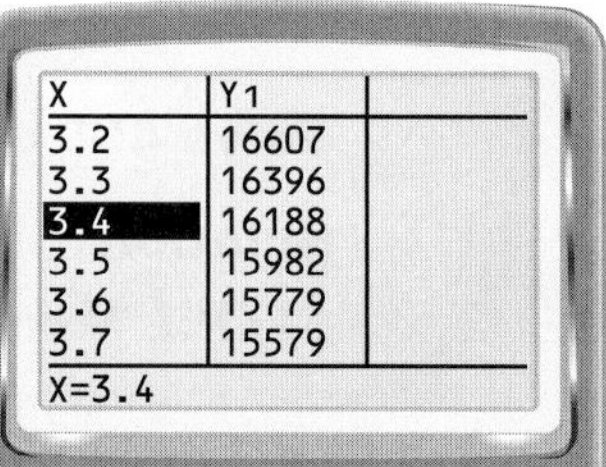

STEP 2 **Use** the *table* feature to create a table of values. Scrolling through the table shows that $y > 16{,}000$ when $0 \le x \le 3.4$.

The car's value exceeds \$16,000 for about the first 3.4 years after it is purchased.

METHOD 2 Use a graph.

STEP 1 **Graph** $y = 25{,}000(0.88)^x$ and $y = 16{,}000$ in the same viewing window. Set the viewing window to show $0 \le x \le 8$ and $0 \le y \le 25{,}000$.

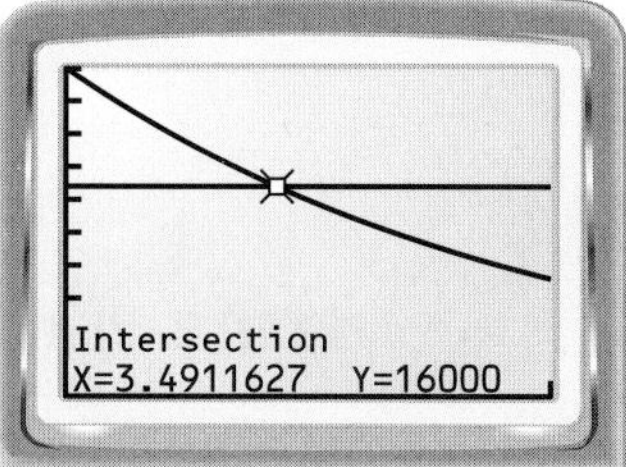

STEP 2 **Use** the *intersect* feature to determine where the graphs intersect. The graphs intersect when $x \approx 3.49$.

The graph of $y = 25{,}000(0.88)^x$ is above the graph of $y = 16{,}000$ when $0 \le x < 3.49$. So, the car's value exceeds \$16,000 for about the first 3.5 years after it is purchased.

Guided Practice for Examples 1 and 2

Solve the exponential inequality.

1. $5^{x-4} \ge 625$ **2.** $32^{x-1} \le 4$ **3.** $7^{3x-4} < 18$

4. **Car Value** In Example 2, during what interval of time does the car's value fall below \$10,000?

Example 3 Solve a logarithmic inequality analytically

Solve the logarithmic inequality.

a. $\log_5 x < 2$ **b.** $\log_4 x + 8 \geq 11$

Solution

a. ***STEP 1*** **Write** and solve the equation obtained by replacing < with =.

$\log_5 x = 2$ Write equation that corresponds to inequality.

$5^{\log_5 x} = 5^2$ Exponentiate each side using base 5.

$x = 25$ $b^{\log_b x} = x$

STEP 2 **Plot** the solution from Step 1 using an open dot. The value x must be a positive number, so the number line should show only positive numbers. The solution $x = 25$ represents the critical x-value of the inequality $\log_5 x < 2$. Test an x-value in each interval to see if it is a solution of the inequality.

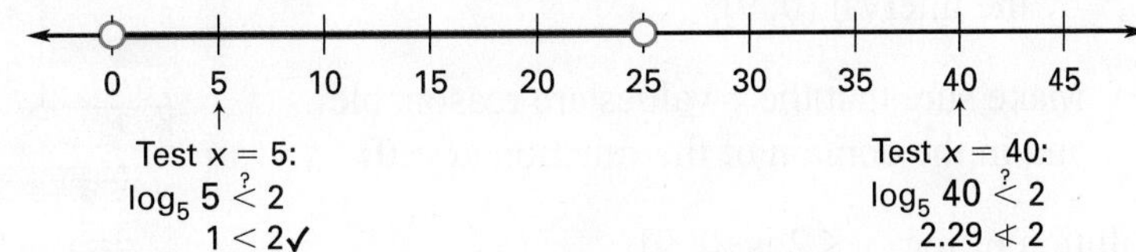

The solution consists of all real numbers in the interval (0, 25).

b. ***STEP 1*** **Write** and solve the equation obtained by replacing ≥ with =.

$\log_4 x + 8 = 11$ Write equation that corresponds to inequality.

$\log_4 x = 3$ Subtract 8 from each side.

$4^{\log_4 x} = 4^3$ Exponentiate each side using base 4.

$x = 64$ $b^{\log_b x} = x$

STEP 2 **Plot** the solution from Step 1 using a solid dot. The solution $x = 64$ represents the critical x-value of the inequality $\log_4 x + 8 \geq 11$. Test an x-value in each interval to see if it is a solution of the inequality.

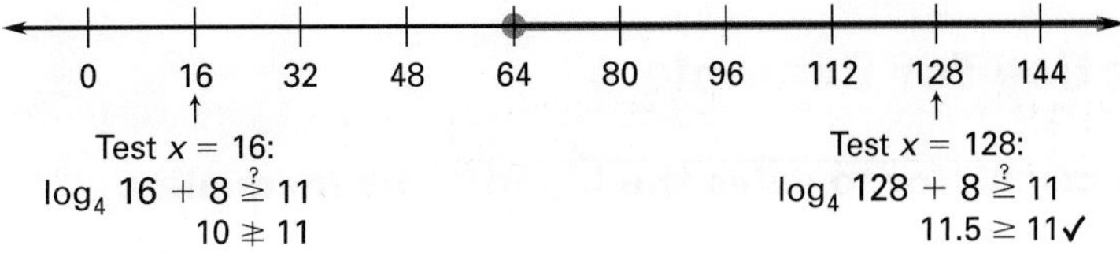

The solution consists of all real numbers in the interval $[64, +\infty)$.

Guided Practice for Example 3

Solve the logarithmic inequality.

5. $\log_3 x - 3 > 1$ **6.** $\log_6 2x + 7 < 10$ **7.** $\log_9(x - 8) \geq \frac{3}{2}$

Example 4 Solve a logarithmic inequality using technology

Solve $\log_3 x \le 2$.

Solution

METHOD 1 Use a table.

STEP 1 **Enter** the function $y = \log_3 x$ into a graphing calculator as $y = \frac{\log x}{\log 3}$.

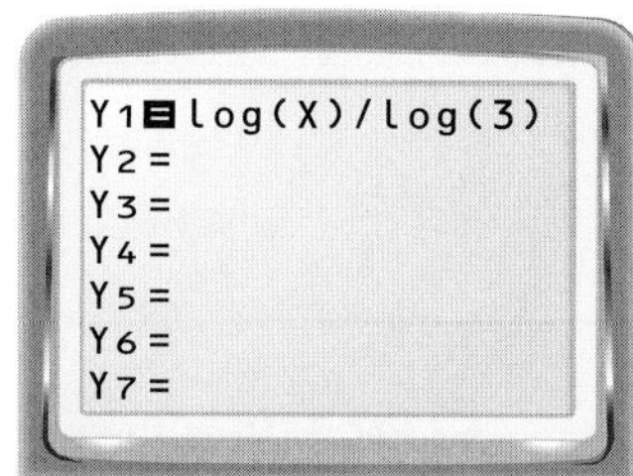

STEP 2 **Use** the *table* feature to create a table of values. Identify the interval for which $y \le 2$. These x-values can be represented by the interval (0, 9].

Make sure that the x-values are reasonable and in the domain of the function ($x > 0$).

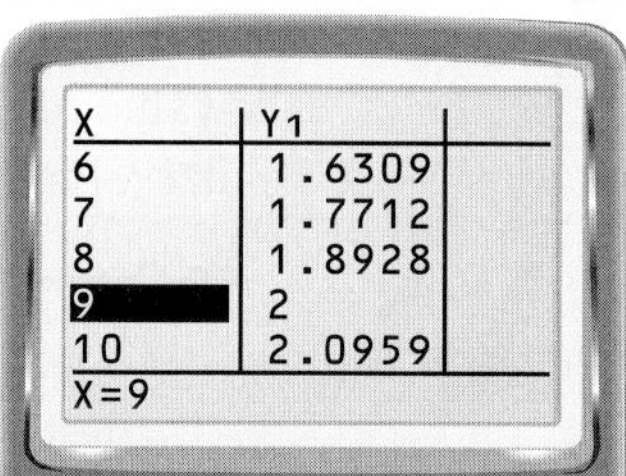

The solution of $\log_3 x \le 2$ is (0, 9].

METHOD 2 Use a graph.

STEP 1 Graph $y = \log_3 x$ and $y = 2$ in the same viewing window.

STEP 2 Using the *intersect* feature, you can determine that the graphs intersect when $x = 9$.

The graph of $y = \log_3 x$ is on or below the graph of $y = 2$ during the x interval (0, 9].

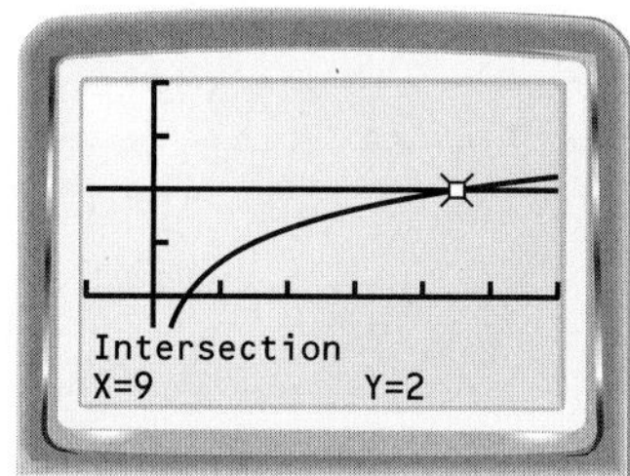

So, the solution of $\log_3 x \le 2$ is (0, 9].

Guided Practice for Example 4

Use a graphing calculator to solve the logarithmic inequality.

8. $\log_2 x < 3$

9. $\log_5(x - 2) \ge \frac{1}{3}$

10. $\log_4 3x > \frac{2}{5}$

LESSON 4.8 **Exercise Set A**

MM3A3c Solve polynomial, exponential, and logarithmic inequalities analytically, graphically, and using appropriate technology. Represent solution sets of inequalities using interval notation.

Solve the exponential inequality analytically.

1. $4^x < 64$

2. $\left(\frac{1}{4}\right)^x \geq 16$

3. $3^x < 81$

4. $25 \leq 5^{x+1}$

5. $4^{x+1} > 64$

6. $27\left(\frac{2}{3}\right)^x \leq \frac{16}{3}$

Use a graphing calculator to solve the exponential inequality.

7. $3 \leq 8\left(\frac{3}{4}\right)^x$

8. $244(0.35)^x > 100$

9. $5(0.4)^{x-2} \geq 5$

Solve the logarithmic inequality analytically.

10. $\log_3 x < 2$

11. $\log_5 x \leq 1$

12. $\log_7 x < 2$

13. $\log_4 x \leq \frac{3}{2}$

14. $\log_5 x - 7 \geq -6$

15. $\log_6 x + 4 < 5$

Use a graphing calculator to solve the logarithmic inequality.

16. $8 \ln x \geq 1$

17. $6 \log_2 x > 14$

18. $-2 \log_7 x + 9 > 11$

19. **Finance** You deposit \$2000 in an account that pays 5% annual interest compounded monthly. During which time interval will your balance exceed \$2500?

20. **Finance** You deposit \$800 in an account that pays 4.5% annual interest compounded continuously. During which time interval will your balance be less than \$900?

21. **Multiple Representations** Suppose the annual rate of inflation averages 4% over the next 20 years.

a. **Writing a Model** Let P represent the present cost of an item. Write a model that gives the cost C (in dollars) of an item after t years.

b. **Using a Table** A can of corn currently costs \$.99. Write an inequality that gives the time interval for which the cost of a can of corn is between \$.99 and \$1.50. Then use a table to predict when this will occur.

c. **Using a Graph** Write an inequality that gives the time interval in which the cost of a can of corn exceeds \$2.00. Then use a graph to predict when this will occur.

22. **Tornadoes** The wind speed s (in miles per hour) near the center of a tornado can be modeled by $s = 93 \log d + 65$, where d is the distance (in miles) that the tornado travels.

a. Approximate the distances for which a tornado must travel to have a center wind speed between 150 miles per hour and 200 miles per hour.

b. Approximate the distances for which a tornado must travel to have a center wind speed of at least 175 miles per hour.

LESSON 4.8 **Exercise Set B**

MM3A3c Solve polynomial, exponential, and logarithmic inequalities analytically, graphically, and using appropriate technology. Represent solution sets of inequalities using interval notation.

Solve the exponential inequality analytically.

1. $7^{x-2} \leq 1.5$

2. $\left(\frac{3}{2}\right)^{x+1} < 10$

3. $14\left(\frac{5}{6}\right)^{x} \geq 9$

4. $-135\left(\frac{9}{7}\right)^{x} \geq -475$

5. $-3e^{x} < -7$

6. $4^{5x+1} \geq 0.5$

Use a graphing calculator to solve the exponential inequality.

7. $-(0.82)^{5x} \leq -10$

8. $20(1.4)^{3.5x} > 1000$

9. $50e^{-0.02x} < 70$

Solve the logarithmic inequality analytically.

10. $\log_2 x < 3.5$

11. $\ln x + 1 \geq 2$

12. $\log_3 4x + 7 \leq 12$

13. $\log_9(x - 1) \geq 1.5$

14. $2 \log_4(x + 3) - 1 > 5$

15. $4 \log_7 3x - 4 \leq 7$

Use a graphing calculator to solve the logarithmic inequality.

16. $\log_5(x - 4) + 6 \leq 8$

17. $\ln 3x + 3 < 8$

18. $-4 \log_2 x > 2x - 7$

19. **Radioactive Decay** Two hundred grams of radium are stored in a container. The amount R (in grams) of radium present after t years can be modeled by $R = 200e^{-0.00043t}$. Write and solve an inequality that can be used to determine when the mass of the radium will be less than 10 grams.

20. **Newton's Law of Cooling** Newton's law of cooling states that the temperature T of a cooling substance at time t (in minutes) can be modeled by the equation $T = (T_0 - T_R)e^{-rt} + T_R$, where T_0 is the initial temperature of the substance, T_R is the room temperature, and r is a constant that represents the cooling rate of the substance.

a. You take a pot of soup off the stove. It has an initial temperature of 212°F, and the room temperature is 72°F. The soup is cooling at a rate of 0.03. You want to eat the soup when the temperature is between 130°F and 140°F. Write an inequality that gives the time interval in which this would occur.

b. Solve the inequality to find the time interval described in part (a).

c. Will the temperature ever drop below 70°F? *Explain.*

21. **Business** The demand equation for a certain product is modeled by the equation

$$p = 6000\left(1 - \frac{4}{4 + e^{-0.002x}}\right)$$

where p is the price and x is the number of units. In order to make a profit, the company cannot sell its product for less than \$80. Approximate the prices in which the company will make a profit and yield a demand of at least 1000 units.

LESSON 4.9

Write and Apply Exponential and Power Functions

Georgia Performance Standards: MM3A2g

Goal Write exponential and power functions.

Example 1 Write an exponential function

Write an exponential function $y = ab^x$ whose graph passes through (1, 6) and (2, 18).

STEP 1 Substitute the coordinates of the two given points into $y = ab^x$.

$6 = ab^1 \qquad 18 = ab^2$

STEP 2 Solve for a in the first equation and substitute into the second equation.

$18 = \left(\frac{6}{b}\right)b^2$ Substitute $\frac{6}{b}$ for a.

$3 = b$ Solve for b.

STEP 3 Because $b = 3$, it follows that $a = \frac{6}{3} = 2$. So, $y = 2 \cdot 3^x$.

Transforming Exponential Data A set of more than two points (x, y) fits an exponential pattern if and only if the set of transformed points $(x, \ln y)$ fits a linear pattern.

Example 2 Find an exponential model

Insects The table shows the number of insects y in a controlled experiment during the xth month of the experiment. Draw a scatter plot of the data pairs $(x, \ln y)$. Then find an exponential model for the original data.

Month, x	1	2	3	4	5	6
Population, y	2.73	5.73	12.04	25.28	53.09	111.50

STEP 1 Use a calculator to find the data pairs $(x, \ln y)$; (1, 1.004), (2, 1.746), (3, 2.488), (4, 3.230), (5, 3.972), and (6, 4.714).

STEP 2 Plot the new points and observe that they lie close to a line. So, an exponential model should be a good fit for the original data.

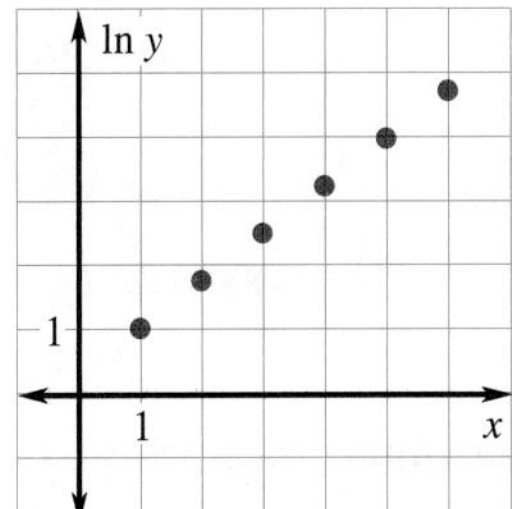

STEP 3 To find an exponential model $y = ab^x$, choose two points (1, 1.004) and (6, 4.714) and find an equation of a line. Then solve for y.

$\ln y - 1.004 = 0.742(x - 1)$ Equation of line

$\ln y = 0.742x + 0.262$ Simplify.

$y = e^{0.742x + 0.262}$ Exponentiate each side using base e.

$y = e^{0.262}(e^{0.742})^x$ Use properties of exponents.

$y \approx 1.3(2.1)^x$ Exponential model

UNIT 4

Georgia Performance Standards

MM3A2g Explore real phenomena related to exponential and logarithmic functions including half-life and doubling time.

Guided Practice for Examples 1 and 2

Write an exponential function $y = ab^x$ whose graph passes through the given points.

1. (1, 8), (2, 16) **2.** (2, 8), (3, 32) **3.** (1, 15), (2, 75)

4. How would the exponential model in Example 2 change if the insect population increased as shown in the table below?

Month, x	1	2	3	4	5	6
Population, y	3	6	12	24	48	96

Example 3 Write a power function

Write a power function $y = ax^b$ whose graph passes through (2, 1) and (4, 3).

Solution

STEP 1 Substitute the coordinates of the two given points into $y = ax^b$.

$1 = a \cdot 2^b$ Substitute 1 for y and 2 for x.

$3 = a \cdot 4^b$ Substitute 3 for y and 4 for x.

STEP 2 Solve for a in the first equation and substitute into the second equation.

$3 = \frac{1}{2^b} \cdot 4^b$ Substitute $\frac{1}{2^b}$ for a.

$3 = 2^b$ Simplify.

$\log_2 3 = b$ Take $\log_2$ of each side.

$\frac{\log 3}{\log 2} = b$ Change-of-base formula

$1.58 \approx b$ Use a calculator.

STEP 3 Because $b \approx 1.58$, it follows that $a \approx \frac{1}{2^{1.58}} \approx 0.33$. So, $y = 0.33x^{1.58}$.

Transforming Power Data A set of more than two points (x, y) fits a power pattern if and only if the set of transformed points $(\ln x, \ln y)$ fits a linear pattern.

Guided Practice for Example 3

Write a power function $y = ax^b$ whose graph passes through the given points.

5. (2, 9), (3, 27) **6.** (1, 8), (2, 32) **7.** (1, 1), (4, 8)

LESSON 4.9 **Exercise Set A**

MM3A2g Explore real phenomena related to exponential and logarithmic functions including half-life and doubling time.

Write an exponential function $y = ab^x$ whose graph passes through the given points.

1. $\left(0, \frac{1}{2}\right), \left(2, \frac{9}{2}\right)$

2. $\left(1, \frac{2}{5}\right), \left(3, \frac{8}{5}\right)$

3. $(1, 12), \left(-1, \frac{3}{4}\right)$

4. $(2, 2), (3, 1)$

5. $(0, 5), \left(2, \frac{20}{9}\right)$

6. $\left(0, \frac{3}{4}\right), \left(1, \frac{1}{4}\right)$

Find an exponential model by solving for *y*.

7. $\ln y = 1.924x + 3.634$

8. $\ln y = 0.283x - 6.275$

9. $\ln y = -3.5x + 4.129$

10. Use the points (x, y) to draw a scatter plot of the points $(x, \ln y)$. Then find an exponential model for the data.

x	1	2	3	4	5	6
y	3.36	9.41	26.34	73.76	206.52	578.27

Write a power function $y = ax^b$ whose graph passes through the given points.

11. $(1, 3), (2, 24)$

12. $(1, 0.5), (4, 8)$

13. $(1, 2), (4, 16)$

14. $(1, -4), (4, -64)$

15. $(4, 0.5), (9, 0.75)$

16. $(3, -7.794), (7, -64.82)$

Find a power model by solving for *y*.

17. $\ln y = 3.3 \ln x + 2.56$

18. $\ln y = 1.05 \ln x - 4.28$

19. $\ln y = 2 \ln 2x + 3.15$

20. Use the points (x, y) to draw a scatter plot of the points $(\ln x, \ln y)$. Then find a power model for the data.

x	1	2	3	4	5	6
y	2.1	7.313	15.172	25.464	38.051	52.831

21. Minimum Wage The table shows the minimum hourly wage in the United States since 1960. Let $x = 1$ represent the year 1960, $x = 2$ represent the year 1965, and so on. Let y represent the minimum hourly wage. Use a graphing calculator to find a power model for the data. Use the model to estimate the minimum hourly wage in 2020.

Year	1960	1965	1970	1975	1980	1985	1990	1995	2000	2005
Wage	\$1.00	\$1.25	\$1.60	\$2.10	\$3.10	\$3.35	\$3.80	\$4.25	\$5.15	\$5.15

UNIT 4

LESSON 4.9 **Exercise Set B**

MM3A2g Explore real phenomena related to exponential and logarithmic functions including half-life and doubling time.

UNIT 4

Write an exponential function $y = ab^x$ whose graph passes through the given points.

1. (1, 2.88), (3, 16.589)
2. (2, 7.35), (4, 90.038)
3. (3, 200.04), (6, 14,820.386)

Use the points (x, y) to draw a scatter plot of the points $(x, \ln y)$. Then find an exponential model for the data.

4.

x	1	2	3	4	5	6
y	5.4	9.72	17.496	31.493	56.687	102.04

5.

x	1	2	3	4	5	6
y	3.6	14.4	57.6	230.4	921.6	3686.4

Write a power function $y = ax^b$ whose graph passes through the given points.

6. (1, 0.3), (4, 2.4)
7. (2, 27.292), (5, 809.86)
8. (6, 17.2), (14, 24.14)

In Exercises 9–12, use the following information.

Gas Prices The data gives the average cost of gasoline in dollars per gallon in the United States during August 2005. Each increment of x represents six days with the first data point, $x = 1$, corresponding to August 3, the second data point, $x = 2$, corresponding to August 9, and so on.

x	1	2	3	4	5	6
y	2.30	2.39	2.54	2.59	2.59	3.08

9. Use the points (x, y) to draw a scatter plot of the points $(\ln x, \ln y)$. Then find a power model for the data.
10. Use your graphing calculator to find an exponential model for the data.
11. Use your graphing calculator to find a power model for the data.
12. Which model is the better fitting model? *Explain* your answer.

TEST | for Unit 4

Graph the function. State the domain and range.

1. $y = 7^x$ **2.** $f(x) = 0.25 \cdot 2^{x+3}$ **3.** $f(x) = 3(0.75)^x$

4. $f(x) = 8 \cdot (0.25)^x$ **5.** $y = (0.8)^x - 3$ **6.** $y = e^{x+3} + 1$

Find the inverse of the function.

7. $y = \log_3 x$ **8.** $f(x) = \ln x$ **9.** $y = \log(x + 5)$

Graph the function. State the domain and range.

10. $y = \log_4 x$ **11.** $y = \log(x - 1) + 5$ **12.** $f(x) = \ln x - 4$

Analyze the graph. (a) Identify the zeros of the function, if any. (b) Determine the intervals for which the function is increasing and decreasing. (c) Determine whether the average rate of change is greater between points *A* and *B* or between *C* and *D*.

13.

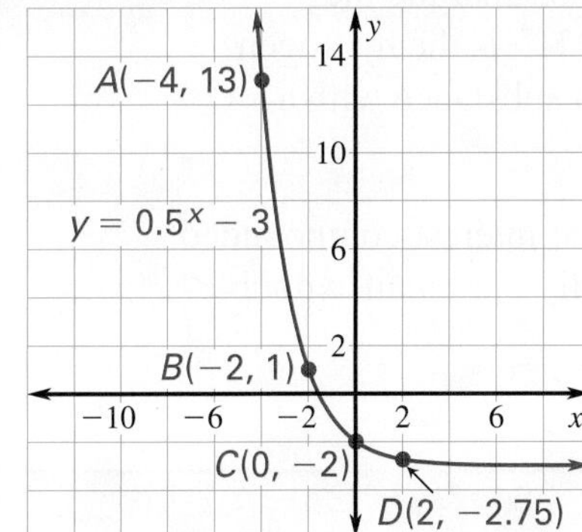

14.

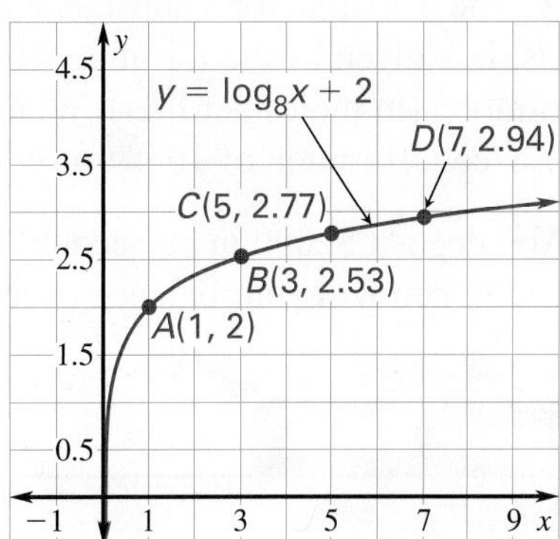

Expand the expression.

15. $\log_3 4x$ **16.** $\log_2 \frac{x^2}{5}$ **17.** $\ln \frac{4}{x^3}$

Condense the expression.

18. $\ln x - 2\ln 4 + \ln 5$ **19.** $\log_4 5 - \log_4 3$ **20.** $3\log x - \log 5 - \log y$

Use the change-of-base formula to evaluate the logarithm. Round your result to three decimal places.

21. $\log_{12} 122$ **22.** $\log_{0.2} 492$ **23.** $\log_{50} 1420$

Solve the equation. Check for extraneous solutions. Round the result to three decimal places if necessary.

24. $e^{2x} = 4$ **25.** $4^x + 1 = 0.5$ **26.** $\log_2 4x = \log_2(x + 15)$

Solve the inequality using any method.

27. $\left(\frac{2}{3}\right)^x \geq 4$ **28.** $5^{x+2} < 6280$ **29.** $-0.5\log_3 x + 5 \leq 4.5$

Write a power function $y = ax^b$ whose graph passes through the given points.

30. (1, 2), (4, 256) **31.** (1, 0.2), (2, 51.2) **32.** (−1, −5), (3, −405)

33. Half-life Models The half-life of nitrogen-13 is about 10 minutes. The amount A (in grams) of radioactive nitrogen-13 that remains in a sample after t minutes is given by $A = 2000\left(\frac{1}{2}\right)^{t/10}$.

a. What is the initial amount of nitrogen-13? ($t = 0$)

b. How much nitrogen-13 is present after half an hour?

c. In about how many hours will 500 grams of nitrogen-13 remain?

34. Bacteria Growth A population of bacteria can be modeled by the function $P = 60e^{0.3t}$ where t is the time (in hours). Graph the model and use the graph to estimate the population after 5 hours.

35. Chemistry The pH value for a substance measures how acidic or alkaline the substance is. It is given by the formula $\text{pH} = -\log\,[H^+]$ where H^+ is the hydrogen ion concentration (in moles per liter). What is the pH value of a substance with a hydrogen ion concentration of $10^{-5.7}$ moles per liter?

36. Finance You deposit \$2000 in an account that pays 3.5% annual interest compounded continuously. When will your balance exceed \$2500? When will your balance double?

Performance Task

Finance

You have \$500 to invest, and you are trying to decide between two different banks. The first bank pays 5% annual interest compounded monthly.

a. Write a model giving the account balance A after t years for the first bank.

b. Make a table of values and graph the model for the first bank. In about how many years will your balance double in the first bank?

c. Analyze the graph in part (b). Identify the zeros of the function, and determine the intervals for which the function is increasing and decreasing. *Explain* what these mean in the context of the problem.

d. A bank representative from the second bank provides the following table of how your money will perform over the next 5 years if deposited in that bank. Draw a scatter plot of the data. Then find an exponential model for the data.

Time, t	1	2	3
Account balance, A	530.00	561.80	595.51

e. If you deposit your money in the second bank, when will your balance exceed \$750? Which bank seems to be the better choice? *Explain.*

UNIT 5
Geometry

5.1 Graph and Write Equations of Parabolas (MM3G2b, MM3G2c)

5.2 Graph and Write Equations of Circles (MM3G1a, MM3G1b, MM3G1c)

5.3 Graph and Write Equations of Ellipses (MM3G2b, MM3G2c)

5.4 Graph and Write Equations of Hyperbolas (MM3G2b, MM3G2c)

5.5 Translate and Classify Conic Sections (MM3G2a, MM3G2b, MM3G2c)

5.6 Solve Quadratic Systems (MM3G1d, MM3G1e)

5.7 Use Figures in Three-Dimensional Space (MM3G3a, MM3G3b, MM3G3c)

LESSON 5.1

Graph and Write Equations of Parabolas

Georgia Performance Standards: MM3G2b, MM3G2c

Goal Graph and write equations of parabolas.

Vocabulary

A **parabola** is the set of points equidistant from a point called the **focus** and a line called the **directrix.** The line perpendicular to the parabola's directrix and passing through its focus is the **axis of symmetry.** The point on the parabola that lies on the axis of symmetry is the **vertex.**

The standard form of the equation of a parabola with vertex at (0, 0) is as follows:

Equation	Focus	Directrix	Axis of Symmetry
$x^2 = 4py$	$(0, p)$	$y = -p$	Vertical ($x = 0$)
$y^2 = 4px$	$(p, 0)$	$x = -p$	Horizontal ($y = 0$)

UNIT 5

Example 1 Graph an equation of a parabola

Graph $x = \frac{1}{4}y^2$. Identify the focus, directrix, and axis of symmetry.

STEP 1 **Rewrite** the equation in standard form.

$x = \frac{1}{4}y^2$ Write original equation.

$4x = y^2$ Multiply each side by 4.

STEP 2 **Identify** the focus, directrix, and axis of symmetry. The equation has the form $y^2 = 4px$ where $p = 1$. The focus is $(p, 0)$, or $(1, 0)$. The directrix is $x = -p$, or $x = -1$. Because y is squared, the axis of symmetry is the x-axis.

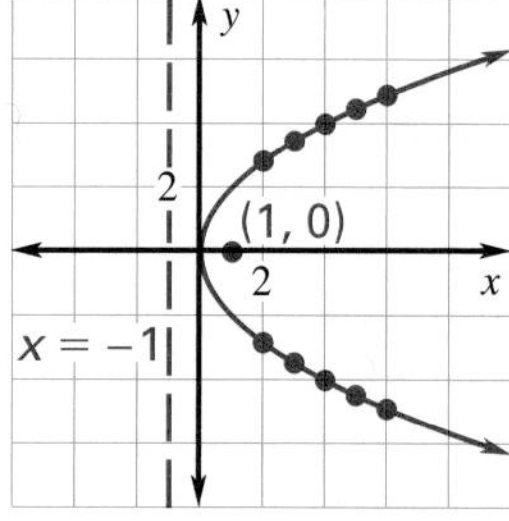

STEP 3 **Draw** the parabola by making a table of values and plotting points. Because $p > 0$, the parabola opens to the right. Use only positive x-values.

x	2	3	4	5	6
y	±2.83	±3.46	±4	±4.47	±4.90

Guided Practice for Example 1

Graph the equation. Identify the focus, directrix, and axis of symmetry of the parabola.

1. $x^2 = \frac{1}{4}y$ **2.** $y^2 = -2x$ **3.** $x = \frac{1}{2}y^2$ **4.** $y = -\frac{1}{3}x^2$

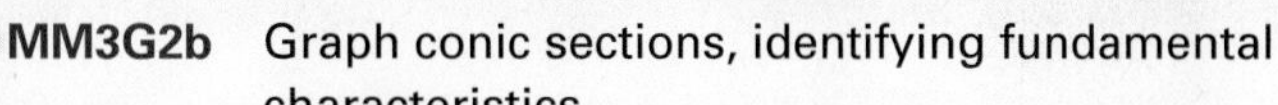

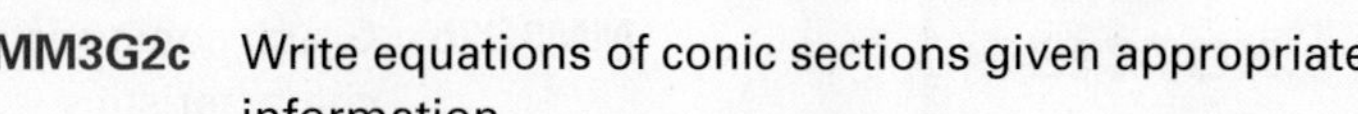

Example 2 Write an equation of a parabola

Write an equation of the parabola shown.

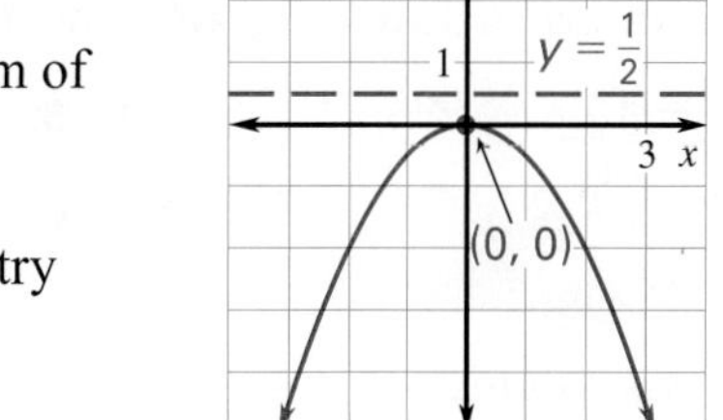

The graph shows that the vertex is (0, 0) and the directrix is $y = -p = \frac{1}{2}$. Substitute $-\frac{1}{2}$ for p in the standard form of the equation of a parabola.

$x^2 = 4py$ Standard form, vertical axis of symmetry

$x^2 = 4\left(-\frac{1}{2}\right)y$ Substitute $-\frac{1}{2}$ for p.

$x^2 = -2y$ Simplify.

Example 3 Solve a multi-step problem

Parabolic Reflector The cross section of a parabolic reflector is 10 yards across and the focus of the reflector is located 4 yards above the vertex. Write an equation for the cross section of a reflector opening upward with its vertex at (0, 0). What is the depth of the reflector?

STEP 1 **Write** an equation for the cross section. Because the focus is above the vertex, p is positive, so $p = 4$. An equation for the cross section of the reflector with its vertex at the origin is as follows.

$x^2 = 4py$ Standard form, vertical axis of symmetry

$x^2 = 4(4)y$ Substitute 4 for p.

$x^2 = 16y$ Simplify.

STEP 2 **Find** the depth of the reflector. The depth is the y-value at the reflector's outer edge. The reflector extends 5 yards to either side of the vertex (0, 0), so substitute 5 for x in the equation from Step 1.

$x^2 = 16y$ Equation for the cross section

$5^2 = 16y$ Substitute 5 for x.

$1.56 \approx y$ Solve for y.

The reflector is about 1.56 yards deep.

Guided Practice for Examples 2 and 3

5. Write the standard form of the equation of the parabola with vertex at (0, 0) and directrix $x = 3$.

6. The cross section of parabolic reflector is 14 meters across and the focus of the reflector is 5 meters above the vertex. Write an equation for the cross section of a reflector opening upward with its vertex at (0, 0). What is the reflector's depth?

LESSON 5.1

Exercise Set A

MM3G2b Graph conic sections, identifying fundamental characteristics.

MM3G2c Write equations of conic sections given appropriate information.

Tell whether the parabola opens *up, down, left,* or *right*.

1. $x^2 = -4y$ **2.** $y^2 = 7x$ **3.** $y^2 = -2x$

Graph the equation. Identify the focus and directrix of the parabola.

4. $x^2 = 12y$ **5.** $y^2 = -4x$ **6.** $x^2 = -y$

7. $y^2 - 6x = 0$ **8.** $x^2 + 8y = 0$ **9.** $2x^2 - y = 0$

10. **Error Analysis** *Describe* and correct the error in graphing $-5x + y^2 = 0$.

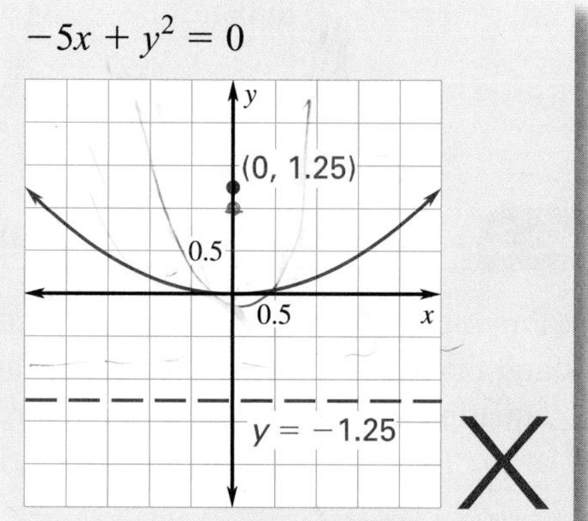

Write the standard form of the equation of the parabola with the given focus and vertex at (0, 0).

11. $(2, 0)$ **12.** $(0, 1)$ **13.** $(-1, 0)$

14. $\left(0, \frac{1}{2}\right)$ **15.** $(3, 0)$ **16.** $(0, -6)$

Write the standard form of the equation of the parabola with the given directrix and vertex at (0, 0).

17. $x = 3$ **18.** $y = -2$ **19.** $x = -1$

20. $y = 4$ **21.** $x = \frac{1}{4}$ **22.** $y = -\frac{1}{2}$

23. **Television Antenna Dish** The cross section of a television antenna dish is a parabola. The receiver is located at the focus, 2.5 feet above the vertex. Assume the vertex is at the origin. Write an equation for the cross section of the dish opening upward.

24. **Headlight** The filament of a light bulb is a thin wire that glows when electricity passes through it. The filament of a car headlight is at the focus of a parabolic reflector, which sends light out in a straight beam. Given that the filament is 1.5 inches from the vertex, write an equation for the cross section of the reflector opening to the right with vertex at (0, 0).

LESSON 5.1 **Exercise Set B**

MM3G2b Graph conic sections, identifying fundamental characteristics.

MM3G2c Write equations of conic sections given appropriate information.

Graph the equation. Identify the focus and directrix of the parabola.

1. $x^2 = 12y$
2. $y^2 = -16x$
3. $8x^2 = -y$
4. $2y^2 - 8x = 0$
5. $4x^2 + y = 0$
6. $4x^2 - 6y = 0$
7. $x^2 - 40y = 0$
8. $x + \left(\frac{1}{20}\right)y^2 = 0$
9. $3x^2 = 4y$

Write the standard form of the equation of the parabola with the given focus and vertex at (0, 0).

10. $(3, 0)$
11. $(0, 6)$
12. $(-2, 0)$
13. $(5, 0)$
14. $\left(-\frac{1}{4}, 0\right)$
15. $\left(0, -\frac{3}{8}\right)$
16. $\left(0, \frac{1}{4}\right)$
17. $\left(-\frac{3}{2}, 0\right)$
18. $\left(0, -\frac{1}{8}\right)$

Write the standard form of the equation of the parabola with the given directrix and vertex at (0, 0).

19. $x = 2$
20. $y = -12$
21. $x = -6$
22. $y = -5$
23. $x = 4$
24. $x = -\frac{1}{12}$
25. $y = \frac{5}{8}$
26. $x = -\frac{7}{4}$
27. $y = -\frac{5}{2}$

28. Solar Energy Cross sections of parabolic mirrors at a solar-thermal complex can be modeled by the equation $\frac{1}{20}x^2 = y$ where x and y are measured in feet. The oil-filled heating tube is located at the focus of the parabola. How high above the vertex of the mirror is the heating tube?

29. Storage Building A storage building for rock salt has the shape of a paraboloid which has vertical cross sections that are parabolas. The equation of a vertical cross section is $y = -\frac{1}{8}x^2$. If the building is 24 feet high, how much rock salt will it hold? (*Hint:* The volume of a paraboloid is $v = \frac{1}{2}\pi r^2 h$ where r is the radius of the base and h is the height.)

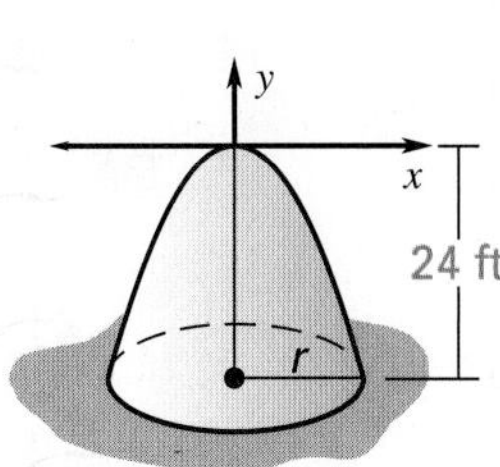

UNIT 5

LESSON 5.2

Graph and Write Equations of Circles

Georgia Performance Standards: MM3G1a, MM3G1b, MM3G1c

Goal Graph and write equations of circles.

Vocabulary

A **circle** is the set of all points (x, y) in a plane that are equidistant from a fixed point, called the **center** of the circle. The distance r between the center and any point (x, y) on the circle is the **radius.** The standard form of the equation of a circle with center at $(0, 0)$ and radius r is $x^2 + y^2 = r^2$.

Example 1 Graph the equation of a circle

Graph $x^2 = 25 - y^2$. Identify the radius of the circle.

STEP 1 **Rewrite** the equation $x^2 = 25 - y^2$ in standard form as $x^2 + y^2 = 25$.

STEP 2 **Identify** the center and radius. From the equation, the graph is a circle centered at the origin with radius $r = \sqrt{25} = 5$.

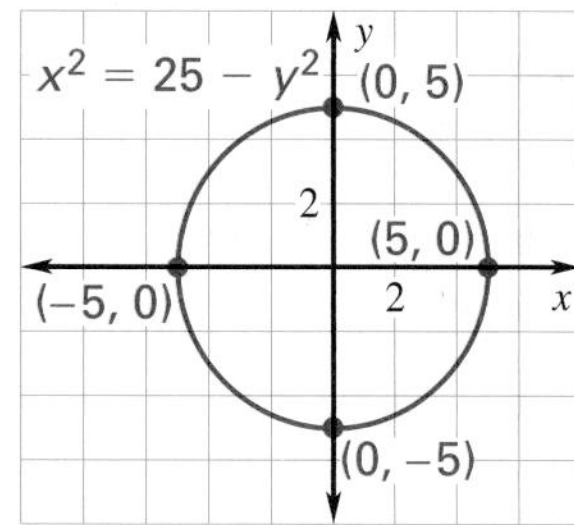

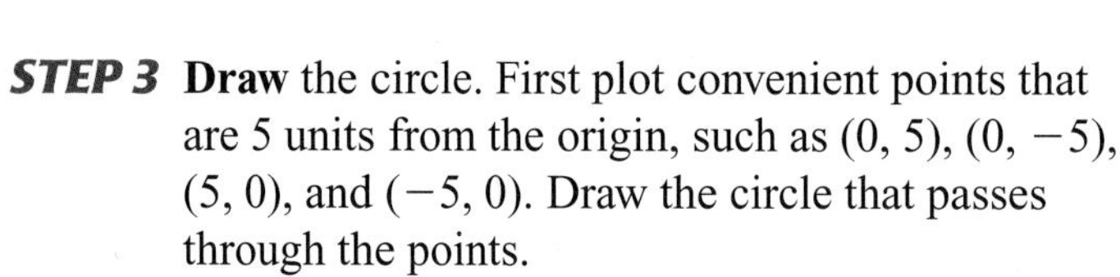

STEP 3 **Draw** the circle. First plot convenient points that are 5 units from the origin, such as $(0, 5)$, $(0, -5)$, $(5, 0)$, and $(-5, 0)$. Draw the circle that passes through the points.

Example 2 Write an equation of a circle

The point (6, 2) lies on a circle whose center is the origin. Write the standard form of the equation of the circle.

Because the point $(6, 2)$ lies on the circle, the circle's radius must be the distance between the center $(0, 0)$ and the point $(6, 2)$. Use the distance formula.

$r = \sqrt{(6 - 0)^2 + (2 - 0)^2} = \sqrt{36 + 4} = \sqrt{40}$ The radius is $\sqrt{40}$.

Use the standard form with $r = \sqrt{40}$ to write an equation of the circle.

$x^2 + y^2 = r^2$ Standard form

$x^2 + y^2 = (\sqrt{40})^2$ Substitute $\sqrt{40}$ for r.

$x^2 + y^2 = 40$ Simplify.

Guided Practice for Examples 1 and 2

Graph the equation. Identify the radius of the circle.

1. $x^2 + y^2 = 16$ **2.** $x^2 = 81 - y^2$ **3.** $y^2 - 9 = -x^2$

4. Write the standard form of the equation of the circle that passes through $(3, 2)$ and whose center is the origin.

Georgia Performance Standards

MM3G1a Find equations of circles. 

MM3G1b Graph a circle given an equation in general form. ☑

MM3G1c Find the equation of a tangent line to a circle at a given point. ☑

Example 3 Find an equation of a line tangent to a circle

Find an equation of the line tangent to the circle $x^2 + y^2 = 10$ at $(-1, 3)$.

Solution

A line tangent to a circle is perpendicular to the radius at the point of tangency. Because the radius to the point $(-1, 3)$ has slope $m = \frac{3 - 0}{-1 - 0} = -3$, the slope of the tangent line at $(-1, 3)$ is the negative reciprocal of -3, or $\frac{1}{3}$. An equation of the tangent line is as follows:

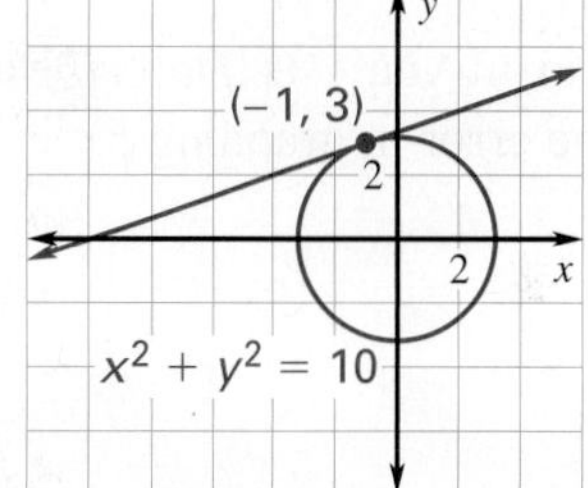

$y - 3 = \frac{1}{3}(x - (-1))$ Point-slope form

$y - 3 = \frac{1}{3}x + \frac{1}{3}$ Distributive property

$y = \frac{1}{3}x + \frac{10}{3}$ Solve for y.

Example 4 Write a circular model

Store Delivery A furniture store advertises free delivery up to a 50 mile radius from the store. If a customer lives 28 miles east and 41 miles north of the store, does the customer qualify for free delivery?

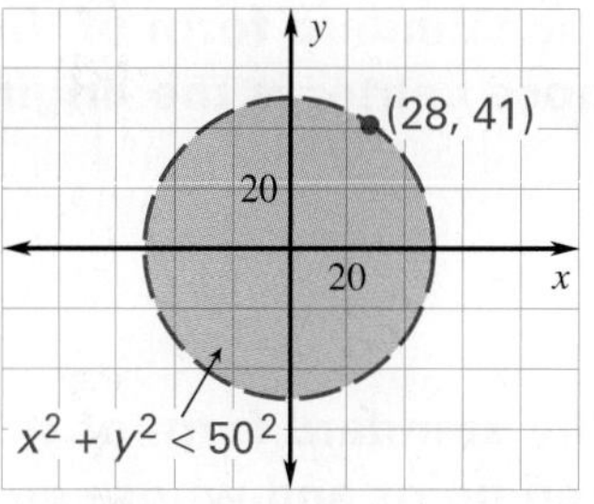

In the diagram above, the origin represents the store and the positive y-axis represents north.

STEP 1 **Write** an inequality for the region covered by free delivery. From the diagram, this region is all points that satisfy the inequality $x^2 + y^2 < 50^2$.

STEP 2 **Substitute** the coordinates (28, 41) into the inequality.

$x^2 + y^2 < 50^2$ Inequality from Step 1

$28^2 + 41^2 \stackrel{?}{<} 50^2$ Substitute for x and y.

$2465 < 2500$ The inequality is true.

The customer does qualify for free delivery.

Guided Practice for Examples 3 and 4

5. Write an equation of the line tangent to the circle $x^2 + y^2 = 20$ at (2, 4).

6. In Example 4, determine if a customer who lives 30 miles west and 41 miles south qualifies for free delivery.

LESSON 5.2 **Exercise Set A**

MM3G1a	Find equations of circles.
MM3G1b	Graph a circle given an equation in general form.
MM3G1c	Find the equation of a tangent line to a circle at a given point.

Graph the equation. Identify the radius of the circle.

1. $x^2 + y^2 = 9$ **2.** $x^2 + y^2 = 20$ **3.** $x^2 + y^2 = 64$

4. $x^2 + y^2 = 50$ **5.** $5x^2 + 5y^2 = 80$ **6.** $3x^2 + 3y^2 = 120$

7. Error Analysis *Describe* and correct the error in graphing $5x^2 + 5y^2 = 80$.

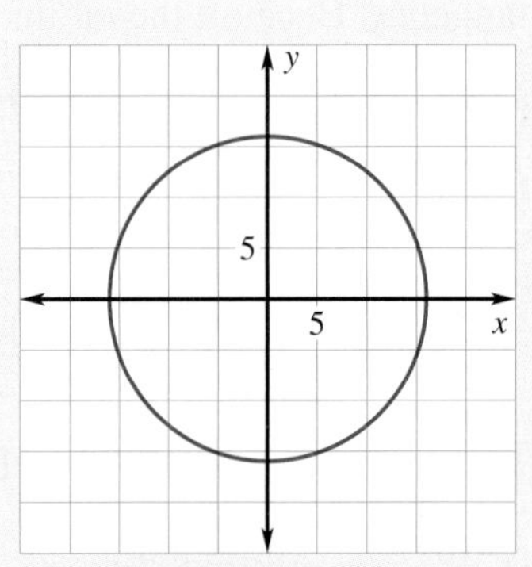

The radius of the circle is 16.

Write the standard form of the equation of the circle with the given radius and whose center is the origin.

8. 11 **9.** $4\sqrt{5}$ **10.** $2\sqrt{7}$

11. $\sqrt{7}$ **12.** $2\sqrt{5}$ **13.** $3\sqrt{10}$

Write the standard form of the equation of the circle that passes through the given point and whose center is the origin.

14. $(0, -10)$ **15.** $(-3, -4)$ **16.** $(-4, -1)$

17. $(2, 3)$ **18.** $(-3, 5)$ **19.** $(4, -6)$

The equations of both circles and parabolas are given. Graph the equation.

20. $x^2 + 3y = 0$ **21.** $2x^2 + 2y^2 = 8$ **22.** $x^2 - 8y = 0$

Write an equation of the line tangent to the given circle at the given point.

23. $x^2 + y^2 = 17; (1, 4)$ **24.** $x^2 + y^2 = 52; (-4, 6)$

25. Capitol Dome The Capitol Dome sits atop the Capitol Building in Washington, D.C. The base of the dome is a circle with a diameter of 96 feet. Suppose a coordinate plane was placed over the base of the dome with the origin at the center of the dome. Write an equation in standard form for the outside boundary of the base of the dome.

LESSON 5.2

Exercise Set B

MM3G1a Find equations of circles.

MM3G1b Graph a circle given an equation in general form.

MM3G1c Find the equation of a tangent line to a circle at a given point.

Graph the equation. Identify the radius of the circle.

1. $x^2 + y^2 = 100$

2. $\frac{1}{3}x^2 + \frac{1}{3}y^2 = 12$

3. $2x^2 + 2y^2 = 98$

4. $4x^2 + 4y^2 = 96$

5. $3x^2 + 3y^2 = 54$

6. $7x^2 + 7y^2 = 196$

Write the standard form of the equation of the circle with the given radius and whose center is the origin.

7. $\sqrt{13}$

8. $2\sqrt{7}$

9. $4\sqrt{17}$

Write the standard form of the equation of the circle that passes through the given point and whose center is the origin.

10. $(7, -4)$

11. $(10, 2)$

12. $(2, -12)$

13. $(-2, -4)$

14. $(3, \sqrt{5})$

15. $\left(\frac{1}{2}, -5\right)$

Write an equation of the line tangent to the given circle at the given point.

16. $x^2 + y^2 = 13; (3, -2)$

17. $x^2 + y^2 = 40; (2\sqrt{6}, 4)$

18. Length of a Chord A circle has a radius of 4 and is centered at the origin. The line $y = 2$ intersects the circle to form a chord. What is the length of the chord? Round your answer to two decimal places.

19. Multiple Representations The Modified Mercalli Intensity Scale rates an earthquake's "shaking strength." Suppose an earthquake has a 5.0 rating at its epicenter, a 4.6 rating 20 miles away from the epicenter, and a 4.2 rating 35 miles away.

a. Drawing Graphs Draw circles in a coordinate plane that represent the locations with a 4.6 rating and the locations with a 4.2 rating. Place the epicenter at the origin.

b. Writing Inequalities For the circles in part (a), write inequalities describing the coordinates of locations with a rating of 4.6 or greater and with a rating of 4.2 or greater.

c. Making a Prediction What can you predict about the rating of locations 16 miles east and 18 miles north of the epicenter? *Explain.*

20. Semicircle In the diagram to the right, the semicircle has a radius of $x + 5$ and the center C is the origin. The point $(15, x)$ lies on the semicircle. Find the value of x.

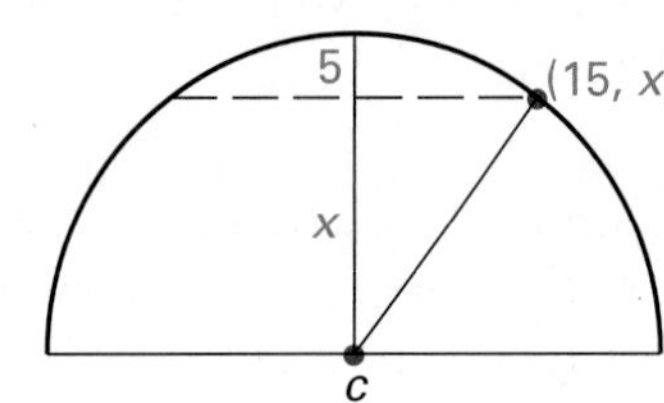

UNIT 5

LESSON 5.2

Problem Solving Workshop

Problem An air traffic control tower can detect airplanes up to 50 miles away. A plane is 38 miles east and 41 miles south of the control tower. Is the plane in the tower's range?

STEP 1 **Read and Understand**

What do you know? The radius of the tower's range

What do you want to find out? Whether the plane is in the tower's range

STEP 2 **Make a Plan** Use what you know to write and solve an inequality.

STEP 3 **Solve the Problem** Write an inequality for the region covered by the tower. From the diagram, this region is all points that satisfy the following inequality: $x^2 + y^2 \le 50^2$

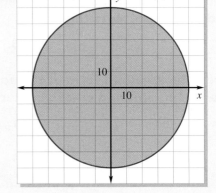

Substitute the coordinates (38, 41) into the inequality.

$x^2 + y^2 \le 50^2$ Write inequality.

$38^2 + 41^2 \overset{?}{\le} 50^2$ Substitute for x and y.

$3125 \not\le 2500$ The inequality is false.

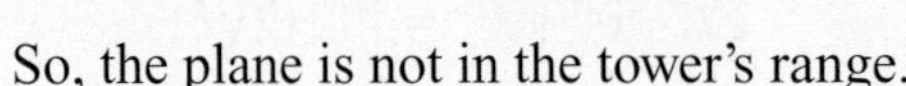

So, the plane is not in the tower's range.

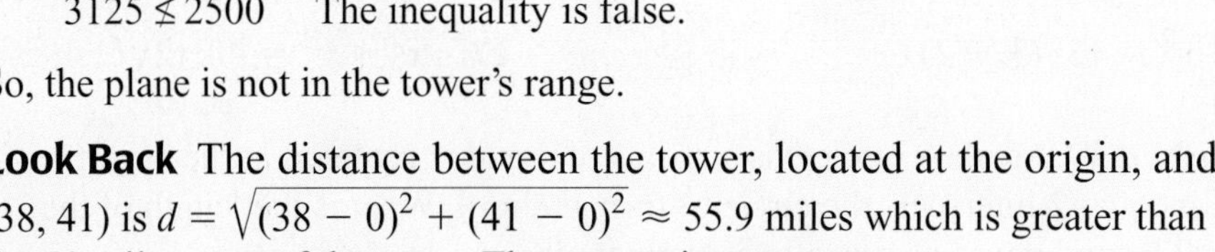

STEP 4 **Look Back** The distance between the tower, located at the origin, and (38, 41) is $d = \sqrt{(38 - 0)^2 + (41 - 0)^2} \approx 55.9$ miles which is greater than the 50 mile range of the tower. The answer is correct.

Practice

1. **Earthquakes** Suppose an earthquake can be felt up to 80 miles from its epicenter. You are located at a point 65 miles west and 50 miles south of the epicenter. Do you feel the earthquake?
2. **Radio Signals** The signals of a radio station can be received up to 65 miles away. Your house is 30 miles east and 56 miles south of the radio station. Can you receive the radio station's signals?
3. **What If?** Suppose in Exercise 2 that you want to drive west from your house. For how many miles will you be able to receive the radio station's signal?
4. **Lawn Sprinklers** A sprinkler can water a region with an 8 foot radius. A plant is 4 feet east and 6 feet north of the sprinkler. Is the plant in the sprinkler's range?
5. **What If?** Suppose in Exercise 4 that there is another plant located 3 feet west and 7 feet south of the sprinkler. Is this plant in the sprinkler's range?
6. **Ocean Navigation** The beam of a lighthouse can be seen for up to 25 miles. You are on a ship that is 19 miles east and 21 miles north of the lighthouse. Can you see the lighthouse beam?

Georgia Performance Standards

MM3G2b Graph conic sections, identifying fundamental characteristics.

Investigating Math Activity
Draw an Ellipse

Use before Lesson 5.3

Materials **thumbtacks, string, cardboard, and tape**

Question

What is the relationship between an ellipse and its foci?

Explore

Draw an ellipse.

Read through the following steps on how to draw an ellipse and the questions that follow. You will need to make some observations as you are drawing your ellipse.

STEP 1 Get two thumbtacks, a piece of string, a piece of cardboard, and tape from your teacher.

STEP 2 Use the tape to attach a piece of paper to the piece of cardboard.

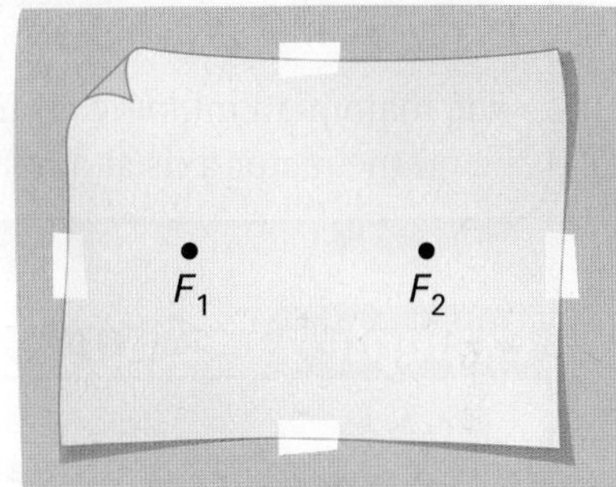

STEP 3 Use your pencil to mark two points on the paper, and label them F_1 and F_2. These will be your *foci*.

STEP 4 Place one thumbtack on each point.

STEP 5 Tie each end of the string to a thumbtack.

STEP 6 Place your pencil in the string and pull it until it is tight.

STEP 7 Carefully move your pencil around the foci until you reach your starting point. Remember to keep the string tight.

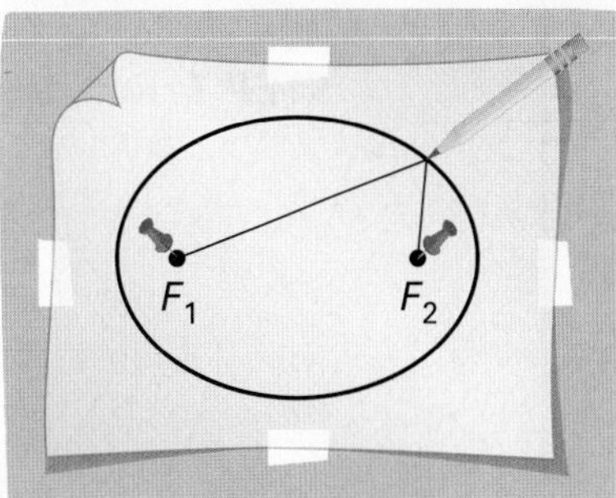

Draw Conclusions

1. What happened to the length of the string from F_2 to a point on the ellipse as the length of the string from F_1 to the same point on the ellipse increased?

2. What happened to the length of the string from F_2 to a point on the ellipse as the length of the string from F_1 to the same point on the ellipse decreased?

3. Did the total length of the string ever change?

4. **Writing** F_1 and F_2 are the *foci* of the ellipse. What must be true about the sum of the distances from the foci to any point on the ellipse? Write a definition for an ellipse in terms of the relationship of the points on the ellipse to the foci.

LESSON 5.3

Graph and Write Equations of Ellipses

Georgia Performance Standards: MM3G2b, MM3G2c

Goal Graph and write equations of ellipses.

Vocabulary

An **ellipse** is the set of all points P in a plane such that the sum of the distances between P and two fixed points, called the **foci,** is a constant. The line through the foci intersects the ellipse at two **vertices.** The **major axis** joins the vertices. Its midpoint is the ellipse's **center.** The line perpendicular to the major axis at the center intersects the ellipse at the two **co-vertices,** which are joined by the **minor axis.**

The standard form of the equation of an ellipse with center at the origin is as follows:

Equation	Major Axis	Vertices	Co-Vertices
$\frac{x^2}{a^2} + \frac{y^2}{b^2} = 1$	Horizontal	$(\pm a, 0)$	$(0, \pm b)$
$\frac{x^2}{b^2} + \frac{y^2}{a^2} = 1$	Vertical	$(0, \pm a)$	$(\pm b, 0)$

The major and minor axes are of lengths $2a$ and $2b$, respectively, where $a > b > 0$. The foci lie on the major axis at a distance of c units from the center, where $c^2 = a^2 - b^2$.

UNIT 5

Example 1 Graph an equation of an ellipse

Graph the equation $9x^2 + y^2 = 36$. Identify the vertices, co-vertices, and foci of the ellipse.

STEP 1 **Rewrite** the equation in standard form.

$9x^2 + y^2 = 36$ Write original equation.

$\frac{9x^2}{36} + \frac{y^2}{36} = \frac{36}{36}$ Divide each side by 36.

$\frac{x^2}{4} + \frac{y^2}{36} = 1$ Simplify.

STEP 2 **Identify** the vertices, co-vertices, and foci. Note that $b^2 = 4$ and $a^2 = 36$, then $b = 2$ and $a = 6$. The denominator of the y^2-term is greater than that of the x^2-term, so the major axis is vertical. The vertices of the ellipse are at $(0, \pm a) = (0, \pm 6)$. The co-vertices are at $(\pm b, 0) = (\pm 2, 0)$. Find the foci.

$c^2 = a^2 - b^2 = 6^2 - 2^2 = 32$, so $c = \sqrt{32} = 4\sqrt{2}$

The foci are at $(0, \pm 4\sqrt{2})$, or about $(0, \pm 5.7)$.

STEP 3 **Draw** the ellipse that passes through each vertex and co-vertex.

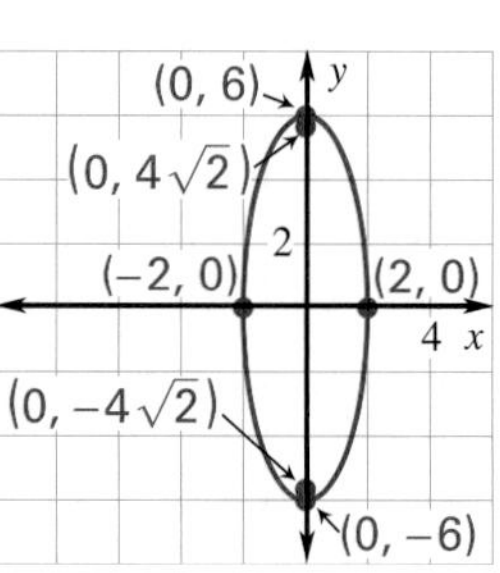

Georgia Performance Standards

MM3G2b Graph conic sections, identifying fundamental characteristics. ☑

MM3G2c Write equations of conic sections given appropriate information. ☑

Guided Practice for Example 1

Graph the equation. Identify the vertices, co-vertices, and foci of the ellipse.

1. $\frac{x^2}{16} + \frac{y^2}{25} = 1$ **2.** $\frac{x^2}{25} + \frac{y^2}{9} = 1$ **3.** $4x^2 + 9y^2 = 36$

Example 2 Write an equation given a vertex and co-vertex

Write an equation of the ellipse that has a vertex at (5, 0), a co-vertex at (0, 4), and center at (0, 0).

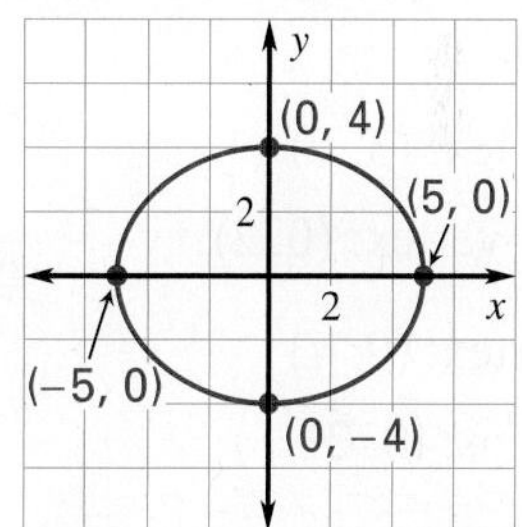

By symmetry, the ellipse must also have a vertex at $(-5, 0)$ and a co-vertex at $(0, -4)$. The major axis is horizontal with $a = 5$, and the minor axis is vertical with $b = 4$.

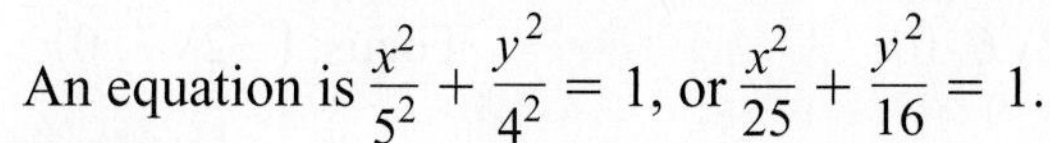

An equation is $\frac{x^2}{5^2} + \frac{y^2}{4^2} = 1$, or $\frac{x^2}{25} + \frac{y^2}{16} = 1$.

Example 3 Write an equation given a vertex and a focus

Write an equation of the ellipse that has a vertex at (0, 13), a focus at (0, −5), and center at (0, 0).

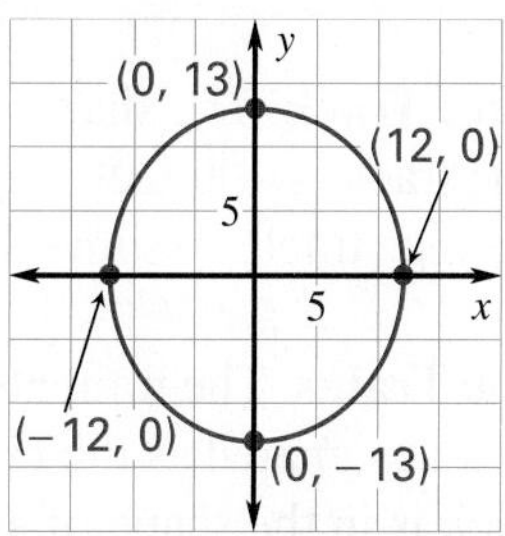

Make a sketch of the ellipse. Because the given vertex and focus lie on the y-axis, the major axis is vertical, with $a = 13$ and $c = 5$. To find b, use the equation $c^2 = a^2 - b^2$.

$5^2 = 13^2 - b^2$

$b^2 = 13^2 - 5^2$

$b^2 = 144$

$b = \sqrt{144}$

$b = 12$

An equation is $\frac{x^2}{12^2} + \frac{y^2}{13^2} = 1$, or $\frac{x^2}{144} + \frac{y^2}{169} = 1$.

Guided Practice for Examples 2 and 3

Write an equation of the ellipse with the given characteristics and center at (0, 0).

4. Vertex: $(0, 3)$; Co-vertex: $(-1, 0)$ **5.** Vertex: $(8, 0)$; Focus: $(-6, 0)$

6. Vertex: $(0, -3)$; Co-vertex: $(2, 0)$ **7.** Vertex: $(-6, 0)$; Focus: $(2, 0)$

UNIT 5

LESSON 5.3

Exercise Set A

MM3G2b Graph conic sections, identifying fundamental characteristics.

MM3G2c Write equations of conic sections given appropriate information.

Graph the equation. Identify the vertices, co-vertices, and foci of the ellipse.

1. $\frac{x^2}{16} + \frac{y^2}{36} = 1$

2. $\frac{x^2}{49} + \frac{y^2}{4} = 1$

3. $\frac{x^2}{64} + \frac{y^2}{100} = 1$

4. $\frac{x^2}{25} + \frac{y^2}{81} = 1$

5. $16x^2 + y^2 = 16$

6. $49x^2 + 4y^2 = 196$

7. $9x^2 + 4y^2 = 36$

8. $16x^2 + 25y^2 = 400$

9. $4x^2 + 81y^2 = 324$

Write an equation of the ellipse with the given characteristics and center at (0, 0).

10. Vertex: $(3, 0)$
Co-vertex: $(0, 2)$

11. Vertex: $(0, 5)$
Co-vertex: $(1, 0)$

12. Vertex: $(-6, 0)$
Co-vertex: $(0, -3)$

13. Vertex: $(0, 4)$
Focus: $(0, 2\sqrt{3})$

14. Vertex: $(-7, 0)$
Focus: $(2\sqrt{6}, 0)$

15. Co-vertex: $(0, 6)$
Focus: $(-2\sqrt{7}, 0)$

The equations of a parabola, a circle, and an ellipse are given. Graph the equation.

16. $x^2 + 12y = 0$

17. $3x^2 + 3y^2 = 48$

18. $6x^2 + 8y^2 = 96$

19. **Swimming Pool** An elliptical pool is 20 feet long and 16 feet wide. Write an equation for the boundary of the swimming pool. Assume the major axis of the pool is vertical.

20. **Race Track** The shape of a dirt race track for car racing is approximately an ellipse. The track is 400 feet long and 250 feet wide. Write an equation for the boundary of the race track. Assume the major axis of the track is horizontal.

21. **Zoo Trains** The train at a zoo encloses an area designated as the children's zoo. The track is in the shape of an ellipse that is 500 yards long and 300 yards wide.

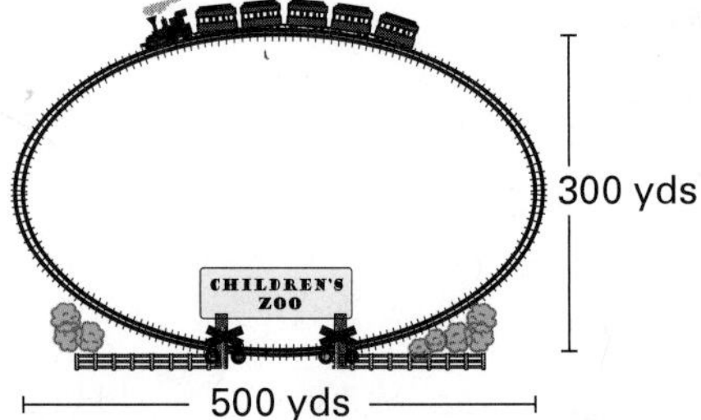

a. Write an equation for the track. Assume the major axis of the track is horizontal.

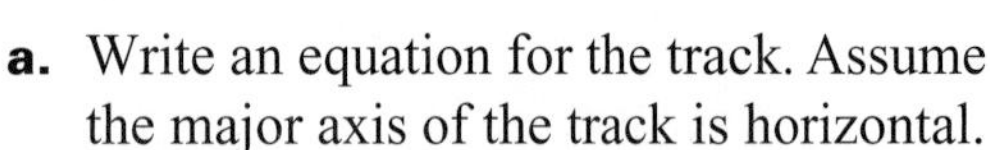

b. The area of an ellipse is $A = \pi ab$. What is the area of the children's zoo?

22. **Australian Football** The playing field for Australian football is an ellipse that is between 135 and 185 meters long and between 110 and 155 meters wide. Write equations of ellipses with vertical major axes that model the largest and smallest fields described. Then write on inequality that describes the possible areas of these fields. (The area of an ellipse is $A = \pi ab$.)

LESSON 5.3 **Exercise Set B**

MM3G2b Graph conic sections, identifying fundamental characteristics.

MM3G2c Write equations of conic sections given appropriate information.

Graph the equation. Identify the vertices, co-vertices, and foci of the ellipse.

1. $\frac{x^2}{3} + 3y^2 = 3$

2. $\frac{9x^2}{16} + \frac{4y^2}{25} = 1$

3. $\frac{x^2}{48} + \frac{y^2}{27} = 3$

4. $4x^2 + 5y^2 = 40$

5. $9x^2 + 6y^2 = 72$

6. $\frac{28x^2}{81} + \frac{63y^2}{25} = 7$

Write an equation of the ellipse with the given characteristics and center at (0, 0).

7. Vertex: $(8, 0)$
Co-vertex: $(0, -5)$

8. Vertex: $(0, -7)$
Co-vertex: $(3, 0)$

9. Vertex: $(13, 0)$
Co-vertex: $(0, \sqrt{31})$

10. Vertex: $(6, 0)$
Focus: $(2\sqrt{3}, 0)$

11. Co-vertex: $(0, 9)$
Focus: $(2\sqrt{22}, 0)$

12. Co-vertex: $(-1, 0)$
Focus: $(0, -\sqrt{35})$

13. Gears In some industrial machines, elliptical gears are used instead of circular ones. One of these elliptical gears is 12 centimeters tall and 8 centimeters wide. Write an equation for the outline of this elliptical gear. Assume the major axis of the gear is vertical.

14. Company Logo You are in charge of designing a company logo similar to the figure at the right. The only stipulations are that the border must be an ellipse and the width of the ellipse must be three times the height. Write an equation in standard form for the outline of the logo in terms of the height h.

15. Boat Tours A tour boat travels between two islands that are 12 miles apart. For a trip between the islands, there is enough fuel for a 20-mile tour.

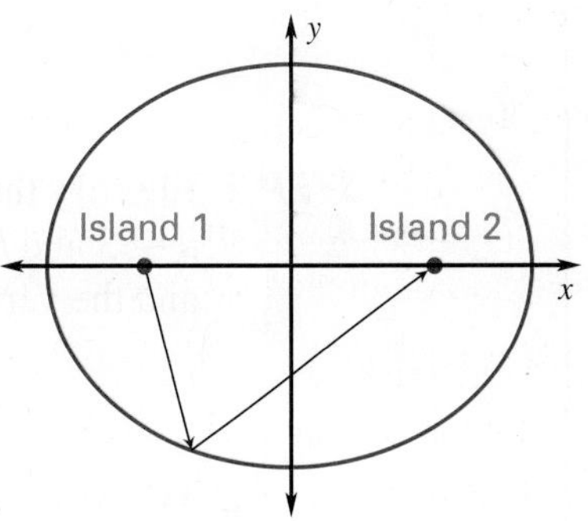

a. The region in which the boat can travel is bounded by an ellipse. *Explain* why this is so.

b. Let (0, 0) represent the center of the ellipse. Find the coordinates of each island.

c. Suppose the boat travels from one island, straight past the other island to the vertex of the ellipse and back to the second island. How many miles does the boat travel? Use your answer to find the coordinates of the vertices.

d. Write an equation of the ellipse.

UNIT 5

LESSON 5.4

Graph and Write Equations of Hyperbolas

Georgia Performance Standards: MM3G2b, MM3G2c

Goal Graph and write equations of hyperbolas.

Vocabulary

A **hyperbola** is the set of all points P in a plane such that the *difference* of the distances between P and two fixed points, again called the **foci,** is a constant. The line through the foci intersects the hyperbola at the two **vertices.** The **transverse axis** joins the vertices. Its midpoint is the hyperbola's **center.**

The standard form of the equation of a hyperbola with center at the origin is as follows:

Equation	Transverse Axis	Asymptotes	Vertices
$\frac{x^2}{a^2} - \frac{y^2}{b^2} = 1$	Horizontal	$y = \pm\frac{b}{a}x$	$(\pm a, 0)$
$\frac{y^2}{a^2} - \frac{x^2}{b^2} = 1$	Vertical	$y = \pm\frac{a}{b}x$	$(0, \pm a)$

The foci lie on the transverse axis, c units from the center, where $c^2 = a^2 + b^2$.

UNIT 5

Example 1 Graph an equation of a hyperbola

Graph $4x^2 - 9y^2 = 36$. Identify the vertices, foci, and asymptotes of the hyperbola.

STEP 1 **Rewrite** the equation in standard form.

$4x^2 - 9y^2 = 36$ Write original equation.

$\frac{4x^2}{36} - \frac{9y^2}{36} = \frac{36}{36}$ Divide each side by 36.

$\frac{x^2}{9} - \frac{y^2}{4} = 1$ Simplify.

STEP 2 **Identify** the vertices, foci, and asymptotes. Note that $a^2 = 9$ and $b^2 = 4$, then $a = 3$ and $b = 2$. The x^2-term is positive, so the transverse axis is horizontal and the vertices are at $(\pm 3, 0)$. Find the foci.

$c^2 = a^2 + b^2 = 3^2 + 2^2 = 13$, so $c = \sqrt{13}$

The foci are at $(\pm\sqrt{13}, 0) \approx (\pm 3.6, 0)$.

The asymptotes are $y = \pm\frac{b}{a}x$, or $y = \pm\frac{2}{3}x$.

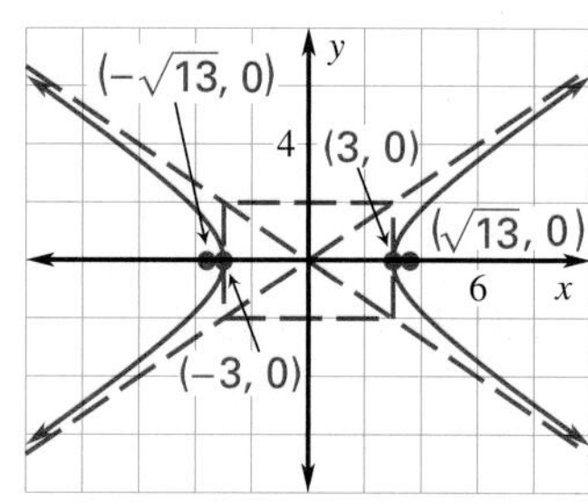

STEP 3 **Draw** the hyperbola. First draw a rectangle centered at the origin that is $2b = 4$ units high and $2a = 6$ units wide. The asymptotes pass through opposite corners of the rectangle. Draw the hyperbola passing through the vertices and approaching the asymptotes.

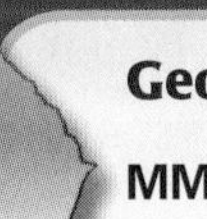

Georgia Performance Standards

MM3G2b Graph conic sections, identifying fundamental characteristics. 

MM3G2c Write equations of conic sections given appropriate information. ☑

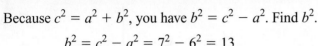

Example 2 Write an equation of a hyperbola

Write an equation of the hyperbola with foci at (0, 7) and (0, −7) and vertices at (0, 6) and (0, −6).

The foci and vertices lie on the *y*-axis equidistant from the origin, so the transverse axis is vertical and the center is the origin. The foci are each 7 units from the center, so $c = 7$. The vertices are each 6 units from the center, so $a = 6$.

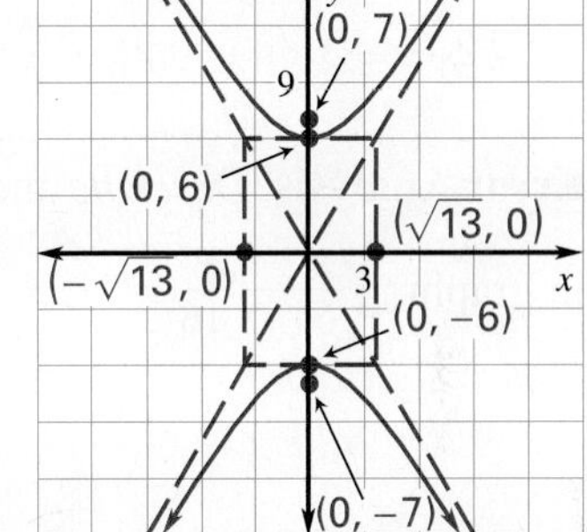

Because $c^2 = a^2 + b^2$, you have $b^2 = c^2 - a^2$. Find b^2.

$$b^2 = c^2 - a^2 = 7^2 - 6^2 = 13$$

Because the transverse axis is vertical, the standard form of the equation is as follows:

$\frac{y^2}{6^2} - \frac{x^2}{13} = 1$ Substitute 6 for a and 13 for b^2.

$\frac{y^2}{36} - \frac{x^2}{13} = 1$ Simplify.

Example 3 Solve a multi-step problem

Hyperbolic Mirror The focus of hyperbolic mirror has coordinates (15, 0). Find the vertex $(a, 0)$ of the mirror, if the point (15, 16) is on the mirror.

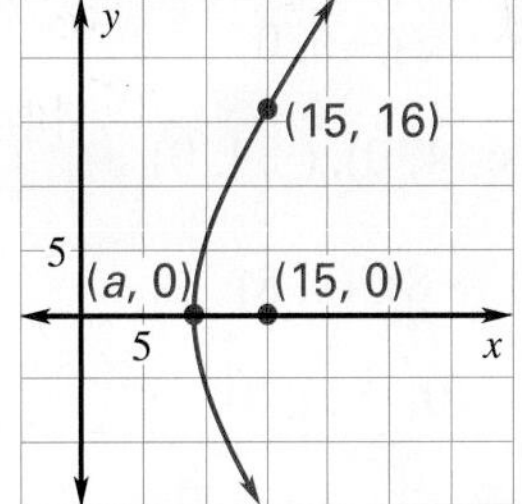

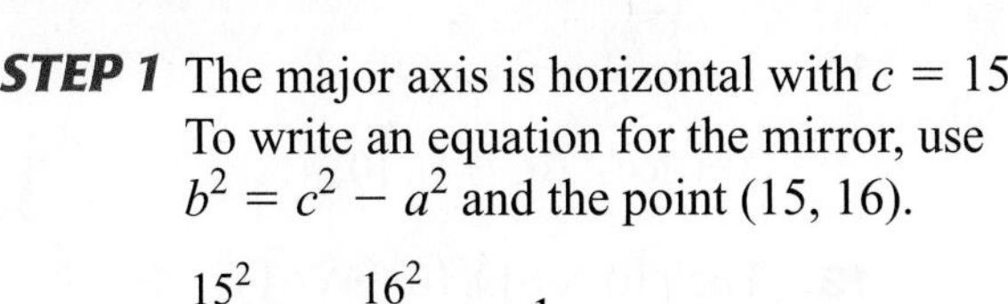

STEP 1 The major axis is horizontal with $c = 15$. To write an equation for the mirror, use $b^2 = c^2 - a^2$ and the point (15, 16).

$$\frac{15^2}{a^2} - \frac{16^2}{c^2 - a^2} = 1$$

STEP 2 Solve $\frac{15^2}{a^2} - \frac{16^2}{15^2 - a^2} = 1$ for a. Because the mirror is represented by the right branch of the hyperbola and the vertex lies between the center (0, 0) and the focus (15, 0), use the solution $a = 9$.

The vertex is (9, 0).

Guided Practice for Examples 1, 2, and 3

1. Graph $x^2 - 4y^2 = 16$. Identify the vertices, foci, and asymptotes.
2. Write an equation of the hyperbola with foci at $(0, \sqrt{13})$ and $(0, -\sqrt{13})$ and vertices at (0, 3) and (0, −3).
3. In Example 3, find the vertex if the focus is (20, 0) and the point on the mirror is (15, 12).

UNIT 5

LESSON 5.4 **Exercise Set A**

MM3G2b Graph conic sections, identifying fundamental characteristics.

MM3G2c Write equations of conic sections given appropriate information.

Graph the equation. Identify the vertices, foci, and asymptotes of the hyperbola.

1. $\frac{x^2}{16} - \frac{y^2}{4} = 1$

2. $\frac{x^2}{9} - \frac{y^2}{36} = 1$

3. $\frac{y^2}{25} - \frac{x^2}{4} = 1$

4. $x^2 - 4y^2 = 4$

5. $2y^2 - 10x^2 = 40$

6. $16y^2 - 4x^2 = 64$

7. **Error Analysis** *Describe* and correct the error in graphing $\frac{x^2}{64} - \frac{y^2}{16} = 1$.

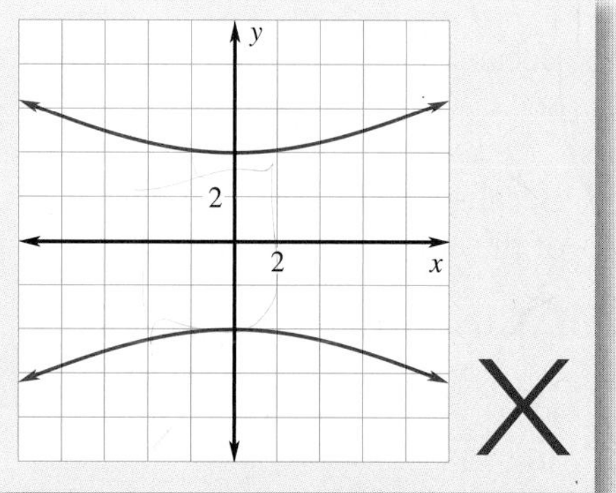

Write an equation of the hyperbola with the given foci and vertices.

8. Foci: $(6, 0), (-6, 0)$
Vertices: $(4, 0), (-4, 0)$

9. Foci: $(0, 8), (0, -8)$
Vertices: $(0, 7), (0, -7)$

10. Foci: $(0, -8), (0, 8)$
Vertices: $(0, -5), (0, 5)$

11. Foci: $(0, -2\sqrt{5}), (0, 2\sqrt{5})$
Vertices: $(0, -4), (0, 4)$

12. Foci: $(\sqrt{13}, 0), (-\sqrt{13}, 0)$
Vertices: $(2, 0), (-2, 0)$

13. Foci: $(0, \sqrt{61}), (0, -\sqrt{61})$
Vertices: $(0, 6), (0, -6)$

14. Foci: $(16, 0), (-16, 0)$
Vertices: $(14, 0), (-14, 0)$

15. Foci: $(0, 12), (0, -12)$
Vertices: $(0, 6\sqrt{3}), (0, -6\sqrt{3})$

The equations of a parabola, an ellipse, and a hyperbola are given. Graph the equation.

16. $25x^2 + 4y^2 = 100$

17. $25x^2 + 4y = 0$

18. $25x^2 - 4y^2 = 100$

19. **Machine Shop** A machine shop needs to make a small automotive part by drilling four holes of radius r from a flat circular piece of radius R. The area of the resulting part is eight square inches. Write an equation of a hyperbola in standard form that relates r and R.

LESSON 5.4

Exercise Set B

MM3G2b Graph conic sections, identifying fundamental characteristics.

MM3G2c Write equations of conic sections given appropriate information.

Graph the equation. Identify the vertices, foci, and asymptotes of the hyperbola.

1. $\frac{x^2}{64} - \frac{y^2}{21} = 1$

2. $\frac{x^2}{32} - \frac{y^2}{48} = 1$

3. $\frac{y^2}{18} - \frac{x^2}{81} = 1$

4. $24x^2 - 13y^2 = 312$

5. $12y^2 - 40x^2 = 480$

6. $16y^2 - 9x^2 = 160$

Write an equation of the hyperbola with the given foci and vertices.

7. Foci: $(8, 0), (-8, 0)$

Vertices: $(6, 0), (-6, 0)$

8. Foci: $\left(0, \frac{5}{2}\right), \left(0, -\frac{5}{2}\right)$

Vertices: $(0, 2), (0, -2)$

The equations of a parabola, an ellipse, and a hyperbola are given. Graph the equation.

9. $121x^2 + 81y^2 = 9801$

10. $108y^2 - 81x = 0$

11. $121x^2 - 81y^2 = 9801$

Write an equation of the hyperbola with the given vertices and asymptotes.

12. Vertices: $(1, 0), (-1, 0)$

Asymptotes: $y = 3x, y = -3x$

13. Vertices: $(0, 4), (0, -4)$

Asymptotes: $y = 2x, y = -2x$

14. Rope Pulley The center cross section of a rope pulley forms a hyperbolic shape for the outline of the concaved groove. The horizontal transverse axis of the hyperbolic outline has a distance of 8 centimeters from vertex to vertex and the foci are $2\sqrt{6}$ centimeters from the center. Write an equation that models the concaved groove.

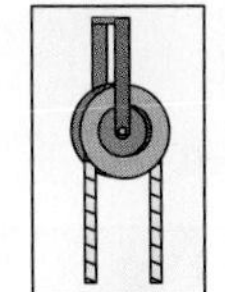

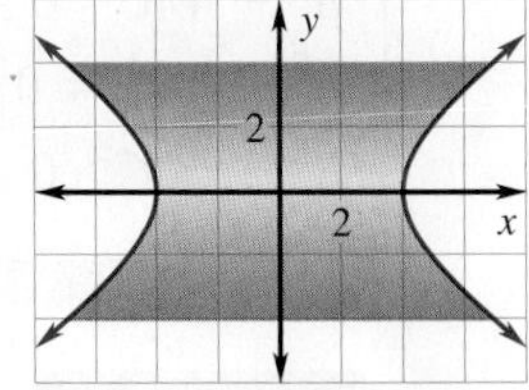

15. Multiple Representations A circular walkway is to be built around a fountain in a park. There is enough concrete available for the walkway to have an area of 500 square feet.

a. Writing an Equation Let the inside and outside radii of the walkway be x feet and y feet, respectively. Draw a diagram of the situation. Then write an equation relating x and y.

b. Making a Table Give four possible pairs of dimensions x and y that satisfy the equation from part (a).

c. Drawing a Graph Graph the equation from part (a). What portion of the graph represents solutions that make sense in this situation?

d. Reasoning How does the width of the walkway, $y - x$, change as both x and y increase? *Explain* why this makes sense.

UNIT 5

LESSON 5.5

Translate and Classify Conic Sections

Georgia Performance Standards: MM3G2a, MM3G2b, MM3G2c

Goal Translate conic sections.

Vocabulary

Because parabolas, circles, ellipses, and hyperbolas are formed when a plane intersects a double-napped cone, they are called **conic sections** or **conics.**

In the following standard form of equations for translated conics, the point (h, k) is the *vertex* of the parabola and the *center* of other conics.

Circle $(x - h)^2 + (y - k)^2 = r^2$

	Horizontal axis	**Vertical axis**
Parabola	$(y - k)^2 = 4p(x - h)$	$(x - h)^2 = 4p(y - k)$
Ellipse	$\frac{(x-h)^2}{a^2} + \frac{(y-k)^2}{b^2} = 1$	$\frac{(x-h)^2}{b^2} + \frac{(y-k)^2}{a^2} = 1$
Hyperbola	$\frac{(x-h)^2}{a^2} - \frac{(y-k)^2}{b^2} = 1$	$\frac{(y-k)^2}{a^2} - \frac{(x-h)^2}{b^2} = 1$

Any conic can be described by a **general second-degree equation** in x and y: $Ax^2 + Bxy + Cy^2 + Dx + Ey + F = 0$. The expression $B^2 - 4AC$ is the **discriminant** of the equation and can be used to identify the type of conic.

Discriminant	**Type of Conic**
$B^2 - 4AC < 0$, $B = 0$, and $A = C$	Circle
$B^2 - 4AC < 0$ and either $B \neq 0$ or $A \neq C$	Ellipse
$B^2 - 4AC = 0$	Parabola
$B^2 - 4AC > 0$	Hyperbola

Example 1 Graph the equation of a translated ellipse

Graph $\frac{(x + 2)^2}{9} + \frac{(y - 1)^2}{16} = 1$.

STEP 1 **Compare** the given equation to the standard form of an ellipse. The graph is an ellipse with center at $(h, k) = (-2, 1)$.

STEP 2 **Plot** the center, vertices $(-2, 5)$ and $(-2, -3)$, and co-vertices $(-5, 1)$ and $(1, 1)$.

STEP 3 **Draw** the ellipse through the points.

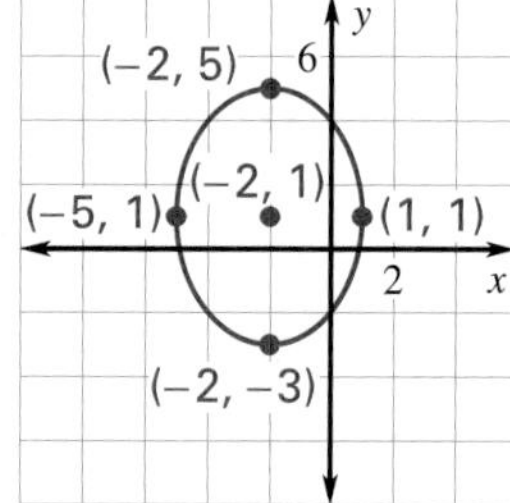

Guided Practice for Example 1

Graph the equation. Identify the important characteristics of the graph.

1. $\frac{(x - 2)^2}{4} - \frac{(y - 2)^2}{5} = 1$

2. $(x - 4)^2 = 4(y + 1)$

Georgia Performance Standards

MM3G2a	Convert equations of conics by completing the square.	
MM3G2b	Graph conic sections, identifying fundamental characteristics.	
MM3G2c	Write equations of conic sections given appropriate information.	

Example 2 Write an equation of a translated circle

Write an equation of the circle with center at (3, −1) and radius $r = \sqrt{10}$.

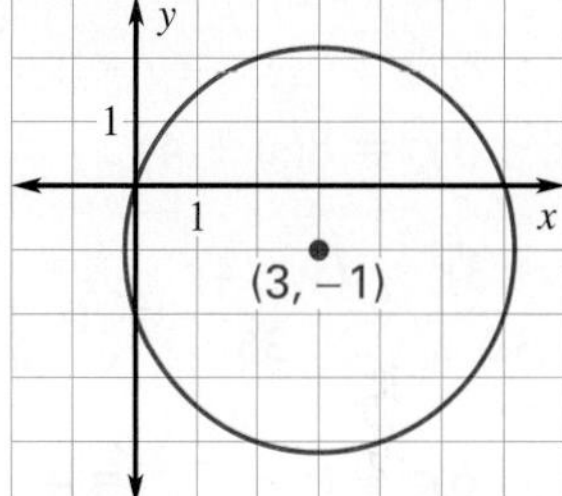

STEP 1 **Determine** the form of the equation. The equation has the form $(x - h)^2 + (y - k)^2 = r^2$.

STEP 2 **Identify** h and k. The center is at $(3, -1)$, so $h = 3$ and $k = -1$.

STEP 3 **Find** r^2. Because $r = \sqrt{10}$, $r^2 = 10$.

The standard form of the equation is $(x - 3)^2 + (y + 1)^2 = 10$.

Example 3 Classify a conic

Classify the conic $4x^2 - 24x + 9y^2 = 0$. Then graph the equation.

Note that $A = 4$, $B = 0$, and $C = 9$, so the value of the discriminant is:

$B^2 - 4AC = 0^2 - 4(4)(9) = -144$

Because $B^2 - 4AC < 0$ and $A \neq C$, the conic is an ellipse.

To graph the ellipse, first complete the square in x.

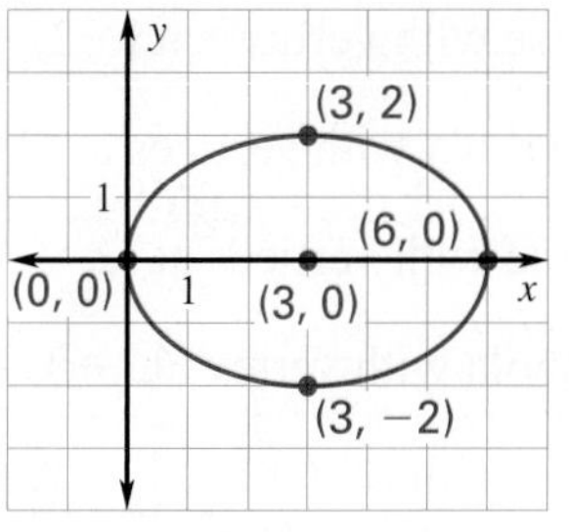

$$4x^2 - 24x + 9y^2 = 0$$
$$4(x^2 - 6x) + 9y^2 = 0$$
$$4(x^2 - 6x + \underline{\ ?\ }) + 9y^2 = 0 + 4(\underline{\ ?\ })$$
$$4(x^2 - 6x + 9) + 9y^2 = 4(9)$$
$$4(x - 3)^2 + 9y^2 = 36$$
$$\frac{(x-3)^2}{9} + \frac{y^2}{4} = 1$$

From the equation, the axis is horizontal, $(h, k) = (3, 0)$, $a = 3$, and $b = 2$. Use these facts to draw the ellipse.

Guided Practice for Examples 2 and 3

3. Write an equation of a circle with center $(-4, 2)$ and radius $r = 3$.

Classify the conic and write its equation in standard form. Then graph the equation.

4. $x^2 + 4y^2 + 2x - 8y + 1 = 0$

5. $x^2 - 4x - 4y = 0$

LESSON 5.5 **Exercise Set A**

MM3G2a Convert equations of conics by completing the square.

MM3G2b Graph conic sections, identifying fundamental characteristics.

MM3G2c Write equations of conic sections given appropriate information.

Graph the equation. Identify the important characteristics of the graph.

1. $x^2 + (y - 3)^2 = 9$

2. $\dfrac{(x-4)^2}{16} + \dfrac{(y-2)^2}{4} = 1$

3. $(x - 3)^2 = 8(y + 4)$

4. $\dfrac{(y+2)^2}{18} - \dfrac{(x+1)^2}{25} = 1$

5. $\dfrac{(x+3)^2}{32} + \dfrac{(y-4)^2}{36} = 1$

6. $(x - 5)^2 + (y + 2)^2 = 28$

7. $(x - 6)^2 + (y - 2)^2 = 4$

8. $\dfrac{(y-8)^2}{16} - \dfrac{(x+3)^2}{4} = 1$

9. $(y - 4)^2 = 3(x + 2)$

10. $\dfrac{(x+1)^2}{16} + \dfrac{(y+3)^2}{4} = 1$

11. $(x + 7)^2 + (y - 1)^2 = 1$

12. $(x + 7)^2 = 12(y - 3)$

Write an equation of the conic section.

13. Circle with center at $(2, -6)$ and a radius of 4

14. Parabola with vertex at $(3, 3)$ and focus at $(3, 0)$

15. Ellipse with vertices at $(-2, -1)$ and $(-2, 7)$ and co-vertices at $(-4, 3)$ and $(0, 3)$

16. Hyperbola with vertices at $(2, 4)$ and $(8, 4)$ and foci at $(-2, 4)$ and $(12, 4)$

17. Ellipse with vertices at $(2, -3)$ and $(2, 6)$ and foci at $(2, 0)$ and $(2, 3)$

18. Parabola with vertex at $(-8, 1)$ and focus at $(-8, 3)$

19. Circle with center at $(3, -4)$ and radius of $4\sqrt{3}$

20. Hyperbola with vertices at $(0, -2\sqrt{6})$ and $(0, 2\sqrt{6})$ and foci at $(0, -5)$ and $(0, 5)$

21. Parabola with vertex at $(6, 2)$ and directrix $x = 2$

22. Error Analysis *Describe* and correct error in writing the standard form of an equation of the circle with center $(3, 7)$ and radius 5.

Center: $(h, k) = (3, 7)$; radius $= 5$

Equation: $(x + 3)^2 + (y + 7)^2 = 25$

UNIT 5

Exercise Set A *(continued)*

Use the discriminant to classify the conic section.

23. $2x^2 + 5x + y + 14 = 0$

24. $4x^2 + 4y^2 - 6x + 8y - 10 = 0$

25. $5x^2 - 5y^2 + 4x - 3y + 4 = 0$

26. $x^2 + 4y^2 - 8x - 12y - 2 = 0$

27. $9x^2 + 4y^2 + 36x - 24y + 36 = 0$

28. $x^2 - 4y^2 + 3x - 26y - 30 = 0$

29. $4x^2 - 9y^2 + 18y + 3x = 0$

30. $x^2 + y^2 - 10x - 2y = -10$

31. $62x^2 + 81y^2 - 868x - 1984 = 0$

32. $y^2 - 6x - 16y + 52 = 0$

33. $x^2 + y^2 + 14x - 2y + 49 = 0$

34. $4x^2 - 25y^2 - 32x - 150y - 261 = 0$

Classify the conic section and write its equation in standard form. Then graph the equation.

35. $y^2 + 8x - 2y - 15 = 0$

36. $x^2 + y^2 - 12x + 2y + 15 = 0$

37. $x^2 - 9y^2 + 54y - 90 = 0$

38. $9x^2 + 36y^2 + 54x - 144y - 99 = 0$

39. $x^2 + 10x - 6y + 7 = 0$

40. $-2x^2 + 5y^2 + 24x - 20y - 102 = 0$

41. $y^2 - 12y + 4x + 4 = 0$

42. $x^2 + y^2 - 6x - 8y + 24 = 0$

43. $9x^2 - y^2 - 72x + 8y + 119 = 0$

44. $4x^2 + y^2 - 48x - 4y + 48 = 0$

45. **Racetrack** A race track is in the shape of a figure eight, which consists of two externally tangent circles. Write equations for the circles if each is 450 feet in diameter, the circles intersect at the origin, and the centers are on the y-axis. Then graph the equations.

46. **Designing a Menu** As part of the graphics art department, your job is to create various art pieces and graphical models for your documents. Your newest project is to design a menu that incorporates the picture of a tree. The equation used to model the tree trunk is $9x^2 - y^2 + 8y - 52 = 0$. Write this equation in standard form and then graph the equation.

47. **Astronomy** An asteroid's path is modeled by $20x^2 - 30y^2 - 60x - 55 = 0$ where x and y are in astronomical units from the sun. Classify the path and write its equation in standard form. Then graph the equation.

48. **Long Jump** A competitor's first long jump can be modeled by $x^2 - 20x + 20y = 0$ where x and y are measured in feet, and the origin marks the start of the jump. Write the equation in standard form. How far was the first jump?

LESSON 5.5 **Exercise Set B**

MM3G2a Convert equations of conics by completing the square.

MM3G2b Graph conic sections, identifying fundamental characteristics.

MM3G2c Write equations of conic sections given appropriate information.

Graph the equation. Identify the important characteristics of the graph.

1. $(y + 4)^2 = -16(x - 5)$

2. $\frac{(x-2)^2}{20} + \frac{(y+5)^2}{9} = 1$

3. $(x - 3)^2 + (y + 4)^2 = 18$

4. $\frac{(y+7)^2}{26} - \frac{(x-4)^2}{12} = 1$

5. $\frac{(x+6)^2}{11} + \frac{(y+5)^2}{27} = 1$

6. $(x - 8)^2 = 6(y + 3)$

7. $\frac{(x-5)^2}{100} + \frac{(y+1)^2}{9} = 1$

8. $(x + 2)^2 + (y - 4.5)^2 = 16$

Write an equation of the conic section.

9. Ellipse with foci at $(3, -4)$ and $(5, -4)$ and vertices at $(-1, -4)$ and $(9, -4)$

10. Parabola with vertex at $(3, -2)$ and focus at $(3, -4)$

11. Circle with center at $(-3, -7)$ and radius of $\sqrt{7}$

12. Parabola with vertex at $(2, 6)$ and directrix $y = 8$

13. Ellipse with vertices at $(2, -1)$ and $(10, -1)$ and foci at $(6 - \sqrt{3}, -1)$ and $(6 + \sqrt{3}, -1)$

14. Hyperbola with vertices at $(-3, 0)$ and $(-3, 4)$ and foci at $(-3, 2 - \sqrt{7})$ and $(-3, 2 + \sqrt{7})$

15. Circle with center at $\left(-\frac{1}{2}, \frac{3}{4}\right)$ and radius of $\frac{2}{3}$

16. Hyperbola with vertices at $\left(-\frac{5}{6}, -1\frac{1}{3}\right)$ and $\left(-\frac{5}{6} \text{ and } 2\frac{2}{3}\right)$ and foci at $\left(-\frac{5}{6}, \frac{2}{3} - \sqrt{13}\right)$ and $\left(-\frac{5}{6}, \frac{2}{3} + \sqrt{13}\right)$

Use the discriminant to classify the conic section.

17. $2x^2 + 8xy + y - 4 = 0$

18. $9x^2 - 4y^2 - x - 12y - 1 = 0$

19. $7x^2 + 7y^2 - 14x + 34 = 0$

20. $3x^2 + 5y^2 + x - 2y = 0$

21. $36x^2 + 16y^2 - 25x + 22y + 2 = 0$

22. $9y^2 - x^2 + 2x + 54y + 62 = 0$

UNIT 5

Exercise Set B *(continued)*

Classify the conic section and write its equation in standard form. Then graph the equation.

23. $x^2 - 14x - 9y + 22 = 0$

24. $x^2 + y^2 + 10x - 12y + 40 = 0$

25. $18x^2 + 10y^2 - 108x - 100y + 232 = 0$

26. $8x^2 - 25y^2 + 32x + 150y - 393 = 0$

27. $4x^2 + 14y^2 + 8x + 56y + 4 = 0$

28. $-32x^2 + 20y^2 + 256x - 280y - 172 = 0$

29. **Machining** As part of a computer program, the programmer must input an equation to tell a machine the exterior shape of the part the machine is producing. The equation used to model the shape is $9x^2 + 36y^2 - 108x - 216y + 324 = 0$. Classify the conic. Write the equation in standard form and then graph the equation.

30. **Golf Shot** A golfer has 125 yards left to the hole. The approach shot can be modeled by $2x^2 - 240x + 180y = 0$ where x and y are measured in yards, and the origin is the point of impact. Write the equation in standard form for the path of the shot. Assuming the shot was straight at the hole, how many yards from the hole does the ball land?

31. **Multiple Representations** Each cable of a suspension bridge is suspended (in the shape of a parabola) between two towers that are 120 meters apart. The top of each tower is 30 meters above the roadway. The cables touch the roadway halfway between the towers.

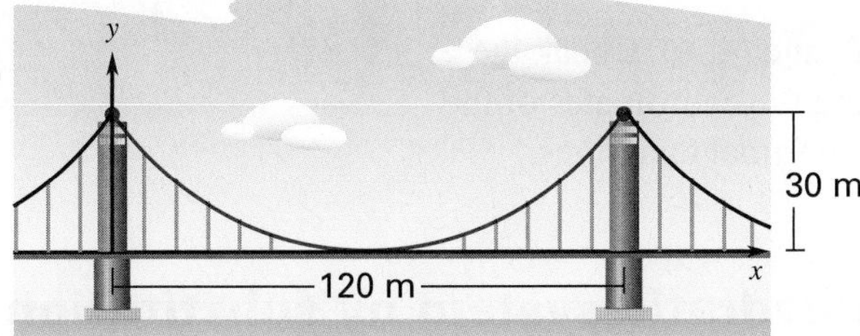

a. **Drawing a Graph** Represent the situation described above using a parabola in a coordinate plane. Assume the base of one of the towers is located at the origin.

b. **Finding Coordinates** The directrix of the parabola is $y = -30$. Find the coordinates of the focus.

c. **Writing an Equation** Write an equation in standard form of the parabola.

d. **Finding the Height** What is the height of the suspension cable 30 meters from the base of a tower?

32. **Communication Towers** A cellular phone transmission tower has a range of 20 miles. A second tower that is located 5 miles south and 10 miles west of the first tower has a range of 15 miles. Write an inequality that describes each tower's range. Assume that the first tower is located at the origin. Do the regions covered by the towers overlap? *Explain* your reasoning.

UNIT 5

LESSON 5.6

Solve Quadratic Systems

Georgia Performance Standards: MM3G1d, MM3G1e

Goal Solve quadratic systems.

Vocabulary

Systems that include one or more equations of conics are called **quadratic systems.**

Example 1 Solve a linear-quadratic system by graphing

Solve the system using a graphing calculator.

$x^2 = 5x - y$ Equation 1

$y - x = 0$ Equation 2

STEP 1 **Solve** each equation for y.

$x^2 = 5x - y$ $\qquad$ $y - x = 0$

$y = 5x - x^2$ Equation 1 $\qquad$ $y = x$ Equation 2

STEP 2 **Graph** the equations $y = 5x - x^2$ and $y = x$. Use the *intersect* feature of the calculator to find the coordinates of the intersection points. The graphs of $y = 5x - x^2$ and $y = x$ intersect at (0, 0) and (4, 4).

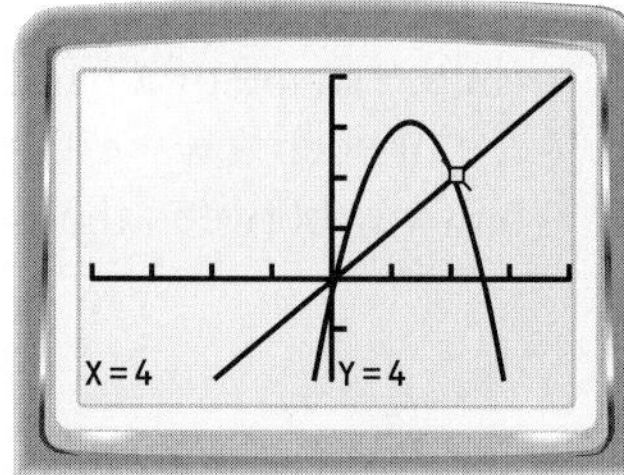

The solutions are (0, 0) and (4, 4). Check the solutions by substituting the coordinates of the points into each of the original equations.

Example 2 Solve a linear-quadratic system by substitution

Solve the system using substitution.

$x^2 + y^2 = 25$ Equation 1

$y = x + 1$ Equation 2

Solution

$x^2 + y^2 = 25$	Equation 1
$x^2 + (x + 1)^2 = 25$	Substitute $x + 1$ for y.
$2x^2 + 2x - 24 = 0$	Simplify.
$2(x + 4)(x - 3) = 0$	Factor trinomial.
$x = -4$ or $x = 3$	Zero product property

To find each y-coordinate, substitute each x-value in Equation 2. The solutions are $(-4, -3)$ and $(3, 4)$. Check the solutions by graphing the equations of the system.

Georgia Performance Standards

MM3G1d	Solve a system of equations involving a circle and a line.	☑
MM3G1e	Solve a system of equations involving two circles.	☑

Guided Practice for Examples 1 and 2

1. Solve the system consisting of the equations $y = x^2 - 2x + 3$ and $y = 2x - 1$ using a graphing calculator.

Solve the system using substitution.

2. $y = 5x - x^2$
$y = x$

3. $4(x - 1)^2 + (y + 3)^2 = 4$
$y = -2x - 3$

4. $x^2 + y^2 = 16$
$y = -x - 4$

Example 3 Solve a quadratic system involving two circles

Solve the system by elimination.

$x^2 + y^2 - 25 = 0$ Equation 1

$x^2 - 10x + y^2 + 10y + 25 = 0$ Equation 2

STEP 1 **Multiply** Equation 1 by -1 and add the equations to eliminate the x^2 and y^2 terms.

$$\begin{array}{rl} -x^2 - y^2 \qquad\qquad + 25 = 0 & \text{Multiply Equation 1 by } -1. \\ x^2 + y^2 - 10x + 10y + 25 = 0 & \\ \hline -10x + 10y + 50 = 0 & \text{Add.} \\ y = x - 5 & \text{Solve for } y. \end{array}$$

STEP 2 **Substitute** $x - 5$ for y in Equation 1 and solve for x.

$$\begin{array}{rl} x^2 + y^2 - 25 = 0 & \text{Equation 1} \\ x^2 + (x - 5)^2 - 25 = 0 & \text{Substitute for } y. \\ 2x^2 - 10x = 0 & \text{Simplify.} \\ 2x(x - 5) = 0 & \text{Factor binomial.} \\ x = 0 \text{ or } x = 5 & \text{Zero product property} \end{array}$$

STEP 3 **Substitute** for x in $y = x - 5$.

$y = (0) - 5 = -5$ Substitute 0 for x.

$y = (5) - 5 = 0$ Substitute 5 for x.

The solutions are $(0, -5)$ and $(5, 0)$. Check the solutions by graphing the equations of the system.

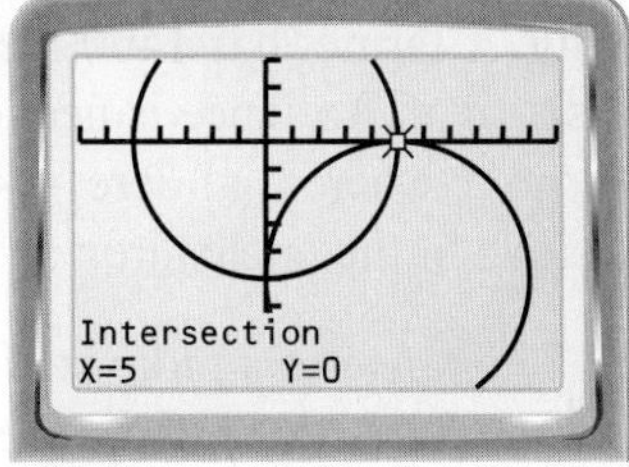

Guided Practice for Example 3

Solve the system by elimination.

5. $x^2 - y^2 - 4 = 0$
$x^2 + y^2 - 10x + 16 = 0$

6. $x^2 + y^2 - 14x + 2 = 0$
$x^2 - y^2 + 8x + 2 = 0$

LESSON 5.6 **Exercise Set A**

MM3G1d Solve a system of equations involving a circle and a line.

MM3G1e Solve a system of equations involving two circles.

Solve the system using a graphing calculator.

1. $x^2 + (y - 3)^2 - 9 = 0$
$x + y - 1 = 0$

2. $2x^2 - y^2 + 4x - 6 = 0$
$2x + y + 4 = 0$

3. $x^2 - y - 4x + 2 = 0$
$x - 2y + 4 = 0$

4. $6x^2 + y^2 = 12$
$3x + y = 1$

5. $(x - 2)^2 + y^2 = 16$
$x = 6$

6. $x - 2x^2 - 3y = 1$
$9x^2 + 4y^2 = 36$

7. **Multiple Choice** Which ordered pair is a solution of the linear-quadratic system below?

$$x^2 - 4x + 4y^2 - 8y = 8$$
$$2x + y = 7$$

A. (1, 5) **B.** (5, −1) **C.** (2, 3) **D.** (−3, 2)

Solve the system using substitution.

8. $x^2 + y^2 = 45$
$y = 2x$

9. $x^2 - 3y - 3 = 0$
$x - y = 1$

10. $x^2 - 2x + y^2 - 2y = 2$
$x + y = 4$

11. $-x^2 + 2y^2 = 16$
$x - y = 0$

12. $3x + y^2 + 2 = 0$
$3x = y - 2$

13. $2x^2 + 6y^2 = 18$
$x + 4y + 8 = 0$

14. $2x^2 + y - 3 = 0$
$3x + y = -6$

15. $4x^2 - x - y^2 + 6 = 0$
$2x - y = 3$

16. $2x + y^2 - 4y + 4 = 0$
$-x + y = 2$

Solve the system.

17. $x^2 - y^2 + 4x - 4 = 0$
$-x^2 + y^2 - 3x + 3 = 0$

18. $x^2 + 2y^2 - 3y = 0$
$x^2 + y^2 - 2 = 0$

19. $2x^2 - y^2 - x - 4 = 0$
$-x^2 + y^2 + 3x - 4 = 0$

20. $x^2 + y^2 = 1$
$x^2 + y^2 + 4x + 4y - 5 = 0$

21. **Farming** A farmer has 1400 feet of fence to enclose a rectangular area that borders a river. No fence is needed along the river. Is it possible for the farmer to enclose five acres? (1 acre = 43,560 square feet) If possible, find the dimensions of the enclosure.

22. **Radio** The range of a radio station is bounded by a circle given by the equation $x^2 + y^2 = 920$ where x and y are measured in miles. A straight highway that passes through the area can be modeled by the equation $y = \frac{1}{2}x + 20$. Find the length of the highway that lies within the range of the radio station.

UNIT 5

LESSON 5.6 **Exercise Set B**

MM3G1d Solve a system of equations involving a circle and a line.

MM3G1e Solve a system of equations involving two circles.

Solve the system using a graphing calculator.

1. $(x + 2)^2 + (y - 3)^2 = 27$
   $x + y - 5 = 0$
2. $x^2 + y^2 + 6x - 16 = 0$
   $2x + y - 1 = 0$
3. $2x^2 - y^2 - 6y + 4 = 0$
   $3x - 4y + 2 = 0$
4. $12x^2 + y^2 = 34$
   $3x - y = 1$
5. $3(x + 5)^2 + y = 6$
   $6x - 2y = 7$
6. $5x^2 - y^2 + 4y = 22$
   $2x^2 + 6y^2 = 42$
7. **Multiple Choice** Which ordered pair is a solution of the quadratic system below?

$$x^2 - x + 5y^2 + 2y = 36$$
$$3x^2 + 4y^2 = 43$$

A. $(1, 5)$ **B.** $(5, -1)$ **C.** $(2, 3)$ **D.** $(-3, 2)$

Solve the system using substitution.

8. $x^2 + y = 16$
   $y = -2x + 1$
9. $x^2 - 3y - 4 = 0$
   $x - y = 2$
10. $x^2 - 2x + y^2 - 2y = 6$
    $x + y = 2$
11. $-x^2 + y^2 = 13$
    $x - y = 1$
12. $x^2 + y^2 + 14 = 0$
    $x^2 = 7y - 2$
13. $x^2 - 8y^2 + 4 = 0$
    $x - 3y + 2 = 0$
14. $2x^2 + y - 3 = 0$
    $-9x + y = -15$
15. $5x^2 - x - y^2 - 25 = 0$
    $12x - y = 10$
16. $x + y^2 + 2y + 9 = 0$
    $-x + 4y = 3$

Solve the system.

17. $x^2 - y^2 + 7x - 12 = 0$
    $-x^2 + y^2 - 2x + 3 = 0$
18. $2x^2 + 2y^2 + 4x - 6y = 0$
    $x^2 + y^2 + 2x - 3y = 1$
19. $5x^2 - y^2 - x + 2y + 2 = 0$
    $-5x^2 + y^2 + 3x - y - 4 = 0$
20. $x^2 + y^2 + 7x - y = 12$
    $x^2 + y^2 + 6x + 3y = 4$
21. **Radio** The range of a radio station is bounded by a circle given by the equation $x^2 + y^2 = 725$ where x and y are measured in miles. A straight highway that passes through the area can be modeled by the equation $y = \frac{2}{3}x - 5$. Find the length of the highway that lies within the range of the radio station.
22. **Aquarium** You want to construct an aquarium with 4 glass sides and a glass top and bottom. The aquarium must hold 35 cubic feet of water and you only have 70 square feet of glass to work with. Is it possible to construct such an aquarium? If possible, find the dimensions of the aquarium.

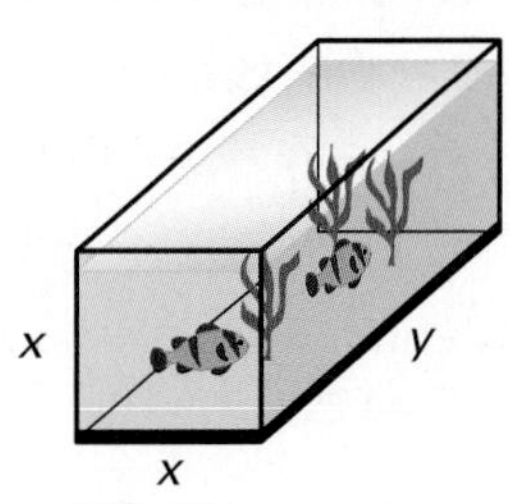

UNIT 5

Georgia Performance Standards

MM3G1d Solve a system of equations involving a circle and a line.

Technology Activity

Solve Quadratic Systems

Use after Lesson 5.6

Question

How can you use a graphing calculator to solve quadratic systems?

The solution(s) to a system is (are) the point(s) of intersection of the graphs of the equations. You can use a graphing calculator to find the point(s) of intersection.

Example

Solve the system of equations. $x^2 + y^2 = 9$
$3x - y = 3$

STEP 1 Solve for *y*

Begin by solving each equation for y.

$x^2 + y^2 = 9$

$y^2 = -x^2 + 9$

$y = \pm\sqrt{-x^2 + 9}$

$3x - y = 3$

$y = 3x - 3$

STEP 2 Enter functions

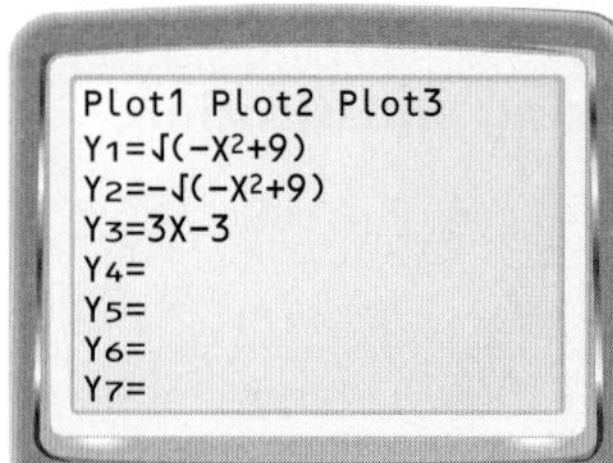

STEP 3 Graph functions

Graph the functions in an appropriate viewing window.

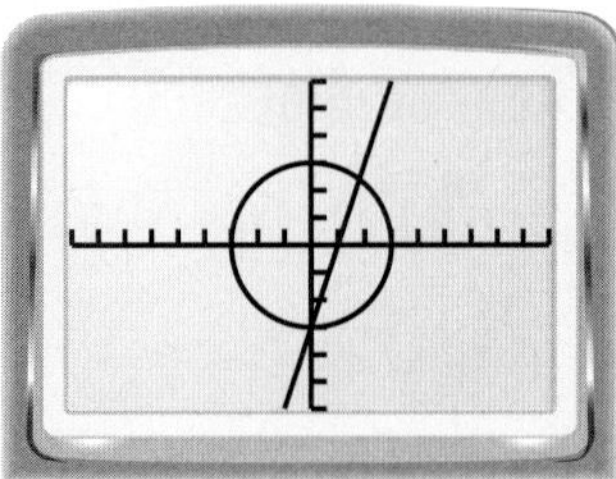

STEP 4 Find points of intersection

Use the *intersect* feature to find both points of intersection.

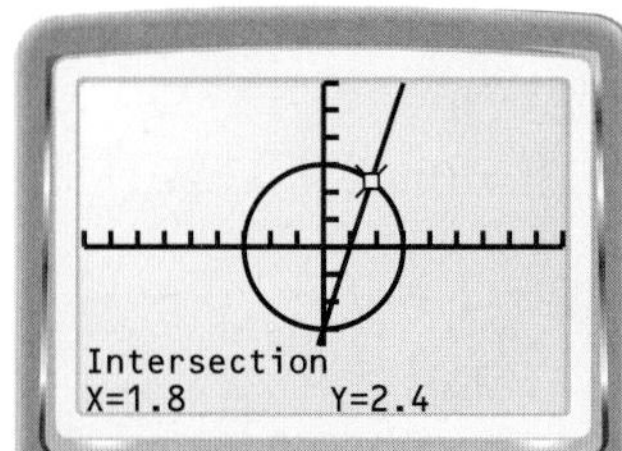

So, the solutions to the system of equations are (1.8, 2.4) and (0, −3).

Practice

Use a graphing calculator to solve the system of equations.

1. $x^2 + y^2 = 18$
$x - y = 0$

2. $-3x^2 + y^2 = 13$
$-3x + y = 1$

3. $x^2 + y^2 = 5$
$y = -2x$

4. $3x^2 - y^2 = -6$
$y = 2x + 1$

5. $x^2 + y^2 = 1$
$x + y = -1$

6. $x^2 = 6y$
$y = -x$

UNIT 5

LESSON 5.7

Use Figures in Three-Dimensional Space

Georgia Performance Standards: MM3G3a, MM3G3b, MM3G3c

Goal Understand the three-dimensional rectangular coordinate system.

Vocabulary

A **three-dimensional coordinate system** or **3-space** is formed by the intersection of an x-axis, a y-axis and a z-axis. The axes determine three coordinate planes: the xy-plane, the xz-plane, and the yz-plane. These planes divide the 3-space into eight octants.

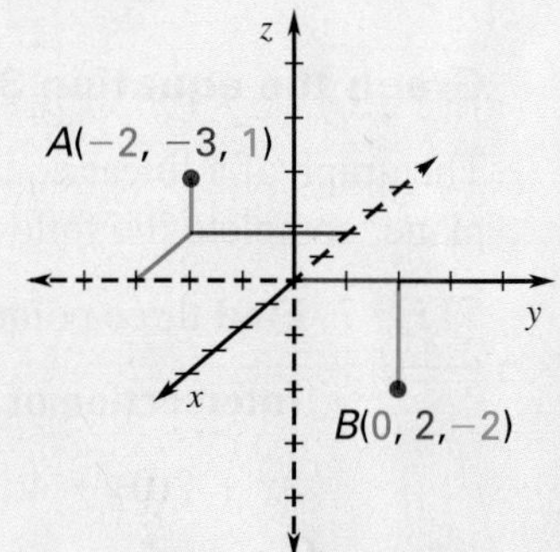

Each point in a 3-space is represented by an ordered triple (x, y, z).

The distance d between (x_1, y_1, z_1) and (x_2, y_2, z_2) is

$d = \sqrt{(x_2 - x_1)^2 + (y_2 - y_1)^2 + (z_2 - z_1)^2}$.

Example 1 Apply distance formula in 3-space

Draw a rectangular prism having a diagonal with endpoints (1, 0, −2) and (2, −1, 3). Find the length of the diagonal.

STEP 1 **Draw** the rectangular prism.

Plot and connect the points $(1, 0, -2)$ and $(2, -1, 3)$. Because the difference of the x-coordinates is $|2 - 1| = 1$, the prism has a length of 1 unit. Because the difference of the y-coordinates is $|-1 - 0| = 1$, the prism has a width of 1 unit. Because the difference of the z-coordinates is $|3 - (-2)| = 5$, the prism has a height of 5 units. Draw the rectangular prism.

STEP 2 **Find** the length of the diagonal.

Let $(x_1, y_1, z_1) = (1, 0, -2)$ and $(x_2, y_2, z_2) = (2, -1, 3)$.

$$d = \sqrt{(x_2 - x_1)^2 + (y_2 - y_1)^2 + (z_2 - z_1)^2}$$
$$= \sqrt{(2 - 1)^2 + (-1 - 0)^2 + [3 - (-2)]^2}$$
$$= \sqrt{(1)^2 + (-1)^2 + (5)^2}$$
$$= \sqrt{1 + 1 + 25}$$
$$= \sqrt{27} = 3\sqrt{3}$$

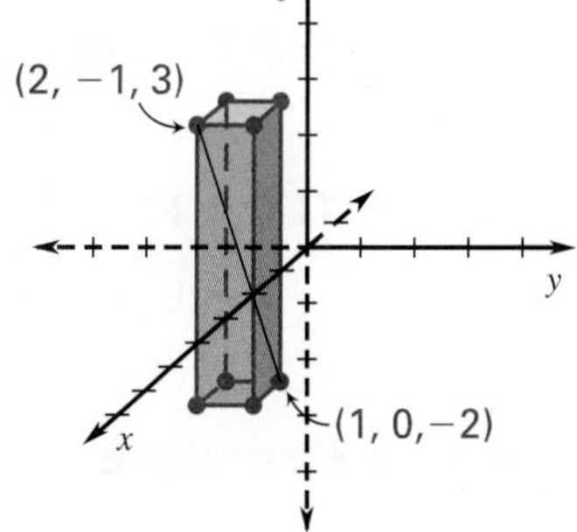

The length of the diagonal is $3\sqrt{3}$ units.

Guided Practice for Example 1

1. Draw a rectangular prism having a diagonal with endpoints $(3, 2, 0)$ and $(0, -1, 3)$. Find the length of the diagonal.

UNIT 5

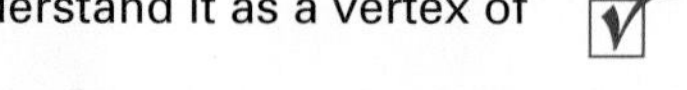

Georgia Performance Standards

MM3G3a Plot the point (x, y, z) and understand it as a vertex of a rectangular prism. 

MM3G3b Apply the distance formula in 3-space. 

MM3G3c Recognize and understand equations of planes and spheres.

Example 2 Recognize and graph the equation of a plane

Graph the equation $3x + 2y + 4z = 12$.

The graph of a linear equation in three variables is a *plane*. In order to sketch a plane, complete the following steps.

STEP 1 **Find** three points at which the plane intersects the axes.

Intersection of *x*-axis:

$3x + 2(0) + 4(0) = 12 \rightarrow x = 4$

The graph intersects the x-axis at (4, 0, 0).

Intersection of *y*-axis:

$3(0) + 2y + 4(0) = 12 \rightarrow y = 6$

The graph intersects the y-axis at (0, 6, 0).

Intersection of *z*-axis:

$3(0) + 2(0) + 4z = 12 \rightarrow z = 3$

The graph intersects the z-axis at (0, 0, 3).

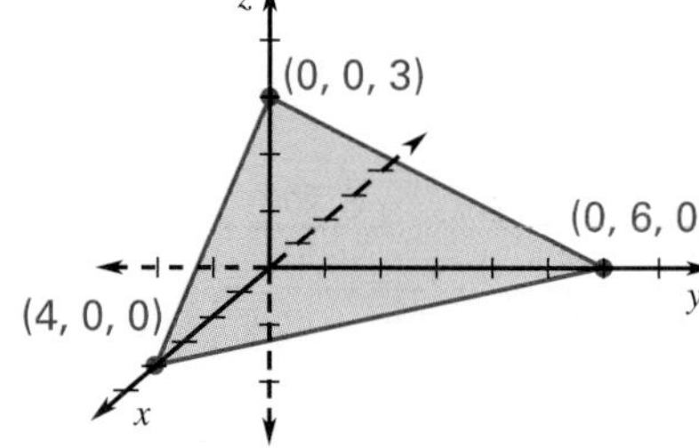

STEP 2 **Plot** and connect the points. Then shade the resulting region.

Example 3 Write an equation for a sphere

Write an equation of a sphere in standard form with center (1, 5, −3) and radius $r = 5$.

STEP 1 **Write** the standard form of an equation for a sphere.

$$(x - x_0)^2 + (y - y_0)^2 + (z - z_0)^2 = r^2$$

STEP 2 **Identify** x_0, y_0, and z_0. The center is at (1, 5, −3), so $x_0 = 1$, $y_0 = 5$, and $z_0 = -3$.

STEP 3 **Find** r^2. Because $r = 5$, $r^2 = 25$.

The standard form of the equation is $(x - 1)^2 + (y - 5)^2 + (z + 3)^2 = 25$.

Guided Practice for Examples 2 and 3

Graph the equation.

2. $x + 2y - 4z = 16$

3. $2x + y - 5z = 10$

4. Write an equation of a sphere in standard form with center (4, −2, 0) and radius $r = 7$.

LESSON 5.7 **Exercise Set A**

MM3G3a Plot the point (x, y, z) and understand it as a vertex of a rectangular prism.

MM3G3b Apply the distance formula in 3-space.

MM3G3c Recognize and understand equations of planes and spheres.

Draw a rectangular prism having a diagonal with the given endpoints. Find the length of the diagonal.

1. (3, 0, 5) and (0, 4, 0)

2. (1, 1, –8) and (–3, 2, 0)

Find the distance between the points.

3. (6, 1, 0) and (9, 4, 0)

4. (7, 4, 1) and (1, 0, 11)

5. (–2, 9, 1) and (4, 4, 2)

6. (–1, –1, 6) and (–5, –8, 4)

Graph the equation of the plane.

7. $x + 6y + 2z + 18 = 0$

8. $2x - 3y + 9z + 36 = 0$

9. $3x + y - 5z - 15 = 0$

10. $-11x + y + 11z + 121 = 0$

11. $-4x + 3y + 2z + 12 = 0$

12. $4x - 5y - 2z - 40 = 0$

Determine whether the equation represents a *plane* or a *sphere*. If it is a plane, graph the equation.

13. $x - 2y + z + 14 = 0$

14. $x^2 + y^2 + z^2 + 100 = 0$

15. $8x^2 + y^2 + z^2 + 8z + 32 = 0$

16. $-6x + 9y + z - 36 = 0$

Write an equation of the sphere in standard form with the given center and radius.

17. (0, 2, 5); $r = 5$

18. (2, 0, 3); $r = 8$

19. (−1, −7, −2); $r = 9$

20. (5, 2, −7); $r = 4$

21. Rectangular Prism Use the graph at the right to complete the following.

a. Find the length, width, and height of the rectangular prism.

b. Find the surface area and the volume of the prism.

c. Suppose the height of the solid is doubled. Give the new coordinates of each vertex.

d. Sketch the new solid in a three-dimensional coordinate system.

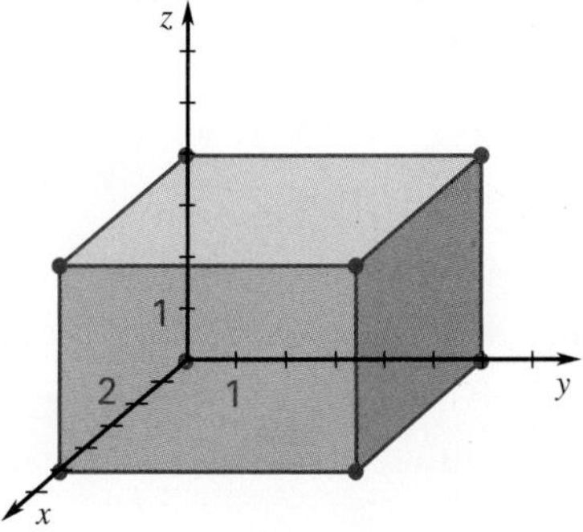

22. **Basketball** Suppose a basketball is sketched in a three-dimensional coordinate system with the origin at the center of the ball. Each axis is given in inches. The point (0, 3.6, 2.7) lies on the surface of the basketball. What is the diameter of the basketball?

UNIT 5

LESSON 5.7 **Exercise Set B**

MM3G3a Plot the point (x, y, z) and understand it as a vertex of a rectangular prism.

MM3G3b Apply the distance formula in 3-space.

MM3G3c Recognize and understand equations of planes and spheres.

Draw a rectangular prism having a diagonal with the given endpoints. Find the length of the diagonal.

1. $(2, 2, 3)$ and $(4, -5, 6)$

2. $(7, 5, 1)$ and $(10, 0, -1)$

Find the distance between the points.

3. $(-12, -4, 5)$ and $(-8, 0, -4)$

4. $(-20, 6, 2)$ and $(4, 4, 1)$

Graph the equation of the plane.

5. $3x + 7y - 3z + 42 = 0$

6. $2x - 4y - 3z + 15 = 0$

7. $x + 2y + 0.5z + 3 = 0$

8. $10x - 5y + 11z + 55 = 0$

Write an equation of the sphere in standard form with the given center and radius.

9. $(2, 2, -2)$; $r = 6$

10. $(8, -2, 0)$; $r = 12$

11. $(15, -1, 6)$; $r = 1.2$

12. $(0, -4, -3)$; $r = 4.5$

13. $(8, 2.5, 0)$; $r = 8\sqrt{3}$

14. $(10, -2, 3)$; $r = 3\sqrt{2}$

Complete the square to write the equation of the sphere in standard form. Identify the center and the radius.

15. $x^2 + y^2 + z^2 - 2x + 6y + 8z + 1 = 0$

16. $x^2 + y^2 + z^2 + 9x - 2y + 10z = -10.25$

17. $9x^2 + 9y^2 + 9z^2 - 6x + 18y + 1 = 0$

18. $4x^2 + 4y^2 + 4z^2 - 4x - 32y + 8z + 33 = 0$

19. **Storage Buildings** A storage building has the shape of a hemisphere. An equation for the outer surface of the storage building is $x^2 + y^2 + z^2 - 40x - 30y + 400 = 0$ when $z \geq 0$. Each axis is given in feet. What is the volume of the storage building? (*Hint:* The volume of a sphere is $V = \frac{4}{3}\pi r^3$ where r is the radius.)

20. Geometry The endpoints of a diameter of a sphere are $(2, 3, 8)$ and $(6, 3, 10)$. Find the center and the radius of the sphere. Then write an equation of the sphere in standard form.

UNIT 5

TEST | for Unit 5

Graph the equation.

1. $y^2 = 16x$

2. $x^2 + y^2 = 36$

3. $x^2 - 8y^2 = 8$

4. $9x^2 + 6y^2 = 18$

5. $(x + 2)^2 + (y - 3)^2 = 49$

6. $(x - 1)^2 = y - 3$

7. $\frac{(x + 1)^2}{100} - \frac{(y - 5)^2}{25} = 1$

8. $\frac{(x - 2)^2}{9} + \frac{y^2}{64} = 1$

9. $\frac{(y + 4)^2}{16} - x^2 = 1$

10. $-x + 4y + 2z + 8 = 0$

11. $4x - 2y - 5z - 20 = 0$

12. $3x - 6y - 3z + 24 = 0$

Write the standard form of the equation of the conic section with the given characteristics.

13. Parabola with vertex at (0, 0) and directrix at $x = 5$

14. Parabola with vertex at (−2, 4) and focus at (3, 4)

15. Circle with center at (3, −1) and radius 4

16. Circle with center at (0, 0) and passing through (12, 9)

17. Ellipse with foci at (4, 2) and (10, 2) and co-vertices at (7, 0) and (7, 4)

18. Ellipse with center at (0, 0), vertex at (±4, 0) and co-vertex at (0, ±2)

19. Hyperbola with vertex at (0, 4), focus at (0, 5), and center at (0, 1)

20. Hyperbola with foci at (0, ±5) and vertices at (0, ±2)

Classify the conic section and write its equation in standard form.

21. $y^2 - 8y - 8x = -24$

22. $x^2 + y^2 - 4x + 2y - 11 = 0$

23. $4x^2 + y^2 - 8x - 8 = 0$

24. $4x^2 - 25y^2 - 100y = 0$

Solve the system.

25. $x^2 + y^2 = 25$

$x + y = 5$

26. $\frac{(x + 1)^2}{100} - \frac{(y - 6)^2}{25} = 1$

$x - 2y = -3$

27. $x^2 + y^2 = 100$

$(x - 14)^2 + y^2 = 16$

28. $\frac{x^2}{9} - y^2 = 1$

$2x + y = 0$

Find the distance between the points.

29. (1, 0, 4) and (0, 8, 0)

30. (2, 2, −9) and (−1, 6, 0)

31. (3, 8, 1) and (−2, 2, 1)

Write an equation of the sphere in standard form with the given center and radius.

32. (0, 3, 2); $r = 6$

33. (4, 0, 2); $r = 8$

34. (−2, 7, 3); $r = 7$

UNIT 5

35. Reflectors The cross section of a parabolic reflector is 25 feet across and the focus of the reflector is located 9 feet above the vertex. Write an equation for the cross section of a reflector opening upward with its vertex at (0, 0). What is the depth of the reflector?

36. Delivery An appliance store advertises free delivery up to a 75 mile radius from the store. If a customer lives 65 miles north and 30 miles west of the store, does the customer qualify for free delivery?

37. Astronomy In its elliptical orbit, an asteroid ranges from 20 million miles to 36 million miles from the sun, which is at one focus of the orbit.

a. Draw a sketch of the situation.

b. Write an equation for the orbit of the asteroid.

38. Radar A radar system reports that a ship is 10 miles away. At the same time, a second station 6 miles east and 7 miles north of the first one reports that the ship is 1 mile away. Write and solve a system of equations to locate the ship relative to the first station.

Performance Task

Campus Parking

To be eligible for a parking pass on a college campus, a student must live at least 1 mile from the campus center.

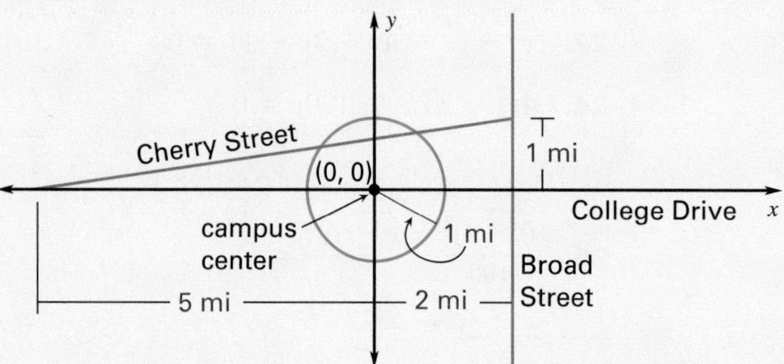

a. Write equations that represent the circle and Cherry Street.

b. Solve the system that consists of the equations from part (a).

c. For what length of Cherry Street are students *not* eligible for a parking pass?

d. Chestnut Lane follows a parabolic arc given by the equation $y = 0.5x^2 - 2x + 2$ when $-2 < x < 3$. Write the equation in standard form. Identify the focus and the directrix.

e. Sketch the circular region and the parabola in the same coordinate plane. Do students living along Chestnut Lane qualify for a parking pass? *Explain.*

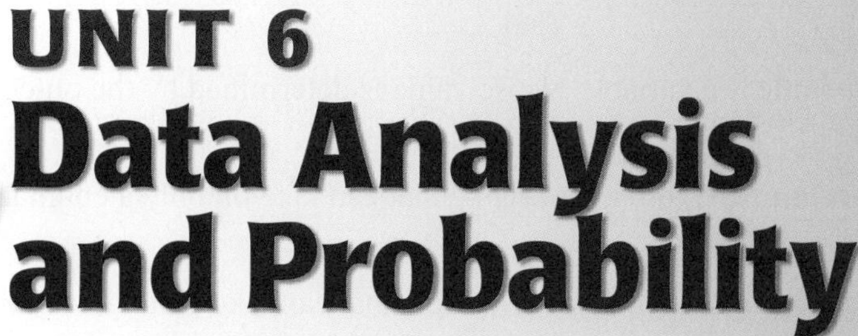

6.1	Construct and Interpret Binomial Distributions (MM3D1)
6.2	Use Normal Distributions (MM3D2a, MM3D2b, MM3D2c)
6.3	Approximate Binomial Distributions and Test Hypotheses (MM3D2b, MM3D2c, MM3D3)
6.4	Select and Draw Conclusions from Samples (MM3D3)
6.5	Experimental and Observational Studies (MM3D3)

LESSON 6.1

Construct and Interpret Binomial Distributions

Georgia Performance Standards: MM3D1

Goal Study probability distributions.

Vocabulary

A **random variable** is a variable whose value is determined by the outcomes of a random event.

A **discrete random variable** is a variable that can take on only a countable number of distinct values.

A **continuous random variable** is a variable that can take on an uncountable, infinite number of possible values, often over a specified interval.

A **probability distribution** is a function that gives the probability of each possible value of a random variable. The sum of all the probabilities in a probability distribution must equal 1.

A **binomial distribution** shows the probabilities of the outcomes of a binomial experiment.

A **binomial experiment** has n independent trials, with two possible outcomes (success or failure) for each trial. The probability for success is the same for each trial. The probability of exactly k successes in n trials is $P(k \text{ successes}) = {}_nC_k p^k(1 - p)^{n-k}$.

A probability distribution is **symmetric** if a vertical line can be drawn to divide the histogram of the distribution into two parts that are mirror images.

A distribution that is not symmetric is called **skewed.**

UNIT 6

Example 1 Construct a probability distribution

Let *X* be a random variable that represents the number of questions that students guessed correctly on a quiz with three true-false questions. Make a table and a histogram showing the probability distribution for *X*.

The possible values of X are the integers 0, 1, 2, and 3. The table shows how many outcomes of answering three questions on a quiz produce each value of X. Divide the number of outcomes for X by the total number of outcomes $1 + 3 + 3 + 1 = 8$ to find $P(X)$.

X (number correct)	0	1	2	3
Outcomes	1	3	3	1
***P*(*X*)**	$\frac{1}{8}$	$\frac{3}{8}$	$\frac{3}{8}$	$\frac{1}{8}$

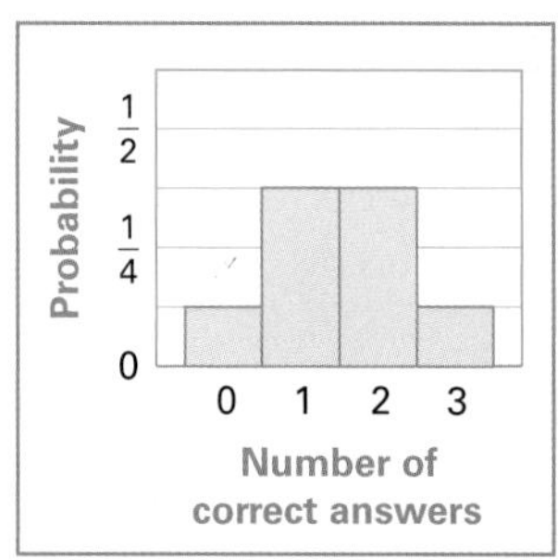

Georgia Performance Standards

MM3D1 Students will create probability histograms of discrete random variables, using both experimental and theoretical probabilities.

Example 2 Interpret a probability distribution

Use the probability distribution in Example 1 to find the probability that a student guesses at least two questions correctly.

Solution

The probability that a student guesses at least two questions correctly is:

$$P(X \geq 2) = P(X = 2) + P(X = 3)$$

$$= \frac{3}{8} + \frac{1}{8} = \frac{4}{8} = \frac{1}{2} = 0.5$$

Example 3 Construct a binomial distribution

In a standard deck of cards, 25% are hearts. Suppose you choose a card at random, note whether it is a heart, then replace it. You conduct the experiment 5 times. Draw a histogram of the binomial distribution for your experiment.

Solution

The probability that a randomly selected card is a heart is $p = 0.25$. Because you conduct the experiment 5 times, $n = 5$.

$P(k = 0) = {}_5C_0(0.25)^0(0.75)^5 \approx 0.237$

$P(k = 1) = {}_5C_1(0.25)^1(0.75)^4 \approx 0.396$

$P(k = 2) = {}_5C_2(0.25)^2(0.75)^3 \approx 0.264$

$P(k = 3) = {}_5C_3(0.25)^3(0.75)^2 \approx 0.088$

$P(k = 4) = {}_5C_4(0.25)^4(0.75)^1 \approx 0.015$

$P(k = 5) = {}_5C_5(0.25)^5(0.75)^0 \approx 0.001$

A histogram of the distribution is shown.

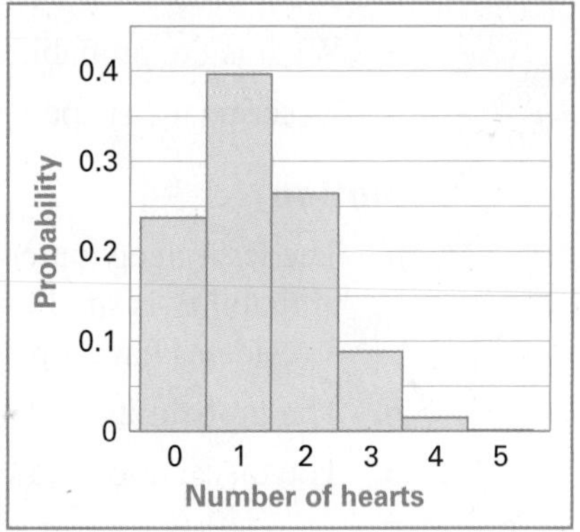

Guided Practice for Examples 1, 2, and 3

1. Use the data to construct a table and a histogram showing the probability distribution for X, a random variable that represents the number of cell phones per household.

***X* (number of cell phones)**	0	1	2	3
Number of households	19	28	37	16

2. What is the probability that a household has at least two cell phones?

3. In Example 3, $P(k = 1)$ is the greatest probability. Is this still the case if you conduct the experiment 8 times? *Explain.*

Example 4 Construct a binomial distribution

According to a survey, about 40% of residents on your street have a pet. Suppose you ask 3 random residents whether they have a pet. Draw a histogram of the binomial distribution showing the probability that exactly *k* of the residents have a pet.

Solution

The probability that a randomly selected resident has a pet is $p = 0.4$. Because you ask 3 residents, $n = 3$.

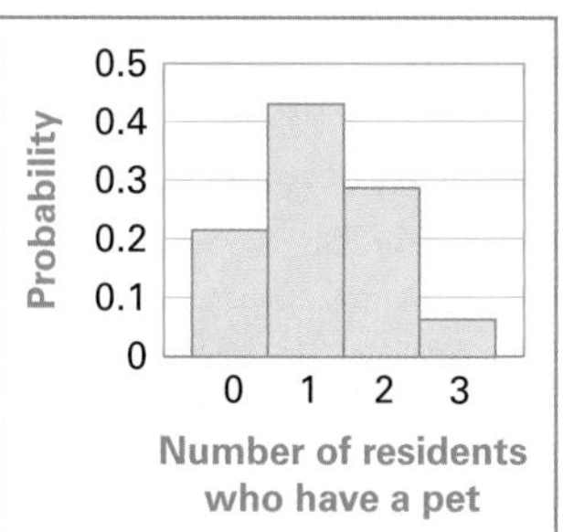

$P(k = 0) = {}_3C_0(0.4)^0(0.6)^3 = 0.216$

$P(k = 1) = {}_3C_1(0.4)^1(0.6)^2 = 0.432$

$P(k = 2) = {}_3C_2(0.4)^2(0.6)^1 = 0.288$

$P(k = 3) = {}_3C_3(0.4)^3(0.6)^0 = 0.064$

A histogram of the distribution is shown.

Example 5 Interpret and classify a binomial distribution

Use the binomial distribution in Example 4 to answer each question.

a. What is the least likely outcome of the survey?

b. What is the probability that $k = 1$?

c. Describe the shape of the binomial distribution.

Solution

a. The least likely outcome is the value of k for which $P(k)$ is smallest. This probability is smallest for $k = 3$. So, the least likely outcome is that all 3 residents have a pet.

b. The probability that $k = 1$ is 0.432.

c. The distribution is skewed because it is not symmetric about any vertical line.

Guided Practice for Examples 4 and 5

In Exercises 4–6 use the following information. A binomial experiment consists of $n = 4$ trials with probability 0.1 of success on each trial.

4. Construct a binomial distribution that shows the probability of exactly k successes and draw a histogram of the distribution.

5. Find the most likely outcome.

6. *Describe* the shape of the binomial distribution.

LESSON 6.1 **Exercise Set A**

MM3D1 Students will create probability histograms of discrete random variables, using both experimental and theoretical probabilities.

Decide whether the random variable *X* is discrete or continuous. *Explain.*

1. X represents the amount of time it takes to brush your teeth.

2. X represents the number of days with a low temperature below freezing in January.

Make a table and a histogram showing the probability distribution for the random variable. *Describe* the distribution as either *symmetric* or *skewed.*

3. B = the number on an index card randomly chosen from a bag that contains 3 cards labeled "1", 4 cards labeled "2", and 3 cards labeled "3".

4. D = the absolute value of the difference when two eight-sided number cubes are rolled.

Calculate the probability of tossing a coin 25 times and getting the given number of heads.

5. 2 **6.** 10 **7.** 18 **8.** 25

Calculate the probability of *k* successes for a binomial experiment consisting of *n* trials with probability *p* of success on each trial.

9. $k \geq 4, n = 8, p = 0.16$

10. $k \leq 5, n = 10, p = 0.45$

11. $k \geq 3, n = 5, p = 0.34$

12. $k \leq 8, n = 12, p = 0.60$

UNIT 6

Match the values of *n* and *p* for a binomial distribution with the histogram that shows the probability of exactly *k* successes.

13. $n = 4, p = 0.45$ **14.** $n = 5, p = 0.75$ **15.** $n = 6, p = 0.83$

A.

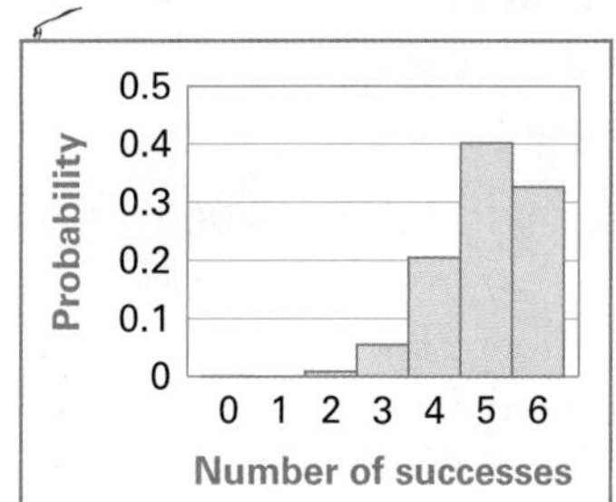

B.

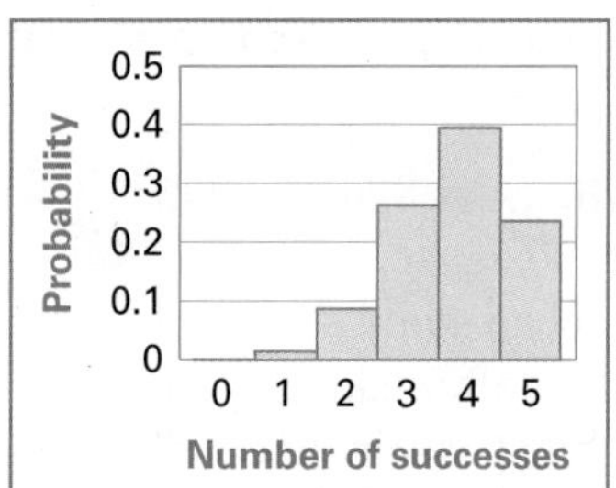

C.

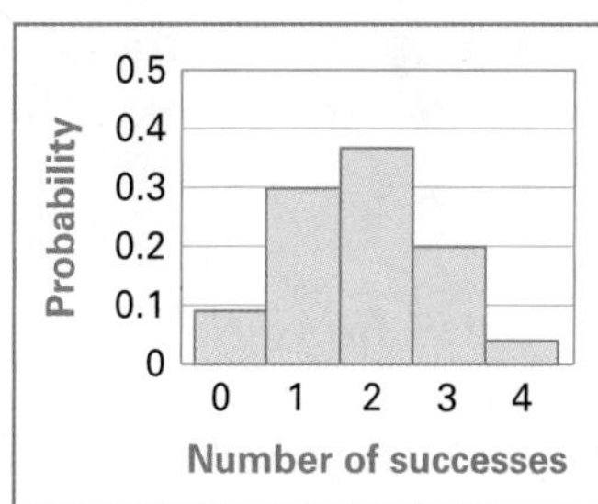

16. Multiple Representations A golden retriever has a litter of 7 puppies. Assume that the probability of a puppy being male is 0.5. Let k be the number of males.

a. Calculating Probabilities Find $P(k)$ for $k = 0, 1, 2, \ldots, 7$.

b. Making a Table Make a table showing the binomial distribution.

c. Making a Histogram Make a histogram showing the binomial distribution. *Describe* the distribution as either *symmetric* or *skewed.*

LESSON 6.1 **Exercise Set B**

MM3D1 Students will create probability histograms of discrete random variables, using both experimental and theoretical probabilities.

In Exercises 1 and 2, make a table and a histogram showing the probability distribution for the random variable. *Describe* the distribution as either *symmetric* or *skewed*.

1. C = the color of a marble chosen from a bag that contains 4 red marbles, 5 blue marbles, 8 green marbles, and 3 orange marbles.
2. X = the product of the numbers spun on two spinners with the numbers 0 through 4. (For each spinner, assume that the probability of spinning each number is the same.)
3. In Exercise 2, what is the probability that the product of the spins is greater than 5?

Calculate the probability of tossing a coin 30 times and getting the given number of heads.

4. 8
5. 15
6. 20
7. 26

Calculate the probability of randomly guessing the given number of correct answers on a 30-question multiple choice exam that has choices A, B, C, and D for each question.

8. 10
9. 20
10. 25
11. 30

Calculate the probability of *k* successes for a binomial experiment consisting of *n* trials with probability *p* of success on each trial.

12. $k \geq 3, n = 8, p = 0.42$
13. $k \leq 4, n = 7, p = 0.18$

A binomial experiment consists of *n* trials with probability *p* of success on each trial. Draw a histogram of the binomial distribution that shows the probability of exactly *k* successes. *Describe* the distribution as either *symmetric* or *skewed*. Then find the most likely number of successes.

14. $n = 6, p = 0.76$
15. $n = 8, p = 0.245$
16. $n = 10, p = 0.066$

17. **Side Effects** According to a medical study, 40% of people will experience an adverse side effect within one hour after taking a particular experimental drug. Suppose you survey 15 people who participated in the study. What is the most likely number of these people who experienced an adverse effect in the study?

18. **Entertainment** An entertainment system has n speakers. Each speaker will function properly with probability p, independent of whether the other speakers are functioning. The system will operate effectively if at least 50% of its speakers are functioning. For what values of p is a 4-speaker system more likely to operate than a 5-speaker system?

Georgia Performance Standards

MM3D1 Students will create probability histograms of discrete random variables, using both experimental and theoretical probabilities.

Technology Activity
Create a Binomial Distribution

Use after Lesson 6.1

Question

How can you use a graphing calculator to calculate binomial probabilities?

Some calculators have a binomial probability distribution function that you can use to calculate binomial probabilities. You can then use the calculator to draw a histogram of the distribution.

Example

Calculate binomial probabilities.

Football According to a recent survey, 62% of people agree with the statement that a team lost a football game because of poor officiating. Suppose you survey 5 people at random. Draw a histogram of the binomial distribution showing the probability that exactly k people agree with the statement. What is the most likely number of people in your survey who agree with the statement?

STEP 1 **Enter values of k**

Let $p = 0.62$ be the probability that a person agrees. Enter the k-values 0 through 5 into list L_1 on the graphing calculator.

STEP 2 **Find values of $P(k)$**

Enter the binomial probability command to generate $P(k)$ for all six k-values. Store the results in list L_2.

STEP 3 **Draw histogram**

Set up the histogram to use the numbers in L_1 as x-values and the numbers in L_2 as frequencies. Draw the histogram in a suitable viewing window.

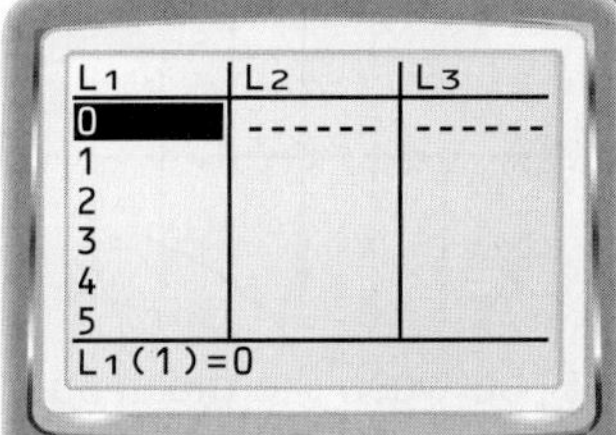

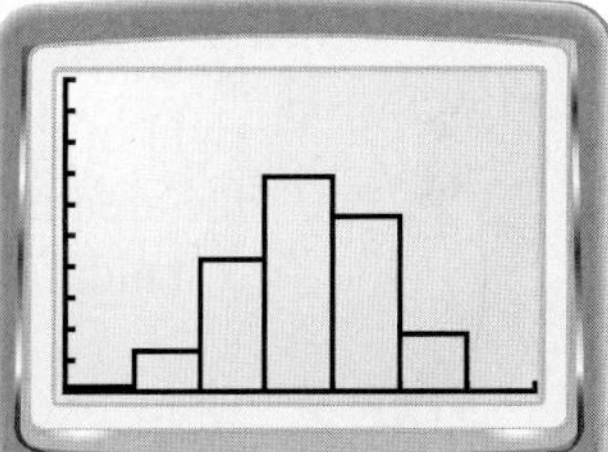

From the histogram in Step 3, you can see that $k = 3$ is the most likely number of the 5 people surveyed who agree that the team lost the game because of poor officiating.

Practice

A binomial experiment consists of n trials with probability p of success on each trial. Use a graphing calculator to draw a histogram of the binomial distribution that shows the probability of exactly k successes. Then find the most likely number of successes.

1. $n = 12, p = 0.28$
2. $n = 15, p = 0.56$
3. $n = 16, p = 0.825$
4. **What If?** In the example, how does the most likely number of people who agree change if you survey 10 adults at random?

UNIT 6

Georgia Performance Standards

MM3D2a Determine intervals about the mean that include a given percent of data. 

Investigating Math Activity
Explore a Normal Curve

Use before Lesson 6.2

Materials **graph paper, salt, spray paint, newspaper, and music stand**

Question

What is the percent of the area under a normal curve within 1, 2, and 3 standard deviations of the mean?

One type of probability distribution is a *normal distribution*. A *normal distribution* is modeled by a bell-shaped curve called a *normal curve* that is symmetric about the mean.

Explore

Create a normal curve.

STEP 1 Cover the music stand with newspaper. Place a piece of graph paper on the stand. Tilt the stand to the desired angle, and pour salt from a point near the middle of the graph paper until enough salt has accumulated to make a bell-shaped curve. Spray the grid and salt with the paint. Discard the salt.

STEP 2 Once the paint has dried, approximate and record the area under the curve by counting the squares and portions of squares on the graph paper.

STEP 3 The mean is the value corresponding to the highest point of the curve. Draw a vertical line at the approximate mean $\bar{x}$.

STEP 4 Draw vertical lines ℓ_1 and ℓ_2 at the ends of the curve. Lines ℓ_1 and ℓ_2 represent 3 standard deviations to the left and the right of the mean. Approximate and record the area under the curve that is within 3 standard deviations of the mean.

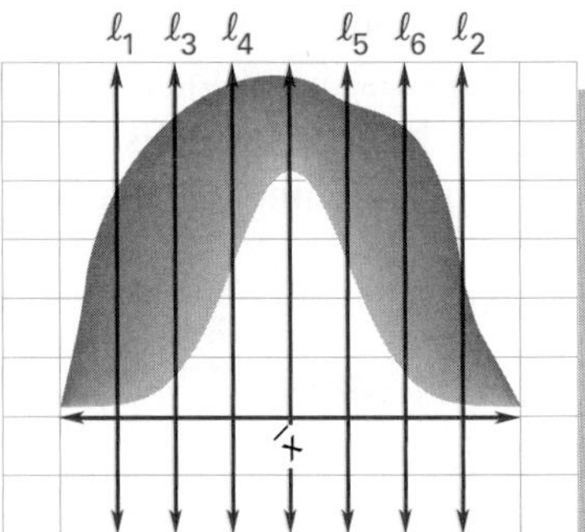

STEP 5 Draw two equally spaced vertical lines ℓ_3 and ℓ_4 between the mean and ℓ_1. Draw two equally spaced vertical lines ℓ_5 and ℓ_6 between the mean and ℓ_2. Lines ℓ_4 and ℓ_5 represent 1 standard deviation from the mean. Lines ℓ_3 and ℓ_6 represent 2 standard deviations from the mean. Approximate and record the area under the curve that is within 1 and 2 standard deviations of the mean.

Draw Conclusions

1. Calculate the percent of the area under the normal curve that is within 1, 2, and 3 standard deviations of the mean.
2. Reasoning *Compare* your answers with those of your classmates, and then write a rule describing the percent of the area under a normal curve that is within 1, 2, and 3 standard deviations of the mean.

LESSON 6.2

Use Normal Distributions

Georgia Performance Standards: MM3D2a, MM3D2b, MM3D2c

Goal Study normal distributions.

Vocabulary

A **normal distribution** is modeled by a bell-shaped curve called a **normal curve** that is symmetric about the mean. A normal distribution with mean $\bar{x}$ and standard deviation σ has the following properties. The total area under the related normal curve is 1. The percent of the area covered by each standard deviation is shown in the graph.

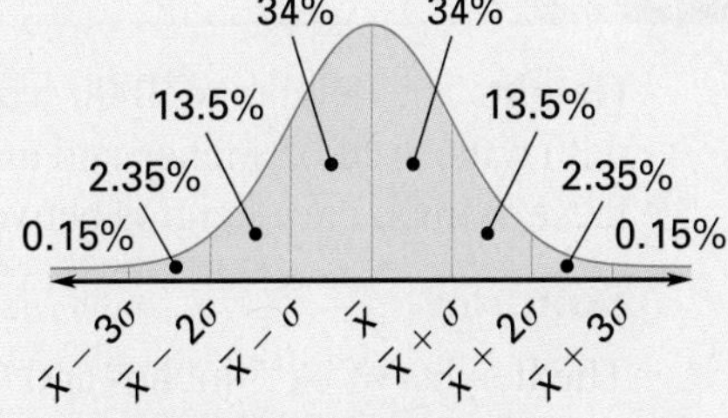

The **standard normal distribution** is the normal distribution with mean 0 and standard deviation 1. The formula below can be used to transform x-values from a normal distribution with mean $\bar{x}$ and standard deviation σ into z-values having a standard normal distribution.

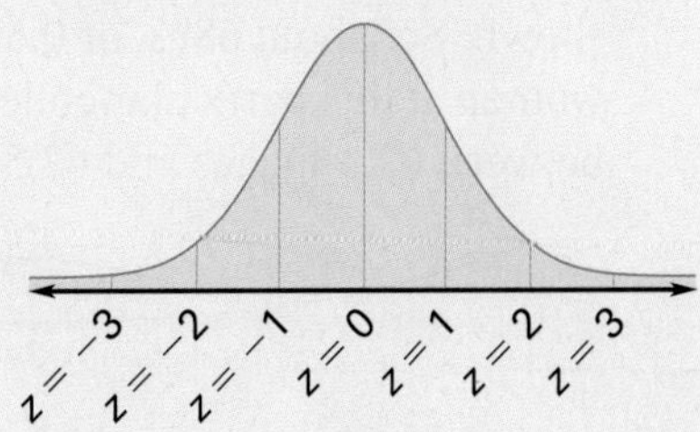

$$z = \frac{x - \bar{x}}{\sigma}$$

The z-value for a particular x-value is called the **z-score** for the x-value and is the number of standard deviations the x-value lies above or below the mean $\bar{x}$. To find the probability that z is less than or equal to some given value, use the standard normal table on page 248.

Example 1 Find a normal probability

A normal distribution has mean $\bar{x}$ and standard deviation σ. For a randomly selected x-value from the distribution, find $P(\bar{x} \le x \le \bar{x} + 3\sigma)$.

Solution

The probability that a randomly selected x-value lies between $\bar{x}$ and $\bar{x} + 3\sigma$ is the shaded area under the normal curve shown.

$$P(\bar{x} \le x \le \bar{x} + 3\sigma) = 0.34 + 0.135 + 0.0235$$
$$= 0.4985$$

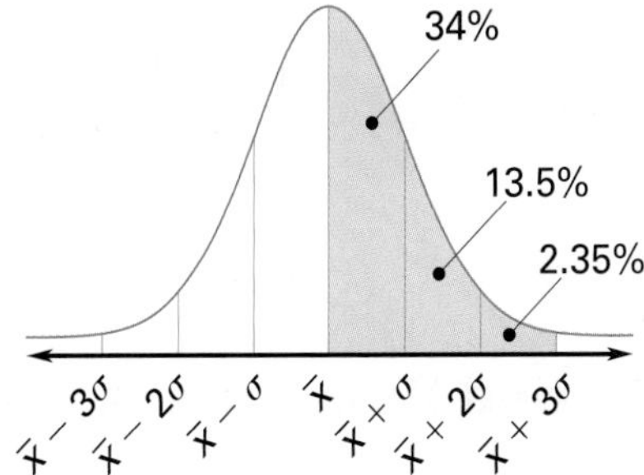

Guided Practice for Example 1

A normal distribution has mean $\bar{x}$ and standard deviation σ. Find the indicated probability for a randomly selected x-value from the distribution.

1. $P(x \le \bar{x} - 2\sigma)$ **2.** $P(x \ge \bar{x} + 2\sigma)$ **3.** $P(\bar{x} - 2\sigma \le x \le \bar{x} + \sigma)$

UNIT 6

Georgia Performance Standards

MM3D2a Determine intervals about the mean that include a given percent of data. 

MM3D2b Determine the probability that a given value falls within a specified interval.

MM3D2c Estimate how many items in a population fall within a specified interval.

Example 2 Interpret normally distributed data

Height The heights of 3000 women at a particular college are normally distributed with a mean of 65 inches and a standard deviation of 2.5 inches. About how many of these women have heights between 62.5 inches and 67.5 inches?

Solution

The heights of 62.5 inches and 67.5 inches represent one standard deviation on either side of the mean, as shown. So, about 68%, or 0.68(3000) = 2040, of the women at this particular college have heights between 62.5 inches and 67.5 inches.

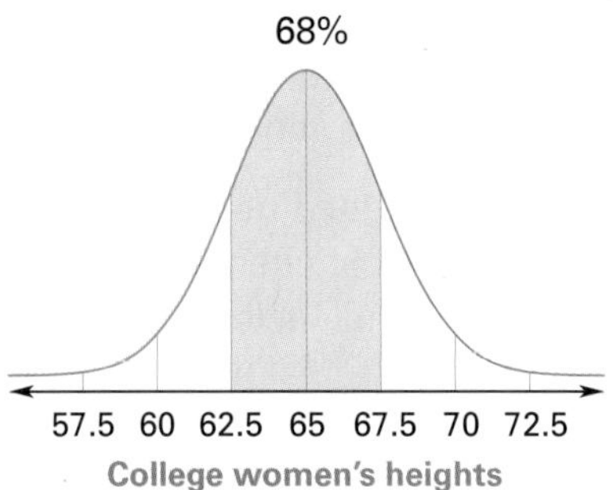

Example 3 Use a *z*-score and the standard normal table

In Example 2, find the probability that a randomly selected college woman has a height of at most 68 inches.

Solution

STEP 1 **Find** the *z*-score corresponding to an *x*-value of 68.

$$z = \frac{x - \bar{x}}{\sigma} = \frac{68 - 65}{2.5} = 1.2$$

STEP 2 **Use** the standard normal table on page 248 to find $P(x \le 68) = P(z \le 1.2)$.

The table shows that $P(z \le 1.2) = 0.8849$. So, the probability that a randomly selected college woman has a height of at most 68 inches is 0.8849.

z	.0	.1	.2
−3	.0013	.0010	.0007
−2	.0228	.0179	.0139
−1	.1587	.1357	.1151
−0	.5000	.4602	.4207
0	.5000	.5398	.5793
1	.8413	.8643	.8849

Guided Practice for Examples 2 and 3

In the following exercises, refer to Example 2.

4. About what percent of college women have heights below 70 inches?

5. About how many of the college women have heights between 60 inches and 65 inches?

6. Find the probability that a randomly selected college woman has a height of at most 61 inches.

LESSON 6.2

Exercise Set A

MM3D2a Determine intervals about the mean that include a given percent of data.

MM3D2b Determine the probability that a given value falls within a specified interval.

MM3D2c Estimate how many items in a population fall within a specified interval.

A normal distribution has mean $\bar{x}$ and standard deviation σ. Find the indicated probability for a randomly selected *x*-value from the distribution.

1. $P(x \leq \bar{x} + \sigma)$
2. $P(x \geq \bar{x} - 2\sigma)$
3. $P(\bar{x} - \sigma \leq x \leq \bar{x} + \sigma)$

Give the percent of the area under the normal curve represented by the shaded region.

4. 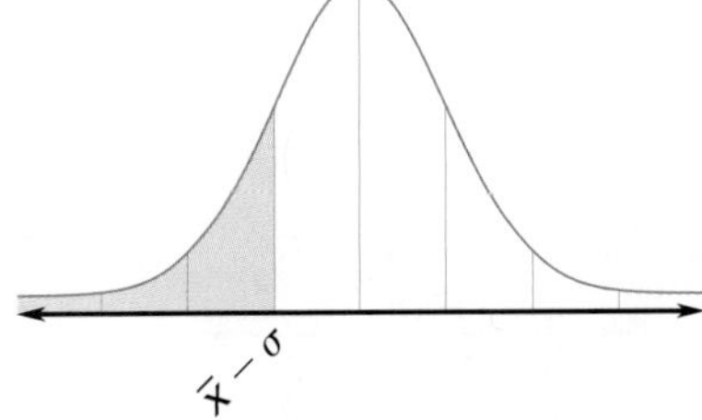

5. 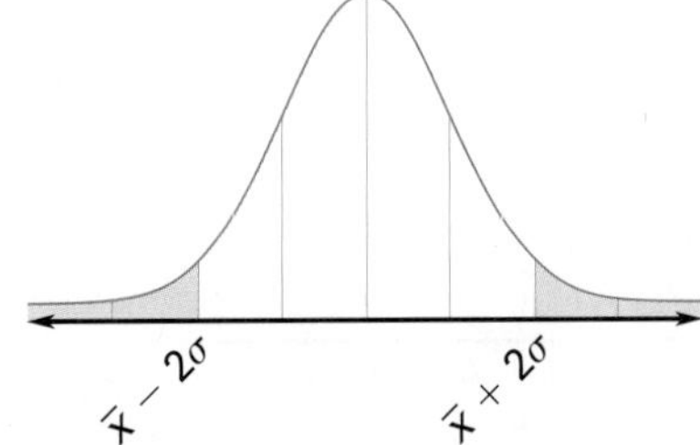

A normal distribution has a mean of 25 and a standard deviation of 5. Find the probability that a randomly selected *x*-value from the distribution is in the given interval.

6. Between 20 and 30
7. Between 10 and 25
8. Between 15 and 35
9. At least 20
10. At least 35
11. At most 30

A normal distribution has a mean of 70 and a standard deviation of 10. Use the standard normal table on page 248 to find the indicated probability for a randomly selected *x*-value from the distribution.

12. $P(x \leq 65)$
13. $P(x \leq 47)$
14. $P(x \leq 73)$
15. $P(x \leq 91)$
16. $P(x \leq 39)$
17. $P(x \leq 101)$

18. **Error Analysis** In a study, the wheat yields (in bushels) for several plots of land were normally distributed with a mean of 5 bushels and a standard deviation of 0.3 bushel. *Describe* and correct the error in finding the probability that a plot yielded at most 4.73 bushels.

$$z = \frac{\bar{x} - x}{\sigma} = \frac{5 - 4.73}{0.3} = 0.9$$

From the standard normal table, $P(z \leq 0.9) = 0.8159$. So, the probability that a plot yielded at most 4.73 bushels is 0.8159.

19. **Biology** The weights of 1800 fish in a lake are normally distributed with a mean of 3 kilograms and a standard deviation of 0.6 kilogram. About how many of the fish have a weight less than or equal to 2.4 kilograms?

UNIT 6

LESSON 6.2

Exercise Set B

MM3D2a Determine intervals about the mean that include a given percent of data.

MM3D2b Determine the probability that a given value falls within a specified interval.

MM3D2c Estimate how many items in a population fall within a specified interval.

A normal distribution has mean $\bar{x}$ and standard deviation σ. Find the indicated probability for a randomly selected *x*-value from the distribution.

1. $P(x \leq \bar{x} + 2\sigma)$ **2.** $P(x \geq \bar{x} + 3\sigma)$ **3.** $P(\bar{x} - 2\sigma \leq x \leq \bar{x} + 3\sigma)$

Give the percent of the area under the normal curve represented by the shaded region.

4.

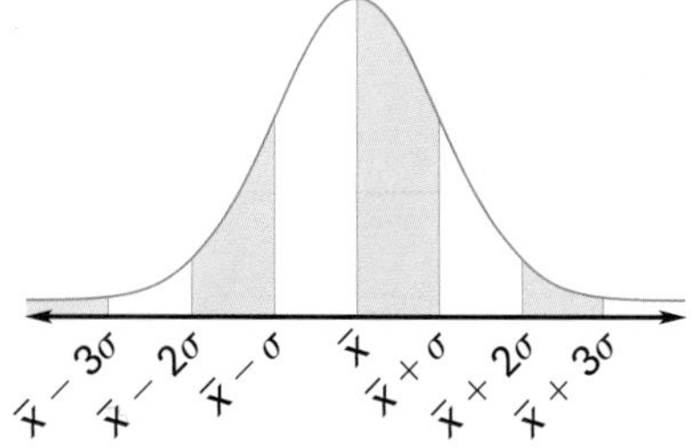

5.

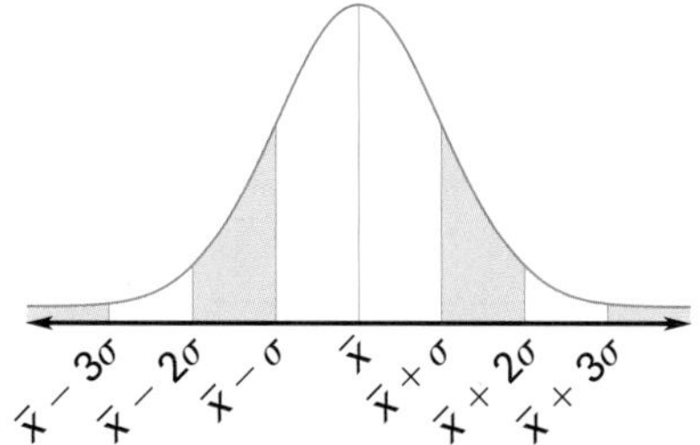

UNIT 6

A normal distribution has a mean of 64.6 and a standard deviation of 2.4. Find the probability that a randomly selected *x*-value from the distribution is in the given interval.

6. Between 64.6 and 69.4 **7.** Between 62.2 and 71.8 **8.** Between 59.8 and 67

9. At least 67 **10.** At least 59.8 **11.** At most 69.4

A normal distribution has a mean of 112.8 and a standard deviation of 9.3. Use the standard normal table on page 248 to find the indicated probability for a randomly selected *x*-value from the distribution.

12. $P(x \leq 104.3)$ **13.** $P(x \leq 79.6)$ **14.** $P(x \leq 127.1)$

15. $P(x \geq 118.7)$ **16.** $P(x \geq 140.7)$ **17.** $P(x \geq 90.9)$

18. $P(111 \leq x \leq 132.6)$ **19.** $P(86.8 \leq x \leq 99.3)$ **20.** $P(123.1 \leq x \leq 142.3)$

In Exercises 21–23, use the following information.

Fitness Two different one-mile run routes were set up for 1200 physical education students. The times to complete uphill course A are normally distributed with a mean of 480 seconds and a standard deviation of 90 seconds. The times to complete level course B are normally distributed with a mean of 420 seconds and a standard deviation of 75 seconds. All students ran both courses.

21. About how many students finished course A in 390 seconds or less?

22. John completed course A in 525 seconds. Shawn completed course B in 470 seconds. Find the *z*-score for both runners.

23. Which student had the better time? *Explain.*

Georgia Performance Standards

MM3D3 Students will understand the differences between experimental and observational studies by posing questions and collecting, analyzing, and interpreting data.

Investigating Math Activity
Collecting Data

Use before Lesson 6.3

Materials **paper, pencil, and a coin**

Question

How can you collect and analyze data from an experiment?

Explore

A quiz has 6 true-false questions. You do not get to see the questions, but instead will flip a coin for each of your answers. Perform the following steps to see how many questions you can answer correctly without seeing the questions.

STEP 1 **Flip** a coin for each question. Let heads represent "true" and tails represent "false." Record your answers. How many of your answers do you think will be correct? What is the probability of answering the first question correctly? What is the probability of answering all 6 questions correctly?

STEP 2 **Determine** your quiz score. The correct answers for the quiz are:

1. true **2.** true **3.** false **4.** true **5.** false **6.** false

Compare your score to the guess you made in Step 1.

STEP 3 **Collect** the individual scores from everyone in your class.

Draw Conclusions

1. Use the scores collected from your class to make a table and a histogram that show the probability distribution.
2. From your results, what is the most likely number of questions to be answered correctly? What is the least likely number of questions to be answered correctly?
3. Reasoning *Compare* the experimental probabilities represented in your histogram with the theoretical probabilities of answering one question correctly, two questions correctly, and so on.

UNIT 6

LESSON 6.3

Approximate Binomial Distributions and Test Hypotheses

Georgia Performance Standards: MM3D2b, MM3D2c, MM3D3

Goal Use normal distributions to approximate binomial distributions.

Vocabulary

Consider the binomial distribution consisting of n trials with probability p of success on each trial. If $np \geq 5$ and $n(1 - p) \geq 5$, then the binomial distribution can be approximated by a normal distribution with the following mean and standard deviation.

Mean: $\bar{x} = np$ **Standard Deviation:** $\sigma = \sqrt{np(1 - p)}$

To test a hypothesis about a statistical measure for a population, use the following steps:

STEP 1 **State** the hypothesis you are testing. The hypothesis should make a statement about some statistical measure of a population.

STEP 2 **Collect** data from a random sample of the population and compute the statistical measure of the sample.

STEP 3 **Assume** the hypothesis is true and calculate the resulting probability P of obtaining the sample statistical measure *or a more extreme* sample statistical measure. If this probability is small (typically $P < 0.05$), you should reject the hypothesis.

UNIT 6

Example 1 Find a binomial probability

Surveys According to a survey conducted by the Harris Poll, 23% of adults in the United States favor abolishing the penny and making the nickel the lowest denomination coin. You are conducting a random survey of 500 adults. What is the probability that you will find at most 106 adults who favor abolishing the penny?

Solution

The number x of adults in your survey who favor abolishing the penny has a binomial distribution with $n = 500$ and $p = 0.23$. Solving the problem using the binomial probability formula is tedious. Instead, approximate the answer using a normal distribution with the mean and standard deviation calculated below.

$\bar{x} = np = 500(0.23) = 115$ Find mean.

$\sigma = \sqrt{np(1 - p)} = \sqrt{500(0.23)(0.77)} \approx 9$ Find standard deviation.

For this normal distribution, 106 is about one standard deviation to the left of the mean. So,

$$P(x \leq 106) \approx 0.0015 + 0.0235 + 0.135 = 0.16.$$

The probability that at most 106 of the people surveyed favor abolishing the penny is about 0.16.

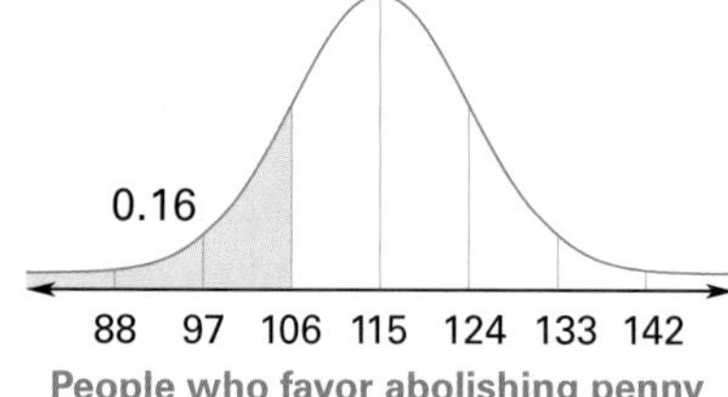

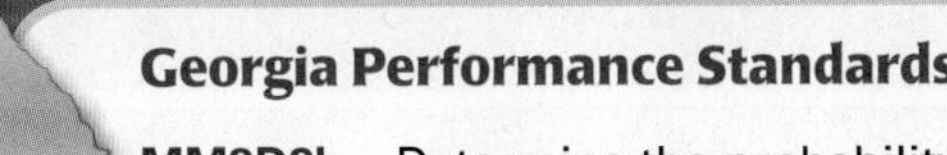

Georgia Performance Standards

MM3D2b	Determine the probability that a given value falls within a specified interval.	☑
MM3D2c	Estimate how many items in a population fall within a specified interval.	☑
MM3D3	Students will understand the differences between experimental and observational studies by posing questions and collecting, analyzing, and interpreting data.	☑

Example 2 Test a hypothesis

Consumer Spending A recent Harris Poll claimed that 44% of adults cut back on their spending in order to pay the increased price of gasoline. To test this finding, you survey 60 adults and find that 21 of them cut back on their spending in order to pay the increased price of gasoline. Should you reject the Harris Poll's findings? Explain.

STEP 1 **State** the hypothesis: 44% of adults cut back on their spending in order to pay the increased price of gasoline.

STEP 2 **Collect** data and calculate a statistical measure. In your survey, 21 out of 60, or 35%, cut back on their spending in order to pay the increased price of gasoline.

STEP 3 **Assume** that the hypothesis in Step 1 is true. Find the resulting probability that you could randomly select 21 *or fewer* adults out of 60 who have cut back on their spending to pay the increased price of gasoline. This probability is

$$P(x \le 21) = P(x = 0) + P(x = 1) + P(x = 2) + \cdots + P(x = 21)$$

where each term in the sum is a binomial probability with $n = 60$ and $p = 0.44$.

You can approximate the binomial distribution with a normal distribution having the following mean and standard deviation:

$$\bar{x} = np = 60(0.44) = 26.4 \qquad \sigma = \sqrt{np(1 - p)} = \sqrt{60(0.44)(0.56)} \approx 3.84$$

Using a z-score and the standard normal table on page 248 gives:

$$P(x \le 21) \approx P\left(z \le \frac{21 - 26.4}{3.84}\right) \approx P(z \le -1.4) = 0.0808$$

So, if it is true that *44% of adults cut back on their spending to pay the increased price of gasoline*, then there is about an 8% probability of finding 21 or fewer adults who cut back on their spending to pay the increased price of gasoline in a random sample of 60 adults. With a probability this large, you should *not* reject the hypothesis.

Guided Practice for Examples 1 and 2

1. Use the fact that hyperopia, or farsightedness, is a condition that affects approximately 25% of the adult population in the United States. Consider a random sample of 280 U.S. adults. What is the probability that 63 or more people are farsighted? What is the probability that 84 or fewer people are farsighted?

2. Rework Example 2 if 18 people in the survey cut back on their spending.

LESSON 6.3 **Exercise Set A**

MM3D2b Determine the probability that a given value falls within a specified interval.

MM3D2c Estimate how many items in a population fall within a specified interval.

MM3D3 Students will understand the differences between experimental and observational studies by posing questions and collecting, analyzing, and interpreting data.

Find the mean and standard deviation of a normal distribution that approximates the binomial distribution with *n* trials and probability *p* of success on each trial.

1. $n = 30, p = 0.4$

2. $n = 50, p = 0.6$

3. $n = 42, p = 0.3$

4. $n = 65, p = 0.15$

5. $n = 72, p = 0.2$

6. $n = 38, p = 0.7$

7. Error Analysis According to a medical study, 20% of all patients with high blood pressure have adverse side effects from a new medication. Suppose 220 patients are treated with the new medication. You want to find the probability that more than 50 patients will have adverse side effects. *Describe* and correct the error in finding the mean and standard deviation.

$$\bar{x} = np = 50(0.2) = 10$$
$$\sigma = \sqrt{np(1-p)}$$
$$= \sqrt{50(0.2)(0.8)} \approx 3$$

X

UNIT 6

Use the fact that approximately 12% of people wear contact lenses. Consider a high school with 1075 students.

8. What is the probability that at least 151 students wear contact lenses?

9. What is the probability that at most 118 students wear contact lenses?

10. What is the probability that between 96 and 140 students wear contact lenses?

A bank loan application may be rejected if a borrower does not have enough assets or has too much debt based on their income. Suppose a bank rejects 15% of their loan applications. This month, there were 180 applications.

11. What is the probability that at most 22 applications will be rejected?

12. What is the probability that at least 27 applications will be rejected?

13. What is the probability that between 17 and 42 applications will be rejected?

Use the fact that approximately 30% of U.S. adults have high blood pressure. Consider a random sample of 190 U.S. adults.

14. What is the probability that 51 or more people have high blood pressure?

15. What is the probability that 69 or fewer people have high blood pressure?

16. What is the probability that between 45 and 75 people have high blood pressure?

17. **Class Rings** You read an article that claims 35% of seniors will buy a class ring. To test this claim, you survey 55 randomly selected seniors in your school and find that 11 are planning to buy a class ring. Should you reject the claim? *Explain.*

LESSON 6.3 Exercise Set B

MM3D2b Determine the probability that a given value falls within a specified interval.

MM3D2c Estimate how many items in a population fall within a specified interval.

MM3D3 Students will understand the differences between experimental and observational studies by posing questions and collecting, analyzing, and interpreting data.

Find the mean and standard deviation of a normal distribution that approximates the binomial distribution with *n* trials and probability *p* of success on each trial.

1. $n = 100, p = 0.37$

2. $n = 135, p = 0.45$

3. $n = 150, p = 0.75$

4. $n = 120, p = 0.08$

5. $n = 240, p = 0.01$

6. $n = 130, p = 0.79$

Use the fact that approximately 2% of people have blood type B−. Consider a random sample of 850 students.

7. What is the probability that at least 13 students have blood type B−?

8. What is the probability that at most 9 students have blood type B−?

9. What is the probability that between 17 and 25 students have blood type B−?

10. Approximately 1% of people have blood type AB−. Consider a random sample of 450 students. Is it reasonable to use a normal distribution to approximate a probability using this information? *Explain.*

According to a medical study, 24% of all patients with high cholesterol have adverse side effects from a certain kind of medication. Consider a random sample of 250 patients.

11. What is the probability that at most 46 patients have adverse side effects from the medication?

12. What is the probability that at least 39 patients have adverse side effects from the medication?

13. What is the probability that between 53 and 67 patients have adverse side effects from the medication?

14. Surveys A survey that asked people in the United States about their feelings of personal well-being found that 85% are generally happy. To test this finding, you question 110 people at random and find that 83 consider themselves generally happy. Would you reject the survey's findings? *Explain.*

15. Computers A manufacturer of laptop computers claims that under normal work use only 2% of its computers will fail to operate at some point during a month. A business uses 500 of the manufacturer's computers under normal work use and has 15 failures in a month. Would you reject the manufacturer's claim? *Explain.*

16. Energy Drink Preferences A company that makes energy drinks has created a new brand of energy drink. The company claims that 80% of people prefer the new energy drink over a competitor's energy drink. A taste test is conducted to test this claim. Of 150 people, 108 prefer the new energy drink. Would you reject the company's claim? *Explain.*

LESSON 6.4

Select and Draw Conclusions from Samples

Georgia Performance Standards: MM3D3

Goal Study different sampling methods for collecting data.

Vocabulary

A **population** is a group of people or objects that you want information about.

A **sample** is a subset of the population.

In a *self-selected sample,* members of a population can volunteer to be in the sample.

In a *systematic sample,* a rule is used to select members of a population, such as selecting every other person.

In a *convenience sample,* easy-to-reach members of a population are selected, such as those in the first row.

In a *random sample,* each member of a population has an equal chance of being selected.

An **unbiased sample** is representative of the population you want information about. A sample that overrepresents or underrepresents part of the population is a **biased sample.**

The **margin of error** gives a limit on how much the responses of a sample would differ from the responses of a population. When a random sample of size n is taken from a large population, the margin of error is approximated by this formula:

$$\text{Margin of error} = \pm\frac{1}{\sqrt{n}}$$

This means that if the percent of the sample responding a certain way is p (expressed as a decimal), then the percent of the population that would respond the same way is likely to be between

$$p - \frac{1}{\sqrt{n}} \text{ and } p + \frac{1}{\sqrt{n}}.$$

UNIT 6

Example 1 Classify samples

Education A teacher wants to find out how many hours students studied for a history quiz. Identify the type of sample described.

a. Before leaving the room, the teacher asks students to write the number of hours they studied for the quiz on the chalkboard if they want to participate.

b. The teacher selects students randomly from an alphabetical list and asks the selected students how many hours they studied for the quiz.

Solution

a. The students can choose whether or not to respond. So, the sample is a self-selected sample.

b. The teacher selects students randomly. So, the sample is a random sample.

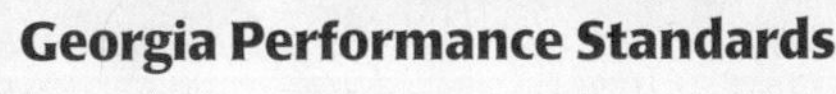

Georgia Performance Standards

MM3D3 Students will understand the differences between experimental and observational studies by posing questions and collecting, analyzing, and interpreting data.

Example 2 Identify biased samples

Tell whether each sample in Example 1 is *biased* or *unbiased*. Explain your reasoning.

Solution

a. The sample is biased because the sample is self-selected and it may not be representative of the entire class.

b. The sample is not biased because it is representative of the population.

Example 3 Find a margin of error

Haircuts In a survey of 800 people, 20% said they get a haircut once per month.

a. What is the margin of error for the survey?

b. Give an interval that is likely to contain the exact percent of all people who get a haircut once per month.

Solution

a. Use the margin of error formula.

Margin of error $= \pm \frac{1}{\sqrt{n}}$ Write margin of error formula.

$= \pm \frac{1}{\sqrt{800}}$ Substitute 800 for n.

$\approx \pm 0.035$ Use a calculator.

The margin of error for the survey is about $\pm 3.5\%$.

b. To find the interval, subtract and add 3.5% to the percent of people who get a haircut once per month.

$20\% - 3.5\% = 16.5\%$ $\quad$ $20\% + 3.5\% = 23.5\%$

It is likely that the exact percent of all people who get a haircut once per month is between 16.5% and 23.5%.

Guided Practice for Examples 1, 2, and 3

1. An electronics company wants to know which aspect of their MP3 player is the consumers' favorite. Technicians are required to ask the question to all customers calling for technical support. Identify the type of sample described.

2. Tell whether the sample in Exercise 1 is *biased* or *unbiased*. *Explain* your reasoning.

3. In a survey of 1100 home buyers, 90% said they used a real-estate agent to research home listings. What is the margin of error? Give an interval that is likely to contain the exact percent of all home buyers who used a real-estate agent to research home listings.

LESSON 6.4

Exercise Set A

MM3D3 Students will understand the differences between experimental and observational studies by posing questions and collecting, analyzing, and interpreting data.

Identify the type of sample described. Then tell if the sample is biased. *Explain* your reasoning.

1. Kevin wants to find out the opinions of college students about the availability of parking spaces. He surveys students as they walk by his car.

2. A yearbook editor wants to know what type of cover the students prefer for the new yearbook. Every fifth student on an alphabetical list is surveyed.

3. A mall supervisor wants to know how often people in the community shop at the mall. The supervisor randomly asks 50 people in the mall how often they shop at the mall.

Find the margin of error for a survey that has the given sample size. Round your answer to the nearest tenth of a percent.

4. 125
5. 250
6. 300
7. 1500
8. 3200
9. 585
10. 166
11. 4000

Find the sample size required to achieve the given margin of error. Round your answer to the nearest whole number, if necessary.

12. $\pm 3\%$
13. $\pm 5\%$
14. $\pm 2.5\%$
15. $\pm 0.8\%$

16. **Error Analysis** In a survey of students, 18% said they like all of their classes. The margin of error in the survey is $\pm 2\%$. *Describe* and correct the error in calculating the sample size.

$$\pm 0.18 = \pm\frac{1}{\sqrt{n}}$$

$$0.0324 = \frac{1}{n}$$

$$n \approx 31$$

X

17. **Multiple Representations** A survey reported that 52% of respondents recommend a skateboarding game for teens 15 and older.

    a. **Calculating Sample Size** If 364 people recommend the game for teens 15 and older, how many people were surveyed?

    b. **Making a Circle Graph** If 126 people do not recommend the game for teens 15 and older, and the remaining replied to let the parents decide, make a circle graph that displays the results of the survey.

    c. **Drawing Conclusions** To the nearest tenth of a percent, what is the margin of error for the survey? Give an interval that is likely to contain the exact percent of people that recommend the skateboarding game for teens 15 and older.

LESSON 6.4 **Exercise Set B**

MM3D3 Students will understand the differences between experimental and observational studies by posing questions and collecting, analyzing, and interpreting data.

Identify the type of sample described. Then tell if the sample is biased. *Explain* your reasoning.

1. A baseball league wants to know who the fans think was the league's best pitcher. Fans are asked to vote on the league's website.
2. The owner of a miniature golf course wants to find the number of times people in the community play a round of miniature golf each year. The owner has the front desk employee survey customers when they pay for a round.
3. An online vendor wants to know how people that purchased a new product feel about changes from the older models. A computer is used to randomly generate a list of 100 customers to survey from a list of all customers that bought the product.

Find the margin of error for a survey that has the given sample size. Round your answer to the nearest tenth of a percent.

4. 482
5. 664
6. 801
7. 773
8. 1252
9. 2498
10. 3444
11. 8417

Find the sample size required to achieve the given margin of error. Round your answer to the nearest whole number.

12. $\pm 1.8\%$
13. $\pm 2.3\%$
14. $\pm 4.8\%$
15. $\pm 3.7\%$
16. $\pm 6.2\%$
17. $\pm 2.9\%$
18. $\pm 4.4\%$
19. $\pm 0.6\%$

In Exercises 20 and 21, use the following information.

Computers A survey reported that 2048 respondents out of 3200 had detected a virus on their computer at least once during the last two years.

20. What is the margin of error for the survey? Round your answer to the nearest tenth of a percent.
21. Give an interval that is likely to contain the exact percent of people that have detected a virus on their computer at least once during the last two years.

In Exercises 22 and 23, use the following information.

Environment A survey claims that the percent of the population that makes purchasing decisions based on the effect it will have on the environment is between 88.75% and 91.25%. The remainder of the people in the survey do not let effects on the environment influence their purchasing decisions.

22. How many people were surveyed?
23. Give an interval that is likely to contain the exact number of people in the population that do not let effects on the environment influence their purchasing decisions.

Georgia Performance Standards

MM3D3 Students will understand the differences between experimental and observational studies by posing questions and collecting, analyzing, and interpreting data. 

LESSON 6.4

Problem Solving Workshop

Problem In a survey of 1600 voters, 51% said they voted for candidate A. What is the margin of error? Give an interval that is likely to contain the exact percent of all voters who voted for candidate A.

STEP 1 **Read and Understand**

What do you know? The number of voters and the percent that voted for candidate A

What do you want to find out? The margin of error for the survey

STEP 2 **Make a Plan** Use the formula for margin of error to solve the problem.

STEP 3 **Solve the Problem** Use the formula for margin of error.

$\text{Margin of error} = \pm\frac{1}{\sqrt{n}}$ Write margin of error formula.

$= \pm\frac{1}{\sqrt{1600}} = \pm 0.025$ Substitute 1600 for n and simplify.

The margin of error is $\pm 2.5\%$.

To find the interval, subtract and add 2.5% to the percent of people surveyed who voted for candidate A (51%).

$51\% - 2.5\% = 48.5\%$ $\qquad$ $51\% + 2.5\% = 53.5\%$

It is likely that the exact percent of all voters who voted for candidate A is between 48.5% and 53.5%.

STEP 4 **Look Back** The answer seems reasonable. In Example 3 on page 229, there were 800 people surveyed and a margin of error of $\pm 3.5\%$. Because more people are surveyed in the problem above, the percent should be lower.

Practice

1. **Juice** In a survey of 400 people, 18% named grape as their favorite juice. What is the margin of error? Give an interval that is likely to contain the exact percent of all people who named grape as their favorite juice.

2. **Gym Class** A survey of 2100 students found that 65% prefer having gym class during the last period of the day. What is the margin of error? Give an interval that is likely to contain the exact percent of all students who prefer to have gym class during the last period.

3. **What If?** In Exercise 2, 35% of the students did not prefer gym class during the last period of the day. What is the margin of error? Give an interval that is likely to contain the exact percent of all students who did not prefer to have gym class during the last period.

4. **Pizza Toppings** In a survey of 500 people, 64% said their favorite pizza topping was pepperoni. What is the margin of error? Give an interval that is likely to contain the exact percent of all people who said their favorite pizza topping was pepperoni.

LESSON 6.5

Experimental and Observational Studies

Georgia Performance Standards: MM3D3

Goal Identify types of studies and flaws in experiments.

Vocabulary

A study is often conducted with two groups. One group, called the **experimental group,** undergoes some procedure or treatment. The other group, called the **control group,** does not undergo the procedure or treatment.

In a well designed experiment, everything else about the experimental group and control group is as similar as possible so that the effect of the procedure or treatment can be determined.

In an **experimental study,** the investigator assigns the individuals to the experimental group or the control group.

In an **observational study,** the assignments of individuals to the experimental group and the control group are outside of the control of the investigator.

Example 1 Identify studies

Tell whether the study is an *experimental study* or an *observational study*. Explain your reasoning.

a. You want to study the effects of regular exercise on a person's heart rate. You measure the heart rate of a person at rest and again after jogging in place for 5 minutes. The control group is students who are not on a school athletic team. The experimental group is students who are on a school athletic team.

b. You want to study the effects that music has on the ability to recall knowledge. Each individual in your study is given material to read on the same unfamiliar topic and then asked to take a factual quiz on the material. The control group is individuals who read the material and take the quiz in a quiet room. The experimental group is individuals who read the material and take the quiz in a room that has classical music playing.

Solution

a. This study is an observational study because the assignments of the individuals to the experimental group and the control group are outside of your control. The students "sort themselves" into the two groups based on their previously-made decisions about whether to participate in school sports.

b. This study is an experimental study because you are assigning individuals to the control group and the experimental group.

Georgia Performance Standards

MM3D3 Students will understand the differences between experimental and observational studies by posing questions and collecting, analyzing, and interpreting data.

Example 2 Identify flaws in an experiment

Research A manufacturing company conducts an experiment to test how effective a new foot cushion for shoes is at relieving back pain. The experimental group consists of young college athletes who are given the foot cushions to use during athletic practices and games. The control group consists of non-athletic college students who are not given the foot cushions.

The company finds that the people in the experimental group experience less back pain than those people in the control group. As a result, the company concludes that the foot cushions are effective. Identify any flaws in this experiment, and describe how they can be corrected.

Solution

College athletes are likely to be more physically active than non-athletic students. So, it could be physical activity rather than the foot cushions that explains why the experimental group had less back pain than the control group.

To correct this flaw, the manufacturing company could redesign the experiment so that the physical activity of the people in the experimental group is simiar to the physical activity of the people in the control group.

Guided Practice for Examples 1 and 2

In Exercises 1 and 2, tell whether the study is an *experimental study* or an *observational study*. *Explain* your reasoning.

1. A scientist wants to study the effects that a nutritional supplement has on the growth of mice. The weight of each mouse is recorded daily. The control group consists of mice that do not receive the supplement. The experimental group consists of mice that receive a safe amount of the supplement.

2. You want to study the effects that using a calculator has on the time it takes to complete a math test. You record how long it takes a student to complete the test. The control group is students that choose not to use calculators. The experimental group is students that choose to use calculators.

3. **Medicine** A researcher conducts an experiment to see if a new medication is effective in preventing strokes. An experimental group of lawyers suffers more strokes than a control group of professional tennis players. Identify any flaws in this experiment and describe how they can be corrected.

4. **Seat Belts** You conduct an experiment to see if parents make their children wear seat belts. You have a police officer ask the question to a large group of parents. Identify any flaws in the experiment, and describe how they can be corrected.

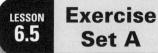

LESSON 6.5 Exercise Set A

MM3D3 Students will understand the differences between experimental and observational studies by posing questions and collecting, analyzing, and interpreting data.

In Exercises 1–3, tell whether the study is an *experimental study* or an *observational study*. *Explain* your reasoning.

1. A professor wants to study the effects that teaching outdoors has on test scores. Each individual in the study is given the same lectures for a month and then tested. The control group is individuals who were lectured and tested indoors. The experimental group is individuals who were lectured and tested outdoors.

2. You want to study the effects that yawning has on other individuals' yawning. Each individual in your study is placed in a room to watch an instructional video. You record the total number of yawns in each group. The control group is individuals who watch the video without a yawning scene. The experimental group is individuals who watch the same video with the addition of one yawning scene.

3. Dr. Smith and Dr. Jones want to study the effects on a patient's arthritis that occur when the patient believes that he or she has used a new ointment. The control group consists of the patients that choose to visit Dr. Smith about arthritis and they receive an ointment with no medicinal value. The experimental group consists of the patients that choose to visit Dr. Jones about arthritis and they receive the new ointment.

4. **Math Anxiety** A company conducts an experiment to determine whether college students suffer from math anxiety. The experimental group consists of students enrolled in a mathematics program. The control group consists of students enrolled in an art history program. Identify any flaws in the experiment, and describe how they can be corrected.

5. **Government** A researcher conducts a survey to determine the approval rating of the current mayor of a city. The experimental group consists of registered voters in the same party as the mayor. The control group consists of registered voters in a different party from the mayor. Identify any flaws in the experiment, and describe how they can be corrected.

6. **Education** A company conducts an experiment to determine whether the use of educational software in an elementary classroom will increase test scores of students. The experimental group consists of students enrolled in third grade who are given the software. The control group consists of students enrolled in first grade who are not given the software.

   The company finds that the students in the experimental group test higher than the students in the control group and concludes that the educational software is effective at increasing test scores. Identify any flaws in the experiment, and describe how they can be corrected.

LESSON 6.5

Exercise Set B

MM3D3 Students will understand the differences between experimental and observational studies by posing questions and collecting, analyzing, and interpreting data.

In Exercises 1–3, tell whether the study is an *experimental study* or an *observational study*. *Explain* your reasoning.

1. A health teacher at a large school wants to study the effects of regular swimming on a student's ability to hold his or her breath. The teacher measures the length of time that a student can hold his or her breath. The control group consists of students who are not on the swim team. The experimental group consists of students who are on the swim team.

2. You want to study the ability of students to talk at a normal tone while listening to loud music with their MP3 player headphones. You measure how loud a student talks normally, then you measure how loud the student talks while listening to loud music with their MP3 player headphones. The control group is students who do not regularly use an MP3 player. The experimental group is students who regularly use an MP3 player.

3. A manager wants to study the effects that positive reinforcement has on an employee's willingness to work overtime. The control group is employees who are given no reinforcement. The experimental group is employees who are given positive reinforcement during their weekly meeting with the manager.

4. **Health** A research company conducts a survey to determine the public's perception of how fast a cold virus would spread in a metropolitan area. The experimental group consists of trained medical professionals. The control group consists of college students. Identify any flaws in the experiment, and describe how they can be corrected.

5. **Statistics** A company that produces mathematics textbooks conducts an experiment to determine how effective an online help tutorial for their statistics book is for college students. The experimental group consists of first year mathematics majors. The control group consists of students from other majors required to take an introductory statistics course. Identify any flaws in the experiment, and describe how they can be corrected.

6. **Dance** A dance company conducts an experiment to determine whether the use of an instructional dance video will increase the skill level of dance students. The experimental group consists of fourth year dance students who are given the video. The control group consists of second year dance students who are not given the video.

   The company finds that the students' skill level in the experimental group has increased while the students' skill level in the control group has not increased. The company concludes that the instructional dance video is effective at increasing skill levels. Identify any flaws in the experiment, and describe how they can be corrected.

TEST | for Unit 6

1. The random variable C represents the color of a pen chosen from a bag that contains 1 red pen, 5 black pens, and 4 blue pens. Make a table and a histogram showing the probability distribution for C. *Describe* the distribution as either *symmetric* or *skewed*.

Calculate the probability of *k* successes for a binomial experiment consisting of *n* trials with probability *p* of success on each trial.

2. $k \le 3, n = 6, p = 0.3$
3. $k \ge 6, n = 10, p = 0.55$
4. $k \le 5, n = 8, p = 0.81$
5. $k \ge 2, n = 5, p = 0.12$

Give the percent of the area under the normal curve represented by the shaded region.

6.

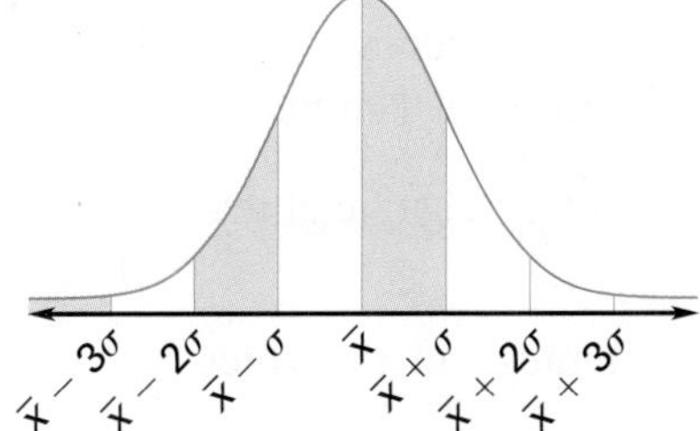

7.

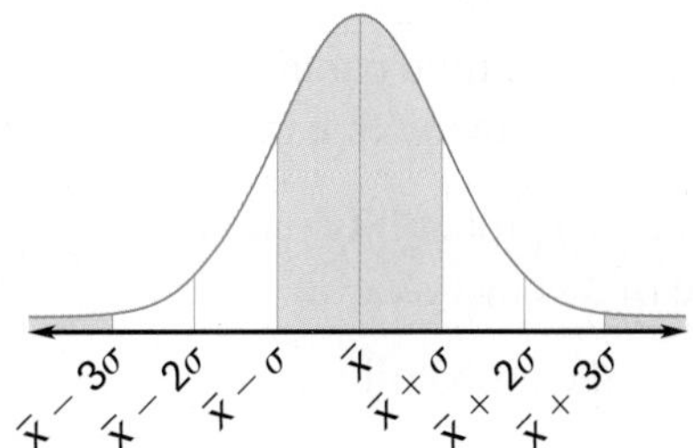

Find the mean and standard deviation of a normal distribution that approximates the binomial distribution with *n* trials and probability *p* of success on each trial.

8. $n = 75, p = 0.15$
9. $n = 96, p = 0.2$
10. $n = 180, p = 0.75$

Find the margin of error for a survey that has the given sample size. Round your answer to the nearest tenth of a percent.

11. 165
12. 475
13. 1450
14. 3540

Find the sample size required to achieve the given margin of error. Round your answer to the nearest whole number, if necessary.

15. $\pm 1.4\%$
16. $\pm 3.8\%$
17. $\pm 5.2\%$
18. $\pm 0.5\%$

19. Tell whether the study below is an *experimental study* or an *observational study*. *Explain* your reasoning.

    You want to study the effects that prior playoff experience has on a player's ability to perform well in the playoffs. The performance of each individual in the playoffs is analyzed. The control group is individuals who have no prior playoff experience. The experimental group is individuals who have prior playoff experience.

UNIT 6

20. **Fruit** According to a farmer's study, 10% of his oranges are too damaged to sell. Which probability is greater: (a) the probability of choosing 40 oranges and getting 3 that are too damaged to sell, or (b) the probability of choosing 50 oranges and getting at most 3 that are too damaged to sell?

In Exercises 21–23, use the fact that approximately 6% of people have blood type A−. Consider a class of 450 students.

21. What is the probability that 17 or fewer students have blood type A−?

22. What is the probability that 32 or more students have blood type A−?

23. What is the probability that between 12 and 37 students have blood type A−?

24. **Paramedics** The time paramedics take to arrive at the scene of an emergency is normally distributed with a mean of 7 minutes and a standard deviation of 1 minute.

a. What is the probability that the paramedics take at most 9 minutes to arrive at the scene of an emergency?

b. What is the probability that the paramedics take between 5 minutes and 8 minutes to arrive at the scene of an emergency?

25. **Water Park** A research company conducts a survey to determine how popular a new indoor water park is among residents. The experimental group consists of young adults from 16 to 29 years of age. The control group consists of adults from 30 to 50 years of age. Identify any flaws in the experiment, and describe how they can be corrected.

Performance Task

Restaurants

Surveys were conducted on two samples of 850 restaurant employees to determine their hand washing habits while working. Sample A consisted of individuals that completed and mailed in the survey. Sample B consisted of phone calls to random restaurant employees.

a. What type of sample is sample A? Sample B? Which is most appropriate for the survey?

b. The question "Do you wash your hands every time you change duties at work?" was among the questions asked. In Sample B, there were 799 responses of "Yes" and the remaining replied "No." Find the margin of error. Round to the nearest tenth. Give an interval that is likely to contain the exact percent that responded "No."

c. If the question is asked to 50 more employees, what is the probability that fewer than 5 of these employees answer "No"?

d. Identify a flaw in the experiment if the surveyed employees are not told that their responses will remain anonymous.

Student Resources

- Tables p. 240
- English–Spanish Glossary p. 250
- Index p. 276
- Selected Answers p. SA1

Tables

Table of Symbols

Symbol	Meaning	Page
$\cdot$	multiplication, times	2
$\approx$	is approximately equal to	2
$-a$	opposite of a	3
(x, y)	ordered pair	6
$\lvert x \rvert$	absolute value of x	10
$<$	is less than	17
$>$	is greater than	17
$\leq$	is less than or equal to	17
$\geq$	is greater than or equal to	17
(x, y, z)	ordered triple	34
$\begin{bmatrix} 1 & 0 \\ 0 & 1 \end{bmatrix}$	matrix	38
$\lvert A \rvert$	determinant of matrix A	49
A^{-1}	inverse of matrix A	54
$x \to +\infty$	x approaches positive infinity	66
$x \to -\infty$	x approaches negative infinity	66
$\sqrt{a}$	the nonnegative square root of a	66
$[a, b]$	$a \leq x \leq b$	81
(a, b)	$a < x < b$	81
$[a, b)$	$a \leq x < b$	81
$(a, b]$	$a < x \leq b$	81
i	imaginary unit equal to $\sqrt{-1}$	94
$\sqrt[n]{a}$	nth root of a	108
e	irrational number ≈ 2.718	140
$\log_b y$	log base b of y	145
$\log x$	log base 10 of x	145
$\ln x$	log base e of x	145
$P(A)$	probability of event A	212
${}_nC_r$	number of combinations of r objects chosen from n distinct objects	212
$\bar{x}$	x-bar, the mean of a data set	218
σ	sigma, the standard deviation of a data set	219

Time

60 seconds (sec) = 1 minute (min)	365 days, 52 weeks (approx.), 12 months = 1 year
60 minutes = 1 hour (h)	10 years = 1 decade
24 hours = 1 day	100 years = 1 century
7 days = 1 week	
4 weeks (approx.) = 1 month	

Measures

Metric	*United States Customary*
Length	**Length**
10 millimeters (mm) = 1 centimeter (cm)	12 inches (in.) = 1 foot (ft)
100 cm, 1000 mm = 1 meter (m)	36 in., 3 ft = 1 yard (yd)
1000 m = 1 kilometer (km)	5280 ft, 1760 yd = 1 mile (mi)
Area	**Area**
100 square millimeters (mm^2) = 1 square centimeter (cm^2)	144 square inches ($in.^2$) = 1 square foot (ft^2)
10,000 cm^2 = 1 square meter (m^2)	9 ft^2 = 1 square yard (yd^2)
10,000 m^2 = 1 hectare (ha)	43,560 ft^2, 4840 yd^2 = 1 acre (A)
Volume	**Volume**
1000 cubic millimeters (mm^3) = 1 cubic centimeter (cm^3)	1728 cubic inches ($in.^3$) = 1 cubic foot (ft^3)
1,000,000 cm^3 = 1 cubic meter (m^3)	27 ft^3 = 1 cubic yard (yd^3)
Liquid Capacity	**Liquid Capacity**
1000 milliliters (mL), 1000 cubic centimeters (cm^3) = 1 liter (L)	8 fluid ounces (fl oz) = 1 cup (c)
1000 L = 1 kiloliter (kL)	2 c = 1 pint (pt)
	2 pt = 1 quart (qt)
	4 qt = 1 gallon (gal)
Mass	**Weight**
1000 milligrams (mg) = 1 gram (g)	16 ounces (oz) = 1 pound (lb)
1000 g = 1 kilogram (kg)	2000 lb = 1 ton
1000 kg = 1 metric ton (t)	
Temperature	**Temperature**
Degrees Celsius (°C)	**Degrees Fahrenheit (°F)**
0°C = freezing point of water	32°F = freezing point of water
37°C = normal body temperature	98.6°F = normal body temperature
100°C = boiling point of water	212°F = boiling point of water

Area and Volume Formulas

Area of an equilateral triangle	Area $= \frac{\sqrt{3}}{4}s^2$ where s is the length of a side
Area of an ellipse	Area $= \pi ab$ where a and b are half the lengths of the major and minor axes of the ellipse
Volume and surface area of a right rectangular prism	Volume $= \ell wh$ where ℓ is the length, w is the width, and h is the height Surface area $= 2(\ell w + wh + \ell h)$
Volume and surface area of a right cylinder	Volume $= \pi r^2 h$ where r is the base radius and h is the height Lateral surface area $= 2\pi rh$ Surface area $= 2\pi r^2 + 2\pi rh$
Volume and surface area of a right regular pyramid	Volume $= \frac{1}{3}Bh$ where B is the area of the base and h is the height Lateral surface area $= \frac{1}{2}ns\ell$ where n is the number of sides of the base, s is the length of a side of the base, and ℓ is the slant height Surface area $= B + \frac{1}{2}ns\ell$
Volume and surface area of a right circular cone	Volume $= \frac{1}{3}\pi r^2 h$ where r is the base radius and h is the height Lateral surface area $= \pi r\ell$ where ℓ is the slant height Surface area $= \pi r^2 + \pi r\ell$
Volume and surface area of a sphere	Volume $= \frac{4}{3}\pi r^3$ where r is the radius Surface area $= 4\pi r^2$

Other Formulas

<table>
<tr><th>Name of Formula</th><th>Statement of Formula</th><th>Page</th></tr>
<tr><td>Determinant of a 2 × 2 matrix</td><td>$\det\begin{bmatrix} a & b \\ c & d \end{bmatrix} = \begin{vmatrix} a & b \\ c & d \end{vmatrix} = ad - cb$</td><td>49</td></tr>
<tr><td>Determinant of a 3 × 3 matrix</td><td>$\det\begin{bmatrix} a & b & c \\ d & e & f \\ g & h & i \end{bmatrix} = \begin{vmatrix} a & b & c \\ d & e & f \\ g & h & i \end{vmatrix} = (aei + bfg + cdh) - (gec + hfa + idb)$</td><td>49</td></tr>
<tr><td>Cramer's rule</td><td>Let $A = \begin{bmatrix} a & b \\ c & d \end{bmatrix}$ be the coefficient matrix of this linear system:
$ax + by = e$
$cx + dy = f$
If $\det A \neq 0$, then the system has exactly one solution.
The solution is $x = \dfrac{\begin{vmatrix} e & b \\ f & d \end{vmatrix}}{\det A}$ and $y = \dfrac{\begin{vmatrix} a & e \\ c & f \end{vmatrix}}{\det A}$.</td><td>49</td></tr>
<tr><td>Area of a triangle</td><td>The area of a triangle with vertices (x_1, y_1), (x_2, y_2), and (x_3, y_3) is given by
$\text{Area} = \pm\frac{1}{2}\begin{vmatrix} x_1 & y_1 & 1 \\ x_2 & y_2 & 1 \\ x_3 & y_3 & 1 \end{vmatrix}$
where the appropriate sign ($\pm$) should be chosen to yield a positive value.</td><td>51</td></tr>
<tr><td>Inverse of a 2 × 2 matrix</td><td>The inverse of the matrix $A = \begin{bmatrix} a & b \\ c & d \end{bmatrix}$ is
$A^{-1} = \dfrac{1}{|A|}\begin{bmatrix} d & -b \\ -c & a \end{bmatrix} = \dfrac{1}{ad - cb}\begin{bmatrix} d & -b \\ -c & a \end{bmatrix}$ provided
$ad - cb \neq 0$.</td><td>54</td></tr>
<tr><td>Discriminant of a general second-degree equation</td><td>Any conic can be described by a general second-degree equation in x and y: $Ax^2 + Bxy + Cy^2 + Dx + Ey + F = 0$. The expression $B^2 - 4AC$ is the discriminant of the conic equation and can be used to identify it.
<table>
<tr><th>Discriminant</th><th>Type of Conic</th></tr>
<tr><td>$B^2 - 4AC < 0$, $B = 0$, and $A = C$</td><td>Circle</td></tr>
<tr><td>$B^2 - 4AC < 0$, and either $B \neq 0$ or $A \neq C$</td><td>Ellipse</td></tr>
<tr><td>$B^2 - 4AC = 0$</td><td>Parabola</td></tr>
<tr><td>$B^2 - 4AC > 0$</td><td>Hyperbola</td></tr>
</table>
If $B = 0$, each axis of the conic is horizontal or vertical.</td><td>194</td></tr>
</table>

Other Formulas *(continued)*

Name of Formula	Statement of Formula	Page
Areas under a normal curve	A normal distribution with mean $\overline{x}$ and standard deviation σ has these properties: • The total area under the related normal curve is 1. • About 68% of the area lies within 1 standard deviation of the mean. • About 95% of the area lies within 2 standard deviations of the mean. • About 99.7% of the area lies within 3 standard deviations of the mean.	219
z-score formula	$z = \frac{x - \overline{x}}{\sigma}$ where x is a data value, $\overline{x}$ is the mean, and σ is the standard deviation	219

Theorems

Theorem or Corollary	Statement of Theorem or Corollary	Page
Remainder theorem	If a polynomial $f(x)$ is divided by $x - k$, then the remainder is $r = f(k)$.	85
Factor theorem	A polynomial $f(x)$ has a factor $x - k$ if and only if $f(k) = 0$.	85
Rational root theorem	If $f(x) = a_nx^n + \cdots + a_1x + a_0$ has *integer* coefficients, then every rational zero of f has this form: $\frac{p}{q} = \frac{\text{factor of constant term } a_0}{\text{factor of leading coefficient } a_n}$	89
Fundamental theorem of algebra	If $f(x)$ is a polynomial of degree n where $n > 0$, then the equation $f(x) = 0$ has at least one solution in the set of complex numbers.	94
Corollary to the fundamental theorem of algebra	If $f(x)$ is a polynomial of degree n where $n > 0$, then the equation $f(x) = 0$ has exactly n solutions provided each solution repeated twice is counted as 2 solutions, each solution repeated three times is counted as 3 solutions, and so on.	94
Complex conjugates theorem	If f is a polynomial function with real coefficients, and $a + bi$ is an imaginary zero of f, then $a - bi$ is also a zero of f.	94
Irrational conjugates theorem	Suppose f is a polynomial function with rational coefficients, and a and b are rational numbers such that $\sqrt{b}$ is irrational. If $a + \sqrt{b}$ is a zero of f, then $a - \sqrt{b}$ is also a zero of f.	94
Descartes' rule of signs	Let $f(x) = a_nx^n + a_{n-1}x^{n-1} + \cdots + a_2x^2 + a_1x + a_0$ be a polynomial function with real coefficients. • The number of *positive real zeros* of f is equal to the number of changes in sign of the coefficients of $f(x)$ or is less than this by an even number. • The number of *negative real zeros* of f is equal to the number of changes in sign of the coefficients of $f(-x)$ or is less than this by an even number.	94

TABLES

Properties of Matrices

Property	Statement of Property	Page
	Let A, B, and C be matrices, and let k be a scalar.	
Associative Property of Addition	$(A + B) + C = A + (B + C)$	38
Commutative Property of Addition	$A + B = B + A$	38
Distributive Property of Addition	$k(A + B) = kA + kB$	38
Distributive Property of Subtraction	$k(A - B) = kA - kB$	38
Associative Property of Matrix Multiplication	$(AB)C = A(BC)$	43
Left Distributive Property of Matrix Multiplication	$A(B + C) = AB + AC$	43
Right Distributive Property of Matrix Multiplication	$(A + B)C = AC + BC$	43
Associative Property of Scalar Multiplication	$k(AB) = (kA)B = A(kB)$	43
Multiplicative Identity	An $n \times n$ matrix with 1's on the main diagonal and 0's elsewhere is an identity matrix, denoted I. For any $n \times n$ matrix A, $AI = IA = A$.	54
Inverse Matrices	If the determinant of an $n \times n$ matrix A is nonzero, then A has an inverse, denoted A^{-1}, such that $AA^{-1} = A^{-1}A = I$.	54

Properties of Rational Exponents

Property	Statement of Property	Page
	Let a and b be real numbers, and let m and n be rational numbers.	
Product of Powers Property	$a^m \cdot a^n = a^{m+n}$	113
Power of a Power Property	$(a^m)^n = a^{mn}$	113
Power of a Product Property	$(ab)^m = a^m b^m$	113
Negative Exponent Property	$a^{-m} = \frac{1}{a^m}, a \neq 0$	113
Zero Exponent Property	$a^0 = 1, a \neq 0$	113
Quotient of Powers Property	$\frac{a^m}{a^n} = a^{m-n}, a \neq 0$	113
Power of a Quotient Property	$\left(\frac{a}{b}\right)^m = \frac{a^m}{b^m}, b \neq 0$	113

Properties of Radicals

Property	Statement of Property	Page
Number of Real *n*th Roots	Let n be an integer greater than 1, and let a be a real number. • If n is odd, then a has one real nth root: $\sqrt[n]{a} = a^{1/n}$. • If n is even and $a > 0$, then a has two real nth roots: $\pm\sqrt[n]{a} = \pm a^{1/n}$. • If n is even and $a = 0$, then a has one nth root: $\sqrt[n]{0} = 0^{1/n} = 0$. • If n is even and $a < 0$, then a has no real nth roots.	109
Radicals and Rational Exponents	Let $a^{1/n}$ be an nth root of a, and let m be a positive integer. • $a^{m/n} = (a^{1/n})^m = (\sqrt[n]{a})^m$ • $a^{-m/n} = \frac{1}{a^{m/n}} = \frac{1}{(a^{1/n})^m} = \frac{1}{(\sqrt[n]{a})^m}, a \neq 0$	109
Product and Quotient Properties of Radicals	Let n be an integer greater than 1, and let a and b be positive real numbers. Then $\sqrt[n]{a \cdot b} = \sqrt[n]{a} \cdot \sqrt[n]{b}$ and $\sqrt[n]{\frac{a}{b}} = \frac{\sqrt[n]{a}}{\sqrt[n]{b}}$.	113

Properties of Logarithms

Property	Statement of Property	Page
	Let a, b, c, m, n, x, and y be positive real numbers such that $b \neq 1$ and $c \neq 1$.	
Logarithms and Exponents	$\log_b y = x$ if and only if $b^x = y$	145
Special Logarithm Values	$\log_b 1 = 0$ because $b^0 = 1$ and $\log_b b = 1$ because $b^1 = b$	145
Common and Natural Logarithms	$\log_{10} x = \log x$ and $\log_e x = \ln x$	145
Product Property of Logarithms	$\log_b mn = \log_b m + \log_b n$	155
Quotient Property of Logarithms	$\log_b \frac{m}{n} = \log_b m - \log_b n$	155
Power Property of Logarithms	$\log_b m^n = n \log_b m$	155
Change of Base	$\log_c a = \frac{\log_b a}{\log_b c}$	156

TABLES

Table of Squares and Square Roots

No.	Square	Sq. Root	No.	Square	Sq. Root	No.	Square	Sq. Root
1	1	1.000	51	2601	7.141	101	10,201	10.050
2	4	1.414	52	2704	7.211	102	10,404	10.100
3	9	1.732	53	2809	7.280	103	10,609	10.149
4	16	2.000	54	2916	7.348	104	10,816	10.198
5	25	2.236	55	3025	7.416	105	11,025	10.247
6	36	2.449	56	3136	7.483	106	11,236	10.296
7	49	2.646	57	3249	7.550	107	11,449	10.344
8	64	2.828	58	3364	7.616	108	11,664	10.392
9	81	3.000	59	3481	7.681	109	11,881	10.440
10	100	3.162	60	3600	7.746	110	12,100	10.488
11	121	3.317	61	3721	7.810	111	12,321	10.536
12	144	3.464	62	3844	7.874	112	12,544	10.583
13	169	3.606	63	3969	7.937	113	12,769	10.630
14	196	3.742	64	4096	8.000	114	12,996	10.677
15	225	3.873	65	4225	8.062	115	13,225	10.724
16	256	4.000	66	4356	8.124	116	13,456	10.770
17	289	4.123	67	4489	8.185	117	13,689	10.817
18	324	4.243	68	4624	8.246	118	13,924	10.863
19	361	4.359	69	4761	8.307	119	14,161	10.909
20	400	4.472	70	4900	8.367	120	14,400	10.954
21	441	4.583	71	5041	8.426	121	14,641	11.000
22	484	4.690	72	5184	8.485	122	14,884	11.045
23	529	4.796	73	5329	8.544	123	15,129	11.091
24	576	4.899	74	5476	8.602	124	15,376	11.136
25	625	5.000	75	5625	8.660	125	15,625	11.180
26	676	5.099	76	5776	8.718	126	15,876	11.225
27	729	5.196	77	5929	8.775	127	16,129	11.269
28	784	5.292	78	6084	8.832	128	16,384	11.314
29	841	5.385	79	6241	8.888	129	16,641	11.358
30	900	5.477	80	6400	8.944	130	16,900	11.402
31	961	5.568	81	6561	9.000	131	17,161	11.446
32	1024	5.657	82	6724	9.055	132	17,424	11.489
33	1089	5.745	83	6889	9.110	133	17,689	11.533
34	1156	5.831	84	7056	9.165	134	17,956	11.576
35	1225	5.916	85	7225	9.220	135	18,225	11.619
36	1296	6.000	86	7396	9.274	136	18,496	11.662
37	1369	6.083	87	7569	9.327	137	18,769	11.705
38	1444	6.164	88	7744	9.381	138	19,044	11.747
39	1521	6.245	89	7921	9.434	139	19,321	11.790
40	1600	6.325	90	8100	9.487	140	19,600	11.832
41	1681	6.403	91	8281	9.539	141	19,881	11.874
42	1764	6.481	92	8464	9.592	142	20,164	11.916
43	1849	6.557	93	8649	9.644	143	20,449	11.958
44	1936	6.633	94	8836	9.695	144	20,736	12.000
45	2025	6.708	95	9025	9.747	145	21,025	12.042
46	2116	6.782	96	9216	9.798	146	21,316	12.083
47	2209	6.856	97	9409	9.849	147	21,609	12.124
48	2304	6.928	98	9604	9.899	148	21,904	12.166
49	2401	7.000	99	9801	9.950	149	22,201	12.207
50	2500	7.071	100	10,000	10.000	150	22,500	12.247

Standard Normal Table

If z is a randomly selected value from a standard normal distribution, you can use the table below to find the probability that z is less than or equal to some given value. For example, the table shows that $P(z \leq -0.6) = 0.2743$. You can find the value of $P(z \leq -0.6)$ in the table by finding the value where row -0 and column 6 intersect.

You can also use the standard normal table to find probabilities for any normal distribution by first converting values from the distribution to z-scores.

In the table, the value .0000+ means "slightly more than 0" and the value 1.0000− means "slightly less than 1."

z	.0	.1	.2	.3	.4	.5	.6	.7	.8	.9
−3	.0013	.0010	.0007	.0005	.0003	.0002	.0002	.0001	.0001	.0000+
−2	.0228	.0179	.0139	.0107	.0082	.0062	.0047	.0035	.0026	.0019
−1	.1587	.1357	.1151	.0968	.0808	.0668	.0548	.0446	.0359	.0287
−0	.5000	.4602	.4207	.3821	.3446	.3085	.2743	.2420	.2119	.1841
0	.5000	.5398	.5793	.6179	.6554	.6915	.7257	.7580	.7881	.8159
1	.8413	.8643	.8849	.9032	.9192	.9332	.9452	.9554	.9641	.9713
2	.9772	.9821	.9861	.9893	.9918	.9938	.9953	.9965	.9974	.9981
3	.9987	.9990	.9993	.9995	.9997	.9998	.9998	.9999	.9999	1.0000−

English-Spanish Glossary

A

asymptote **(p. 130)** A line that a graph approaches more and more closely.

asíntota **(pág. 130)** Recta a la que se aproxima una gráfica cada vez más.

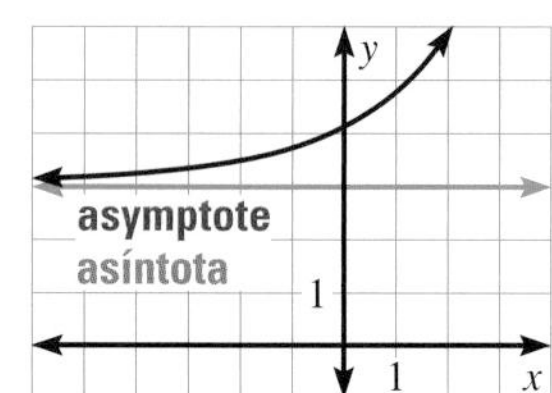

The asymptote for the graph shown is the line $y = 3$.

La asíntota para la gráfica que se muestra es la recta $y = 3$.

---

average rate of change for a nonlinear function **(p. 149)** For a nonlinear function, the average rate of change between any two points (x_1, y_1) and (x_2, y_2) is the slope of the line through the two points.

$$\text{Average rate of change} = \frac{y_2 - y_1}{x_2 - x_1}$$

The average rate of change of $y = 2^x - 4$ from $(2, 0)$ to $(3, 4)$ is $\frac{4 - 0}{3 - 2}$, or 1.

tasa de cambio promedio de una función **(pág. 149)** Para una función, la tasa de cambio promedio entre dos puntos cualesquiera (x_1, y_1) y (x_2, y_2) es la pendiente de la recta que atraviesa los dos puntos.

$$\text{Tasa de cambio promedio} = \frac{y_2 - y_1}{x_2 - x_1}$$

La tasa de cambio promedio de $y = 2^x - 4$ de $(2, 0)$ a $(3, 4)$ es $\frac{4 - 0}{3 - 2}$, ó 1.

---

axis of symmetry of a parabola **(p. 176)** The line perpendicular to the parabola's directrix and passing through its focus and vertex.

See **parabola.**

eje de simetría de una parábola **(pág. 176)** La recta perpendicular a la directriz de la parábola y que pasa por su foco y su vértice.

Ver **parábola.**

B

biased sample **(p. 228)** A sample that overrepresents or underrepresents part of a population.

The members of a school's basketball team would form a biased sample for a survey about whether to build a new gym.

muestra sesgada **(pág. 228)** Muestra que representa de forma excesiva o insuficiente a parte de una población.

Los miembros del equipo de baloncesto de una escuela formarían una muestra sesgada si participaran en una encuesta sobre si quieren que se construya un nuevo gimnasio.

binomial distribution (p. 212) The probability distribution associated with a binomial experiment.

distribución binomial (pág. 212) La distribución de probabilidades asociada a un experimento binomial.

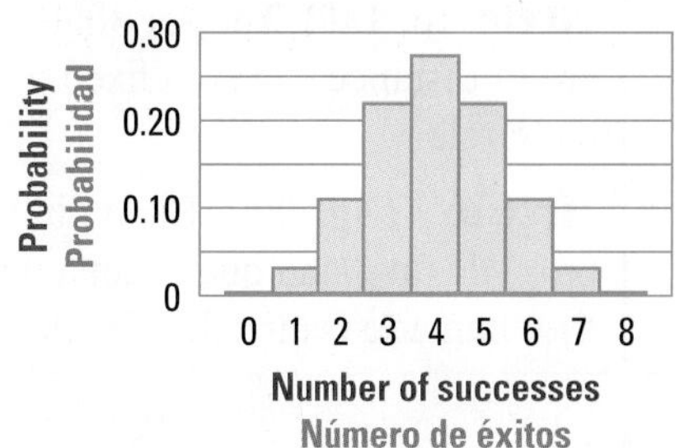

Binomial distribution for 8 trials with $p = 0.5$.

Distribución binomial de 8 pruebas con $p = 0.5$.

---

binomial experiment (p. 212) An experiment that meets the following conditions. (1) There are *n* independent trials. (2) Each trial has only two possible outcomes: success and failure. (3) The probability of success is the same for each trial.

experimento binomial (pág. 212) Experimento que satisface las siguientes condiciones. (1) Hay *n* pruebas independientes. (2) Cada prueba tiene sólo dos resultados posibles: éxito y fracaso. (3) La probabilidad de éxito es igual para cada prueba.

A fair coin is tossed 12 times. The probability of getting exactly 4 heads is as follows:

Una moneda normal se lanza 12 veces. La probabilidad de sacar exactamente 4 caras es la siguiente:

$$\begin{aligned} P(k = 4) &= {}_nC_k p^k(1 - p)^{n-k} \\ &= {}_{12}C_4(0.5)^4(1 - 0.5)^8 \\ &= 495(0.5)^4(0.5)^8 \\ &\approx 0.121 \end{aligned}$$

C

center of a circle (p. 180) *See* circle.

centro de un círculo (pág. 180) *Ver* círculo.

The circle with equation $(x - 3)^2 + (y + 5)^2 = 36$ has its center at $(3, -5)$. *See also* circle.

El círculo con la ecuación $(x - 3)^2 + (y + 5)^2 = 36$ tiene el centro en $(3, -5)$. *Ver también* círculo.

---

center of a hyperbola (p. 190) The midpoint of the transverse axis of a hyperbola.

centro de una hipérbola (pág. 190) El punto medio del eje transverso de una hipérbola.

***See* hyperbola.**

***Ver* hipérbola.**

---

center of an ellipse (p. 186) The midpoint of the major axis of an ellipse.

centro de una elipse (pág. 186) El punto medio del eje mayor de una elipse.

***See* ellipse.**

***Ver* elipse.**

ENGLISH-SPANISH GLOSSARY

circle (p. 180) The set of all points (x, y) in a plane that are of distance r from a fixed point, called the center of the circle.

círculo (pág. 180) El conjunto de todos los puntos (x, y) de un plano que están a una distancia r de un punto fijo, llamado centro del círculo.

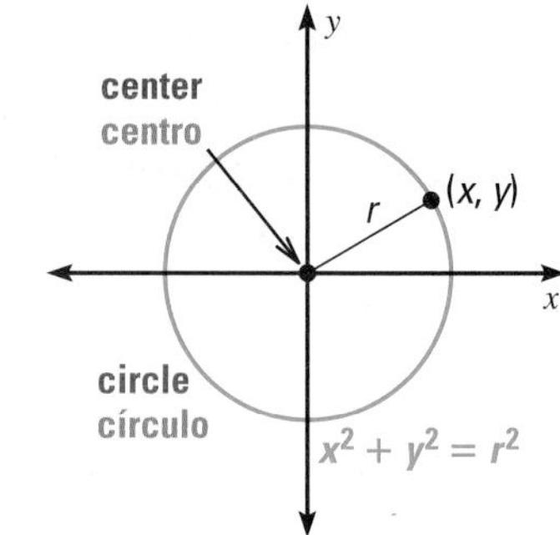

coefficient matrix (p. 49) The coefficient matrix of the linear system $ax + by = e, cx + dy = f$ is $\begin{bmatrix} a & b \\ c & d \end{bmatrix}$.

matriz coeficiente (pág. 49) La matriz coeficiente del sistema lineal $ax + by = e, cx + dy = f$ es $\begin{bmatrix} a & b \\ c & d \end{bmatrix}$.

$$9x + 4y = -6$$
$$3x - 5y = -21$$

coefficient matrix: / **matriz coeficiente:** $\begin{bmatrix} 9 & 4 \\ 3 & -5 \end{bmatrix}$

matrix of constants: / **matriz de constantes:** $\begin{bmatrix} -6 \\ -21 \end{bmatrix}$

matrix of variables: / **matriz de variables:** $\begin{bmatrix} x \\ y \end{bmatrix}$

common logarithm (p. 145) A logarithm with base 10. It is denoted by $\log_{10}$ or simply by log.

$\log_{10} 100 = \log 100 = 2$ because $10^2 = 100$.

logaritmo común (pág. 145) Logaritmo con base 10. Se denota por $\log_{10}$ ó simplemente por log.

$\log_{10} 100 = \log 100 = 2$ ya que $10^2 = 100$.

complex conjugates (p. 94) Two complex numbers of the form $a + bi$ and $a - bi$.

números complejos conjugados (pág. 94) Dos números complejos de la forma $a + bi$ y $a - bi$.

$$2 + 4i, 2 - 4i$$

conic section (p. 194) A curve formed by the intersection of a plane and a double-napped cone. Conic sections are also called conics.

See **circle, ellipse, hyperbola,** *and* **parabola.**

sección cónica (pág. 194) Una curva formada por la intersección de un plano y un cono doble. Las secciones cónicas también se llaman cónicas.

Ver **círculo, elipse, hipérbola** *y* **parábola.**

consistent system (p. 6) A system of equations that has at least one solution.

sistema compatible (pág. 6) Sistema de ecuaciones que tiene al menos una solución.

$$y = 2 + 3x$$
$$6x + 2y = 4$$

The system above is consistent, with solution (0, 2).

El sistema de arriba es compatible, con la solución (0, 2).

ENGLISH-SPANISH GLOSSARY

constraints (p. 30) In linear programming, the linear inequalities that form a system.

See linear programming.

restricciones (pág. 30) En la programación lineal, las desigualdades lineales que forman un sistema.

Ver programación lineal.

continuous random variable (p. 212) A variable that can take on an uncountable, infinite number of possible values, often over a specified interval.

The weight of a person is a continuous random variable.

variable aleatoria continua (pág. 212) Una variable que puede tomar un número incontable e infinito de valores posibles, a menudo durante un intervalo especificado.

El peso de una persona es una variable aleatoria continua.

control group (p. 233) A group that does not undergo a procedure or treatment when an experiment is conducted. *See also* experimental group.

See experimental group.

grupo de control (pág. 233) Grupo que no se somete a ningún procedimiento o tratamiento durante la realización de un experimento. *Ver también* grupo experimental.

Ver grupo experimental.

co-vertices of an ellipse (p. 186) The points of intersection of an ellipse and the line perpendicular to the major axis at the center.

See ellipse.

puntos extremos del eje menor de una elipse (pág. 186) Los puntos de intersección de una elipse y la recta perpendicular al eje mayor en el centro.

Ver elipse.

Cramer's rule (p. 49) A method for solving a system of linear equations using determinants: For the linear system $ax + by = e, cx + dy = f$, let A be the coefficient matrix. If $\det A \neq 0$, the solution of the system is as follows:

$$x = \frac{\begin{vmatrix} e & b \\ f & d \end{vmatrix}}{\det A},\ y = \frac{\begin{vmatrix} a & e \\ c & f \end{vmatrix}}{\det A}$$

regla de Cramer (pág. 49) Método para resolver un sistema de ecuaciones lineales usando determinantes: Para el sistema lineal $ax + by = e, cx + dy = f$, sea A la matriz coeficiente. Si $\det A \neq 0$, la solución del sistema es la siguiente:

$$x = \frac{\begin{vmatrix} e & b \\ f & d \end{vmatrix}}{\det A},\ y = \frac{\begin{vmatrix} a & e \\ c & f \end{vmatrix}}{\det A}$$

$$\begin{aligned} 9x + 4y &= -6 \\ 3x - 5y &= -21; \end{aligned} \quad \begin{vmatrix} 9 & 4 \\ 3 & -5 \end{vmatrix} = -57$$

Applying Cramer's rule gives the following:

Al aplicar la regla de Cramer se obtiene lo siguiente:

$$x = \frac{\begin{vmatrix} -6 & 4 \\ -21 & -5 \end{vmatrix}}{-57} = \frac{114}{-57} = -2$$

$$y = \frac{\begin{vmatrix} 9 & -6 \\ 3 & -21 \end{vmatrix}}{-57} = \frac{-171}{-57} = 3$$

ENGLISH-SPANISH GLOSSARY

decay factor (p. 135) The quantity b in the exponential decay function $y = ab^x$ with $a > 0$ and $0 < b < 1$.

factor de decrecimiento (pág. 135) La cantidad b de la función de decrecimiento exponencial $y = ab^x$, con $a > 0$ y $0 < b < 1$.

The decay factor for the function $y = 3(0.5)^x$ is 0.5.

El factor de decrecimiento de la función $y = 3(0.5)^x$ es 0.5.

---

degree of a polynomial function (p. 66) The exponent in the term of a polynomial function where the variable is raised to the greatest power.

grado de una función polinómica (pág. 66) En una función polinómica, el exponente del término donde la variable se eleva a la mayor potencia.

***See* polynomial function.**

***Ver* función polinómica.**

---

dependent system (p. 6) A consistent system of equations that has infinitely many solutions.

sistema dependiente (pág. 6) Sistema compatible de ecuaciones que tiene infinitas soluciones.

$$2x - y = 3$$
$$4x - 2y = 6$$

Any ordered pair $(x, 2x - 3)$ is a solution of the system above, so there are infinitely many solutions.

Cualquier par ordenado $(x, 2x - 3)$ es una solución del sistema que figura arriba, por lo que hay infinitas soluciones.

---

determinant (p. 49) A real number associated with any square matrix A, denoted by det A or $|A|$.

determinante (pág. 49) Número real asociado a toda matriz cuadrada A, denotada por det A o $|A|$.

$$\det \begin{bmatrix} 5 & 4 \\ 3 & 1 \end{bmatrix} = 5(1) - 3(4) = -7$$

$$\det \begin{bmatrix} a & b \\ c & d \end{bmatrix} = ad - cb$$

---

dimensions of a matrix (p. 38) The dimensions of a matrix with m rows and n columns are $m \times n$.

dimensiones de una matriz (pág. 38) Las dimensiones de una matriz con m filas y n columnas son $m \times n$.

A matrix with 2 rows and 3 columns has the dimensions 2 × 3 (read "2 by 3").

Una matriz con 2 filas y 3 columnas tiene por dimensiones 2 × 3 (leído "2 por 3").

---

directrix of a parabola (p. 176) *See* parabola.

directriz de una parábola (pág. 176) *Ver* parábola.

***See* parabola.**

***Ver* parábola.**

---

discrete random variable (p. 212) A variable that can take on only a countable number of distinct values.

variable aleatoria discreta (pág. 212) Una variable que puede tomar un número contable de valores diferenciados.

The Saturday night attendance at a movie theater is a discrete random variable.

La asistencia de público al cine un sábado a la noche es una variable aleatoria discreta .

ENGLISH-SPANISH GLOSSARY

discriminant of a general second-degree equation (p. 194) The expression $B^2 - 4AC$ for the equation $Ax^2 + Bxy + Cy^2 + Dx + Ey + F = 0$. Used to identify which type of conic the equation represents.

For the equation $4x^2 + y^2 - 8x - 8 = 0$, $A = 4$, $B = 0$, and $C = 1$.

$$B^2 - 4AC = 0^2 - 4(4)(1) = -16$$

Because $B^2 - 4AC < 0$, $B = 0$, and $A \neq C$, the conic is an ellipse.

discriminante de una ecuación general de segundo grado (pág. 194) La expresión $B^2 - 4AC$ para la ecuación $Ax^2 + Bxy + Cy^2 + Dx + Ey + F = 0$. Se usa para identificar qué tipo de cónica representa la ecuación.

Para la ecuación $4x^2 + y^2 - 8x - 8 = 0$, $A = 4$, $B = 0$ y $C = 1$.

$$B^2 - 4AC = 0^2 - 4(4)(1) = -16$$

Debido a que $B^2 - 4AC < 0$, $B = 0$ y $A \neq C$, la cónica es un elipse.

E

edge of a vertex-edge graph (p. 59) A line segment connecting the vertices of a graph.

***See* vertex-edge graph.**

arista de una gráfica de aristas y vértices (pág. 59) Un segmento de recta que conecta los vértices de una gráfica.

***Ver* gráfica de aristas y vértices.**

element of a matrix (p. 38) Each number in a matrix.

***See* matrix.**

elemento de una matriz (pág. 38) Cada número de una matriz.

***Ver* matriz.**

elimination method (p. 13) A method of solving a system of equations by multiplying equations by constants, then adding the revised equations to eliminate a variable.

To use the elimination method to solve the system with equations $3x - 7y = 10$ and $6x - 8y = 8$, multiply the first equation by -2 and add the equations to eliminate x.

método de eliminación (pág. 13) Método para resolver un sistema de ecuaciones en el que se multiplican ecuaciones por constantes y se agregan luego las ecuaciones revisadas para eliminar una variable.

Para usar el método de eliminación a fin de resolver el sistema con las ecuaciones $3x - 7y = 10$ y $6x - 8y = 8$, multiplica la primera ecuación por -2 y suma las ecuaciones para eliminar x.

ellipse (p. 186) The set of all points P in a plane such that the sum of the distances between P and two fixed points, called the foci, is a constant.

elipse (pág. 186) El conjunto de todos los puntos P de un plano tales que la suma de las distancias entre P y dos puntos fijos, llamados focos, es una constante.

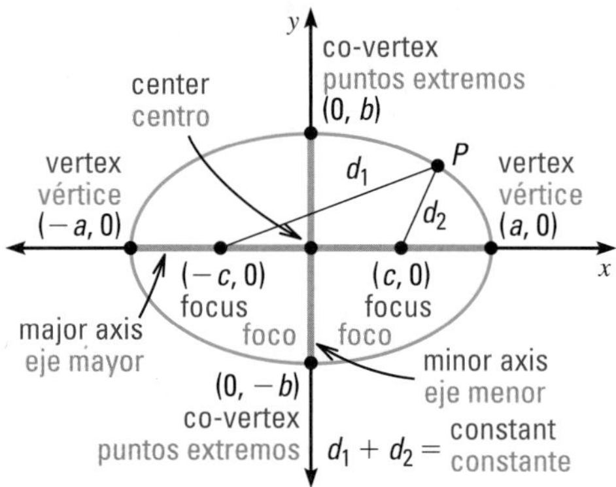

end behavior (p. 66) The behavior of the graph of a function as x approaches positive infinity $(+\infty)$ or negative infinity $(-\infty)$.

comportamiento (pág. 66) El comportamiento de la gráfica de una función al aproximarse x a infinito positivo $(+\infty)$ o a infinito negativo $(-\infty)$.

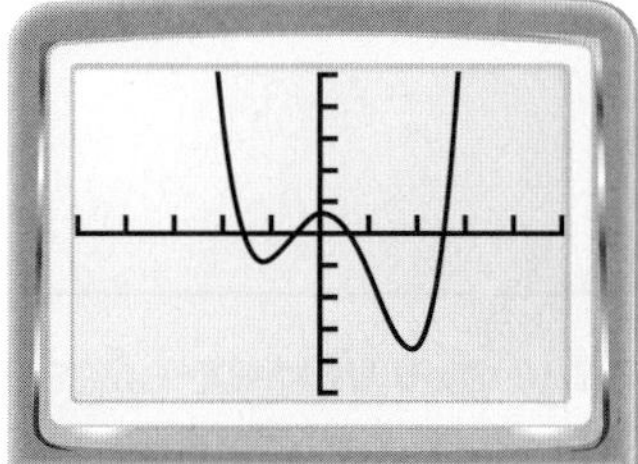

$f(x) \to +\infty$ as $x \to -\infty$ or as $x \to +\infty$.

$f(x) \to +\infty$ según $x \to -\infty$ o según $x \to +\infty$.

equal matrices (p. 38) Matrices that have the same dimensions and equal elements in corresponding positions.

matrices iguales (pág. 38) Matrices que tienen las mismas dimensiones y elementos iguales en posiciones correspondientes.

$$\begin{bmatrix} 6 & 0 \\ -\frac{4}{4} & \frac{3}{4} \end{bmatrix} = \begin{bmatrix} 3 \cdot 2 & -1 + 1 \\ -1 & 0.75 \end{bmatrix}$$

even function (p. 66) A function f is even if $f(-x) = f(x)$.

función par (pág. 66) Una función f es par si $f(-x) = f(x)$.

$f(x) = x^2 + 5$ is an even function.

$f(x) = x^2 + 5$ es una función para.

experimental group (p. 233) A group that undergoes some procedure or treatment when an experiment is conducted. *See also* control group.

One group of headache sufferers, the experimental group, is given pills containing medication. Another group, the control group, is given pills containing no medication.

grupo experimental (pág. 233) Grupo que se somete a algún procedimiento o tratamiento durante la realización de un experimento. *Ver también* grupo de control.

Un grupo de personas que sufren de dolores de cabeza, el grupo experimental, recibe píldoras que contienen el medicamento. Otro grupo, el grupo de control, recibe píldoras sin el medicamento.

experimental study (p. 233) A study in which the investigator assigns the individuals to the experimental group or the control group.

As part of a study on virus-protection software for computers, the investigator installs one brand of virus-protection software on half the computers and a different brand on the other half of the computers being used in the study.

estudio experimental (pág. 233) Un estudio en el cual el investigador asigna a los individuos al grupo experimental o al grupo de control.

Como parte de un estudio sobre software antivirus para computadoras, el investigador instala una marca de software antivirus en la mitad de las computadoras y otra marca en la otra mitad de las computadoras usadas en el estudio.

exponential decay function (p. 135) If $a > 0$ and $0 < b < 1$, then the function $y = ab^x$ is an exponential decay function with decay factor b.

función de decrecimiento exponencial (pág. 135) Si $a > 0$ y $0 < b < 1$, entonces la función $y = ab^x$ es una función de decrecimiento exponencial con factor de decrecimiento b.

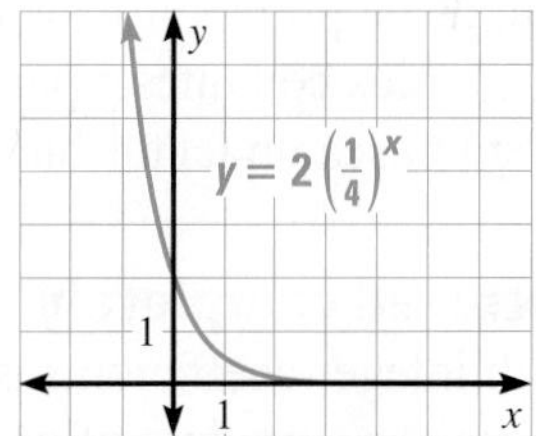

exponential equation (p. 159) An equation in which a variable expression occurs as an exponent.

$4^x = \left(\frac{1}{2}\right)^{x-3}$ is an exponential equation.

ecuación exponencial (pág. 159) Ecuación que tiene como exponente una expresión algebraica.

$4^x = \left(\frac{1}{2}\right)^{x-3}$ es una ecuación exponencial.

exponential function (p. 130) A function of the form $y = ab^x$, where $a \neq 0$, $b > 0$, and $b \neq 1$.

función exponencial (pág. 130) Función de la forma $y = ab^x$, donde $a \neq 0$, $b > 0$ y $b \neq 1$.

***See* exponential growth function *and* exponential decay function.**

***Ver* función de crecimiento exponencial *y* función de decrecimiento exponencial.**

exponential growth function (p. 130) If $a > 0$ and $b > 1$, then the function $y = ab^x$ is an exponential growth function with growth factor b.

función de crecimiento exponencial (pág. 130) Si $a > 0$ y $b > 1$, entonces la función $y = ab^x$ es una función de crecimiento exponencial con factor de crecimiento b.

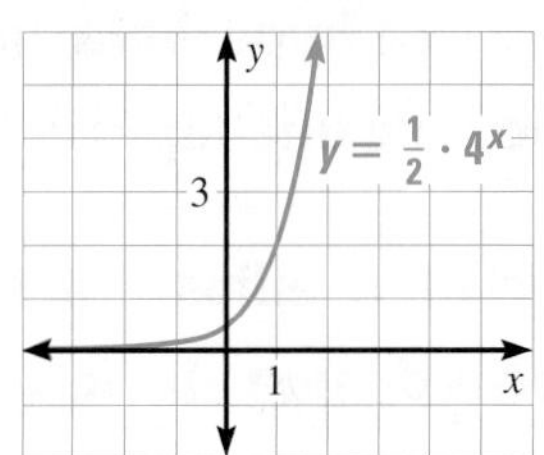

exponential inequality in one variable (p. 163) An inequality that can be written in the form $ab^x + k < 0$, $ab^x + k > 0$, $ab^x + k \leq 0$, or $ab^x + k \geq 0$, where $a \neq 0$, $b > 0$, and $b \neq 1$.

$3(2)^x - 5 \leq 0$ and $-5(0.8)^x + 2 > 0$ are exponential inequalities in one variable.

desigualdad exponencial con una variable (pág. 163) Una desigualdad que puede escribirse en la forma $ab^x + k < 0$, $ab^x + k > 0$, $ab^x + k \leq 0$, o $ab^x + k \geq 0$, donde $a \neq 0$, $b > 0$, y $b \neq 1$.

$3(2)^x - 5 \leq 0$ y $-5(0.8)^x + 2 > 0$ son desigualdades exponenciales con una variable.

F

factor by grouping (p. 76) To factor a polynomial with four terms by grouping, factor common monomials from pairs of terms, and then look for a common binomial factor.

factorizar por grupos (pág. 76) Para factorizar por grupos un polinomio con cuatro términos, factoriza unos monomios comunes a partir de los pares de términos y luego busca un factor binómico común.

$$\begin{aligned} &x^3 - 3x^2 - 16x + 48 \\ &= x^2(x - 3) - 16(x - 3) \\ &= (x^2 - 16)(x - 3) \\ &= (x + 4)(x - 4)(x - 3) \end{aligned}$$

factored completely (p. 76) A factorable polynomial with integer coefficients is factored completely if it is written as a product of unfactorable polynomials with integer coefficients.

$3x(x - 5)$ is factored completely.

$(x + 2)(x^2 - 6x + 8)$ is *not* factored completely because $x^2 - 6x + 8$ can be factored as $(x - 2)(x - 4)$.

completamente factorizado (pág. 76) Un polinomio que puede factorizarse y que tiene coeficientes enteros está completamente factorizado si está escrito como producto de polinomios que no pueden factorizarse y que tienen coeficientes enteros.

$3x(x - 5)$ está completamente factorizado.

$(x + 2)(x^2 - 6x + 8)$ *no* está completamente factorizado ya que $x^2 - 6x + 8$ puede factorizarse como $(x - 2)(x - 4)$.

feasible region (p. 30) In linear programming, the graph of the system of constraints.

***See* linear programming.**

región factible (pág. 30) En la programación lineal, la gráfica del sistema de restricciones.

***Ver* programación lineal.**

foci of a hyperbola (p. 190) *See* hyperbola.

***See* hyperbola.**

focos de una hipérbola (pág. 190) *Ver* hipérbola.

***Ver* hipérbola.**

foci of an ellipse (p. 186) *See* ellipse.

***See* ellipse.**

focos de una elipse (pág. 186) *Ver* elipse.

***Ver* elipse.**

focus of a parabola (p. 176) *See* parabola.

***See* parabola.**

foco de una parábola (pág. 176) *Ver* parábola.

***Ver* parábola.**

ENGLISH-SPANISH GLOSSARY

G

general second-degree equation in *x* and *y* **(p. 194)** The form $Ax^2 + Bxy + Cy^2 + Dx + Ey + F = 0$.

ecuación general de segundo grado en *x* e *y* **(pág. 194)** La forma $Ax^2 + Bxy + Cy^2 + Dx + Ey + F = 0$.

$16x^2 - 9y^2 - 96x + 36y - 36 = 0$ and $4x^2 + y^2 - 8x - 8 = 0$ are second-degree equations in x and y.

$16x^2 - 9y^2 - 96x + 36y - 36 = 0$ y $4x^2 + y^2 - 8x - 8 = 0$ son ecuaciones de segundo grado en x e y.

graph of a linear inequality in two variables **(p. 17)** The set of all points in a coordinate plane that represent solutions of the inequality.

gráfica de una desigualdad lineal con dos variables **(pág. 17)** El conjunto de todos los puntos de un plano de coordenadas que representan las soluciones de la desigualdad.

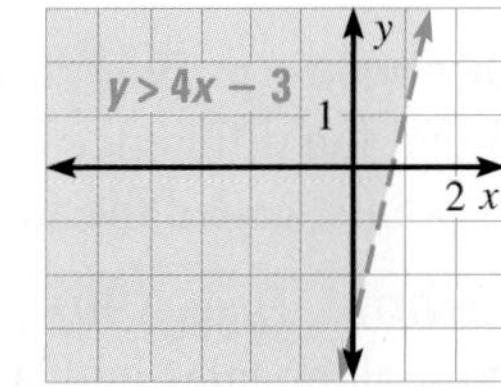

graph of a system of linear inequalities **(p. 23)** The graph of all solutions of the system.

gráfica de un sistema de desigualdades lineales **(pág. 23)** La gráfica de todas las soluciones del sistema.

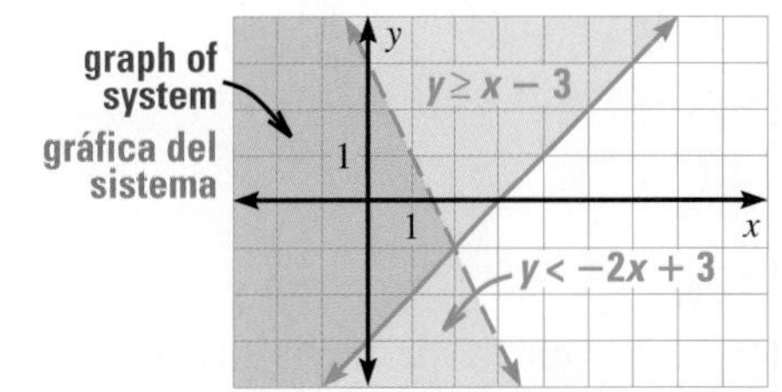

growth factor **(p. 130)** The quantity b in the exponential growth function $y = ab^x$ with $a > 0$ and $b > 1$.

factor de crecimiento **(pág. 130)** La cantidad b de la función de crecimiento exponencial $y = ab^x$, con $a > 0$ y $b > 1$.

The growth factor for the function $y = 8(3.4)^x$ is 3.4.

El factor de crecimiento de la función $y = 8(3.4)^x$ es 3.4.

H

half-life **(p. 135)** The time required for a substance or an amount to fall to half its initial value.

vida media **(p. 135)** El tiempo que requiere una sustancia o una cantidad para alcanzar la mitad de su valor inicial.

A sample of beryllium 11 will decay to half its size in 13.8 seconds. So, beryllium 11 has a half life of 13.8 seconds.

Una muestra de berilio 11 decaerá a la mitad de su tamaño en 13.8 segundos. Por lo tanto, el berilio 11 tiene una vida media de 13.8 segundos.

half-planes (p. 17) The two regions into which the boundary line of a linear inequality divides the coordinate plane.

semiplanos (pág. 17) Las dos regiones en que la recta límite de una desigualdad lineal divide al plano de coordenadas.

The solution of $y < 3$ is the half-plane consisting of all the points below the line $y = 3$.

La solución de $y < 3$ es el semiplano que consta de todos los puntos que se encuentran debajo de la recta $y = 3$.

hyperbola (p. 190) The set of all points P in a plane such that the difference of the distances from P to two fixed points, called the foci, is constant.

hipérbola (pág. 190) El conjunto de todos los puntos P de un plano tales que la diferencia de distancias entre P y dos puntos fijos, llamados focos, es constante.

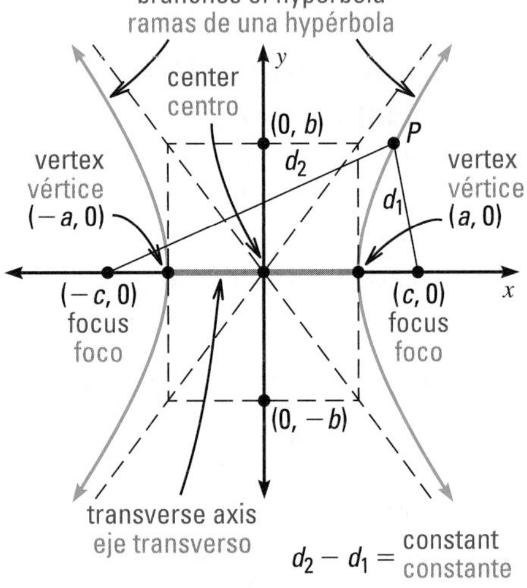

I

identity matrix (p. 54) The $n \times n$ matrix that has 1's on the main diagonal and 0's elsewhere.

matriz identidad (pág. 54) La matriz $n \times n$ que tiene los 1 en la diagonal principal y los 0 en las otras posiciones.

The 2 × 2 identity matrix is $\begin{bmatrix} 1 & 0 \\ 0 & 1 \end{bmatrix}$.

La matriz identidad 2 × 2 es $\begin{bmatrix} 1 & 0 \\ 0 & 1 \end{bmatrix}$.

inconsistent system (p. 6) A system of equations that has no solution.

sistema incompatible (pág. 6) Sistema de ecuaciones que no tiene solución.

$$x + y = 4$$
$$x + y = 1$$

The system above has no solution because the sum of two numbers cannot be both 4 and 1.

El sistema de arriba no tiene ninguna solución porque la suma de dos números no puede ser 4 y 1.

independent system (p. 6) A consistent system that has exactly one solution.

sistema independiente (pág. 6) Sistema compatible que tiene exactamente una solución.

The system consisting of $4x + y = 8$ and $2x - 3y = 18$ has exactly one solution, $(3, -4)$.

El sistema que consiste de $4x + y = 8$ y $2x - 3y = 18$ tiene exactamente una solución, $(3, -4)$.

index of a radical (p. 109) The integer n, greater than 1, in the expression $\sqrt[n]{a}$.

The index of $\sqrt[3]{-216}$ is 3.

índice de un radical (pág. 109) El número entero n, que es mayor que 1 y aparece en la expresión $\sqrt[n]{a}$.

El índice de $\sqrt[3]{-216}$ es 3.

---

interval notation (p. 81) A notation for representing an interval on a number line as a pair of numbers that are the endpoints of the interval. Parentheses are used to show that the endpoints are excluded, and brackets are used to show that the endpoints are included.

[4, 9) represents the interval between 4 and 9 that includes 4 and does not include 9. This interval can also be written as $4 \le x < 9$.

notación de intervalo (pág. 81) Una notación para representar un intervalo sobre una recta numérica como un par de números que son los extremos del intervalo. Los paréntesis se usan para indicar que los extremos se excluyen y los paréntesis cuadrados se usan para indicar que los extremos se incluyen.

[4, 9) representa el intervalo entre 4 y 9 que incluye el 4 y no incluye el 9. Este intervalo también puede escribirse como $4 \le x < 9$.

---

inverse matrices (p. 54) Two $n \times n$ matrices are inverses of each other if their product (in both orders) is the $n \times n$ identity matrix. *See also* identity matrix.

matrices inversas (pág. 54) Dos matrices $n \times n$ son inversas entre sí si su producto (de ambos órdenes) es la matriz identidad $n \times n$. *Ver también* matriz identidad.

$$\begin{bmatrix} -5 & 8 \\ 2 & -3 \end{bmatrix}^{-1} = \begin{bmatrix} 3 & 8 \\ 2 & 5 \end{bmatrix}$$

because
ya que

$$\begin{bmatrix} 3 & 8 \\ 2 & 5 \end{bmatrix} \begin{bmatrix} -5 & 8 \\ 2 & -3 \end{bmatrix} = \begin{bmatrix} 1 & 0 \\ 0 & 1 \end{bmatrix}$$

and
y

$$\begin{bmatrix} -5 & 8 \\ 2 & -3 \end{bmatrix} \begin{bmatrix} 3 & 8 \\ 2 & 5 \end{bmatrix} = \begin{bmatrix} 1 & 0 \\ 0 & 1 \end{bmatrix}.$$

L

leading coefficient (p. 66) The coefficient in the term of a polynomial function that has the greatest exponent.

***See* polynomial function.**

coeficiente inicial (pág. 66) En una función polinómica, el coeficiente del término con el mayor exponente.

***Ver* función polinómica.**

---

like radicals (p. 113) Radical expressions with the same index and radicand.

$\sqrt[4]{10}$ and $7\sqrt[4]{10}$ are like radicals.

radicales semejantes (pág. 113) Expresiones radicales con el mismo índice y el mismo radicando.

$\sqrt[4]{10}$ y $7\sqrt[4]{10}$ son radicales semejantes.

---

linear equation in three variables (p. 34) An equation of the form $ax + by + cz = d$ where a, b, and c are not all zero.

$2x + y - z = 5$ is a linear equation in three variables.

ecuación lineal con tres variables (pág. 34) Ecuación de la forma $ax + by + cz = d$, donde a, b y c no son todos cero.

$2x + y - z = 5$ es una ecuación lineal con tres variables.

ENGLISH-SPANISH GLOSSARY

linear inequality in two variables (p. 17) An inequality that can be written in one of the following forms: $Ax + By < C$, $Ax + By \le C$, $Ax + By > C$, or $Ax + By \ge C$.

$5x - 2y \ge -4$ is a linear inequality in two variables.

desigualdad lineal con dos variables (pág. 17) Desigualdad que puede escribirse de una de las siguientes formas: $Ax + By < C$, $Ax + By \le C$, $Ax + By > C$ o $Ax + By \ge C$.

$5x - 2y \ge -4$ es una desigualdad lineal con dos variables.

linear programming (p. 30) The process of maximizing or minimizing a linear objective function subject to a system of linear inequalities called constraints. The graph of the system of constraints is called the feasible region.

programación lineal (pág. 30) El proceso de maximizar o minimizar una función objetivo lineal sujeta a un sistema de desigualdades lineales llamadas restricciones. La gráfica del sistema de restricciones se llama región factible.

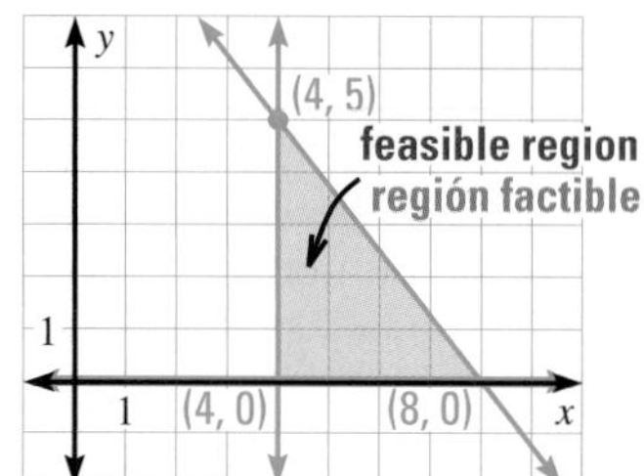

To maximize the objective function $P = 35x + 30y$ subject to the constraints $x \ge 4$, $y \ge 0$, and $5x + 4y \le 40$, evaluate P at each vertex. The maximum value of 290 occurs at (4, 5).

Para maximizar la función objetivo $P = 35x + 30y$ sujeta a las restricciones $x \ge 4$, $y \ge 0$ y $5x + 4y \le 40$, evalúa P en cada vértice. El valor máximo de 290 ocurre en (4, 5).

local maximum (p. 98) The y-coordinate of a turning point of a function if the point is higher than all nearby points.

máximo local (pág. 98) La coordenada y de un punto crítico de una función si el punto está situado más alto que todos los puntos cercanos.

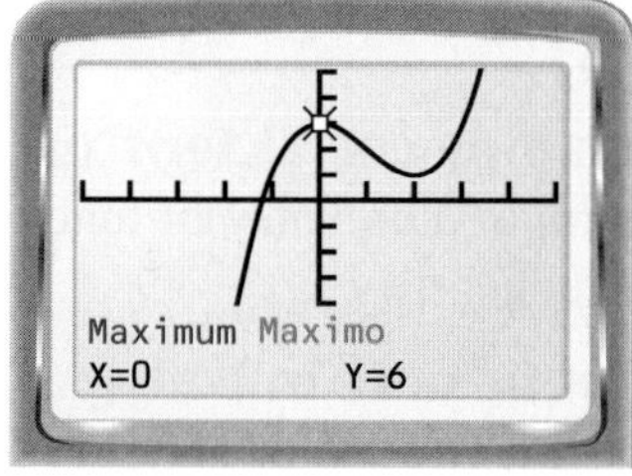

The function $f(x) = x^3 - 3x^2 + 6$ has a local maximum of $y = 6$ when $x = 0$.

La función $f(x) = x^3 - 3x^2 + 6$ tiene un máximo local de $y = 6$ cuando $x = 0$.

ENGLISH-SPANISH GLOSSARY

local minimum (p. 98) The y-coordinate of a turning point of a function if the point is lower than all nearby points.

mínimo local (pág. 98) La coordenada y de un punto crítico de una función si el punto está situado más bajo que todos los puntos cercanos.

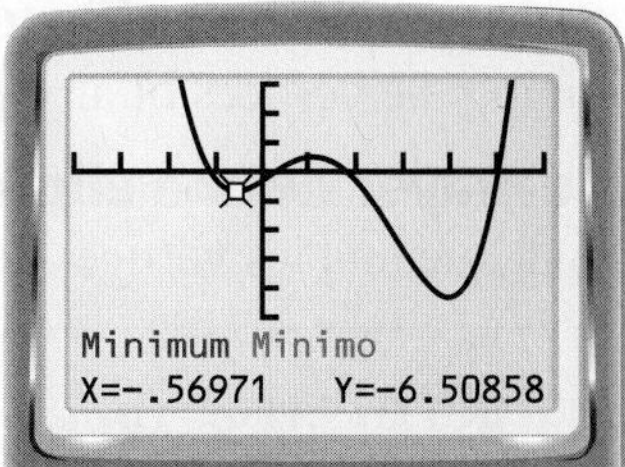

The function $f(x) = x^4 - 6x^3 + 3x^2 + 10x - 3$ has a local minimum of $y \approx -6.51$ when $x \approx -0.57$.

La función $f(x) = x^4 - 6x^3 + 3x^2 + 10x - 3$ tiene un mínimo local de $y \approx -6.51$ cuando $x \approx -0.57$.

---

logarithm of *y* with base *b* (p. 145) Let b and y be positive numbers with $b \neq 1$. The logarithm of y with base b, denoted $\log_b y$ and read "log base b of y," is defined as follows: $\log_b y = x$ if and only if $b^x = y$.

$\log_2 8 = 3$ because $2^3 = 8$.

$\log_{1/4} 4 = -1$ because $\left(\frac{1}{4}\right)^{-1} = 4$.

logaritmo de *y* con base *b* (pág. 145) Sean b e y números positivos, con $b \neq 1$. El logaritmo de y con base b, denotado por $\log_b y$ y leído "log base b de y", se define de esta manera: $\log_b y = x$ si y sólo si $b^x = y$.

$\log_2 8 = 3$ ya que $2^3 = 8$.

$\log_{1/4} 4 = -1$ ya que $\left(\frac{1}{4}\right)^{-1} = 4$.

---

logarithmic equation (p. 159) An equation that involves a logarithm of a variable expression.

$\log_5 (4x - 7) = \log_5 (x + 5)$ is a logarithmic equation.

ecuación logarítmica (pág. 159) Ecuación en la que aparece el logaritmo de una expresión algebraica.

$\log_5 (4x - 7) = \log_5 (x + 5)$ es una ecuación logarítmica.

---

logarithmic function (p. 145) A function of the form $f(x) = \log_b x$.

$f(x) = \log_3 x$ is a logarithmic function.

función logarítmica (pág. 145) Una función de la forma $f(x) = \log_b x$.

$f(x) = \log_3 x$ es una función logarítmica.

---

logarithmic inequality in one variable (p. 163) An inequality that can be written in the form $\log_b x + k < 0$, $\log_b x + k > 0$, $\log_b x + k \leq 0$, or $\log_b x + k \geq 0$, where $b > 0$, $b \neq 1$.

$\log_3 x > 0$ and $\log_5 x - 100 \leq 0$ are logarithmic inequalities in one variable.

desigualdad logarítmica con una variable (pág. 163) Una desigualdad que puede escribirse en la forma $\log_b x + k < 0$, $\log_b x + k > 0$, $\log_b x + k \leq 0$, or $\log_b x + k \geq 0$, donde $b > 0$, $b \neq 1$.

$\log_3 x > 0$ y $\log_5 x - 100 \leq 0$ son desigualdades logarítmicas con una variable.

major axis of an ellipse (p. 186) The line segment joining the vertices of an ellipse.

See ellipse.

eje mayor de una elipse (pág. 186) El segmento de recta que une los vértices de una elipse.

Ver elipse.

---

margin of error (p. 228) The margin of error gives a limit on how much the responses of a sample would be expected to differ from the responses of the population.

If 40% of the people in a poll prefer candidate A, and the margin of error is ±4%, then it is expected that between 36% and 44% of the entire population prefer candidate A.

margen de error (pág. 228) El margen de error indica un límite acerca de cuánto se prevé que diferirían las respuestas obtenidas en una muestra de las obtenidas en la población.

Si el 40% de los encuestados prefiere al candidato A y el margen de error es ±4%, entonces se prevé que entre el 36% y el 44% de la población total prefiere al candidato A.

---

matrix, matrices (p. 38) A rectangular arrangement of numbers in rows and columns. Each number in a matrix is an element.

matriz, matrices (pág. 38) Disposición rectangular de números colocados en filas y columnas. Cada numero de la matriz es un elemento.

$$A = \begin{bmatrix} 4 & -1 & 5 \\ 0 & 6 & 3 \end{bmatrix}$$

Matrix A has 2 rows and 3 columns. The element in the second row and first column is 0.

La matriz A tiene 2 filas y 3 columnas. El elemento en la segunda fila y en la primera columna es 0.

---

matrix of constants (p. 54) The matrix of constants of the linear system $ax + by = e, cx + dy = f$ is $\begin{bmatrix} e \\ f \end{bmatrix}$.

See coefficient matrix.

matriz de constantes (pág. 54) La matriz de constantes del sistema lineal $ax + by = e,$ $cx + dy = f$ es $\begin{bmatrix} e \\ f \end{bmatrix}$.

Ver matriz coeficiente.

---

matrix of variables (p. 54) The matrix of variables of the linear system $ax + by = e, cx + dy = f$ is $\begin{bmatrix} x \\ y \end{bmatrix}$.

See coefficient matrix.

matriz de variables (pág. 54) La matriz de variables del sistema lineal $ax + by = e, cx + dy = f$ es $\begin{bmatrix} x \\ y \end{bmatrix}$.

Ver matriz coeficiente.

---

minor axis of an ellipse (p. 186) The line segment joining the co-vertices of an ellipse.

See ellipse.

eje menor de una elipse (pág. 186) El segmento de recta que une los puntos extremos de una elipse.

Ver elipse.

multiplicity of roots (p. 98) The number of times a given polynomial equation has a value as a root. For the polynomial equation $f(x) = 0$, k is a repeated solution, or a root with a multiplicity greater than 1, if and only if the factor $x - k$ has an exponent greater than 1 when $f(x)$ is factored completely.

−1 is a repeated solution of the equation $(x + 1)^2(x - 3) = 0$. In this equation, −1 is a root with a multiplicity of 2.

multiplicidad de raíces (p. 98) El número de veces que una ecuación polinómica dada tiene un valor como raíz. Para la ecuación polinómica $f(x) = 0$, k es una solución repetida, o una raíz con multiplicidad mayor de 1, si y solo si el factor $x - k$ tiene un exponente mayor de 1 cuando $f(x)$ se descompone completamente en factores.

−1 es una solución repetida de la ecuación $(x + 1)^2(x - 3) = 0$. En esta ecuación, −1 es una raíz con una multiplicidad de 2.

N

natural base *e* (p. 140) An irrational number defined as follows: As n approaches $+\infty$, $\left(1 + \frac{1}{n}\right)^n$ approaches $e \approx 2.718281828$.

***See* natural logarithm.**

base natural *e* (pág. 140) Número irracional definido de esta manera: Al aproximarse n a $+\infty$, $\left(1 + \frac{1}{n}\right)^n$ se aproxima a $e \approx 2.718281828$.

***Ver* logaritmo natural.**

natural logarithm (p. 145) A logarithm with base e. It can be denoted $\log_e$, but is more often denoted by ln.

$\ln 0.3 \approx -1.204$ because $e^{-1.204} \approx (2.7183)^{-1.204} \approx 0.3$.

logaritmo natural (pág. 145) Logaritmo con base e. Puede denotarse $\log_e$, pero es más frecuente que se denote ln.

$\ln 0.3 \approx -1.204$ ya que $e^{-1.204} \approx (2.7183)^{-1.204} \approx 0.3$.

normal curve (p. 219) A smooth, symmetrical, bell-shaped curve that can model normal distributions and approximate some binomial distributions.

***See* normal distribution.**

curva normal (pág. 219) Curva lisa, simétrica y con forma de campana que puede representar distribuciones normales y aproximar a algunas distribuciones binomiales.

***Ver* distribución normal.**

normal distribution (p. 219) A probability distribution with mean $\bar{x}$ and standard deviation σ modeled by a bell-shaped curve with the area properties shown at the right.

distribución normal (pág. 219) Una distribución de probabilidad con media $\bar{x}$ y desviación normal σ representada por una curva en forma de campana y que tiene las propiedades vistas a la derecha.

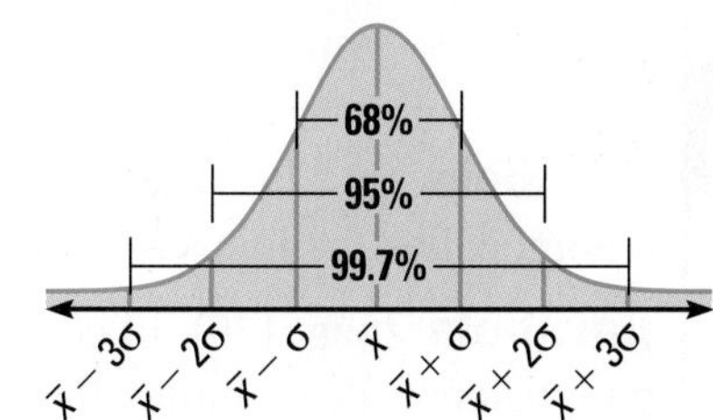

ENGLISH-SPANISH GLOSSARY

nth root of a (p. 109) For an integer n greater than 1, if $b^n = a$, then b is an nth root of a. Written as $\sqrt[n]{a}$.

raíz enésima de a (pág. 109) Para un número entero n mayor que 1, si $b^n = a$, entonces b es una raíz enésima de a. Se escribe $\sqrt[n]{a}$.

$\sqrt[3]{-216} = -6$ because $(-6)^3 = -216$.

$\sqrt[3]{-216} = -6$ ya que $(-6)^3 = -216$.

O

objective function (p. 30) In linear programming, the linear function that is maximized or minimized.

función objetivo (pág. 30) En la programación lineal, la función lineal que se maximiza o minimiza.

***See* linear programming.**

***Ver* programación lineal.**

observational study (p. 233) A study in which the assignments of individuals to the experimental group and the control group are outside the control of the investigator.

estudio observacional (p. 233) Un estudio en el cual las asignaciones de los individuos al grupo experimental y al grupo de control no son controladas por el investigador.

In a study involving headache sufferers, participants are randomly assigned to the control group or the experimental group by a computer.

En un estudio que incluye personas que padecen jaquecas, los participantes son asignados aleatoriamente al grupo de control o al grupo experimental por la computadora.

odd function (p. 66) A function f is odd if $f(-x) = -f(x)$.

función impar (p. 66) Una función f es impar si $f(-x) = -f(x)$.

$f(x) = x^3$ is an odd function.

$f(x) = x^3$ es una función impar.

ordered triple (p. 34) A set of three numbers of the form (x, y, z) that represents a point in space.

terna ordenada (pág. 34) Un conjunto de tres números de la forma (x, y, z) que representa un punto en el espacio.

The ordered triple $(2, 1, -3)$ is a solution of the equation $4x + 2y + 3z = 1$.

La terna ordenada $(2, 1, -3)$ es una solución de la ecuación $4x + 2y + 3z = 1$.

P

parabola (p. 176) The set of all points equidistant from a point called the focus and a line called the directrix.

parábola (pág. 176) El conjunto de todos los puntos equidistantes de un punto, llamado foco, y de una recta, llamada directriz.

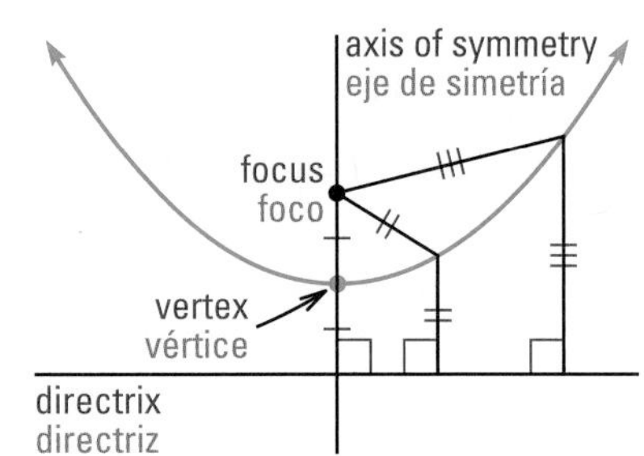

ENGLISH-SPANISH GLOSSARY

polynomial (p. 66) A monomial or a sum of monomials, each of which is called a term of the polynomial.

-14, $x^4 - \frac{1}{4}x^2 + 3$, and $7b - \sqrt{3} + \pi b^2$ are polynomials.

polinomio (pág. 66) Monomio o suma de monomios, cada uno de los cuales se llama término del polinomio.

-14, $x^4 - \frac{1}{4}x^2 + 3$ y $7b - \sqrt{3} + \pi b^2$ son polinomios.

---

polynomial function (p. 66) A function of the form $f(x) = a_n x^n + a_{n-1}x^{n-1} + \cdots + a_1 x + a_0$ where $a_n \neq 0$, the exponents are all whole numbers, and the coefficients are all real numbers.

$f(x) = 11x^5 - 0.4x^2 + 16x - 7$ is a polynomial function. The degree of $f(x)$ is 5, the leading coefficient is 11, and the constant term is -7.

función polinómica (pág. 66) Función de la forma $f(x) = a_n x^n + a_{n-1}x^{n-1} + \cdots + a_1 x + a_0$ donde $a_n \neq 0$, los exponentes son todos números enteros y los coeficientes son todos números reales.

$f(x) = 11x^5 - 0.4x^2 + 16x - 7$ es una función polinómica. El grado de $f(x)$ es 5, el coeficiente inicial es 11 y el término constante es -7.

---

polynomial inequality in one variable (p. 81) An inequality that can be written in the form

$a_n x^n + a_{n-1}x^{n-1} + \ldots + a_1 x + a_0 < 0$,

$a_n x^n + a_{n-1}x^{n-1} + \ldots + a_1 x + a_0 > 0$,

$a_n x^n + a_{n-1}x^{n-1} + \ldots + a_1 x + a_0 \leq 0$, or

$a_n x^n + a_{n-1}x^{n-1} + \ldots + a_1 x + a_0 \geq 0$, where $a_n \neq 0$.

$3x^4 + 2x^3 + 5x - 4 < 0$ and $7x^3 - 8x^2 + 1 \geq 0$ are polynomial inequalities in one variable.

desigualdad polinómica con una variable (pág. 81) Una desigualdad que puede escribirse en la forma

$a_n x^n + a_{n-1}x^{n-1} + \ldots + a_1 x + a_0 < 0$,

$a_n x^n + a_{n-1}x^{n-1} + \ldots + a_1 x + a_0 < 0$,

$a_n x^n + a_{n-1}x^{n-1} + \ldots + a_1 x + a_0 \leq 0$, ó

$a_n x^n + a_{n-1}x^{n-1} + \ldots + a_1 x + a_0 \geq 0$, donde $a_n \neq 0$.

$3x^4 + 2x^3 + 5x - 4 < 0$ y $7x^3 - 8x^2 + 1 \geq 0$ son desigualdades polinómicas con una variable.

---

polynomial long division (p. 85) A method used to divide polynomials similar to the way you divide numbers.

división desarrollada polinómica (pág. 85) Método utilizado para dividir polinomios semejante a la manera en que divides números.

$$
\begin{array}{r}
x^2 + 7x + 7 \\
x - 2\,\overline{)\,x^3 + 5x^2 - 7x + 2} \\
\underline{x^3 - 2x^2} \qquad\qquad \\
7x^2 - 7x \qquad \\
\underline{7x^2 - 14x} \qquad \\
7x + 2 \\
\underline{7x - 14} \\
16
\end{array}
$$

$$\frac{x^3 + 5x^2 - 7x + 2}{x - 2} = x^2 + 7x + 7 + \frac{16}{x - 2}$$

population (p. 228) A group of people or objects that you want information about.

A sportswriter randomly selects 5% of college baseball coaches for a survey. The population is all college baseball coaches. The 5% of coaches selected is the sample.

población (pág. 228) Grupo de personas u objetos acerca del cual deseas informarte.

Un periodista deportiva selecciona al azar al 5% de los entrenadores universitarios de béisbol para que participe en una encuesta. La población son todos los entrenadores universitarios de béisbol. El 5% de los entrenadores que resultó seleccionado es la muestra.

probability distribution (p. 212) A function that gives the probability of each possible value of a random variable. The sum of all the probabilities in a probability distribution must equal 1.

distribución de probabilidades (pág. 212) Función que indica la probabilidad de cada valor posible de una variable aleatoria. La suma de todas las probabilidades de una distribución de probabilidades debe ser igual a 1.

Let the random variable X represent the number showing after rolling a standard six-sided die.

Sea la variable aleatoria X el número que salga al lanzar un dado normal de seis caras.

Probability Distribution for Rolling a Die
Distribución de probabilidad al lanzar un dado

X	1	2	3	4	5	6
$P(X)$	$\frac{1}{6}$	$\frac{1}{6}$	$\frac{1}{6}$	$\frac{1}{6}$	$\frac{1}{6}$	$\frac{1}{6}$

Q

quadratic form (p. 76) The form $au^2 + bu + c$, where u is any expression in x.

The expression $16x^4 - 8x^2 - 8$ is in quadratic form because it can be written as $u^2 - 2u - 8$ where $u = 4x^2$.

forma cuadrática (pág. 76) La forma $au^2 + bu + c$, donde u es cualquier expresión en x.

La expresión $16x^4 - 8x^2 - 8$ está en la forma cuadrática ya que puede escribirse $u^2 - 2u - 8$, donde $u = 4x^2$.

quadratic system (p. 200) A system of equations that includes one or more equations of conics.

sistema cuadrático (pág. 200) Sistema de ecuaciones que incluye una o más ecuaciones de cónicas.

$$y^2 - 7x + 3 = 0 \qquad x^2 + 4y^2 + 8y = 16$$
$$2x - y = 3 \qquad 2x^2 - y^2 - 6x - 4 = 0$$

The systems above are quadratic systems.

Los sistemas de arriba son sistemas cuadráticos.

R

radical equation (p. 122) An equation with one or more radicals that have variables in their radicands.

ecuación radical (pág. 122) Ecuación con uno o más radicales en cuyo radicando aparecen variables.

$\sqrt[3]{2x + 7} = 3$

radical function (p. 118) A function that contains a radical with a variable in its radicand.

función radical (pág. 118) Función que tiene un radical con una variable en su radicando.

$f(x) = \frac{1}{2}\sqrt{x}, g(x) = -3\sqrt[3]{x + 5}$

radius of a circle (p. 180) The distance from the center of a circle to a point on the circle. Also, a line segment that connects the center of a circle to a point on the circle. *See also* circle.

The circle with equation $(x - 3)^2 + (y + 5)^2 = 36$ has radius $\sqrt{36} = 6$. *See also* circle.

radio de un círculo (pág. 180) La distancia desde el centro de un círculo hasta un punto del círculo. También, es un segmento de recta que une el centro de un círculo con un punto del círculo. *Ver también* círculo.

El círculo con la ecuación $(x - 3)^2 + (y + 5)^2 = 36$ tiene el radio $\sqrt{36} = 6$. *Ver también* círculo.

random variable (p. 212) A variable whose value is determined by the outcomes of a random event.

The random variable X representing the number showing after rolling a six-sided die has possible values of 1, 2, 3, 4, 5, and 6.

variable aleatoria (pág. 212) Variable cuyo valor viene determinado por los resultados de un suceso aleatorio.

La variable aleatoria X que representa el número que sale al lanzar un dado de seis caras tiene como valores posibles 1, 2, 3, 4, 5 y 6.

repeated solution (p. 94) For the polynomial equation $f(x) = 0$, k is a repeated solution if and only if the factor $x - k$ has an exponent greater than 1 when $f(x)$ is factored completely.

-1 is a repeated solution of the equation $(x + 1)^2(x - 2) = 0$.

solución repetida (pág. 94) Para la ecuación polinómica $f(x) = 0$, k es una solución repetida si y sólo si el factor $x - k$ tiene un exponente mayor que 1 cuando $f(x)$ está completamente factorizado.

-1 es una solución repetida de la ecuación $(x + 1)^2(x - 2) = 0$.

S

sample (p. 228) A subset of a population. ***See* population.**

muestra (pág. 228) Subconjunto de una población. ***Ver* población.**

scalar (p. 38) A real number by which you multiply a matrix. ***See* scalar multiplication.**

escalar (pág. 38) Número real por el que se multiplica una matriz. ***Ver* multiplicación escalar.**

scalar multiplication (p. 38) Multiplication of each element of a matrix by a real number, called a scalar.

multiplicación escalar (pág. 38) Multiplicación de cada elemento de una matriz por un número real llamado escalar.

$$-2\begin{bmatrix} 4 & -1 \\ 1 & 0 \\ 2 & 7 \end{bmatrix} = \begin{bmatrix} -8 & 2 \\ -2 & 0 \\ -4 & -14 \end{bmatrix}$$

simplest form of a radical (p. 113) A radical with index n is in simplest form if the radicand has no perfect nth powers as factors and any denominator has been rationalized.

$\sqrt[3]{135}$ in simplest form is $3\sqrt[3]{5}$.
$\frac{\sqrt[5]{7}}{\sqrt[5]{8}}$ in simplest form is $\frac{\sqrt[5]{28}}{2}$.

forma más simple de un radical (pág. 113) Un radical con índice n está escrito en la forma más simple si el radicando no tiene como factor ninguna potencia enésima perfecta y el denominador ha sido racionalizado.

$\sqrt[3]{135}$ en la forma más simple es $3\sqrt[3]{5}$.
$\frac{\sqrt[5]{7}}{\sqrt[5]{8}}$ en la forma más simple es $\frac{\sqrt[5]{28}}{2}$.

skewed distribution (p. 212) A probability distribution that is not symmetric. *See also* symmetric distribution.

distribución asimétrica (pág. 212) Distribución de probabilidades que no es simétrica. *Ver también* distribución simétrica.

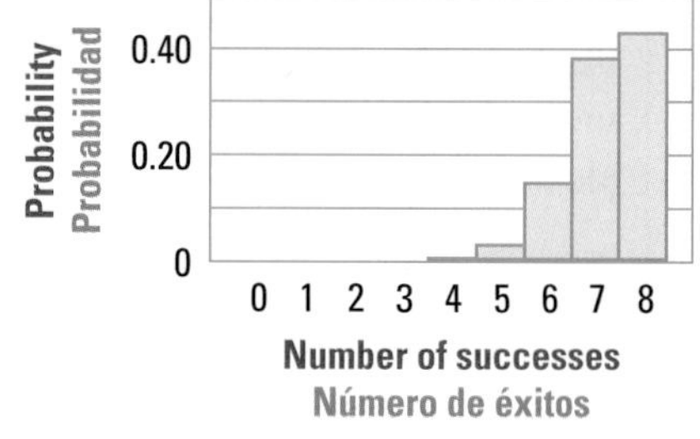

solution of a linear inequality in two variables (p. 17) An ordered pair (x, y) that produces a true statement when the values of x and y are substituted into the inequality.

The ordered pair (1, 2) is a solution of $3x + 4y > 8$ because $3(1) + 4(2) = 11$, and $11 > 8$.

solución de una desigualdad lineal con dos variables (pág. 17) Par ordenado (x, y) que produce un enunciado verdadero cuando x e y se sustituyen por sus valores en la desigualdad.

El par ordenado (1, 2) es una solución de $3x + 4y > 8$ ya que $3(1) + 4(2) = 11$, y $11 > 8$.

solution of a system of linear equations in three variables (p. 34) An ordered triple (x, y, z) whose coordinates make each equation in the system true.

solución de un sistema de ecuaciones lineales en tres variables (pág. 34) Terna ordenada (x, y, z) cuyas coordenadas hacen que cada ecuación del sistema sea verdadera.

$$\begin{aligned} 4x + 2y + 3z &= 1 \\ 2x - 3y + 5z &= -14 \\ 6x - y + 4z &= -1 \end{aligned}$$

$(2, 1, -3)$ is the solution of the system above.

$(2, 1, -3)$ es la solución del sistema de arriba.

---

solution of a system of linear equations in two variables (p. 6) An ordered pair (x, y) that satisfies each equation of the system.

solución de un sistema de ecuaciones lineales en dos variables (pág. 6) Par ordenado (x, y) que satisface cada ecuación del sistema.

$$\begin{aligned} 4x + y &= 8 \\ 2x - 3y &= 18 \end{aligned}$$

$(3, -4)$ is the solution of the system above.

$(3, -4)$ es la solución del sistema de arriba.

---

solution of a system of linear inequalities in two variables (p. 23) An ordered pair (x, y) that is a solution of each inequality in the system.

solución de un sistema de desigualdades lineales en dos variables (pág. 23) Par ordenado (x, y) que es una solución de cada desigualdad del sistema.

$$\begin{aligned} y &> -2x - 5 \\ y &\le x + 3 \end{aligned}$$

$(-1, 1)$ is a solution of the system above.

$(-1, 1)$ es una solución del sistema de arriba.

---

standard form of a polynomial function (p. 66) The form of a polynomial function that has terms written in descending order of exponents from left to right.

forma general de una función polinómica (pág. 66) La forma de una función polinómica en la que los términos se ordenan de tal modo que los exponentes disminuyen de izquierda a derecha.

The function $g(x) = 7x - \sqrt{3} + \pi x^2$ can be written in standard form as $g(x) = \pi x^2 + 7x - \sqrt{3}$.

La función $g(x) = 7x - \sqrt{3} + \pi x^2$ escrita en la forma general es $g(x) = \pi x^2 + 7x - \sqrt{3}$.

---

standard normal distribution (p. 219) The normal distribution with mean 0 and standard deviation 1. *See also* z-score.

distribución normal típica (pág. 219) La distribución normal con media 0 y desviación típica 1. *Ver también* puntuación z.

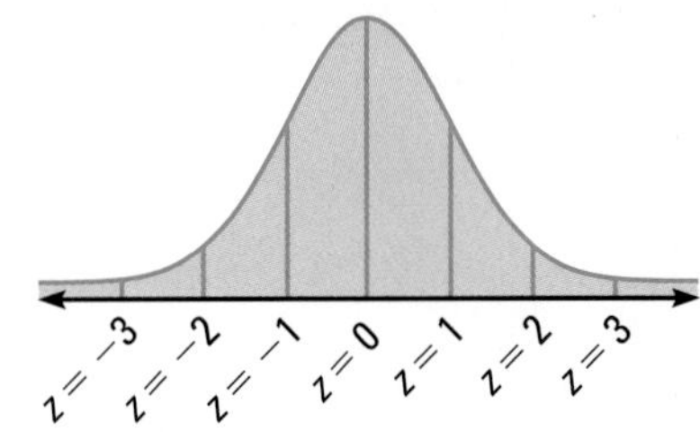

ENGLISH-SPANISH GLOSSARY

substitution method (p. 13) A method of solving a system of equations by solving one of the equations for one of the variables and then substituting the resulting expression in the other equation(s).

método de sustitución (pág. 13) Método para resolver un sistema de ecuaciones mediante la resolución de una de las ecuaciones para una de las variables seguida de la sustitución de la expresión resultante en la(s) otra(s) ecuación (ecuaciones).

$$2x + 5y = -5$$
$$x + 3y = 3$$

Solve equation 2 for x: $x = -3y + 3$. Substitute the expression for x in equation 1 and solve for y: $y = 11$. Use the value of y to find the value of x: $x = -30$.

Resuelve la ecuación 2 para x: $x = -3y + 3$. Sustituye la expresión para x en la ecuación 1 y resuelve para y: $y = 11$. Usa el valor de y para hallar el valor de x: $x = -30$.

symmetric distribution (p. 212) A probability distribution, represented by a histogram, in which you can draw a vertical line that divides the histogram into two parts that are mirror images.

distribución simétrica (pág. 212) Distribución de probabilidad representada por un histograma en la que se puede trazar una recta vertical que divida al histograma en dos partes; éstas son imágenes especulares entre sí.

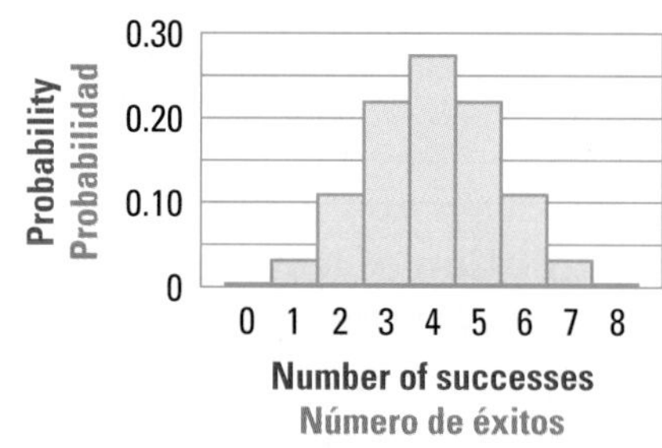

synthetic division (p. 85) A method used to divide a polynomial by a divisor of the form $x - k$.

división sintética (pág. 85) Método utilizado para dividir un polinomio por un divisor en la forma $x - k$.

−3	2	1	−8	5
		−6	15	−21
	2	−5	7	−16

$$\frac{2x^3 + x^2 - 8x + 5}{x + 3} = 2x^2 - 5x + 7 - \frac{16}{x + 3}$$

synthetic substitution (p. 66) A method used to evaluate a polynomial function.

sustitución sintética (pág. 66) Método utilizado para evaluar una función polinómica.

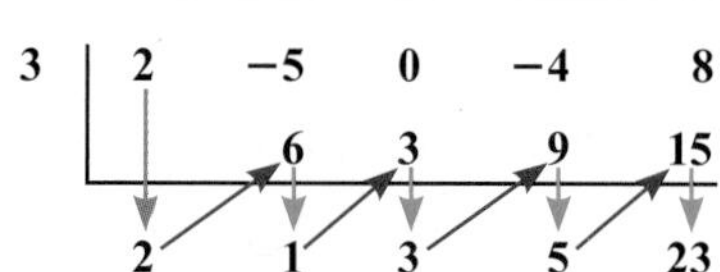

The synthetic substitution above indicates that for $f(x) = 2x^4 - 5x^3 - 4x + 8$, $f(3) = 23$.

La sustitución sintética de arriba indica que para $f(x) = 2x^4 - 5x^3 - 4x + 8$, $f(3) = 23$.

system of linear inequalities in two variables **(p. 23)** A system consisting of two or more linear inequalities in two variables. *See also* linear inequality in two variables.

sistema de desigualdades lineales con dos variables **(pág. 23)** Sistema que consiste de dos o más desigualdades lineales con dos variables. *Ver también* desigualdad lineal con dos variables.

$$x + y \le 8$$
$$4x - y > 6$$

system of three linear equations in three variables **(p. 34)** A system consisting of three linear equations in three variables. *See also* linear equation in three variables.

sistema de tres ecuaciones lineales en tres variables **(pág. 34)** Sistema formado por tres ecuaciones lineales con tres variables. *Ver también* ecuación lineal con tres variables.

$$2x + y - z = 5$$
$$3x - 2y + z = 16$$
$$4x + 3y - 5z = 3$$

system of two linear equations in two variables **(p. 6)** A system consisting of two equations that can be written in the form $Ax + By = C$ and $Dx + Ey = F$ where x and y are variables, A and B are not both zero, and D and E are not both zero.

sistema de dos ecuaciones lineales con dos variables **(pág. 6)** Un sistema que consiste en dos ecuaciones que se pueden escribir de la forma $Ax + By = C$ y $Dx + Ey = F$, donde x e y son variables, A y B no son ambos cero, y D y E tampoco son ambos cero.

$$4x + y = 8$$
$$2x - 3y = 18$$

three-dimensional coordinate system **(p. 205)** Three-dimensional space defined by the x-, y-, and z-axes. The three dimensional coordinate system is also called 3-space.

sistema de coordenadas tridimensional **(pág. 205)** Espacio tridimensional definido por los ejes x, y, y z. El sistema de coordenadas tridimensional también llamado espacio tridimensional.

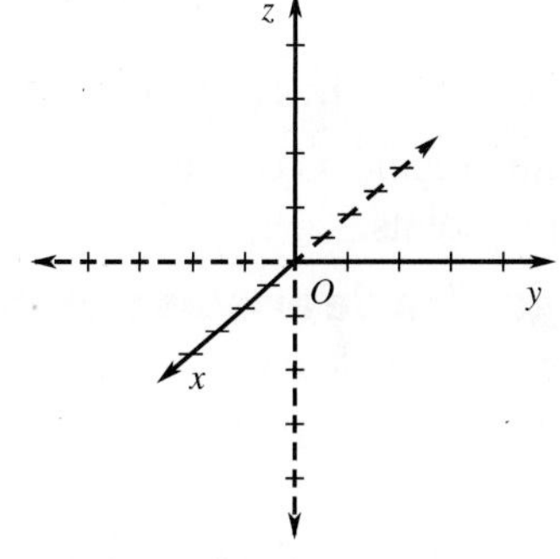

transverse axis of a hyperbola **(p. 190)** The line segment joining the vertices of a hyperbola.

eje transverso de una hipérbola **(pág. 190)** El segmento de recta que une los vértices de una hipérbola.

See **hyperbola.**

Ver **hipérbola.**

ENGLISH-SPANISH GLOSSARY

unbiased sample (p. 228) A sample that is representative of the population you want information about.

You want to poll members of the senior class about where to hold the prom. If every senior has an equal chance of being polled, then the sample is unbiased.

muestra no sesgada (pág. 228) Muestra que es representativa de la población acerca de la cual deseas informarte.

Quieres encuestar a algunos estudiantes de último curso sobre el lugar donde organizar el baile de fin de año. Si cada estudiante de último curso tiene iguales posibilidades de ser encuestado, entonces es una muestra no sesgada.

verbal model (p. 2) A word equation that represents a real-life problem.

Distance (miles) = Rate (miles/hour) • Time (hours)

modelo verbal (pág. 2) Ecuación expresada mediante palabras que representa un problema de la vida real.

Distancia (millas) = Velocidad (millas/hora) • Tiempo (horas)

vertex of a parabola (p. 176) The point on a parabola that lies on the axis of symmetry.

***See* parabola.**

vértice de una parábola (pág. 176) El punto de una parábola que se encuentra en el eje de simetría.

***Ver* parábola.**

vertex of a vertex-edge graph (p. 59) A point on a vertex-edge graph that is either the endpoint of an edge or not part of an edge.

***See* vertex-edge graph.**

vértice de una gráfica de aristas y vértices (pág. 59) Un punto de una gráfica de aristas y vértices que es el extremo de una arista o que no es parte una arista.

***Ver* gráfica de aristas y vértices.**

vertex-edge graph (p. 59) A collection of points and line segments connecting some (possibly empty) subset of the points.

gráfica de aristas y vértices (pág. 59) Una colección de puntos y segmentos de recta que conectan algún subconjunto (posiblemente vacío) de los puntos.

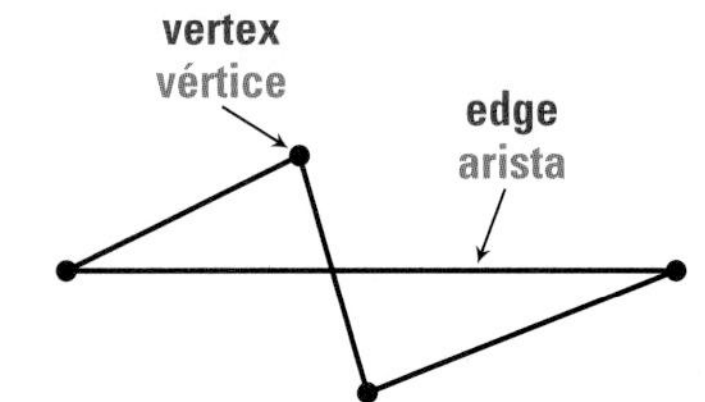

vertices of a hyperbola (p. 190) The points of intersection of a hyperbola and the line through the foci of the hyperbola.

***See* hyperbola.**

vértices de una hipérbola (pág. 190) Los puntos de intersección de una hipérbola y la recta que pasa por los focos de la hipérbola.

***Ver* hipérbola.**

ENGLISH-SPANISH GLOSSARY

vertices of an ellipse (p. 186) The points of intersection of an ellipse and the line through the foci of the ellipse.

See **ellipse.**

vértices de una elipse (pág. 186) Los puntos de intersección de una elipse y la recta que pasa por los focos de la elipse.

Ver **elipse.**

Z

zero of a function (p. 149) A number k is a zero of a function f if $f(k) = 0$.

The zeros of the function $f(x) = 2(x + 3)(x - 1)$ are -3 and 1.

cero de una función (pág. 149) Un número k es un cero de una función f si $f(k) = 0$.

Los ceros de la función $f(x) = 2(x + 3)(x - 1)$ son -3 y 1.

z-score (p. 219) The number z of standard deviations that a data value lies above or below the mean of the data set: $z = \frac{x - \bar{x}}{\sigma}$.

A normal distribution has a mean of 76 and a standard deviation of 9. The z-score for $x = 64$ is $z = \frac{x - \bar{x}}{\sigma} = \frac{64 - 76}{9} \approx -1.3$.

puntuación z (pág. 219) El número z de desviaciones típicas que un valor se encuentra por encima o por debajo de la media del conjunto de datos: $z = \frac{x - \bar{x}}{\sigma}$.

Una distribución normal tiene una media de 76 y una desviación típica de 9. La puntuación z para $x = 64$ es $z = \frac{x - \bar{x}}{\sigma} = \frac{64 - 76}{9} \approx -1.3$.

Index

A

Absolute value inequality
  graphing, 18, 20, 21
    in a system, 24, 25, 27
Activities, *See also* Technology Activities
  algebra
    exponential and logarithmic equations, 144
    inverse matrices, 53
    radicals and rational exponents, 108
    systems with many or no solutions, 12
    zeros of a polynomial function, 93
  data analysis
    collecting data, 223
    explore a normal curve, 218
  geometry, draw an ellipse, 185
Addition
  of like radicals, 114–116
  of like roots, 114–116
Algebra, *See* Equation(s); Exponential equation(s); Exponential function(s); Function(s); Linear system(s); Logarithmic equation(s); Logarithmic inequality (inequalities); Polynomial equation(s); Polynomial function(s); Polynomial inequality (inequalities); Radical equation(s)
Approximation, *See also* Estimation
  of binomial distribution using normal distribution, 224–227
  of *n*th roots, 109–112
Assessment
  Performance Task, 64, 106, 128, 174, 210, 238
  Unit Test, 63–64, 105–106, 127–128, 173–174, 209–210, 237–238
Associative property of addition, 38
  applied to matrices, 38–42
Associative property of matrix multiplication, 43
  applying, 43–47
Associative property of scalar multiplication, 43
  applying, 43–47
Asymptote(s)
  of the graph of an exponential function, 130
  of a hyperbola, 190
Average rate of change
  exponential functions and, 149–154
  logarithmic functions and, 150–154
Axis of symmetry, of a parabola, 176

B

Base
  of a common logarithm, 145
  of an exponential expression, 144
  of an exponential function
    decay, 135
    growth, 130
  of a logarithmic expression, 144
  of a natural logarithm, 145
Biased sample, 228
Binomial distribution(s), 212
  approximating using normal distribution, 224–227
  constructing and interpreting, 212–217
  creating on a graphing calculator, 217
  histogram of, 212–217
  skewed, 212
  symmetrical, 212
Binomial experiment, 212
  probability and, 212–217
Break-even analysis, 7, 9, 11

C

Calculator, *See also* Graphing calculator
  approximating roots with, 109–112
Center
  of a circle, 180
  of an ellipse, 186
  of a hyperbola, 190
Change-of-base formula, 156–158
Checking reasonableness, 9, 11
Checking solutions
  algebraically, 6–11
  using a calculator, 117, 160
  graphically, 84
  using substitution, 122, 123
  using synthetic substitution, 67
Circle(s), *See also* Conic section(s), 180
  center of, 180
  discriminant of an equation of, 194
  finding equations of lines tangent to, 181–183
  graphing equations of, 180–183
  radius of, 180
  writing equations of, 180–183
Classifying
  binomial distributions, 214
  conic sections, 194–199
  linear systems, 7–11
  samples, 228–231
  zeros of polynomial functions, 94–97
Coefficient matrix, 49
Common logarithm, *See also* Logarithm(s), 145
Communication, describing in words, *Throughout. See for example* 5, 9, 20, 21, 25, 33, 35, 70, 75, 78, 83, 84
Commutative property of addition, 38
  applied to matrices, 38–42
Complex conjugates theorem, 94
  applying, 94–97

INDEX

Compound interest, 131–133, 161
continuously, 141, 161
Conics, *See also* Conic section(s), 194
Conic section(s), *See also* Circle(s); Ellipse(s); Hyperbola(s); Parabola(s)
classifying, 194–199
general second-degree equation, 194
discriminant of, 194
translating, 194–199
equations of, 194–199
Conjugates, 113
Consistent system, 6
dependent, 6
independent, 6
Constant(s), matrix of, 54
Constraints, 30
linear programming and, 30–33
Continuously compounded interest, 141, 161
Continuous random variable, 212
Control group, 233
Convenience sample, 228
Corollary, to the fundamental theorem of algebra, 94
Co-vertices, of an ellipse, 186
Cramer's rule, 49
to solve linear systems, 49–52
Critical thinking, exercises, 70, 79, 84, 92, 97, 103, 112
Critical *x*-value, 163, 165
Cube root function(s), 118–121

D

Data
analyzing
using binomial distribution, 212–217, 224–227
using break-even analysis, 7, 9, 11
finding margin of error, 229–232
identifying bias, 229–231
using normal distribution, 219–222, 224–227
collecting
identifying flaws in an experiment, 234–236
identifying studies, 233–236
sampling methods, 228–231
displaying, in histograms, 212–217
Decay factor, 135
Decay function(s), *See also* Exponential function(s)
exponential, 135
decay factor, 135
depreciation and, 138, 139
domain of, 136–138
evaluating on a graphing calculator, 139
graphing, 135–138
half-life and, 136–138
range of, 136–138
translation and, 136–138
Decreasing on an interval, 149–154
Degree of a polynomial function, 66
Dependent system, 6
Depreciation, exponential decay functions and, 138, 139
Descartes' rule of signs, 94
Determinatant
of a matrix, 49
evaluating, 49–52
rules for, 49
Dimensions of a matrix, 38
Directrix, 176
Discrete random variable, 212
Discriminant
of an equation of a circle, 194
of an equation of an ellipse, 194
of a general second-degree equation of a conic section, 194
of an equation of a hyperbola, 194
of an equation of a parabola, 194
Distance formula, 4
equation of a circle and, 180
to find distance in space, 205, 207–208
Distance between two points
in a coordinate plane, 180
in three-dimensional space, 205, 207–208
Distributive property of addition, 38
applied to matrices, 38–42
Distributive property of subtraction, 38
applied to matrices, 38–42
Domain
of an exponential growth function, 131–133
of a function involving natural base *e*, 140–143
of a logarithmic function, 146–148
Doubling time, exponential growth functions and, 131, 132, 133
Draw conclusions, 12, 53, 93, 108, 144, 185, 218, 223
Draw a diagram, problem-solving strategy, 3–5

E

Edge, of a vertex-edge graph, 59
Element(s), of a matrix, 38
Elimination method, for solving linear systems, 14–16, 34–37
Ellipse(s), *See also* Conic section(s), 186
area of, 188
center of, 186
co-vertices of, 186
discriminant of an equation of, 194
drawing, 185
foci of, 186
graphing equations of, 186–189
major axis of, 186
minor axis of, 186
vertices of, 186
writing equations of, 186–189
End behavior
of a polynomial function, 66
describing, 68–70
Equal matrices, 38
Equation(s), *See also* Formulas; Function(s); Linear-quadratic system; Linear system(s); Quadratic system(s)
of circles, 180–184
of ellipses, 186–189

exponential, 159, 161–162
general second-degree of a conic section, 194
discriminant of, 194
of hyperbolas, 190–193
linear, 34
logarithmic, 159–162
matrix, 40–42
of parabolas, 176–179
polynomial, 77–80, 98
radical, 122–125
of translated conic sections, 194–199
Error analysis, *Throughout. See for example* 4, 8, 19, 21, 25, 33, 75, 78, 83, 100, 116, *See also* Margin of error
Estimation, *See also* Approximation
from graphs, 6, 8, 10, 11, 131, 132, 133, 134, 136, 137, 138, 141, 153, 154
Euler number, 140
Even function, 66
Experiment(s)
identifying flaws in, 234–236
observational results and, 223
Experimental group, 233
Experimental study, 233
identifying, 233, 235, 236
Exponent(s)
rational
evaluating expressions with, 108–117
solving equations with, 123–125
Exponential equation(s), 159
as logarithmic equations, 144, 145, 147–148
solving, 159, 161–162
using a graphing calculator, 159
Exponential expression(s)
base of, 144
evaluating, 108–117, 144
Exponential function(s), 130
asymptote, 130
decay, 135
decay factor, 135
depreciation and, 138, 139
domain of, 136–138
evaluating on a graphing calculator, 139
graphing, 135–138
half-life and, 136–138
range of, 136–138
translation and, 136–138
graphs of
average rate of change, 149–154
intervals of increase and decrease, 149–154
zeros, 149–154
growth, 130
compound interest and, 131–133
domain of, 131–133
doubling time and, 131, 132, 133
graphing, 130–134
growth factor, 130
range of, 131–133
translations and, 131–133
involving natural base *e*, 140–143
continuously compounded interest and, 141
domain of, 140–143
graphing, 140–143
range of, 140–143
translations and, 140, 142, 143
logarithmic functions and, 145–148
natural base, 140–143
writing, 169–172
Exponential inequalities in one variable, 163
critical *x*-value of, 163
solving, 163–164, 167–168
using a graphing calculator, 164
Expression(s)
conjugates, 113
exponential, 108–117
logarithmic, 155–158
natural base, 140, 142, 143
in quadratic form, 76
radical, 108–121

F

Factor(s)
decay, 135
growth, 130
Factoring
completely, 76
polynomials, 76–79
using the factor theorem, 85–88
by grouping, 76
using the remainder theorem, 85–88
to solve polynomial equations, 77–79
Factor theorem, 85
applying, 85–88
Feasible region, 30
maximum value and, 30
minimum value and, 30
Focus (foci)
of an ellipse, 186
of a hyperbola, 190
of a parabola, 176
Formulas
area
of an ellipse, 188
of a parallelogram, 4
of a rectangle, 2
change of base, 156
compound interest, 131
continuously compounded interest, 141
depreciation, 138
distance, 4
in space, 205
lateral surface area
of a cone, 125, 128
of a cylinder, 125
margin of error, 228
table of, 242–243
volume
of a paraboloid, 179
of a sphere, 208
z-score, 219
Function(s), *See also* Exponential function(s); Graphing; Polynomial function(s)
cube root, 118–121
even, 66

INDEX

involving natural base *e*, 140–143
linear objective, 30–33
logarithmic, 144–148, 150–154
natural base, 140–143, 151–152
objective, 30–33
odd, 66
radical, 118
graphing, 118–121
square root, 118–121
Fundamental theorem of algebra, 94
applying, 94–97
corollary to, 94

G

General second-degree equation
of a conic section, 194
discriminant of, 194
Geometry, *See* Circle(s); Conic section(s); Ellipse(s); Formulas; Hyperbola(s); Parabola(s); Three-dimensional coordinate system
Graph(s)
of polynomial functions, analyzing, 98–104
vertex edge, 59
using, 59–62
Graphing
absolute value inequalities, 18, 20, 21
in a system, 24, 25, 27
equations
of circles, 180–184
of ellipses, 186–189
of hyperbolas, 190–193
of parabolas, 176–179
of a plane, 206–208
functions
cube root, 118–121
exponential decay, 135–138
exponential growth, 130–134
involving natural base *e*, 140–143
logarithmic, 146–148, 151–152
natural base, 140–143
polynomial, 68–70, 71–75, 98–104
radical, 118–121
square root, 118–121
linear inequalities, 17–22
systems of, 23–29
linear programming and, 30–33
linear systems, 6–11
to solve quadratic systems, 200–204
Graphing calculator
create a binomial distribution, 217
evaluating exponential decay models, 139
evaluating radicals and rational exponents, 108
finding the inverse of a matrix, 55, 57, 58
finding local maximums and minimums, 104
finding turning points, 98
finding zeros of a polynomial function, 93, 96, 97
graphing natural base functions, 141
graphing radical functions, 119
graphing systems of linear equations, 12
to make a table of values, 117
matrices representing vertex-edge graphs and, 60
maximizing a polynomial function, 99
to perform matrix operations, 48
to solve an exponential equation, 159
to solve an exponential inequality, 164
to solve a logarithmic equation, 160
to solve a logarithmic inequality, 166
to solve quadratic systems, 200, 202–204
solving polynomial equations using a graph, 80
solving radical equations using a graph, 126
Growth factor, 130
Growth function(s), *See also* Exponential function(s)
exponential, 130
compound interest and, 131–133
domain of, 131–133
doubling time and, 131, 132, 133
graphing, 130–134
range of, 131–133
translations and, 131–133

H

Half-life, 135
exponential decay functions and, 136–138
Half-plane, 17
Histogram, probability, 212–217
Hyperbola(s), *See also* Conic section(s), 190
center of, 190
discriminant of equation of, 194
foci of, 190
graphing equations of, 190–193
transverse axis of, 190
vertices of, 190
writing equations of, 191–193
Hypothesis (hypotheses), testing, 225–227

I

Identity matrix, 54
Inconsistent system, 6
Increasing on an interval, 149–154
Independent system, 6
Index of a radical, 108, 109
Inequalities, *See* Linear inequalities; Logarithmic inequality (inequalities); Polynomial inequality (inequalities); Systems of linear inequalities
Interest
compound, 131–133
continuously compounded, 141

INDEX

Interval(s)
of decrease, 149–154
of increase, 149–154
Inverse matrices, 54
identifying, 53
to solve linear systems, 56–58
Inverses, exponential and logarithmic functions, 144–148
Irrational conjugates theorem, 94
applying, 94–97

L

Left distributive property, 43
applying, 43–47
Linear equation(s), *See also* Linear system(s)
in three variables, 34
Linear inequalities, *See also* Systems of linear inequalities
constraints as, 30–33
in two variables, 17
graphing, 17–22
half-plane and, 17
solution of, 17
Linear objective function, 30
linear programming and, 30–33
Linear programming, 30–33
constraints and, 30–33
feasible region and, 30
linear objective function and, 30–33
Linear-quadratic system
solving
by graphing, 200–204
by substitution, 200–203
Linear system(s), 6
classifying, 7–11
consistent, 6
dependent, 6
independent, 6
inconsistent, 6
with many or no solutions, 12, 14–16
solution of, 6
solving
algebraically, 13–16, 34–37
using Cramer's rule, 49–52
by graphing, 6–11
using inverse matrices, 56–58
in three variables, 34–37
solution of, 34
writing, 7, 9, 11
Local maximum, 98
finding, 98–104
on a graphing calculator, 104
Local minimum, 98
finding, 98–104
on a graphing calculator, 104
Log, 144, 145
Logarithm(s), 144, 145
common, 145
evaluating, 145–148
natural, 145
properties of, 155
applying, 155–158
Logarithmic equation(s), 159
exponential equations and, 144, 145, 147–148
solving, 160–162
using a graphing calculator, 160
Logarithmic expression(s)
base of, 144
change-of-base formula and, 156–158
condensing, 156–158
expanding, 155, 157, 158
Logarithmic function(s), 145
domain of, 146–148
exponential functions and, 144–148
graphing, 146–148, 151–152
graphs of
average rate of change, 150–154
intervals of increase and decrease, 150–154
zeros, 150–154
natural
graphing, 151–152
translating, 151–152
power, writing, 170–172
range of, 146–148
translation and, 146–148, 151–152
Logarithmic inequality (inequalities) in one variable, 163
critical x-value of, 165
solving, 165–168
using a graphing calculator, 166
Logarithm of y with base b, 145
Logical reasoning, *See also* Error analysis; Properties; Reasoning; Theorem(s)
identifying bias, 229–231
testing hypotheses, 224–227
Look for a pattern, problem-solving strategy, 2–5

M

Major axis, of an ellipse, 186
Margin of error, 228
finding, 229–232
Matrix (matrices), 38
adding, 38–42, 48
coefficient, 49
of constants, 54
determinant of, 49
evaluating, 49–52
dimensions of, 38
elements of, 38
equal, 38
identity, 54
inverse, 54
identifying, 53
to solve linear systems, 55–58
multiplying, 43–48
by a scalar, 38–42
properties of operations, 38, 43
applying, 38–47
to represent a vertex-edge graph, 60–62
subtracting, 38–42, 48
of variables, 54
Matrix equation(s), 40–42
Measurement, *See also* Formulas
distance, in space, 205, 207–208
Measures, table of, 241
Minor axis, of an ellipse, 186
Multiple representations, *Throughout. See for example* 5, 9, 11, 26, 28, 57, 58, 69, 75, 84
Multiplication, scalar, 38–42
Multiplicity of a root, 98

Multi-step problems, *Throughout. See for example* 12, 13, 14, 18, 23, 24, 29, 31, 34, 35, 39, 44

N

Natural base *e*, 140
functions involving, 140–143
graphing, 140–143
Natural base expression(s), simplifying, 140, 142, 143
Natural base function(s), 140–143
domain of, 140, 142, 143
graphing, 140–143
on a graphing calculator, 141
range of, 140, 142, 143
translations and, 140, 142, 143
Natural logarithm, 145
Normal curve, 218, 219
Normal distribution, 218, 219
to approximate binomial distribution, 224–227
interpreting, 219–222
normal curve and, 218
probability and, 219–222, 224–227
standard, 219
***n*th root(s),** 108, 109
approximating, 109–112
evaluating, 108–112

O

Objective function, 30
linear programming and, 30–33
Observational study, 233
identifying, 233, 235, 236
Odd function, 66
Ordered pair, as solution of a linear inequality, 17
Ordered triple, 205
as solution of a system with three variables, 34

P

Parabola(s), See also Conic section(s), 176
axis of symmetry of, 176
directrix of, 176
discriminant of an equation of, 194
focus of, 176
graphing equations of, 176–179
writing equations of, 177–179
Parent function
cube root, 118
square root, 118
Performance Tasks
art, 106
campus parking, 210
finance, 174
MP3 players, 64
park design, 128
restaurants, 238
Plane, graphing the equation of, 206–208
Polynomial(s), *See also* Polynomial equation(s); Polynomial function(s), 66
degree of, 66
dividing, 85–88
factoring, 76–79
using the factor theorem, 85–88
using the remainder theorem, 85–88
Polynomial curve fitting, 37
Polynomial equation(s)
multiplicity of a root of, 98
solving
by factoring, 77–79
using a graph, 80
Polynomial function(s), 66
characteristics of, 68–70
complex conjugates theorem and, 94–97
Descartes' rule of signs and, 94
end behavior of, 66
describing, 68–70
evaluating, 66–70
even, 66
fundamental theorem of algebra and, 94–97
graphing, 68–70, 98–104
as translations, 71–75
graphs of, analyzing, 98–104
identifying, 66, 69, 70
irrational conjugates theorem and, 94–97
local maximum of, 98
finding, 98–104
local minimum of, 98
finding, 98–104
multiplicity of a root of, 98
odd, 66
repeated solution and, 94
standard form of, 66
translating, 71–75
zeros of
classifying, 94–97
finding, 86–97
Polynomial inequality (inequalities), 81
solving
algebraically, 81, 83, 84
using a graph, 82–84
Polynomial long division, 85
using, 85–88
Population, 228
sampling, 228–231
Power property
of logarithms, 155
applying, 155–158
Probability
binomial distribution and, 212–217, 224–227
binomial experiment, 212–217
continuous random variable, 212
discrete random variable, 212
normal distribution and, 218–222
random variable, 212
Probability distribution(s), 212
binomial, 212–217, 224–227
histogram of, 212–217
normal, 218–222, 224–227
skewed, 212
symmetric, 212
Probability histogram, 212–217
Problem solving
break-even analysis, 7, 9, 11
strategies, 2–5
draw a diagram, 3–5
use a formula, 2, 4–5
look for a pattern, 2–5
Problem Solving Workshop, 29, 80, 117, 134, 184, 232
Product property of logarithms, 155
applying, 155–158

Properties
of exponents, 113
applying, 113–117
of logarithms, 155
applying, 155–158
of matrix operations, 38, 43
applying, 38–47
of radicals, 113
applying, 113–117
table of, 245–246
Proportional reasoning, *See* Exponential function(s); Function(s); Polynomial function(s)

Q

Quadratic form
of an expression, 76
factoring polynomials in, 76–79
Quadratic system(s), 200
solving
by graphing, 200–204
using substitution, 200–203
Quotient property of logarithms, 155
applying, 155–158

R

Radical(s), *See also* Radical equation(s); Radical expression(s); Radical function(s)
adding, 114–116
properties of, 113
applying, 113–117
simplest form, 113
subtracting, 114–116
Radical equation(s), 122
solving, 122–125
using a graphing calculator, 126
Radical expression(s)
evaluating, 108–116, 118–121
involving variables, 114–116
Radical function(s), 118
graphing, 118–121
on a graphing calculator, 119, 121
Radius, of a circle, 180
Random sample, 228
Random variable, 212
continuous, 212
discrete, 212
probability distribution, 212
Range
of an exponential growth function, 131–133
of a function involving natural base *e*, 140–143
of a logarithmic function, 146–148
Rational exponent(s)
applying properties of, 113–117
evaluating expressions with, 108–112
solving equations with, 123–125
variable expressions and, 114–116
Rational root theorem, 89
Reasoning, *See also* Logical reasoning
exercises, 93, 218, 223
Rectangular prism, in the three-dimensional coordinate system, 207
Remainder theorem, 85
applying, 85–88
Repeated solution, 94
Right distributive property, 43
applying, 43–47
Root(s)
adding, 114–116
*n*th
approximating, 109–112
evaluating, 108–112
subtracting, 114–116

S

Sample(s), 228
biased, 228
classifying, 228–231
convenience, 228
margin of error, 228
finding, 229–232
random, 228
self-selected, 228
systematic, 228
unbiased, 228
Scalar, 38
multiplying by, 38–42
Scalar multiplication, 38–42
Self-selected sample, 228
Simplest form radical, 113
Skewed probability distribution, 212
Solution
of a linear inequality in two variables, 17
of a system of linear equations, 6, 12
of a system of linear inequalities, 23
of a system with three variables, 34
Sphere, writing the equation for, 206–208
Square root function(s), 118–121
Square roots, table of, 247
Squares, table of, 247
Standard form
equation of a circle, 180–183
equation of a parabola, 176–179
of a polynomial function, 66
Standard normal distribution, *See also* Normal distribution, 219
Standard normal table, 248
using, 220–222
Statistics
binomial distribution, 212–217, 224–227
margin of error, 228–232
normal curve, 218, 219
normal distribution, 219–222, 224–227
samples and, 228–232
Substitution method
for solving linear systems, 13–16
for solving quadratic systems, 200–203
Subtraction
of like radicals, 114–116
of like roots, 114–116
Symbols, table of, 240

INDEX

Symmetric probability distribution, 212
Synthetic division, 85
using, 85–88
Synthetic substitution, 66
to evaluate polynomials, 66–70
Systematic sample, 228
Systems of linear inequalities
graphing, 23–29
solution of, 23
System of three linear equations, *See also* Linear system(s), 34–37
System of two linear equations, *See also* Linear system(s), 6–11

T

Table of formulas, 242–243
Table of measures, 241
Table of properties, 245–246
Table of squares and square roots, 247
Table of symbols, 240
Table of theorems, 244
Tangent line, finding equations of, 181–183
Technology activities, *See also* Graphing calculator
graphing calculator
creating a binomial distribution, 217
evaluating exponential decay models, 139
finding local maximums and minimums, 104
matrix operations, 48
solving quadratic systems, 204
solving radical equations using a graph, 126
Theorem(s)
complex conjugates, 94
applying, 94–97
factor, 85
applying, 85–88
table of, 244
fundamental theorem of algebra, 94
applying, 94–97
corollary to, 94
irrational conjugates, 94
applying, 94–97
rational root, 89
remainder, 85
applying, 85–88
Three-dimensional coordinate system, 205
distance between two points, 205, 207–208
graphing the equation of a plane, 206–208
ordered triple, 205
rectangular prism in, 207
writing the equation of a sphere, 206–208
3-space, 205
Transformation, *See* Translation(s)
Translation(s)
of conic sections, 194–199
of exponential decay functions, 136–138
of exponential growth functions, 131–133
of functions involving natural base *e*, 140, 142, 143
of logarithmic functions, 146–148, 151–152
of polynomial functions, 71–75
of radical functions, 118–121
Transverse axis, of a hyperbola, 190

U

Unbiased sample, 228
Use a formula, problem solving strategy, 2, 4–5

V

Variable(s), matrix of, 54
Verbal model, 2
examples, 2, 77, 90
Vertex (vertices)
of an ellipse, 186
of a hyperbola, 190
of a parabola, 176
of a vertex-edge graph, 59
Vertex-edge graph(s), 59
edge of, 59
representing with a matrix, 60–62
using, 59–62
vertex of, 59
Visual thinking, *See* Circle(s); Conic section(s); Ellipse(s); Graph(s); Graphing; Hyperbola(s); Parabola(s); Three-dimensional coordinate system
Vocabulary, lesson introduction, *Throughout. See for example* 2, 6, 13, 17, 23, 30, 34, 38, 43, 49, 54, 59

W

Writing, *See also* Communication
equations
of circles, 180–183
of ellipses, 187–189
of hyperbolas, 191–193
of parabolas, 177–179
of spheres in three-dimensional space, 206–208
of translated conic sections, 195–199
exponential functions, 169–172
linear systems, 7, 9, 11
power functions, 170–172

X

***x*-value,** critical, 163, 165

Z

Zero(s)
of an exponential function, 149–154
of a logarithmic function, 150–154
of a polynomial function, 86–97
***z*-score,** 219
finding, 220–222

INDEX

Selected Answers

UNIT 1

1.1 Exercise Set A (p. 4)

1. 315 mi **3.** 63 mi/h **5.** 54 ft^2 **7.** 13 m

9. In the table the inputs increase by 5. An equation that represents the table is $y = 2x + 9$.

11. $y = 3x + 34$ **13.** $y = 58 - 11x$ **15.** 5 **17.** 3

1.1 Exercise Set B (p. 5)

1. $y = 6x + 22$

3. a. \$57; \$62; \$67; \$72; *Sample answer:* 175 text messages **b.** $69.2 = 0.1x + 52$; 172 text messages. **c.** *Sample answer:* Yes; the estimate in part (a) was comparable to the exact answer in part (b).

5.

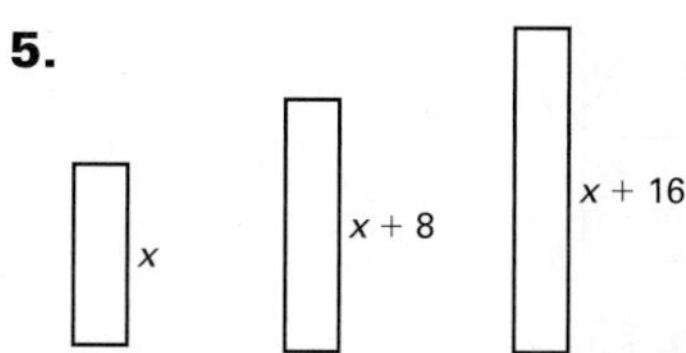

$3x + 24 = 84$; 20 in., 28 in., 36 in.

7.

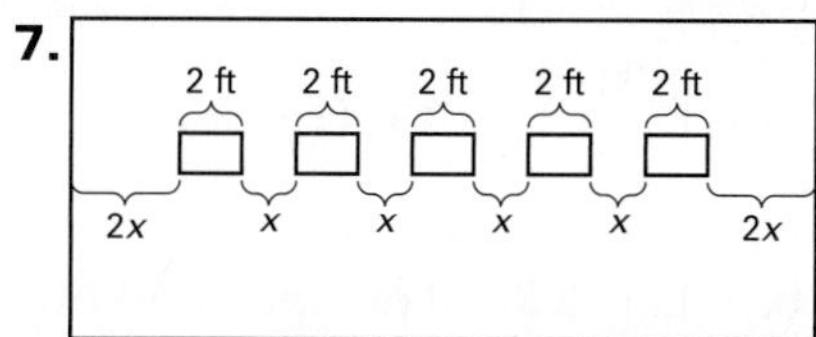

$8x + 10 = 24$; $x = 1.75$; So the paintings should be 1.75 feet apart and the spaces on the left and right should be 3.5 feet.

1.2 Exercise Set A (pp. 8–9)

5.

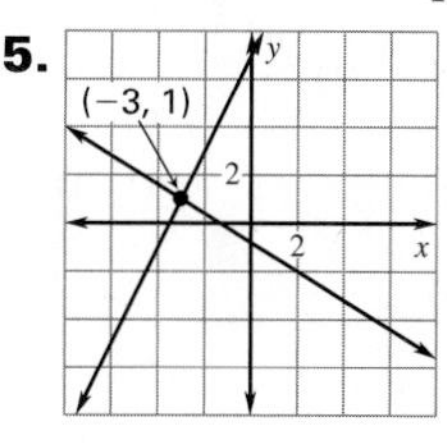

$(-3, 1)$

7.

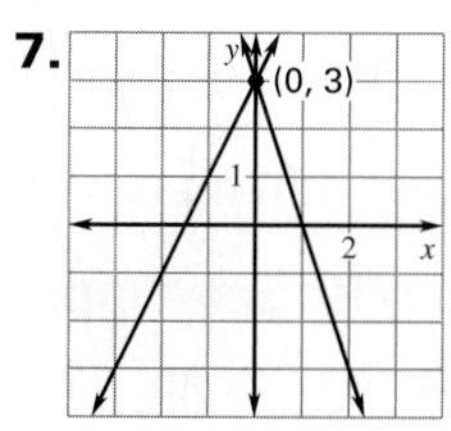

$(0, 3)$

9.

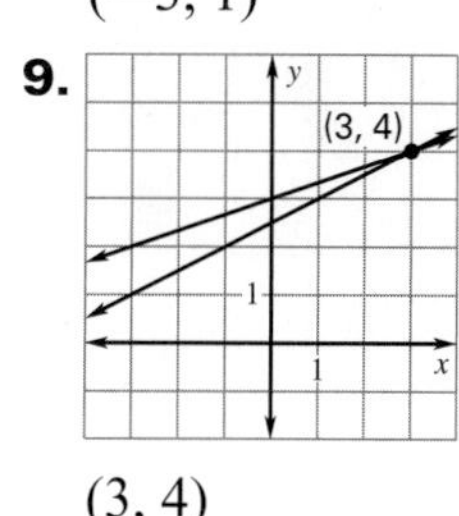

$(3, 4)$

11.

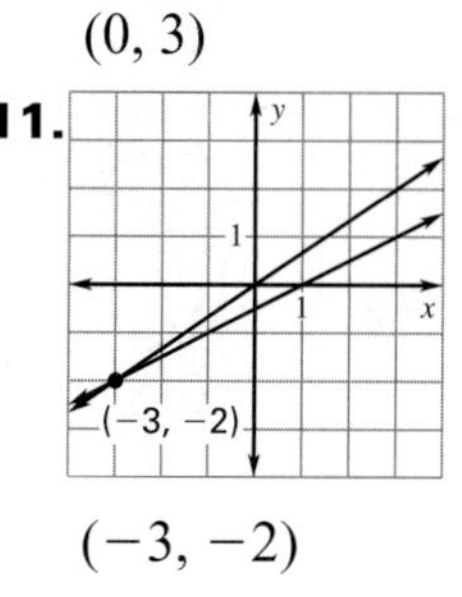

$(-3, -2)$

13.

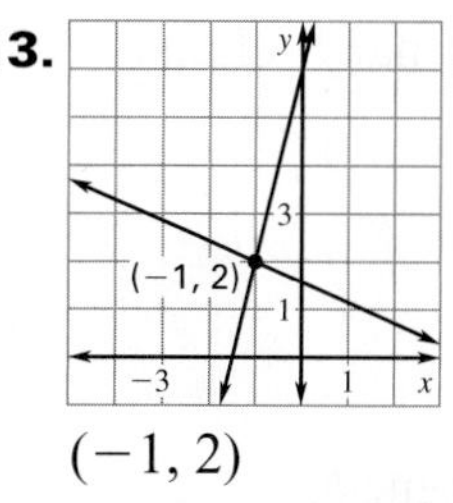

$(-1, 2)$

15.

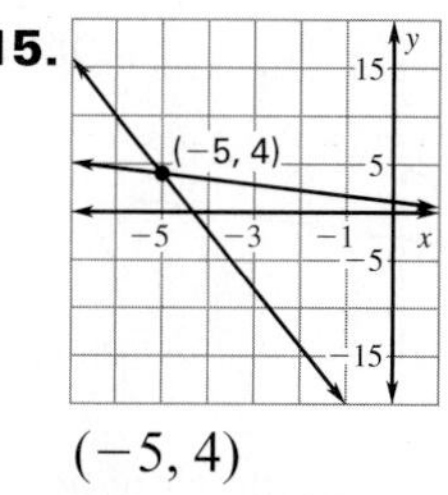

$(-5, 4)$

17. $(2, -1)$; consistent and independent

19. no solution; inconsistent **21.** infinitely many solutions; consistent and dependent **23.** $(3, 0)$; consistent and independent **25.** $(2, -1)$; consistent and independent **27.** $(2, 6)$; consistent and independent **29.** lifeguard; 8 h, cashier: 10 h

31. 60 tickets at \$36; 140 tickets at \$28

33. $R = 5500t$

35.

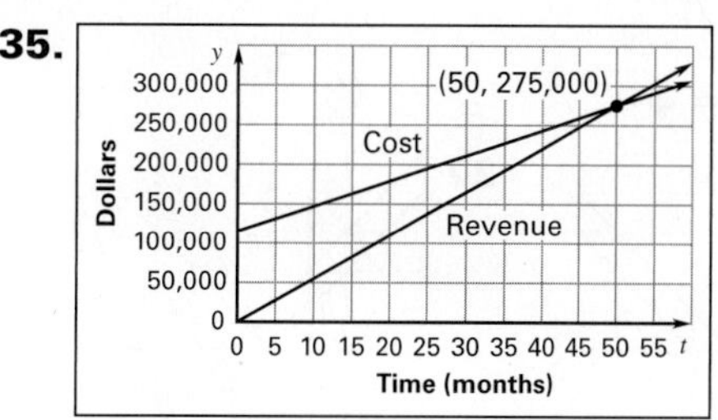

1.2 Exercise Set B (pp. 10–11)

1.

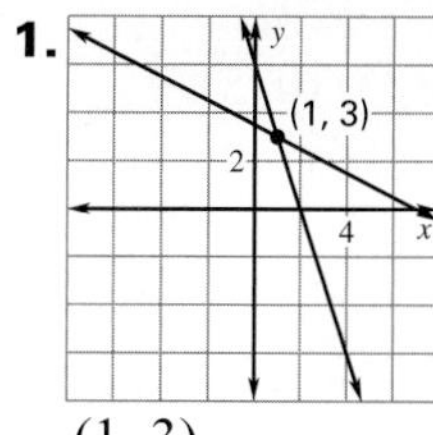

$(1, 3)$

3.

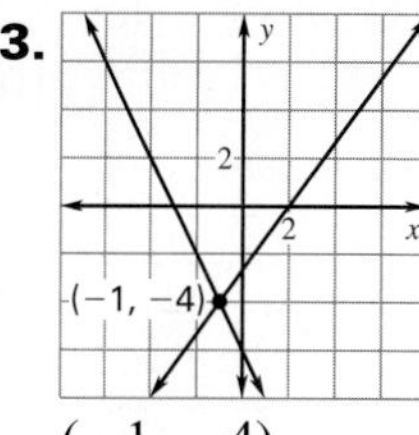

$(-1, -4)$

5.

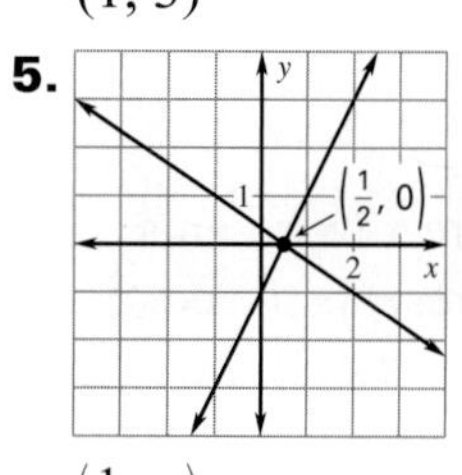

$\left(\frac{1}{2}, 0\right)$

7.

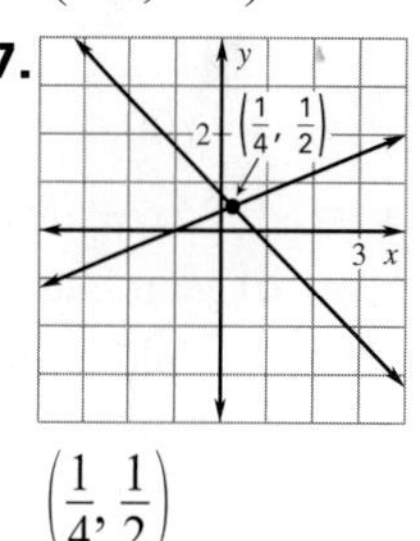

$\left(\frac{1}{4}, \frac{1}{2}\right)$

9.

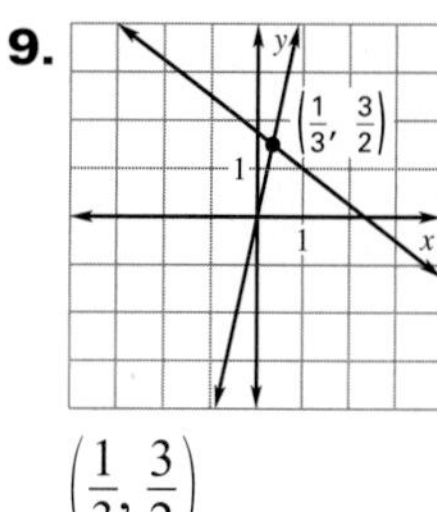

$\left(\frac{1}{3}, \frac{3}{2}\right)$

11. 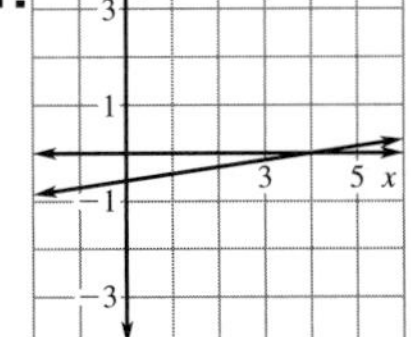

; infinitely many solutions

13. (3, 1); consistent and independent

15. (1, −4); consistent and independent

17. $\left(\frac{4}{5}, -\frac{13}{5}\right)$; consistent and independent

19. infinitely many solutions; consistent and dependent

21. $\left(-\frac{16}{5}, \frac{7}{5}\right)$; consistent and independent

23. *Sample answer:*
$x + y = 2$
$2x + 2y = 4$

25. 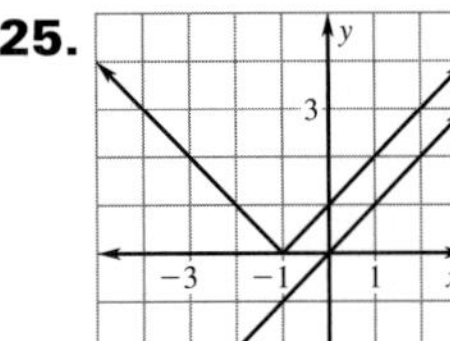

no solution

27. 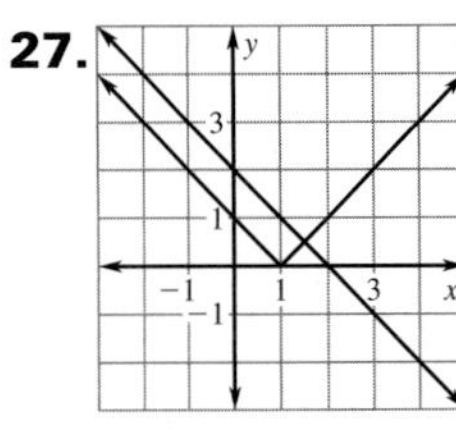

(1.5, 0.5)

29. 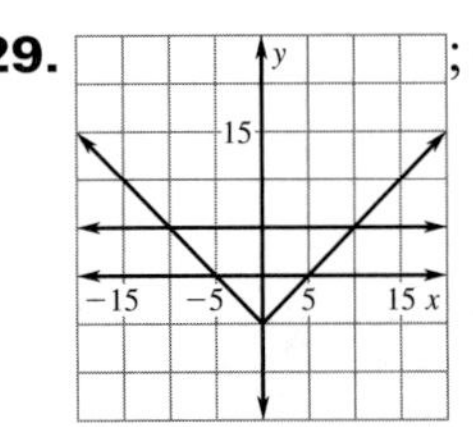

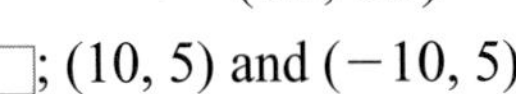
; (10, 5) and (−10, 5)

31. $x + y = 20$
$4x + 6y = 100$

33. a. $y = 90.25x + 756$, where x represents the number of years, and y represents the cost; $y = 48.50x + 1424$, where x represents the number of years, and y represents the cost

b. 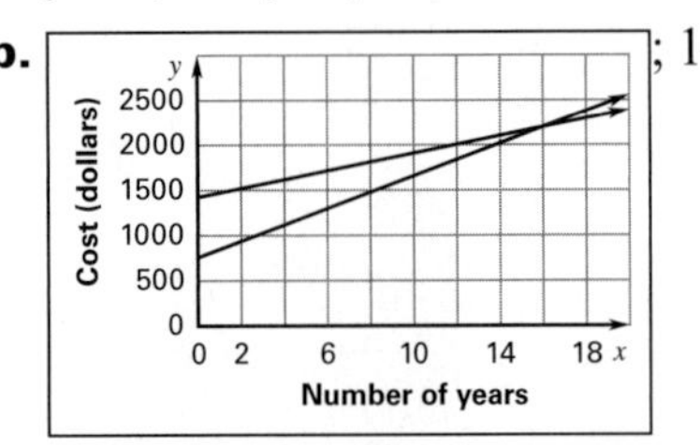

; 16 years

c. Yes, a washer can last 16 years.

35. 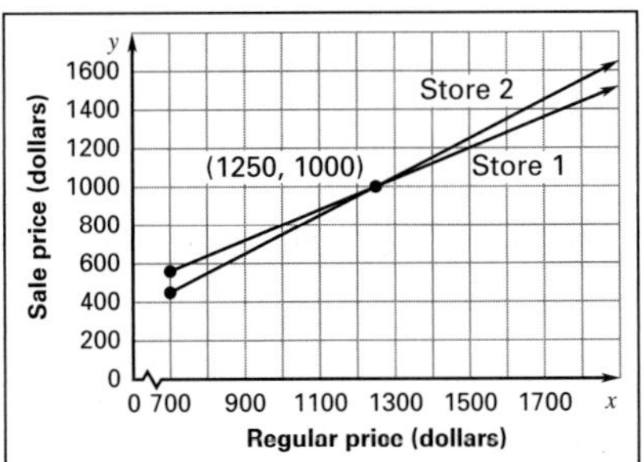

37. $R = 1.25x$

39. 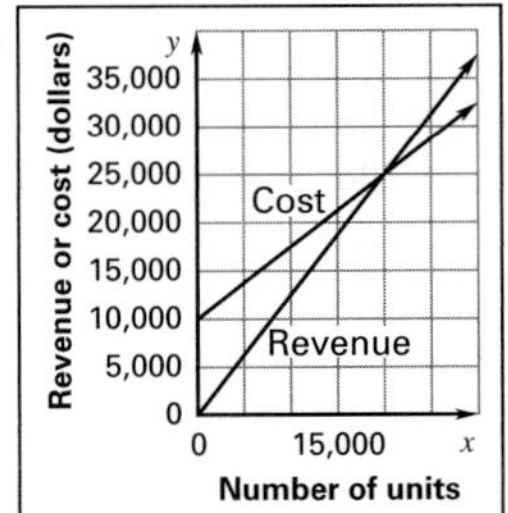

1.3 Exercise Set A (p. 15)

1. (2, 2) **3.** (2, −1) **5.** $\left(\frac{2}{3}, -2\right)$ **7.** (2, 3)

9. (−16, −5) **11.** $\left(-\frac{4}{5}, \frac{17}{10}\right)$ **13.** (1, −1)

15. no solution **17.** (16, 6) **19.** infinitely many solutions **21.** (6, −12) **23.** 60 of type A, 24 of type B

1.3 Exercise Set B (p. 16)

1. (4, −3) **3.** infinitely many solutions

5. (−3, 7) **7.** (3, −4) **9.** (1, −2) **11.** (6, 2)

13. (10, 10) **15.** $\left(\frac{17}{7}, \frac{9}{7}\right)$ **17.** $\left(\frac{14}{3}, 0\right)$

19. plane: 150 mi/h, wind: 50 mi/h **21.** $20.00

1.4 Exercise Set A (pp. 19–20)

1. yes; yes **3.** no; no **5.** yes; yes

11. 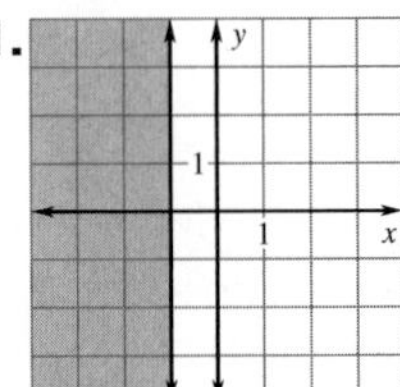

13. 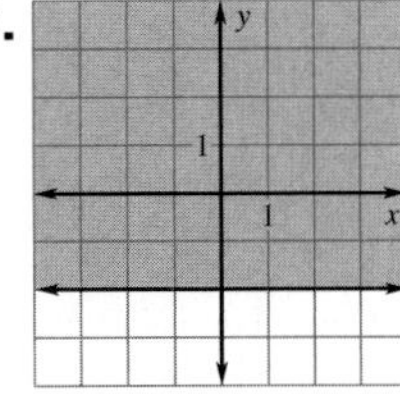

15. 
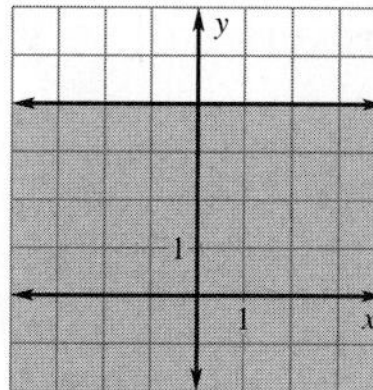

17.
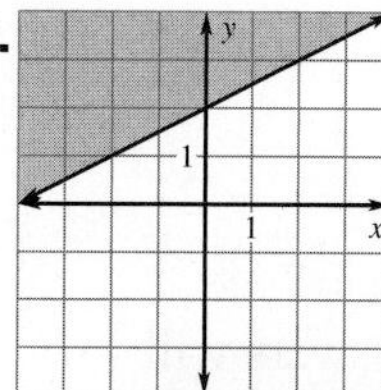

19.
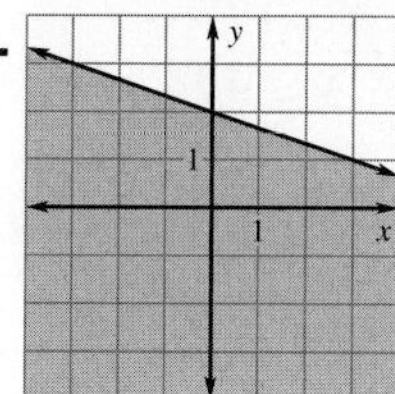

21.
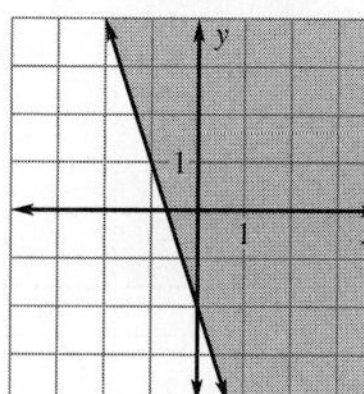

23. The other side of the boundary line should be shaded.

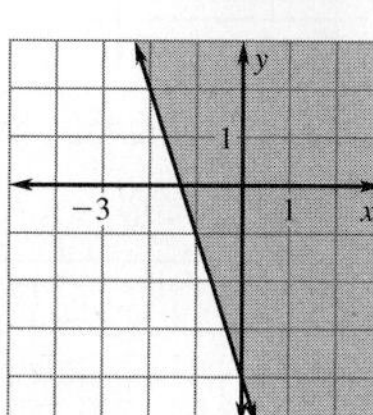

25. $y \leq 5$

27. 
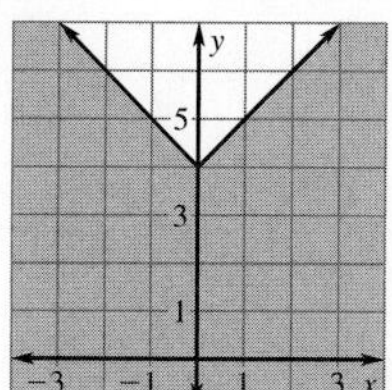

29. $20x + 10y \geq 1500$ **31.** $25x + 20y \leq 550$

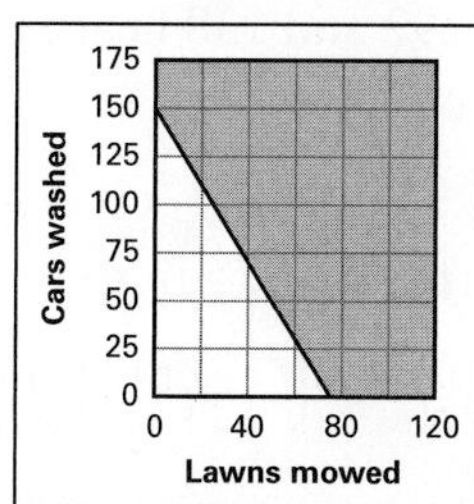

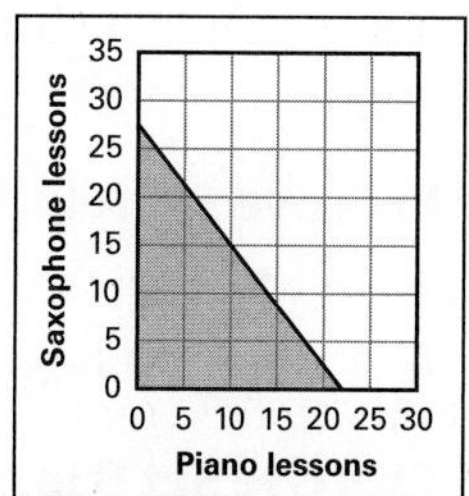

33. 10

1.4 Exercise Set B (pp. 21–22)

1. yes **3.** yes

9. 
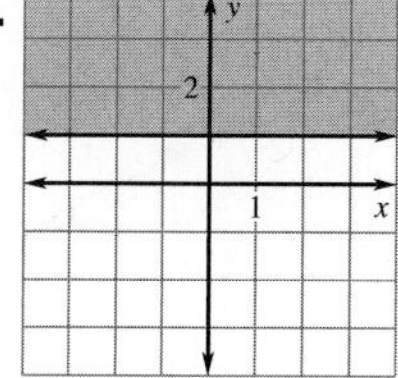

11.
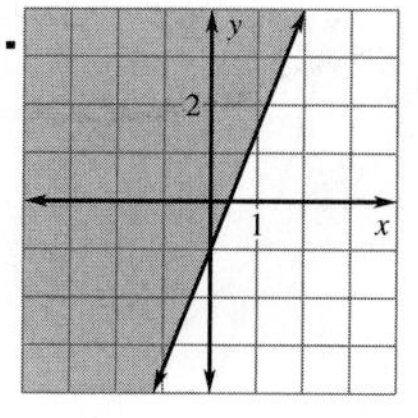

13.
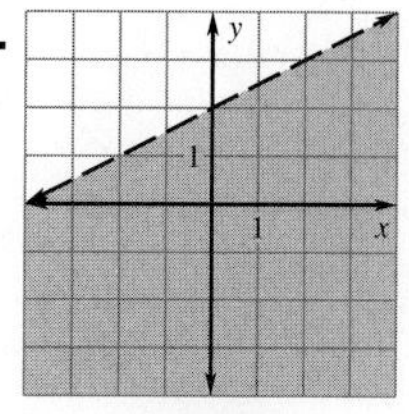

15.
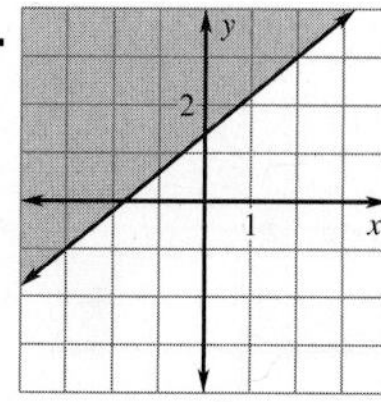

17.
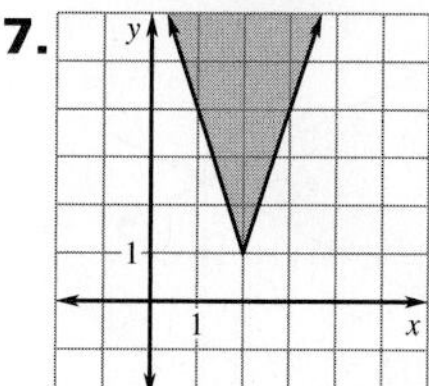

19.
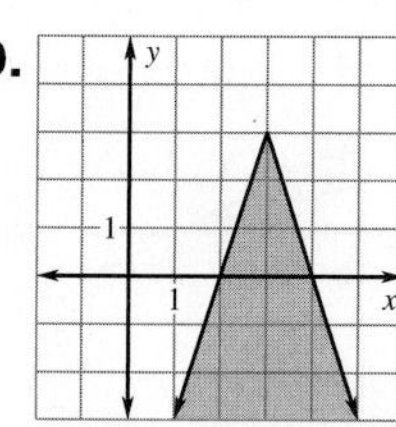

21. The other side of the boundary line should be shaded.

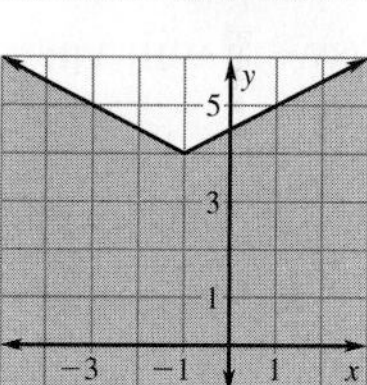

23. $y < -\frac{3}{4}x + \frac{3}{2}$ **25.** $y \geq |x| + 2$

27.
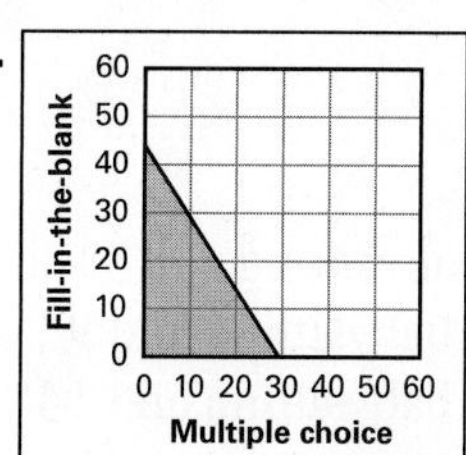

29. $c = 5t + 10$ **31.** no; The initial cost will be less but as the hours increase the cost will eventually surpass the music teachers cost due to the higher hourly rate.

1.5 Exercise Set A (pp. 25–26)

5.

7.
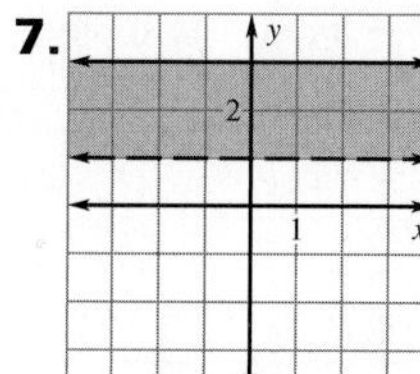

9.

11.
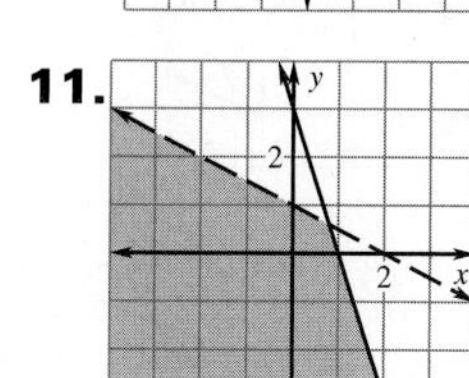

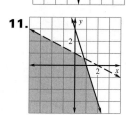

13.

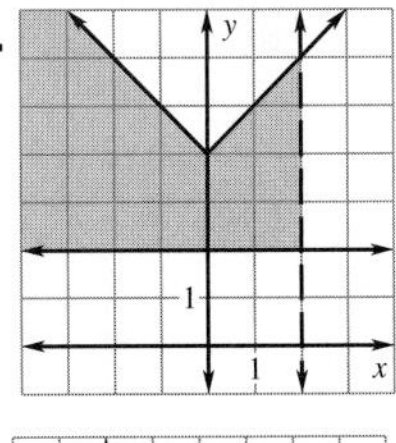

15.

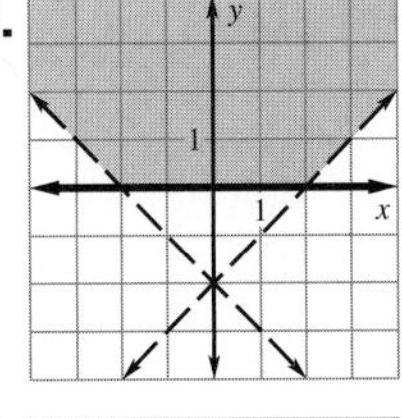

17.

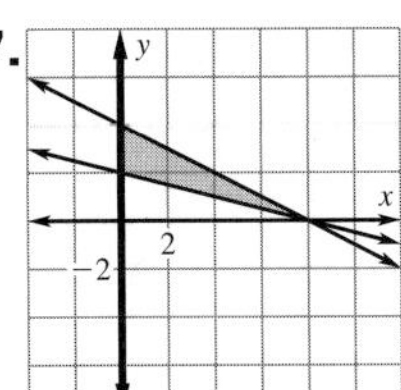

19.

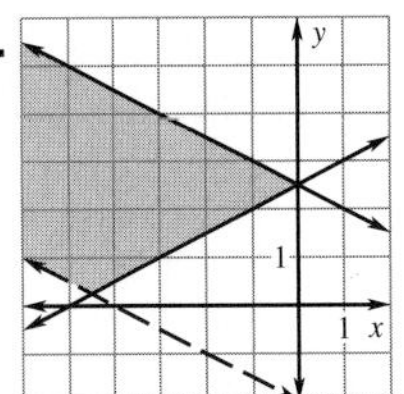

21. Answers will vary. **23.** Answers will vary.

25. $t \leq 3$
$d \leq 55t$

27. a. $x + y \leq 24$, $7x + 6.5y \geq 100$

b.

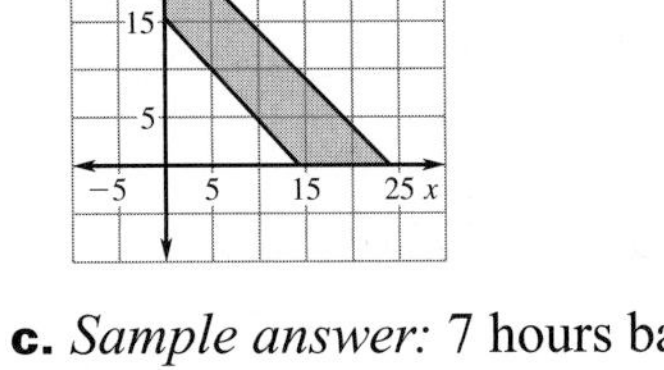

c. *Sample answer:* 7 hours babysitting and 11 hours at the grocery store, 9 hours babysitting and 9 hours at the grocery store, 5 hours babysitting and 14 hours at the grocery store

1.5 Exercise Set B (pp. 27–28)

5.

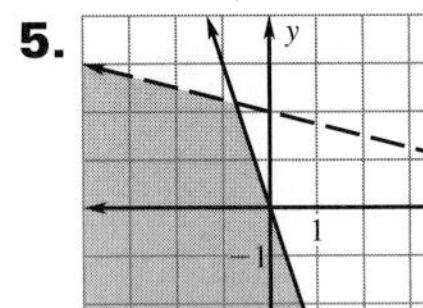

7.

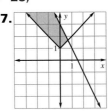

9.

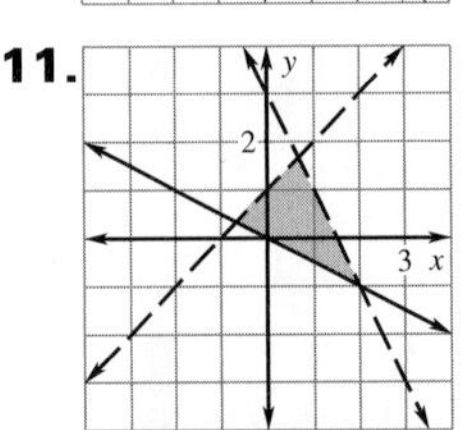

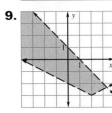

11.

13.

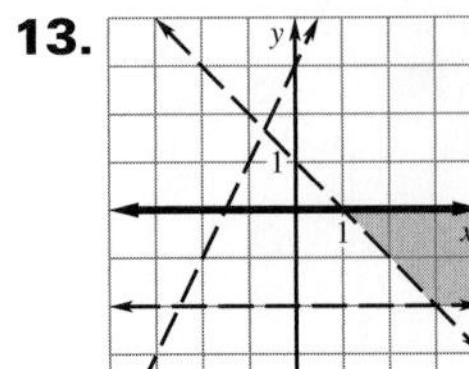

15.

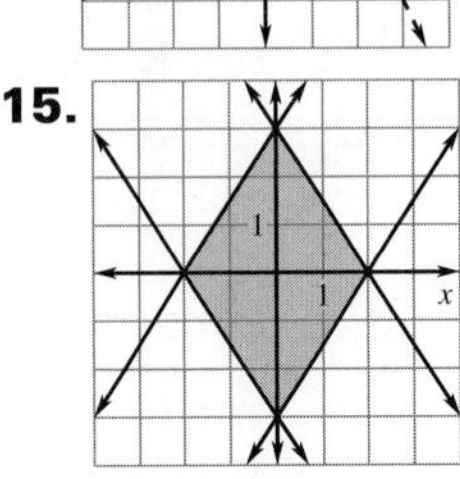

17. Answers will vary. **19.** Answers will vary.

21. $y \leq 4$
$y \geq -x - 2$
$y \geq x - 2$

23. Answers will vary.

25.

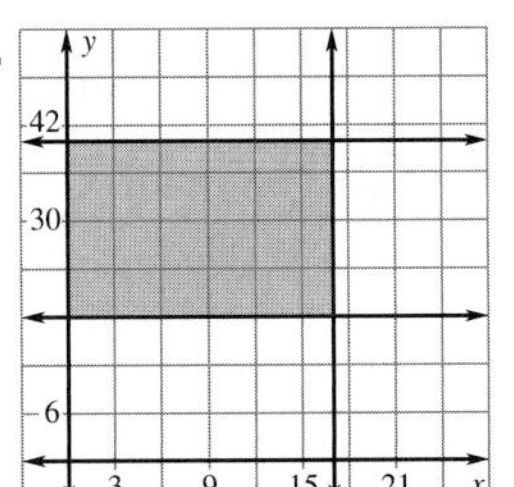

$x \geq 0, x \leq 17,$
$y \geq 18, y \leq 40$

27. a. $x \geq 20$, $x \leq 65$, $y \geq 0.5(220 - x)$, $y \leq 0.75(220 - x)$

b.

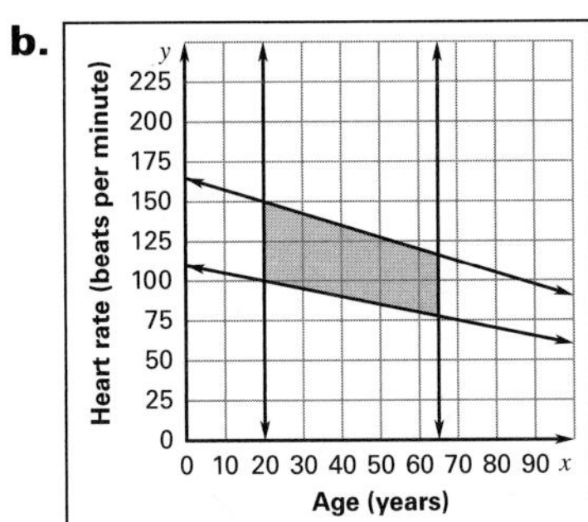

c. No, the person's heart rate is above the recommended range. A 36-year old person's heart rate should be between 92 and 138 heartbeats per minute.

1.6 Exercise Set A (p. 32)

1. 1; 16 **3.** 270; 920 **5.** 10; 50 **7.** 24; 72

9. 9; 27 **11.** 30 inkjet printers, 30 laser printers

1.6 Exercise Set B (p. 33)

1. 46; 100 **3.** 0; 38 **5.** 0; no maximum

7. The graph should have a vertex at (3, 2), not (4, 2). The maximum value of C is 74. It occurs when $x = 2$ and $y = 14$.

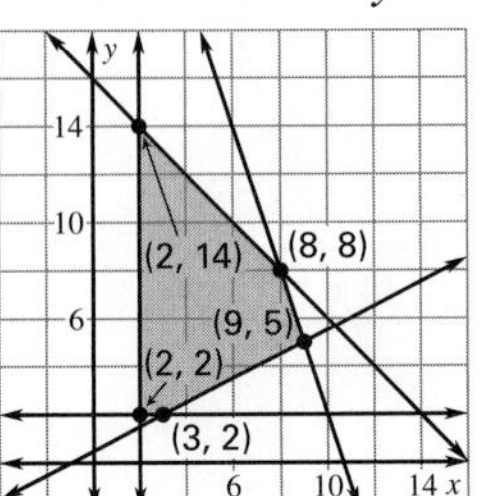

1.7 Exercise Set A (p. 36)

1. no **3.** no **5.** (2, 1, 4) **7.** (3, 1, −2)

9. (5, −3, 6) **11.** $\left(-\frac{5}{2}z + \frac{19}{2}, 2z - 12, z\right)$

13. $0.5x + 0.75y + 0.4z = 2885$
$0.3x + 0.1y + 0.3z = 1335$
$0.2x + 0.15y + 0.3z = 1230$;
1st delivery: 1800, 2nd delivery: 1500, 3rd delivery: 2150

1.7 Exercise Set B (p. 37)

1. (2, 1, −3) **3.** no solution **5.** $\left(\frac{1}{2}, 1, -\frac{3}{2}\right)$

7. $\left(\frac{3}{2}, -2, -1\right)$ **9.** (7, −21, 18) **11.** $\left(\frac{4}{3}, -\frac{1}{4}, -\frac{2}{3}\right)$

13. (1, 1, 1, 1) **15.** $(2 - y, 0, y, -2)$

17. $a + b + c = -2$
$4a - 2b + c = 7$
$25a - 5b + c = -2$; $a = -1, b = -4, c = 3$

1.8 Exercise Set A (p. 41)

1. $\begin{bmatrix} 4 & 0 \\ 10 & 4 \end{bmatrix}$ **3.** $\begin{bmatrix} 2 & -1 & 7 \\ -4 & -4 & 2 \\ 2 & 3 & -6 \end{bmatrix}$

5. $\begin{bmatrix} 3 & 9 & 13 \\ 2 & 0 & -4 \\ 10 & 3 & 9 \end{bmatrix}$ **7.** $\begin{bmatrix} -12 & -6 \\ -9 & -6 \end{bmatrix}$

9. $\begin{bmatrix} -16 & -4 \\ 20 & 0 \\ -4 & 12 \end{bmatrix}$

11. $x = 2, y = -7$ **13.** 15,000 more **15.** more

1.8 Exercise Set B (p. 42)

1. $\begin{bmatrix} 5 & -2 \\ 4 & 8 \end{bmatrix}$ **3.** $\begin{bmatrix} -4 & -20 \\ 6 & -18 \end{bmatrix}$ **5.** $\begin{bmatrix} 1 \\ 1 \end{bmatrix}$

7. $\begin{bmatrix} \frac{5}{3} & 0 & 2 \\ \frac{4}{3} & 3 & 2 \\ \frac{19}{3} & \frac{26}{3} & 2 \end{bmatrix}$ **9.** $\begin{bmatrix} -4 & 18 \\ 33 & -20 \\ -1 & -24 \end{bmatrix}$

11. $x = -3, y = 1$

13.
$$\begin{array}{l} \\ \text{Store A} \\ \text{Store B} \end{array} \begin{array}{c} \begin{array}{ccc} \text{May} & \text{June} & \text{July} \end{array} \\ \begin{bmatrix} x & 2x & 3x - 150 \\ y & 1.5y + 220 & 3y - 60 \end{bmatrix} \end{array}$$

1.9 Exercise Set A (p. 46)

1. A: 3 × 2; B: 1 × 3; *not* defined

3. $[11]$ **5.** $\begin{bmatrix} -2 & 6 \\ 1 & -3 \\ -3 & 9 \end{bmatrix}$ **7.** $\begin{bmatrix} -5 & 15 & -11 \\ 4 & 10 & 20 \\ 8 & 6 & 16 \end{bmatrix}$

9. $[1]$ **11.** $\begin{bmatrix} -3 \\ -6 \\ -16 \\ 8 \end{bmatrix}$ **13.** $\begin{bmatrix} 8 & -10 \\ -2 & 6 \end{bmatrix}$

15. $\begin{array}{l} \text{Game 1} \\ \text{Game 2} \end{array} \begin{bmatrix} \$1361 \\ \$1625 \end{bmatrix}$

1.9 Exercise Set B (p. 47)

1. $\begin{bmatrix} -2 & 6 \\ -2 & -1 \\ 9 & 8 \end{bmatrix}$ **3.** $\begin{bmatrix} 1 & 2 \\ -17 & 12 \\ -9 & 5 \end{bmatrix}$

5. $\begin{bmatrix} -4 & -8 \\ -2 & 3 \end{bmatrix}$ **7.** $\begin{bmatrix} -1 & -21 \\ 2 & 6 \\ -2 & -22 \end{bmatrix}$

9. $\begin{bmatrix} 14 & 35 \\ 8 & 2 \\ 8 & 30 \end{bmatrix}$ **11.** $x = 3, y = 4$

13. $AB = \begin{bmatrix} 0 & -2 & -4 \\ -1 & -3 & -1 \end{bmatrix}$;
reflection through the origin

1.10 Exercise Set A (p. 51)

1. −12 **3.** $-\frac{3}{2}$ **5.** −91 **7.** 6 **9.** 2 **11.** (−5, 3)

13. (1, −1, 2) **15.** $\left(\frac{1}{2}, \frac{1}{4}, -1\right)$

17. Premium: \$2.15,
Regular: \$1.95

SELECTED ANSWERS

1.10 Exercise Set B (p. 52)

1. 22 **3.** -10 **5.** -72 **7.** 9 **9.** (4, 6)

11. (7, −8) **13.** $\left(-\frac{61}{8}, \frac{3}{8}, \frac{43}{8}\right)$ **15.** (−7, 3, 9)

17. (−3, −4, −1) **19.** (297, 240, 1)

1.11 Exercise Set A (p. 57)

1. $\begin{bmatrix} 2 & -7 \\ -1 & 4 \end{bmatrix}$ **3.** $\begin{bmatrix} \frac{1}{10} & \frac{1}{5} \\ -\frac{3}{10} & \frac{2}{5} \end{bmatrix}$ **5.** $\begin{bmatrix} 1 & 1 \\ -\frac{5}{2} & -2 \end{bmatrix}$

7. $\begin{bmatrix} 1 & -1 & 0 \\ 0 & \frac{1}{3} & -\frac{1}{3} \\ 0 & 0 & \frac{1}{5} \end{bmatrix}$ **9.** $\begin{bmatrix} 8 & 1 \\ -11 & -1 \end{bmatrix}$

11. $\begin{bmatrix} -1 & 4 & -1 \\ 4 & -8 & 1 \end{bmatrix}$ **13.** (2, 2) **15.** (1, −2, 4)

17. a. $x + y + z = 1011$
$x + 2y + 3z = 1669$
$x - y = -305$

b. $\begin{bmatrix} 1 & 1 & 1 \\ 1 & 2 & 3 \\ 1 & -1 & 0 \end{bmatrix} \begin{bmatrix} x \\ y \\ z \end{bmatrix} = \begin{bmatrix} 1011 \\ 1669 \\ -305 \end{bmatrix}$

c. 1-point: 353, 2-point: 658, 3-point: 0

1.11 Exercise Set B (p. 58)

1. no inverse **3.** $\begin{bmatrix} \frac{2}{13} & -\frac{7}{13} \\ \frac{1}{13} & \frac{3}{13} \end{bmatrix}$

5. $\begin{bmatrix} -0.2\overline{2} & 0.2\overline{7} & 0.8\overline{8} \\ -0.1\overline{1} & -0.1\overline{1} & 0.4\overline{4} \\ 0.1\overline{1} & 0.1\overline{1} & 0.5\overline{5} \end{bmatrix}$

7. $\begin{bmatrix} 18 & 30 & -44 \\ 7 & 11 & -\frac{31}{2} \end{bmatrix}$

9. (−7, 7) **11.** $\left(\frac{1}{2}, -1\right)$

13. (6, −7, 4) **15.** $A = (A^{-1})^{-1}$

1.12 Exercise Set A (p. 61)

1. 5 vertices; 7 edges **3.** 5 vertices; 8 edges

5. false

7. *Sample answer:* 2 tanks: one tank with gouramis, tetras, and black mollies; another tank with just angelfish; 2 tanks: one tank with gouramis and angelfish; another tank with tetras and black mollies

9. $\begin{array}{c} \\ C \\ D \\ E \\ F \\ G \end{array} \begin{array}{c} \begin{array}{ccccc} C & D & E & F & G \end{array} \\ \begin{bmatrix} 0 & 1 & 0 & 0 & 0 \\ 1 & 0 & 0 & 1 & 2 \\ 0 & 0 & 0 & 2 & 0 \\ 0 & 1 & 2 & 0 & 1 \\ 0 & 2 & 0 & 1 & 0 \end{bmatrix} \end{array}$

11. *Sample answer:*

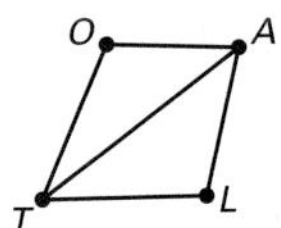

1.12 Exercise Set B (p. 62)

1. false **3.** true **5.** The shortest route is to the pizza shop, to your friend's house, then to your cousin's house, a distance of 7 miles.

7. $\begin{array}{c} \\ R \\ S \\ T \\ U \\ V \end{array} \begin{array}{c} \begin{array}{ccccc} R & S & T & U & V \end{array} \\ \begin{bmatrix} 0 & 2 & 0 & 0 & 1 \\ 2 & 0 & 0 & 1 & 2 \\ 0 & 0 & 0 & 2 & 0 \\ 0 & 1 & 2 & 0 & 1 \\ 1 & 2 & 0 & 1 & 0 \end{bmatrix} \end{array}$

9. a. 4 **b.** 2 **c.** 3 **d.** 9

11. *Sample answer:*

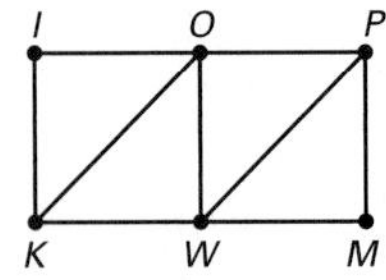

UNIT 2

2.1 Exercise Set A (p. 69)

1. yes; $f(x) = -2x + 7$; 1; −2

3. no **5.** −283 **7.** 3 **9.** $-\infty, +\infty$

11. even; The graph is symmetric with respect to the y-axis.

13. odd; The graph is symmetric with respect to the origin.

15.

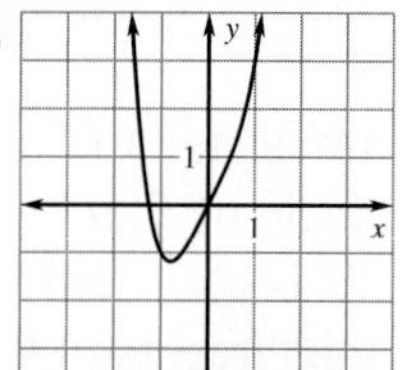

17. a.

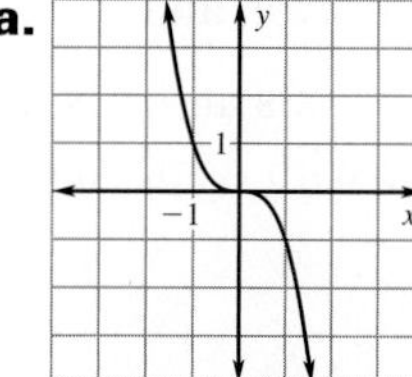

b. domain: all real numbers; range: all real numbers

c. degree: 3; leading coefficient: -1

d. decreasing over all real numbers

19. a.

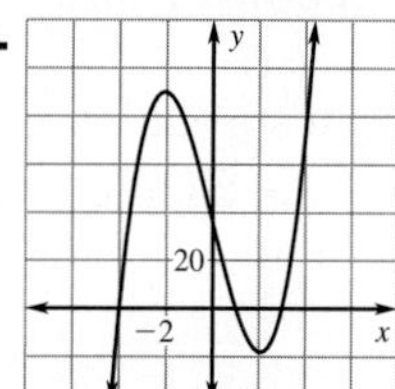

b. domain: all real numbers; range: all real numbers

c. degree: 3; leading coefficient: 3

d. increasing for about $x < -2$ and about $x > 2$; decreasing for $-2 < x < 2$

2.1 Exercise Set B (p. 70)

1. yes; $f(x) = \sqrt{5}x^3 - 2x^2 + 7$; 3; $\sqrt{5}$

3. 32 **5.** $+\infty, -\infty$ **7.** $+\infty, +\infty$

9. odd; The graph is symmetric with respect to the origin.

11.

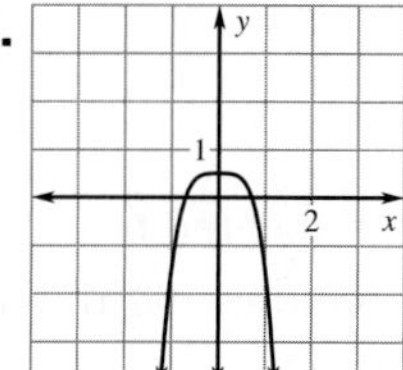

13.

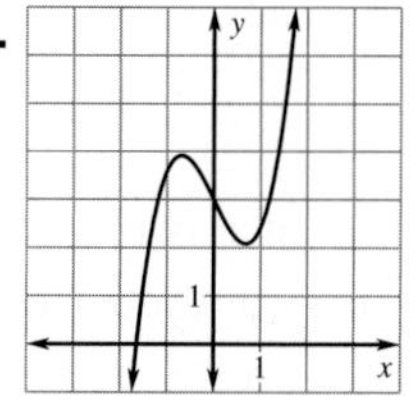

15. a.

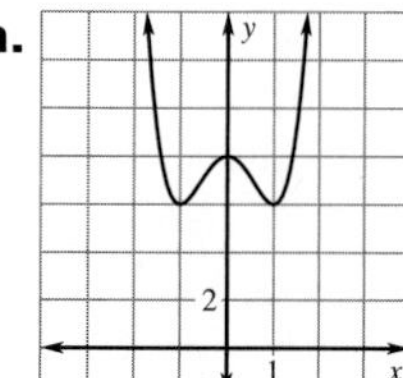

b. domain: all real numbers; range: $y \geq 6$

c. degree: 4; leading coefficient: 2

d. y-axis symmetry

e. increasing for $-1 < x < 0$ and $x > 1$; decreasing for $x < -1$ and $0 < x < 1$

17. *Sample answer:* $f(x) = -x^4 + 2x^3$

2.2 Exercise Set A (p. 74)

5. The graph of g is the graph of f translated down 6 units.

7.

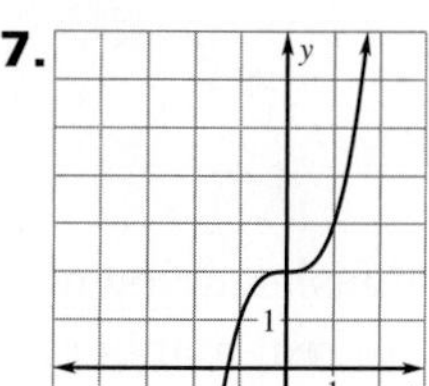

The graph of g is the graph of f translated up 2 units; the domains and ranges of both functions are all real numbers; f has x- and y-intercepts of 0 and g has an x-intercept of about -1.3 and a y-intercept of 2; f is odd and symmetric with respect to the origin and g is neither even nor odd and is symmetric with respect to the point (0, 2).

9.

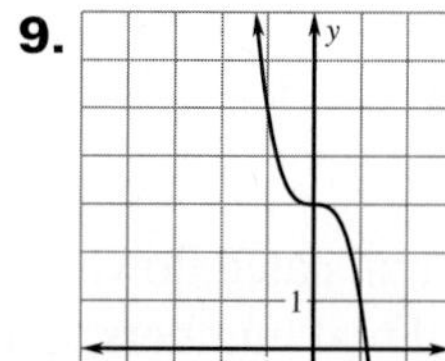

The graph of g is the graph of f translated up 3 units; the domains and ranges of both functions are all real numbers; f has x- and y-intercepts of 0 and g has an x-intercept of about 1.1 and a y-intercept of 3; f is odd and symmetric with respect to the origin and g is neither even nor odd and is symmetric with the respect to the point (0, 3).

11. 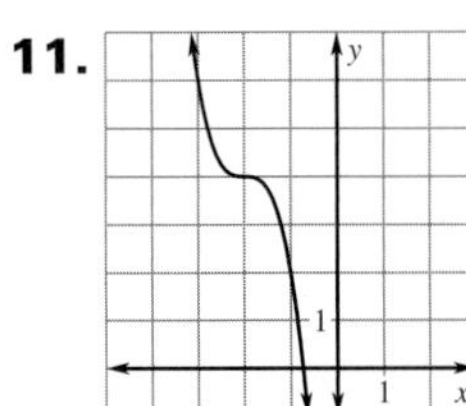

The graph of g is the graph of f translated to the left 2 units and up 4 units; the domains and ranges of both functions are all real numbers; f has x- and y-intercepts of 0 and g has an x-intercept of about -0.74 and a y-intercept of -12; f is odd and symmetric with respect to the origin and g is neither even nor odd and is symmetric with the respect to the point $(-2, 4)$.

13. 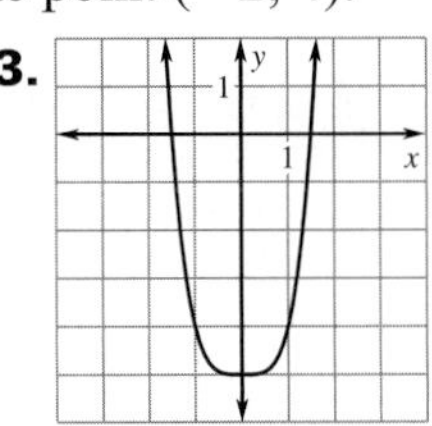

The graph of g is the graph of f translated down 5 units; the domain of f and g is all real numbers and the range of f is $y \geq 0$ and the range of g is $y \geq -5$; f has x- and y-intercepts of 0 and g has x-intercepts of about -1.5 and 1.5 and a y-intercept of -5; f and g are even and symmetric with respect to the y-axis.

15. 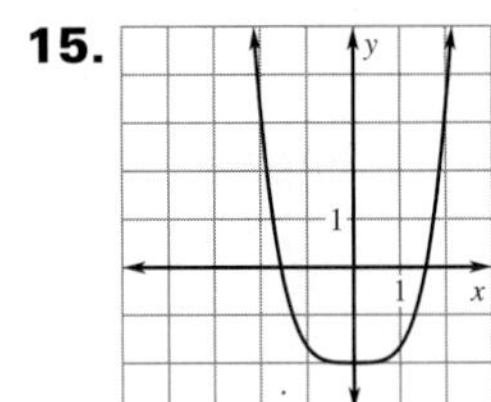

The graph of g is the graph of f translated down 2 units; the domain of f and g is all real numbers and the range of f is $y \geq 0$ and the range of g is $y \geq -2$; f has x- and y-intercepts of 0 and g has x-intercepts of about -1.6 and 1.6 and a y-intercept of -2; f and g are even and symmetric with respect to the y-axis.

17. 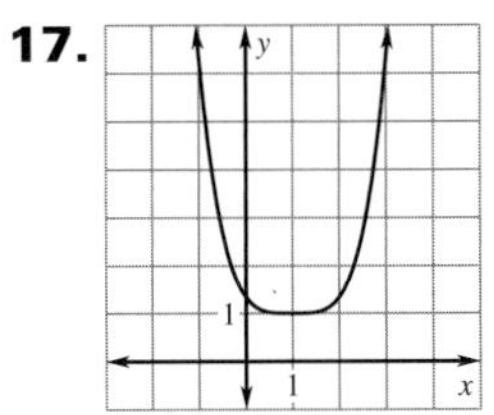

The graph of g is the graph of f translated to the right 1 unit and up 1 unit; the domain of f and g is all real numbers and the range of f is $y \geq 0$ and the range of g is $y \geq 1$; f has x- and y-intercepts of 0 and g has a y-intercept of $\frac{4}{3}$; f is even and symmetric with respect to the y-axis and g is neither even nor odd and is symmetric with respect to the line $x = 1$.

19. $y = (x + 5)^4$

2.2 Exercise Set B (p. 75)

1. The graph of g is the graph of f translated down 7 units. **3.** The graph of g is the graph of f translated to the left 3 units and down 1 unit.

5. 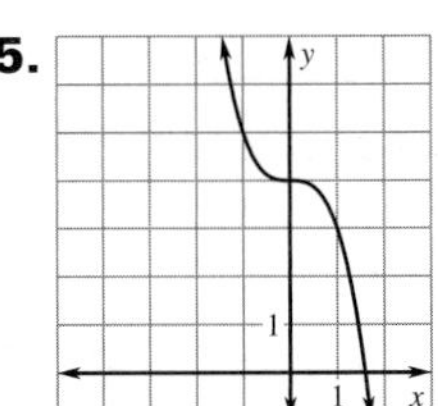

The graph of g is the graph of f translated up 4 units; the domains and ranges of both functions are all real numbers; f has x- and y-intercepts of 0 and g has an x-intercept of about 1.6 and a y-intercept of 4; f is odd and symmetric with respect to the origin and g is neither even nor odd and is symmetric with respect to the point $(0, 4)$.

7. 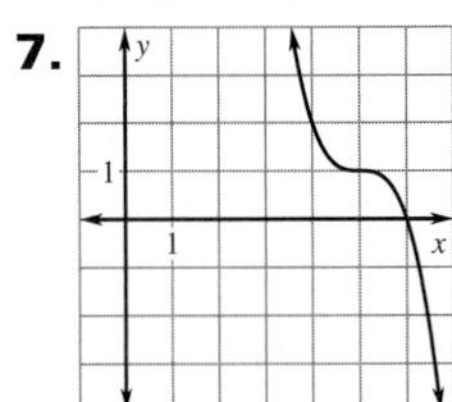

The graph of g is the graph of f translated to the right 5 units and up 1 unit; the domains and ranges of both functions are all real numbers; f has x- and y-intercepts of 0 and g has an x-intercept of 6 and a y-intercept of 126; f is odd and symmetric with respect to the origin and g is neither even nor odd and is symmetric with respect to the point $(5, 1)$.

9. 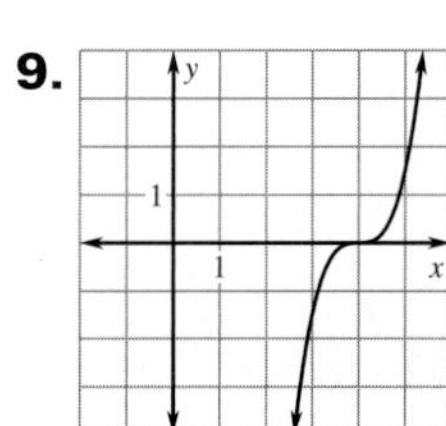

The graph of g is the graph of f translated to the right 4 units; the domains and ranges of both functions are all real numbers; f has x- and y-intercepts of 0 and g has an x-intercept of 4 and a y-intercept of -96; f is odd and symmetric with respect to the origin and g is neither even nor odd and is symmetric with respect to the point (4, 0).

11. 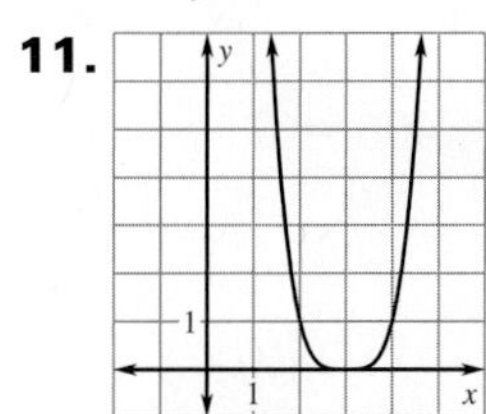

The graph of g is the graph of f translated to the right 3 units; the domain of f and g is all real numbers and the range of f and g is $y \geq 0$; f has x- and y-intercepts of 0 and g has an x-intercept of 3 and a y-intercept of 81; f is even and symmetric with respect to the y-axis and g is neither even nor odd and is symmetric with respect to the point $x = 3$.

13. 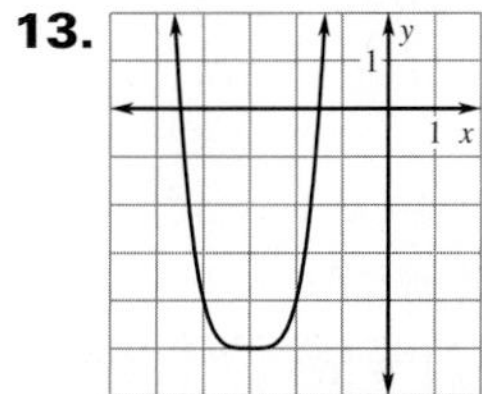

The graph of g is the graph of f translated to the left 3 units and down 5 units; the domain of f and g is all real numbers and the range of f is $y \geq 0$ and the range of g is $y \geq -5$; f has x- and y-intercepts of 0 and g has x-intercepts of about -4.5 and -1.5 and a y-intercept of 76; f is even and symmetric with respect to the y-axis and g is neither even nor odd and is symmetric with respect to the point $x = -3$.

15. 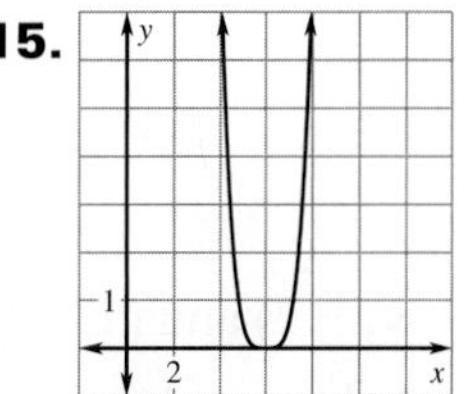

The graph of g is the graph of f translated to the right 6 units; the domain of f and g is all real numbers and the range of f and g is $y \geq 0$; f has x- and y-intercepts of 0 and g has an x-intercept of 6 and a y-intercept of 648; f is even and symmetric with respect to the y-axis and g is neither even nor odd and is symmetric with respect to the point $x = 6$.

17. The student described the direction of the translation incorrectly. The graph of $g(x) = -2(x - 5)^3 + 4$ is the graph of $f(x) = -2x^3$ translated right 5 units and up 4 units. **19.** $y = 3(x + 7)^4 + 1$

2.3 Exercise Set A (p. 78)

1. $(x + 5)(x^2 - 5x + 25)$
3. $(4n - 3)(16n^2 + 12n + 9)$
5. $(w + 3)(w^2 - 3w + 9)$ **7.** $(r^2 + 6)(r - 3)$
9. $(c + 3)(c - 3)(c + 4)$ **11.** $(x^2 - 6)(x^2 + 6)$
13. $(2y^3 + 1)(3y^3 - 4)$ **15.** $(d^2 - 5)(d^2 - 2)$
17. $(a^3 + 6)(a + 1)(a^2 - a + 1)$
19. $2(b + 7)(b - 2)(b^2 + 2b + 4)$ **21.** $0, \frac{9}{4}$
23. $-5, -\sqrt{3}, \sqrt{3}$ **25.** $-1, 0, 1$
27. 6 ft by 3 ft by 1 ft

2.3 Exercise Set B (p. 79)

1. $(x - 8)(x^2 + 8x + 64)$
3. $7(h + 4)(h^2 - 4h + 16)$ **5.** $(6x^2 + 1)(2x - 1)$
7. $(n + 4)(n - 4)(3n - 10)$
9. $(y^2 + 9)(y + 3)(y - 3)$
11. $(3a^2 - 1)(2a^2 + 5)$
13. $(r - 1)(r^2 + r + 1)(r^2 + 1)$
15. $(a^2b + 5)(a^4b^2 - 5a^2b + 25)$
17. -10 **19.** 4 **21.** $-\frac{3}{5}, 1$ **23.** $-\frac{1}{3}, \frac{1}{3}$
25. $-1, 0, 1$ **27.** $-\frac{\sqrt{6}}{2}, 0, \frac{\sqrt{6}}{2}$

SELECTED ANSWERS

29. *Sample answer:*
$x^4 + 5x^3 + x + 5$; $(x + 5)(x + 1)(x^2 - x + 1)$

2.4 Exercise Set A (p. 83)

1. $(-\infty, -5)$ and $(0, 4)$ **3.** $(-\infty, -2)$ and $(2, \infty)$ **5.** $(-\infty, -2)$ and $(2, \infty)$ **7.** $[-4, 1]$ and $[4, \infty)$ **9.** $\left(-4, \frac{3}{2}\right)$ and $(4, \infty)$ **11.** $[-3, -1.4]$ and $[1.4, 3]$ **13.** $(-2.4, 0)$ and $(2.4, \infty)$ **15.** $(-\infty, 0]$ and $\left[\frac{2}{3}, \frac{5}{2}\right]$ **17.** $(-\infty, -0.5]$ and $[0.5, 8]$ **19.** The open dots on the graph mean that the values do not satisfy the inequality. The solution set is $(0, 1)$ and $(3, \infty)$. **21. a.** $1000(1 + r)^3 > 1200$ **b.** The interest rate must be greater than 6.3%.

2.4 Exercise Set B (p. 84)

1. $(-4, 2)$ and $(6, \infty)$ **3.** $\left[-2, -\frac{1}{2}\right]$ and $\left[\frac{1}{2}, 2\right]$ **5.** $\left(-3, -\frac{3}{2}\right)$ and $(3, \infty)$ **7.** $(-4, 2)$ and $(7, \infty)$ **9.** $(-\infty, -1.6]$ and $[-0.4, 1.5]$ **11.** $(-2.4, -1.3)$ and $(1, \infty)$ **13.** $(4, \infty)$ **15.** $[6, \infty)$ **17.** $(-\infty, -0.3]$ and $[0.3, 1]$ **19.** If $<$ is replaced with $\leq$, then the solution set changes from $(-\infty, -7)$ and $(-1, 1)$ to $(-\infty, -7]$ and $[-1, 1]$. **21.** The height of the box is greater than 3 inches and less than 9.6 inches.

2.5 Exercise Set A (p. 87)

1. $x + 7$ **3.** $x^2 - 3x + 10$ **5.** $8x + 5 + \frac{12x + 25}{x^2 - 3}$ **7.** $x + 3$ **9.** $x^3 + 2x^2 - 3x + 3 - \frac{4}{x - 2}$ **11.** $2x^3 - 5x^2 + 6$ **13.** $(x - 6)(x + 1)(x + 2)$ **15.** $(x - 9)(x - 2)(x - 7)$ **17.** $(x - 1)(2x + 3)(2x - 3)$ **19.** 2 **21.** $-5, -\frac{1}{2}$ **23.** 5 **25.** $x - 2$

2.5 Exercise Set B (p. 88)

1. $2x^2 - 4x + 9 - \frac{28}{2x + 3}$ **3.** $2x - \frac{9}{x^3 + x^2 - 5}$ **5.** $x^3 + 2x^2 - 8x + 20 - \frac{56}{x + 3}$ **7.** $2x^2 + 5x - 1$ **9.** $(x - 5)(x + 3)(x + 11)$ **11.** $(x + 7)(2x - 1)(2x^2 + 3)$ **13.** $-\frac{5 - \sqrt{17}}{2}, -\frac{5 + \sqrt{17}}{2}$ **15. a.** $1, -8$ **b.** $x - 4, x - 1, x + 8$ **c.** $x = 4, x = 1, x = -8$

2.6 Exercise Set A (p. 91)

1. $\pm 1, \pm 3, \pm 7, \pm 21$ **3.** $\pm 1, \pm 2, \pm 5, \pm 10, \pm\frac{1}{5}, \pm\frac{2}{5}$ **5.** $-2, 1, 4$ **7.** $-4, 3, 6$ **9.** $-\frac{3}{2}, \frac{1}{2}, 3$ **11.** $-2, -1, 1$ **13.** $-3, -1, \frac{1}{2}, 1$ **15. a.** $t^4 - 18t^3 + 89t^2 - 32t - 400 = 0$ **b.** 1, 2, 4, 5, 8 **c.** 4; 1999 **d.** about 6.4 or 2001

2.6 Exercise Set B (p. 92)

1. $-2, 1, 5$ **3.** $-3, -\sqrt{2}, -1, \sqrt{2}$ **5.** $-3 - 2\sqrt{2}, -1, -3 + 2\sqrt{2}, 3$ **7.** $-\frac{3}{4}, -\frac{1}{2}, \frac{1}{3}, 2$ **9.** $-\sqrt{3}, -\frac{5}{3}, \frac{1}{2}, \sqrt{3}$ **11.** *Sample answer:* $f(x) = 6x^3 - 7x^2 + 10x + 2$ **13. a.** for each function: $-5, -1, 4$ **b.** The zeros of $f(x)$ are also the zeros of $af(x)$. **c.** To apply the rational zero theorem, the coefficients must be integers. **d.** $-3, -\frac{1}{4}, 1$

2.7 Exercise Set A (p. 96)

1. 3 **3.** 7 **5.** $-1, 1, 3$ **7.** $-5, -i, i$ **9.** $-3, 2 + \sqrt{3}, 2 - \sqrt{3}$ **11.** $f(x) = x^2 + 11x + 28$ **13.** $f(x) = x^3 + 2x^2 - 3x$ **15.** $f(x) = x^4 + 5x^3 + 4x^2 + 20x$ **17.** The polynomial function should be written as a product of three factors because $2 - i$ must also be a zero by the complex conjugates theorem.

$$\begin{aligned} f(x) &= (x - 3)[x - (2 + i)][x - (2 - i)] \\ &= (x - 3)(x^2 - 4x + 5) \\ &= x^3 - 7x^2 + 17x - 15 \end{aligned}$$

19. $-0.62, -0.50, 1.62$ **21.** $-4.09, -0.98, 1.47, 4.60$ **23.** 3 and 9 years after opening

2.7 Exercise Set B (p. 97)

1. $-3, -1, 3$ **3.** $-2, 0, 2 + i\sqrt{3}, 2 - i\sqrt{3}$

5. $-3, -1, 3, \frac{9}{2}$ **7.** $-i, i, -1 + \sqrt{2}, -1 - \sqrt{2}$

9. $f(x) = 2x^4 - 4x^3 - 32x^2 + 64x$

11. $f(x) = 2x^3 + 10x^2 - 6x - 30$

13. $f(x) = 2x^4 - 22x^3 + 80x^2 - 116x + 56$

15. 2 or 0; 1; 2 or 0 **17.** 4, 2, or 0; 1; 4, 2, or 0

19. $-0.75, 0.75$ **21.** $-1.06, 3.98$

23. *Sample answer:* One zero is a repeated zero.

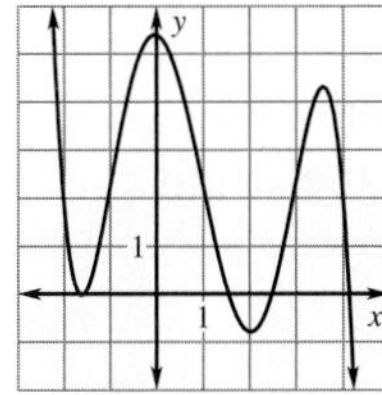

25. a. $R = -315t^5 + 5554t^4 + 1932t^3 - 709{,}619t^2 + 6{,}441{,}145t + 49{,}246{,}365$ **b.** 2001

2.8 Exercise Set A (pp. 100–101)

1. The error is in calling -6 a factor. The correct statement is *If* -6 *is a solution of the polynomial equation* $f(x) = 0$, *then* $(x + 6)$ *is a factor of* $f(x)$.

3. 4 **5.** 3 **7.** $-4, 6, 8$ **9.** $-5, -1, 7$ **11.** 8

13. zeros: -2 (multiplicity 2), 5; turning points: 2

15. zeros: -6 (multiplicity 2), $\frac{2}{3}$ (multiplicity 2); turning points: 3 **17.** zeros: 0 (multiplicity 2), $-4, \frac{3}{2}$ (multiplicity 3); turning points: 4

19.

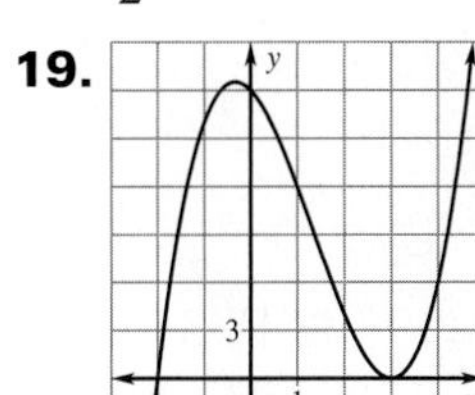

21.

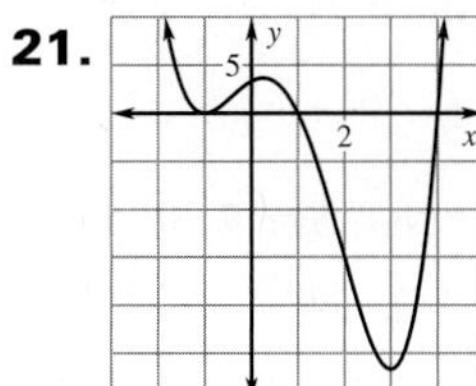

23.

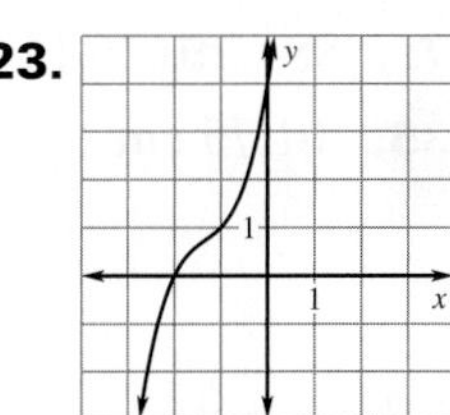

25. $(-2, 0)$: min, $(-0.5, 5)$: max, $(1, 0)$: min; $-2, 1; 4$

27.

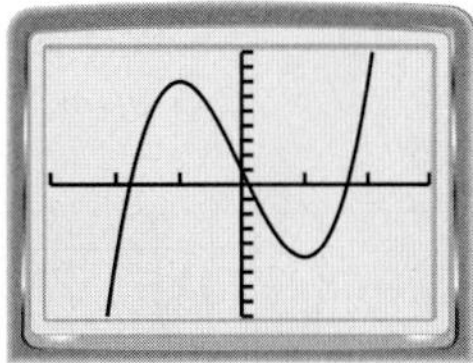

x-int: $-1.79, 0.11, 1.67$; max: $(-1, 7)$; min: $(1, -5)$

29.

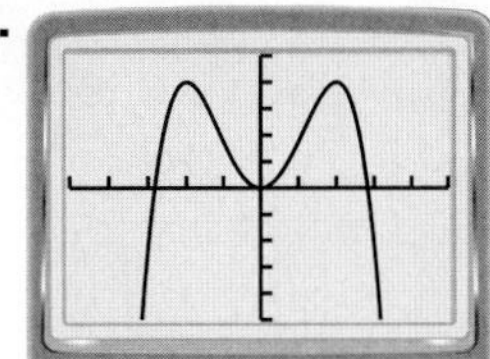

x-int: $-2.83, 0, 2.83$; max: $(-2, 4), (2, 4)$; min: $(0, 0)$

31.

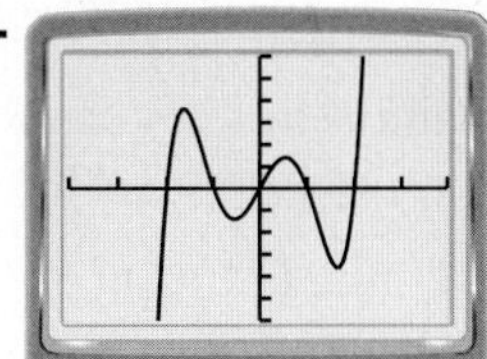

x-int: $-2, -1, 0, 1, 2$; max: $(-1.64, 3.63)$, $(0.54, 1.42)$; min: $(-0.54, -1.42)$, $(1.64, -3.63)$

33. about 5 in. by 7 in. by 1.5 in.; about 52.5 in.^{3}

35. a.

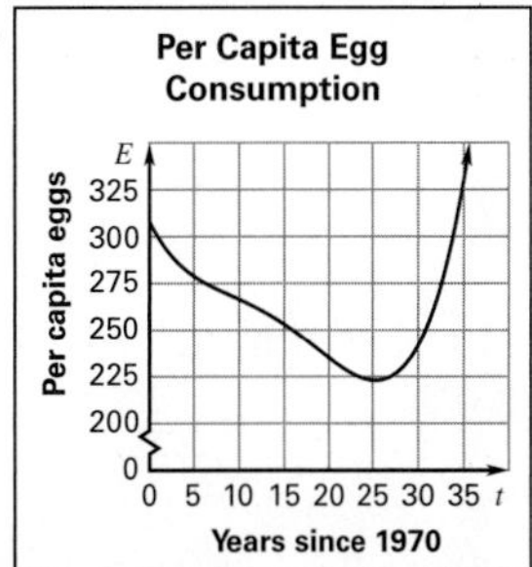

b. (25.33, 222.93); *Sample answer:* From 1970 to 1995, per capita egg consumption decreased to about 223 eggs, then began to increase again.

2.8 Exercise Set B (pp. 102–103)

1. 8

3. zeros: -2 (multiplicity 2), $3, \frac{9}{2}$; turning points: 3

5. zeros: 0 (multiplicity 3), -1 (multiplicity 2), 1; turning points: 3 **7.** zeros: $-3, -2, 2$ (multiplicity 2); turning points: 3

9. 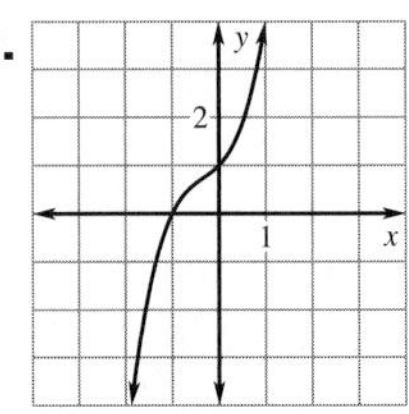

domain: $-\infty < x < \infty$
range: $-\infty < y < \infty$

11. 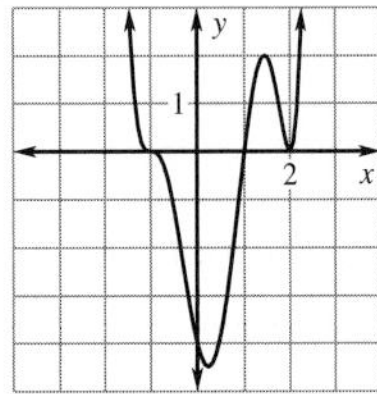

domain: $-\infty < x < \infty$
range: $y \geq -4.489$

13. 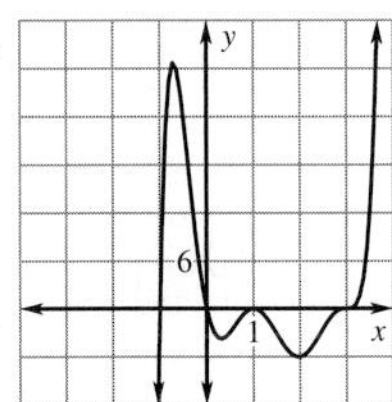

domain: $-\infty < x < \infty$
range: $-\infty < y < \infty$

15. 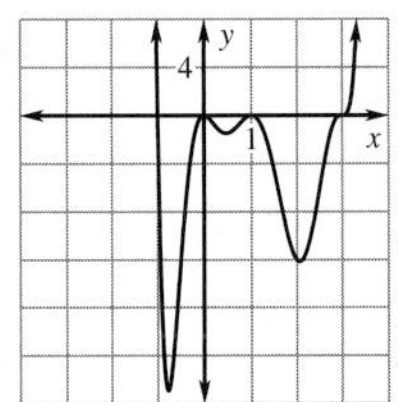

domain: $-\infty < x < \infty$
range: $y \geq -22.9$

17. $(-2, 2.4)$: max, $(0, -1.2)$: min, $(1, -1)$: max, $(2.2, -2)$: min; $-2.5, -1, 2.6$; 5

19. $(-1.5, -2.25)$: min, $(0, 3)$: max, $(2, -3)$: min, $(3.5, 2)$: max; $-2, -1, 1, 3, 4$; 5

21. 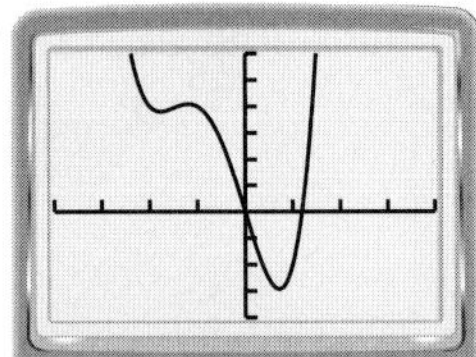

x-int: 0, 1.2; max: $(-1.19, 4.09)$; min: $(-1.77, 3.8)$, $(0.71, -2.93)$

23. 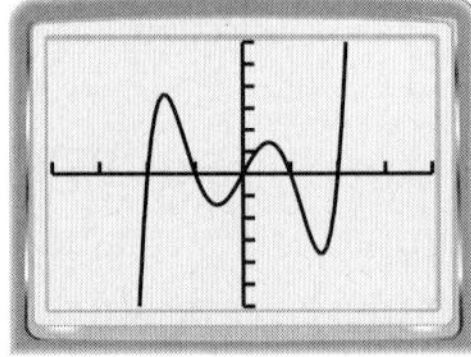

x-int: $-2, -1, 0, 1, 2$; max: $(-1.64, 3.63)$, $(0.54, 1.42)$; min: $(-0.54, -1.42)$, $(1.64, -3.63)$

25. 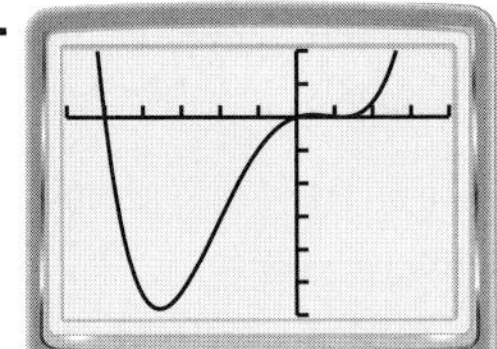

x-int: $-5, 0, 1.2$; max: $(0.42, 1.38)$; min: $(-3.57, -116.16)$, $(1.2, 0)$

27. *Sample answer:* $f(x) = x^3 - 6x^2 + 5x + 12$, $g(x) = x^4 - 5x^3 - x^2 + 17x + 12$, $h(x) = x^5 - 8x^4 + 14x^3 + 20x^2 - 39x - 36$

29. 2, 4

31. If n is even, there is a turning point. If n is odd, the graph passes through the x-axis.;

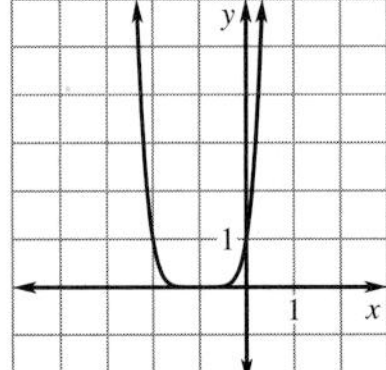

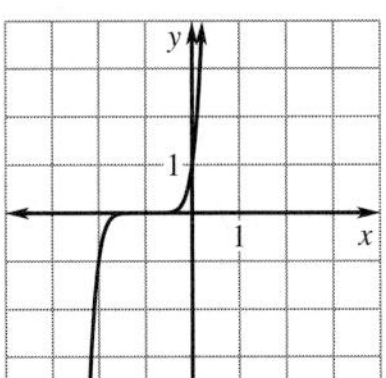

33. a. 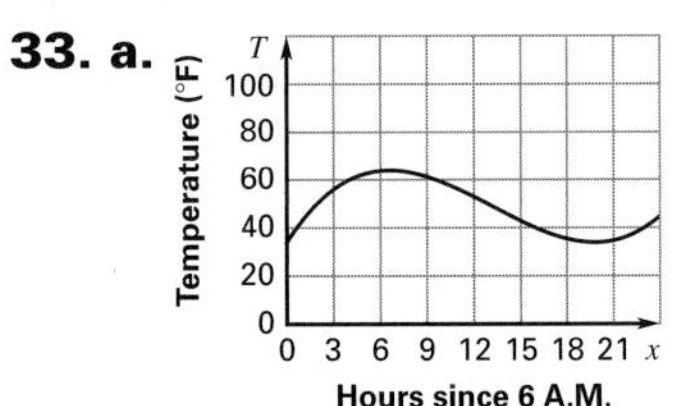

b. (6.6, 63.9), (19.8, 34.0); the high temperature for the 24-hour period was 63.9°F, which occurred at about 12:36 P.M. and the low temperature for the 24-hour period was 34°F, which occurred at about 1:48 A.M. **c.** $34 \leq y \leq 63.9$

UNIT 3

3.1 Exercise Set A (p. 111)

1. $7^{1/3}$ **3.** $14^{4/5}$ **5.** $11^{7/8}$ **7.** $\sqrt[3]{17}$ **9.** $(\sqrt[3]{33})^2$ **11.** $(\sqrt[5]{-28})^7$ **13.** 4 **15.** 81 **17.** 32 **19.** 625 **21.** -8 **23.** 2.20 **25.** 3.00 **27.** 2.88 **29.** 26.15 **31.** about 5.2 cm **33.** -1.58 **35.** 601.75 cm^3; 8.44 cm

3.1 Exercise Set B (p. 112)

1. $63^{3/5}$ **3.** $124^{7/6}$ **5.** $(\sqrt{13})^3$ **7.** 9 **9.** 16 **11.** $\frac{1}{125}$ **13.** $-\frac{1}{8}$ **15.** $-\frac{1}{3125}$ **17.** 22.89

19. 132.26 **21.** 32 **23.** 0.09 **25.** 4.21
27. 0.18, 5.82 **29.** ±2.06 **31.** 1.32
33. −3.58 **35.** about 1.81 in.

3.2 Exercise Set A (p. 115)

1. $7^{5/3}$ **3.** $6^{1/2}$ **5.** 2 **7.** $11^{3/4}$ **9.** 27 **11.** 2
13. x^3 **15.** $x^{1/7}$ **17.** $2x\sqrt[3]{2x}$ **19.** $x^{3/5}$
21. $x^{5+\sqrt{3}}$ **23.** $\frac{x^{2\sqrt{3}}}{2}$ **25.** $8\sqrt[3]{5}$ **27.** $-6\sqrt{3}$
29. $2xy^6$ **31.** $xy^2\sqrt[4]{3x^3yz^3}$ **33.** $\frac{3\sqrt[3]{3xy^2z^2}}{2yz}$
35. about 10 ft

3.2 Exercise Set B (p. 116)

1. $16 \cdot 5^{9/4}$ **3.** $7^{6/5}$ **5.** 4 **7.** $\frac{\sqrt{6}}{3}$ **9.** $\frac{\sqrt{70}}{35}$
11. $\frac{x^4\sqrt[4]{x}}{y^2}$ **13.** $x^{1/3}y^{1/6}$ **15.** $\frac{\sqrt{3}z^{1/4}}{x^{1/2}y^{1/3}}$
17. $9x^4\sqrt[4]{x^3}$
19. Addition was used to combine the exponents instead of subtraction; $\frac{y^{1/2}}{y^{-3/4}} = y^{1/2-(-3/4)} = y^{5/4}$
21. $3x^2z\sqrt[3]{xyz^2}$ **23.** $\frac{\sqrt[3]{50x + 25\sqrt{x}}}{5}$
25. $4x^2z\sqrt{xyz}$ **27.** about 4.3 in.

3.3 Exercise Set A (p. 120)

1.

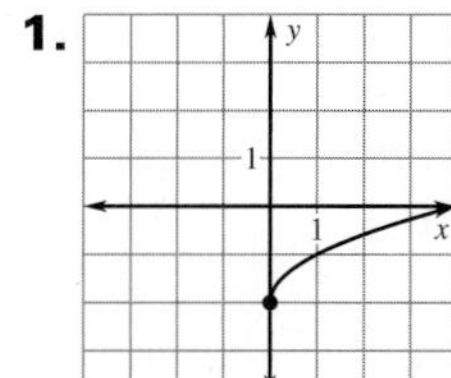

domain: $x \ge 0$,
range: $y \ge -2$

3.

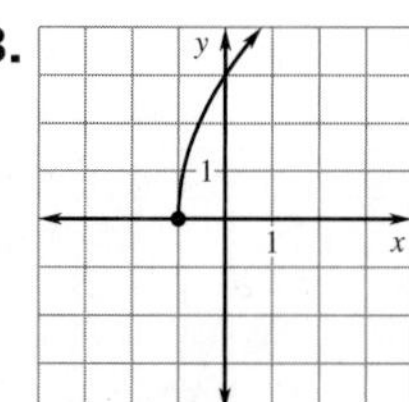

domain: $x \ge -1$,
range: $y \ge 0$

5.

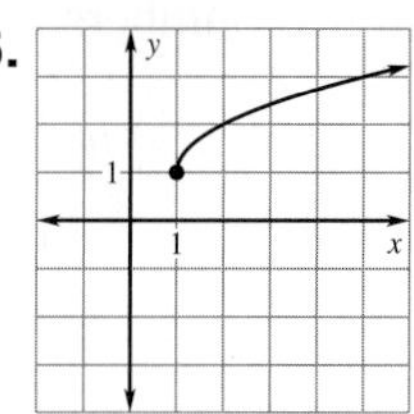

domain: $x \ge 1$,
range: $y \ge 1$

7.

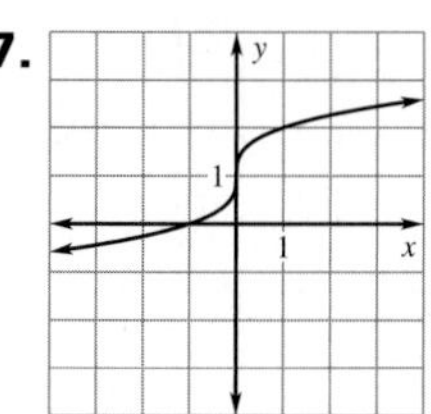

domain and range:
all real numbers

9.

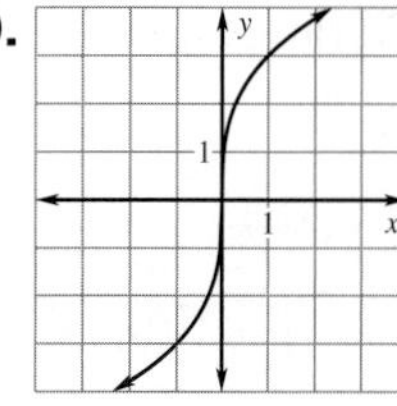

domain and range:
all real numbers

11.

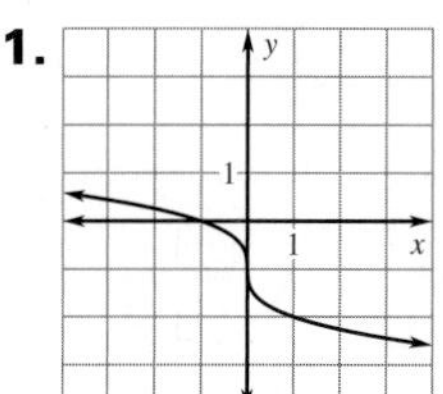

domain and range:
all real numbers

13. domain: $t \ge -273$, range: $V \ge 0$

15. domain: $0 \le h \le 200$; range: $0 \le t \le 3.5$

17. a. $v_t = 33.7\sqrt{\frac{175}{A}}$

b. *Sample answer:*

A	2	4	6	8	10
v_t	315.23	222.90	182.00	157.62	140.98

c.

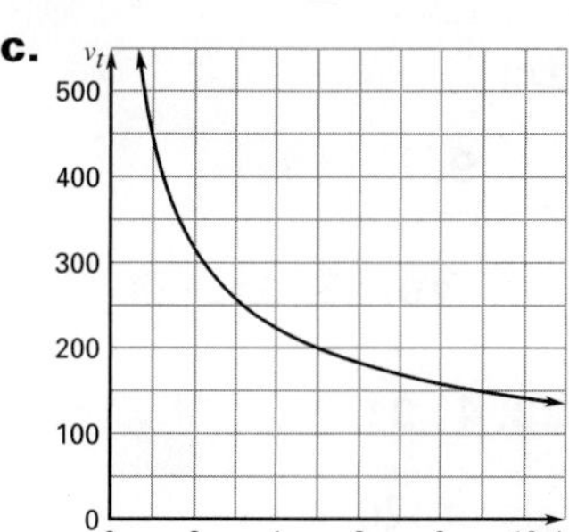

3.3 Exercise Set B (p. 121)

1.

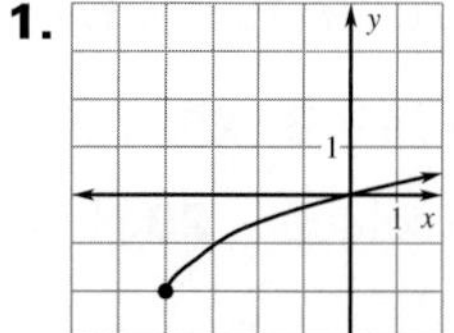

domain: $x \ge -4$,
range: $y \ge -2$

3.

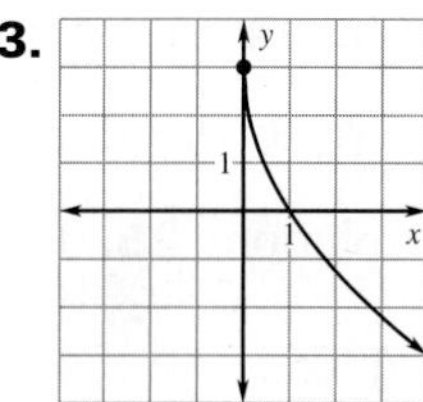

domain: $x \ge 0$,
range: $y \le 3$

5.

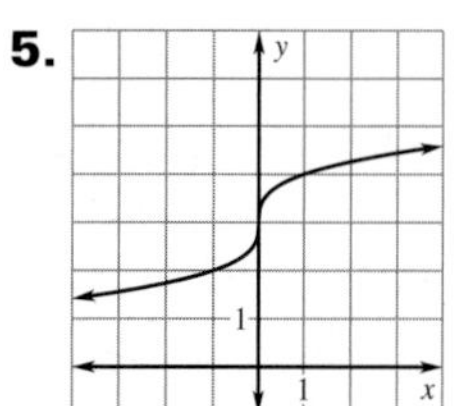

domain and range:
all real numbers

7.

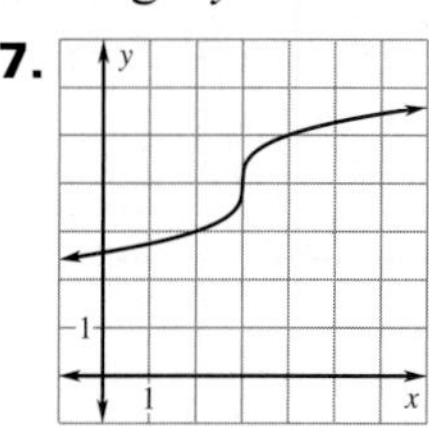

domain and range:
all real numbers

9. 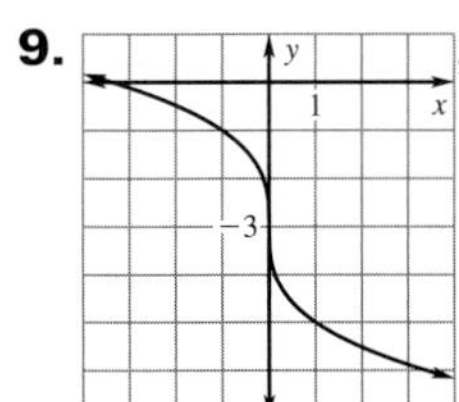; domain and range: all real numbers

11. (0, 0) and (1, 1)

13.

15. On the interval $(-1, 1)$, the larger the root, the steeper the graph. On the intervals $(-\infty, -1)$ and $(1, \infty)$, the larger the root, the less steep the graph.

17. domain: $0 \le h \le 175$; range: $0 \le t \le 3.3$

19. 31 ft

3.4 Exercise Set A (p. 124)

1. 81 **3.** 2 **5.** 3 **7.** 173 **9.** 26 **11.** $-\frac{1}{8}$

13. -68 **15.** $-\frac{8}{27}$ **17.** $\frac{26}{5}$ **19.** 27 **21.** -8

23. -1 **25.** 4 **27.** $\frac{5}{2}$ **29.** 4 **31.** 1

33. about 45.87 m **35.** about 120.97 m

3.4 Exercise Set B (p. 125)

1. $\frac{15}{2}$ **3.** -4 **5.** $\pm\sqrt{39}$ **7.** -6 **9.** 120 **11.** $\frac{397}{81}$

13. 25 **15.** 9 **17.** no solution **19.** 3 **21.** -5

23. no solution **25.** 0 **27.** no solution **29.** 12 in.

UNIT 4

4.1 Exercise Set A (p. 132)

5. 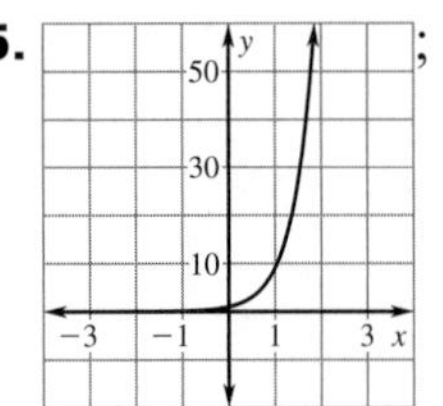; domain: all real numbers; range: $y > 0$

7. 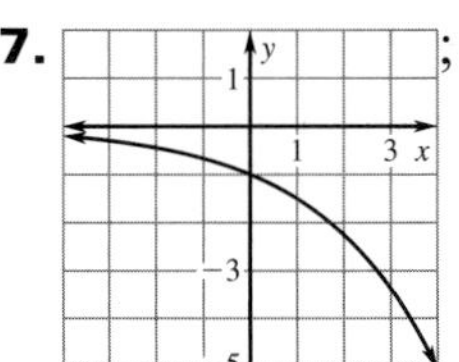; domain: all real numbers; range: $y < 0$

9. 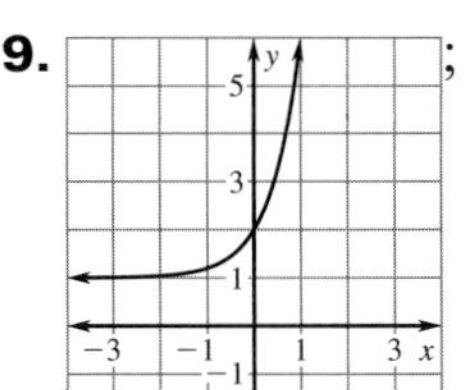; domain: all real numbers; range: $y > 1$

11. 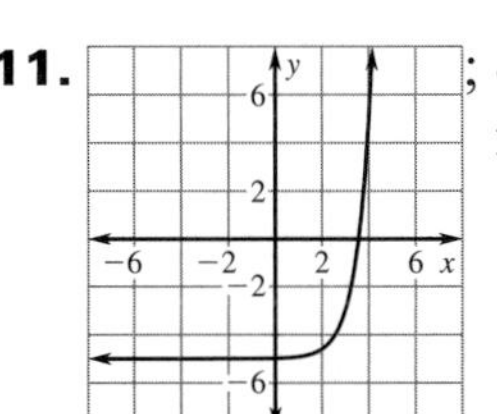; domain: all real numbers; range: $y > -5$

13. The function was not evaluated correctly when $x = 0$. The correct point is (0, 0.5), not (0, 1).

15. a. $E = 1350(1.09)^t$; about 1748 students
b. 2016

4.1 Exercise Set B (p. 133)

1. 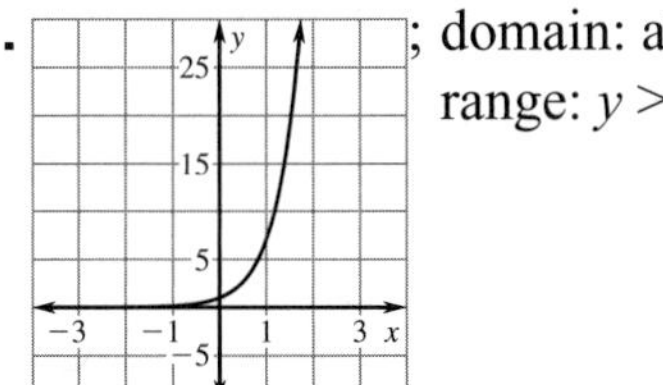; domain: all real numbers; range: $y > 0$

3. 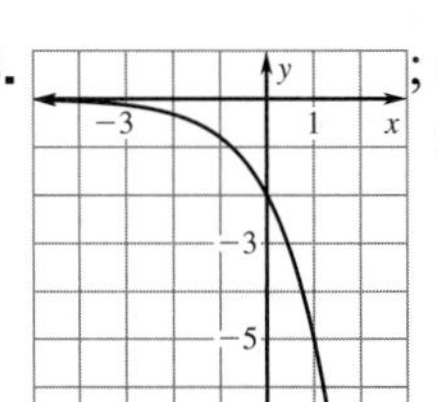; domain: all real numbers; range: $y < 0$

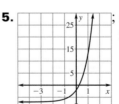

5. 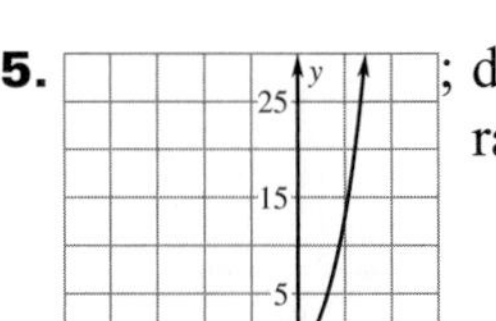; domain: all real numbers; range: $y > -7$

7. 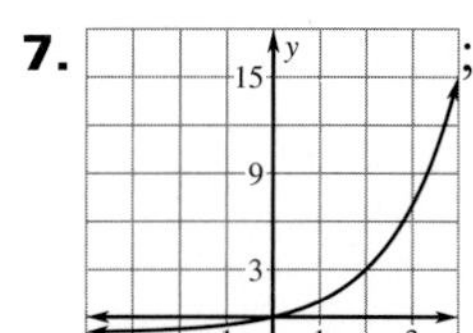; domain: all real numbers; range: $y > -1$

9. 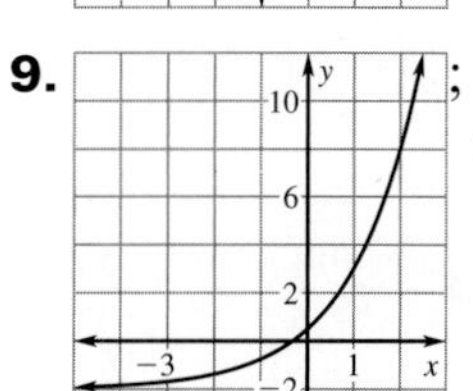; domain: all real numbers; range: $y > -2$

11. \$4660.05

13. a. $P = 494{,}290(1.03)^t$; 664,284

b. 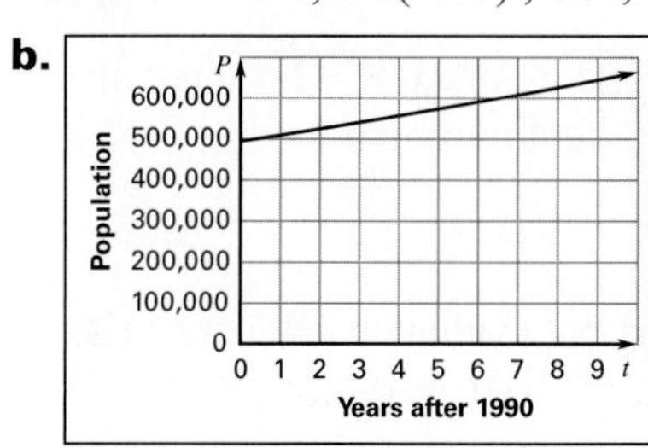

domain: $0 \le t \le 10$;
range: $494{,}290 \le P \le 664{,}284$

c. 1993

15. a. $n = 41(1.089)^t$

b.

n	0	1	2	3
t	41	44.65	48.62	52.95

c. 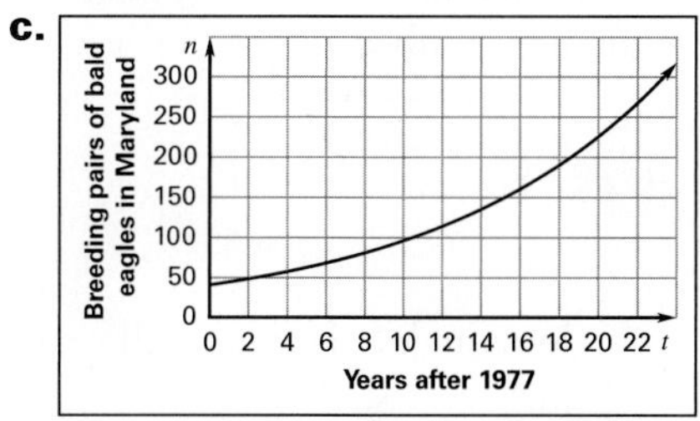

d. 1985

4.2 Exercise Set A (p. 137)

1. exponential decay **3.** exponential decay

7. 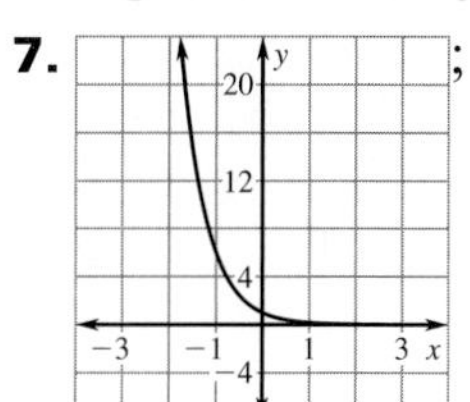; domain: all real numbers; range: $y > 0$

9. 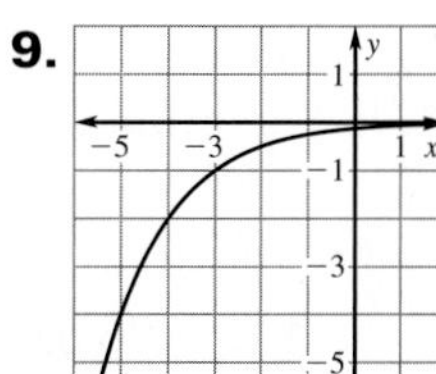; domain: all real numbers; range: $y < 0$

11. 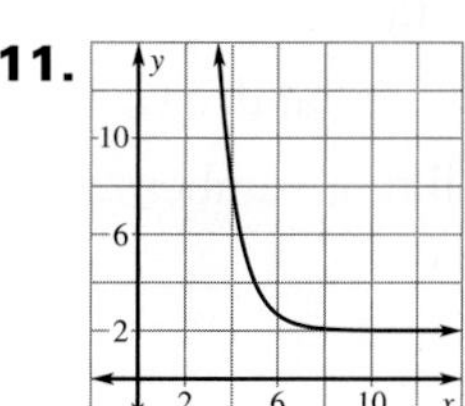; domain: all real numbers; range: $y > 2$

13. 3 h

4.2 Exercise Set B (p. 138)

1. 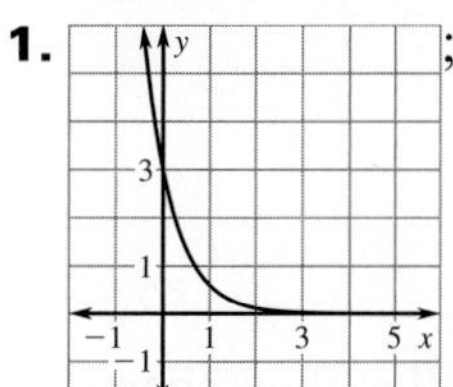; domain: all real numbers; range: $y > 0$

3. 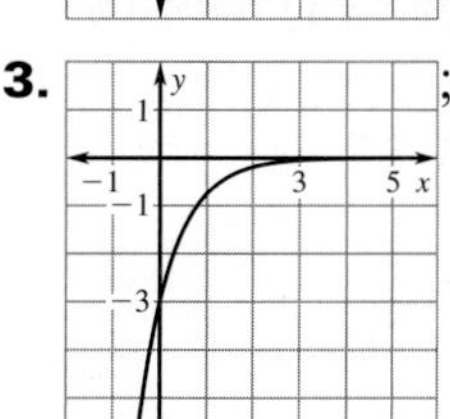; domain: all real numbers; range: $y < 0$

5. 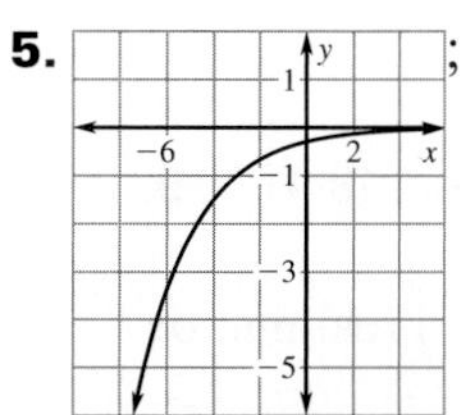; domain: all real numbers; range: $y < 0$

7. 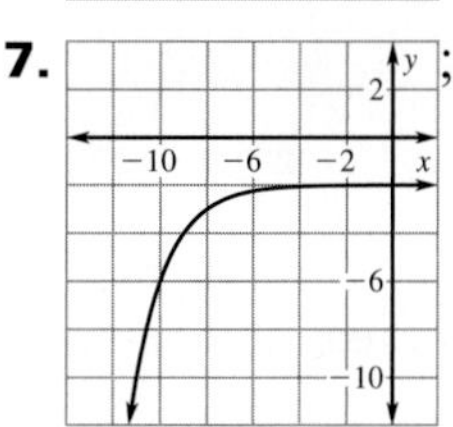; domain: all real numbers; range: $y < -2$

9. 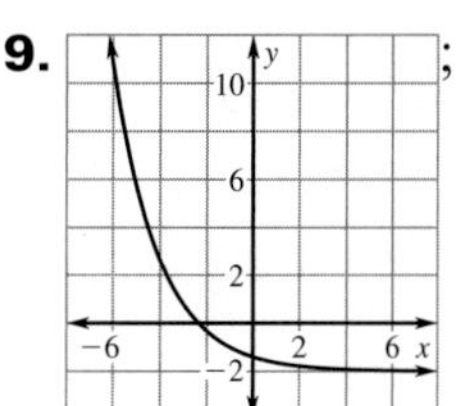; domain: all real numbers; range: $y > -2$

11. The decay factor should be $1 - 0.03 = 0.97$, not 0.03. **13. a.** 400 g **b.** about 243.8 g **c.** 28 days

4.3 Exercise Set A (p. 142)

1. $\frac{1}{e^3}$ **3.** $\frac{1}{e^{12}}$ **5.** $\frac{e^2}{4}$ **7.** $6e^{5x}$ **9.** $\frac{1}{e^x}$ **11.** 1096.633 **13.** 1.822 **15.** exponential growth **17.** exponential decay **19.** exponential decay

21. ; domain: all real numbers; range: $y > 0$

23. ; domain: all real numbers; range: $y < 3$

25. ; domain: all real numbers; range: $y > -3$

27. \$3444.50

4.3 Exercise Set B (p. 143)

1. $4e^{10}$ **3.** $27e^{12}$ **5.** $\frac{e^{9x-3}}{8}$ **7.** 148.413 **9.** 0.202

11. ; domain: all real numbers; range: $y > -3$

13. 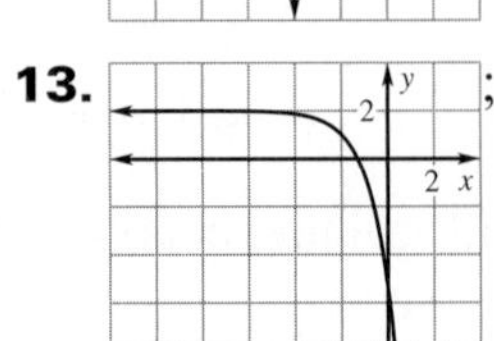 ; domain: all real numbers; range: $y < 2$

15. 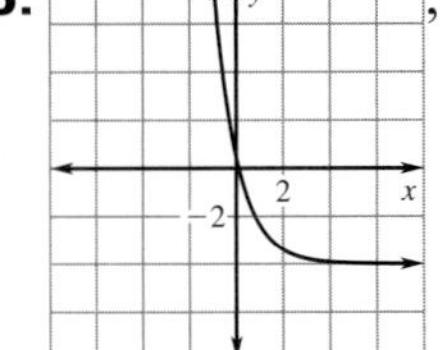 ; domain: all real numbers; range: $y > -4$

17. exponential growth **19.** 3 **21.** 21

4.4 Exercise Set A (p. 147)

1. $7^2 = 49$ **3.** $5^3 = 125$ **5.** $4^{-1} = \frac{1}{4}$ **7.** 2 **9.** -1 **11.** $\frac{1}{3}$ **13.** 0.805 **15.** -0.693 **17.** $f^{-1}(x) = e^x$ **19.** $f^{-1}(x) = 2(10^x)$ **21.** $f^{-1}(x) = 3^{x-2}$

23. ; domain: $x > -2$; range: all real numbers

25. about 129

4.4 Exercise Set B (p. 148)

1. $4^{1/2} = 2$ **3.** $\left(\frac{1}{4}\right)^{-3} = 64$ **5.** $\frac{3}{2}$ **7.** $\frac{2}{3}$ **9.** $\frac{3}{2}$ **11.** 7.974 **13.** $f^{-1}(x) = 7^x$ **15.** $f^{-1}(x) = \left(\frac{1}{2}\right)^{x-2}$ **17.** $f^{-1}(x) = e^{x+3} + 1$

19. 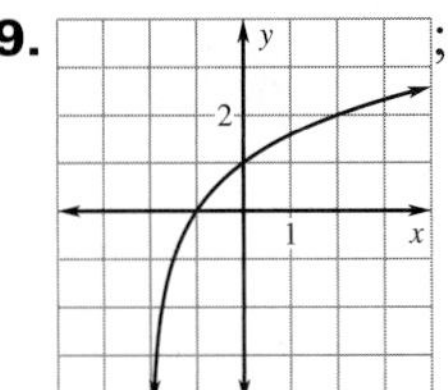 ; domain: $x > -2$; range: all real numbers

21. ; domain: $x > 1$; range: all real numbers

23. 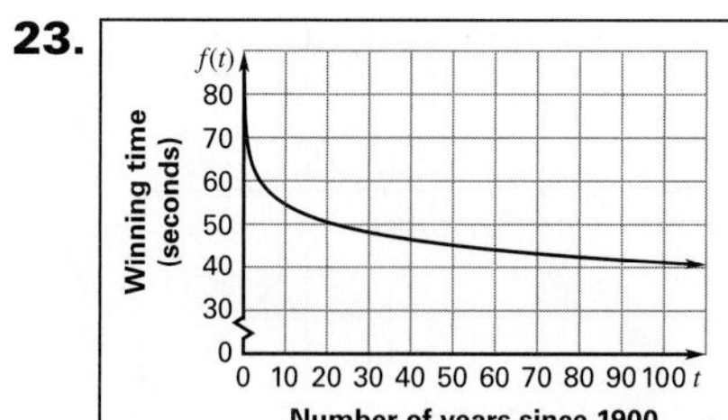

4.5 Exercise Set A (p. 153)

1. a. y-intercept: 1; no x-intercept; no zeros **b.** increasing: $(-\infty, \infty)$ **c.** C and D

3. The zero is the x-coordinate of the x-intercept, not the y-coordinate of the y-intercept. The zero is $x = 2$.

5. 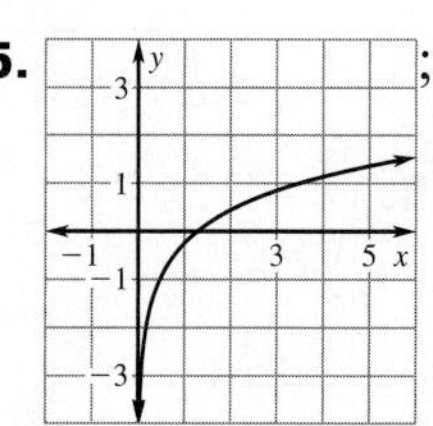 ; domain: $x > 0$; range: all real numbers

7. a. no zeros **b.** decreasing: $(-\infty, \infty)$

9. a. $x = 1$ **b.** decreasing: $(0, \infty)$

4.5 Exercise Set B (p. 154)

1. a. $x = 0$ **b.** increasing: $(-\infty, \infty)$ **c.** C and D

3. a. no zeros **b.** increasing: $(-\infty, \infty)$

5. a. no zeros **b.** increasing: $(-\infty, \infty)$

7. a. $x = 9$ **b.** increasing: $(-1, \infty)$

9. 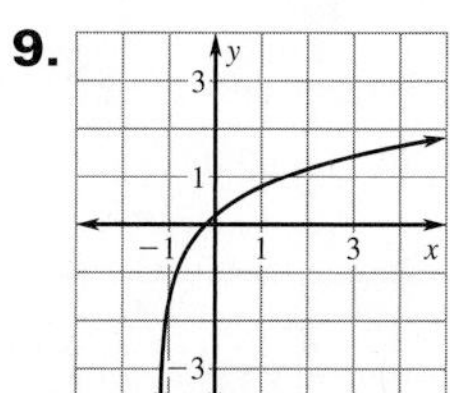 domain: $x > -1.2$; range: all real numbers

11. ; domain: $x > -7.8$; range: all real numbers

13. a. 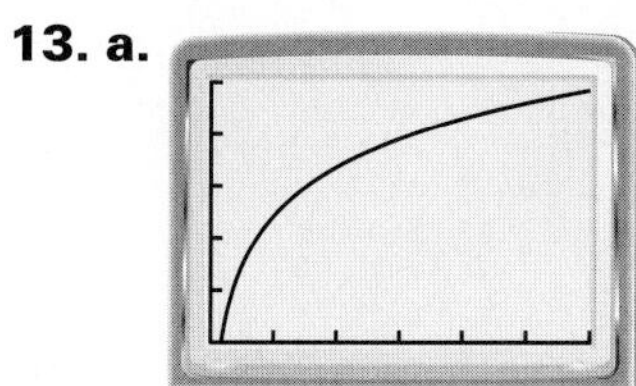 ; no zeros (the function is only defined for $x > 4$.)

b. increasing: $(4, \infty)$; The alligator's length increases as its weight increases.

4.6 Exercise Set A (p. 157)

5. 1.447 **7.** 1.204 **9.** -0.602

11. $2 \log_7 x + \log_7 y$ **13.** $\log 5 + \frac{1}{3} \log x$

15. $\log_9 2 + 3 \log_9 x - \frac{1}{2}$ **17.** $\log_3 16$

19. $\log \frac{2x^2}{3}$ **21.** 1.277 **23.** 0.139 **25.** 2.018

27. a. $\text{pH} = 6.1 + \log B - \log C$ **b.** about 7.38 **c.** just below normal

4.6 Exercise Set B (p. 158)

1. 3.332 **3.** 2.772 **5.** 1.659

7. $3 \log_2 x - \log_2 y - 2 \log_2 z$

9. $\log 2 + \frac{1}{2} \log x - 2 \log y$

11. $5[\log_9 2 + 2 \log_9 x + \log_9 y + \log_9 z]$

13. $\log_3 \frac{5}{3}$ **15.** $\log_2 \frac{9}{x^3 y}$ **17.** $\log \frac{\sqrt{(x+4)^3}}{6x^3}$

19. 1.869 **21.** 2.665

4.7 Exercise Set A (p. 161)

1. 0 **3.** 1.544 **5.** 0.462 **7.** $\frac{5}{2}$ **9.** 2.243 **11.** 5

13. 2 **15.** $\frac{4}{5}$ **17.** 2.730 **19.** 0.327

21. no solution **23.** 54.598 **25.** $\frac{1}{3}$ **27.** 30.375

29. 39.121 **31.** $\frac{10}{7}$ **33.** 4 **35.** 36.399

39. about 28.1 yr **41.** about 22.88

4.7 Exercise Set B (p. 162)

1. 1.609 **3.** 0.973 **5.** 2.096 **7.** 2.473 **9.** 6.091

11. -4.420 **13.** -0.135 **15.** 0 **17.** $-\frac{9}{2}$

19. 9998 **21.** 12 **23.** 1 **25.** 1 **27.** no solution

29. $2, \frac{5}{2}$ **31.** 4, 8 **33.** 0.656 **35.** -9.110

37. \$206,400

4.8 Exercise Set A (p. 167)

1. $(-\infty, 3)$ **3.** $(-\infty, 4)$ **5.** $(2, \infty)$

7. $(-\infty, 3.409]$ **9.** $(-\infty, 2]$ **11.** $(0, 5]$ **13.** $(0, 8]$

15. (0, 6) **17.** (5.04, ∞) **19.** after about 4.5 years
21. a. $C = P(1.04)^t$ **b.** $0.99 < 0.99\,(1.04)^t < 1.5$; in the first 10.5 years, (0, 10.5) **c.** $0.99\,(1.04)^t > 2$; over 18.0 years, (18.0, ∞)

4.8 Exercise Set B (p. 168)

1. $(-\infty, 2.21]$ **3.** $[-\infty, 2.42)$ **5.** $(0.85, +\infty)$
7. $(-\infty, -2.32]$ **9.** $(-16.82, +\infty)$
11. $[2.72, +\infty)$ **13.** $[28, +\infty)$ **15.** $(0, 70.29]$
17. $(0, 49.47)$
19. $200e^{-0.00043t} < 10$; after about 6966.8 years
21. $80 \le p \le 196.36$

4.9 Exercise Set A (p. 171)

1. $y = \frac{1}{2}(3)^x$ **3.** $y = 3(4)^x$ **5.** $y = 5\left(\frac{2}{3}\right)^x$
7. $y = 37.86(6.85)^x$ **9.** $y = 62.12(0.03)^x$
11. $y = 3x^3$ **13.** $y = 2x^{1.5}$ **15.** $y = \frac{1}{4}x^{0.5}$
17. $y = 12.94x^{3.3}$ **19.** $y = 93.34x^2$
21. $y = 0.81x^{0.79}$; \$6.14

4.9 Exercise Set B (p. 172)

1. $y = 1.2(2.4)^x$ **3.** $y = 2.7(4.2)^x$

5.
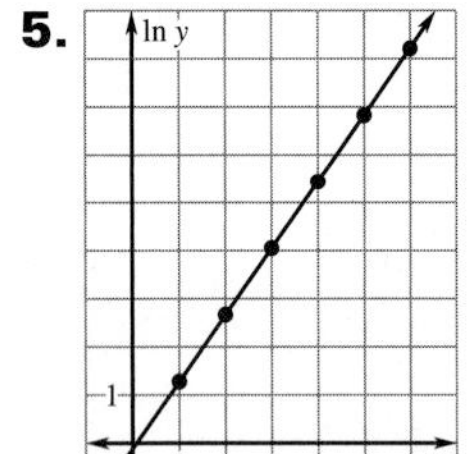

$y = 0.9(4^x)$

7. $y = 2.1x^{3.7}$

9.
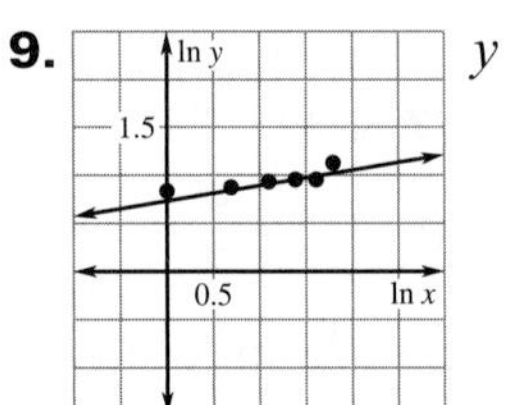

$y = 2.2x^{0.13}$

11. $y = 2.232x^{0.129}$

UNIT 5

5.1 Exercise Set A (p. 178)

1. down
3. left

5.
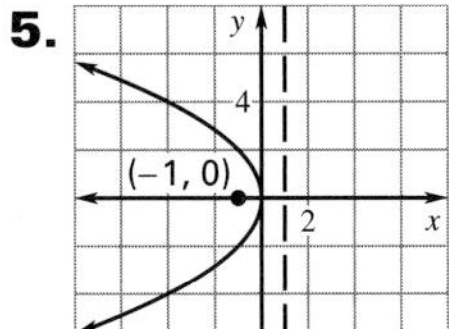

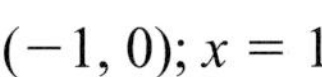
$(-1, 0); x = 1$

7.
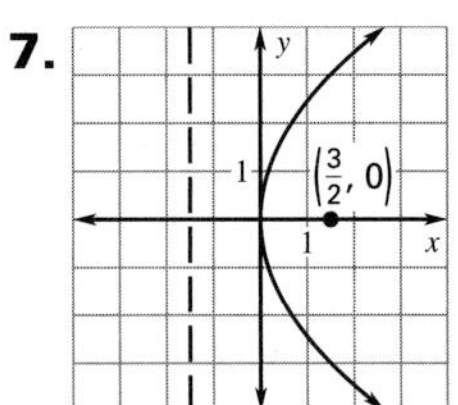

$\left(\frac{3}{2}, 0\right); x = -\frac{3}{2}$

9.
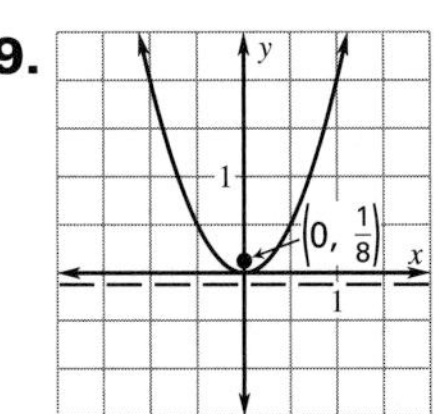

$\left(0, \frac{1}{8}\right); y = -\frac{1}{8}$

11. $y^2 = 8x$ **13.** $y^2 = -4x$ **15.** $y^2 = 12x$
17. $y^2 = -12x$ **19.** $y^2 = 4x$ **21.** $y^2 = -x$
23. $x^2 = 10y$

5.1 Exercise Set B (p. 179)

1. 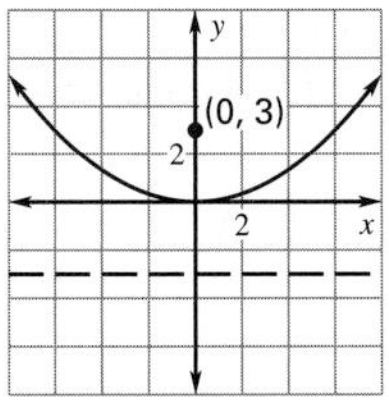 $(0, 3); y = -3$

3.
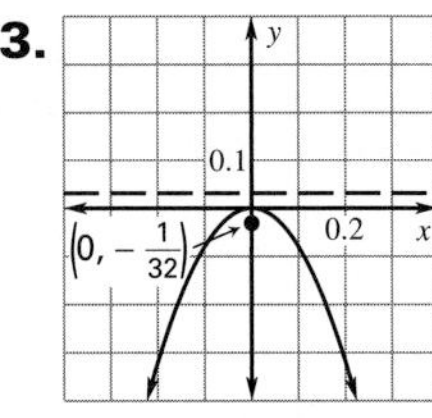

$\left(0, -\frac{1}{32}\right); y = \frac{1}{32}$

5.
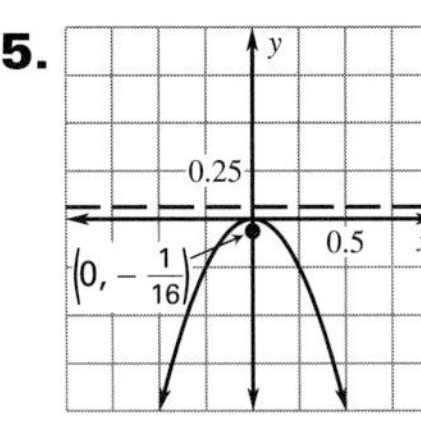

$\left(0, -\frac{1}{16}\right); y = \frac{1}{16}$

7.
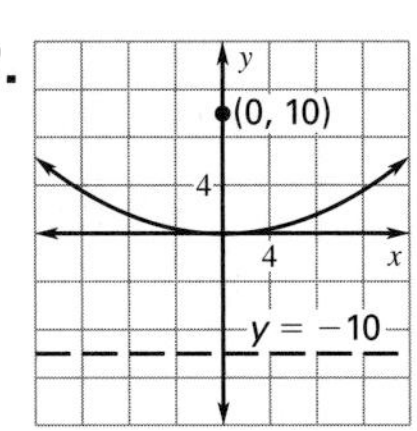

$(0, 10); y = -10$

9.
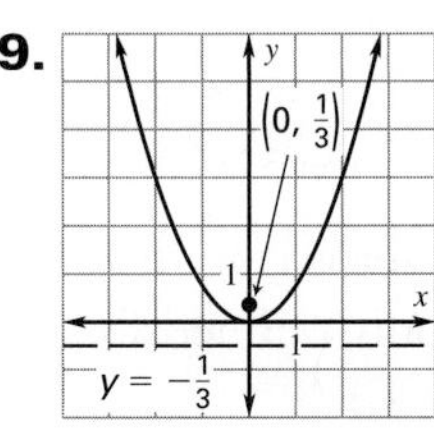

$\left(0, \frac{1}{3}\right); y = -\frac{1}{3}$

11. $x^2 = 24y$ **13.** $y^2 = 20x$ **15.** $x^2 = -\frac{3}{2}y$
17. $y^2 = -6x$ **19.** $y^2 = -8x$ **21.** $y^2 = 24x$
23. $y^2 = -16x$ **25.** $x^2 = -\frac{5}{2}y$ **27.** $x^2 = 10y$
29. about 7238.2 ft^3

5.2 Exercise Set A (p. 182)

1.

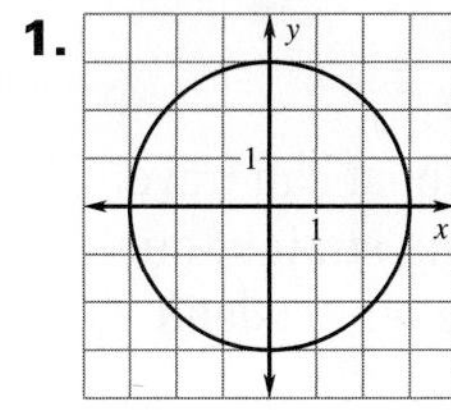

3

3.

8

5.

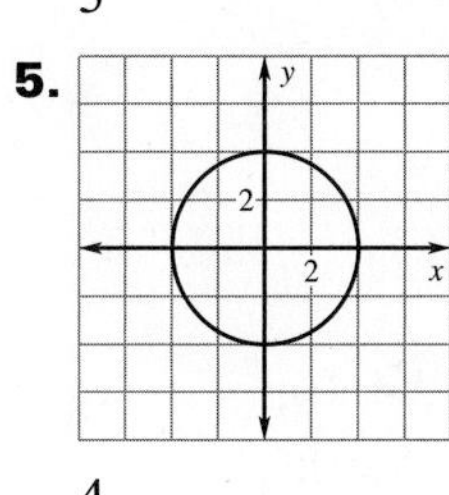

4

7. The radius of the circle should be 4, not 16.

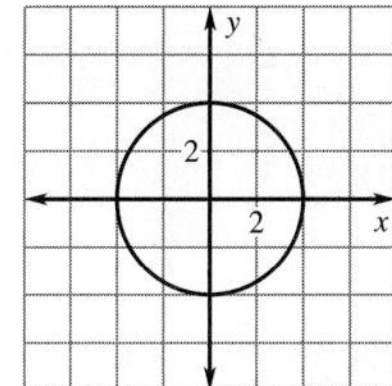

9. $x^2 + y^2 = 80$ **11.** $x^2 + y^2 = 7$
13. $x^2 + y^2 = 90$ **15.** $x^2 + y^2 = 25$
17. $x^2 + y^2 = 13$ **19.** $x^2 + y^2 = 52$

21.

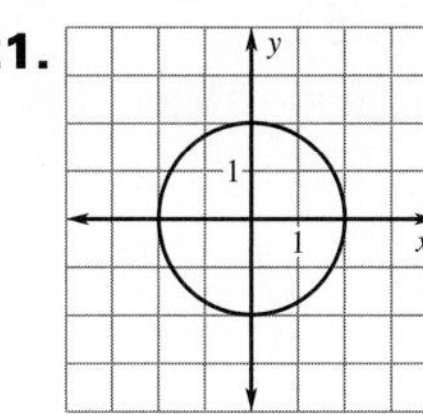

23. $y = -\frac{1}{4}x + \frac{17}{4}$ **25.** $x^2 + y^2 = 2304$

5.2 Exercise Set B (p. 183)

1.

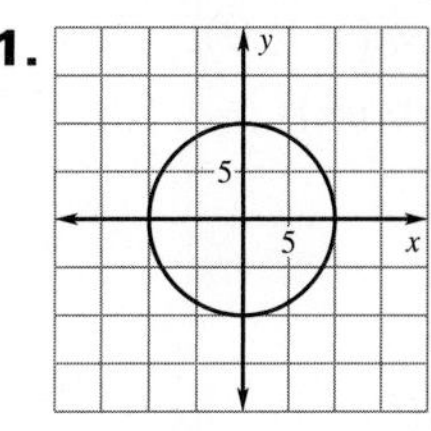

10

3.

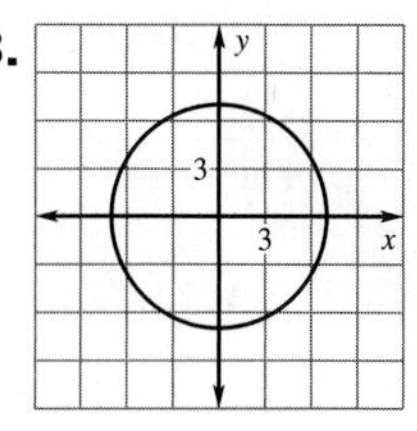

7

5.

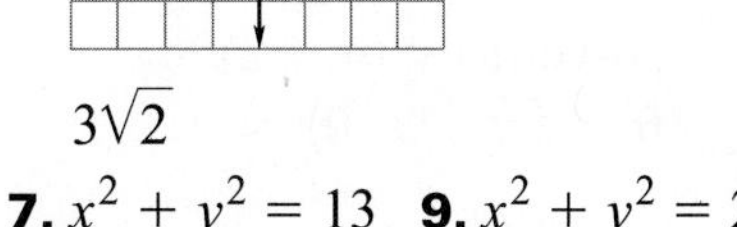

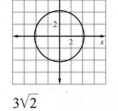

$3\sqrt{2}$

7. $x^2 + y^2 = 13$ **9.** $x^2 + y^2 = 272$
11. $x^2 + y^2 = 104$ **13.** $x^2 + y^2 = 20$
15. $x^2 + y^2 = \frac{101}{4}$ **17.** $y = \frac{-\sqrt{6}}{2}x + 10$

19. a.

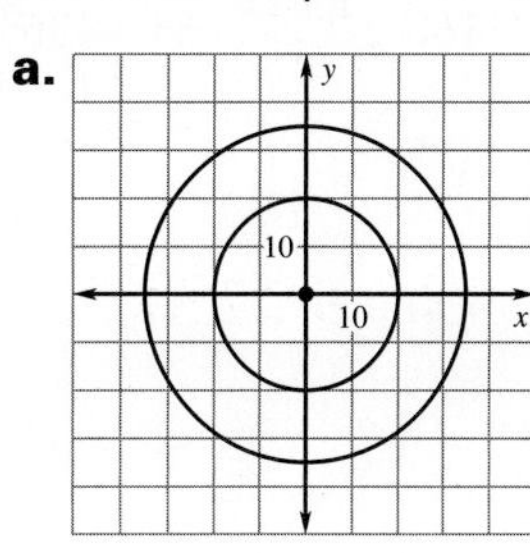

b. $x^2 + y^2 \leq 400$
$x^2 + y^2 \leq 1225$

c. The rating is between 4.2 and 4.6. The location is outside of the circle with a rating of 4.6, but inside the circle with a rating of 4.2.

5.3 Exercise Set A (p. 188)

1.

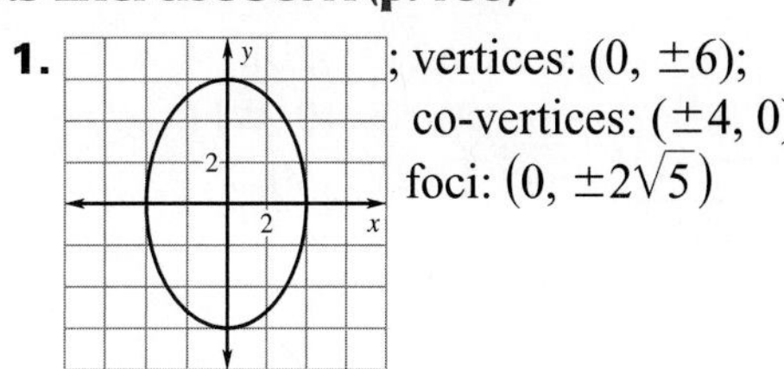

; vertices: $(0, \pm 6)$; co-vertices: $(\pm 4, 0)$; foci: $(0, \pm 2\sqrt{5})$

3.

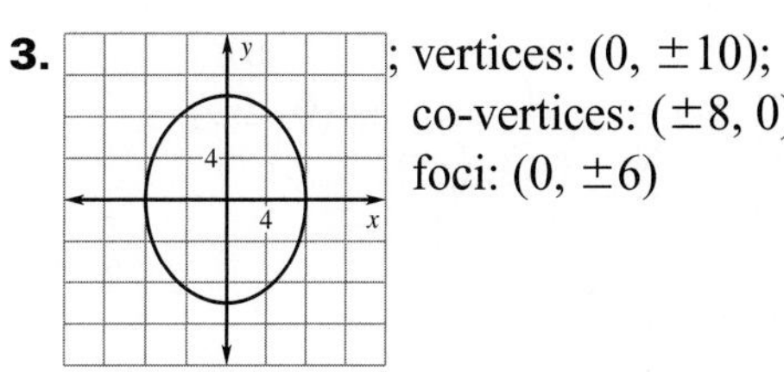

; vertices: $(0, \pm 10)$; co-vertices: $(\pm 8, 0)$; foci: $(0, \pm 6)$

5. 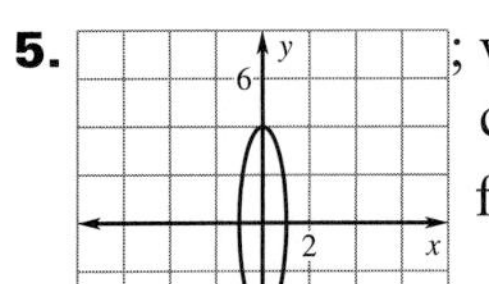 ; vertices: $(0, \pm 4)$; co-vertices: $(\pm 1, 0)$; foci: $(0, \pm\sqrt{15})$

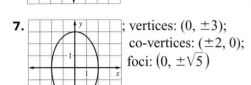

7. ; vertices: $(0, \pm 3)$; co-vertices: $(\pm 2, 0)$; foci: $(0, \pm\sqrt{5})$

9. 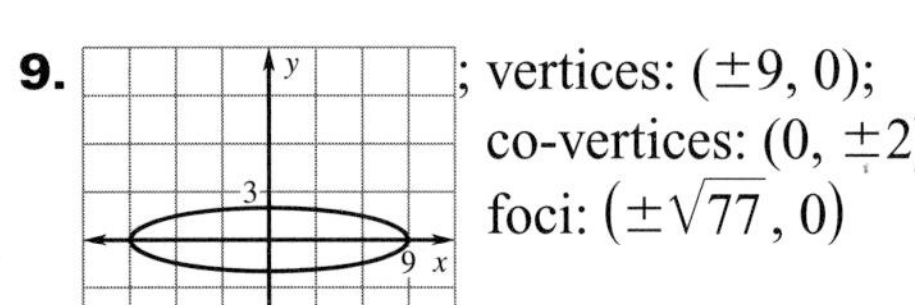 ; vertices: $(\pm 9, 0)$; co-vertices: $(0, \pm 2)$; foci: $(\pm\sqrt{77}, 0)$

11. $\frac{x^2}{1} + \frac{y^2}{25} = 1$ **13.** $\frac{x^2}{4} + \frac{y^2}{16} = 1$ **15.** $\frac{x^2}{64} + \frac{y^2}{36} = 1$

17. 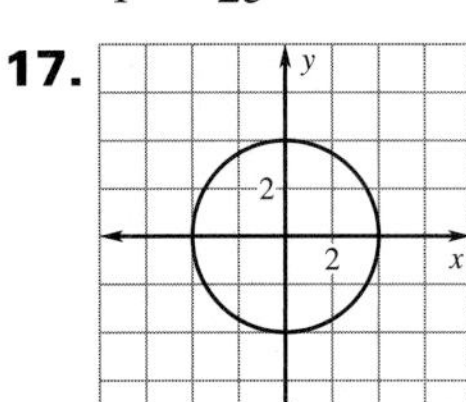

19. $\frac{x^2}{64} + \frac{y^2}{100} = 1$

21. a. $\frac{x^2}{62{,}500} + \frac{y^2}{22{,}500} = 1$ **b.** $37{,}500\pi$ yd^2

5.3 Exercise Set B (p. 189)

1. 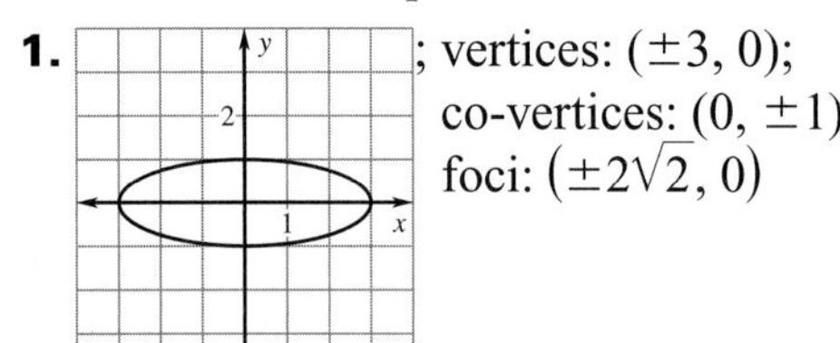 ; vertices: $(\pm 3, 0)$; co-vertices: $(0, \pm 1)$; foci: $(\pm 2\sqrt{2}, 0)$

3. 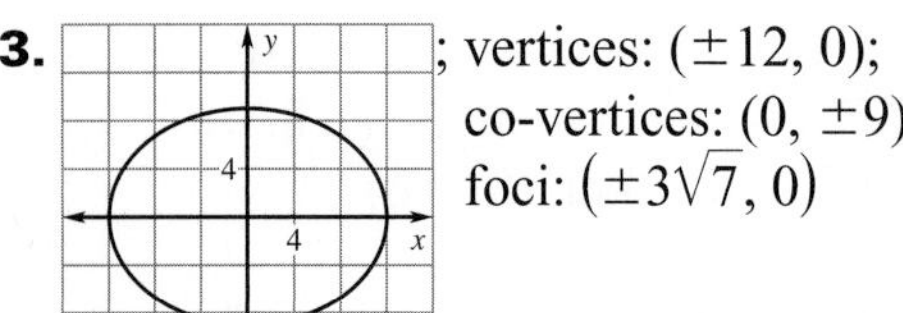 ; vertices: $(\pm 12, 0)$; co-vertices: $(0, \pm 9)$; foci: $(\pm 3\sqrt{7}, 0)$

5. 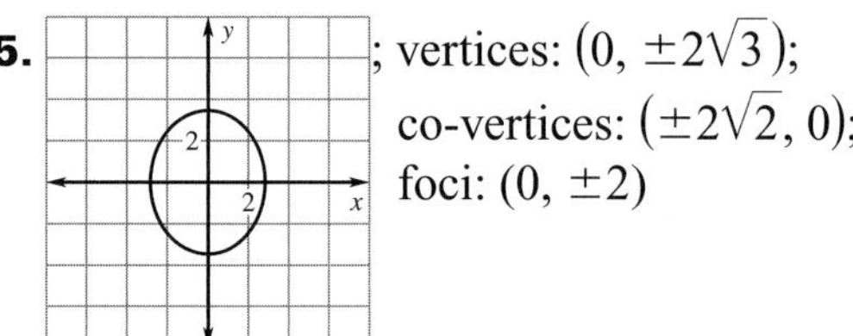 ; vertices: $(0, \pm 2\sqrt{3})$; co-vertices: $(\pm 2\sqrt{2}, 0)$; foci: $(0, \pm 2)$

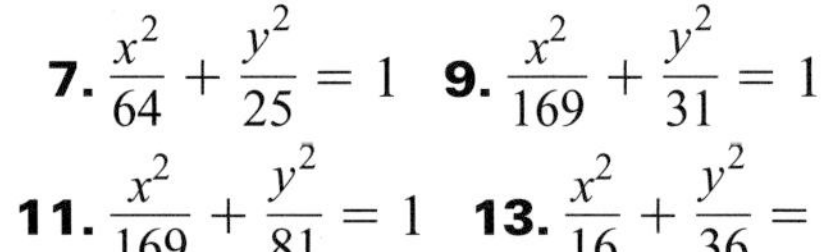

7. $\frac{x^2}{64} + \frac{y^2}{25} = 1$ **9.** $\frac{x^2}{169} + \frac{y^2}{31} = 1$

11. $\frac{x^2}{169} + \frac{y^2}{81} = 1$ **13.** $\frac{x^2}{16} + \frac{y^2}{36} = 1$

15. a. The greatest distance the boat can travel between islands is 20 miles, going straight out to a point and then straight to the other island. This is the definition of an ellipse.
b. Island 1: $(-6, 0)$; Island 2: $(6, 0)$
c. 20 mi; $(\pm 10, 0)$
d. $\frac{x^2}{100} + \frac{y^2}{64} = 1$

5.4 Exercise Set A (p. 192)

1. 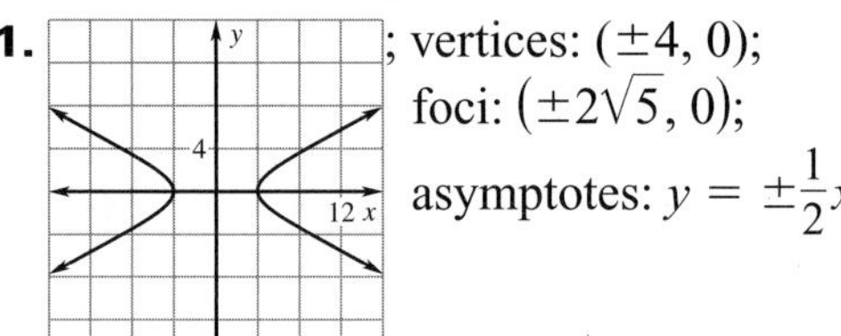 ; vertices: $(\pm 4, 0)$; foci: $(\pm 2\sqrt{5}, 0)$; asymptotes: $y = \pm\frac{1}{2}x$

3. 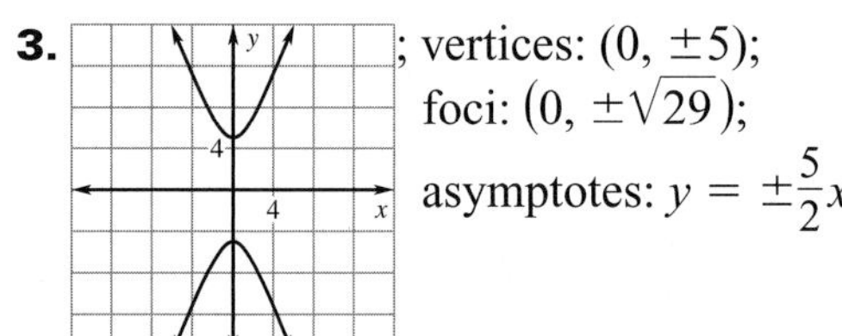 ; vertices: $(0, \pm 5)$; foci: $(0, \pm\sqrt{29})$; asymptotes: $y = \pm\frac{5}{2}x$

5. 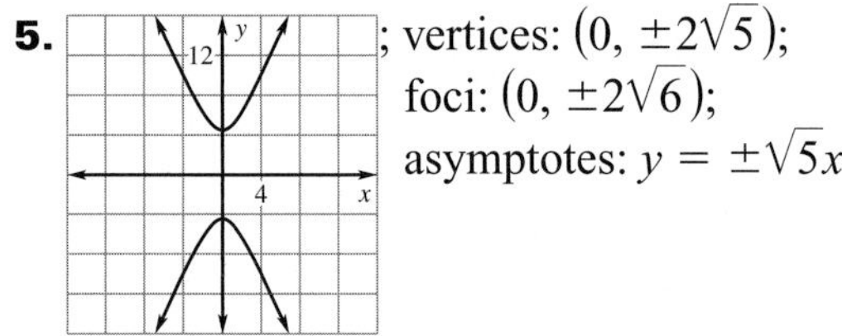 ; vertices: $(0, \pm 2\sqrt{5})$; foci: $(0, \pm 2\sqrt{6})$; asymptotes: $y = \pm\sqrt{5}x$

7. The transverse axis should be horizontal, not vertical.

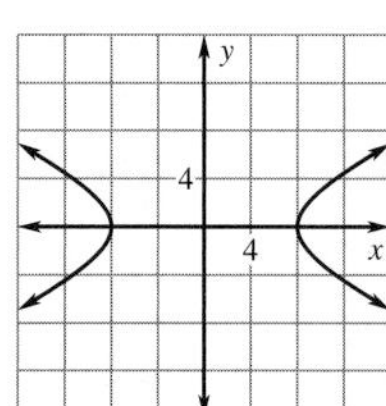

9. $\frac{y^2}{49} - \frac{x^2}{15} = 1$ **11.** $\frac{y^2}{16} - \frac{x^2}{4} = 1$

13. $\dfrac{y^2}{36} - \dfrac{x^2}{25} = 1$ **15.** $\dfrac{y^2}{108} - \dfrac{x^2}{36} = 1$

17.

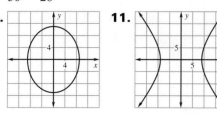

19. $\dfrac{R^2}{\left(\frac{8}{\pi}\right)} - \dfrac{r^2}{\left(\frac{2}{\pi}\right)} = 1$

5.4 Exercise Set B (p. 193)

1. ; vertices: $(\pm 8, 0)$; foci: $(\pm\sqrt{85}, 0)$; asymptotes: $y = \pm\dfrac{\sqrt{21}}{8}x$

3. ; vertices: $(0, \pm 3\sqrt{2})$; foci: $(0, \pm 3\sqrt{11})$; asymptotes: $y = \pm\dfrac{\sqrt{2}}{3}x$

5. ; vertices: $(0, \pm 2\sqrt{10})$; foci: $(0, \pm 2\sqrt{13})$; asymptotes: $y = \pm\dfrac{\sqrt{30}}{3}x$

7. $\dfrac{x^2}{36} - \dfrac{y^2}{28} = 1$

9.

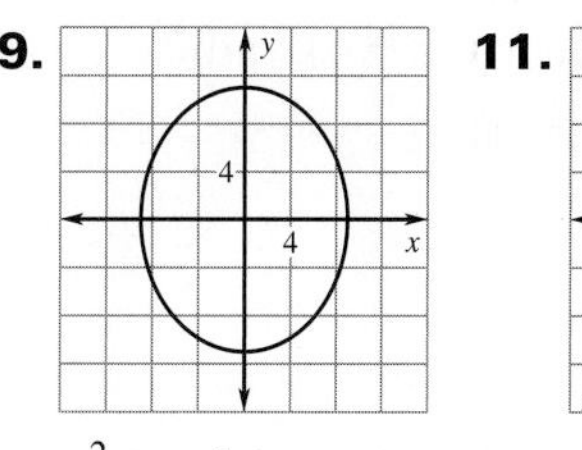

11.

13. $\dfrac{y^2}{16} - \dfrac{x^2}{4} = 1$

15. a. $\pi y^2 - \pi x^2 = 500$

b. *Sample answer:* (2, 12.8), (4, 13.2), (6, 14.0), (8, 14.9)

c. ; the part of the hyperbola in the first quadrant

d. It gets smaller; because the area of the concrete remains constant as the radii increase, the width decreases.

5.5 Exercise Set A (pp. 196–197)

1. ; center: (0, 3); radius: 3

3.

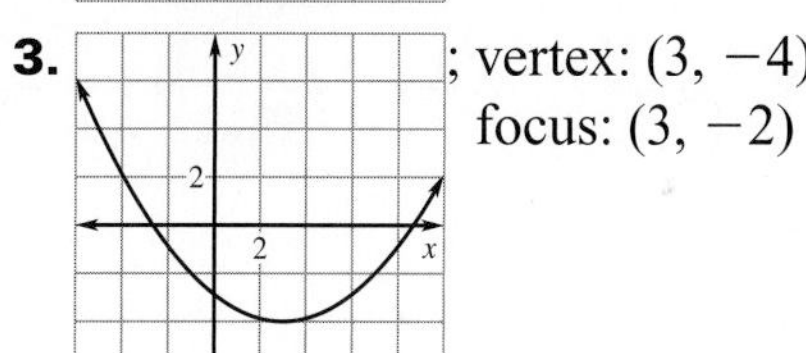

; vertex: $(3, -4)$; focus: $(3, -2)$

5.

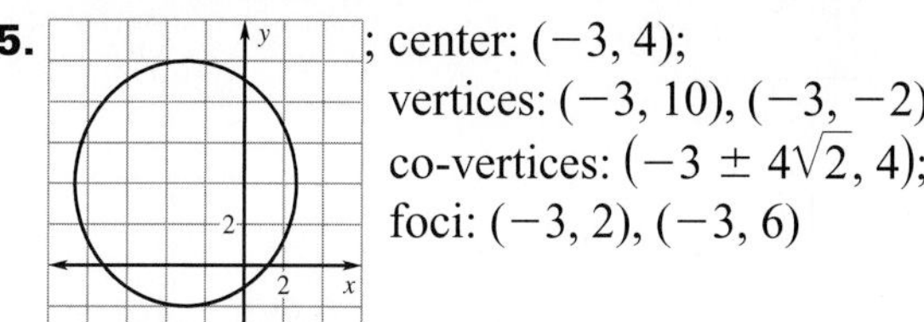

; center: $(-3, 4)$; vertices: $(-3, 10)$, $(-3, -2)$; co-vertices: $(-3 \pm 4\sqrt{2}, 4)$; foci: $(-3, 2)$, $(-3, 6)$

7.

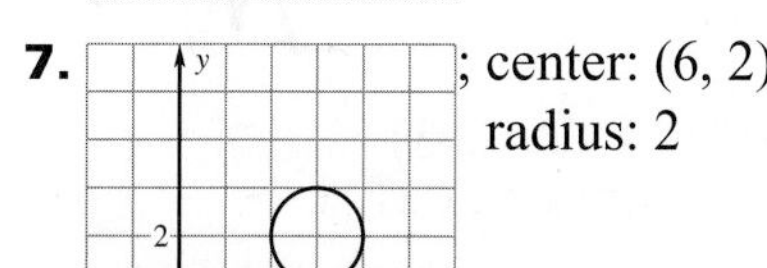

; center: (6, 2); radius: 2

9.

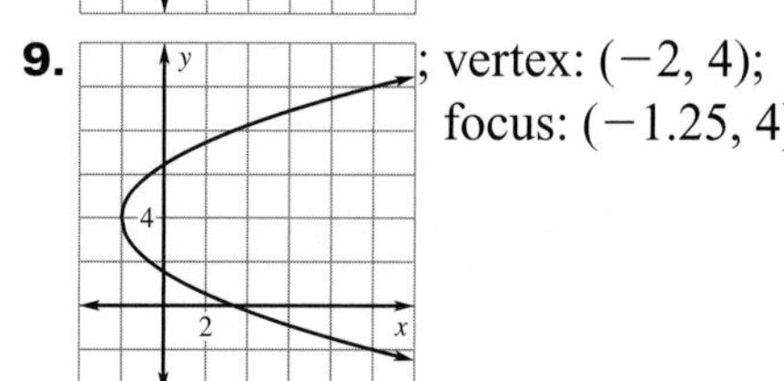

; vertex: $(-2, 4)$; focus: $(-1.25, 4)$

11. 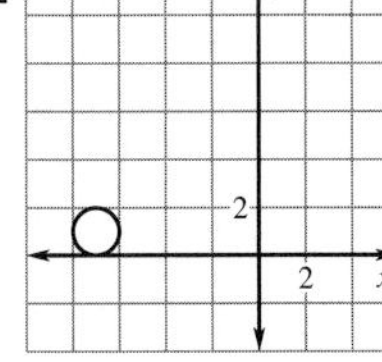

; center: $(-7, 1)$; radius: 1

13. $(x-2)^2 + (y+6)^2 = 16$

15. $\dfrac{(x+2)^2}{4} + \dfrac{(y-3)^2}{16} = 1$

17. $\dfrac{(x-2)^2}{18} + \dfrac{(y-1.5)^2}{20.25} = 1$

19. $(x-3)^2 + (y+4)^2 = 48$

21. $(y-2)^2 = 16(x-6)$ **23.** parabola

25. hyperbola **27.** ellipse **29.** hyperbola

31. ellipse **33.** circle

35. parabola; $(y-1)^2 = -8(x-2)$

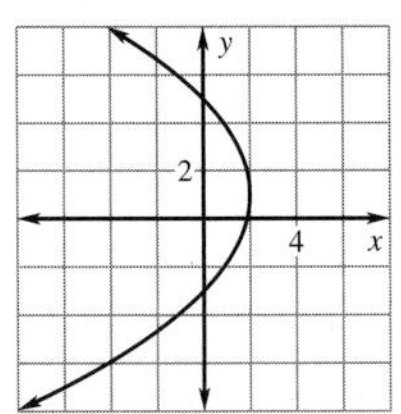

37. hyperbola; $\dfrac{x^2}{9} - \dfrac{(y-3)^2}{1} = 1$

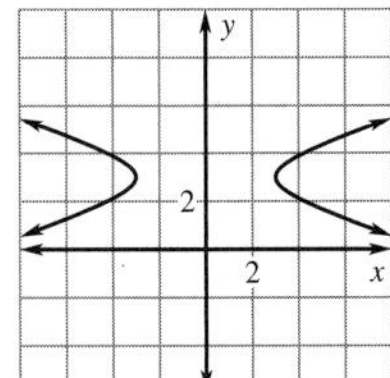

39. parabola; $(x+5)^2 = 6(y+3)$

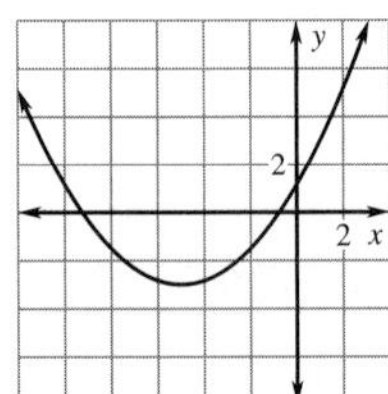

41. parabola; $(y-6)^2 = -4(x-8)$

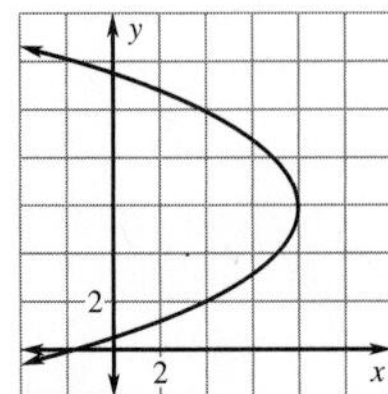

43. hyperbola; $\dfrac{(x-4)^2}{1} - \dfrac{(y-4)^2}{9} = 1$

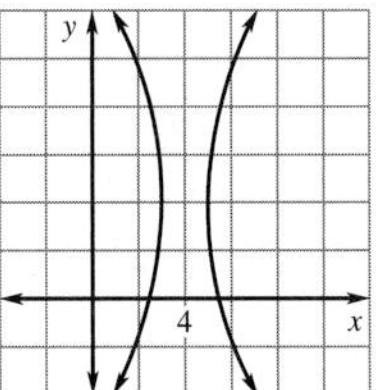

45. $x^2 + (y+225)^2 = 50{,}625$;
$x^2 + (y-225)^2 = 50{,}625$

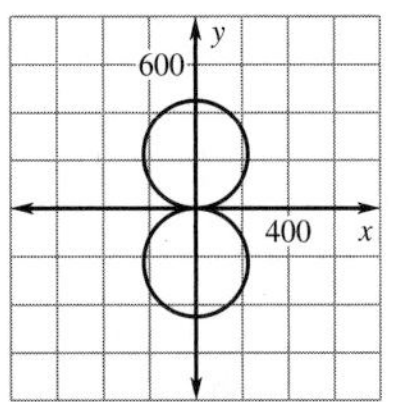

47. hyperbola; $\dfrac{(x-1.5)^2}{5} - \dfrac{y^2}{\left(\frac{10}{3}\right)} = 1$

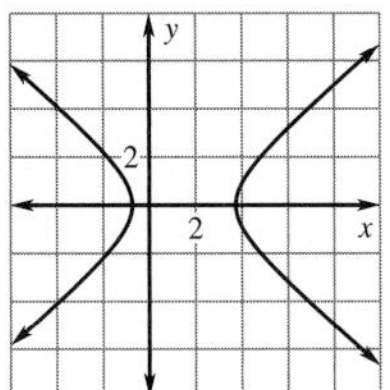

5.5 Exercise Set B (pp. 198–199)

1. 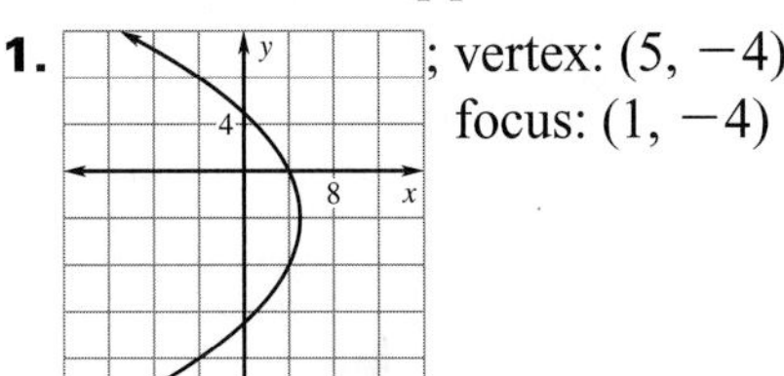

; vertex: $(5, -4)$; focus: $(1, -4)$

3. 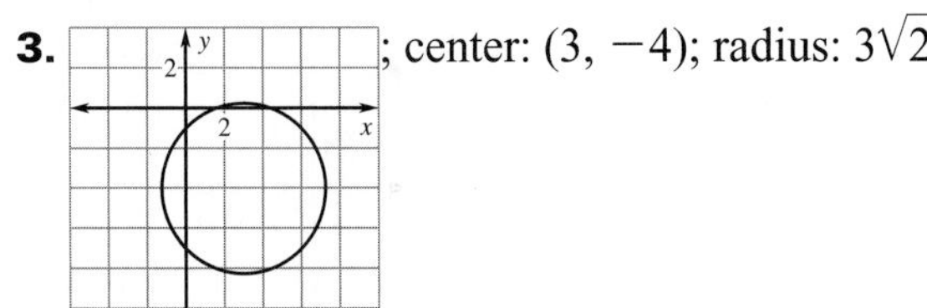

; center: $(3, -4)$; radius: $3\sqrt{2}$

5. 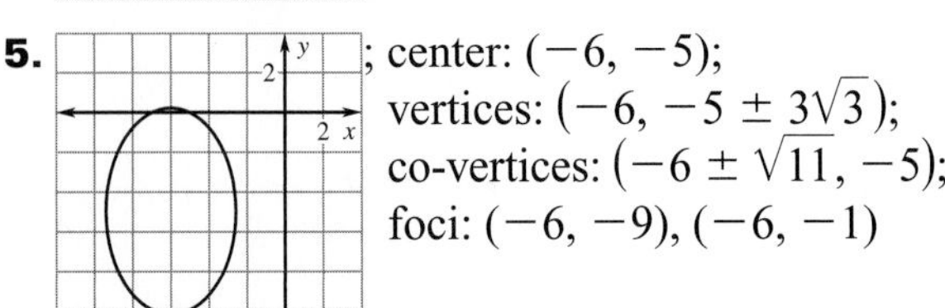

; center: $(-6, -5)$; vertices: $(-6, -5 \pm 3\sqrt{3})$; co-vertices: $(-6 \pm \sqrt{11}, -5)$; foci: $(-6, -9)$, $(-6, -1)$

7. 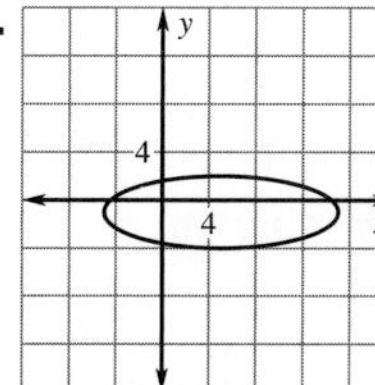

; center: $(5, -1)$; vertices: $(15, -1)$ and $(-5, -1)$; co-vertices: $(5, 2)$ and $(5, -4)$; foci: $(5 \pm \sqrt{91}, -1)$

9. $\frac{(x-4)^2}{25} + \frac{(y+4)^2}{24} = 1$

11. $(x+3)^2 + (y+7)^2 = 7$

13. $\frac{(x-6)^2}{16} + \frac{(y+1)^2}{13} = 1$

15. $\left(x + \frac{1}{2}\right)^2 + \left(y - \frac{3}{4}\right)^2 = \frac{4}{9}$

17. hyperbola **19.** circle **21.** ellipse

23. parabola; $(x-7)^2 = 9(y+3)$

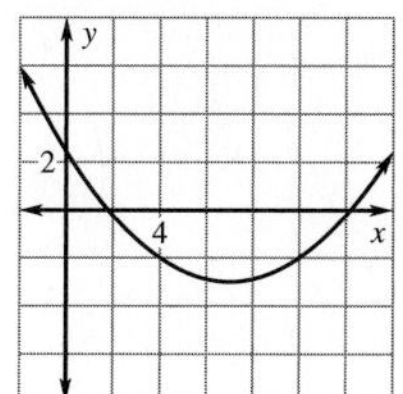

25. ellipse; $\frac{(x-3)^2}{10} + \frac{(y-5)^2}{18} = 1$

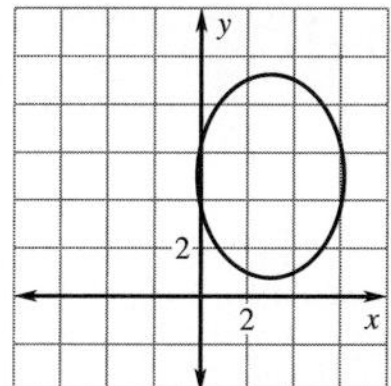

27. ellipse; $\frac{(x+1)^2}{14} + \frac{(y+2)^2}{4} = 1$

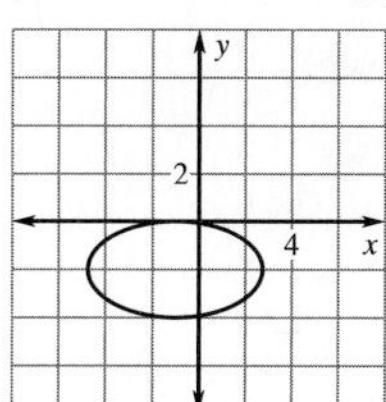

29. ellipse; $\frac{(x-6)^2}{36} + \frac{(y-3)^2}{9} = 1$

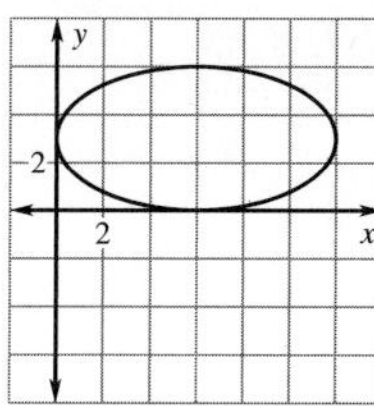

31. a. 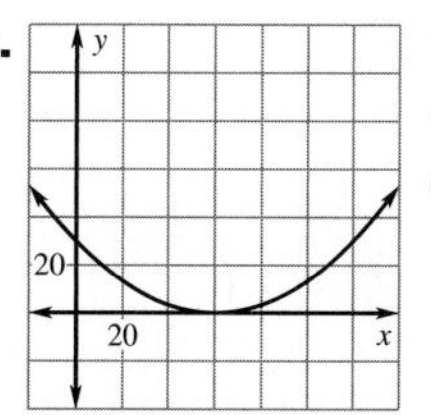

b. (60, 30)
c. $(x-60)^2 = 120y$
d. 7.5 m

5.6 Exercise Set A (p. 202)

1. (−2.87, 3.87), (0.87, 0.13) **3.** (0, 2), (4.5, 4.25) **5.** (6, 0) **9.** (0, −1), (3, 2) **11.** (−4, −4), (4, 4) **13.** no solution **15.** $\left(\frac{3}{11}, -\frac{27}{11}\right)$ **17.** (1, 1), (1, −1) **19.** $(-4, \pm 4\sqrt{2}), (2, \pm\sqrt{2})$ **21.** yes; 466.6 ft by 466.8 ft, or 233.4 ft by 933.2 ft

5.6 Exercise Set B (p. 203)

1. (−3.08, 8.08), (3.08, 1.92) **3.** (0.15, 0.61), (3.50, 3.13) **5.** (−2.60, −11.30), (−8.40, −28.70) **9.** (2, 0), (1, −1) **11.** (−6, −7) **13.** $(16 + 6\sqrt{7}, 6 + 2\sqrt{7}), (16 - 6\sqrt{7}, 6 - 2\sqrt{7})$ **15.** no solution **17.** $\left(\frac{9}{5}, \pm\frac{4\sqrt{6}}{5}\right)$ **19.** (−2, 6), (−1, 4) **21.** about 53.2 mi

5.7 Exercise Set A (p. 207)

1. 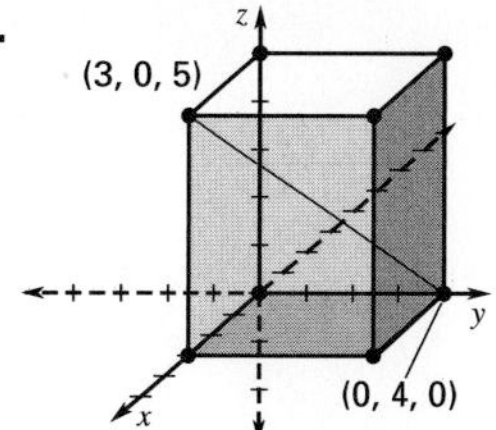

$5\sqrt{2}$

3. $3\sqrt{2}$ **5.** $\sqrt{62}$

7. 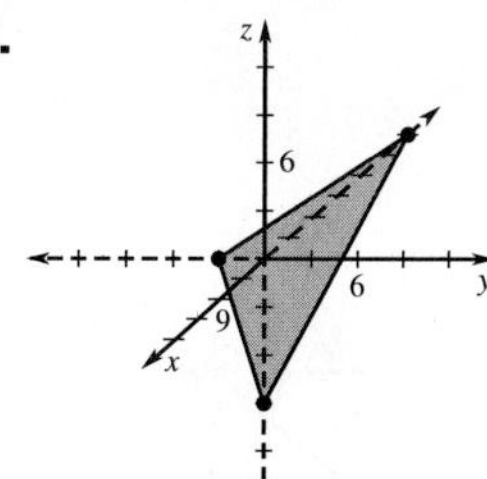

9. 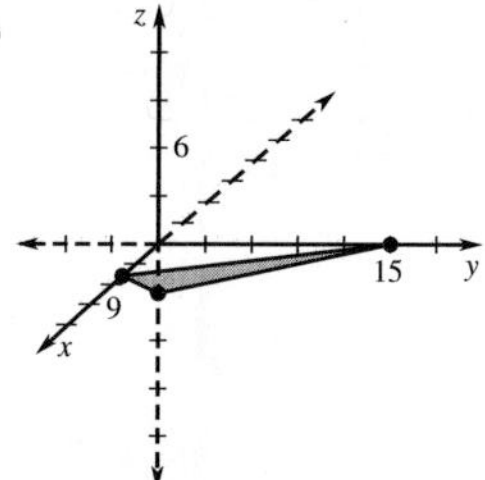

11. 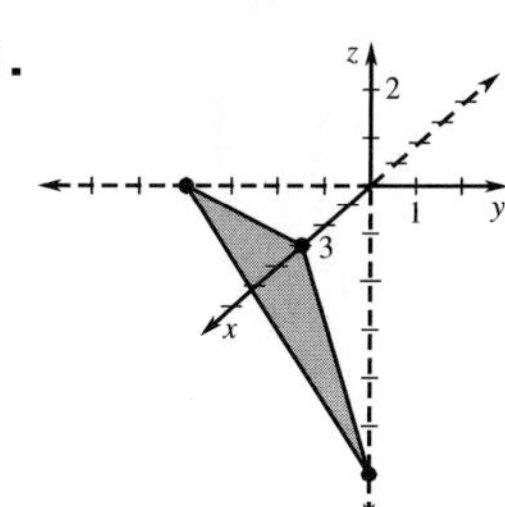

13. plane;

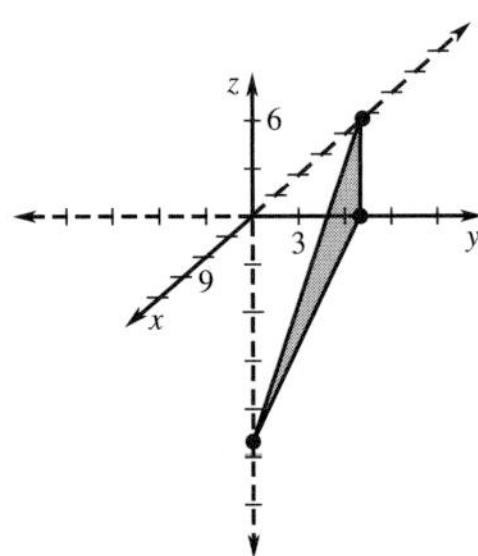

15. sphere **17.** $x^2 + (y - 2)^2 + (z - 5)^2 = 25$

19. $(x + 1)^2 + (y + 7)^2 + (z + 2)^2 = 81$

21. a. length = 6; width = 5; height = 5

b. $SA = 148$ units^2; $V = 120$ units^3

c. (0, 0, 0), (0, 6, 0), (5, 6, 0), (5, 0, 0), (0, 0, 8), (0, 6, 8), (5, 6, 8), (5, 0, 8)

d.

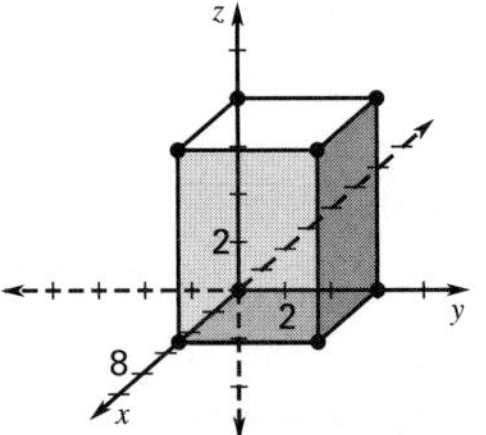

5.7 Exercise Set B (p. 208)

1.

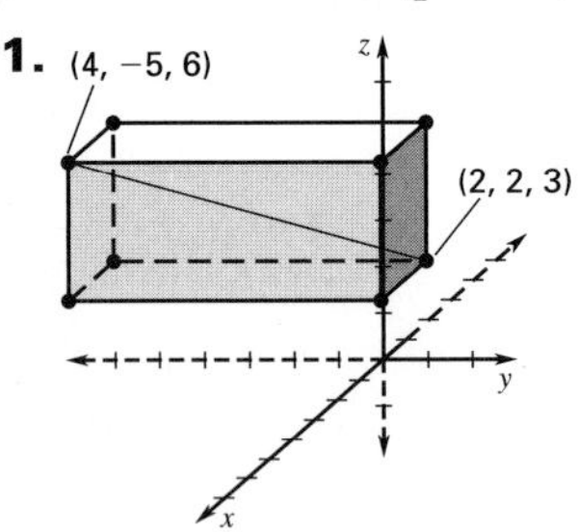

$\sqrt{62}$

3. $\sqrt{113}$

5. **7.**

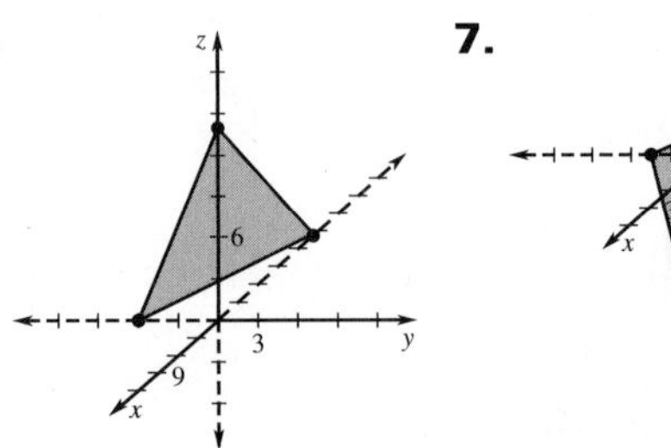

9. $(x - 2)^2 + (y - 2)^2 + (z + 2)^2 = 36$

11. $(x - 15)^2 + (y + 1)^2 + (z - 6)^2 = 1.44$

13. $(x - 8)^2 + (y - 2.5)^2 + z^2 = 192$

15. $(x - 1)^2 + (y + 3)^2 + (z + 4)^2 = 25$; center: $(1, -3, -4)$; radius: 5

17. $\left(x - \frac{1}{3}\right)^2 + (y + 1)^2 + z^2 = 1$;

center: $\left(\frac{1}{3}, -1, 0\right)$; radius: 1

19. 2250π ft^3

UNIT 6

6.1 Exercise Set A (p. 215)

1. continuous; Length of time is a random variable that has an infinite number of possible values, so it is uncountable.

3.

B	1	2	3
***P*(*B*)**	0.3	0.4	0.3

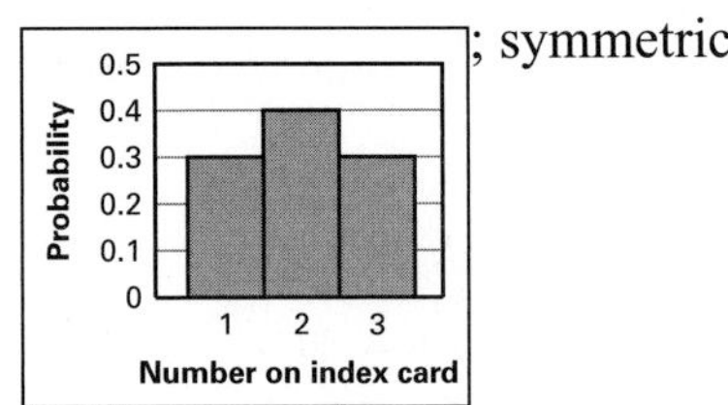

; symmetric

5. about 0.00000894 **7.** about 0.0143

9. about 0.0267 **11.** about 0.220

6.1 Exercise Set B (p. 216)

1.

C	red	blue	green	orange
***P*(*C*)**	0.2	0.25	0.4	0.15

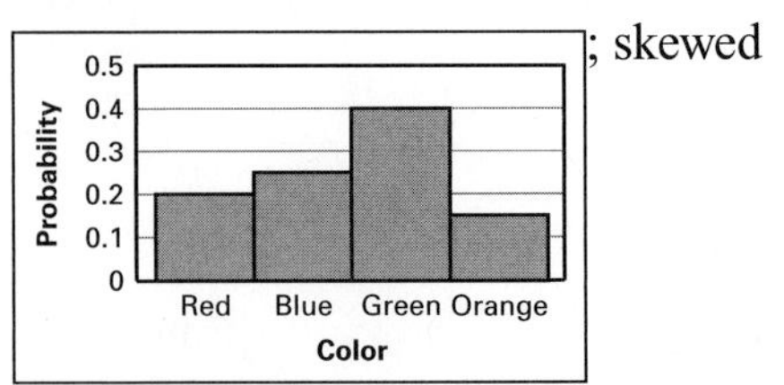

; skewed

3. 0.32 **5.** about 0.144 **7.** about 0.0000255

9. about 0.00000154 **11.** about 8.67×10^{-19}

13. about 0.997

15. 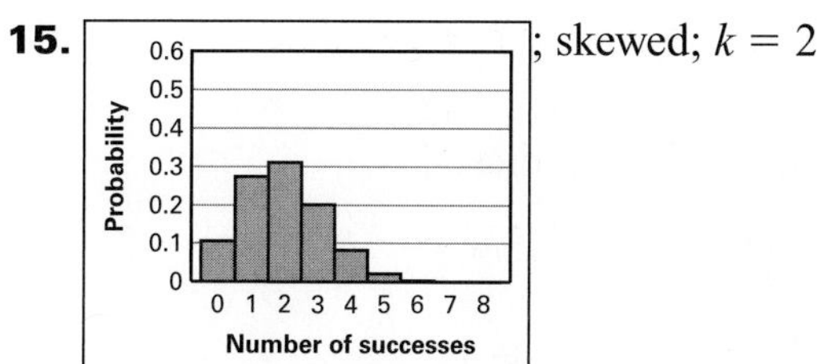

; skewed; $k = 2$

17. 6

6.2 Exercise Set A (p. 221)

1. 84% **3.** 68% **5.** 5% **7.** 0.4985

9. 0.84 **11.** 0.84 **13.** 0.0107 **15.** 0.9821

17. 0.9990 **19.** 288

6.2 Exercise Set B (p. 222)

1. 97.5% **3.** 97.35% **5.** 27.3% **7.** 0.8385

9. 0.16 **11.** 0.975 **13.** 0.0002 **15.** 0.2743

17. 0.9918 **19.** 0.0642 **21.** 192 **23.** John; In a standard normal distribution, John's time is lower which is better when running a mile.

6.3 Exercise Set A (p. 226)

1. 12; about 2.7 **3.** 12.6; about 3.0

5. 14.4; about 3.4 **7.** The value of n should be 220, not 50. So, $\bar{x} = 44$ and $\sigma \approx 6$. **9.** about 0.16

11. 0.16 **13.** 0.9735 **15.** about 0.975

17. Yes; $P(x \le 11) \approx P(z \le -2.3) \approx 0.0107$, which is less than 0.05.

6.3 Exercise Set B (p. 227)

1. 37; about 4.8 **3.** 112.5; about 5.3

5. 2.4; about 1.5 **7.** about 0.84 **9.** about 0.475

11. about 0.025 **13.** about 0.68

15. No; $P(x \ge 15) \approx 1 - P(z \le 1.6) \approx 1 - 0.9452 = 0.0548$, which is greater than 0.05.

6.4 Exercise Set A (p. 230)

1. convenience; biased; The sample is not representative of the population. **3.** random; biased; People currently at the mall are more likely to shop at the mall than people in the community in general.

5. $\pm$6.3% **7.** $\pm$2.6% **9.** $\pm$4.1% **11.** $\pm$1.6%

13. 400 **15.** 15,625

17. a. 700

b. 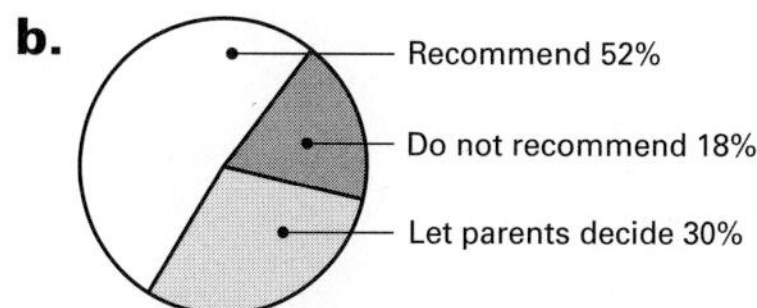

c. $\pm$3.8%; between 48.2% and 55.8%

6.4 Exercise Set B (p. 231)

1. self-selected; unbiased; People visiting the league website would not be biased toward any one particular player. **3.** random; unbiased; Selecting customers at random would eliminate bias.

5. $\pm$3.9% **7.** $\pm$3.6% **9.** $\pm$2.0% **11.** $\pm$1.1%

13. 1890 **15.** 730 **17.** 1189 **19.** 27,778

21. between 62.2% and 65.8%

23. between 560 and 720 people

6.5 Exercise Set A (p. 235)

1. Experimental study; The professor is assigning individuals to the control group and the experimental group.

3. Observational study; The assignments of the patients to the experimental group and the control group are outside the doctor's control.

5. *Sample answer:* The approval rating of the registered voters in the same party as the mayor is likely to be higher than that of the registered voters in a different party from the mayor. To correct the flaw, the company should redesign the experiment so that the political affiliations in both groups are similar.

6.5 Exercise Set B (p. 236)

1. Observational study; The assignments of the students to the experimental group and the control group are outside of the teacher's control.

3. Experimental study; The manager is assigning employees to the control group and the experimental group.

5. *Sample answer:* The mathematical knowledge of the students enrolled as math majors is likely to be higher than that of the mathematical knowledge of students enrolled in other majors. To correct the flaw, the company should redesign the experiment so that the mathematical backgrounds in both groups are similar.